THE HOLLYWOOD MUSICAL THE HOLLYWOOD MUSICAL

THE
HOLLYWOOD MUSICAL

CLIVE HIRSCHHORN

CROWN PUBLISHERS INC.
New York

Published in Great Britain 1981 by
Octopus Books Limited
59 Grosvenor Street
London WI

First published in the US 1981 by Crown Publishers Inc.
Inquiries should be addressed to Crown Publishers Inc.,
One Park Avenue, New York 10016

© 1981 Octopus Books Limited

Third impression 1983

Library of Congress Cataloging in Publication Data

Hirschhorn, Clive.
    The Hollywood musical.

    I. Moving-pictures, Musical — United States — History
and criticism.   I. Title.
PNI995.9.M86H5 1981   791.43'09'09357 81-3122
ISBN 0-5I7-54044-4   AACR2

Produced by Mandarin Publishers Limited
22a Westlands Road,
Quarry Bay, Hong Kong

Printed in Hong Kong

Designers: Design 23
Research Consultant: Arthur Jackson
Photographic Consultant
and prelim pictures: Ian Cook

page I Radio City, New York
page 2/3 Pantages foyer, Hollywood
page 4/5 Mann's Cinema, Hollywood

CONTENTS

FOREWORD

A book such as this surely deserves to be credited with that most wonderful cliché – 'an idea whose time has come', and those of us who have worked hard and long in the field of music and dance will welcome it warmly. True, many good books have been written before, but as far as I know none is as all-embracing as this one. I know it will prove indispensable to the thousands of young people who are studying film seriously in colleges and universities throughout the world, as well as being a source of great joy to every film buff. Like *The Guinness Book of Records* and the Wallace family's *Book of Lists*, I can see it now, being thumbed through to settle bets made in bars, classrooms, or even after academic lectures. Just thinking of all the fights it may stop stamps it as worthwhile.

Then, too, there will be the fanatics like myself who will just love to pick it up and browse through titles, credits and the years the films were produced, saying to themselves 'Was it that long ago?', or 'Why, I must have seen that when I was eighteen – that was *our* song'. How many of us remember old loves, school days, even war-time, through the songs and dances of the musicals of the periods involved. Perhaps nothing else does more to revive memories of faces and places – and for me they are very pleasant memories.

The members of the group who worked at MGM during my tenure there were very serious about musicals. That is not to say that we didn't make them to entertain and uplift the spirit, but we thought that to do this effectively they had to be superbly crafted; and that meant the closest kind of collaboration among the choreographers, directors, producers, musicians, conductors, musical arrangers, designers, costumiers – the list is endless. There were probably more assembled talents in this field at Metro than anywhere else at any other time. Yet we mustn't forget that, overwhelming as MGM was in numbers, other studios possessed a great share of entertainers and creators, and also contributed immensely to the world of musical pictures.

Again, each studio contributed much to the historical changes in the field, starting with **The Jazz Singer**, progressing into European-style operetta, lavish extravaganzas, then more and more into shows that integrated story, song and dance with ever-developing skills.

An all-encompassing reference book of this kind does one other important thing – it illuminates the source from which many of the finished works sprang. This has been, I think, one of the major gaps in many previous publications. If one adds up all the people who worked in this field since the beginning of sound pictures the total is much more, I believe, than the average film-goer realizes. And now this same film-goer, through this book, will be able to comprehend more fully the contribution of all those people who are often forgotten.

So here it is at last – a complete source book; one that will not only serve as the ultimate in reference guides but will rectify and remedy many of the things that have been overlooked in the past.

Gene Kelly

This book
is dedicated to

the many talented men and women whose particular skills behind the scenes have enhanced the good name of the Hollywood musical. To most of them you will not be able to attach a face but their contributions to the genre were incalculable. First and foremost were the musical men themselves: arrangers, conductors and orchestrators who took the tunes provided by the composers and embellished them with a 'sound' unique to their own studio. At MGM Herbert Stothart, Conrad Salinger, Skip Martin, Adolph Deutsch, Saul Chaplin, Georgie Stoll, vocal arranger Ken Darby (who later went to 20th Century-Fox), Kay Thompson, Johnny Green, Leo Arnaud, Lennie Hayton and André Previn helped many a song to achieve immortality; while doing the same at 20th Century-Fox were Alfred Newman, Herbert Spencer, Charles Henderson, Earl Hagen, Emil Newman, Louis Silver, Edward B. Powell and Arthur Lange. Paramount had Robert Emmett Dolan, Victor Young, Joseph J. Lilley and Van Cleave; and Warner Bros. had Leo Forbstein, Max Steiner, Heinz Roemheld and Ray Heindorf. Helping to set the fashions of the day were the studios' brilliant and versatile costume designers, the best of them being Irene Sharaff, Adrian, Helen Rose, Walter Plunkett (all of whom worked for MGM, Plunkett joining the studio in 1947 after eleven years at RKO), Orry-Kelly (Warner Bros. and 20th Century-Fox), Royer, Yvonne Wood, Travis Banton, William Travilla and Gwen Wakeling (20th Century-Fox), Edith Head (Universal) and Jean Louis at Columbia. Cedric Gibbons was the name on almost every MGM film for decades as art director; Richard Day and Lyle Wheeler were responsible for the way many of the musicals at 20th Century-Fox looked; and Van Nest Polglase and Carroll Clarke for the art deco sheen of the Astaire/Rogers offerings at RKO. Anton Grot and Carl Jules Weyl were the two heavyweight art directors at Warner Bros. in the thirties and forties, and Paramount's top man was Hans Dreier. Finally, as in the last moments of **Singin' In The Rain** (MGM, 1952), I'd like to pull back the curtain and pay tribute to those unseen heroes and heroines who dubbed the voices for so many of the stars, who would not otherwise have made names for themselves in the musical cinema. They include Nan Wynn, Martha Mears, Jo Ann Greer, Anita Ellis (all of whom dubbed for Rita Hayworth – Miss Ellis also vocalizing for Vera-Ellen), Betty Wand, Trudy Erwin, Carole Richards, Marni Nixon, Lisa Kirk, Bill Lee and Bill Shirley. Without them, and all the other 'behind the camera' talents, the Hollywood musical would simply not have been possible.

AUTHOR'S ACKNOWLEDGEMENTS

This book has been made possible by the invaluable assistance of many people who have given unstintingly of their time and expertise.

First and foremost I should like to acknowledge the efforts of Robyn Karney who, in an editorial capacity, supervised every stage from inception to completion with a sharp and critical eye.

I am also greatly indebted to Tom Vallance who gave so generously of his own extensive knowledge – and his enthusiasm – in helping to make the book as complete a record as possible. To George Baxt in New York my heartfelt thanks for bringing his specialized knowledge of musicals to bear on both the text and the illustrations; and to Arthur Jackson in Cornwall my gratitude for putting his extensive list of credits and song titles at my disposal. The efforts of my researcher, Corin Moore, who spent literally hundreds of hours ferreting out obscure information, cannot be over-estimated either. In this regard my thanks also to Karen Press. Gilbert Adair and Ronald Bergan both contributed substantially to the book, and other much appreciated assistance was given by Tony Slide, Lucy Saroyan and Sam

Gill of the Academy of Motion Picture Arts and Sciences in Beverly Hills; Monty Arnold, Paul Myers, Dorothy Swerdlove, David Bartholomew, Donald Fowle, Dr Roderick Bladel, Dan Patrie and Max Silverman of the Library of Performing Arts, Lincoln Centre, New York; Peter Seward, Susan Julian-Huxley, Linda Wood, Brenda Davies, Gillian Hartnoll, Pat Terilli, Janice Headland and Sandra Archer of the British Film Institute; The American Film Institute; Mary Corliss of the Museum of Modern Art, New York; the Stills Archive of the British Film Institute. My thanks also to Gene Kelly, Lois McClelland, Ray Block, Eddie Brandt's Saturday Matinee, Movie Star News, Erik Spilker, Jim Simpson, Madeleine Harmsworth, Barbara Roett, Dick Vosburgh, Frank Lazarus, Maxine Andrews, Bill Bast, Tony Sloman, Bernard Hrusa-Marlow, Reginald Wright, Neil Stevens, Miles Kreuger, Chris Hahn, Lois Butlin, Susan Wallis, David Watkinson, Bob Grimes, Rodger Hambleton, Ken Sephton, Howard Mandelbaum, Vyvyan Cole, Allen L. Salyers and Peter McKriel. I am indebted too, to the following publications: The New York Times, The Motion Picture Herald, Kine Weekly, The Monthly Film Bulletin and Variety.

AUTHOR'S NOTE

Despite my lifelong love and experience of the Hollywood musical I really did not appreciate just how mammoth a number of films over the past 50 years could have a strong case made for their inclusion when I began writing this book. *The Hollywood Musical* aims to be as complete a record of the genre as possible, but clearly it was essential, very early on, to establish workable guidelines as to what constitutes a 'musical'. The decision was a difficult one to make and, necessarily, had to be subjective.

There are no problems with films like **Top Hat** (RKO, 1935), **Coney Island** (20th Century-Fox, 1943), **Singin' In The Rain** (MGM, 1952) or **The Band Wagon** (MGM, 1953). They are quintessential Hollywood musicals whose inclusion in such a book is both automatic and obvious. But what of a film like **Rhapsody** (MGM, 1954)? To many it might be considered a romantic drama with music, rather than a musical. The point is debatable. I believe its inclusion to be justified because its musical content is sufficiently important to the story. On the other hand, a film such as Robert Altman's **A Perfect Couple** (20th Century-Fox, 1979) is not listed as a main entry despite the many songs featured in it. In my opinion the music is not central to the plot, and the film's fundamental concern would in no way be altered had the female protagonist been a model or an actress rather than a pop singer.

Yet, despite exercising all possible care, grey areas still remain. I have attempted to clarify these by including a section at the back of the book which lists films, like **A Perfect Couple**, whose musical content cannot, in all fairness, be overlooked but which, in my personal judgement, can hardly be labelled as a musical. Into this category (which I have called 'fringe' musicals) I have also placed Republic's **Magic Fire** (1956) – a biopic of Richard Wagner—whereas Columbia's **A Song To Remember** (1945) and **Song Without End** (1960) – biopics of Chopin and Liszt—appear as fully-fledged entries. My reason for this is that the excerpts in the first film are too abbreviated to do justice to their composer and are unsatisfying, whereas in the Chopin and Liszt biopics the musical content is altogether more representative of the two composers.

Certain films whose musical programme is fairly substantial do not feature in the book at all: films such as **The Roaring Twenties** (Warner Bros, 1939), **Road House** (20th Century-Fox, 1948), and Paramount's **Dark City** (1950) which has a total of five songs in it. None of these films can be considered a musical. The songs in them exist merely as interludes and are in no way integral to the plot.

The same, I realize, might be said of films such as **You'll Find Out** (RKO, 1940), which *does* appear in the main text. The reason for its inclusion is that its star, Kay Kyser, was a popular band leader whose music-making, together with Ginny Simms, Ish Kabibble, Harry Babbit and Sully Mason, were what the audiences of 1943 paid to see.

Musicals such as **Happy-Go-Lovely** (1950), **A Hard Day's Night** (1964), **Help!** (1965), **The Yellow Submarine** (1968), **Oliver!** (1968), **Chitty Chitty Bang Bang** (1969), **Tommy** (1970), **Scrooge** (1970) and **The Slipper And The Rose** (1976) are not listed in the book at all; for although in some instances they involved American finance, or, in others, American creative talent, they were essentially British,

having been made by British technicians at British studios. At the same time, I have made four exceptions to the rule: **I Could Go On Singing** (United Artists, 1963), **Half A Sixpence** (Paramount, 1971), **The Boy Friend** (MGM, 1971) and **The Rocky Horror Picture Show** (20th Century-Fox, 1975). All four, strictly speaking, do not belong in a book such as this. Yet how could I omit Judy Garland's last film, which also happened to be a musical? **Half A Sixpence** appears solely because it was directed by George Sidney, another of the genre's heavyweights; while **The Boy Friend** justifies its inclusion because it paid homage to the Hollywood musical in general and to Busby Berkeley in particular. Similarly, my decision to include **The Rocky Horror Picture Show** was based on the fact that it too drew its inspiration from Hollywood – in this instance from the vintage Universal horror movie. That it has also become something of a cult film in the United States further influenced my decision.

Films such as **A Funny Thing Happened On The Way To The Forum** (United Artists, 1966), **Dr Dolittle** (20th Century-Fox, 1967), **Goodbye Mr Chips** (MGM, 1969), **Song Of Norway** (ABC, 1970), **Willie Wonka And The Chocolate Factory** (David Wolper Productions, 1971), **Fiddler On The Roof** (United Artists, 1971), **The Little Prince** (Paramount, 1972), **Man of La Mancha** (United Artists, 1972), **Jesus Christ Superstar** (Universal, 1973) etc. are included, as they are all American projects filmed on location outside the USA.

Because of their limited release I have completely omitted the dozens of all-black low-budget musicals made throughout the forties – films such as Herald's **Miracle In Harlem** (1948), **Boy What A Girl** (1947), Famous Films' **Hi-De-Ho** (1947) with Cab Calloway, and Astor Pictures' **Look Out Sister** (1948). Nor are featurettes (such as Walt Disney's **Saludos Amigos**, RKO, 1943) included, nor the plethora of Western musicals starring singing cowboys Gene Autry, Dick Foran, Roy Rogers and Tex Ritter.

Apart from the previously mentioned 'fringe' musicals, the book contains two further appendices: a catalogue of American International and other low-budget rock 'n' roll, twist and 'beach party' musicals of the fifties and sixties; and a list of important documentaries, such as **Woodstock** (Warner Bros, 1970) and **Gimme Shelter** (Cinema V, 1970).

Academy Award winners and nominations are not, as a rule, specifically mentioned in the text, but a special panel containing the lists of Academy Awards (and nominations), the New York Film Critics' Awards, the New York Times Annual 'Ten Best' Awards and the top moneymaking films, all pertaining to musicals mentioned in the main body of the book, appears at the beginning of each year. The first Academy Awards were presented on 16th May 1929 for the years 1927 and 1928. This practice continued until 1934 when the awards were no longer presented on a split year basis; hence those in 1935 covered the year 1934 only.

Despite my efforts to make careful and sensible distinctions as to what should be included in the various sections of the book, I remain painfully aware that there will always be room for disagreement. To those readers who may sometimes be disappointed by the choices I have opted for, I can only repeat that choices had to be made, and I crave their indulgence accordingly.

Clive Hirschhorn London, 1980

INTRODUCTION

The musical was the only new cinematic genre to be born with the coming of the 'talkers' (as the first sound pictures were initially called) and, like many an infant, among the first words it uttered was 'Mammy'. Though there were better films in 1927 than **The Jazz Singer** (Warner Bros.), it was Samson Raphaelson's shamelessly sentimental story, and Al Jolson in blackface singing that famous song, that brought the Hollywood musical into being. If we are still touched by **The Jazz Singer** today, it is largely because of its pioneering aspect.

Though initially dependent on its parents – operetta and musical comedy – for inspiration, the screen musical was soon recognized as a vital art form in its own right, and the many changes of public taste, which more than once threatened its survival, have never managed to kill it off completely. In the 50 years or so since its birth, the musical has proved itself to be the phoenix of the film industry. Unlike perennials such as Westerns and war and crime films, it is the musical alone that periodically disappears, only to rise again from the ashes to prove that reports of its demise are greatly exaggerated. Thanks to some creative genius who has always been there to impart the kiss of life when it was most needed, Hollywood has produced at least one excellent musical every year up until the sixties. Among the greatest of these *auteurs* were Ernst Lubitsch, Rouben Mamoulian, Busby Berkeley, Arthur Freed, Vincente Minnelli, Gene Kelly and Stanley Donen. And even in the seventies, a decade characterized by radical upheavals in taste and form, there have been produced several felicities such as **Cabaret** (Allied Artists, 1972), the second remake of **A Star Is Born** (Warner Bros., 1976), **New York, New York** (United Artists, 1977), **The Rose** (20th Century-Fox, 1979) – a brilliant recreation of the sixties rock scene, and **All That Jazz** (Columbia, 1979). Along with these movies came another wave of names and personalities to revitalize respect for the genre: Bob Fosse, Barbra Streisand, Liza Minnelli and Bette Midler.

IN THE BEGINNING

Most film musicals of the late twenties and early thirties were stagy and static, and the novelty of sound, even with two-colour Technicolor, was not enough to hold the public. As in the fifties when Hollywood thought that new technical advances would coax people out of the comfort of their homes, so it was with the arrival of sound in the twenties. The major studios believed in the talisman of the new toy but they neglected to learn how to use it properly. It was Irving Thalberg, the 'boy wonder' at MGM, who foresaw the possibilities inherent in the film musical – possibilities undreamed of in the philosophy of those who were indiscriminately flooding the screen with mindless 'all talking, all singing, all dancing' attractions. Thalberg asked composer Nacio Herb Brown and lyricist Arthur Freed to create new songs especially for **The Broadway Melody**, thereby starting a tradition that would spawn not only some of the best musicals ever made but also an impressive number of skilled songwriting teams. It was not long before the giants of popular music – George and Ira Gershwin, Irving Berlin, Cole Porter, Jerome Kern, Richard Rodgers and Lorenz Hart – were writing screen originals.

Thalberg's thinking bore other important fruit: in 1929, when the screen musical was a mere two years old, **The Broadway Melody** won the first Oscar for a sound movie and, with it, the brash *parvenu* had arrived to stay. **The Broadway Melody** was significant in several ways, not least for the approval it won from the Academy of Motion Picture Arts and Sciences. It was also MGM's first venture into sound and the first of what was to become the most durable stand-by of the entire genre, the 'backstage musical'.

Because there were so many obstacles to overcome in the industry's conversion to sound, it was an exciting period for anyone willing to accept the challenge. Among the major problems were the cumbersome and stationary camera, and the poor quality of the sound recording. Before the camera became more mobile, dancing could not really be conceived spatially and most dance routines seemed flat and lifeless. Singers had fewer problems in that they could just stand still and sing, and hope that the sensitive recording equipment would survive their high notes.

As well as the technical difficulties, there were contextual problems. What worked on the musical stage would not work in the musical film, so new aesthetics had to be conceived. The realistic eye of the camera, through which the subjective eye of the director stared, demanded more than simply filmed theatre. Musical numbers, if they were to break from their stage conventions, had to be structured in the cutting-room. Dance directors now needed to be more than choreographers: they had to possess an understanding of the visual demands of film, while directors needed a definite musical sensibility. Filmed theatre was quickly rejected by artists and the public alike, and stories and screenplays were sought which were created specifically with the screen in mind, and whose music was integral to the plot.

Few film makers, however, realized that the musical numbers, no matter how good, ought to grow naturally out of the texture of the work. It was Rouben Mamoulian and Ernst Lubitsch who first recognized that the film musical could have a freedom and a flexibility unacceptable in most other, more 'realistic' genres. Their European backgrounds helped bring a much needed sophistication to Hollywood and, being well-versed in the tradition of operetta, they knew that characters did not need a naturalistic excuse to burst into song. Lubitsch's **The Love Parade** (Paramount, 1929) pointed the way forward, and two more excellent examples of the technique followed: Mamoulian's **Love Me Tonight** (Paramount, 1932) and Lubitsch's **The Merry Widow** (MGM, 1934). Most film makers, however, felt that the only way to introduce song and dance numbers into the narrative was in the context of a show – a belief which led to the popularity and proliferation of the backstage musical and the 'show-within-a-show' format. Nonetheless, there *were* other attempts at originality. King Vidor filmed much of **Hallelujah** (MGM, 1929) on location, proving that sound – which he dubbed in afterwards – and visual poetry need not be contradictory; while David Butler in **Sunnyside Up** (Fox, 1929) imparted a refreshing spontaneity to the story of a Manhattan slum girl's romance with a handsome millionaire.

Broadway, vaudeville, and even opera stars were lured west by the 'talkers'. But it soon became apparent that stars in one medium did not necessarily shine in another, even though they were musical or dramatic artists. Among those from the musical stage who did achieve screen stardom were Helen Morgan, Eddie Cantor, Jeanette MacDonald, Maurice Chevalier and the Marx Brothers, while some notable casualties included George Jessel, Ann Pennington and Irene Bordoni. But whether they succeeded or not, there were so many performers in Hollywood hoping to immortalize themselves on celluloid between 1929 and 1930 that the studios tried to squeeze as many of them at a time into one film. Thus the film revue was born, consisting usually of a string of unrelated numbers and serving as little more than a showcase for its stars. The revue, which from time to time appeared disguised as another popular musical stand-by, the biographical picture (biopic), was never very satisfactory as it tended to lack artistic unity. The very first movie revue was **Hollywood Revue of 1929** (MGM), and it introduced the Nacio Herb Brown/Arthur Freed hit 'Singin' In The Rain', which was to feature in three more movies before finally giving its name to one of the greatest screen musicals ever made. Two of the best examples of the film revue were **Paramount On Parade** (1930), in which Lubitsch directed Chevalier in three sequences, and the extraordinary **King Of Jazz** (Universal, 1930). John Murray Anderson's innovative direction of the latter proved a forerunner to Busby Berkeley's remarkable inventiveness, and the film, shot in beautiful two-colour Technicolor, was also notable in that it marked the feature film debut of Bing Crosby.

THE EARLY THIRTIES
By 1930, four distinct types of movie musical were emerging: the backstage musical, the film revue, the operetta, and the campus musical. The latter genre was typified by **Good News** (MGM, 1930), whose cast of college kids needed little excuse to go into their dance, and in which the hero scored the winning touchdown in the last few seconds of the Big Match (a climax which was to become a regular feature of such movies for the next twenty-odd years).

Songs, however, were not confined to musicals alone, and as soon as the movies found a voice, even non-musicals felt obliged to include a song or two: Marlene Dietrich sang Leo Robin and Karl Hajos's 'Give Me The Man' and 'What Am I Bid?' in Von Sternberg's *Morocco* (Paramount, 1930) – and undeniably enhanced the inherent eroticism of the film.

It was the independent producer Samuel Goldwyn who gave Busby Berkeley his first chance in movies, appointing him as dance director on **Whoopee** (Goldwyn-United Artists, 1930). By so doing, Goldwyn also gave the cinema one of its few undisputed geniuses. Berkeley immediately began to experiment with space and movement and overhead shots, and almost single-handedly liberated the musical from its stagy confines. **Whoopee** was notable, too, in that its leading man, Eddie Cantor, became one of Hollywood's top stars in the early thirties. It also introduced Betty Grable (aged 15) to the screen.

Because so many all-talking, all-dancing, all-singing pictures had been rushed into production in 1929 and

1930, it was inevitable that saturation point would soon be reached, and it was. The public, choking on a surfeit of mindless musicals, turned apathetic, and the major studios declared a moratorium on the genre. By 1931, with the Depression affecting the film industry, there simply wasn't the money to spend on lavish productions, and many projects were shorn of most of their musical numbers, such as Jerome Kern's **Men Of The Sky** (Warner Bros., 1931), or abandoned altogether.

All the same, Paramount – the honey-pot which attracted many European directors – found itself in quixotic mood and took a chance in presenting the scintillating **Love Me Tonight** (1932), directed by Rouben Mamoulian with a score by Richard Rodgers and Lorenz Hart. Maurice Chevalier increased his popularity in this, and in two of Lubitsch's most sophisticated *boudoir* operettas, **The Smiling Lieutenant** (1931) and **One Hour With You** (1932), both also for Paramount. Busby Berkeley staged the numbers in two more Eddie Cantor vehicles, **Palmy Days** (Goldwyn-United Artists, 1931) and **The Kid From Spain** (Goldwyn-United Artists 1932) – both calculated to cheer up the most depressed of the Depression-hit people of America.

But despite its occasional felicities, 1931 and 1932 were two lean years for the musical. Then, just as the genre seemed to be *passé*, Darryl F. Zanuck, head of production at Warner Bros., gave the nod to screenwriters Rian James and James Seymour, dance director Busby Berkeley, director Lloyd Bacon and composers Al Dubin and Harry Warren to go ahead with a song and dance show that would be sufficiently different to attract audiences all over again. The result was **42nd Street** (1933) whose great success led the studio to follow it up with two more backstage extravaganzas in the same year: **Gold Diggers Of 1933** and **Footlight Parade**. Though it was Berkeley's kaleidoscopic production numbers that were the really revolutionary aspect of these musicals – making the parts infinitely greater than the whole – the plots nonetheless moved at a brisk pace, the performances were full of verve, and the screenplays abrasive and witty. Nor was the Depression ignored, and the effective 'My Forgotten Man' number from **Gold Diggers Of 1933** – which owed much to German expressionism – was one of the rare social comment numbers to emerge from a musical, balanced by the same film's optimistic opening – 'We're In The Money'. The only musical to use the Depression as its central subject matter and not merely as background was **Hallelujah I'm A Bum** (United Artists, 1933) which starred Al Jolson in his first film for over two years. A box-office failure, it consolidated the opinion expressed in the well known Hollywood aphorism that Western Union, not the movies, was for sending messages.

In 1933, RKO, having faced bankruptcy the previous year, found prosperity with two magnificent pairings – Fay Wray and King Kong; and Fred Astaire and Ginger Rogers, the latter dancing together for the first time in **Flying Down To Rio**. This was the first musical in which the immaculate dancing of the performers took precedence over the actual staging of the numbers. And, although the nine films they made together for RKO contained several elaborate set pieces, it was not the spectacle, but the Astaire-Rogers magic the customers paid to see. Knowing they were on to a good thing, RKO hired the best composers, designers and supporting actors to back up their money-making team, and with 'The

Continental' by Con Conrad and Herb Magidson (from **The Gay Divorcee**, 1934) made history by winning the first Oscar to be awarded to a song.

Along with Ginger Rogers, two blondes emerged to dominate the screen: Mae West, seen at her outrageous best in **I'm No Angel** and **She Done Him Wrong** (both Paramount, 1933) until the interfering Hays Code threw a wet blanket over her innuendos and quenched her fire; and Shirley Temple who, at the age of seven, was as old as the musical itself. Four of her films were released in 1934, making her not only a top box-office draw, but an institution.

The marriage of Ernst Lubitsch to **The Merry Widow** (MGM, 1934) was, indeed, an occasion for rejoicing for, despite the lavish production values provided by the studio, it nonetheless managed to retain that delicate and insouciant 'Lubitsch touch' which characterized his best work both before and after the coming of sound. **The Merry Widow** also marked the end of what many consider to be the most interesting part of Jeanette MacDonald's career, when she was the only singer in pictures who could sing with her tongue in her cheek. And although she still retained a certain amount of sauce, albeit diluted with sugar, her profitable eight-operetta partnership with Nelson Eddy (beginning in 1935 with MGM's **Naughty Marietta**) was no longer characterized by sexual innuendo but by sentimentality.

Over at RKO Irving Berlin provided some top drawer songs for Astaire and Rogers's **Top Hat**; at Paramount Rodgers and Hart were doing the same for Bing Crosby in **Mississippi** (1935), while at Warner Bros. the prolific team of Al Dubin and Harry Warren wrote for Al Jolson and his wife Ruby Keeler in **Go Into Your Dance** (1935). Dubin and Warren, two of the greatest of all Hollywood composers, had previously written the score for **Dames** (Warner Bros. 1934), and for **Gold Diggers Of 1935** (Warner Bros. 1935) they supplied the perennial 'Lullaby of Broadway' which, in turn, inspired Busby Berkeley to new heights of invention and creativity in one of the greatest production numbers in the history of the genre. It was Hollywood's golden era as far as the songs written especially for movies were concerned, many of them becoming part of the folklore of popular American music.

RUN-UP TO THE FORTIES

In 1936 MGM offered the world **The Great Ziegfeld**, a sumptuous, no-expense-spared biopic of the legendary showman in which Luise Rainer became the first actress to win an Oscar for a musical. In the same year MGM scored a second time with the joyous **Born to Dance**, which made a star of the stylish tap-dancer, Eleanor Powell.

At Warner Bros. Berkeley continued to create illusions of space and multiple resources with his intricate and fantastical dance routines, but MGM was fast establishing itself as *the* studio for the musical spectacular, and Jack Warner began to lose interest in the genre, concentrating instead on melodramas and non-musical biopics. The last major Warner Bros. musical of the decade was **Gold Diggers Of 1937** (1936), the feeblest of the series, and it was no accident that Berkeley terminated his contract with the studio in 1939 and headed straight for MGM.

A new genre – the animated musical – was created in 1937 with Walt Disney's **Snow White And The Seven Dwarfs** (RKO). Apart from that, there was little that was new or exciting in the Hollywood musical, and its lack of

creative energy cued in its second fall from grace. Except for **Snow White**, the only other innovative musical in 1937 was Mamoulian's **High, Wide And Handsome** (Paramount), a musical western with a Jerome Kern/Oscar Hammerstein II score, which successfully fused the naturalistic with the theatrical.

At MGM Jeanette MacDonald and the doggedly unanimated Nelson Eddy continued their series of operettas with **Maytime** (1937), their most lavish movie yet; and the studio continued along the giant's causeway with **Rosalie** (1937). For RKO, Astaire and Rogers asked the rhetorical question, **Shall We Dance?** (1937) and were answered with a resounding affirmative from their adoring public. But after seven films together, Fred and Ginger developed the seven-film itch and went their separate ways for a while. Astaire made **A Damsel In Distress** (RKO, 1937) with the non-dancing, non-singing Joan Fontaine, while Rogers appeared in three straight films for the studio.

1937 was also the year in which Universal was rescued from the economic doldrums by a new star, Deanna Durbin who, in her debut in **Three Smart Girls**, sang in an appealingly plummy soprano and became everybody's favourite teenage daughter. There had, of course, been child stars before: Shirley Temple, Jane Withers, and boy soprano Bobby Breen. But Miss Durbin was no tiny tot and, with the emergence of Judy Garland, Mickey Rooney and Donald O'Connor, a new phenomenon was born— the teenage star.

Despite the popularity of the movies, radio was the great mass medium in the thirties and forties, and instead of fighting off this heavyweight competitor, Hollywood wisely used it to let the fans see as well as hear their air wave favourites on the screen. Among the most popular entertainers of the late thirties were Jack Benny, Fred Allen, Kenny Baker, Eddie (Rochester) Anderson, Ben Bernie, George Burns and Gracie Allen, Kate Smith, Frances Langford, and ventriloquist Edgar Bergen with his talking doll Charlie McCarthy. These, and many, many others appeared in a multitude of musicals with a radio background, most notably Paramount's successful *Big Broadcast* series, the 1938 edition giving the world Ralph Rainger and Leo Robin's 'Thanks For The Memory' sung by Bob Hope and Shirley Ross. It became Hope's theme song and the title of a non-musical film he made in the same year.

In 1938 Busby Berkeley, with only one year left to go on his contract at Warner Bros., turned **Hollywood Hotel**, based on the popular radio programme of the same name, into a modest but successful musical entertainment that traversed no new territory, but which gave Hollywood its unofficial theme song in the Johnny Mercer/Richard Whiting number, 'Hooray For Hollywood'. Not one radio-inspired musical turned out to be a world-beater, but several of them did contain incidental pleasures, especially when an effective comedy routine or a catchy song surfaced from the dross.

1938 saw the emergence of the 20th Century-Fox big-budget black and white musical with **Alexander's Ragtime Band**, starring Alice Faye and Tyrone Power; while the two major musicals of the year at MGM were **The Great Waltz**, a luxurious biopic of Johann Strauss II, and **Sweethearts**, the first Jeanette MacDonald/Nelson Eddy vehicle in Technicolor. Though all three were box-office successes, it wasn't until **The Wizard Of Oz** (MGM) the following year, that the musical received its much-needed shot in the arm. The first musical masterpiece in Technicolor, it brilliantly integrated sets, costumes, screenplay and score (by Harold Arlen and E.Y. Harburg), featured one of the most popular songs ever to emerge from Hollywood ('Over The Rainbow') and turned 17-year-old Judy Garland into a major star. The same year, songwriter Arthur Freed, who was the assistant producer to Mervyn LeRoy on **Oz**, was given his first assignment as a fully-fledged producer with **Babes In Arms** (MGM), a move which resulted, a few years later, in his becoming the greatest producer of musicals in Hollywood's history.

At 20th Century-Fox, Al Jolson, now at the end of his career, trundled out his old routines for **Rose Of Washington Square** (1939) and for the same year's Stephen Foster biopic, **Swanee River**, in which he played minstrel impresario E.P. Christy. Astaire and Rogers starred in **The Story Of Vernon And Irene Castle** (RKO) then called the whole thing off, giving audiences a ten-year wait for their one-off return in MGM's **The Barkleys Of Broadway** (1949). As the new decade began, that other famous Hollywood pair, Jeanette MacDonald and Nelson Eddy were still singing cheek by jowl in the sweet-sweet **Bitter Sweet** (MGM, 1940) and the old **New Moon** (MGM, 1940); while a brand new team was setting off on the first of several roads – all of which led directly to the bank. Bob Hope, Bing Crosby and sarong girl Dorothy Lamour starred in **Road To Singapore** (Paramount, 1940) and, for the remainder of the decade, continued to convulse audiences from Rio to Morocco. America's 'good neighbour' policy with Latin America found strong support at 20th Century-Fox, who introduced the beguilingly original Carmen Miranda to American audiences in **Down Argentine Way** (1940), and then starred her in **That Night In Rio** (1941) and **Weekend In Havana** (1941).

Busby Berkeley made what turned out to be the best film of his new career at MGM with **Babes On Broadway** (1941) – his third with Judy Garland and Mickey Rooney, and the one in which Garland movingly sang 'Chin Up, Cheerio, Carry On' (by Burton Lane and E.Y. Harburg) to a group of refugee British kids, indicating that at last the Hollywood musical was becoming less isolationist and was beginning to face up to the fact that there was a war on in Europe.

MUSICALS AT WAR
The bombing of Pearl Harbour in 1941 changed everything. From then on, throughout the rest of the war, musicals were not merely decorative, but functioned as an integral part of the war effort. In **Yankee Doodle Dandy** (Warner Bros. 1942) James Cagney whipped up patriotic fervour with George M. Cohan's 'You're A Grand Old Flag', and won an Oscar for his efforts; Bing Crosby sang a tribute to the same banner in **Star-Spangled Rhythm** (Paramount, 1942) and delivered a patriotic oration atop a studio-built Mount Rushmore; while in MGM's **For Me And My Gal** (1942), Gene Kelly became a soldier in World War I and learned to sacrifice his egotism to his country's needs. Most of the major studios helped to boost morale during the war by mustering all the available talent under contract and displaying them in all-star revues such as **Stage Door Canteen** (United Artists, 1943), **Thank Your Lucky Stars** (Warner Bros. 1943) and **Hollywood Canteen** (Warner Bros. 1944).

Irving Berlin's **This Is The Army** (Warner Bros. 1943)

featured real servicemen in its cast; while **Thousands Cheer** (MGM, 1943), with its pin-prick of a plot, staged a grand finale featuring such guest stars as Mickey Rooney, Judy Garland, Lena Horne, Lucille Ball, Eleanor Powell, Red Skelton and Margaret O'Brien. The war years also produced several B-musicals set in munitions factories – which may account for the popularity of such belters as Betty Hutton, Martha Raye and Cass Daley. At least they could be heard through all the din!

As the guns and tanks came off the assembly lines, so musicals slid off the conveyor belts of Hollywood's dream factories in an attempt to satisfy the public's insatiable demand for more and more escapist entertainment. Helping in no small way to alleviate some of the gloom of those war-torn years were The Andrews Sisters, as well as America's big bands. Some of the most popular of these (Tommy Dorsey, Kay Kyser, Harry James, Glenn Miller, Benny Goodman, Jimmy Dorsey, Xavier Cugat) found their way into eight out of ten musicals. America in the forties had caught swing fever and Hollywood was quick to exploit it, despite the generally colourless personalities of the bandleaders themselves. As the decade reached its half-way mark, one was left with the distinct impression that most Americans spent their leisure time in nightclubs listening to band music.

In 1943, Vincente Minnelli made his debut as a film director (thanks to the talent-spotting of Arthur Freed) in MGM's all-black **Cabin In The Sky**. Another all-black offering in the same year was 20th Century-Fox's **Stormy Weather**. Though both were criticized for propagating the negro stereotype, they at least allowed black artists to express themselves more than they would otherwise have been permitted to do in the segregation-conscious movies of the time, and left their mark with such memorable numbers as 'Happiness Is A Thing Called Joe' (by Harold Arlen and E.Y. Harburg) sung by Ethel Waters in **Cabin In The Sky**, and the title number of **Stormy Weather** (by Arlen and Ted Koehler), sung by Lena Horne. In 1944, Minnelli established himself as a major director with the enchanting **Meet Me In St Louis** (MGM), and the same film's leading lady, Judy Garland, graduated from star to superstar.

Original songs were still being written by all the top composers, among the best of the period being Jerome Kern's 'Long Ago And Far Away' from **Cover Girl** (Columbia, 1944), the film that marked Gene Kelly's promotion from hoofer to dancer, and which saw the beginning of the innovative work he would soon be doing at MGM.

In the forties Broadway shows were frequently manhandled by Hollywood. Storylines were changed and the original Broadway scores were ditched in favour of inferior but more 'popular' material. Cole Porter (**Panama Hattie**, MGM, 1942; **Dubarry Was A Lady**, MGM, 1943; **Mexican Hayride**, Universal, 1949), and Kurt Weill (**Knickerbocker Holiday**, United Artists, 1944; **Lady In The Dark**, Paramount, 1944; **One Touch Of Venus**, Universal, 1948) were the hardest-hit victims of the system. Danny Kaye, who had appeared in *Lady in the Dark* on Broadway, and caused a minor sensation in it, made his screen debut for Sam Goldwyn in **Up In Arms** (1944) and achieved instant movie stardom. Betty Grable, who had replaced Alice Faye at 20th Century-Fox, remained the forces' favourite even when the troops were on their way home, appearing in feather-light Technicolor frolics such as **Pin-Up Girl** (1944) and **The**

Dolly Sisters (1945). At MGM, producer Arthur Freed, and his celebrated Freed unit – as his talented production team came to be known – overreached themselves in attempting to explore new frontiers of the musical with a fantasy called **Yolanda And The Thief** (1945). Though the film was a box-office failure, its heart was in the right place and, if nothing else, it pointed the way to the more adventurous MGM musicals of the late forties and early fifties.

POST-WAR PRODUCTIONS
By 1946 Al Jolson was considered a has-been. But he came to the rescue of an ailing studio in the shape of Larry Parks, who himself became a major star, albeit a short-lived one – thanks to McCarthyism – after the release of Columbia's **The Jolson Story** – one of the most popular of all biopics. Nineteen years after Jolson's first words on the screen were the last words in modernity, his voice was again heard by a whole new generation for, though Parks acted the role, the musical soundtrack was dubbed entirely by Jolson.

Biopics of composers or musical performers continued to proliferate in the forties and, in most cases, were little more than a feeble excuse for a series of song and dance numbers which often lacked an appropriate sense of period; and although the music was generally distinguished, the lives depicted were almost interchangeable, most of them adopting a clichéd, rags-to-riches format, and often mercilessly bending or distorting the facts. After Gershwin in **Rhapsody In Blue** (Warner Bros. 1945), other major composers to receive the biopic treatment were Cole Porter in the lamentable **Night And Day** (Warner Bros. 1946), Jerome Kern in the lavish **Till The Clouds Roll By** (MGM, 1946) and Richard Rodgers and Lorenz Hart in the ludicrous **Words And Music** (MGM, 1948). Porter was able to see himself portrayed by Cary Grant but Kern had died the previous year shortly after completing his score for 20th Century-Fox's **Centennial Summer**.

In **Holiday In Mexico** (MGM, 1946), another contribution to Hollywood's 'good neighbour' policy, producer Joseph Pasternak – who had master-minded the career of Deanna Durbin at Universal in the thirties – starred his latest nightingale, Jane Powell. Most of Pasternak's musicals for MGM were sweet, naive and thoroughly conventional, usually featuring nubile young sopranos such as Powell, Ann Blyth and Kathryn Grayson. He also seemed to have a penchant for films with numbers in their titles and came up with no fewer than twelve of them, including **One Hundred Men And A Girl** (Universal, 1937), **Thousands Cheer** (MGM, 1943), **Music For Millions** (MGM, 1944) and **Ten Thousand Bedrooms** (MGM 1957).

In 1947, as the spectre of television began to loom large over film production, the musical once again suffered a decline – both in quality and quantity. There was no news in 1947, except **Good News** (MGM), a remake of the 1930 campus musical, and the only song and dance show of any consequence. It starred June Allyson and Peter Lawford and marked the directorial debut of Charles Walters, who hitherto had functioned only as a choreographer. An integral member of the Arthur Freed unit, Walters, like Stanley Donen, Vincente Minnelli, George Sidney, Robert Alton, Roger Edens and Gene Kelly, helped impart to the MGM musical its distinctive style and 'look'.

The major new face of 1948 was the all-American girl next door, Doris Day, a band singer who rocketed to stardom after her first movie, **Romance On The High Seas** (Warner Bros.). But it was Rouben Mamoulian with **Summer Holiday** (MGM), a musical version of Eugene O'Neill's *Ah Wilderness!*, and Vincente Minnelli with **The Pirate** (MGM), adapted from the Broadway play by S.N. Behrman, who created the most interesting work of the year. Neither film was a commercial success, and both were artistically flawed. But at least, like the ill-fated **Yolanda And The Thief**, they took risks.

In 1948, Gene Kelly, who had partnered Judy Garland in **The Pirate** and danced through the non-musical **The Three Musketeers** (MGM, 1948), broke an ankle playing volley ball and persuaded Fred Astaire to take over his role in **Easter Parade** (MGM) opposite Garland. It was like asking a tenor to replace a baritone, yet, despite the stylistic disparity between the two dancers, director Charles Walters and choreographer Robert Alton made it work.

As the decade drew to an end, TV's continuing grip on audiences resulted in a sharp decline in cinema attendances. The situation was aggravated by the McCarthy communist witch-hunts which did nothing to help the prestige of an industry already humiliated by TV, and battered about the ears by numerous economic upheavals within the movie colony itself. In looking back to a less turbulent period of its past, a wave of nostalgic musicals inundated the screen: **Look For The Silver Lining** (Warner Bros. 1949), **Oh You Beautiful Doll** (20th Century-Fox, 1949), **In The Good Old Summertime** (MGM, 1949), and **Take Me Out To The Ball Game** (MGM, 1949), to name a few. As a final bow to remembrance of things past, Astaire and Rogers danced for the last time together in **The Barkleys Of Broadway** (MGM, 1949). A notable exception to this nostalgic trend, and one of the epoch-making Hollywood musicals, was **On The Town** (MGM, 1949) directed – partially on location in New York – by Gene Kelly and Stanley Donen, with choreography by Kelly.

INTO THE FIFTIES
The musicals of 1950 weren't exactly characterized by originality. 20th Century-Fox churned out the same old fluff for Betty Grable (**Wabash Avenue**, a remake of the same studio's **Coney Island**, 1943, that had also starred Grable; and **My Blue Heaven**), and June Haver (**I'll Get By**); while Warner Bros. continued with their series of nostalgic sweet nothings whose titles were borrowed from popular songs (Universal had done the same thing throughout the forties), and whose stars were that rhyming couple, Doris Day and Gordon MacRae. Their films included **Tea For Two** (1950), **On Moonlight Bay** (1951), **Lullaby Of Broadway** (1951) and **By The Light Of The Silvery Moon** (1953). In 1950 Betty Hutton, on loan to MGM from Paramount, stepped in to play the title role in **Annie Get Your Gun** after Judy Garland was fired from the production, and gave it everything she had. But for most people, Hutton, like The Andrews Sisters, will mainly be remembered as a typical product of the forties.

Summer Stock (1950) – a 'let's put on a show' anachronism – turned out to be Judy Garland's last film for MGM. Charles Walters directed it, and although it was beset with production problems, it contained one of the best numbers Garland ever committed to film – Harold Arlen and Ted Koehler's 'Get Happy'. Though Gene Kelly had one excellent solo in **Summer Stock**, it was a retrograde step for him, coming so soon after his more innovative work. The other great male dancer, Fred Astaire, was still on top in 1950, and after accepting an Oscar in 1949 for 'raising the standard of screen musicals' co-starred with Red Skelton and Vera-Ellen in the delightful **Three Little Words** (MGM), a biopic based on the lives of songwriters Burt Kalmar and Harry Ruby, in which he played Kalmar.

In 1950, MGM began to reap the benefits of their latest discovery, Mario Lanza, whose teaming with Kathryn Grayson in **That Midnight Kiss** (1949) and **The Toast Of New Orleans** (1950) spelled box-office dynamite. And if the public believed Lanza to be a great opera singer, that didn't worry MGM one bit. On the contrary, they encouraged this belief by casting him in and as **The Great Caruso** (1951), one of the most successful biopics of the fifties.

Despite the colourful George Sidney remake of **Showboat** (1951), and Astaire's dancing on the ceiling in Stanley Donen's solo directorial debut, **Royal Wedding** (MGM), the best musical of 1951 was Vincente Minnelli's **An American In Paris** (MGM), which was itself overtaken the following year by **Singin' In The Rain** (MGM), another Kelly-Donen collaboration and the pinnacle of the genre. After that, the musical went into another decline. Warner Bros. went back to square one with their impoverished remake of **The Jazz Singer** (1952). MGM, in turn, remade a not-so-merry **Merry Widow** (1952) as well as the RKO 1934 release **Roberta**, this time calling it **Lovely To Look At** (1952). The hey-day was over, and while **Singin' In The Rain** miraculously managed to fuse the past with the present, most of the other attempts to recapture the musical's first early rapture were anaemic failures. Yet, though there were to be fewer and fewer musicals over the next twenty years, some masterpieces were still to come. Minnelli's **The Band Wagon** (MGM, 1953) was one of them, giving Fred Astaire the most challenging role of his long and distinguished career. In **Gentlemen Prefer Blondes** (20th Century-Fox, 1953) directed by Howard Hawks, Marilyn Monroe became a major musical star and forever immortalized the dictum that 'Diamonds Are A Girl's Best Friend'. The latest in a long line of Fox blondes, her quality was incandescent and this film brought out the best in her. Its success, as well as that of **Kiss Me Kate** (MGM, 1953) and **Call Me Madam** (20th Century-Fox), sounded the death knell for the original screen musical and helped clear a path for the arrival of one Broadway import after another.

But the shape of things to come was also a large rectangle. CinemaScope made its appearance in 1953 and swallowed up anything approaching taste and charm. At first the giant screen was filled with Demetrius and thousands of gladiators, as well as with Richard and his Crusaders and King Arthur and his Knights. But the musical did not escape for long, and it suffered in the new process in much the same way that a play conceived for a proscenium arch suffers on an open stage. A remake of **Rose Marie** (MGM, 1954) was the first victim of the distorting lens, whose wide-open spaces not even Busby Berkeley could adequately fill. Sigmund Romberg's **The Student Prince**, (MGM, 1954), directed by Richard Thorpe and with an oversized Mario Lanza lending his oversized voice to the mini-talented Edmund Purdom (as the Prince) fared marginally better than Friml's heroine, but **Jupiter's Darling** (MGM, 1954) with Esther Williams

and Howard Keel, and **Lucky Me** (Warner Bros. 1954) were disasters.

Paramount had its own wide-screen technique – the less obtrusive Vistavision – and it was seen to good advantage in Irving Berlin's **White Christmas** (1954), a sort of **Holiday Inn** (Paramount, 1942) revisited.

Two directors, however, managed to make a positive virtue out of the long, narrow strip in which they were forced to operate: Stanley Donen in the exuberant **Seven Brides For Seven Brothers** (1954), choreographed by Michael Kidd; and George Cukor in the first remake of **A Star Is Born** (Warner Bros. 1954) – which, with **Singin' In The Rain**, must rank as one of the supreme achievements of the genre. Judy Garland was its star and, like the lady in the Stephen Sondheim song from 'Follies' she could, after its successful release, triumphantly proclaim, 'I'm Still Here!'

1954 saw two more musical biopics: Stanley Donen's entertaining but inaccurate **Deep In My Heart** (MGM, 1954) in which most of the musical stars still under contract to the studio were trotted out in the service of the show's subject, Sigmund Romberg (played by Jose Ferrer); and the altogether more impressive **The Glenn Miller Story** (Universal-International), Anthony Mann's moving tribute to one of America's best-loved band leaders. James Stewart and June Allyson starred.

The year ended with Irving Berlin's **There's No Business Like Show Business** (20th Century-Fox), a quintessential backstage story which filled the CinemaScope screen with the starry presences of Ethel Merman, Dan Dailey, Marilyn Monroe, Johnnie Ray, Donald O'Connor and Mitzi Gaynor.

Broadway shows began to infiltrate Hollywood in earnest in 1955 with **Brigadoon** (MGM), **Kismet** (MGM), **Guys And Dolls** (A Sam Goldwyn Production released by MGM), **Hit The Deck** (MGM) and **Oklahoma!** (20th Century-Fox). But, as usual, it was an original that emerged as the best musical of the year: Gene Kelly and Stanley Donen's **It's Always Fair Weather** (MGM), with a sparkling screenplay by Betty Comden and Adolph Green (who also wrote the lyrics) and a score to match by André Previn. The film took a few satirical swipes at television, but today television gets its revenge by lopping off a third of the wide-screen image. The following year several more Broadway shows reached the screen, the best being Rodgers and Hammerstein's **Carousel** and **The King And I** (20th Century-Fox), and Cole Porter's **Silk Stockings** (MGM) in which Cyd Charisse again proved she was Fred Astaire's best partner since Ginger Rogers. The stylish direction was by Rouben Mamoulian, whose last film it was.

1956 was also the year in which the movies and the world of popular music was revolutionized by the advent of rock 'n' roll – the first being Columbia's **Rock Around The Clock** which starred Bill Haley and His Comets. Elvis Presley – Hollywood's latest money-making acquisition – launched his career in 1956 with **Love Me Tender** (20th Century-Fox), his contribution to the rock scene the following year being the popular and profitable **Jailhouse Rock** (MGM). Only Frank Tashlin's **The Girl Can't Help It** (20th Century-Fox) starring the studio's latest blonde, Jayne Mansfield, demonstrated that rock and a sense of humour could co-exist in the same frame.

It was, however, another Broadway import, **The Pajama Game** (Warner Bros.) directed by Stanley Donen and with Doris Day heading the cast, that saved 1957 from hitting rock bottom where its musicals were concerned. Not since 1931 had there been a year quite like it.

1958 saw even fewer musicals than 1957 – but among them was one of the best of the decade – Vincente Minnelli's enchanting **Gigi** (MGM), based on the novel by Colette, and with book and lyrics by Alan Jay Lerner and a rapturous score by Frederick Loewe. Leslie Caron, Louis Jourdan, Maurice Chevalier and Hermione Gingold starred – and, at a stroke, one's flagging faith in the screen musical was revived. The year's other major musical was Rodgers and Hammerstein's **South Pacific** (20th Century-Fox), directed with altogether too heavy a hand by Joshua Logan.

SIXTIES, SEVENTIES AND SO ON

In 1961, **West Side Story** reached Hollywood via United Artists, and despite a clash of intentions between directors Jerome Robbins and Robert Wise, was one of the most effective of all Broadway imports, and far superior to the previous year's leaden **Can-Can** (20th Century-Fox), or Vincente Minnelli's pleasant, but not particularly resourceful handling of the Judy Holliday showcase **Bells Are Ringing** (MGM, 1960).

By 1962 rock 'n' roll was *passé*, the current craze being the twist, and we were now invited to **Twist Around The Clock** (Columbia).

But 1962 offered some weightier musicals as well, with Broadway's **Gypsy** and **The Music Man** reaching the screen via Warner Bros. and with admirable fidelity to the original shows. All the same, the Hollywood musical had now become something it had never been before (except, possibly, for a brief moment in its infancy): a Broadway parasite.

Billy Rose's Jumbo (MGM, 1962), a stage hit from 1935, saw the end of Busby Berkeley's movie career. He was the second unit director, but his personal imprint on the sequences he directed was unmistakeable. 1962 also saw the end of the Crosby/Hope 'road' shows with **Road To Hong Kong** released, not by Paramount, but by United Artists, and with Joan Collins in the role usually played by Dorothy Lamour, though Lamour was also in it. It was a lamentable experience, as was the undistinguished end to Judy Garland's exciting up-and-down career in the British-made, and optimistically titled, **I Could Go On Singing** (United Artists, 1963).

The next few years offered very little to sing about. Elvis Presley swivelled his hips through a cycle of innocuous vehicles – some better than others – and there were the usual Broadway imports, the best being the Warner Bros. production of Lerner and Loewe's **My Fair Lady** (1964) directed by George Cukor. Twist gave way to a series of equally inane 'beach party' musicals from American International, aimed largely at the teenage market, teenagers having become a viable economic force in the sixties, and a major part of the ticket-buying public.

In 1964, Julie Andrews became the second woman to win a Best Actress Oscar in a musical for her work in Walt Disney's **Mary Poppins** (Buena Vista) and, overnight, became the new superstar Hollywood had been waiting for. The following year she scaled ever greater heights of stardom with her appealing performance in the saccharine but extremely successful screen adaptation of Rodgers and Hammerstein's long-running Broadway hit, **The Sound Of Music** (20th Century-Fox), one of the most profitable films in Hollywood's history.

As a direct result of the monumental box-office returns of **The Sound Of Music**, 20th Century-Fox invested heavily in two more big-budget musicals: **Dr. Dolittle** (1967) with Rex Harrison; and **Star!** (1968), a biopic of the late Gertrude Lawrence and another starring vehicle for Julie Andrews. Both lost millions.

In 1967 Julie Andrews appeared for Universal in **Thoroughly Modern Millie**, a lavishly produced twenties romp which more than recouped its costs. But it was the failure of **Star!** (even a shortened, re-edited version called **Those Were The Happy Times** failed to find a public) coupled with the disastrous **Darling Lili** (Paramount, 1970) which she made for her director husband Blake Edwards, that exacerbated her decline in popularity; a decline which coincided with the spectacular rise of Barbra Streisand.

After her award-winning debut as Fanny Brice in William Wyler's **Funny Girl** (Columbia, 1968)—first seen as a Broadway musical in 1964, also starring Streisand— Hollywood's latest superstar was soon being directed by two giants of the genre: Gene Kelly in **Hello Dolly!** (20th Century-Fox, 1969) and Vincente Minnelli in **On A Clear Day You Can See Forever** (Paramount, 1969) – both via Broadway.

The only other star to equal Streisand, if not quite in popularity, then certainly in talent, was Liza Minnelli, the daughter of Vincente Minnelli and Judy Garland, whose Oscar-winning performance in Bob Fosse's stunningly directed screen translation of the Broadway hit **Cabaret** was the quintessence of star quality.

In 1970, **Woodstock** (Warner Bros.) ushered in a decade of documentary musicals and filmed pop concerts such as **Elvis, That's The Way It Is** (MGM, 1970), **Gimme Shelter** (Cinema V), **The Song Remains The Same** (Warner Bros. 1972) and **Medicine Ball Caravan** (Warner Bros. 1974) to name only a handful. Broadway blockbusters such as **Fiddler On The Roof** (United Artists, 1971), **Man Of La Mancha** (United Artists, 1972), **1776** (Columbia, 1972), **Jesus Christ Superstar** (Universal, 1973), **Mame** (Warner Bros. 1974) and **The Wiz** (Paramount, 1979) also dominated the scene, though on balance it was not a great decade for musicals. One notable exception was Bob Fosse's vastly restructured **Cabaret** (Allied Artists, 1972). Other oases in the wastelands of the genre were the Streisand remake of **A Star Is Born** (Warner Bros., 1976), Martin Scorcese's **New York, New York** (United Artists, 1977), Bette Midler in **The Rose** (20th Century-Fox, 1979) and Fosse's indulgent but visually stunning **All That Jazz** (Columbia, 1979).

In 1974, MGM produced a lavish compilation film comprising scores of clips from its past musical glories and called – simply and aptly – **That's Entertainment**. A sequel followed in 1976, and both films served to remind us, with their evocation of the thirties, forties and fifties, that things ain't what they used to be. The enthusiastic public response to these bumper compendiums of nostalgia perhaps augurs well for the future of the screen musical in which new generations are beginning to take an interest. As the eighties get under way, the future of the film musical is uncertain, and one hopes that, as has always been the case in the past, the genre will continue to be served, rescued and revivified by new creative talent. For – as the ads for **That's Entertainment** so succinctly put it—'Boy, do we need it now!'.

1927/8

Academy Awards

Writing (Adaptation)
NOMINATIONS INCLUDED: *The Jazz Singer* (WB)
Alfred Cohn

Engineering Effects
(Award not given after this year)
The Jazz Singer Nugent Slaughter

Special Awards
Warner Bros. for producing *The Jazz Singer*,
the outstanding pioneer talking picture
which revolutionised the industry.
(statuette)

Following the success of their *Don Juan* on 6 August 1926 – which starred John Barrymore and was the first feature film to use the Vitaphone sound-on-disc system – Warner Bros. decided to take a gamble on a feature in which the characters actually spoke and sang. In reality it was a calculated risk for, despite the success of *Don Juan* (which had a specially commissioned score by William Axt, appropriate sound effects, but no dialogue), the studio was on the verge of bankruptcy anyway; and without a blockbuster to help turn the tide of their declining fortunes, the four Warners – Sam, Jack, Harry and Albert – fully realized that the last reel of their careers as movie moguls was fast unspooling, and that it would only be a matter of time before The End appeared. So they sank everything they had into a property called **The Jazz Singer** whose author, Samson

Raphaelson, had first written it as a short story called *The Day of Atonement*, then turned it into a successful stage vehicle for George Jessel. The story of Jakie Rabinowitz, a cantor's son torn between a life in the theatre and a life in the synagogue, it struck the Warners as the perfect subject with which to launch the first 'talker', as it was to become known in the industry. Its star would be George Jessel, who had already appeared for the brothers in a silent called *Private Izzy Murphy* (1926), and whose impact as Jakie Rabinowitz was the talk of Broadway. But when Jessel realized that songs were to be added, he doubled his initial fee and was turned down flat. In an attempt to salvage the situation, Jack Warner offered the role to Eddie Cantor but, fearing the adverse effect on his career should the 'experiment' fail, Cantor refused it. Rather than return to Jessel and pay what he had asked, the brothers decided to approach the man they considered to be the greatest entertainer in the world: Al Jolson. Jolson accepted, and the salary negotiated was $75,000, a third to be paid in cash, the rest in weekly instalments of $6,250, a proportion of which would be reinvested in the picture in order to earn Jolson a percentage of the profits. It was a brilliant piece of casting, endorsed by the wildly enthusiastic cheers of everyone present at the film's historic premiere on 6 October 1927. Though the narrative of **The Jazz Singer** was undiluted *schmaltz* from start to finish, director Alan Crosland, by taking his

cameras on location into the predominantly Jewish areas of New York's lower East Side, managed to convey an accurate picture of ghetto life and, ethnically, offered a fascinating glimpse of a community of aliens desperately trying to assimilate themselves into a new society while, at the same time, clinging fervently to their Middle-European traditions. The contrast between life on Hester and Orchard streets, and life on Broadway, was equally marked. As Jakie Jolson was tremendous, and his singing of 'Toot Toot Tootsie Goodbye' by Gus Kahn, Ernie Erdman and Dan Russo, and of 'Mammy' by Sam Lewis, Joe Young and Walter Donaldson, which he performed in blackface (left), allowed audiences hitherto denied the chance to see for themselves, why Jolson was considered to be the greatest performer in the world. His tremendous personality was also evident in the one major dialogue scene: an ad-libbed conversation with his mother (Eugenie Besserer, right) as he sits at the piano in their humble home demonstrating (to Irving Berlin's 'Blue Skies') what 'jazz' is all about. The scene is interrupted by the sudden appearance of Cantor Rabinowitz (Warner Oland) with just one word: 'Stop!' After that the film becomes silent again until Jolson's next song. May McAvoy was cast as Mary Dale, the showgirl in Jakie's life, with other roles going to Otto Lederer, Bobby Gordon (Jakie at 13), Richard Tucker, Nat Carr, William Demarest, Anders Randolf, Will Walling, Roscoe Karns, Myrna Loy (as a chorus girl), and Cantor Joseff Rosenblatt who, as himself, sang the Jewish 'Yahrzeit'. The holy 'Kol Nidre', sung in synagogues on the eve of The Day of Atonement, was featured twice, 'sung' once by Jolson and once by Oland but, on both occasions, with the voices dubbed. Alfred A. Cohn adapted Raphaelson's play for the screen, and the titles ('God made her a woman and love made her a mother!') were by Jack Jarmuth. The film grossed $3,500,000. Other songs: *My Gal Sal* (Bobby Gordon) Paul Dresser; *Waiting For The Robert E. Lee* L. Wolfe Gilbert, Lewis E. Muir; *Dirty Hands, Dirty Face* (Jolson) Edgar Leslie, Grant Clarke, Jolson, James V. Monaco; *Mother, I Still Have You* (Jolson) Jolson, Louis Silvers. By some terrible irony of fate, none of the four Warner brothers was able to attend the New York premiere of **The Jazz Singer**. Sam Warner, the brother most instrumental in pioneering sound, died of a sinus infection (the result of a broken nose suffered years earlier), on 5 October 1927 – one day before the premiere, and after six operations undertaken in an attempt to save his life. Harry, Albert and Jack Warner immediately took a train to Los Angeles to be in time for the funeral on 9 October.

Fanny Brice made her movie debut in **My Man** (1928), a part-talkie, and the only film she made for Warner Bros. She played a Broadway hopeful who, *en route* to the Great White Way, has an unfulfilling love affair with Guinn Williams (an elastic exerciser in a shop window). The romance might have worked had her selfish sister (Edna Murphy) not wooed him away from her just as the couple were about to be married. Andre De Segurola appeared as the Broadway producer responsible for removing Miss Brice (illustrated) from her unhappy private life and introducing her into the world of the footlights, with other roles under Archie Mayo's tentative direction going to Richard Tucker, Billy Seay, Arthur Hoyt, Ann Brody and Clarissa Selwynne. They, however, were all overshadowed by Miss Brice, whose way with a song (such as 'My Man', an English adaptation by Channing Pollock from Maurice Yvain's French ballad 'Mon Homme'), or a funny sketch (such as 'Mrs Cohen At The Beach') was the only
▽

reason for putting up with a rather novelettish story by Mark Canfield (alias Darryl F. Zanuck), which Robert Lord adapted and Joe Jackson scripted. Other songs: *Second Hand Rose* Grant Clarke, James Hanley; *If You Want A Rainbow (You Must Have The Rain)* Billy Rose, Mort Dixon, Oscar Levant; *I'm An Indian* Blanche Merrill, Leo Edwards; *I Was A Florodora Baby* Ballard MacDonald, Harry Carroll; *I'd Rather Be Blue* Billy Rose, Fred Fisher.

△

Until the arrival in 1939 of *Gone With The Wind* (Selznick International), the most financially successful sound picture in Hollywood's history was **The Singing Fool** (1928), Al Jolson's second part-talkie for Warner Bros. Even more sentimental in its story than *The Jazz Singer*, Jolson, in an extremely self-congratulatory piece of acting, starred as a singer-composer who not only loses his wife (a singularly unanimated performance from Josephine Dunn), but also his adored little Sonny Boy (Davey Lee, seen here on Jolson's lap). He is comforted in his grief and misery by cigarette girl Betty Bronson, whose genuine concern for his well-being helps him to face life afresh. The team of Buddy De Sylva, Lew Brown and Ray Henderson supplied their star with three enormous song hits including 'Sonny Boy', a lachrymose little item which Jolson sang at his ailing son's deathbed and which, allegedly, was written in jest by the composers who simply could not take such a blatant attack on the tear ducts seriously. Whatever the circumstances surrounding the song's creation might have been, its recording sold over three million copies, making it the number one pop song of its time. Jolson received $150,000 for his work on the film, and the three Warner brothers reaped profits in excess of $4,000,000. C. Graham Baker's scenario (from a story by Leslie S. Barrows) allowed Jolson to appear at times in blackface, and also gave parts to Reed Howes, Edward Martindel, Arthur Housman and Robert Emmett O'Connor. The tear-jerking direction was by Lloyd Bacon. Other songs: *It All Depends On You; I'm Sittin' On Top Of The World* Sam Lewis, Joe Young, Henderson; *There's A Rainbow Round My Shoulder* Billy Rose, Jolson, Dave Dreyer; *Keep Smiling At Trouble* De Sylva, Lewis Gensler; *Golden Gate* Maurice Rubens, Nat and Max Lief; *The Spaniard Who Blighted My Life* Billy Merson (all sung by Jolson).

1929

Academy Awards

Best Picture
The Broadway Melody (MGM) produced by
Harry Rapf
NOMINATIONS INCLUDED: *The Hollywood Revue*
(MGM) produced by Harry Rapf

Direction
NOMINATIONS INCLUDED: Harry Beaumont
The Broadway Melody

Art Direction
NOMINATIONS INCLUDED: *The Hollywood Revue*
Cedric Gibbons

The New York Times Annual 'Ten Best'
1st *The Love Parade* (Paramount). 3rd
Hallelujah (MGM). 10th *Sally* (First National).

With **The Broadway Melody** (MGM), produced
by Lawrence Weingarten and premiered at
Grauman's Chinese Theatre in Hollywood on 1
February 1929, the movie musical was spectacularly launched. The first of the all-talking, all-singing, all-dancing entertainments to revolutionize the industry (and which, for the next
two years, would proliferate until, by the end of
1930, they had sung and danced their way out of
favour), it was an impressive achievement for
MGM, whose skilled technicians showed the rest
of Hollywood that with a bit of ingenuity and
imagination, the cumbersome sound equipment
so restricting to directors weaned on the man-oeuverability of the silent camera, need not be
the millstone to creativity which it was generally considered to be. Originally conceived by
director Harry Beaumont and scenarist Edmund

Goulding as a loosely disguised biopic of the
Duncan Sisters, the storyline of **The Broadway
Melody** changed direction as it was developed
(Norman Houston and James Gleason wrote the
dialogue), and became the backstage saga – a
springboard which would be used for the stories
of countless musicals to come – of a vaudeville
sister act and the romantic entanglements that
beset it. The movie starred Anita Page (right)
and Bessie Love (left), with Miss Love delivering
a brave, highly-charged performance as the
sister who loses her stage partner as well as the
man she loves. Miss Love's emoting re-instated
her as a star, but she never again did anything as
impressive in her career. Charles King (centre)
was the man she loses to her sister, with Jed
Prouty, Kenneth Thomson, Edward Dillon,
Mary Doran and singer James Burroughs excellent in support. Arthur Freed (later to make such
an indelible mark on MGM as their top producer
of musicals) and Nacio Herb Brown, a pair of
West Coast songwriters, were signed to compose
the score – the first ever to be conceived and
written especially for the screen – and they came
up with a forty-carat stunner which included, of
course, the catchy title song which they themselves appeared on screen to demonstrate, and
which the studio would reprise several more
times in its history, and which would lend its
name to a popular series of musical extravaganzas starring Eleanor Powell in the following
decade. Charles King was fortunate enough to
get the best of the score, including the title song
which he warbled on three different occasions,
and the melodious 'You Were Meant For Me',
while the Misses Page and Love were seen at their
best in 'Harmony Babies'. Other songs included
The Wedding Of The Painted Doll, used in a
Technicolor production number; a second number for the two leading ladies called *The Boy
Friend*; *Love Boat* (Burroughs and chorus); *Truthful Parson Brown* by Willard Robinson, performed
by The Biltmore Trio and Orchestra, and George
M. Cohan's famous *Give My Regards To Broadway*,
also heard on screen for the first time (in a
fragment over the credits).

Though black actor Stepin Fetchit (illustrated)
was outstanding in **Hearts In Dixie**
(Fox) playing a lazy, work-shy layabout in a
poor Negro cotton community shortly after the
Civil War, there was a lot else to admire in
producer-director Paul Sloane's technically proficient, dramatically touching tale of the sacrifice a father (Clarence Muse) makes to ensure
the education of his son (Eugene Jackson). The
naturalness of the performances – especially as
the majority of the cast (all black except for
Richard Carlyle as a physician) had never before
appeared in a talkie – as well as the expressiveness of the direction and skilful manipulation of
the camera, were striking. Sloane's use of music,
mainly traditional Negro spirituals, revealed a
genuinely creative feeling for the medium in
general and musicals in particular, and he never
allowed the music to impose on the narrative
unless it made a specific point. The result was a
prestigious triumph for William Fox and his
team, and a delightful and touching contribution to the art of the Hollywood musical. It
was photographed by Glen Williams, written by
Walter Weems and choreographed by Fanchon
and Marco. Also cast: Bernice Pilot, Clifford
Ingram, Mildred Washington, Zack Williams
and Gertrude Howard. There was an original
title song by Howard Jackson, who also did the
scoring for the film.

Lucky In Love (Pathe), a vapid comedy with
songs, was particularly deficient in the leading
man department. For, as played by Morton
Downey (left), the hero of Gene Markey's screenplay – an American stable boy in love with the
granddaughter of an Irish earl – was a monumental bore, unworthy of his sweetheart's affections or of the audience's concern. Betty Lawford
was the object of Downey's desires; and the
villain of the piece, complete with *East Lynne*
moustache, was Colin Keith-Johnston. Also cast
were Halliwell Hobbes as the Earl, J.M. Kerrigan,
Edward McNamara, Richard Taber and Edward
O'Connor. It was directed by Kenneth Webb and
supervised by Robert Kane. Songs: *Love Is A
Dreamer*; *For The Likes O' You And Me*; *When They
Sing 'The Wearing Of The Green' In Syncopated
Blues* Bud Green, Sammy Stept.

Giving a performance that fell mid-way between George M. Cohan and Al Jolson, in a film that had more than a passing similarity to *The Jazz Singer* (Warner Bros. 1927), George Jessel (left), star of **Lucky Boy** (Tiffany-Stahl) was unable to impart to this Norman Taurog-Charles C. Wilson directed comedy the kiss of life that it so desperately needed. Lacking a freshness of approach both in execution and content, the story (by Viola Brothers Shore, dialogue by Jessel) of a Jewish jeweler's son's attempts to become a Broadway star against the wishes of his family, just refused to play. The fact that it was basically a silent film with dialogue and music sequences added to it, didn't help matters either, although there was a generous helping of songs. Rosa Rosanova (right) and William Strauss were Jessel's parents; Margaret Quimby and Mary Doran the women in his life. Songs: *Lucky Boy*; *My Mother's Eyes* L. Wolfe Gilbert, Abel Baer; *Old Man Sunshine*; *My Real Sweetheart*; *In My Bouquet Of Memories* Sam M. Lewis, Joe Young, Harry Akst; *My Blackbirds Are Bluebirds Now* Irving Caesar, Cliff Friend; *California Here I Come* Al Jolson, B.G. De Sylva, Joseph Meyer.

▽

Whether or not it was due to the unsympathetic ▷ nature of the role he played (a composer who shamelessly uses his friends and lovers to further his career), leading man Charles Kaley (centre) made a hasty exit from feature films after **Lord Byron of Broadway** (MGM) was released. Another casualty was his leading lady, Ethelind Terry, whose complete misuse of the medium, both vocally and physically, resulted in an equally hasty departure back to Broadway whence she had come. With the central roles so unappealingly cast, and a story (from the novel by Nell Martin, dialogue by Crane Wilbur and Willard Mack) of only minimal interest, **Lord Byron of Broadway** didn't stand a chance at the box office despite an Arthur Freed-Nacio Herb Brown score which included 'A Bundle Of Old Love Letters' and 'Should I'. Technicolor was used in two sequences: Dimitri Tiomkin's 'Blue Daughter Of Heaven', sung off-screen by James Burroughs, and complete with overhead shots a year before Busby Berkeley's *Whoopee*; and for a fantasy item called 'The Woman In The Shoe'. Sammy Lee was the dance director, with Albertina Rasch in charge of the Tiomkin ballet sequence; and the film was directed by William Nigh and Harry Beaumont. Also cast were Marion Shilling (left), Cliff Edwards (right), Gwen Lee, Benny Rubin, Drew Demarest and John Byron. Other songs: *Only Love Is Real*; *When I Met You*; *You're The Bride And I'm The Groom* Freed, Brown; *Love Ain't Nothing But The Blues* Joe Goodwin, Louis Alter.

△

Syncopation (RKO) was very much in step with the current vogue of backstage musicals, and traversed no new territory in the recounting of its oh-so-familiar tale of a husband and wife vaudeville act that breaks up because one partner is dissatisfied with something or other. In this instance it was the wife who outgrows her unsophisticated husband – but only temporarily. By the final fade they're together again, both privately and professionally. Barbara Bennett (left) and Bobby Watson were top-starred, with Ian Hunter (as the man Miss B. almost leaves Bobby for), Morton Downey (right), Osgood Perkins (father of Anthony), Mackenzie Ward, Verree Teasdale, Dorothy Lee and, best of all, Fred Waring and His Pennsylvanians – whose 'Tin Pan Parade' was a high spot in a film not endowed with an abundance of them – completing the cast. Robert Kane produced, Bert Glennon directed and the screenplay was an adaptation by Frances Agnew of Gene Markey's novel *Stepping High*. Songs: *Jericho* Leo Robin, Richard Myers; *Mine Alone* Herman Ruby, Myers; *Do Something*; *I'll Always Be In Love With You* Bud Green, Sammy Stept, Ruby.

◁

Another backstage story, **Close Harmony** (Paramount) starred a versatile Charles 'Buddy' Rogers as a warehouse clerk-cum-bandleader who, through the determined conniving of chorus girl Nancy Carroll (making her musical debut), is given the opportunity to hit the big time with his band. The plot had little going for it, but with Rogers doing all that could humanly be expected of a musical comedy star, and then some, it didn't seem to matter at all. John V.A. Weaver and Percy Heath's screenplay (story by Elsie Janis and Gene Markey) propped up the narrative's carbon-copy situations with a fair quota of gags; and with Jack Oakie (right) and Richard 'Skeets' Gallagher (left) on hand as a singing team called Barney and Bay, audiences went home happy. Also featured were Jesse Stafford and His Orchestra, Matty Roubert, Ricca Allen, Wade Boteler, Baby Mack, Oscar Smith, Greta Granstedt, Harry Green, and Gus Partos. It was directed by John Cromwell and Edward Sutherland. Songs: *She's So I Dunno*; *I Want To Go Places And Do Things*; *I'm All A-Twitter, I'm All A-Twirl* Richard A. Whiting, Leo Robin; *Twelfth Street Rag* Euday L. Bowman, Spencer Williams.

Coincidence took pride of place in the screenplay which Frances Agnew, Eddie Dowling and George J. Crone fashioned for **The Rainbow Man** (Sono Art/Paramount), a vehicle for Eddie Dowling which was heavily reminiscent of Al Jolson's *The Singing Fool* (Warner Bros., 1928), but not nearly as financially successful. Dowling (centre) played a minstrel man called Rainbow Riley who, after the death of an acrobat friend, adopts his son Billy, then falls in love with Mary, a hotel keeper's daughter, only to discover that Mary's dead sister was none other than little Billy's late mother! Too maudlin by half, this overtly sentimental *ragôut* was just about made palatable by the engaging presence of Marian Nixon who, as Mary, was alone in bringing a patina of credibility to the screenplay that the rest of the cast, including Dowling, were quite unable to manage. Both lovely to look at and delightful to hear (her speaking voice was among the best to grace a talking picture in 1929), Miss Nixon's rescuing presence went some distance to counteract the cloying effect of little Frankie Darro as the orphan. Dowling broke into song when you least expected him to, further reducing the credibility of an already far-fetched scenario. Also involved in the tearjerker were Sam Hardy as a minstrel manager, Lloyd Ingraham and Billy Hayes. George W. Weeks and O.E. Goebel produced, and the director was Fred Newmayer. Songs: *Little Pal*; *Rainbow Man* Dowling, James Hanley; *Sleepy Valley* Andrew B. Sterling, Hanley.

TWENTIES MUSICALS

The saga of Margot, a French girl who is ▷ unaware that her somewhat unprepossessing boyfriend and The Red Shadow, mysterious leader of the Riffs, are one and the same man, **The Desert Song** (Warner Bros.) was the first all-talking, all-singing operetta to come to the screen. The story – by Otto Harbach, Laurence Schwab, Frank Mandel and Oscar Hammerstein II – suffered from an underlying improbability, and Harvey Gates's screenplay unintentionally provoked mirth. Nonetheless, Sigmund Romberg's romantically tuneful score (lyrics by Hammerstein II) overcame these disadvantages, and John Boles (left) was a sufficiently dashing Red Shadow to keep audiences' minds off the banality of the plot. Carlotta King (right) played the gullible Margot, with brave support on offer from Louise Fazenda, John Miljan, Johnny Arthur, Marie Wells, Edward Martindel, Jack Pratt, Otto Hoffman, Robert E. Guzman and Myrna Loy. Directed by Roy Del Ruth and photographed by Barney McGill partly in two-colour Technicolor, the movie proved a success and was remade in 1943 with Dennis Morgan and in 1953 with Gordon MacRae. Songs: *Riff Song* (Boles); *French Marching Song* (King); *Then You Will Know* (Boles, King); *Desert Song* (King, Boles); *Song Of The Brass Key* (Wells, Pratt); *Sabre Song* (King, Boles); *Romance* (King); *One Alone* (Boles); *One Flower* (Guzman, Pratt); *My Little Castagnette* (Wells).

△

Though saddled with a trite and cumbersome script by Ernest Vajda, C.E. Andrews and Ethel Doherty, and working in a language that was not his own (in a medium still teething where sound was concerned), Maurice Chevalier's success in his first full-length American feature, **Innocents of Paris** (Paramount), was a resounding example of style triumphing over content. The story of a junk merchant (Chevalier, right) who rescues a child from drowning in the Seine, then falls in love with the child's Aunt Louise, the plot ultimately forced the hero to choose between romance and a career in the theatre. He chooses love – but not before singing three Richard A. Whiting–Leo Robin songs including the famous 'Louise'. He also sang 'It's A Habit Of Mine' which opened with a short routine for chorus girls, then developed into the quintessential Chevalier number, performed by the star with a straw hat and a cocky demeanour, oozing his characteristic sexual confidence and legendary Gallic charm. Sylvia Beecher (left) as his inamorata was nowhere as convincing as her leading man in a performance that owed more to the art of elocution than it did to acting. Completing the cast were Russell Simpson, Mr and Mrs George Fawcett, John Miljan, Margaret Livingston, David Durand, Jack Luden and Johnnie Morris. The director was Richard Wallace. Other songs: *Wait Till You See 'Ma Cherie'*; *On Top Of The World Alone* Whiting, Robin; *Valentine* Henri Christine, Herbert Reynolds; *Les Ananas* (a French version of *Yes, We Have No Bananas*); *Dites-Moi Ma Mere* (from Chevalier's Paris repertoire).

Minnie's Boys, better known to Broadway audiences as the Marx Brothers – Groucho (centre left), Chico (centre right), Harpo (right) and Zeppo (left) – made their all-talking, all-singing, all-dancing debut with **The Cocoanuts** (in 1921 they had appeared in a silent comedy called *Humor Risk*, prints of which no longer exist), and were as enthusiastically welcomed on the screen as they had been on stage. Virtually a filmed version of the Sam Harris Broadway presentation, the Paramount film bore several of the hallmarks (or scars) of the early talkies. The sound reproduction left much to be desired and the camera work was static. All the same, the refreshing zaniness of the quartet helped to override these technical liabilities, and in their 'Viaduct' sketch gave the movies one of its classic
▽

comedy scenes. Mary Eaton and Oscar Shaw co-starred as the obligatory young lovers, the formidable Margaret Dumont was on hand as Mrs Potter, a haughty guest at the *Hotel de Cocoanut*, with Kay Francis (her debut), Cyril Ring, Basil Ruysdael and Sylvan Lee completing the cast. It was adapted from the George S. Kaufman–Morrie Ryskind–Irving Berlin play by Ryskind, photographed by George Folsey, supervised by Monta Bell for producer Walter Wanger, and directed by Joseph Santley and Robert Florey. The score was by Irving Berlin and included *When My Dreams Come True* (not in the original production), *Florida By The Sea*, *Monkey-Doodle-Doo*, and *The Tale Of A Shirt*, which was ingeniously set to the famous *Toreador Song* from Bizet's *Carmen*.

△
Minstrel headliner Eddie Leonard (centre) made his talkie debut with **Melody Lane** (Universal), a rather lachrymose musical about a vaudeville dancer and his partner, Leonard, and Josephine Dunn, right) and the travails that overtake them. As was generally the way with such plots, the team – who also happen to be married to each other – split when the lady of the act is offered a role in a stock company, and three years pass before they are reunited in New York. He has become a down-and-out prop man, she a successful dramatic star. Their young daughter Jane La Verne inadvertently effects a happy ending for them, in spite of their differences, when she hurts herself in a fall and is sung (literally) back to health by her pa. Huntley Gordon (left) was also in it. The paying customers avoided it in droves – despite the inclusion of one of Leonard's famous 'trademark' numbers, 'Roly Boly Eyes' (his own composition). It was written by J.G. Hawks and Robert F. Hill from a play by Jo Swerling, with Hill also directing. Songs: *The Song Of The Islands* Charles King; *Here I Am*; *There's Sugar Cane Round My Door*; *The Boogy Man Is Here* Eddie Leonard, Grace Stern, Jack Stern.

A typical case, prevalent at the time, of songs ▷ in search of a good storyline, **William Fox Movietone Follies of 1929** (GB: **Movietone Follies of 1929**), concerned itself with the slim-line tale of a southerner from Virginia (John Breeden) who travels to New York in order to buy up a show which is still in rehearsal just so that he can fire his girlfriend Lila (Lola Lane) from the cast because he disapproves of the stage as a career. It doesn't quite work out that way and, pre-dating *42nd Street* (Warner Bros., 1933) by four years, young Lila finds herself catapulted to stardom when the leading lady indulges in a spot of temperament and refuses to go on. With the show an established hit, Breeden sells his interest in it at a profit, and persuades Lila to return to Virginia and marry him. Sue Carol (right), who led the striking 'Breakaway' number, was featured; so were Dixie Lee and David Rollins (left), and the rest of the cast included De Witt Jennings, Sharon Lynn, Arthur Stone, adagio dancers Harriet and John Griffith, and Stepin Fetchit. It was written and directed for producer William Fox by David Butler (dialogue by William K. Wells), the musical numbers were staged by Marcel Silver and Fanchon, the score was by Con Conrad, Sidney Mitchell and Archie Gottler (who played a stage manager in it), and the musical director, Arthur Kay, did the on-screen conducting. Songs and musical numbers: *Walking With Susie*; *Why Can't I Be Like You?*; *Legs*; *That's You, Baby*; *Look What You've Done To Me*; *Big City Blues*; *Pearl Of Old Japan*. Interesting sideline: As well as normal photography, the film was made in Fox's 70mm Grandeur System which was well received at a preview. The soundtrack was three times as wide as on 35mm film, resulting in superior sound quality, but movie managements, already in debt through conversion to sound, were not receptive since it required new projectors and screens with ground glass surfaces.

Will pretty Lois Moran (centre) agree to ▷ appear in student impresario David Percy's (centre right) musical numbers in the forthcoming college revue? Or will she decide, instead, to appear in the numbers being created for her by Percy's rival, Duke Morrison (later to be known as John Wayne)? That was the basic idea on which **Words and Music** (Fox) hung, and if ever there was a tenuous excuse for a series of songs and dances, this was it. In fact, the reason it happened at all was to use Lois Moran's numbers which had been cut from William Fox's *Movietone Follies of 1929* to bring that film down to manageable length! Helen Twelvetrees, William Orlamond, Elizabeth Patterson, Ward Bond, Richard Keene, Frank Albertson, Tom Patricola, the dancing Collier Sisters, plus adagio dancers Vina Gale, Arthur Springer, Harriet and John Griffith, and Helen and Charles Huff also appeared; the musical numbers were staged by Frank Merlin and Edward Royce, it was presented by William Fox, and directed by James Tinling from a screenplay by Andrew Bennison (story by Frederick Hazlitt Brennan and Jack McEdwards). Songs included: *Stepping Along* William Kernell; *Too Wonderful For Words* Kernell, Dave Stamper, Edmund Joseph, Paul Gerard Smith; *Shadows* Con Conrad, Sidney Mitchell, Archie Gottler.

In bringing Phillip Dunning and George Abbot's 1927 stage hit **Broadway** to the screen, director Paul Fejos devised a camera crane (at a cost of $75,000) capable of travelling at every conceivable angle and at a speed of six hundred feet a minute. His object? To impart a greater fluidity to the tale of an innocent Broadway hoofer who finds himself involved in a bootlegging murder. Producer Carl Laemmle Jr's $1,000,000 production for Universal contained an elaborate cabaret setting (the film's visual *pièce de resistance*) which was a trifle out of kilter with the sleazy, hard-hitting atmosphere purveyed in the Broadway original; while the addition of several musical numbers gave the material even further gloss – but not enough to diminish the undeniable impact of the tense backstage melodrama being played out among the protagonists. Glenn Tryon (illustrated centre) was excellent as the innocent hoofer, Merna Kennedy somewhat less so as the girl he loves. Repeating the roles they had created on stage were Thomas E. Jackson as sleuth Dan McCorn, and Paul Porcasi as the owner of *The Paradise Night Club* where much of the action takes place. Robert Ellis was the bad guy of the piece, with Evelyn Brent effective as Pearl, the vengeful showgirl who, with a bullet aimed at point-blank range, puts an end to Ellis's criminal activities. Others in the cast were Otis Harlan, Marion Lord, Fritz Feld, Leslie Fenton, and Gus Arnheim and His Cocoanut Grove Ambassadors. The screenplay was by Edward T. Lower Jr and Charles Furthman, and the splashy but routine dance numbers the work of Maurice L. Kusell. Hal Mohr was the cameraman, and the nightclub sequences were in 'natural' colour. The film was remade in 1942. Songs and musical numbers: *Broadway; The Chicken Or The Egg; Hot Footin' It; Hittin' The Ceiling; Sing A Little Love Song* Con Conrad, Sidney Mitchell, Archie Gottler.

Honky Tonk (Warner Bros.) was memorable mainly for the central performance of Sophie Tucker – 'the last of the red-hot mommas' – with songs by Jack Yellen (who also wrote the dialogue) and Milton Ager, as well as 'Some Of These Days' by Shelton Brooks, the number now indivisible from the star who made it famous. Tucker (illustrated) starred as a nightclub singer who sacrifices her all to educate her daughter. But the ungrateful girl, on learning of her mother's profession, denounces her, thus giving Miss Tucker ample opportunity to tug at the audience's heartstrings, which she did to great effect. The film, adapted by C. Graham Baker from a story by Leslie S. Barrows, offered something for everyone, and everyone was duly enthusiastic. Lila Lee was featured as the daughter, and the supporting cast included Audrey Ferris, George Duryea, Mahlon Hamilton and John T. Murray. The dances were directed by Larry Ceballos, and the film by Lloyd Bacon who did full justice to the aggressive talent of his star. Songs: *I'm The Last Of The Red Hot Mommas; I'm Doin' What I'm Doin' For Love; He's A Good Man To Have Around; I'm Feathering A Nest (For A Little Bluebird); I Don't Want To Get Thin.* Remade as *Lullaby Of Broadway* (Warner Bros., 1951). ▽

◁ **Smiling Irish Eyes** (First National) starred James Hall as a fiddle-playing songwriter who deserts the Irish mist to pursue the bright lights of Broadway, leaving behind him the girl with whom he has written the film's well-known title song (actual composers Ray Perkins and Herman Ruby). The neglected lass who follows her love to America, only to suffer disillusionment before living happily ever after, was played by Colleen Moore in her first all-singing, all-dancing picture, produced by her husband John McCormick. Heavy handed and prosaic, the screenplay was by Tom Geraghty and the direction by William A. Seiter with choreography by Larry Ceballos (see illustration). Also in it were Claude Gillingwater, Robert Homans, Aggie Herring and Betty Francisco. Songs included *A Wee Bit Of Love; Then I'll Ride Home With You; Old Killarney Fair* Norman Spencer, Herman Ruby.

First National's **Broadway Babies** was another runner from the popular backstage stable. Although fairly predictable, it had enough twists and turns to sustain interest, and leading lady Alice White (illustrated) emerged with credit. Not hitherto renowned as a musical comedy star, Miss White displayed a surprisingly good voice, and convinced both as a dancer and as an actress in this tale of a pure-hearted chorus girl in love with her stage manager (Charles Delaney). Their romance is disrupted by the arrival of a Detroit rum-runner (Fred Kohler) who almost succeeds in winning Alice's heart. Her love for her stage-manager prevails, however, the situation being assisted by Kohler's convenient demise at the hands of a trigger-happy gangster. The sprightly direction was by Mervyn LeRoy, whose cast was completed by Sally Eilers and Marion Byron (doing well as Miss White's co-chorines), Tom Dugan, Bodil Rosing, Louis Natheaux, Jocelyn Lee and Maurice Black. It was written by Monte Katterjohn and Humphrey Pearson from a story by Jay Gelzer, and the songs included: *Wishing And Waiting For Love; Jig Jigaloo* Grant Clarke, Harry Akst; *Broadway Baby Doll* Al Bryan, George W. Meyer.

The Time, The Place And The Girl (Warner Bros.), a lively campus musical, followed the career of a college football hero (Grant Withers) whose inflated ego takes a knock after his graduation when he becomes a less than successful bond salesman. Withers (right) however, has a way with the ladies – which his boss capitalizes on by getting him to offload bad bonds on to naive females, one of whom turns out to be the boss's wife! Written by Robert Lord from the W.M. Hough-Joseph E. Howard-Frank R. Adams play, it was directed by Howard Bretherton with a cast that featured Betty Compson (left), James R. Kirkwood, Vivian Oakland, Gretchen Hartman and Irene Haisman. The Vitaphone sound-on-disc system employed the roar of football crowds to good effect. Songs: *I Wonder Who's Kissing Her Now* Frank Adams, Harold Orlob, Will Hough, Joe Howard; *Collegiate* Mo Jaffe, Nat Bonx; *Doin' The Racoon* Raymond Klages, J. Fred Coots, Herb Magidson; *Fashionette* Robert King, Jack Glogau; *Jack And Jill* Larry Spier, Sam Coslow; *How Many Times* Irving Berlin; *Everything I Do I Do For You* Al Sherman; *If You Could Care* E. Ray Goetz, Arthur Wimperis, Herman Darewski. ▽

Silent star Betty Compson, whose numerous accomplishments also included playing the violin, got a chance to do just that in **Street Girl** (Radio Pictures). And to prove that she could also act, she lumbered herself with a Hungarian accent – or what passed for one – and never faltered. She played a destitute violinist called Freddie Joyzelle who improves the fortunes of a quartet of jazz musicians. As the boys scratch, bang, thump and blow nightly at a run-down East Side restaurant, Freddie is scheming to change their venue to a smart Hungarian restaurant and to up their salary from a lousy hundred bucks a week to an impressive three thousand. Needless to say, she has a romantic involvement with one of the boys in the band but, after a few obligatory complications, Jane Murfin's serviceable screenplay ended happily ever after. Miss Compson was delightful and there was good work from Ned Sparks (right) who had all the best lines as the most pessimistic member of the group. John Harron (centre) played Betty's beau, with Jack Oakie (2nd left) and Guy Buccola (left) completing the combo. Joseph Cawthorn (2nd right) and Ivan Lebedeff (as Prince Nicolas of Aragon) were also in it; so were Doris Eaton and the Radio Pictures Beauty Chorus, Raymond Maurel and the Cimini Male Chorus, and Gus Arnheim and His Cocoanut Grove Ambassadors. William Le Baron produced, and the director was the talented Wesley Ruggles. Pearl Eaton staged the dances, and Oscar Levant and Sidney Clare wrote the songs which included: *Huggable And Sweet; My Dream Memory; Broken Up Tune.*

Carl Laemmle's part-talking production of the Jerome Kern–Oscar Hammerstein II Broadway success **Show Boat** (Universal) was something of a curiosity, and it failed to find a responsive public. Originally filmed as a silent picture – with songs and dialogue being added for the sound version – it also contained an 18-minute prologue, introduced by Laemmle and Florenz Ziegfeld, featuring (for no reason that made any sense) three extracts from the original stage production with the original stage cast. Tess Gardella and the Jubilee Singers sang 'C'Mon Folks' and 'Hey Feller'; Helen Morgan sang 'Bill' and 'Can't Help Lovin' Dat Man' and Jules Bledsoe, with the same chorus that accompanied him on Broadway, performed 'Ol Man River'. The film version of the show that followed these extracts suffered by comparison. Laura La Plante (centre), whose singing voice was dubbed by Eva Olivetti, starred as an excessively lachrymose Magnolia; Joseph Schildkraut (left), speaking with more than just a trace of an accent, played Gaylord Ravenal, looking better than he sounded, and overacting shamelessly; Otis Harlan as Cap'n Andy was totally defeated by the comedy in the role and in no way matched up to Charles Winninger's already legendary Broadway performance, while Emily Fitzroy as the Cap'n's martinet wife,

For their production of **Dance of Life**, based on a play by George Manker Watters and Arthur Hopkins called *Burlesque*, Paramount recruited Hal Skelly (centre) from Broadway to recreate the role of Ralph 'Skid' Johnson, a burlesque entertainer who takes to drink when he allows success on Broadway to go to his head, and his pretty dancer wife Bonny (Nancy Carroll, centre right, in the role played on stage by Barbara Stanwyck), to divorce him after he resumes an affair with a former flame (Dorothy Revier). But it all comes right in the end when Miss Carroll, who has remarried, decides that her old husband needs her more than her wealthy new one and unselfishly returns to him. As in the original play, audiences were given a no-punches-pulled glimpse at backstage life, and a graphic – even

painful – account of a performer on the skids. Skelly was first rate throughout; so were his two leading ladies. The associate producer was David O. Selznick, it was directed by John Cromwell and Edward Sutherland (from a screenplay by Benjamin Glazer, dialogue by George Manker Watters), and the cast included Ralph Theodore, Charles D. Brown, Al St John, May Boley and Oscar Levant. A scene in The Ziegfeld Follies was photographed in two-colour Technicolor. Songs: *True Blue Lou; King of Jazzmania; Cuddlesome Baby; Flippity Flop; Ladies Of The Dance* Sam Coslow, Richard A. Whiting, Leo Robin. The source play *Burlesque* was later filmed again as *Swing High, Swing Low* (Paramount, 1937), and as *When My Baby Smiles At Me* (20th Century-Fox, 1948).

Parthenia Hawks, was generally considered to be wildly eccentric. The best and most consistent performance was given by Alma Rubens as the tragic Julie. (A tragic figure in real life too, Miss Rubens, a drug addict, died in 1931 at the age of 33 after being committed to the California Institute for the Insane.) **Show Boat's** screenplay – a rambling and diffuse effort by Charles Kenyon – was one of the chief reasons for the film's disappointing critical reception; so were Harry Pollard's over-earnest direction and Edward J. Montaigne's sloppy editing. Others in the cast were Elise Bartlett, Jack McDonald Stepin Fetchit, Neely Edwards, Theodore Lorch and Jane La Verne (right) plus the combined voices of the Billbrew Chorus, Silvertone Quartet, The Four Emperors of Harmony, Claude Collins, and Jules Bledsoe singing a series of Negro spirituals off-screen. Other songs: *Ol' Man River; Can't Help Lovin' Dat Man* Kern, Hammerstein II; *The Lonesome Road* Gene Austin, Nathaniel Shilkret; *Here Comes That Show Boat* Maceo Pinkard, Billy Rose; *Love Sings A Song In My Heart* Joseph Cherniavsky, Clarence J. Marks; *Coon, Coon, Coon* Gene Jefferson, Leo Friedmann; *Down South* Sigmund Spaeth, William H. Myddleton; *I've Got Shoes; Deep River* (traditional). **Show Boat** was remade by Universal (1936) and MGM (1951).

The first of the no-plot, all-star movie revues, **The Hollywood Revue of 1929** came to the screen with all MGM's manifold resources lavished upon it. The result was an over-produced (by Harry Rapf) extravaganza that attempted to out-Ziegfeld Ziegfeld in the sheer scope of its presentation. Though uneven in quality, it had its moments – notably Cliff Edwards introducing Arthur Freed and Nacio Herb Brown's 'Singin' In The Rain' (illustrated), Marion Davies doing 'Tommy Atkins On Parade' (also Freed and Brown), and the Gus Edwards–Joe Goodwin number called 'While Strolling Through The Park One Day' which featured Cliff Edwards, Gus Edwards, Polly Moran, Marie Dressler and Bessie Love. The movie also offered audiences a chance to see John Gilbert, Norma Shearer and Lionel Barrymore in an extract from *Romeo and Juliet*. The show was compered by Conrad Nagel and Jack Benny, included two Technicolor sequences, and called on Buster Keaton and Laurel and Hardy to provide the bulk of the laughs. It was directed by Charles F. Riesner, with Sammy Lee and George Cunningham in charge of the dance direction. Al Boasberg and Robert Hopkins wrote it; Cedric Gibbons and Richard Day dreamed up the sets. The very full musical programme also featured the following songs and musical numbers: *You Were Meant For Me* (Conrad Nagel dubbed by Charles King) Freed, Brown; *Low-Down Rhythm* (Jane Purcell, dancers) Raymond Klages, Jesse Greer; *For I'm The Queen* (Marie Dressler) Andy Rice, Martin Broones; *Gotta Feelin' For You* (Joan Crawford, Paul Gibbons, Biltmore Trio) Jo Trent, Louis Alter; *Bones And Tambourines* (Ensemble); *Strike Up the Band* (Brox Sisters, dancers); *Tableau Of Jewels* (James Burroughs, girls) Fred Fisher; *Lon Chaney Will Get You If You Don't Watch Out* (Gus Edwards, dancers); *Your Mother And Mine* (illustrated left, Jack Benny, Karl Dane, George K. Arthur); *Orange Blossom Time* (Charles King, Albertina Rasch Ballet, Belcher Child Dancers); *Minstrel Days* (Gus Edwards, chorus); *Nobody But*

You (Cliff Edwards); *I Never Knew I Could Do A Thing Like That* (Bessie Love, Boys); *Marie, Polly And Bess* (Dressler, Moran, Love) Gus Edwards, Joe Goodwin.

TWENTIES MUSICALS

'Rough and profane' was how one reviewer described **The Cock-Eyed World** (Fox) – a sequel to Laurence Stallings and Maxwell Anderson's *What Price Glory* (Fox, 1926) which again starred Victor McLaglen (left) and Edmund Lowe (right), with Raoul Walsh directing, as he had the first time round. Lacking the irony of the earlier film, or its deep involvement with the subject of war, **The Cock-Eyed World** was a moderately entertaining comedy with several songs scattered throughout the narrative. The screenplay, by Walsh and William K. Wells, was based on an unpublished play by Stallings and Anderson, and focused mainly on the friendly rivalry that existed between Sergeant Flagg (McLaglen) and Quirt (Lowe), particularly where women were concerned. And the women concerned were a Russian minx (Jeanette Dagna), a Brooklyn flapper (Jean Bary) and a Spanish spitfire named Elenita (Lily Damita, centre). Also in the cast were El Brendel, Bob Burns, Joe Brown and Stuart Erwin. The film was a moderate success. Songs: *Semper Fidelis* John Philip Sousa; *Over There* George M. Cohan; *Rose Of No Man's Land* James Caddigan, James Brennan; *Ka-Ka-Katy* Geoffrey O'Hara; *What Has Become Of Hinky Dinky Parlay Voo* Al Dubin, Irving Mills, Jimmy McHugh, Irwin Dash; *You're The Cream In My Coffee* Buddy De Sylva, Lew Brown, Ray Henderson; *Glorianna* Sidney Clare, Lew Pollack; *So Long*; *So Dear To Me* Con Conrad, Sidney Mitchell, Archie Gottler.

Apart from the usual suspension of disbelief without which the musical as a genre could not exist, **Broadway Scandals** (Columbia) asked audiences to accept Carmel Myers (left), an actress of average ability, as Valeska, a Broadway superstar whose incandescence alone could light up the Great White Way. The plot has Myers coming between a young song-and-dance man (Jack Egan, right) and his sweetheart (Sally O'Neil) when she asks the former, who is in the process of devising a new act with the latter, to become her leading man. Egan at first refuses, but accepts when girlfriend Sally agrees to join the chorus of the show. Through Egan's influence Sally scores a personal triumph when given a spot of her own, as a result of which Miss Myers throws a jealous tantrum and has the talented young upstart fired. Predictably Egan packs his bags and temporarily exits the big-time, until he and Sally can, quite literally, get their act together. Harry Cohn produced, George Archainbaud directed, Gladys Lehman wrote the scenario, and Norman Huston and Howard J. Green the dialogue (from a story by Green). Others in the cast were Tom O'Brien, J. Barney Sherry, John Hyams and Charles Wilson. Songs included: *What Is Life Without Love?* Fred Thompson, David Franklin, Jack Stone; *Does An Elephant Love Peanuts?* James Hanley; *Can You Read In My Eyes* Sam Coslow; *Love's The Cause Of All My Blues* Jo Trent, Charles Daniels; *Would I Love To Love You* Dave Dreyer, Sidney Clare; *Rhythm Of The Tambourine*; *Kickin' The Blues Away* David Franklin.

Warner Bros. attempted to repeat the success of *The Jazz Singer* and *The Singing Fool* by drawing on the same ingredients for **Say It With Songs**. This time Al Jolson (foreground) starred as a radio singer who is jailed for having accidentally killed a man who flirted with his (Jolson's) wife. Jolson was paid the astronomical sum of half a million dollars to appear in what turned out to be an unmitigated disaster – with the songwriting team of Buddy De Sylva, Lew Brown and Ray Henderson providing yet another funereal air *à la* 'Sonny Boy', this time called 'Little Pal', which completely failed to repeat the success of the earlier song. Darryl F. Zanuck and Harvey Gates were responsible for the story, with Joseph Jackson receiving credit for adaptation and dialogue. The director was Lloyd Bacon. Jolson's wife was played by Marian Nixon, and Davey Lee (Little Pal) appeared in a featured role, with other parts going to Holmes Herbert, Fred Kohler, John Bowers and Kenneth Thomson. Songs included: *Why Can't You; Used To You; I'm In Seventh Heaven; One Sweet Kiss* De Sylva, Brown, Henderson; *Back In Your Own Backyard; I'm Ka-razy About You* Dave Dreyer, Al Jolson, Billy Rose.

A hit for Warner Bros. and a personal triumph for Winnie Lightner (whose career had started in vaudeville), **Gold Diggers of Broadway** was adapted from Avery Hopwood's stage play *Gold Diggers*, first filmed by Warner Bros. in 1923. Robert Lord's scenario provided some genuine love interest and a fair amount of comedy in the familiar story of three girls and the wealthy trio of chumps who fall for their charms; and under Roy Del Ruth's direction, it zinged along, substantially enhanced by the imaginative use made of Technicolor, and by a clutch of Al Dubin–Joe Burke songs. These included two hit numbers (crooned by Nick Lucas), 'Tiptoe Through The Tulips', and 'Painting The Clouds With Sunshine', the latter lending its name to the 1951 remake of the movie starring Virginia Mayo. Larry Ceballos staged the musical numbers (illustrated) with the accent on tap; Nancy Welford and Ann Pennington played Miss Lightner's fellow 'gold diggers'; with other featured roles going to Conway Tearle, Lilyan Tashman, William Bakewell, Helen Foster and Albert Gran. Other songs included: *In A Kitchenette; Go To Bed; And Still They Fall In Love; What Will I Do Without You?; Mechanical Man; Song Of The Gold Diggers.*

Marianne is the only musical in the history of the genre in which the leading lady and a pig attempt to upstage one another. In this instance, the leading lady was Marion Davies (left) with the pig the main fulcrum of Dale Van Every's silly World War I comedy (dialogue by Gladys Unger and Laurence Stallings). For without the animal – whom Miss Davies befriends and attempts to save from the slaughterhouse – she would never have met Private Lawrence Gray (right) and fallen in love. Actually, in a rather desperate attempt to keep the movie buoyant, Miss Davies did a lot else besides fall in love – she sang, she danced, she emoted and, for her *pièce de resistance*, impersonated Sarah Bernhardt and Maurice Chevalier! She even encumbered herself with a French accent throughout the film's seven reels, but to little avail. With **Marianne**, Cosmopolitan Productions and MGM failed to bring home the bacon and the film's luke-warm reception was not entirely surprising. Cliff Edwards (Ukelele Ike) and Benny Rubin provided some boisterous comedy, with Scott Kolk, Robert Edeson, George Baxter and Emile Chautard in support. A silent version of the film was also shot, with Oscar Shaw and Robert Castle featured in the roles played in the sound version by Lawrence Gray and George Baxter. Robert Z. Leonard directed. Songs: *When I See My Sugar*; *Marianne*; *Oo-La-La* Roy Turk, Fred Ahlert; *Hang On To Me*; *Just You, Just Me* Raymond Klages, Jesse Greer; *Blondy* Arthur Freed, Nacio Herb Brown.

Adapted by Hugh Herbert from a story by Ben Hecht, **The Great Gabbo** (James Cruze Productions) gave the celebrated Austrian actor-director Erich von Stroheim (illustrated) a heaven-sent opportunity to chew up the scenery – which he did to stunning effect. He played Gabbo, a ventriloquist whose unbridled egotism results in his losing the one girl he loves (Betty Compson), his sanity and, finally, his dummy and soulmate Otto, whom he smashes up in an outburst of jealous rage. Dramatic stuff, directed a trifle crudely by James Cruze (real-life husband of Miss Compson), and vigorously performed by a cast that included Donald Douglas and Marjorie 'Babe' Kane. The choreography was by Maurice Kusell, and the songs by Paul Titsworth, Lynn Cowan, Donald McNamee and King Zany. These were: *The New Step*; *I'm In Love With You*; *I'm Laughing*; *Ickey*; *Every Now And Then*; *The Web Of Love*; *The Ga-Ga Bird*.

Because of the huge risk factor involved in an all-black presentation, Nicholas Schenck, the President of MGM, refused to allow **Hallelujah** to proceed until its producer/director King Vidor agreed to invest his salary in the production itself. The result was an impressive music drama about a poor cotton-picking family in the South, and one of the year's best films. It starred Daniel L. Haynes as Zeke (centre) and Nina Mae McKinney as Chick, the harlot whose link with a disreputable bunch of craps shooters brings about Zeke's downfall and his ultimate search for religion. Victoria Spivey played the good girl Haynes really loves, William Fountaine was Chick's conniving lover and Everett McGarrity the younger brother Haynes accidentally shoots after being cheated out of his money in a rigged game of craps. The first full-length, all-black, all-talking feature, **Hallelujah** made stunning use of negro spirituals in the telling of its somewhat melodramatic story (by Vidor, dialogue by Ransom Rideout) and, against Vidor's wish, also

The first Viennese operetta to be filmed as an all-talking, all-singing, all-dancing extravaganza, **Married in Hollywood** (Fox) by Oscar Straus, with additional music by Dave Stamper and Arthur Kay and lyrics by Harlan Thompson, was a well-recorded effort in which its leading players, Norma Terris (right) and J. Harold Murray – both Broadway recruits from Ziegfeld shows – sang better than they acted. Considering the paucity of plot (American girl vocalist, while on a European tour, falls in love with a Balkan prince much to the chagrin of his parents), this was no liability at all. It was the music that mattered and audiences did not go home disappointed. The final sequences were filmed in 'natural' colour and showed the prince and his showgirl united in Hollywood where she has become a star of motion pictures, and where he has fled following a palace revolution, about to live happily ever after. If vocally the film belonged to its two Broadway visitors, the acting honours went to Walter Catlett in the role of a film producer whose talent spotting results in Miss Terris's Hollywood contract. Also cast were Irene Palasty (left), Lennox Pawle, Tom Patricola, Evelyn Hall and Herman Bing. It was produced by William Fox, written by Harlan Thompson, choreographed by Edward Royce and directed by Marcel Silver with a pleasing sense of rhythm and pace. The songs included: *Dance Away The Night*; *Peasant Love Song*; *A Man, A Maid*; *Deep In Love*; *Bridal Chorus*; *National Anthem*; *Once Upon A Time*.

had a couple of Irving Berlin songs tacked on to the completed picture. The first, called 'Waiting At The End Of The Road', was sung by the Dixie Jubilee Singers at a market place while waiting for the cotton they have just picked to be weighed; while the second, 'Swanee Shuffle', provided Nina Mae McKinney with a jazzy come-hither dance as part of her plan to entice Haynes. Though Vidor disapproved acutely of the studio's interference with his work, his film remains an honest depiction of the kind of life lived by the American negro in a particular period of history and, fifty years later, retains its power to move audiences profoundly. The innovative camera set-ups (especially evident in a chase through a swamp), the subtlety of the direction, the exemplary deployment of sound, and the conviction of all the central performances combined to make **Hallelujah** a watershed in the development of the screen musical. The film was shot 'silent' on location, the sound being dubbed in in Hollywood.

William Fox's **Sunnyside Up** (Fox), one of the most inventive and original musicals of the year, successfully attempted to break away from the familiar backstage musical to tell the simple, uncluttered (and, it must be said, unoriginal) story of a poor girl from Yorkville, Manhattan, and her romance with a handsome young millionaire from Long Island. Janet Gaynor (illustrated in background) was the girl, Charles Farrell (foreground left) the beau, and it mattered not a jot that neither performer was particularly talented as a musical comedy star nor, if you closed your eyes, that their singing voices sounded identical. What they did have was charm and appeal, plus a first-rate score by De Sylva, Brown and Henderson behind which to hide their conspicuous lack of ability. Two-colour 'Multicolor' also came to their rescue in an entertainment sequence staged, for charity, in Farrell's Long Island retreat; so did a rather remarkable (for its time) production number called 'Turn On The Heat' sung by Sharon Lynn, in which a bevy of girls, clad in Eskimo furs, slowly shed their winter garments as their igloos melt, and the freezing Arctic setting changes to a tropical paradise complete with palm trees that miraculously materialize, fully grown, from little holes in the ground. The heat intensifies, everything in sight catches fire, and the girls make a spectacular exit by diving into a surrounding ornamental

pool. The scene ends with a sheet of water sprouting upwards in place of the more traditional curtain. The film's other production number, while more modest in scale, featured the hit song 'If I Had A Talking Picture Of You' rendered first by Gaynor and Farrell, then by an entire kindergarten of tots. The score produced two further hits, 'I'm A Dreamer', sung by Gaynor to her own accompaniment on a zither, and the rousing title song, which climaxed a neighbourhood party in a poor section of New York's East Side. The slender sub-plot was provided by Marjorie White and Frank Richardson as a couple of ordinary tenement dwellers, who also got a crack at the title song, as well as one of their own, a ditty called 'You've Got Me Pickin' Petals Off O' Daisies'. The score contained two more songs, 'You Find The Time, I'll Find The Place' sung by Sharon Lynn, and 'It's Great To Be Necked', sung by Marjorie White as 'It's Great To Be Necht (on a braw brecht moonlicht nicht)', the sequence being an unacknowledged parody of Sir Harry Lauder's songs. The story and dialogue were by De Sylva, Brown and Henderson, and the dance numbers the brainchild of Seymor Felix. The director was David Butler, and his supporting cast included El Brendel, Mary Forbes, Joe Brown, Peter Cawthorne and Jackie Cooper. **Sunnyside Up**, without doubt, was one of the formative musicals of the early talkies.

As was typical of most campus musical comedies, the students on view in **So This Is College** (MGM) didn't so much as open a book throughout the eleven reels it took to unspool – study clearly being the least important item on scenarists Al Boasberg, Delmer Daves and Joe Farnham's agenda. They were far more concerned with the friendship between two football-playing buddies and the romance each is having with a scheming college girl whose duplicity is revealed at the big USC–Stanford match. Elliott Nugent (left, sitting), Robert Montgomery (foreground right) and Sally Starr (centre) were recruited from Broadway by producer-director Sam Wood to breathe freshness into the workaday plot, but despite the inclusion of some exciting stock footage of an actual football match between the two universities (filmed in 1928) and the addition of four songs, the movie – like Miss Starr – came and went. Cliff Edwards (foreground, 2nd right), Polly Moran, Phyllis Crane, Dorothy Dehn, Max Davidson and Ann Brody were also cast. Songs: *Sophomore Prom* Jesse Greer; *College Days*; *Campus Capers* Martin Broones; *I Don't Want Your Kisses* Fred Fisher, Martin Broones.

Paramount should have found a stronger vehicle for Gertrude Lawrence's talkie debut than **The Battle of Paris**, a woebegone effort in which the star fought valiantly against the inanities of the plot (story and screenplay by Gene Markey) – and lost. She played a street singing Parisienne who, after teaming up with a pickpocket called Zizi (Charles Ruggles), falls in love with Walter Petrie (left) an American artist whose pocket Zizi has picked, and decides to become his model. Miss Lawrence (right) demonstrated her unique way with a couple of undistinguished Cole Porter songs (his movie debut), but the film as a whole found no takers and was a dismal flop. Gladys Du Bois, Arthur Treacher and Joe King were also cast and the director was Robert Florey. Songs: *They All Fall In Love*; *Here Comes The Bandwagon* Porter; *What Makes My Baby Blue*; *Housekeeping For You* Howard Dietz, Jay Gorney.

The Love Parade (Paramount), with music and lyrics by Victor Schertzinger and Clifford Grey, was Ernst Lubitsch's first sound film and Jeanette MacDonald's (centre) screen debut. It was also the first of four films Chevalier and MacDonald were to make together, and the first full-scale musical conceived by a director of genius. The story concerns Queen Louise of Sylvania (MacDonald) who, while waiting for her dream lover to come along, learns of the sexual proclivities of her foreign emissary, Count Alfred (Chevalier), in Paris. Titillated, she calls for him in order to prove his prowess on home ground. She is satisfied and marries him. But the count doesn't really enjoy playing the role of Prince Consort, for not only does MacDonald wear the crown, but also the trousers. In the end, however, male chauvinism wins the day, and the queen agrees to make him her king. Although the film lacked the fluidity of movement Lubitsch was to achieve in later musicals such as *Monte Carlo* (Paramount, 1930) and *The Merry Widow* (MGM, 1934), there was sufficient imagination in the handling of the scenario and the score was integrated into the action to breathtaking effect. It was written by Ernest Vajda and Guy Bolton from a play by Leon Xanrof and Jules Chancel, and produced by Lubitsch with a supporting cast that included Lupino Lane, Lillian Roth, Edgar Norton, Lionel Belmore and Eugene Pallette. Songs: *Nobody's Using It Now* (Chevalier – the first musical soliloquy in a talking picture); *Paris, Stay The Same* (Chevalier, Lupino Lane); *Dream Lover* (MacDonald, chorus); *Anything To Please The Queen* (MacDonald, Chevalier); *Wedding March* (chorus); *Let's Be Common* (Lane, Lillian Roth); *March Of The Grenadiers* (Macdonald, men); *Champagne* (Lane); *My Love Parade* (MacDonald, Chevalier); *Sylvania's Queen* (chorus); *The Queen Is Always Right* (Roth, Lane, chorus); *Valse Tatjana* (ballet music by O. Potoker).

With **Applause** (Paramount), filmed at the Astoria Studios in New York, 29-year-old torch singer Helen Morgan was given the finest screen role of her career, and director Rouben Mamoulian a chance to turn his considerable talents to talking pictures. The result was an unqualified artistic success for both of them. The story of an ageing Broadway burlesque queen called Kitty Darling, it showed Morgan sharing a squalid, drunken existence with Hitch, an unscrupulous comedian, and the effect her 17-year-old daughter, April, has on her when she arrives from a convent to take up residence in the big city. April's appearance results in Morgan (right) marrying the no-good Hitch out of a sense of propriety, but the marriage is a disaster and in no time at all Hitch is making passes at April who rejects them and, instead, becomes engaged to a sailor. Distressed, however, at her mother's rapid decline, April decides to give up the sailor in order to look after her. But Morgan takes poison rather than allow her daughter to ruin her happiness by becoming her 'meal ticket'. Showing tremendous cinematic flair, Mamoulian contrasted the relentlessly sordid aspects of his story (from the novel by Beth Brown) with lengthy passages depicting a more serene existence at the convent and, in both milieus, allowed his camera to move with more fluidity than was customary for early talking pictures. His use of sound was equally innovative, and instead of using only one mic-

rophone insisted, for certain scenes, on two, the sound from both being mixed together later. Because of the uncompromisingly unglamorous view it took of its subject, **Applause** was not the box-office success Mamoulian and his producers Jesse L. Lasky and Walter Wanger had hoped for, yet it remains one of the most striking of all the early talkies – and the apogee of its star's up-and-down career. Certainly she did nothing finer, and the four songs she sings in the film are superbly rendered. Joan Peers co-starred as her daughter, and was splendid; but Fuller Mellish Jr's performance as Hitch (left) was unfortunately not up to their high standard, being melodramatic and over-stated. The scenario and dialogue were by Garrett Fort and the cameraman was George Folsey. The rest of the cast included Henry Wadsworth, Jack Cameron and Dorothy Cumming. Songs: *What Wouldn't I Do For That Man* E.Y. Harburg, Jay Gorney; *Yaka Hula Hickey Dula* E. Ray Goetz, Joe Young, Pete Wendling; *Give Your Little Baby Lots Of Lovin'* Dolly Morse, Joe Burke; *I've Got A Feelin' I'm Fallin'* Billy Rose, Harry Link, Fats Waller (all sung by Helen Morgan); *Pretty Baby* Gus Kahn, Egbert Van Alstyne, Tony Jackson; *Turkey Trot* Robin Hood Bowers, Edgar Smith; *Waiting For The Robert E. Lee* Lewis F. Muir, L. Wofe Gilbert; *Doin' The New Raccoon* Dolly Morse, Joe Burke; *Smiles* J. Will Callahan, Lee Roberts; *Sweetheart Of All My Dreams* Art and Kay Fitch, Bert Lowe; *That's My Weakness Now* Bud Green, Sammy Stept.

A lavish, if somewhat uncinematic screen transplant of Ziegfeld's 1927 stage hit, **Rio Rita** (RKO), directed (in 24 days) by Luther Reed for producer William Le Baron, retained the spirit and spectacle of the Broadway production and was the most successful movie adaptation of a musical comedy – and one of the most remunerative – to date. Like the stage show, in which a basically flimsy plot chased a pleasing score without ever catching up with it, the film's narrative line was hardly its trump card, and the story, which mainly concerned itself with the mysterious identity of a bandit known as Kinkajou – and the distinct possibility that he may even be Rio Rita's brother – took third billing to the opulence of the production (the latter half being filmed in Technicolor) and the attractive presence of John Boles (right) and Bebe Daniels (centre) for whom Harry Tierney and Joseph McCarthy's melodious score presented no problems at all. Bert Wheeler and Robert Woolsey (making their talking picture debuts) were the obligatory comic relief, with other roles going to Don Alvarado (left), Dorothy Lee, George Renevant (who turns out to be the dreaded Kinkajou), Helen Kaiser, Fred Burns and Tiny Sandford. The dance director was Pearl Eaton. The songs included *You're Always In My Arms (But Only In My Dreams)*; *Sweetheart We Need Each Other*; *Following The Sun Around*; *Rio Rita*; *If You're In Love You'll Waltz*; *The Kinkajou*; *The Ranger's Song* Tierney, McCarthy. Remade by MGM in 1942 as an Abbott and Costello vehicle.

Burnt-cork comedians George Moran and Charles Mack (illustrated left and right) known to their fans as The Black Crows, made their talkie debut in **Why Bring That Up?** (Paramount), a well-crafted comedy by George Abbott, who directed and wrote the dialogue from a story by Octavus Roy Cohen, which gave Messrs M and M several opportunities to reprise some of their better-known sketches – including the one about the early bird and the worm. The story itself wasn't much (the duo find themselves involved with a minx who, in cahoots with her shady lover, attempts to fleece Moran of all he owns), but it served its purpose as a comic springboard for its two popular stars. The denouement, however, in which Mack, after being knocked unconscious by the minx's lover, is nursed back to health by Moran, who in desperation goes through some of their act together, was mawkish in the extreme and derivative of at least two other films in 1929 employing a similar device. Evelyn Brent starred as the minx, with Freeman S. Wood as her accomplice, and Harry Green, Bert Swor, Lawrence Leslie and Henry Lynch completed the cast. Songs included: *Do I Know What I'm Doing While In Love* Richard A. Whiting, Leo Robin; *Shoo Shoo Boogie Boo* Whiting, Sam Coslow.

Vaudevillian Belle Baker (centre) scored a personal success in **The Song of Love** (Columbia), a mawkish backstage story by Howard Green, Henry McCarthy and Dorothy Howell which reunites her with her husband (and former stage partner) after she retires from the business, and he fools around with a flirtatious blonde called Maizie. Actually, it is their young son (David Durand, right) who is responsible for the reconciliation, and were he not so unpalatably cute one might almost have been happy for him. Ralph Graves (left) played the philandering father, Eunice Quedens (to become better known as Eve Arden) was Maizie. Harry Cohn supervised the production, Erle C. Kenton directed, and the supporting cast included Arthur Housman and Charles Wilson. Songs: *I'm Somebody's Baby Now* Mack Gordon, Max Rich; *I'm Walking With The Moonbeams (Talking To The Stars)* Gordon, Rich, Maurice Abrahams; *I'll Still Go On Wanting You* Bernie Grossman; *White Way Blues* Gordon, Rich, George Weist.

Another all-star revue, but one which concentrated more on the personalities of the numerous performers involved than on spectacle, **Paramount on Parade** was an entertaining showcase for the studio's remarkable roster of talents, both in front of and behind the camera. After its Technicolored opening title number featuring Virginia Bruce and the Paramount Publix Ushers (danced by Mitzi Mayfair), Jack Oakie, Leon Errol and Skeets Gallagher introduced themselves as the occasion's masters of ceremony, and then introduced, in turn, practically every star under contract to Paramount at the time including (in alphabetical order) Iris Adrian, Richard Arlen, Jean Arthur, Mischa Auer, William Austin, George Bancroft, Clara Bow, Evelyn Brent, Mary Brian, Clive Brook, Nancy Carroll, Ruth Chatterton, Maurice Chevalier, Gary Cooper, Cecil Cunningham, Stuart Erwin, Henry Fink, Kay Francis, Mitzi Green, Phillips Holmes, Helen Kane, Dennis King, Abe Lyman and His Band, Fredric March, Nino Martini, Mitzi Mayfair, the Marion Morgan Dancers, David Newell, Warner Oland, Zelma O'Neal, Eugene Pallette, Joan Peers, Jack Pennick, William Powell, Charles 'Buddy' Rogers, Lillian Roth, Rolfe Sedan and Stanley Smith. Though eleven directors had a hand in steering the film to its success – Dorothy Arzner, Otto Brower, Edmund Goulding, Victor Heerman, Edwin H. Knopf, Rowland V. Lee, Lothar Mendes, Victor Schertzinger, Edward Sutherland, Frank Tuttle, and Ernst Lubitsch who was responsible for the three Chevalier sequences ('Sweeping The Clouds Away', illustrated) including the Technicolor finale – the overall production supervisor was Elsie Janis, with Albert S. Kaufman credited as producer. David Bennett was the dance director. Needless to say, the songs and musical numbers were numerous, and included: *Anytime's The Time To Fall In Love* (Charles 'Buddy' Rogers, Lillian Roth, chorus); *What Did Cleopatra Say?* (Helen Kane); *I'm True To The Navy Now* (Clara Bow, men) Elsie Janis, Jack King; *We're The Masters Of Ceremony* (Jack Oakie, Leon Errol, Skeets Gallagher) Ballard MacDonald, Dave Dreyer; *Come Back To Sorrento* (Nino Martini) Ernesto de Curtis, Leo Robin; *I'm In Training For You* (Jack Oakie, Zelma O'Neal; danced by Mitzi Mayfair and girls); *Dancing To Save Your Sole* (Nancy Carroll, Abe Lyman's Band, chorus; danced by Al Norman); *Let Us Drink To The Girl Of My Dreams* (Richard Arlen, Jean Arthur, Virginia Bruce, Mary Brian, Gary Cooper, James Hall, Phillips Holmes, David Newell, Joan Peers, Fay Wray) L. Wolfe Gilbert, Abel Baer; *My Marine* (Ruth Chatterton) Richard A. Whiting, Ray Egan; *All I Want Is Just One Girl* (Maurice Chevalier) Richard A. Whiting, Leo Robin; *I'm Isadore The Toreador* (Harry Green, Kay Francis) David Franklin; *Sweeping The Clouds Away* (Maurice Chevalier, girls) Sam Coslow; *Nichavo* (Dennis King) Mme Mana-Zucca, Helen Jerome. Inset right: Charles 'Buddy' Rogers, Lillian Roth. Inset Below: Helen Kane.

THIRTIES MUSICALS

△
The screen version of the 1925 operetta by Oscar Hammerstein II, Otto Harbach, Herbert Stothart and George Gershwin. **Song of the Flame** (First National) was given an elaborate Technicolor production which even went into wide screen at one point. But its story of a peasant (Bernice Claire, left) known as 'The Flame', who incites the mob to revolution in Russia with her 'Song of the Flame', was a tedious exercise. Gordon Rigby's rather flat adaptation of the material – which involved 'The Flame' in a love affair with a Russian prince (Alexander Gray, right) whose life she saves by agreeing to sacrifice her virginity to an evil fellow-conspirator (a singing Noah Beery), only had vitality in the musical numbers felicitously staged by Jack Haskell. Alan Crosland's direction was, on the other hand, unremarkable. The songs, which included some extra new numbers composed for the movie, were: *The Cossack Love Song*; *Song Of The Flame* Hammerstein II, Stothart, Gershwin, Harbach; *Petrograd*; *Liberty Song*; *The Goose Hangs High*; *Passing Fancy*; *One Little Drink* Grant Clarke, Harry Akst, Ed Ward; *When Love Calls* Ed Ward.

Probably the worst of all the early campus musicals, **Sunny Skies** (Tiffany Productions) gave top billing to comedian Benny Rubin (centre) who, as a college student called upon to undergo a blood transfusion, gave an unpalatable performance that veered uneasily between farce and pathos. The finale had the hero (Rex Lease) redeeming a bout of drunkenness by making a winning touchdown in the last minutes of an all-important game. Ho-hum . . . Marceline Day (right), Marjorie 'Babe' Kane (left), Greta Granstedt, Wesley Barry and Robert Randall lent support. It was written by Erle Snell and George Cleveland (story by A.P. Younger), and the director was Norman Taurog. Songs included: *Wanna Find A Boy*; *Must Be Love*; *You For Me*; *Sunny Days*.
▽

For almost half of its running time, a farcical plot involving a butler (El Brendel) who pretends to be a lumberman, and a wealthy blade (William Collier Jr) who fancies himself as the Casanova of the showgirl circuit, all but sabotaged the efforts of **Movietone Follies of 1930** (Fox) to entertain. Fortunately, the situation improved in the second half, with music coming to the rescue via Marjorie White, Frank Richardson, and erstwhile Ziegfeld girl Noel Francis, whose singing of a Con Conrad–Jack Meskill ditty called 'Cheer Up And Smile' was the vocal highlight of the film. A blackface routine called 'Here Comes Emily Brown', also by Conrad and Meskill, performed by Frank Richardson and Marjorie White (both illustrated), ran it a close second. It was written by William K. Wells, directed by Benjamin Stoloff, choreographed by Danny Dare and Maurice Kusell, and also featured Miriam Seegar, Huntly Gordon, Paul Nicholson, and Yola d'Avril as a French maid much given to tantrums. Other songs included: *You'll Give In* Joseph McCarthy, James Hanley; *I Wanna Be A Talking Picture Queen* McCarthy, Hanley, James Brockman; *Doin' The Derby* Conrad, Meskill; *I Feel A Certain Feeling Coming On*; *Bashful* Cliff Friend, James V. Monaco.
▽

◁ **Showgirl in Hollywood** (First National), based on J.P. McEvoy's novel *Hollywood Girl*, was an attempt to satirize the movie industry, but the satire went badly off-course in this Harvey Thew-James A. Starr adaptation. Nevertheless, in taking a behind-the-scenes look at the mechanics of movie-making, the film did provide an accurate view of how early sound films were made. The plot, such as it was, concerned a comedy performer's rise to Hollywood stardom after being spotted by a film producer in a New York nightclub. Alice White (left) was top cast, with support from Jack Mulhall (right), John Miljan, Ford Sterling, Virginia Sale, Herman Bing and, notably, Blanche Sweet. The director was Mervyn LeRoy, the songsmiths Bud Green and Sammy Stept, the dance director Jack Haskell, and it was photographed (by Sol Polito) in black and white with Technicolor sequences. Robert Lord produced. Songs included: *Hang On To The Rainbow*; *I've Got My Eye On You* (not to be confused with the later Cole Porter standard from *Broadway Melody of 1940*); *There's A Tear For Every Smile In Hollywood* Green, Stept; *My Sin* Buddy De Sylva, Lew Brown, Ray Henderson.

One of the previous year's stage shows by Richard Rodgers, Lorenz Hart and Owen Davis, **Spring is Here** (First National) was rewritten for the screen by James A. Starr with a reasonable ration of witty dialogue. Which was just as well, considering the unconvincing plot: father (Ford Sterling) of a pretty young thing (Bernice Claire, illustrated) disapproves of her romantic attachment to Lawrence Gray, favouring Alexander Gray instead. Dad banishes Lawrence from the family manse, but he returns to elope with Bernice. Alexander, however, intervenes, and finally carries her off. There was support from Louise Fazenda, Inez Courtney, Frank Albertson (illustrated) and Natalie Moorhead, and the direction was by John Francis Dillon. Songs: *Spring Is Here In Person* – not to be confused with the more famous *Spring Is Here* (*Why Doesn't My Heart Go Dancing?*) which Rodgers and Hart later wrote for the film *I Married An Angel*; *Yours Sincerely*; *Rich Man, Poor Man*; *Baby's Awake Now*; *With A Song In My Heart* Rodgers and Hart; *Cryin' For The Carolines*; *Have A Little Faith In Me*; *Bad Baby*; *How Shall I Tell?* Sam Lewis, Joe Young, Harry Warren.
▷

△

Bride of the Regiment (First National) was another filmed operetta and, like so many of its predecessors, was characterized by a tediousness which no amount of Technicolor and spectacle could relieve. Its nonsensical plot told of a countess who saves her husband from the firing squad by flirting with a lecherous Austrian colonel. The colonel passes out from too much champagne, dreams that the countess has willingly submitted to him, and sets her husband free. John Francis Dillon directed, Ray Harris and Humphrey Pearson wrote the screenplay, Jack Haskell staged the musical numbers and the songs were by Al Dubin, Al Bryan and Ed Ward. The protagonists were Vivienne Segal, Walter Pidgeon (as the colonel, centre), and Allen Prior, with support from Louise Fazenda, Ford Sterling, Lupino Lane, Claude Fleming (right) and Myrna Loy (left). Songs included: *Brokenhearted Lover; Cook's Song; Dream Away; Heart Of Heaven; I'd Like To Be A Happy Bride; One Kiss And Then Goodbye Sweetheart.* Remade as *That Lady in Ermine* (20th Century-Fox, 1948).

Hold Everything was yet another Broadway original – by Buddy De Sylva, Ray Henderson, Lew Brown and John McGowan – that came to the screen via Warner Bros. in an adaptation by Robert Lord with a score by Al Dubin and Joe Burke. A vehicle for Joe E. Brown, top-cast as Gink Schiner, an indolent and mediocre prizefighter, it was the comedy rather than the music that won on points, and which kept the comedian's fans happy as he went about upsetting his sweetheart (Winnie Lightner, foreground) by flirting with all the pretty girls, busybodying himself around a fighter's training camp where Georges La Verne (real-life champ Georges Carpentier) is preparing for a heavyweight title bout, and astounding everyone by making a success of his own fight at the tournament. There were various threads of sub-plot, one of which involved Carpentier with a pushy society girl (Dorothy Revier); and another which had a crooked promoter trying to 'fix' a fight only to be foiled by Brown. It was photographed in Technicolor, zippily directed by Roy Del Ruth, and had a cast that also featured Sally O'Neil, Bert Roach, Edmund Breese, Tony Stabeneau and Jimmie Quinn. Songs: *Take It On The Chin; When Little Red Roses Get The Blues For You; Sing A Little Theme Song; Physically Fit; Girls We Remember; All Alone Together; Isn't This A Cockeyed World.*

▽

◁ After the sheen and sophistication which Ernst Lubitsch imparted to *The Love Parade*, **The Big Pond** (Paramount), produced by Monta Bell and directed by Hobart Henley, which also starred Maurice Chevalier, was a disappointingly pedestrian effort that not even the four songs imposed onto Robert Presnell and Garrett Fort's narrative (dialogue by Preston Sturges) could redeem. Based on the play by George Middleton and A.E. Thomas, it had Chevalier (right) working as a guide in Venice and falling in love with an American tourist (Claudette Colbert, left) whose father, believing Chevalier to be nothing more than an opportunist, offers him a job in his New York chewing gum factory. Complications arise and Chevalier is fired, but saves the day by inadvertently inventing rum-flavoured gum. So much for the plot. The star's perky personality was an undoubted plus in a film littered with minuses, and his singing of 'You Brought A New Kind Of Love To Me' by Irving Kahal, Pierre Norman and Sammy Fain, offered cinemagoers three minutes of magic out of the movie's total 85-minute running time. George Barbier and Marion Ballou played Miss Colbert's parents, with Andrée Corday, Frank Lyons, Nat Pendleton and Elaine Koch completing the cast. It was filmed at Paramount's Astoria Studios on Long Island, in both English and French. Other songs: *Livin' In The Sunlight, Lovin' In The Moonlight* Al Lewis, Al Sherman; *This Is My Lucky Day* Buddy De Sylva, Lew Brown, Ray Henderson; *Mia Cara* Kahal, Norman, Fain.

△

Director Harry Beaumont attempted to infuse MGM's **The Florodora Girl** (GB: **The Gay Nineties**) with as much period atmosphere and detail as possible, and succeeded. He succeeded, too, in drawing from its star Marion Davies (right) a genuinely funny performance as Daisy, a man-shy Florodora girl who, after being taken in hand by her colleagues, finds love in the arms of a millionaire (Lawrence Gray, left). Gene Markey's screenplay (additional dialogue by Ralph Spence, Al Boasberg and Robert Hopkins) was affectionately satirical about the milieu it set out to recreate, and provided good roles for Walter Catlett, Claud Allister and Sam Hardy. Ilka Chase, Jed Prouty, Louis John Bartels and Nance O'Neil were also cast. A stage sequence (*Tell Me Pretty Maiden* by Owen Hall and Leslie Stuart) was filmed in Technicolor, and the songs included: *My Kind Of Man; Pass The Beer And Pretzels; Swingin' In The Lane* Herbert Stothart, Clifford Grey.

△

Charles 'Buddy' Rogers fans had a field day with their idol in **Safety in Numbers** (Paramount), a witless little musical which left non-admirers groaning at the antics of both the hero (centre), and the three Follies girls who are ordered by the lad's guardian uncle to educate him in the ways of the world – prior to his inheriting $25,000,000. Kathryn Crawford (right), Josephine Dunn (left) and Carole Lombard (centre right) comprised the trio, with Miss Crawford eventually hooking Rogers for herself. Geneva Mitchell, Roscoe Karns, Francis McDonald and Virginia Bruce (centre left) had parts in it as well; it was written by Marion Dix (from a story by George Marion Jr and Percy Heath), and directed by Victor Schertzinger with David Bennett in charge of the dances. Songs: *My Future Just Passed; The Pick-Up; Do You Play, Madame?; I'd Like To Be A Bee In Your Boudoir; You Appeal To Me; Business Girl; Pepola* George Marion Jr, Richard A. Whiting.

The undisputed hero of Universal's lavish Technicolor revue **King of Jazz** was its director John Murray Anderson who, in an astonishing motion picture debut, revealed a creative imagination that was as refreshing as it was rare. And although the film's quality varies, its best moments are bold and unforgettable. Watching the film today, one is struck by the sheer originality of Anderson's concepts and the way in which subsequent musicals have borrowed from them (see illustrations). For example, the A Bench In The Park' number (by Jack Yellen and Milton Ager), performed by The Brox Sisters, The Rhythm Boys, George Chiles, and Paul Whiteman and His Orchestra, predated Busby Berkeley's 'Pettin' In The Park' (from *Gold Diggers Of 1933*) by a couple of years, yet the similarities between the two sequences are striking. In Yellen and Ager's 'Happy Feet', performed by The Sisters G, there is a moment that recalls Berkeley's '42nd Street' routine in the use it makes of cut-out New York skyscrapers. And there can be no mistaking the resemblance between the final tableau of 'The Melting Pot Of Jazz' and the final tableau of MGM's *Till The Clouds Roll By* (1946); or the finale of the 'Bridal Veil' sequence (music by Yellen and Ager) with the moment in MGM's *The Great Ziegfeld* (1941) when a garment of equal proportions is shown to breathtaking effect. Anderson's staging of Gershwin's 'Rhapsody In Blue' vies in originality with 'The Melting Pot Of Jazz' (in which the music of various nationalities is mixed in one giant cauldron to produce a new sound called Jazz), and is perhaps the most dazzlingly inventive sequence in the entire film. To contemporary audiences used to the garishness of many of the current colour processes, the two-colour Technicolor used in **King of Jazz** makes a welcome change and is one of the chief assets of an extraordinary entertainment. Other musical numbers: *So The Bluebirds And The Blackbirds Got Together*, by Harry Barris and Billy Moll, performed by Bing Crosby and The Rhythm Boys, Al Rinker, and Harry Barris; *It Happened In Monterey* by Mabel Wayne and Billy Rose, sung by John Boles; *Ragamuffin Romeo* by Mabel Wayne and Harry De Costa, performed by Jeannie Lang, George Chiles, Don Rose and Marian Statler; Yellen and Ager's *The Song Of The Dawn* also sung by John Boles; *Mississippi Mud* by Harry Barris and James Cavanaugh, performed by Crosby and The Rhythm Boys; *Music Hath Charms* by Yellen and Ager, performed by Crosby; *When Day Is Done* by Buddy De Sylva and Robert Katscher (used by Ferde Grofé as part of his arrangement for the *A Bench In The Park* sequence). Also of note is the fact that Paul Whiteman's band at that time included such great jazz musicians as guitarist Eddie Lang and violinist Joe Venuti, and in addition to his arrangements for the principal numbers, orchestrator Ferde Grofé's scoring involved several medleys designed to give solo specialty spots to members of the band. In these, segments were heard from Kreisler's *Caprice Viennoise*, *Nola* by Felix Arndt and James Burns, *Linger Awhile* by Harry Owens and Vincent Rose, and *Aba Daba Honeymoon* by Arthur Fields and Walter Donovan. There were several folk, classical, and light classical pieces: *A-Hunting We Will Go*; Luigini's *Ballet Egyptien*; *Rule Britannia*; *D'Ye Ken John Peel*; *Santa Lucia*; *Funiculi-Funicula*; *Comin' Through The Rye*; *Wiener Blut*; *Fair Killarney*; *The Irish Washerwoman*; *Ay-yi Ay-yi-yi*; *Song Of The Volga Boatmen*; *Otchichornya*; some Sousa marches, and a couple of parodies called *Has Anybody Seen Our Nelly?* and *Oh, How I'd Like To Own A Fishstore*. Carl Laemmle produced, Frederick T. Lowe Jr wrote it, with sketches by Harry Ruskin, and Hal Mohr, Jerome Ash and Ray Rennahan photographed it.

THIRTIES MUSICALS

Director Leo McCarey, still a novice where sound was concerned, came a cropper with **Let's Go Native** (Paramount), a punchdrunk comedy that dissipated a potentially amusing idea in a welter of trite dialogue, triter lyrics, soporific choreography and undistinguished photography. What it *did* have going for it though, was a fairly pleasant score by Richard A. Whiting (lyrics by George Marion Jr who, incidentally, was an erstwhile writer of silent-screen titles) and a pleasing performance from Jack Oakie as a taxi-driver. Jeanette MacDonald (centre) received second billing to Oakie and was passable in the role of a modiste who, in order to escape her creditors, sets sail for South America. She never gets there, for the ship founders during a storm and, together with several other members of the *dramatis personae*, she finds herself marooned on a tropical island. What happens on the island formed the kernel of George Marion Jr and Percy Heath's screenplay, and it should have been far more diverting than it was. James Hall (centre foreground) played Miss MacDonald's boyfriend, with Kay Francis (left foreground), Charles Sellon, David Newell, Eugene Pallette, Skeets Gallagher and The King's Men in it too. Songs: *Let's Go Native*; *My Mad Moment*; *It Seems To Be Spring*; *Joe Jazz*; *I've Gotta Yen For You.*

Grant Withers and Sue Carol brought more conviction to **Dancing Sweeties** (Warner Bros.) than this tepid romance, boringly directed by Ray Enright, deserved. Written by Gordon Rigby and Joseph Jackson (from a story by Harry Fried) it concerned a young couple who meet during a dance contest, fall in love and marry. The husband is ambitious and they part when the wife is unable to learn complicated new dance routines, but they get together again and settle for a life of domestic bliss. Also featured in this

pitifully thin plot were Edna Murphy, Tully Marshall, Eddie Phillips, Kate Price and Ada Mae Vaughan. Songs: *Wishing And Waiting For Love* Grant Clarke, Harry Akst; *Hullabaloo* Bobby Dolan, Walter O'Keefe; *I Love You, I Hate You* Al Bryan, Joseph Meyer; *The Kiss Waltz* Al Dubin, Joe Burke. *Dancing With Tears In My Eyes*, also by Dubin and Burke, was removed from the final print because the front office didn't think it good enough. It later became an enduring hit for Rudy Vallee on radio.

Apart from singing a few songs, Clara Bow did quite a bit of heavy-duty emoting in **Love Among The Millionaires** (Paramount). She played a waitress in a railroad cafe who finds herself in the midst of a romance with a brakeman called Jerry (Stanley Smith). Except that Jerry isn't a brakeman at all – he's a junior executive out to learn the business, as his father happens to be president of the railroad company. At a Palm Beach gathering Miss Bow, believing herself to be too common for the likes of him, attempts to sabotage the romance by deliberately singing in a manner likely to offend the guests. She almost succeeds, but true love wins through and Clara's martyrdom is short-lived. So was the film. It was adapted by Grover Jones and William Conselman from a story by Keene Thompson, with dialogue by Herman J. Mankiewicz, was directed by Frank Tuttle, and also featured 9-year-old Mitzi Green (right) whose impersonation of Clara Bow (centre), her elder sister in the story, was the film's high-spot. Also cast were Skeets Gallagher, Stuart Erwin, Charles Sellon (left) and Theodore Von Eltz. Songs included: *Believe It Or Not I've Found My Man*; *That's Worth Waiting For*; *Love Among The Millionaires*; *Rarin' To Go*; *Don't Be A Meanie* L. Wolfe Gilbert, Abel Baer.

A circus melodrama with songs, **Swing High** (Pathe) didn't. Its leaden, convoluted, intrigue-filled tale of circus life and love remained moribund while the heroine (Helen Twelvetrees, foreground) of James Seymour and Ray B. McCarey's screenplay – story by Seymour, and Joseph Santley who also directed – manages to save her sweetie (Fred Scott, centre, holding her hand) from the local siren (Dorothy Burgess) but not, alas, the film. Also on hand: John Sheehan, Daphne Pollard, Stepin Fetchit, Chester Conklin and Ben Turpin. E.B. Derr produced. Songs: *Do You Think I Could Grow On You?*; *It Must Be Love*; *With My Guitar And You*; *Shoo The Hoodoo Away*; *There's Happiness Over The Hill* Mack Gordon, Abner Silver, Ted Snyder.

Another campus musical, but this time set in ▷
Spain, **In Gay Madrid** (MGM) starred heart-
throb Ramon Novarro (left) whose amorous
exploits result in his being sent from Madrid to
Santiago where his father hopes he will settle
down and study. But there are pretty girls in
Santiago too – especially Carmina (Dorothy
Jordan, right), and in no time at all lover boy is
wooing her with half a dozen romantic ballads.
Competent performances from a cast that in-
cluded Lottice Howell, Claude King, Eugenie
Besserer, William V. Mong and Beryl Mercer,
with a screenplay (Bess Meredyth, Salisbury
Field and Edwin Justus Mayer, story by
Alejandro Perez Lugin) and direction (by Robert
Z. Leonard) to match, all added up to a pleasing,
lightweight entertainment. Songs included: *Dark
Night* Herbert Stothart, Clifford Grey, Xavier
Cugat; *Santiago*; *Smile While We May* Roy Turk,
Grey; *Into Your Heart* Turk, Fred Ahlert.

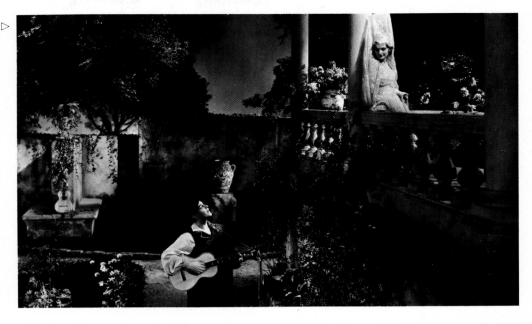

Golden Dawn, an operetta by Otto Harbach,
Oscar Hammerstein II, Emmerich Kalman and
Herbert Stothart, was first seen on the stage in
1927. Warner Bros. brought it to the screen,
complete with East African setting and
Technicolor photography, neither of which was
able to blur the absurdities of the subject matter.
An incredible story about a native uprising
against the British and the Germans in World
War I, it seemed to defeat the judgement of both
scenarist Walter Anthony and director Ray
Enright, and the best that can be said of Larry
Ceballos's musical numbers is that, nowadays,
they can be regarded as a piece of camp.
Vivienne Segal (illustrated) and Walter Woolf
King were inoffensive in the leads, but the same
cannot be said of a blacked-up Noah Beery
Muddling along between these extremes were
Alice Gentle, Lupino Lane, Dick Henderson, Otto
Matiesen and Marion Byron. Most of the dialogue
was accompanied by music, a device the critics
found tiresome. Harbach, Hammerstein and
Kalman contributed four songs – *Whip Song*;
Dawn; *My Bwana* and *We Too* – and the Grant
Clarke–Harry Akst combo wrote *My Heart's Love
Call*; *Africa Smiles No More*; *Mooda's Song*; *In A
Jungle Bungalow*.
▽

Boop-a-doop girl Helen Kane (centre) and Victor ▷
Moore starred as the star and owner of a
medicine show in **Dangerous Nan McGrew**
(Paramount), a feeble musical which flickered
into life only when Miss Kane gurgled out her
songs. For the rest it was a tedious non-starter
which squandered the talents of James Hall,
Stuart Erwin, Frank Morgan and Louise Closser
Hale. It was written by Paul Gerard Smith and
Pierre Collings (from a story by Charles Beahan
and Garrett Fort) and incohesively directed by
Malcolm St Clair – who was clearly more at
home with Rin-Tin-Tin at Warner Bros. Songs:
Dangerous Nan McGrew; *I Owe You* Don
Hartman, Al Goodhart; *Aw! C'mon, Whatta Ya
Got To Lose?* Richard A. Whiting, Leo Robin; *Once
A Gypsy Told Me (You Were Mine)* Irving Kahal,
Sammy Fain, Pierre Norman.

As part of his fraternity initiation, Eddie Fripp
(Arthur Lake, left) had to kick the first man he
met, and kiss the first girl. This led to all sorts of
complications – mainly romantic – in **Cheer Up
and Smile** (Fox), a youth-orientated romp in
which the hero, amidst several other improbable
occurrences, becomes a singing sensation after
taking the place of 'Whispering' Jack Smith
(centre) who has been knocked unconscious in a
New York nightspot! The female lead, and the
girl of Lake's dreams, was Dixie Lee (right), with
Howard J. Green's screenplay (from a story by
Richard Connell) giving roles to Johnny Arthur,
Charles Judels, John Darrow, Sumner Getchell
and Franklin Pangborn. William Fox produced
and the director was Sidney Lanfield. Songs: *The
Shindig*; *Where Can You Be?*; *The Scamp Of The
Campus*; *When You Look In My Eyes*; *You May
Not Like It But Its A Great Idea* Raymond Klages,
Jesse Greer.
▽

One Mad Kiss (Fox) was one bad musical. All
about a Spanish Robin Hood who single-
handedly does battle with corrupt government
officials in the interest of the oppressed, it starred
Jose Mojica (left) as the outlaw, Mona Maris
(centre) as a dancehall girl, and Antonio Moreno
(centre right) as the hissable dictator Don Es-
trada. It was written by Dudley Nichols from a
play by Adolph Paul, presented by William Fox
and directed by Marcel Silver and James Tinling.
It was also made in Spanish and, if nothing else,
offered an abundance of songs. These were: *Oh,
Where Are You*; *One Mad Kiss* Jose Mojica, Troy
Saunders; *Behind The Mask*; *Monkey On A String*;
Oh! Have I A Way With The Girls! James Hanley,
Joseph McCarthy; *Only One*; *The Gay Heart* Dave
Stamper, Clare Kummer; *Once In A While* Stam-
per, Kummer, Cecil Arnold; *In My Arms*; *I Am
Free* William Kernell; *Lament* Dudley Nichols,
Jose Mojica.
▽

THIRTIES MUSICALS

Ernst Lubitsch's astonishing mastery of every ▷ aspect of the cinema was in generous evidence in **Monte Carlo**, a sophisticated melding of music, romance and comedy. All about a beautiful countess (Jeanette MacDonald, left) who abandons her would-be husband on the day of their wedding, takes the famous *Blue Express* to Monte Carlo, and falls in love with a count disguised as a barber (Jack Buchanan, right), it was another supremely effective demonstration of the efficacy of the integrated musical (Paramount's *The Love Parade* and *Love Me Tonight* being earlier examples) compared to the boring predictability of the many photoplays passing for musicals at the time. Not as overtly carnal in atmosphere as *The Love Parade*, the film substituted romance for sex and charm for passion – due largely to the casting of Jack Buchanan who, unlike Maurice Chevalier, exuded, in everything he did, a sense of propriety. The result was utterly delightful and caused one critic to remark that with *The Love Parade* and **Monte Carlo** safely preserved on celluloid, the rest of the year's musicals could be burned without anyone noticing the loss. Musically, the sequence that received most recognition (and rightly so) was the one aboard the *Blue Express*, in which MacDonald, in perfect counterpoint to the jets of steam emanating from under the speeding wheels of the train and the rhythmic movement of the pistons, sings 'Beyond The Blue Horizon' to a landscape of peasants who momentarily abandon their labours on the land and join her in the second chorus. Another musical highlight was an operatic sequence in which the opera's plot closely paralleled the one being played out between the protagonists. Entitled *Monsieur Beaucaire*, it was especially written by Whiting, Harling and Robin who based it on a story of the same name by Booth Tarkington and Eleanor G. Sutherland. Other highlights: a love duet sung over a telephone (called 'Give Me A Moment Please'), and the melodious 'Always In All Ways' beautifully sung by MacDonald and Buchanan. The music was by Richard A. Whiting and W. Franke Harling and the lyrics by Lubitsch's favourite lyricist, the talented and innovative Leo Robin. Ernest Vajda wrote the screenplay (from the play *The Blue Coast* by Hans Mueller), with additional dialogue by Vincent Lawrence. The cast was completed by Claud Allister, ZaSu Pitts, Tyler Brooke, John Roche, Lionel Belmore, Albert Conti and Helen Garden, and the appropriately attractive settings were by Hans Dreier. Other songs: *Day Of Days* (chorus); *She'll Love Me And Like It* (Allister, MacDonald); *Trimmin' The Women* (Buchanan, Roche, Brooke); *Whatever It Is, It's Grand* (Buchanan, MacDonald).

The famous comedy team of Ole Olsen and Chic ▷ Johnson (left) made their Warner Bros. debut in **Oh! Sailor Behave!** as a couple of American sailors on the Bay of Naples (a convincing reconstruction on the studio backlot) who, among other things, are searching for a man with a wooden leg guilty of robbing a Navy storehouse. Typical of their particular brand of comedy was aiming a pea-shooter at the legs of possible suspects, then clearing from suspicion anyone who jumps on being hit. The screenplay, by Joseph Jackson with dialogue by Jackson and Sid Silvers, was adapted from an unsuccessful Broadway comedy by Elmer Rice, and the movie itself chalked up only moderate returns at the box office. This may well have been because the prevailing decline in interest in musicals led Warner Bros. to delay the release of this one. It was directed by Archie Mayo, with Charles King (right) and Irene Delroy providing the love interest; and the supporting cast included Lotti Loder, Noah Beery, Lowell Sherman, Vivien Oakland and Charles Judels. Olsen and Johnson wrote a song of their own for it ('The Laughing Song') with Al Dubin and Joe Burke on hand to provide the others. They included: *Love Comes In The Moonlight*; *Leave A Little Smile*; *Tell Us Which One Do You Love*; *Highway To Heaven*.

Nothing of any consequence happened in **Sweethearts On Parade** (Columbia). As Photoplay succinctly put it: 'Another nice little girl from the country goes to the big city. Another suave millionaire, with more money than morals, lures the little girl to his yacht. Another poor but honest hero saves her. And another movie is born.' And dies, they might have added. Alice White (right) was the 'nice girl', Kenneth Thomson the millionaire, and Lloyd Hughes the poor but honest hero. Marie Prevost was in it too – so were Ray Cooke (left), Wilbur Mack, Ernest Wood and Max Asher. Al Cohn and James Starr provided the story, Colin Clements wrote the screenplay; it was produced by Al Christie and directed by Marshall Neilan. Songs: *Sweethearts On Parade* Charles Newman, Carmen Lombardo; *Dream Of Me* Henry Cohen, Irving Bibo; *Yearning Just For You* Benny Davis, Joe Burke; *Misstep* Irving Bibo. ◁

The plot devised by George S. Kaufman and Morrie Ryskind for the Marx Brothers (Harpo, left, Chico, centre left) in **Animal Crackers** (Paramount) was, as usual, of little importance compared to the distinctly surreal antics of the team, and in their second talkie the quartet firmly established themselves as the screen's most outrageous purveyors of mirth. Set on a large estate belonging to the redoubtable Margaret Dumont (centre), and pivoting on the theft of a valuable painting, Ryskind's scenario allowed Groucho (right) to run riot as Captain Jeffrey Spaulding, an African explorer who makes his entrance sitting in a bamboo and tiger-skin hammock carried by four strapping Nubian warriors. Director Victor Heerman's cast included Lillian Roth and Hal Thompson as the young lovers, Louis Sorin as an art connoisseur, as well as Kathryn Reece, Richard Greig, Edward Metcalf and The Music Masters (as six footmen). Several songs were imposed upon the unorthodox proceedings and they included: *Why Am I So Romantic?*; *Hooray For Captain Spaulding* Bert Kalmar, Harry Ruby; *Collegiate* Mo Jaffe, Nat Bonx; *Some Of These Days* Shelton Brooks.

Paramount took no gambles with their production of **Queen High**, and played it safe by casting Frank Morgan and Charles Ruggles as business partners who manufacture garters but are always at loggerheads with one another. Their particular brand of comedy and skilful handling of dialogue kept Frank Mandel's undemanding screenplay (from a 1917 play by Edward Henry Peple, and the Laurence Schwab–Buddy De Sylva–Lewis Gensler 1926 musical reworking of it) simmering with laughs, and made the musical interpolations seem almost superfluous. Ginger Rogers (left) and Stanley Smith (right) provided the love interest and sang several of the songs with gusto, with Helen Carrington, Theresa Maxwell Canover, Nina Olivette, Tom Brown and Betty Garde in support. Mandel and Schwab produced and the director was Fred Newmeyer. Songs: *I Love The Girls In My Own Peculiar Way* E.Y. Harburg, Henry Souvaine; *It Seems To Me*; *I'm Afraid Of You* Edward Eliscu, Arthur Schwartz, Ralph Rainger; *Everything Will Happen For The Best* B.G. De Sylva, Lewis Gensler.

Based on James Gleason's play *Mr Bones*, **Mammy** (Warner Bros.) starred Al Jolson as an end-man in a travelling minstrel show and was a smash hit. Gordon Rigby's screenplay (dialogue by Joseph Jackson) didn't exactly sparkle, but with an Irving Berlin score to go with it, who cared? As it was, the story was a slightly melodramatic hodge-podge dealing with the desperate financial straits of the minstrel show, Al's love for Lois Moran which provokes the jealousy of her current beau (Lowell Sherman), and a card game which leads to Sherman being wounded for which Al is blamed and arrested. But all comes right in the end and, apart from Jolson himself (left), the film was memorable mainly for recreating the world of the minstrel show in all its aspects: from the blacking-up procedure in the dressing rooms to the street parades before the big event. The musical high point was an extended minstrel revue featuring about 60 performers and filmed in good-looking Technicolor (the rest of the film was black and white). It was directed by Michael Curtiz for producer Walter Morosco, and the cast, who did their best to make their presences felt in the overwhelming scene-hogging company of Jolson, included Louise Dresser (right), Mitchell Lewis, Hobart Bosworth and Tully Marshall. The Berlin songs were: *To My Mammy*; *Across The Breakfast Table Looking At You*; *Let Me Sing And I'm Happy*; *Knights Of The Road*; *Yes, We Have No Bananas* by Frank Silver and Irving Cohn sung to the tunes of several well-known operatic arias.

Top Speed (First National), from the play by Bert Kalmar, Harry Ruby and Guy Bolton, and written for the screen by Humphrey Pearson and Henry McCarty, was a real gas for Joe E. Brown fans and even quite tolerable to those who couldn't stand him. A musical comedy, with the emphasis on the comedy, it featured Brown as a lowly clerk who pretends to be a millionaire and wins a boat race in a craft owned by his girlfriend's father. There was a villain thrown in for good measure (and who, thanks to Brown's intervention, gets his come-uppance), plus some well-staged dance numbers by Larry Ceballos. It was directed by the relative newcomer Mervyn LeRoy, whose efficiency and sense of comic timing was nowhere better demonstrated than in his inventive handling of the climactic boat race. LeRoy's attractive and talented cast included Bernice Claire (right), Jack Whiting (left), Laura Lee, Rita Flynn, Edmund Breese and, making his debut for Warner Bros., Frank McHugh, one of the studio's most durable character actors. Songs: *As Long As I Have You And You Have Me*; *Looking For The Lovelight In The Dark* Al Dubin, Joe Burke; *Knock Knees*.

THIRTIES MUSICALS

Sweet Kitty Bellairs (Warner Bros.) was, on the face of it, just another operetta-style romp, set this time in 18th-century England, and not immediately noticeable for the drawing power of its stars or a score of obvious hit tunes. On examination, though, it revealed several virtues not characteristic of Hollywood musicals of the time. While the story, centring on the romance of a coquette and a highwayman during one summer in fashionable Bath, was slight, the telling of it was done in an authentic period style and played by actors who were clearly cast for their understanding of high comedy. Very much a traditional ballad opera in musical flavour, the package was a seductive and undisguisedly romantic one, whose origins dated back to a novel, *The Bath Comedy* by Agnes and Egerton Castle, which became a stage play by David Belasco in 1903, from which it was adapted for the silent screen as a vehicle for Mae Murray. This Technicolor musical version had a screenplay by J. Grubb Alexander, and a rich crop of salty and clever songs by Bobby Dolan and Walter O'Keefe (who later became famous for his updating of the 1868 song 'The Man On The Flying Trapeze'). Alfred E. Green directed, capturing the intended flavour of the piece to charming perfection, with an excellent cast that included Claudia Dell (centre right) as the warm-hearted, flirtatious heroine, Perry Askam (right) as a fop, Ernest Torrence as an elderly and irascible cuckold and Walter Pidgeon (centre left), June Collyer, Lionel Belmore (left) and Arthur Edmund Carewe lending first class support. The Dolan–O'Keefe musical numbers were *Tally Ho*; *Highwayman Song*; *Song Of The City Of Bath*; *Drunk Song*; *Pump Song*; *Duelling Song*; *My Love*; *You-oo, I Love But You*; *Peggy's Leg*.

An operetta, with sequences in Technicolor, **Dixiana** (RKO) starred Bebe Daniels (right) as a circus performer in the New Orleans of the 1840s, and Everett Marshall (left, from the Metropolitan Opera) as the wealthy Southerner she falls for. Marshall's mother (Jobyna Howland) disapproves of her prospective daughter-in-law's background and prolongs the plot by separating the couple. But after some treacherous goings-on perpetrated by a gambler sporting the name of Royal Montague (Ralf Harolde, centre) it all came right in the end. Some broad-comedy was supplied by the irrepressible team of Bert Wheeler and Robert Woolsey and, in one of the film's more genuinely spontaneous moments, Bill Robinson tap-danced. For the rest, it was a pleasant, well-sung, attractively directed (by Luther Reed who also adapted it from a short story by Anne Caldwell) piece of romantic fiction that whiled away the time painlessly enough. William Le Baron produced, the cast including Joseph Cawthorn, Dorothy Lee, Edward Chandler, Raymond Maurel and George Herman. Songs: *Dixiana* Benny Davis, Harry Tierney; *Here's To The Old Days*; *A Tear, A Kiss, A Smile*; *My One Ambition Is You*; *A Lady Loved A Soldier*; *Mr and Mrs Sippi*; *Guiding Star* Anne Caldwell, Harry Tierney.

Based on a 1925 play by Vincent Lawrence, and a remake of the 1927 comedy *Spring Fever* (MGM), **Love in the Rough** (MGM) was an amiable enough musical which gave Robert Montgomery and his co-star Dorothy Jordan (right-hand couple) a chance to prove how pleasantly they sang – especially in the Dorothy Fields–Jimmy McHugh number 'Go Home And Tell Your Mother'. Montgomery played a golfer who helps his sweetheart (Miss Jordan) to win a wager of $3,000 by beating an opponent in a climactic golf tournament. There wasn't a great deal more to it than that, but the songs, all by Fields and McHugh, were pleasant enough, and for those who liked Benny Rubin's particular brand of comedy, he was on hand to provide it, together with a cast that also included J.C. Nugent, Dorothy McNulty and Tyrrell Davis (left-hand couple), Harry Burns and Allan Lane. It was adapted by Sarah Y. Mason and scripted by Joe Farnham and Robert E. Hopkins, and the director was Charles F. Riesner. Other songs: *I'm Doing That Thing*; *I'm Learning A Lot From You*; *Like Kelly Can*; *One More Waltz*.

By the time the 1927 Laurence Schwab–Lew Brown–Frank Mandel–Buddy De Sylva musical **Good News** came to the screen via MGM, it was old news, and its tired story (football hero threatens the chances of his college team by neglecting his studies, but is successfully coached by an ugly duckling astronomy student who blossoms – *mirabile dictu* – into a beauty) certainly needed all the help it could get from the score by De Sylva, Brown and Henderson, and the other first-league composers, which went with it. Stanley Smith and an insipid Mary Lawlor starred as the footballer and the girl who helps him improve his grades, with Bessie Love (illustrated), Cliff Edwards, Lola Lane, Dorothy McNulty (she would become known as Penny Singleton), Thomas Jackson, specialty dancer Al (Rubberlegs) Norman and Delmer Daves also on hand to lend stalwart support to this rah-rah musical. It was adapted for the screen by Frances Marion, and directed by Nick Grinde with some assistance from Edgar McGregor, the show's original Broadway director. Due to the moratorium being imposed on musicals towards the end of 1930, the release print of **Good News** had several numbers excised from it, notably the duets of 'The Best Things In Life Are Free' and 'Lucky In Love'; and a Lola Lane number called 'That's How You Know We're Co-Eds'. The standout number was the ever-popular 'Varsity Drag'. Other songs: *He's A Lady's Man*; *Good News*; *Tait Song*; *Students Are We* De Sylva, Lew Brown, Henderson; *If You're Not Kissing Me*; *Football* Arthur Freed, Nacio Herb Brown; *I Feel Pessimistic* J. Russell Robinson, George Waggner; *Gee But I'd Like To Make You Happy* Reggie Montgomery. Remade in 1947.

Another unashamed dollop of romance for Ramon Novarro fans, **Call of the Flesh** (MGM), also known as *The Singer From Seville*, again placed the Mexican idol (illustrated) in a Spanish setting – this time as a would-be opera singer who captures the heart of convent girl Dorothy Jordan (illustrated). Novarro's singing, and a sequence in Technicolor, were the highlights of John Colton's rather workaday screenplay (story by Dorothy Farnum) though Renée Adorée, whose last film this was to be, was delightful as a Spanish dancer in love with Novarro. Less happily cast was Russell Hopton as Enrique, Miss Jordan's brother, whose big moment, when he tries to persuade Novarro not to marry his sister, went for nothing. Also in it were Ernest Torrence, Nance O'Neil, and Mathilde Comont. The competent direction was by Charles Brabin, with dance direction from Eduardo Cansino. Songs: *Just For Today*; *Not Quite Good Enough For Me* Herbert Stothart, Clifford Grey; *Lonely* Stothart, Grey, Novarro. Operatic excerpts, all sung by Novarro, included 'Vesti la Giubba' *Pagliacci* Leoncavallo; 'Cavatina' *L'Elisir d'Amore* Donizetti; 'Questa o quella' *Rigoletto* Verdi.
▽

△

◁ An all-Technicolor musical with a golfing background, **Follow Thru** (Paramount) featured Jack Haley in the role he created the previous year on Broadway – though top billing went to Nancy Carroll as a golf pro's daughter out to beat her rival in love in a golfing tournament, and Charles 'Buddy' Rogers as the golf instructor who coaches her to victory. Haley played a girl-shy millionaire and in this, his first screen appearance, holed in one with both audiences and critics and launched his movie career. Zelma O'Neal (illustrated), Eugene Pallette, Thelma Todd, Claude King and Kathryn Givney were also in it; it was written and directed by Laurence Schwab and Lloyd Corrigan (from the stage show by Schwab, Buddy De Sylva, Lew Brown and Ray Henderson) and produced by Schwab and Frank Mandel. Songs: *A Peach Of A Pair* George Marion Jr, Richard A. Whiting; *It Must Be You* Edward Eliscu, Manning Sherwin; *Button Up Your Overcoat*; *Then I'll Have Time For You*; *I Want To Be Bad* De Sylva, Brown, Henderson.

With the bulk of its original score removed, RKO's **Leathernecking** (G.B.: **Present Arms**), partly filmed in colour, was the celluloid transposition of a Rodgers and Hart–Herbert Fields stage musical, *Present Arms*, the musical numbers of which had been directed on Broadway in 1928 by Busby Berkeley. The hackneyed story was of an army private (Ken Murray, 2nd left) who decides to impress society in general and his sweetheart (Irene Dunne) in particular by pretending to be a captain. Sprightly performances from Murray, Benny Rubin (right), Lilyan Tashman, Eddie Foy Jr (2nd right), Ned Sparks, Fred Santley (left) and Louise Fazenda kept it bearable; ditto director Edward Cline's pleasing lightness of touch. Pearl Eaton was responsible for the dance routines, the associate producer was Louis Sarecky, and the screenplay by Jane Murfin from an adaptation by Alfred Jackson. Songs: *You Took Advantage Of Me*; *A Kiss For Cinderella* Rodgers and Hart; *All My Life*; *Careless Kisses*; *Evening Star*; *Nice And So Peculiar* Benny Davis, Harry Akst; *Shake It Off And Smile* Sidney Clare, Oscar Levant.

Al Jolson (illustrated) starred in the movie version of his 1925 stage success, **Big Boy** (Warner Bros.), again playing the part of a negro jockey who triumphs over adversity and eventually wins the Kentucky Derby. Although there wasn't a great deal of mileage left in William K. Wells, Perry Vekroff and Rex Taylor's screenplay (from a play by Harold Atteridge), it was larded with wise-cracks, making up in humour what it lacked in originality. Alan Crosland directed with a refreshing lightness of touch after his *sturm-und-drang* approach to *The Jazz Singer* (Warner Bros. 1927) and, in supporting roles cast Claudia Dell, Louise Closser Hale, Lloyd Hughes, Eddie Phillips, John Harron and Noah Beery. But it was Jolson the customers wanted – and it was Jolson they got. With a vengeance! Songs: *What Will I Do Without You?* Al Dubin, Joe Burke; *Tomorrow Is Another Day*; *Liza Lee* Bud Green, Sammy Stept; *Down South* Sigmund Spaeth, William H. Myddleton; *The Handicap March* Dave Reed Jr, George Rosey; *Sonny Boy* Buddy De Sylva, Lew Brown, Ray Henderson.
▽

THIRTIES MUSICALS

Heads Up (Paramount) was a routine musical starring Charles 'Buddy' Rogers as an officer with the Coast Guards who goes through no end of bother to win the love of pretty Margaret Breen (against her mother's wishes), and to expose his rival as a fugitive bootlegger. Originally seen as a 1929 Broadway musical with music and lyrics by Richard Rodgers and Lorenz Hart, it was adapted for the screen by John McGowan and Jack Kirkland, directed by Victor Schertzinger with uneasy shifts of emphasis between comedy and melodrama, and featured Victor Moore and Helen Kane (foreground) as the comic support, with Helen Carrington, Gene Cowing, Harry Shannon, Preston Foster and Billy Taylor also cast. The dances were staged by George Hale. Songs included: *My Man Is On The Make*; *A Ship Without A Sail* Rodgers, Hart; *If I Knew You Better* Victor Schertzinger.

Like the Broadway hit on which it was based, **Whoopee** (Goldwyn) starred Eddie Cantor who, having previously made two unsuccessful films, became a Hollywood star with this one. It also introduced Busby Berkeley to screen audiences, and was one of the first musicals to use two-colour Technicolor really effectively. Based on a story by E.J. Ruth, a play by Owen Davis called *The Nervous Wreck*, and on the stage musical by William Anthony McGuire, Walter Donaldson and Gus Kahn (and written for the screen by William Conselman), it concerned itself with a hypochondriac (Cantor) who finds himself on an Arizona ranch peopled with cowboys, Indians, and a multitude of Broadway chorus girls. It provided plenty of scope for Cantor's comic persona, as well as giving him four Donaldson–Kahn numbers to sing, most notably 'Making Whoopee', the one song to have survived the transition from Broadway, and Cantor's biggest-ever hit. Berkeley, who staged the dances for **Whoopee**, cut his teeth on the numbers, all of which bore his unmistakable imprint (see illustration), and made quite a debut for himself. Believing that the film musical was 'terribly static and restricted', Berkeley came to Hollywood at the behest of Sam Goldwyn, who promised him complete artistic freedom. Taking advantage of this promise, and with the confidence of youth on his side, he immediately eliminated three of the four camera crews usually employed in the filming of production numbers and concentrated on only one camera – a practice he continued throughout

his career. In **Whoopee**'s opening sequence, 'Cowboy Number', a young Betty Grable leads the chorus and becomes the centre of Berkeley's first abstract pattern of dancers. For the first time ever the chorus girls were filmed in close-up, the camera becoming the surrogate for the average male out front in the stalls. As Berkeley commented to Goldwyn, 'We've got these beautiful girls, why not let the public see them?' In addition, the girls provided the perfect counter-point to Berkeley's abstract forms and, as such, would in future humanize all his choreographic flights of fantasy. **Whoopee** was produced by Samuel Goldwyn and Florenz Ziegfeld, directed by Thornton Freeland, and also starred Eleanor Hunt. Its supporting cast included Paul Gregory, John Rutherford, Ethel Shutta, Spencer Charters, Chief Caupolican, Albert Hackett and William H. Philbrick – all from the original stage production. Other songs: *Mission Number*; *A Girlfriend Of A Boyfriend Of Mine*; *Makin' Waffles*; *My Baby Just Cares For Me*; *Stetson*; *The Song Of The Setting Sun* Donaldson, Kahn; *I'll Still Belong To You* Nacio Herb Brown, Edward Eliscu.

Interesting sideline: Florenz Ziegfeld's participation in the production was, for the most part, nominal. Following the 1929 crash, Ziegfeld and Goldwyn formed a joint corporation to film **Whoopee** and *Kid Boots*, but Ziegfeld alienated Goldwyn by insisting that his name be first in the corporation, with the result that Goldwyn restricted his access to the sound stages, and *Kid Boots* did not get made (except for the silent version, with Cantor, in 1926).

60

Thankfully the only musical to be attempted by the epic-orientated Cecil B. De Mille, **Madam Satan** (MGM) was a curious entertainment that cost a great deal of money to make and laid a brick at the box office. Set aboad a giant dirigible, its acorn of a plot (by Jeanie MacPherson, Gladys Unger and Elsie Janis) had a wealthy socialite (Kay Johnson, right) attempting to win back the love of her husband (Reginald Denny, left) by assuming the identity of a mysterious 'Madam Satan'. The climax of this hodge-podge was a spectacular costume party given aboard the dirigible, the floor show being an electrical ballet (staged by LeRoy Prinz and composed by Herbert Stothart) in which the participants, among other things, pretend to be spark plugs. A bolt of lightning, doubtless offended by the bad taste of it all, wrathfully strikes the floating airship, forcing its occupants to descend to the relative safety of New York via parachute. Husband and wife, by the way, were blissfully reunited. No less than forty-six players were credited, and they included Lillian Roth as the wild showgirl Denny temporarily leaves his wife for, Roland Young, Elsa Peterson, Irwin Boyd, Tyler Brooke, Wilfred Lucas, Albert Conti and, in a small part, composer Jack King. Cedric Gibbons and Mitchell Leisen dreamed up the sets, the gowns were by Adrian, and it was photographed by Robert Rosson. Songs and musical numbers included: *We're Going Somewhere*; *The Cat Walk*; *This Is Love* Herbert Stothart, Clifford Grey; *All I Know Is You Are In My Arms*; *Low Down*; *Auction Number*; *Satan's Song*; *Live And Love Today* Elsie Janis, Jack King.

One of the worst musicals of the year, **The Lottery Bride** (United Artists) – about a Norwegian lass who becomes the lottery bride of a miner only to discover that her husband is the older brother of the man she *really* loves – starred Jeanette MacDonald (right), had a score especially written for the occasion by Rudolf Friml, and settings by the great William Cameron Menzies. To no avail, alas. The film, hastily and carelessly directed by Germany's Paul L. Stein, only fuelled the flames of the public's fast-growing antipathy to musicals and it was a monumental failure, bringing naught but embarrassment to its participants. They included the British John Garrick (left), Broadway's Robert Chisholm (whose fine voice was the film's one redeeming feature), ZaSu Pitts and Joe E. Brown. It was adapted by Horace Jackson from a story by Herbert Stothart called *Bride 66* and scripted by Howard Emmett Rogers. Songs: *You're An Angel*; *My Northern Light*; *Yubla*; *Round She Whirls*; *High And Low*; *Shoulder To Shoulder*; *Napoli*; *I'll Follow The Trail*; *Come Drink To The Girl That You Love* Friml, J. Keirn Brennan.

A highly romantic and greatly fictionalized account of the life of Jenny Lind ('the Swedish nightingale') reached the screen in an MGM musical drama called **A Lady's Morals** (GB: **Jenny Lind**). It also marked the successful debut in pictures of the Metropolitan Opera's Grace Moore. Intent on giving the facts of Miss Lind's life a novelettish veneer, screenwriters Hans Kraly, Claudine West, John Meehan and Arthur Richman (story by Dorothy Farnum) partnered the Swedish soprano with a cocky young composer called Paul Brandt (Reginald Denny), who, in the course of the narrative, is hurt in a riot and goes blind. But none of this mattered very much (except possibly to the fictional Mr Brandt), since the film's *raison d'être* was the glowing presence of Miss Moore (illustrated, with Gilbert Emery) – and the arias and songs she sang throughout. They included a selection from Donizetti's *The Daughter Of The Regiment*, the 'Casta Diva' from Bellini's *Norma*, 'Is It Destiny?', 'The Student's Song' and 'I Hear Your Voice' by Clifford Grey and Oscar Straus, 'Oh Why' by Arthur Freed, Herbert Stothart and Henry M. Woods, 'Lovely Hour' by Carrie Jacobs Bond, and 'Swedish Pastorale' by Howard Johnson and Herbert Stothart. Wallace Beery played P.T. Barnum, with other parts going to Jobyna Howland as Miss Lind's companion, Gus Shy, George F. Marion, Paul Porcasi and Judith Vosselli, Sidney Franklin directed.

Maurice Chevalier's fourth film for Paramount – excluding *Paramount on Parade* – was **Playboy of Paris**, and it desperately needed the magic touch of Ernst Lubitsch to bring it to life. What it got, instead, was the leaden one of Ludwig Berger, who also produced. (A French version, called *Le Petit Café*, starring Chevalier, Françoise Rosay and an all-French cast fared better and was generally considered to be the superior of the two.) The story had Chevalier being a waiter by day (illustrated) and a playboy by night, much to the distress of his employer (O.P. Heggie) and his employer's daughter (Frances Dee), who is in love with him. Complications abound and, in the end, Chevalier finds himself being challenged to a duel. Vincent Lawrence's screenplay (adapted by Percy Heath from Tristan Bernard's play *Le Petit Café*) made quite sure that it all ended happily, without, alas, being able to guarantee the same good fortune at the box office. One sequence, however, which became a classic, featured Chevalier tasting and appraising the heady contents of several barrels of wine. It was the best thing in a film that always promised more than it delivered. Others in the cast were Stuart Erwin, Eugene Pallette, Dorothy Christy, Cecil Cunningham, and Tyler Brooke. Songs: *My Ideal*; *It's A Great Life If You Don't Weaken*; *In The Heart Of Old Paree*; *Yvonne's Song* Richard A. Whiting, Newell Chase, Leo Robin.

THIRTIES MUSICALS

◁ Warner Bros.' predilection for operettas, more often than not taken from established stage successes, often resulted in catastrophe. With **Viennese Nights**, however, they acquired something specially written for the screen by Oscar Hammerstein II and Sigmund Romberg, and it turned out just fine. Filmed entirely in two-colour Technicolor, the story spanned 40 years, telling of a young composer (Alexander Gray, 2nd right) and the attractive woman (Vivienne Segal, centre right) who ought to have married him, but who weds a philanderer (Walter Pidgeon, centre left) instead. It had its over-*schmaltzy* moments and a profusion of plot but, nonetheless, made for a melodious and pleasing entertainment rich in Romberg waltzes. Alan Crosland directed a cast which included Bert Roach (right), Milton Douglas, Jean Hersholt, June Purcell and Louise Fazenda, and Jack Haskell directed the dances. Songs included: *I Bring A Love Song*; *I'm Lonely*; *You Will Remember Vienna*; *Here We Are*; *Regimental March*; *Yes, Yes, Yes*; *Goodbye My Love*; *Viennese Nights*.

Jeanette MacDonald, on loan to Fox from Paramount who didn't quite know what to do with her in the face of the negative reaction to musicals, sang opera for the first time in **Oh, For a Man!** beginning, no less, with the 'Liebestod' from Wagner's *Tristan and Isolde*. A slender but enjoyable trifle about an opera star (MacDonald, right) whose apartment is invaded by a burglar with a penchant for singing, it had MacDonald not only arranging for the rogue (Reginald Denny, left) to have his voice professionally trained, but falling in love with him as well! All very improbable, but adequately scripted (by Philip Klein and Lynn Starling), and delightfully performed by Miss MacDonald who was on top of the flimsy material all the way. Director Hamilton MacFadden made quite sure that his star always looked good and, in addition, drew enjoyable performances from vivacious Marjorie White and haughty Alison Skipworth. Completing the cast were Bela Lugosi, Albert Conti, Andre Cheron and William Davidson. Songs: *Believe Me If All Those Endearing Young Charms* (Matthew Locke, lyrics by Thomas Moore); *On A Summer Night*; *I'm Just Nuts About You* William Kernell; and a German art song (composer uncertain).

▽

Two of the best voices to grace the screen in 1930 – those of Lawrence Tibbett (left) and Grace Moore (centre) – brought glory to the Sigmund Romberg–Oscar Hammerstein II operetta **New Moon** which MGM presented in a no-expense-spared production, and which was a heartening box-office success. Transposed from its original French setting to Russia, its typical operetta-type plot (by Frank Mandel and Laurence Schwab) had the Princess Tanya (Moore) falling for a dashing lieutenant (Tibbett) despite the fact that she is already engaged to a Russian governor called Brusiloff (Adolphe Menjou, right). Roland Young, Guy Shy and Emily Fitzroy were in it too; adapted by Sylvia Thalberg and Frank Butler (dialogue by Cyril Hume), with Jack Conway directing. Songs: *Lover Come Back To Me*; *One Kiss*; *Stout-Hearted Men*; *Wanting You*; *Marianne*; *Funny Little Sailor Men*; *Farmer's Daughter*; *What Is Your Price Madame*.

The talkies helped to establish a lot more stars than they ruined – comedian Ed Wynn (illustrated) being a prime example. His distinctive, if somewhat squeaky, voice responded excellently to the machinations of the movie microphone, as audiences discovered in **Follow the Leader** (Paramount), a screen adaptation by Gertrude Purcell and Sid Silvers of a William K. Wells–George White–Buddy De Sylva–Lew Brown–Ray Henderson musical comedy called *Manhattan Mary*. In it, Wynn played a former acrobat turned waiter who, through a series of mishaps, finds himself elected the leader of a notorious gang called 'The Hudson Dusters'. Ginger Rogers was cast opposite him as a singer aching for a crack at Broadway, with Stanley Smith as the man she loves. Also cast were Lou Holtz, Lida Kane and newcomer Ethel Merman, who was brought in as a last-minute replacement for Ruth Etting, and got to sing the Sammy Fain–Irving Kahal number 'Satan's Holiday'. The director was Norman Taurog. Other songs included De Sylva, Brown and Henderson's *Broadway, The Heart Of The World*, retained from the original stage show; and *Brother, Just Laugh It Off* by E.Y. Harburg, Arthur Schwartz and Ralph ◁ Rainger.

Another casualty of the cinema-going public's ▷
declining interest in musicals was **Are You
There?** (Fox), a vehicle for Canadian comedienne
Beatrice Lillie (centre), which had four of its
songs dropped after completion. Initial press
reaction was not favourable and so the film
never went out on full general release. A pity, as
its rediscovery a few years ago revealed it to be
the perfect showcase for its irrepressible star's
outrageously zany sense of fun. She played a
private eye who is hired by the son of a duke to
prevent his father from marrying the Countess
Helenka. Disguised as Lady Diana, a big game
hunter, Miss Lillie gets to work on the case and
exposes the duke's intended as a fraud – winning
in the process the love of the old boy for herself.
Harlan Thompson wrote it, Hamilton Mac-
Fadden directed it and an excellent cast
included John Garrick as the duke's son, George
Grossmith as the duke, and Olga Baclanova as
the phoney countess. Surviving songs: *Lady
Detective*; *Queen Of The Hunt Am I*; *Baghdad Daddies*
Grace Henry, Morris Hamilton.

△
Melville Crossman's (a pseudonym for Darryl F.
Zanuck) story about two shopgirls who embark
on a gold-digging search for a rich old man
benefitted from an excellent screenplay by
Arthur Caesar, and reached the screen as **The
Life of the Party** (Warner Bros.) with Winnie
Lightner as the star. Filmed in Technicolor and
crisply directed by Roy Del Ruth, the movie's
appearance unfortunately coincided with the
current wave of unpopularity that was affecting
screen musicals, so that what had been conceived as a full-scale musical lost all but one of
its numbers to the cutting-room floor.
Nevertheless, Miss Lightner (left) together with
Irene Delroy as her friend, were backed up by a
collection of effectively amusing performances
from Charles Butterworth (right), Jack Whiting,
Arthur Hoyt and, notably, Charles Judels as a
hot-tempered couturier. The song that remained
was *Can It Be Possible?* Sidney Mitchell, Archie
Gottler, Joseph Mayer. Casualties were *One Robin
Doesn't Make A Spring*; *Somehow* Frederick Loewe,
Earle Crooker.

Sunny, the Otto Harbach–Oscar Hammerstein
II–Jerome Kern stage success in which the
effervescent Marilyn Miller (illustrated, below
left, with Jerome Kern) had so delighted
audiences on Broadway, was picked up for the
movies, complete with its star and its
Harbach–Hammerstein–Kern melodies, by First
National. The plot was quite nonsensical:
English circus bareback rider dresses up as a boy,
stows away on board a New York-bound ship, is
discovered, and, after being taken care of by
some sympathetic passengers, marries one of
them. But the story, adapted by Humphrey
Pearson and Henry McCarty, was secondary to
the gaiety of Miss Miller's singing and dancing.
Joe Donahue played the man whom Sunny
marries; and others featured in the cast were
Lawrence Gray, O.P. Heggie, Inez Courtney,
Barbara Bedford, Judith Vosselli and Clyde Cook.
William A. Seiter made a good job of the direction,
and the movie was embellished by ballet sequences directed by Theodore Kosloff. The songs
included: *Sunny*; *Who?*; *Two Little Love Birds*; *D'ya
Love Me?*; *I Was Alone*.
▽

Kiss Me Again (First National), originally
known as *The Toast Of The Legion*, was a
Technicolor screen adaptation of Victor
Herbert's famous operetta *Mademoiselle Modiste*.
Julian Josephson and Paul Perez reworked the
original book by Henry Blossom and provided
star parts for Walter Pidgeon (right) and Bernice
Claire (left) in a story which led the pair of
them, as a French lieutenant and his inamorata
Mademoiselle Fifi, along the rocky road to love,
encountering a number of Victor Herbert me-
lodies (lyrics by Henry Blossom) on their way.
William A. Seiter directed with a cast that also
included Edward Everett Horton, Claude
Gillingwater, Frank McHugh, Judith Vosselli,
June Collyer and Albert Gran. Songs: *Kiss Me
Again*; *The Time, The Place And The Girl*; *When
The Cat's Away*; *I Want What I Want When I Want
It*; *Mascot Of The Troop*; *If I Were On The Stage*;
◁ *Love Me, Love My Dog*.

Buddy De Sylva, Lew Brown and Ray Henderson
followed their 1929 hit *Sunnyside Up* with **Just
Imagine** (Fox), the first science fiction musical
which, though fascinating in the way it predicted such things as automatic doors, space
exploration, test-tube babies, food-substitute
pills, televisual telephones and, most alarm-
ingly, names replaced by numbers, suffered from
an inferior screenplay, some pedestrian direction (by David Butler), and a score that in no
way matched *Sunnyside Up* or the same team's
Good News. The performances by El Brendel
(centre right, as Single O), Maureen O'Sullivan
(as LN-18), John Garrick (centre left, as J-21),
Marjorie White (right, as D-6), Frank Albertson
(left, as RT-42), Hobart Bosworth (as Z-4) and
Mischa Auer (as B-36) were serviceable enough,
but as the boldness of the concept was never
reflected in anything they had to do or say, none
of them was able to make much impact. The
dance director was Seymour Felix and the
imaginative settings the work of Stephen
Goosson and Ralph Hammeras. Songs: *The
Drinking Song*; *The Romance Of Elmer
Stremmingway*; *Never Never Wed*; *There's
Something About An Old-Fashioned Girl*; *Mothers
Ought To Tell Their Daughters*; *I Am The Words,
You Are The Melody*; *Dance Of Victory*; *Never Swat
A Fly*.
▽

1931

Academy Awards

Art Direction
NOMINATIONS INCLUDED: *Just Imagine* (Fox) Stephen Goosson & Ralph Hammeras. *Whoopee* (Goldwyn, UA) Richard Day.

The New York Times Annual 'Ten Best'
3rd *The Smiling Lieutenant* (Paramount)

The Annual Top Moneymaking Films
INCLUDING (In alphabetical order): *Animal Crackers* (Paramount). *Check And Double Check* (RKO).

The Hot Heiress (First National) was a totally negative contribution to the screen musical. The public failed entirely to respond to the story of a riveter (Ben Lyon, left) who is taken up by a society woman from Port Chester (Ona Munson, right) and passed off as an architect; and even some original songs by Richard Rodgers and Lorenz Hart didn't help – a particular pity since the tunes themselves were well received, and critics remarked that a few more wouldn't have been amiss. The story and screenplay were by Herbert Fields, and the cast included Walter Pidgeon, Thelma Todd, Tom Dugan, Inez Courtney and Holmes Herbert, all of whom remained obstinately inert under the direction of Clarence 'Badger, whose limited acquaintance with musicals was all too evident. As a result of the film's artistic as well as commercial failure, the composers withdrew from their next two assignments for the studio. Songs included: *You're The Cats*; *Nobody Loves A Riveter*; *Like Ordinary People Do*; *Too Good To Be True* (deleted before the film's release). Remade in 1934 as *Happiness Ahead*, and again in 1941.
▽

Though the critics were respectful about MGM's ▷ **The Prodigal** (originally called *The Southerner*), this Lawrence Tibbett vehicle – in which the booming baritone played a self-imposed hobo who, after traversing the highways and byways of life for five years in the company of two other self-made tramps, returns to the bosom of his genteel Southern family and falls in love with his brother's wife – was not a success. In it, Tibbett (left) sang the famous 'Without A Song' by Vincent Youmans, Edward Eliscu and Billy Rose (the one thing he was never without!). But as the film was without an audience, it was of no consequence to anyone that it was the best moment in this Harry Pollard-directed curiosity. Bess Meredyth and Wells Root wrote it, with parts for Roland Young and Cliff Edwards as Tibbett's hobo buddies, and Esther Ralston as the sister-in-law he falls for. Also: Purnell Pratt, Emma Dunn, Hedda Hopper (right), Stepin Fetchit, and Theodore von Eltz. Other songs included: *Life Is A Dream* Arthur Freed, Oscar Straus; *Home Sweet Home* John Howard Payne, Sir Henry Bishop.

A remake of Ludwig Berger's *Ein Walzertraum* (*A Waltz Dream*), **The Smiling Lieutenant** (Paramount) reunited Maurice Chevalier with director Ernst Lubitsch, and gave the ailing screen musical a temporary respite that was hailed by critics and public alike as a welcome watering-hole in a desert of mediocrity. The story of an officer of the guards who, due to circumstances entirely out of his control, finds himself married to the rather plain-looking Princess Anna, it featured Chevalier (left) as the officer, Miriam Hopkins as his wife, and Claudette Colbert (right) as Nikki, the beautiful woman he really loves. Ironically, it is Nikki who, taking pity on the princess, teaches her how to improve her appearance, with the result that overnight she becomes a ravishing beauty whose good looks more than satisfy the man she has married. A wry and enchanting fairy-tale, its screenplay (by Ernest Vajda and Samson Raphaelson) frothed along, bringing out the best in its director and his three principal players. Enhanced by a melodious Oscar Straus score (lyrics by Clifford Grey), it simply couldn't miss – and didn't. Also cast were Charles Ruggles, George Barbier, Hugh O'Connell, Robert Strange and Con MacSunday. Songs: *Toujours L'Amour In The Army* (Chevalier); *Breakfast Table Love*; *Jazz Up Your Lingerie* (Colbert, Hopkins); *Live For Today*; *While Hearts Are Singing* (introduced by ◁ Colbert); *One More Hour Of Love* (Chevalier).

△

Beguiled by the British musical comedy star Evelyn Laye, Sam Goldwyn prevailed upon two Pulitzer Prize-winning writers, Louis Bromfield and Sidney Howard, to fashion a story that would do justice to her American screen debut. What they actually came up with was a rather mindless operetta called **One Heavenly Night** (United Artists) which, as it turned out, was anything but. Miss Laye (right) played a flower girl from Budapest who spends most of the time masquerading as a cabaret star. She falls in love with the dashing if somewhat roguish Count Mirko Tabor (John Boles, left) and, after a few elementary complications, marries him. Goldwyn's faith in his leading lady was justified. She scored a personal success and emerged from the venture unscathed. So did comedian Leon Errol who, in the course of the film's 82-minute running time, managed to air his entire repertoire of comic *shtick*. The film itself, directed by George Fitzmaurice, was dismissed as old-fashioned hogwash, and Goldwyn never again turned his hand to operetta. Miss Laye made only one more film in America before returning to Britain where she continued to charm London West End audiences for several decades. Others in the cast were Lilyan Tashman, Hugh Cameron, Marion Lord, Luis Alberni and Lionel Belmore. Songs: *I Belong To Everybody*; *Along The Road of Dreams*; *My Heart Is Beating*; *Goodnight Serenade*; *Heavenly Night* Nacio Herb Brown, Bruno Granichstaedten, Edward Eliscu, Clifford Grey.

Bright Lights (Warner Bros./First National) was another backstage musical filmed in Technicolor in which its star, Dorothy Mackaill (right), was at her best as a Hula dancer. Unfortunately, there was nothing else to be said in favour of this story about an actress who gives up her career for marriage, only to find a series of obstacles obstructing her path to happiness. Humphrey Pearson wrote the banal screenplay for producer Robert North and director Michael Curtiz, and Larry Ceballos staged the musical numbers. Noah Beery, Frank Fay (left), Inez Courtney, Eddie Nugent, Edmund Breese, Daphne Pollard and Frank McHugh were also featured and the songs included: *I'm Crazy For Cannibal Love* Al Bryan, Ed Ward; *Chinatown, My Chinatown* William Jerome, Jean Schwartz; *Song* ◁ *Of The Congo* Ned Washington, Benny Rubens.

It all began when Dorothy Jordan, deciding that marriage to executive producer Merian C. Cooper was preferable to dancing the Carioca atop seven white pianos with a relative unknown called Fred Astaire, opted out of her commitment to RKO, and was replaced by Ginger Rogers. It took only one number – the aforementioned Carioca (illustrated) – to make the world realize that in Astaire and Rogers, the musical had found a dance team of incomparable dazzle, and it was no accident that the last shot of **Flying Down to Rio** is not of its two stars – Dolores Del Rio and Gene Raymond – but of Astaire and Rogers. Clearly the studio knew a good thing when it saw one. The film itself – despite a threadbare plot (exotic Brazilian beauty cannot decide whom she loves more: an American aviator-cum-songwriter, or her fiancé back home in Brazil) – contained a wonderful Vincent Youmans score (his last before retiring to Denver with tuberculosis) and a spectacular finale (staged by Dave Gould) featuring dozens of girls in Rockette-like formation, dancing on the wings of aeroplanes, thousands of feet above the city of Rio de Janeiro. Van Nest Polglase designed the sets, and would continue to do so for all the Astaire–Rogers musicals at RKO, Hermes Pan (uncredited) was the assistant dance director, and the screenplay was by Cyril Hume, H.W. Haneman and Erwin Gelsey, from a play by Anne Caldwell based, in turn, on a story by Lou Brock, the associate producer. Raul Roulien, Blanche Frederici, Walter Walker, Etta Moten, Paul Porcasi, Franklin Pangborn, Eric Blore and Luis Alberni were also in it, and the director was Thornton Freeland. Songs: *Music Makes Me* (Rogers); *The Carioca* (Moten); *Orchids in The Moonlight* (Roulien, Astaire, Del Rio); *Flying Down To Rio* (Astaire, chorus) lyrics by Edward Eliscu and Gus Kahn.

A screenplay (by Gene Fowler and Benjamin Glazer with additional dialogue by Claude Binyon and Frank Butler) composed largely of rhyming couplets did little to help Maurice Chevalier in **The Way To Love**, the last film he made for Paramount before accepting an offer from Irving Thalberg at MGM. In the feeblest of his American efforts so far, Chevalier (right) was cast as a Parisian sidewalk hawker whose one ambition in life is to become a tourist guide. He succeeds, and after rejecting the advances of Nydia Westman, finds true happiness with Ann Dvorak (left). Miss Dvorak, on loan from Warner Bros., replaced Sylvia Sidney who walked out of the picture mid-way through shooting, citing ill-health as the reason. The role was then offered to Carole Lombard who, after reading the script, turned it down, doubtless resorting to some of the foul language for which she was notorious, as she did so. Less fortunate were Edward Everett Horton, Arthur Pierson, Minna Gombell, Blanche Frederici, Douglass Dumbrille, John Miljan, Sidney Toler and a dog called Mutt, who were in it to the bitter end. Benjamin Glazer produced, and the director was Norman Taurog. Songs: *Lover of Paree*; *In A One-Room Flat*; *Lucky Guy*; *The Way To Love*; *Its Oh, It's Ah, It's Wonderful* Ralph Rainger, Leo Robin.

Wholesome James Dunn (left) who specialized in playing Mr Average – from humble soda jerks to jobbing clerks – found himself thinking up slogans for a meat-packing outfit in **Jimmy and Sally** (Fox), a likeable romantic comedy with songs which co-starred Claire Trevor as the girl who provides him with his best ideas but gets no credit for it. Romantic problems intruded but they were all worked out to everyone's satisfaction. Paul Schofield and Marguerite Roberts wrote it; James Tinling directed, and his cast included Harvey Stephens, Lya Lys (right), Jed Prouty, Gloria Roy, Alma Lloyd and John Arledge. Songs included: *You're My Thrill*; *Eat Marlowe's Meat*; *It's The Irish In Me* Sidney Clare, Jay Gorney.

A romantic musical comedy that was a three-time loser – being neither romantic, musical, nor comic – **My Lips Betray** (Fox) betrayed all concerned with its predictably coy plot and, as a vehicle for Lilian Harvey (illustrated), was less good even than her first Hollywood effort, *My Weakness* (Fox). Written by the usually sophisticated S.N. Behrman (from a play by Attila Orbok), its operetta-like plot rooted the action in the mythical country of Ruthania, and concerned the amorous cavortings of an impoverished working girl (Harvey) and the King of Ruthania (John Boles) who, disguised as a songwriting captain, falls in love with her. It was all too much to bear, and under John Blystone's soggy direction, collapsed in a heap – leaving its stars with icing sugar all over their attractive faces. El Brendel was in it too and his continued assault on the English language elicited groans all round. Nor was there much joy to be derived from the performances of Irene Browne (as the Queen Mother), Maude Eburne (mildly amusing as the heroine's guardian), Henry Stephenson and Herman Bing. Songs: *His Majesty's Car; To Romance; Why Am I Happy?; The Band Is Gaily Playing* William Kernell.

Modest but enjoyable, **Going Hollywood** was Bing Crosby's first film for MGM (and his last until *High Society* in 1956), and provided him with one of his biggest hit songs to date – 'Temptation'. It was composed by Arthur Freed and Nacio Herb Brown, who furnished the film with its six other new songs as well. It also starred Marion Davies (left), in one of her best roles, as a French teacher in a girls' school who follows Crosby (right) to Hollywood and, in the best fairy-tale fashion finds herself replacing Fifi D'Orsay as the object of his affections as well as the leading lady in his next film. It could only happen in Hollywood and did – many times. Broadway's Patsy Kelly, making her feature film debut, was in it too, so were Ned Sparks (excellent as a cynical film director), and Stuart Erwin as a show backer. Lennie Hayton appeared as conductor and pianist. It was written by Donald Ogden Stewart from a story by Frances Marion, and was directed by Raoul Walsh with a lightness of touch absent in his tough-guy assignments at Warner Bros. a decade later. Other songs: *We'll Make Hay While The Sun Shines; Our Big Love Scene; Going Hollywood; Cinderella's Fella; After Sundown; Beautiful Girl* Freed, Brown; *Just An Echo In The Valley* Reginald Connelly, Jimmy Campbell, Harry Woods.

Duck Soup was the last film the Marx Brothers made at Paramount before moving to MGM, the last to include Zeppo as part of the team, and their least successful at the box office in spite of the superior quality of its timeless humour and penetrating wit. Furthermore, it was banned in Italy by Mussolini – a fact which filled the brothers with immense pride. The only Marx Brothers comedy to be set in a mythological kingdom (Freedonia) it featured Groucho (right) as Rufus T. Firefly who, possessing the statesmanship of Gladstone, the humility of Lincoln and the wisdom of Pericles, is made dictator of the place. It was written by Bert Kalmar and Harry Ruby (who also supplied the songs) with additional dialogue by Nat Perrin and Arthur Sheekman. Leo McCarey directed it and at least one sequence in which Harpo and Chico, while decked out to look like Groucho, pretend to be his reflection in a mirror, was visually superb. Margaret Dumont (left) was in there pitching again, with Raquel Torres, Louis Calhern and Edgar Kennedy also cast. Songs: *Freedonia Hymn; His Excellency Is Due; The Country's Going To War; When The Clock On The Wall Strikes Ten; The Laws Of My Administration.*

Though the storyline devised by Robert Lord and Delmer Daves (screenplay by Daves) for **Dames** was no *War And Peace* – chorus-girl Joan Blondell wheedles money out of Guy Kibbee so that songwriter Dick Powell can get his show on – its production numbers (see illustrations) by Busby Berkeley were once again mind-bogglingly effective. The best of these was the title number (by Al Dubin and Harry Warren), a paean to feminine pulchritude or, as one of the lyrics puts it, 'What do you go for, go see a show for, tell the truth you go to see those beautiful dames.' Clad in frilly white blouses, headgear to match and black tights, dozens of girls configured into intricate geometric patterns, with Berkeley's innovative trick photography helping to create an overall sense of wonderment and spectacle that none of his contemporaries was able to emulate. With 'The Girl At The Ironing Board', another Dubin–Warren number, Joan Blondell as a laundress serenades a pile of pyjamas and men's underwear which suddenly jerks into life and becomes part of the routine. Though far less elaborate in scale than the 'Dames' sequence, it was visually as inventive as anything Berkeley had done so far, with Miss Blondell's pleasing handling of the vocal providing an added bonus. The film's most popular sequence, however, was

Berkeley's staging of Dubin and Warren's 'I Only Have Eyes For You'. A brilliant song in its own right, it was a literal visualization of Dubin's lyrics, and featured scores of Ruby Keelers as part of a dream Dick Powell is having on a New York subway; a dream in which even the faces in the advertisements turn into his sweetheart. Highspot of the number is the jigsaw made by the girls as each, equipped with a board on her back, bends over so that the boards interlock to form a giant-size picture of Ruby. It was Berkeley at his imaginative best, and the sort of work that helped to rescue the musical once more, and keep it alive and kicking for the rest of the decade. Two other songs were featured: 'When You Were A Smile On Your Mother's Lips' by Irving Kahal and Sammy Fain, and 'Try To See It My Way' by Mort Dixon and Allie Wrubel, and while they were pleasant enough, they never achieved the popularity of the three Dubin–Warren contributions. The director was Ray Enright, whose cast included ZaSu Pitts, Hugh Herbert, Phil Regan, Arthur Vinton, and songwriter Sammy Fain making an appearance as – a songwriter. Top left illustration shows L to R: Keeler, Pitts and Kibbee.

THIRTIES MUSICALS

△

Gift of Gab (Universal) was a shapeless and cumbersome liability about an arrogant radio announcer (Edmund Lowe, right) who redeems himself in the eyes of his girl (Gloria Stuart, centre) when he risks his life to inform his listeners of the whereabouts of a missing plane. Over thirty big name performers tried to salvage it with their respective skills but to no avail, proving, once and for all, that if you're saddled with a stinker, you're saddled with a stinker. For the record, the stars included Ruth Etting, Phil Baker, Ethel Waters, Alice White, Alexander Woollcott, Victor Moore (left), Helen Vinson, Gene Austin, Andy Devine, Wini Shaw, Sterling Holloway, Boris Karloff, Bela Lugosi, Paul Lukas, and Gus Arnheim and His Orchestra. It was directed by Karl Freund from a screenplay by Rian James and Lou Breslow, and a story by Jerry Wald and Philip G. Epstein. Songs: *Talking To Myself*; *I Ain't Gonna Sin No More*; *Gift of Gab* Herb Magidson, Con Conrad; *Somebody Looks Good* George Whiting, Albert von Tilzer; *Don't Let This Waltz Mean Goodbye*; *Walkin' On Air* Jack Meskill, von Tilzer; *What A Wonderful Day* Harry Tobias, Al Sherman; *Tomorrow – Who Cares* Murray Mencher, Charles Tobias.

△

◁ Though censor Will Hays imposed all sorts of strictures on Mae West's **Belle of the Nineties** (Paramount), he was unable to censor the lady's libidinous personality or the walk that launched a thousand female impersonators' hips across the length and breadth of the country. As she had been in her previous two films, Mae (illustrated) was a smash and although her performance as Ruby Carter, the chief attraction at the Sensation House, New Orleans, was fundamentally no different from Lady Lou or Tira, it was once again an object lesson in innuendo. There was a plot of sorts (story and screenplay by Miss West) involving a pair of rivals for her affection ('I prefer two kinds of men – domestic and foreign'), some stolen jewels, and a prize fight, but what mattered were the wisecracks it spawned ('It's better to be looked over than overlooked') rather than the story it told, and its screenplay became the most widely quoted of the year. Roger Pryor played Tiger Kid, the good man Mae falls for, John Miljan was the Sensation House's villainous owner ('His mother should have thrown him away and kept the stork') with Katherine De Mille as his jealous mistress. John Mack Brown was also in it, so were James Donlan (father of Yolande), Tom Herbert, Stuart Holmes, Harry Woods and Edward Gargan. Duke Ellington and His Band accompanied Miss West and, keeping a firm control on it all, was director Leo McCarey. Songs: *My Old Flame*; *Troubled Waters*; *My American Beauty*; *When A St Louis Woman Comes Down To New Orleans* Arthur Johnston, Sam Coslow; *The Memphis Blues* George A. Norton, W.C. Handy.

Jimmy Durante starred in **Student Tour** (MGM) and once again was the victim of a haven't-we-been-here-before plot. Seems his celebrated proboscis just had no talent for smelling out an original idea. He played the trainer of a college rowing team that found itself in serious danger of jeopardising an around-the-world tour to England – and a chance to compete in an important rowing event while over there – because all its members have flunked a philosophy exam. To alleviate the situation, professor Charles Butterworth (left, with Durante) generously offers to accompany them on the cruise and help them with their studies. His plain-Jane niece (Maxine Doyle) comes along for the ride as well – and proves Dorothy Parker right by removing her glasses and instantly finding true love in the hefty arms of the team's personable captain (Phil Regan). A few good Arthur Freed–Nacio Herb Brown songs momentarily helped inject some momentum into Ralph Spence and Philip Dunne's screenplay (story by George Seaton, Arthur Bloch and Samuel Marx) but not enough to make it anything more than the B-picture it was. The cast also included, Florine McKinney, Douglas Fowley, Monte Blue, Betty Grable, Herman Brix (Bruce Bennet) and, in a flashy guest appearance (his last before star-status was accorded him in *Naughty Marietta*, MGM 1935), Nelson Eddy. The director was Charles Riesner. Songs: *A New Moon Is Over My Shoulder*; *From Now On*; *By The Taj Mahal*; *The Snake Dance*; *The Carlo*; *Fight 'Em* Freed, Brown; *I Just Say It With Music* Jimmy Durante.

◁ Grace Moore made opera respectable in **One Night Of Love** (Columbia) – at least as far as the movies were concerned. Cunningly calculated to appeal to audiences who had hitherto regarded opera as a five-letter word of repellent aspect, and a form of entertainment strictly for eggheads, its simple story – of a young soprano's rise to eminence and the faith and patience lavished on her by a celebrated Italian music maestro – captured the imaginations of audiences everywhere and overnight turned Miss Moore (right) into a superstar. Tullio Carminati (left) played her devoted but long-suffering teacher, Lyle Talbot the handsome American she meets, and for whom she almost jettisons her career. Completing the cast were Mona Barrie, Jessie Ralph, Luis Alberni and Andres de Segurola. It was directed by Victor Schertzinger (a composer whose hobby was making movies; or a movie-maker whose hobby was writing songs) who combined his twin interests by providing the film with its appealing title number (lyrics by Gus Kahn). The screenplay was by S.K. Lauren, James Gow and Edmund North from a story by Dorothy Speare and Charles Beahan. Miss Moore sang the famous *Ciri-Biri-Bin* by A. Pestalozza and Rudolf Thaler, and other operatic music included extracts from Donizetti's *Lucia di Lammermoor*, Puccini's *Madame Butterfly* and Bizet's *Carmen*.

Having lured Maurice Chevalier, Jeanette Mac-Donald and Ernst Lubitsch from Paramount, and with a complicated legal situation regarding the rights now satisfactorily settled, MGM's Irving Thalberg mounted the third and best version of **The Merry Widow**, Lehar's enduring masterpiece. The result was one of the great screen musicals of all time, an enchantingly intoxicating mixture of music and romance, sparklingly directed, and performed with style and grace by its two leading players. In as near perfect an adaptation of an operetta as the screen had yet seen, writers Ernest Vajda and Samson Raphaelson took certain liberties with the spirit of the piece. What they helped to create was a musical fairy-tale of incomparable sophistication whose nearest rival in excellence to date was *Love Me Tonight* (Paramount, 1932). Mac-Donald, of course, played the widow (illustrated); Chevalier (who had wanted Grace Moore for the widow) was the irresistably charming and handsome reprobate Count Danilo. Edward Everett Horton played Ambassador Popoff, Una Merkel Queen Dolores, George Barbier King Achmed, with other parts going to Minna Gombell, Ruth Channing, Sterling Holloway, Donald Meek, Akim Tamiroff and Herman Bing. (A French version called *La Veuve Joyeuse* ▽

was simultaneously shot with several cast changes among the supporting performers.) Though Lehar's melodies underscored most of the action throughout the film, the musical and visual highlight was undoubtedly the Grand Ball. As the lilting 'Merry Widow Waltz' (lyrics by Lorenz Hart) reached its climax, the dancers, effectively costumed in sharply contrasting black and white, whirled their way down a large mirrored passageway while an overhead shot charted their melodious progress. The moment was a *tour de force* for its brilliant director and one of breathtaking beauty for the spectator. The brilliant and prolific Lorenz Hart also supplied new lyrics for 'Girls Girls Girls', as well as for the rapturous 'Vilia', 'Maxims', 'Melody Of Laughter', and 'if Widows Are Rich'; with Gus Kahn contributing a lyric of his own to 'Tonight Will Teach Me To Forget'. Despite the high critical praise with which this best of all Merry Widows was received, it is astonishing to note that it failed to find a large audience. And although it took Jeanette MacDonald one step closer to the superstardom she was to enjoy after *Naughty Marietta* (MGM) the following year, it ended Chevalier's brief association with the studio until his triumphant return to it over 20 years later in *Gigi* (1957). Remade in 1952.

Bing Crosby was joined by Miriam Hopkins no less, in **She Loves Me Not** (Paramount), one of the few vehicles so far to come 'the groaner's' way in which the plot was as good as the songs. Aided and abetted by fellow Princeton student Edward Nugent, Crosby takes pity on attractive Curly Flagg (Hopkins), a cabaret dancer who, after witnessing a murder, flees the scene of the crime for fear of being implicated. He gives her sanctuary and, in a reversal of what was expected of Brandon Thomas's Charley's Aunt, insists that she dress up in male attire to avoid detection (see illustration). All the predictable complications ensued – but thanks to the ingenuity of producer Benjamin Glazer's screenplay (from the play by Howard Lindsay and the novel by Edward Hope), some nifty direction by Elliott Nugent, and a clutch of first rate performances – especially from Kitty Carlisle as Crosby's fiancée, and Henry Stephenson as a college Dean – it was an entertaining romp. Remade in 1942 as *True To The Army* (Paramount). Also cast: Lynne Overman, Warren Hymer, Judith Allen, George Barbier and Henry Kolker. Songs: *Love In Bloom* Ralph Rainger, Leo Robin; *After All, You're All I'm After* Edward Heyman, Arthur Schwartz; *Straight From The Shoulder (Right From The Heart)*; *I'm Hummin' (I'm Whistlin'. I'm Singin')*; *Put A Little Rhythm In Everything You Do* Mack Gordon, Harry Revel; *Cocktails For Two* Arthur Johnston, Sam Coslow. ▽

THIRTIES MUSICALS

Jerome Kern and Oscar Hammerstein II's tuneful stage success **Music In The Air** (Fox), though coming uncomfortably close to Viennese operetta in content, managed to avoid the more unpalatable excesses of that genre thanks to a robust screenplay (by Howard I. Young and Billy Wilder) that never took more than one lump of sugar at a time in the telling of its potentially cloying story. Gloria Swanson (left) was given top billing as a temperamental German prima donna who, after quarrelling with the lyricist of her new operetta, punishes him by seducing an innocent young Bavarian schoolmaster (Douglass Montgomery, vocals dubbed by James O'Brien) while the lyricist (John Boles, right), to annoy the prima donna, promises the teacher's sweetheart (June Lang, vocals dubbed by Betty Hiestand) that he will write a show for her, It ends with the two youngsters returning to their little village of Ebendorf, grateful to be free of the selfish connivances of show-folk. A uniformly excellent cast which also included Al Shean (repeating the role he played on Broadway), Reginald Owen, Joseph Cawthorn, Hobart Bosworth and Marjorie Main, garnered uniformly favourable reviews and was generally well received. Joe May directed, and the excellent score included: *I've Told Every Little Star*; *One More Dance*; *The Song Is You*; *We Belong Together*; *There's A Hill Beyond A Hill*; *I'm So Eager*.
▽

Alice Faye (centre left) teamed up with James Dunn (centre) in **365 Nights in Hollywood** (Fox) as a Hollywood hopeful from Peoria who joins a bogus film school but who, through the devotion of a has-been movie director, finds fame, fortune and, of course, romance. Two large-scale production numbers *en route* to the happy ending helped take the curse off William Conselman and Henry Johnson's singularly trite screenplay (story by James Starr), though funnymen Frank Mitchell and Jack Durant as a couple of icemen put the curse straight back on it. John Qualen, John Bradford and Frank Melton were in it too, it was produced by Sol Wurtzel and the director was George Marshall. Songs included: *You're My Future Star*; *Yes To You* Sidney Clare, Richard A. Whiting.
▽

△

Another tailor-made Eddie Cantor vehicle. **Kid Millions**, about a simple-minded 'nebbish' (Cantor, centre) who inherits $77,000,000 from his archaeologist father, cost millions, and made millions. Set for much of its time in Egypt, and with a plot that had various characters contriving to separate Eddie from his fortune, it was a zippy musical with all the usual Cantor ingredients, plus a spectacular Technicolor finale set in an ice-cream factory in Brooklyn, and featuring Broadway's Ethel Merman who, in her third film, almost tucked the show under her ample arms and ran away with it. Merman also featured in the opening number – a ditty called 'An Earful Of Music' (by Gus Kahn and Walter Donaldson) and gave audiences precisely that. Ann Sothern and George Murphy as the obligatory young lovers got to sing the film's big romantic ballad ('Your Head On My Shoulder' by Harold Adamson and Burton Lane) while Cantor, in his traditional blackface sequence (a minstrel show set on board a ship) and playing end man to George Murphy's interlocutor, offered a vigorous rendition of Irving Berlin's 'Mandy'. The musical numbers were the responsibility of Seymour Felix who seemed to rely on the hefty budget for staging them. Arthur Sheekman, Nat Perrin and Nunnally Johnson wrote the original screenplay and Roy Del Ruth called the shots. The extremely serviceable supporting cast included Jesse Block, Eve Sully, Berton Churchill, Warren Hymer, Paul Harvey and Edgar Kennedy. Other songs: *When My Ship Comes In* (Cantor); *Okay Toots* (Cantor, Goldwyn Girls); *Ice Cream Fantasy* (Merman, Goldwyn Girls Cantor, Hymer) Kahn, Donaldson; *I Want To Be A Minstrel Man* (Nicholas, Goldwyn Girls) Adamson, Lane.

△

Little Mitzi Green did her celebrated impersonation of George Arliss, and Nancy Carroll (left) took the mickey out of Garbo *à la Grand Hotel* (MGM 1932) in **Transatlantic Merry Go Round** (United Artists), an 'anything goes' musical into which everything went. A combination thriller, melodrama, farce and revue, it was set, as its title suggested, on board a transatlantic ocean liner, and involved the somewhat bizarre activities of (among others) a pair of shady gamblers, a thief, an unfaithful wife who has no idea her husband has come along for the ride as well, and an escaped convict. It really made no sense at all but was rich in incident, full of good tunes, and had a talented cast that also included Gene Raymond, Jack Benny (right), Sydney Howard, Sid Silvers, Sidney Blackmer, Ralph Morgan, William Boyd, Shirley Grey, and Jimmy Grier and His Orchestra. The screenplay was by Joseph Moncure March and Harry W. Conn from an original story by Leon Gordon. Edward Small produced, and the director was Benjamin Stoloff. Songs: *It Was Sweet Of You*; *Rock and Roll*; *Moon Over Monte Carlo* Sidney Clare, Richard A. Whiting; *If I Had A Million Dollars* Johnny Mercer, Matt Malneck.

One of the few musicals intentionally aimed at children, **Babes in Toyland** (MGM) produced by Hal Roach, was a 79-minute delight. It starred Stan Laurel and Oliver Hardy (as Stannie Dum and Ollie Dee) who, accompanied by a tuneful Victor Herbert score, invaded nurseryland to the merriment of children (and their parents) the world over. Stan and Ollie (illustrated) played a couple of toymakers who, due to Stannie's characteristic ineptitude (instead of making 600 toy soldiers one foot high, he makes 100 soldiers six foot high) inadvertently become the heroes of Toyland when the city's ramparts are stormed by the dreaded Bogeymen. Grateful inhabitants included Little Bo-Peep (Charlotte Henry), Tom-Tom (Felix Knight), Little Boy Blue (Johnny Downs) Curly Locks (Jean Darling), Mother Goose (Virginia Karns), Widow Peep (Florence Roberts) and Little Miss Muffet (Alice Dahl). It was entrancingly directed by Charles Rogers and Gus Meins from a screenplay by Nick Grinde and Frank Butler. Songs included: *Toyland*; *Don't Cry Bo-Peep*; *A Castle In Spain*; *I Can't Do That Sum*; *Go To Sleep, Slumber Deep* Victor Herbert, Glen MacDonough; *Who's Afraid Of The Big Bad Woolf* Ann Ronell, Frank Churchill; *March Of The Toys* Victor Herbert.

▽

△

Radio star Joe ('You nasty man') Penner (foreground) made a cheerful movie debut in **College Rhythm** (Paramount) and, together with his famous duck, served, amongst other things, as a mascot when two department stores go collegiate and compete for the honours in a climactic football game. Such was the nonsensical aspect of George Marion Jr's plot (screenplay by Walter DeLeon, John McDermott and Francis Martin). And if the story didn't actually help the undertaking, it didn't hinder it either, credit having to go to the above-mentioned Mr Penner for being the personable comedian he was, to tenor Lanny Ross for singing so sweetly, to Lyda Roberti (centre) for her inimitable rendition of the title song which Mack Gordon and Harry Revel wrote as part of their bouncy score, to Jack Oakie (right) for the usual purveyance of his humour, to Norman Taurog for his energetic, well-paced direction, and to Helen Mack, Mary Brian, George Barbier and Franklin Pangborn for their stalwart support. Other songs: *Stay As Sweet As You Are*; *Goo-goo I'm Ga-Ga Over You*; *Let's Give Three Cheers For Love*; *Take A Number From One To Ten*.

With each new film, Bing Crosby (right) seemed to enjoy an increasingly comfortable relationship with the camera, and **Here Is My Heart** (Paramount) revealed him to be a light comedian with an enviable sense of timing. He played a millionaire crooner who, bored with what life has been offering him, journeys to Monte Carlo where he falls in love with a disdainful princess. He succeeds in entering her hotel suite by posing as a waiter, and in no time at all (75 minutes to be precise) claims her for his own. Kitty Carlisle (left) was suitably glacial as the princess, but once thawed, proved a most sympathetic partner especially in the duets. It was written by Edwin Justus Mayer and Harlan Thompson from a play by Alfred Savoir and efficiently directed by Frank Tuttle, with Roland Young, Alison Skipworth and Reginald Owen excellent in other roles. Songs: *Love Is Just Around The Corner* Lewis Gensler, Leo Robin; *June In January*; *With Every Breath I Take*; *You Can't Make A Monkey Of The Moon* Ralph Rainger, Leo Robin.

◁

1935

Mae West (left), in modern-dress and with the old *avoirdupois* very much in evidence on those parts of her body hitherto occupied by curves, didn't generate quite the same enthusiasm in **Goin' To Town** (Paramount) as she had in her previous pictures. The potentially amusing story of a cattle queen who inherits an oilfield from a fellow who, in turn, has won her in a dice game (but stops a bullet for cattle rustling), its chief concern was with Miss West's attempts to crash high society and become part of the Newport aristocracy. And although Mae fashioned a screenplay for herself (story by Marion Morgan and George B. Dowell) that, predictably, had its fair quota of wisecracks, the film lacked a sense of fun. West's attack on the *haut monde* seemed too heartfelt for genuine enjoyment and it imparted to the film a decided feeling of unease. It was directed by Alexander Hall for producer William Le Baron, and co-starred Paul Cavanagh (right, as a social asset Miss West sets her sights on, then pursues to South America) and Ivan Lebedeff, with Tito Coral, Marjorie Gateson and Fred Kohler Sr in support. Apart from an amusing sequence in which Mae was seen and heard as Delilah in a performance of Saint-Saëns' *Samson and Delilah* (singing 'Softly Awakes My Heart', an English version of the aria *Mon Coeur S'ouvre A Ta Voix*), she also sang three other songs: *Love Is Love In Any Woman's Heart*; *He's A Bad, Bad Man But He's Good Enough For Me* Sammy Fain, Irving Kahal; *Now I'm A Lady* Fain, Kahal, Sam Coslow.

Lottery Lover (20th Century) chronicled the escapades of a handful of naval cadets in Paris who happen to find a garter belonging to sexy revue star Gaby Aimee (Peggy Fears, right). The sailors draw lots to see who will be the lucky guy to return it to her, and the winner turns out to be a love-shy greenhorn named Frank (Lew Ayres, left). How he coped formed the basis of a patchy screenplay by Franz Schultz and Billy Wilder (story by Sig Herzig and Maurice Hanline) whose entertainment value was minimal. Pat Paterson, Sterling Holloway and Reginald Denny co-starred, with Alan Dinehart, Walter King and Eddie Nugent in support. The director was William Thiele. Songs: *There's A Bit Of Paree In You*; *Ting-A-Ling-A-Ling*; *Close Your Eyes And See*; *All For The Love Of A Girl* Don Hartman, Jay Gorney.

If there was one thing George Raft (right) could do better than anyone else it was the **Rumba** (Paramount). In fact, apart from a slight plot involvement with some gangsters who have reasons for not wanting Mr Raft to dance, Raft occupied most of the film's running time rumbaing with partners Iris Adrian, the exotic Margo, and the lovely Carole Lombard (left), who, to Raft's consternation, falls in love with someone else. It was adapted from a story by Guy Endore and Seena Owen by Howard J. Green, with additional dialogue by Harry Ruskin and Frank Partos; was choreographed by LeRoy Prinz, featured a specialty dance by Veloz and Yolanda, was produced by William Le Baron, and directed by Marion Gering with Monroe Owsley, Samuel S. Hinds, Virginia Hammond and Gail Patrick completing the cast. Songs: *I'm Yours For Tonight*; *The Magic Of You*; *The Rhythm Of The Rumba*; *Your Eyes Have Said*; *If I Knew* Ralph Rainger, Leo Robin.

The sweet music in **Sweet Music** (Warner Bros.) included the title number by Al Dubin and Harry Warren; *I See Two Lovers*; *Fare Thee Well Annabelle* and *The Snake Charmer* by Mort Dixon and Allie Wrubel; *Good Green Acres of Home*; *Ev'ry Day*; *Don't Go On A Diet*; *Winter Overnight*; *There's A Different You In Your Heart*, and *Seltzer Theme Song* by Irving Kahal and Sammy Fain. Indeed, the songs were far better than the plot – by Jerry Wald – that they accompanied, or the film's two leads, Rudy Vallee (right) and Ann Dvorak (left). Miss Dvorak couldn't sing, Mr Vallee couldn't act; a fact which somewhat incapacitated the screenplay (by Wald, Carl Erickson and Warren Duff), and rendered the Beatrice-and-Benedick romance between the two stars totally ineffectual. Far more convincing were the contributions of Ned Sparks, Helen Morgan, Alice White, Allen Jenkins, Joseph Cawthorn and Robert Armstrong. Another plus factor was Bobby Connolly's staging of the dance numbers. Alfred E. Green directed, and the production supervisor was Sam Bischoff.

MGM's irresponsibility in not issuing a health warning to diabetics when it released **The Night Is Young** cannot be over-estimated. For the sugar content of this Sigmund Romberg–Oscar Hammerstein II operetta (book by Vicki Baum, screenplay by Edgar Allan Woolf and Frank Schulz) was lethal. The oh-so-familiar story of an archduke (Ramon Novarro, left) who spurns the love of a princess for that of a common-or-garden ballet dancer (Evelyn Laye, right), it did the movie careers of its two stars no good whatsoever, Miss Laye permanently returning to Britain after its completion, and Novarro deserting Hollywood for the next 14 years. It didn't do audiences much good either, and the wise ones (of whom there were many) stayed away. One song, however, managed to survive both the critics' venom and the ravages of time: 'When I Grow Too Old To Dream'. For the rest, the score was no more inspired than the plot it accompanied, and was soon forgotten. Also cast: Charles Butterworth, Edward Everett Horton, Herman Bing, Una Merkel, Donald Cook, Henry Stephenson, Charles Judels, Albert Conti and, as the Countess Rafay (whoever she was), Rosalind Russell. Harry Rapf produced and the director was Donald Murphy. Other songs: *My Old Mare*; *The Night Is Young*; *The Noble Duchess*; *Lift Your Glass*; *There's A Riot In Havana*.

Sweet Adeline (Warner Bros.) was a pretty dull affair which nevertheless served as an excuse for some heavenly numbers by Jerome Kern and Oscar Hammerstein II. It also starred Irene Dunne as a gay-nineties Hoboken lass whose affections are craved by all the male customers of her father's popular *biergarten*, but whose heart, in the end, is won by a handsome young songwriter (Donald Woods, 2nd right). Erwin S. Gelsey wrote it, Bobby Connolly staged the musical numbers, Edward Chodorov supervised the production, and Mervyn LeRoy directed with a supporting cast that included Phil Regan, Hugh Herbert (centre), Ned Sparks (right), Joseph Cawthorn, Louis Calhern, Nydia Westman, Dorothy Dare and Winifred Shaw (left). Songs included: *Here Am I*; *Why Was I Born?*; *Don't Ever Leave Me*; *'Twas Not Long Ago*; *We Were So Very Young*; *Lonely Feet*.

Part gangster melodrama and part musical, **Stolen Harmony** (Paramount) was a George Raft offering in which the tough guy with the nimble feet even played the saxophone. But he was basically a dancin' man and, after being released from prison, joins up with maestro Ben 'Yowsah' Bernie and His Band and embarks on a cross-country bus tour, eventually helping to perk up the Leon Gordon, Harry Ruskin, Claude Binyon and Lewis Foster screenplay (story by Leon Gordon) by helping the police catch a gang of gunmen led by Lloyd Nolan. Grace Bradley (illustrated with Raft) played his dancing partner, with other roles going to Iris Adrian, Goodee Montgomery, Paul Gerrits, Ralf Harolde, William Cagney, William Pawley and Charlie Arnt. It was produced by Albert Lewis, and the director was Alfred Werker. Songs: *Would There Be Love*; *Let's Spill The Beans*; *I Never Had A Man To Cry Over*; *Fagin Youse A Viper* Mack Gordon, Harry Revel.

Flushed with the critical and financial success of *The Gay Divorcée* (1934), RKO, in between frequent visits to the bank, lost no time in securing yet another hit Broadway property for Fred Astaire (foreground centre) and Ginger Rogers. This time it was Jerome Kern and Otto Harbach's **Roberta** which, despite a ridiculous plot by Alice Duer Miller (all-American football hero inherits his aunt's chic dress salon in Paris) managed, somehow, to inspire Kern to write his most ravishing score since *Show Boat*. The melodies even impressed producer Pandro S. Berman who, treating Kern in a slightly less cavalier manner than he had done Cole Porter in *The Gay Divorcée*, retained four of the show's original numbers ('Let's Begin', 'Smoke Gets In Your Eyes', 'Yesterdays', and 'I'll Be Hard To Handle' with new lyrics by Bernard Dougall), used three more as background music ('You're Devastating', 'The Touch Of Your Hand', and 'Don't Ask Me Not To Sing') and commissioned a further two from Kern and lyricist Dorothy Fields – the haunting 'Lovely To Look At' (prominently featured in the show's fashion parade finale) and the lively 'I Won't Dance', originally written by Kern and Hammerstein II for a London show called *Three Sisters*, now given new lyrics by Fields. Ballard MacDonald and James Hanley's 'Indiana' was interpolated into the score. Four people had a hand in the screenplay (Jane Murfin, Sam Mintz, Glenn Tryon and Allan Scott) providing evidence that four heads were definitely not better than one. They did, however, manage to give Fred and Ginger the best moments in the show, a fact which could not have pleased the aristocratic Irene Dunne, who was billed above Astaire and Rogers but who, unfortunately, had to shoulder the burden of the cumbersome plot. Miss Dunne's musical highspot came with her wistful rendition of the incomparable 'Smoke Gets In Your Eyes' – but it was Fred and Ginger the public came to see. No accident therefore, that they, rather than Miss Dunne, featured in the last shot of the film – just as they had done in *Flying Down To Rio*. Of the five numbers they were given, the best was 'I'll Be Hard To Handle' – and the most interesting in that it was the first time in a dance routine they were able to bait each other competitively. Miss Rogers's handling of the lyric – *à la* Lyda Roberti who had played the role in the original stage production – also happened to be the funniest thing in the show. Randolph Scott was cast as the footballer who unexpectedly finds himself involved in the world of *haute couture* (and the man with whom Miss Dunne falls hopelessly in love), and Helen Westley played his aunt Roberta, with Claire Dodd, Victor Varconi, Luis Alberni and Ferdinand Munier completing the cast. The director was William A. Seiter. It was remade by MGM as *Lovely To Look At* in 1952.

THIRTIES MUSICALS

Darryl F. Zanuck – the man who helped revitalize the musical with *42nd Street* (Warner Bros. 1933) – anxious that 20th Century should not, in any way, be considered inferior to Warner Bros., wasted no time in preparing a musical he hoped would be even more spectacular in scope and achievement than *42nd Street*. The result was **Folies Bergère**, in the event hardly an innovative world-beater but a diverting enough *bon-bon* with two big production numbers – one of which used leading man Maurice Chevalier's boater as its visual motif; the great entertainer's trademark was scaled up to fill the entire set. The other number relied on copious rain, several dozen girls and an equal number of umbrellas. Though the routines were briskly enough staged by Dave Gould (see illustration) they failed to compare with the work Berkeley was pioneering at Warner Bros. and at best were moderately eye-catching. The story itself concerned a Parisian millionaire who, finding it necessary to be in two places at once (a secret business meeting and a ball), engages the professional services of a Folies Bergère comedian to impersonate him at the

ball. The role was perfect for Chevalier (though Zanuck's first choice was Charles Boyer), who played both the business man and the artist, and he sailed through it, picking up excellent reviews. (A more *risqué* French version featuring topless girls at the Folies was made at the same time, and was equally well received.) Merle Oberon co-starred as the businessman's wife and Ann Sothern was his show-girl mistress, with other roles assigned to Walter Byron, Lumsden Hare, Robert Greig, Eric Blore, Halliwell Hobbes and Phillip Dare. William Goetz and Raymond Griffith were the associate producers, it was written by Bess Meredyth and Hal Long from a play by Rudolph Lothar and Hans Adler, and the director was Roy Del Ruth. It was remade as *That Night in Rio* (1941) and again in 1952 as a vehicle for Danny Kaye called *On The Riviera*, both by 20th Century-Fox. Songs: *Singing A Happy Song*; *Rhythm Of The Rain* Jack Meskill, Jack Stern; *You Took The Words Right Out Of My Mouth* Harold Adamson, Burton Lane; *Valentine* Henri Christine, Herbert Reynolds (English lyrics), Albert Willemetz (French lyrics).

Lanny Ross, originally cast as the leading man in **Mississippi** (Paramount) was replaced after a newly-appointed studio head took a look at the lack-lustre rushes. His replacement, at the suggestion of producer Arthur Hornblow Jr, was Bing Crosby (right). Adapted from Booth Tarkington's novel *Magnolia* by Herbert Fields and Claude Binyon, **Mississippi** was the story of a young pacifist who, after refusing on principle to defend his sweetheart's honour and being banished in disgrace, joins a riverboat troupe as a singer, acquires a reputation as a crackshot after a saloon brawl in which the villain of the piece accidentally kills himself with his own gun, falls in love with his former fiancée's sister (Joan Bennett, left), and finally bullies her apprehensive family into accepting him. Though the burden of the plot rested squarely on Crosby's capable shoulders, it was his co-star W.C. Fields as Commodore Jackson, owner of the riverboat, who hogged the limelight. His comic routines – most notably the one in which, to the glaring disapproval of his opponents in a poker game, he deals himself five aces and has somehow to rectify the situation – were vintage Fields and deservedly attracted most of the critical kudos. The screenplay was by Francis Martin and Jack Cunningham, the score, which yielded three hits all sung by Crosby – 'Down By The River', 'Soon', and 'Easy To Remember' – was by Richard Rodgers and Lorenz Hart, although Stephen Foster's 'Swanee River' was also interpolated for Crosby to sing, with a Negro choral accompaniment. Completing the cast were Queenie Smith, Gail Patrick, Claude Gillingwater, John Miljan, Ed Pawley, Fred Kohler Sr and John Larkin. Directed by Edward Sutherland. A remake of *Cameo Kirby* (Fox, 1930).

Carl Brisson played two parts in **All The King's Horses** (Paramount): a Ruritanian monarch and his film-star double. The double doubles as king – both on the throne and in the royal bedroom, thus leaving His Majesty free to take a little jaunt to Vienna. Frank Tuttle and Frederick Stephani's adaptation of the play and the musical on which it was based (the first by Lawrence Clark and Max Giersberg; the second by Frederick Herendeen and Edward Horan) was drenched in tedium, making life especially difficult for Mr Brisson and his co-star Mary Ellis, both of whom, however, sang pleasantly. Edward Everett Horton, Katherine De Mille, Eugene Pallette, Arnold Korff and Marina Schubert were also in it, it was produced by William Le Baron, and directed by Frank Tuttle (production number illustrated). Songs: *A Little White Gardenia*; *Be Careful Young Lady*; *Dancing The Viennese*; *A King Can Do No Wrong*; *When My Prince Charming Comes Along* Sam Coslow.

△

Busby Berkeley not only directed the musical sequences in **Gold Diggers Of 1935** (Warner Bros.), but was given a crack at the entire film. Unfortunately, the story Robert Lord and Peter Milne devised for it (screenplay by Manuel Seff and Peter Milne), and which they set in a New England summer resort hotel (involving the romantic pairings of several guests), was weak even by musical comedy standards. But the two major production numbers (which formed part of a charity show being staged at the hotel) were something else – particularly 'Lullaby Of Broadway' (illustrated), arguably the acme of Berkeley's remarkable career and his own favourite among all the numbers he created. The sad little tale of a 'Broadway baby' who lives by night and sleeps by day, it chronicled the last twenty-four hours in her life prior to her being pushed accidentally, out of a window in a Manhattan nightspot and plunging to her death. The number – by Al Dubin and Harry Warren – begins with Wini Shaw's face as a white speck (on an otherwise black screen) becoming larger and larger until she is seen in full close-up. After finishing the song Miss Shaw turns her head away from the camera and puts a cigarette in her mouth, whereupon the contours of her face become the contours of the Manhattan skyline as seen from the air. The number's climax, set in a massive nightclub and featuring some of the best precision dancing ever filmed, involved over a hundred men and women who, photographed from every conceivable angle, abandoned themselves to the music in a frenzy of movement that had audiences gasping in awe for its entire duration. The sequence ended as it began, with Miss Shaw's face now receding into the background until all that was left was a black screen. The other full-scale production number, 'The Words Are In My Heart' (also by Dubin and Warren) made use of fifty-six miniature pianos and fifty-six girls. Another example of Berkeley's imagination working at full pitch, it necessitated fifty-six men concealing themselves under the pianos as a means of moving them about – and although careful examination of the sequence reveals their exact whereabouts, the effect is nonetheless remarkable – particularly the moment (photographed backwards) in which the pianos group themselves into a perfect oblong, in much the same way that Berkeley's girls formed a jigsaw of Ruby Keeler's face in *Dames* (Warner Bros. 1934). Dubin and Warren wrote one other number for the film, 'I'm Going Shopping With You', first presented in the opening sequence, then later sung by Dick Powell (playing a medical student-cum-hotel clerk) as he accompanies his co-star Gloria Stuart on an expensive shopping expedition. The cast was completed by Frank McHugh, Joseph Cawthorn, Adolphe Menjou, Hugh Herbert, Alice Brady, Glenda Farrell, Grant Mitchell, Dorothy Dare and Thomas Jackson.

101

1936

Academy Awards

Best Picture
The Great Ziegfeld (MGM) produced by Hunt Stromberg
NOMINATIONS INCLUDED: *San Francisco* (MGM) produced by John Emerson and Bernard H. Hyman

Best Actor
NOMINATIONS INCLUDED: Spencer Tracy *San Francisco*

Best Actress
Luise Rainer *The Great Ziegfeld*

Best Supporting Actor
(New category)
NOMINATIONS INCLUDED: Stuart Erwin *Pigskin Parade* (20th Century-Fox)

Direction
NOMINATIONS INCLUDED: Robert Z. Leonard *The Great Ziegfeld*. W.S. Van Dyke *San Francisco*.

Writing (Original story)
NOMINATIONS INCLUDED: *The Great Ziegfeld* William Anthony McGuire. *San Francisco* Robert Hopkins. *Three Smart Girls* (Universal) Adele Commandini.

Art Direction
NOMINATIONS INCLUDED: *The Great Ziegfeld* Cedric Gibbons, Eddie Imazu & Edwin B. Willis

Sound Recording
San Francisco Douglas Shearer
NOMINATIONS INCLUDED: *Banjo On My Knee* (20th Century-Fox) E.H. Hansen. *That Girl From Paris* (RKO) Franklin Hansen. *Three Smart Girls* Homer G. Tasker.

Film Editing
NOMINATIONS INCLUDED: *The Great Ziegfeld* William S. Gray

Song
'The Way You Look Tonight' *Swing Time* (RKO) Jerome Kern *cm*; Dorothy Fields *lyr*.
NOMINATIONS INCLUDED: 'I've Got You Under My Skin' *Born To Dance* (MGM) Cole Porter. 'Pennies Heaven' from *Pennies from Heaven* (Columbia) Arthur Johnston *cm*; Johnny Burke *lyr*. 'When Did You Leave Heaven' *Sing Baby Sing* (20th Century-Fox) Richard A. Whiting *cm*; Walter Bullock *lyr*.

Assistant Director
NOMINATIONS INCLUDED: Joseph Newman for *San Francisco*

Dance Direction
Seymour Felix for 'A Pretty Girl Is Like A Melody' number from *The Great Ziegfeld*.
NOMINATIONS INCLUDED: Busby Berkeley for 'Love And War' number from *Gold Diggers Of 1937* (WB). Bobby Connolly for '1000 Love Songs' number from *Cain and Mabel* (WB). Dave Gould for 'Swingin' The Jinx' number from *Born To Dance*. Jack Haskell for 'Skating Ensemble' number from *One In A Million* (20th Century-Fox). Russell Lewis for 'The Finale' number from *Dancing Pirate* (RKO). Hermes Pan for 'Bo Jangles' number from *Swing Time*.

The New York Times Film Critic Awards
Best Actress
Luise Rainer *The Great Ziegfeld*

The New York Times Annual 'Ten Best' (eleven films this year)
11th *The Great Ziegfeld*

The Annual Top Moneymaking Films
INCLUDING: *Broadway Melody Of 1936* (MGM). *Follow The Fleet* (RKO). *The Great Ziegfeld*. *The King Steps Out* (Columbia). *A Night At The Opera* (MGM). *Rhythm On The Range* (Paramount). *Rose Marie* (MGM). *San Francisco*. *Show Boat* (Universal). *Thanks a Million* (Fox).

△
Paramount's **Collegiate** (GB: **The Charm School**) was the sort of programmer that made the other half of a double bill thoroughly embarrassed at the company it was keeping. Though Joe Penner (left) received top billing, the story (by Alice Duer Miller, screenplay by Walter DeLeon and Frances Martin) revolved around co-star Jack Oakie whose man-about-Broadway life-style is somewhat disrupted when he learns that, thanks to a clause in his aunt's will, he has become the dean of a girl's college. Adding one more 'r' to the three r's – Oakie introduces a course in rhythm, appointing Betty Jane Cooper as dance instructress and tunesmiths Mack Gordon and Harry Revel as song coaches. Cue for several musical numbers (by Gordon and Revel) and not much else. Penner played an amnesiac who finds himself in possession of a large bankroll, with other parts going to Ned Sparks, Lynne Overman (as Oakie's Man Friday), Frances Langford, Betty Grable (right), Henry Kolker and Donald Gallagher. Louis Lighton produced and the director was Ralph Murphy. 'I Feel Like A Feather In The Breeze' and 'You Hit The Spot' were the best two numbers in a score which included 'Rhythmatic' and 'My Grandfather's Clock In The Hallway'.

Strike Me Pink was the sixth and last film Eddie Cantor (left) made for Samuel Goldwyn and, as usual, it contained all the familiar Cantoresque ingredients. Fourteen writers, legend has it, worked on the screenplay (though only three were credited: Frank Butler, Francis Martin and Philip Rapp; story by Clarence Budington Kelland) and what they eventually came up with was the tale of a timid little tailor who, after purchasing a book called: *Man Or Mouse: What Are You?*, becomes (with the help of girlfriend Sally Eilers) king pin on the campus by agreeing to run an amusement park, unaware that several notorious gangsters are more than just slightly interested in the slot-machine concession. How, in a breathless, knockabout finale, he manages to help the police apprehend the heavies, provided the film with its main comic set-piece. For the rest it was the music that counted – with co-star Ethel Merman (right) prominently featured in three of the four numbers written especially for the film by Harold Arlen and Lew Brown (and staged by Robert Alton). Norman Taurog directed it all for the whacky nonsense it was, and his cast was completed by William Frawley, Parkyakarkus (Harry Parke), Helen Lovell, Gordon Jones, Brian Donlevy, Jack La Rue, Sunnie O'Dea, Rita Rio (later Dona Drake), Edward Brophy and the 1936 Goldwyn Girls. Songs: *First You Have Me High, Then You Have Me Low* (Merman); *The Lady Dances* (Cantor, Rio, Goldwyn Girls); *Calabash Pipe* (Cantor, Merman); *Shake It Off With*
◁ *Rhythm* (Merman, Goldwyn Girls).

Darryl F. Zanuck relied on Alice Faye to sell **King of Burlesque** (20th Century-Fox) rather than on costly production numbers, and instructed dance director Sammy Lee to avoid overhead shots and feather boas like the plague. The result was a backstage musical efficiently directed by Sidney Lanfield, fairly modest in scale, but generous in entertainment value. It also benefitted from a first-class screenplay by Harry Tugend (based on a story by Vina Delmar, and adapted by James Seymour), the main business of which concerned the rise, fall and resurrection of a small-time burlesque entrepreneur who, after graduating to Broadway and presenting a string of popular hit shows, marries above his station, produces an ultra-sophisticated flop, divorces his wife, returns to Broadway after a down-and-out period, and, with the help of Miss Faye (left), as well as an elevator operator, a boot-black, telephonist and

an office boy (all with show-business in their ▷ blood) puts on a revue that turns out to be a smash. It was spiritedly performed by a strong cast that included Warner Baxter (centre, as the producer), Jack Oakie (right, as Baxter's right-hand man), Mona Barrie (as the society broad Baxter marries), Arline Judge (as Oakie's intended), Gregory Ratoff (as an impecunious show backer) – as well as Fats Waller, Nick Long Jr, Kenny Baker and Charles Quigley. An excellent score provided Alice Faye with several hits ('I'm Shooting High', 'Whose Big Baby Are You', 'I've Got My Fingers Crossed' and 'Spreading Rhythm Around') by Jimmy McHugh and Ted Koehler. Other songs: *Lovely Lady* (by McHugh and Koehler) and *I Love To Ride The Horses* (by Jack Yellen and Lew Pollack). It was remade in 1943 as *Hello, Frisco, Hello* (20th Century-Fox), with Alice Faye again providing the glamour in the same role as before.

John Boles starred in **Rose of the Rancho** (Paramount) as a government agent out to track down a mysterious character by the name of Don Carlos, whose nocturnal activities involve him in leading a group of Spanish vigilantes against a posse of land-grabbers. Except that Don Carlos isn't a man at all, but lovely Gladys Swarthout (illustrated – her debut) whose daytime activities, as the daughter of Don Pascual – give no indication of the grit of which the girl is made. A sort of distaff *Desert Song* but without, alas, a score to match (although one song, 'If I Should Lose You' by Ralph Rainger and Leo Robin, has stood the test of time) – **Rose of the Rancho** – based on a play by Richard Walton Tully and David Belasco, and written for the screen by Frank P. Partos, Charles Brackett, Arthur Sheekman and Nat Perrin (adaptation by Harlan Thompson and Brian Hooker), was an uneasy mixture of operetta and low-comedy (the latter in the capable hands of Willie Howard, essaying the role of a Jewish cowboy called Pancho Spiegelgass and Herb Williams as an insurance broker) that never knew in what direction it wished to go. Charles Bickford, Grace Bradley, H.B. Warner, Charlotte Granville and Don Alvarado were also in it, William Le Baron produced, and Marion Gering directed. Songs: *If I Should Lose You; Thunder Over The Prairie; Little Rose Of The Rancho; Got A Girl In Cal-i-for-ni-ay; There's Gold In Monterey; Where Is My Love; The Padre And The Bride* Rainger, Robin.
▽

Paramount acquired the rights to Cole Porter's 1934 smash hit musical **Anything Goes** (with a book by Guy Bolton and P.G. Wodehouse which Howard Lindsay and Russel Crouse revised) and brought it to the screen with several of the original Porter songs intact, and with Ethel Merman (centre) repeating the role she created on the stage. Victor Moore and William Gaxton, however, were not on hand to impart to the film version some of the qualities that made the show such a success on Broadway – their roles being played instead by Charles Ruggles and Bing Crosby. All of which meant that the aptly titled **Anything Goes**, while it had quite a lot going for it, did not, alas, have everything. Mr Moore's absence was a grievous body blow to the undertaking, which nothing Ruggles did as the Rev. D. Moon – Public Enemy Number 13 – could disguise. What basically the film lacked, was sparkle – the one ingredient its rather silly

book cried out for if it was to make any kind of musical comedy sense at all. But it *did* have Ethel Merman singing 'You're The Top' and 'I Get A Kick Out Of You' plus two more Porter standards, as well as a few new songs by several other accomplished writers, so all was not lost. The story, which concerned Crosby's shipboard romance with an English heiress (Ida Lupino), the furtherance of which required him to pose as a gangster, was re-worked for the screen by Walter DeLeon, Sidney Salkow, John C. Moffit and Francis Martin. Benjamin Glazer produced it, and the director was Lewis Milestone. Also cast: Arthur Treacher and Margaret Dumont. Other songs included: *Anything Goes; All Through The Night* (background only); *There'll Always Be A Lady Fair* Porter; *Sailor Beware* Richard A. Whiting, Leo Robin; *Shanghi-de Ho; My Heart and I* Frederick Hollander, Robin; *Moonburn* Edward Heyman, Hoagy Carmichael. Remade 1956.

THIRTIES MUSICALS

Colleen was Ruby Keeler's penultimate film for Warner Bros. and the sixth and last time she would co-star with Dick Powell. However, the hitherto popular twosome, with Miss Keeler (left) at her least animated, were unable to rescue Peter Milne, Sig Herzig and F. Hugh Herbert's paltry screenplay (from a story by Robert Lord) and the film failed to find many takers. All about an eccentric millionaire (Hugh Herbert) who, after hiring a gold-digging floozie (Joan Blondell) to run his dress shop for him, finds himself having to contend with nephew Powell's scheme to replace Blondell with honest, sincere Miss Keeler, it featured Jack Oakie, Louise Fazenda, Paul Draper (right), Marie Wilson, Luis Alberni and Hobart Cavanaugh. Alfred E. Green directed, and the dance numbers were staged without much zest or imagination by Bobby Connolly. The score, by Al Dubin and Harry Warren, was one of the least distinguished of their career. Songs: *I Don't Have To Dream Again*; *You've Gotta Know How To Dance*; *An Evening With You*; *A Boulevardier From The Bronx*.

Though Mae West (illustrated) took to religion in **Klondike Annie** (Paramount), she still had to mind her p's and q's as far as the censor was concerned, with the result that the quips in her latest offering were decidedly short of innuendo. ('I can always tell a lady,' remarks co-star Victor McLaglen, to which comes the reply, 'Yeah? What do you tell 'em?') But Mae West functioning at only 60° proof was better than nothing, and there was enough of her intrinsic personality to keep her fans contented in this tale of a Barbary Coast broad (West) who, after murdering her Chinese lover (Harold Huber), hops on a freighter for the Klondike, takes the place of a recently deceased Salvation Army sister, and, once in the Klondike, gives a decided shot in the arm to the religious services at which she officiates. And whatever one might have said about her material, no one complained when she declared, in words and music by Gene Austin, that she was just an 'Occidental Woman In An Oriental Mood For Love'. Philip Reed, Soo Yong, Lucille Webster Gleason, Helen Jerome Eddy, Tetsu Komai, Harry Beresford and Conway Tearle were in it too, it was written by Mae West from her play of the same name (story by Marian Morgan and George B. Dowell) with additional material suggested by Frank Mitchell Dazey. William Le Baron produced and the director was Raoul Walsh. Other songs: *Mister Deep Blue Sea*; *Cheer Up Little Sister*; *I Hear You Knockin' But You Can't Come In*; *It's Never Too Late To Say No*; *This May Not Be Love But It's Wonderful*; *It's Better To Give Than To Receive*; *Open Up Your Heart And Let The Sunshine In* Gene Austin, James Johnson; *My Medicine Man* Sam Coslow.

◁ Originally intended as a vehicle for the increasingly popular Grace Moore, and rewritten to accommodate the soprano's operatic talents, Rudolf Friml's **Rose Marie** (MGM) underwent a change of plans when Miss Moore's commitments clashed with the film's shooting schedule. As it was imperative that the film be shot in summer (much of it on location in Lake Tahoe), Jeanette MacDonald (illustrated) was given the starring role. As she would again be teamed with Nelson Eddy, the studio was justifiably confident that the same people who paid to see *Naughty Marietta* would pay to see **Rose Marie**. Not that much of the original stage version's plot (first seen in 1924) survived the surgery performed on it by screenwriters Frances Goodrich, Albert Hackett and Alice Duer Miller. Instead of the backwoods singer originally intended by librettists Otto Harbach and Oscar Hammerstein II, Rose Marie La Flamme now became Marie de Flor, a Canadian opera singer of renown; and instead of the Mountie existing as a subsidiary character whose function was merely to assist in bringing the lovers together, he now became the hero who gets his woman. A virtual newcomer called James Stewart, in his second screen appearance, was cast as the soprano's errant brother who escapes from a penitentiary and, badly wounded, hides out in the north woods. The question is: who will find him first? His sister, or the Mountie with whom she eventually falls in love? With so much beautiful music and scenery on offer – plus the romantic appeal of the two stars – it didn't really matter much, happy endings being obligatory to plots of this sort anyway. The quintessential operetta, and probably the one most closely associated with MacDonald and Eddy, **Rose Marie** was, as MGM's hierarchy had hoped,

Based on the play by George M. Cohan, **Song and Dance Man** (20th Century-Fox) with a screenplay by Maude Fulton, was a platitudinous backstage story of a song and dance partnership. Claire Trevor (right) and Paul Kelly (left) were the performing duo, with Michael Whalen cast as the man Miss Trevor loves. What little plot there was concerned the unselfish sacrifices Kelly makes in order to ensure his partner's happiness with her handsome beau. Ruth Donnelly, James Burke, Helen Troy, Lester Matthews, Ralf Harolde, Gloria Roy and Margaret Dumont were in it too, Sol M. Wurtzel produced, and the director was Allan Dwan. Songs: *You're My Favourite One*; *On Holiday In My Playroom*; *Join The Party*; *Let's Get Going*; *Ain't He Good Looking?*; *Dancing In The Open* Sidney Clare, Lew Pollack.

▽

another box-office hit, collecting rave reviews and legions of new fans for its singing love-birds wherever it was shown. Apart from its stars, the film also featured Reginald Owen, Allan Jones (one of the studio's fastest-rising new talents), George Regas, Robert Greig, Una O'Connor, Lucien Littlefield, Alan Mowbray, Herman Bing, Gilda Gray and a young Englishman named David Nivens (later to become Niven). Hunt Stromberg produced and the director was again W.S. Van Dyke. Songs and musical numbers: *Rose Marie*; *Indian Love Call* Friml, Harbach, Hammerstein II; *The Mounties*; *Totem Tom Tom* Friml, Harbach, Stothart, Hammerstein II (staged by Chester Hale); *Just For You* (adapted from the original score's 'Finaletto' by Stothart, new lyrics by Gus Kahn); *Pardon Me Madame* Stothart, Gus Kahn; *Dinah* Harry Akst, Sam Lewis, Joe Young; *Some Of These Days* Shelton Brooks; *Tes Yeux* Rene Alphonse Rabey; scenes from Gounod's *Romeo and Juliet* and Puccini's *Tosca*. Remade in 1954.

After *Top Hat* (RKO, 1935) came **Follow the Fleet** (RKO) and it was apparent to all the world that the fabulous team of Fred Astaire, Ginger Rogers and Irving Berlin could do no wrong. Refurbished from a 1922 play by Hubert Osborne called *Shore Leave* which, in turn, provided the inspiration for the 1927 Broadway musical *Hit The Deck* (filmed by RKO in 1930), its adapters Dwight Taylor and Allan Scott concentrated the serious love interest (as was the case in RKO's *Roberta*, 1934) on its two co-stars, leaving Astaire and Rogers free to entertain the customers. Which they did stupendously. He played an ex-dancer turned sailor; she was a former partner of his, now singing for her supper in a San Francisco dance-hall. They meet up at a dance contest and join forces to put on a fund-raising show for the restoration of a schooner. Heaven knows the plot was no masterpiece, but at least it was innovative in that it dispensed with the hitherto obligatory comedians (Blore, Pangborn, Everett Horton *et al*) who usually tagged along on such occasions. It allowed Ginger Rogers to do a solo tap dance (her first and last in an Astaire–Rogers musical), and, for the first time in six movies took Astaire out of formal attire and put him into something more relaxed than top hat, white tie and tails – except for one extremely formal number, the famous 'Let's Face The Music And Dance' (illustrated) first sung by Astaire, then danced by him and Rogers as the finale to their fund-raising effort. The rest of the numbers showed the team in a much more casual mood than audiences had become used to, and the results were enchanting. Then, of course, there was Berlin's seductive score. By alternating his more zingy numbers – such as 'Let Yourself Go', first sung by Ginger, then danced by her and Fred, and 'I'm Putting All My Eggs In One Basket', introduced by Astaire at the piano, then danced by both of them in another of their 'competitive' routines – with such sombre ballads as 'Get Thee Behind Me Satan' and 'But Where Are You' both sung by a lovelorn Harriet Hilliard, Berlin created a perfectly balanced musical programme, every one of whose songs have since become part of America's rich musical heritage. Randolph Scott appeared as Miss Hilliard's love interest, and the man for whom the schooner is being salvaged; with Astrid Allwyn, Ray Mayer, Harry Beresford, Addison Randall and Russell Hicks in support. And if you look closely you'll catch glimpses of Betty Grable, Lucille Ball and Tony Martin. The film was produced by Pandro S. Berman, choreographed by Hermes Pan, and directed by Mark Sandrich. Other songs: *We Saw The Sea*; *I'd Rather Lead A Band*.

Any resemblance between Hal Roach's **The Bohemian Girl** (MGM) and Michael W. Balfe's renowned operetta of the same name was pure luck. But fidelity in this instance didn't matter at all. What did were the comic antics of Laurel and Hardy (left) who were given plenty of scope to indulge themselves as a pair of Gypsy rogues who adopt a little girl unaware that the child (Darla Hood) is a princess. A fair share of laughter and a fair share of the original score guaranteed success at the box office – the slight tremor audiences experienced on leaving the cinema after each performance being Balfe turning in his grave. It was directed by James W. Horne and Charles Rogers, featured Jacqueline Wells, Joy Hodges, James Finlayson, Mae Busch (2nd right), Antonio Moreno (right), Harry Bowers and Thelma Todd (who died tragically

shortly after the film was completed); with additional music by Nathaniel Shilkret and Robert Shayon. No screenwriter was credited but the screenplay utilized the original book by Alfred Bunn, written in 1843. Songs included: *I Dreamt That I Dwelt In Marble Halls*; *Then You'll Remember Me*; *The Heart Bowed Down*; *But Memory Is The Only Friend That Grief Can Call It's Own* Balfe, Bunn; *Heart Of A Gipsy* Shilkret, Shayon.

◁ The only other child star of the period even remotely comparable to Shirley Temple in popularity was Jane Withers (right) whose starring role in **Paddy O'Day** (20th Century-Fox) was a jaunty showcase for her engaging talents. She played an Irish immigrant who, after experiencing problems with the immigration authorities, escapes deportation by running away to the house where she believes her mother is employed as a cook – only to discover that her mother is dead. Pinky Tomlin, however, is conveniently on hand to take care of her and, by marrying a Russian dancer who was on the same ship as young Paddy, is able to adopt her against the wishes of his spinsterish aunts. The dancer was played by Rita Cansino (left), soon to become Rita Hayworth. On the evidence of her nondescript performance here, anyone betting on her chances of superstardom would have been on the receiving end of extremely favourable odds. It was written by Lou Breslow and Edward Eliscu, produced by Sol Wurtzel and directed by Lewis Seiler. The cast was completed by Jane Darwell, George Givot, Francis Ford, Vera Lewis, Louise Carter, Russell Simpson and Michael and Nina Visaroff. Songs: *Keep That Twinkle In Your Eye*; *I Like A Balalaika* Sidney Clare, Edward Eliscu, Harry Akst; *Changing My Ambition* Pinky Tomlin.

115

THIRTIES MUSICALS

Apart from Helen Westley (as Parthenia Hawks) and Queenie Smith (as Ellie) all the principal performers in director James Whale's memorable screen version of Edna Ferber, Jerome Kern and Oscar Hammerstein II's **Show Boat** (Universal) had appeared in various stage productions of the classic musical, and their total familiarity with (and commitment to) their roles was very much in evidence throughout. Irene Dunne (right) played Magnolia Hawks, Allan Jones (left) was her Ravenal, and Charles Winninger Cap'n Andy, with Paul Robeson quite magnificent as Joe, and Helen Morgan ditto as the mulatto Julie. Donald Cook played Morgan's husband Steve, with other roles going to Hattie McDaniel as Joe's wife Queenie, Francis X. Mahoney as Rubberface and Charles Middleton as Sheriff Mahoney. An extremely faithful adaptation (by Hammerstein himself) of the original 1927 Broadway presentation, plus the addition of three new Kern–Hammerstein songs – 'I Have The Room Above Her' (sung by Jones and Miss Dunne); 'Ah Still Suits Me' (Robeson
▽

and McDaniel), and 'Gallivantin' Around' (sung by Miss Dunne in blackface) – the film only falters in its modern section towards the end in which several plot points were arbitrarily and unconvincingly resolved. The loss of 'Why Do I Love You' (relegated in the final release print to the background) was also to be regretted. For the rest, however, Whale's **Show Boat** with its brilliant camerawork by John J. Mescall, the vigorous staging of its musical numbers by LeRoy Prinz, and the visual splendour of its art direction (by Charles D. Hall) offered audiences a most satisfactory version of an undisputed musical comedy masterpiece. The producer was Carl Laemmle Jr. It was remade by MGM in 1951. Other songs: *Cotton Blossom*; *Cap'n Andy's Ballyhoo*; *Where's The Mate For Me?*; *Make Believe*; *Ol' Man River*; *Can't Help Lovin' Dat Man*; *Mis'ry's Comin' Around*; *You Are Love*; *Bill*; as well as *Goodbye Ma Lady Love* Joe Howard; *At A Georgia Camp Meeting* Kerry Mills; *After The Ball* Charles K. Harris; *Washington Post March* John Philip Sousa.

An unusual offering from Warner Bros., and one which brought the studio a great deal of prestige but no money, was Marc Connelly's **The Green Pastures**. The music, which contributed immeasurably to the atmosphere of the film, was comprised of negro spirituals arranged and conducted by Hall Johnson, and impressively sung by his Choir. Connelly saw his story as a fable which would demonstrate 'certain aspects of a living religion in the terms of its believers', and he constructed it as a re-telling of the Bible as seen through the eyes of negro children at a Sunday school in a Southern backwater. Rex Ingram was cast in the central role of 'De Lawd' and delivered a performance of dignity and towering strength. Just before his entrance, the memorable line 'Gangway for de Lawd God Jehovah' was uttered – an example of the tone and flavour of the film's approach to religion. Today **The Green Pastures** would be thought somewhat racist in its depiction of blacks as humble and ingenuous simpletons, but in 1936 it represented a worthy attempt to break new ground in the cinema (see illustration). Henry Blanke supervised the production and William Keighley (with Marc Connelly) directed a cast of excellent players including Eddie 'Rochester' Anderson (as Noah), Oscar Polk, Frank Wilson, George Reed, Abraham Gleaves and Myrtle Anderson. The spirituals sung were: *Joshua Fit De Battle Of Jericho And De Walls Came Tumblin' Down*; *De Old Ark's A-moverin'*; *Let My People Go*; *Run, Sinner, Run*; *Death's Gwinter Lay His Cold Hands On Me*; *When The Saints Come Marchin' In*.
▽

Sitting on the Moon was an innocuous, pleasant little programmer about a couple of songwriters (Roger Pryor and William Newell), who fall for an ex-film star (Grace Bradley, illustrated), and for her comical pal (Pert Kelton). There wasn't much more in it than that, but it was neatly packaged by director Ralph Staub whose cast also included Joyce Compton as a professional blackmailer (claiming that Pryor married her in one of his drunken moments), Henry Kolker, Henry Wadsworth, Pierre Watkin and The Theodores – a dance team who featured prominently in one of the specialty dances. The associate producer was Albert E. Levoy, it was written by Raymond L. Schrock from a story by Julian Field, and adapted by Rex Taylor and Sidney Sutherland. Songs included: *Sitting On The Moon*; *Lost In My Dreams*; *How Am I Doin' With You?* Sidney Mitchell, Sammy Stept.
▽

An enjoyable programmer, **Walking on Air** (RKO) was the story of an impetuous young woman (Ann Sothern) who, to annoy her father, persuades a personable young college student (Gene Raymond, centre, with blond hair) to pretend to fall madly in love with her in the guise of an aristocratic but irritating Frenchman. This way she hopes her stubborn father will finally allow her to marry the man she *really* loves (Alan Curtis). But the inevitable happens and Miss Sothern finds herself walking on air when she realizes that it isn't Mr Curtis she wants, but handsome Mr Raymond. Such was the stuff of romantic musical comedy, and in the capable hands of its attractive cast, it worked well enough. Jessie Ralph and Henry Stephenson played Miss Sothern's parents, with other roles going to Gordon Jones, George Meeker, Maxine Jennings, Anita Colby and Charles Coleman. It was written by Bert Kalmar, Harry Ruby, Viola Brothers Shore and Rian James from a story by Francis M. Cockrell, and directed by Joseph Santley. Songs included: *Cabin On A Hilltop*; *Let's Make A Wish*; *My Heart Wants to Dance* Kalmar, Ruby.

Though Bing Crosby was the official star of **Rhythm on the Range** (Paramount), the first of two Westerns he would appear in during his lengthy career (the other was the 1969 remake of 20th Century-Fox's *Stagecoach*), the real attraction and 'find' of the show was an eccentric newcomer with a voice as big as her mouth called Martha Raye. She played a cowboy's sister (making her entrance on Grand Central Station!) who, although only part of the sub-plot, lit up the screen whenever she was on – particularly in her vigorous, full-throated rendition of a Sam Coslow number called 'Mr Paganini'. Audiences (and critics) loved her, and with her first film her career was triumphantly launched. For the rest – well, it was a pleasing enough musical, low on plot, high on songs (including the popular 'Empty Saddles' by Billy Hill, from a poem by J. Keirn Brennan, and 'I'm An Old Cowhand' by Johnny Mercer, with which Bing scored a huge hit) – with Crosby (illustrated) as a singing cowboy (he even sings a lullaby to a 2000-pound Hereford bull!) who meets a runaway heiress (Frances Farmer) on a freight train, and marries her. Bob Burns, Samuel S. Hinds, Warren Hymer, Lucille Webster Gleason and George E. Stone were also featured, the little pinprick of a screenplay employed the services of Walter DeLeon, Francis Martin, John C. Moffitt and Sidney Salkow (story by Mervin J. Houser), it was breezily directed by Norman Taurog, and the happy producer was Benjamin Glazer – for it was one of Paramount's top money-making films of the year. Other songs: *I Can't Escape From You* Leo Robin, Richard A. Whiting; *Drink It Down* Ralph Rainger, Robin; *Hang Up My Saddle*; *Rhythm On The Range* Walter Bullock, Whiting; *Memories* Whiting, Frederick Hollander; *Round-up Lullaby* Bager Clark, Gertrude Rose.

Just before the release of **Stage Struck** (First National), its stars Joan Blondell and Dick Powell were married. Which was just as well, for the event generated some interest in the movie which might otherwise have passed unnoticed by their fans. Although directed by Busby Berkeley, and with songs by E.Y. Harburg and Harold Arlen, it was a modest effort resting, yet again, on a backstage story which, this time, had Blondell in the (unlikely) guise of an untalented performer who finances her own show for Broadway and hires Powell to direct it. Disagreements spring up between them, but their reconciliation is effected by the ever-smooth Warren William. So much for the plot, enclosed in a disappointing screenplay by Tom Buckingham and Pat C. Flick (from a story by supervisor Robert Lord) which the cast – Frank McHugh, Jeanne Madden (illustrated), Carol Hughes, Hobart Cavanaugh and Spring Byington – were unable to improve. Songs and musical numbers included: *In Your Own Quiet Way*; *Fancy Meeting You*; *You're Kinda Grandish*; *The New Parade*.

A disaster musical (as opposed to a musical disaster), **San Francisco** was an artistic, technical and financial triumph for its studio, MGM, as well as a personal one for its three stars: Clark Gable (left), Jeanette MacDonald (right) and Spencer Tracy (centre right). Relying on such sure-fire ingredients as romance, nostalgia, sex, religion, music and spectacle (all expertly tied with a ribbon of moral retribution to keep the more sinful elements of the package in a neat, and thoroughly acceptable, perspective), it told the story of a midwestern opera singer (MacDonald) who, in 1906, is offered a job along the rough-and-ready Barbary Coast by cabaret owner Blackie Norton (Gable). But it is not long before the *diva*, who has fallen in love with her boss, is discovered by Nob Hill's aristocracy, and deserts Norton's cabaret for a career as an opera star on 'the other side of the tracks'. Norton subbornly refuses to alter his life-style in accordance with the soprano's loftier ambitions; she is equally determined to safeguard her new-found position in society. It is an impossible situation for both of them, and it takes an earthquake – literally – to reconcile them. Spencer Tracy played Father Mullin, the tough but compassionate chaplain of a Barbary Coast mission, with other roles in Anita Loos's stunningly professional, all-purpose screenplay (story by Robert Hopkins and additional dialogue by Erich von Stroheim) going to such vintage performers as Jack Holt (centre left), Edgar Kennedy and Al Shean, as well as Jessie Ralph, Shirley Ross, Ted Healy, Margaret Irving and Harold Huber. Val Raset staged the dances, the impressive musical direction was by Herbert Stothart, and the superb special effects were the work of James Basevi, who was also responsible for the locust plague in MGM's *The Good Earth* (1936), and the hurricane in United Artists' *The Hurricane* (1937). It was produced by John Emerson and Bernard H. Hyman, and directed with the precision and detail of a successful military manoeuvre, by W.S. Van Dyke, with D.W. Griffith in charge of the crowd scenes. It was no surprise to anyone that **San Francisco** was one of the biggest money-makers of the year. Songs: *Happy New Year*; *San Francisco* Bronislau Kaper, Walter Jurmann, Gus Kahn; *Noontime* Ted Healy; *Love Me And The World Is Mine* Ernest R. Ball, David Reed Jr; *A Heart That's Free* A.J. Robyn, T. Railey; *The Holy City* Stephen Adams, F.E. Weatherley; *Would You?* Arthur Freed, Nacio Herb Brown; *Nearer My God To Thee* Lowell Mason, Sarah F. Adams; *The Battle Hymn Of The Republic* William Steffe, Julia Ward Howe; *At A Georgia Camp Meeting* Kerry Mills; *The Philippine Dance* Bob Carleton; *A Hot Time In The Old Town Tonight* Joe Hayden, Theodore Metz, and 'The Jewel Song', 'Soldiers' Chorus'; 'Il Se Fait Tard' and 'Anges Purs' from Gounod's *Faust*; 'Sempre Libera' from Verdi's *La Traviata*.

1937

Academy Awards

Best Picture
NOMINATIONS INCLUDED: *In Old Chicago* (20th Century-Fox) produced by Darryl F. Zanuck with Kenneth MacGowan. *100 Men And A Girl* (Universal) Produced by Charles R. Rogers with Joe Pasternak

Supporting Actress
Alice Brady *In Old Chicago*

Writing (Original Story)
NOMINATIONS INCLUDED: *A Damsel In Distress* (RKO) Carroll Clark. *Every Day's A Holiday* (Major Productions, Paramount) Wiard Ihnen *Manhattan Merry-Go-Round* (Republic) John Victor Mackay. *Vogues Of 1938* (Wanger, UA) Alexander Toluboff. *You're A Sweetheart* (Universal) Jack Otterson.

Sound Recording
NOMINATIONS INCLUDED: *Hitting A New High* (RKO) John O. Aalberg. *In Old Chicago* E.H. Hansen. *Maytime* Douglas Shearer. *100 Men And A Girl* Homer Tasker.

Film Editing
NOMINATIONS INCLUDED: *100 Men And A Girl* Bernard W. Burton

Assistant Director
(Award not given after this year.)
Robert Webb *In Old Chicago*

Music
Song
'Sweet Leilani' *Waikiki Wedding* (Paramount) Harry Owens
NOMINATIONS INCLUDED: 'Remember Me' *Mr Dodd Takes The Air* (WB) Harry Warren *cm*; Al Dubin *lyr*. 'That Old Feeling' *Vogues Of 1938* Sammy Fain *cm*; Lew Brown *lyr*. 'They Can't Take That Away From Me' *Shall We Dance* (RKO) George Gershwin *cm*; Ira Gershwin *lyr*. 'Whispers In The Dark' *Artists And Models* (Paramount) Frederick Hollander *cm*; Leo Robin *lyr*.

Score
(Throughout 1937, Best Score was considered a music department achievement and the award was presented to the department head instead of to the composer.) *100 Men And A Girl* Universal Studio Music Dept.; Charles Previn, head. (No composer credit.)
NOMINATIONS INCLUDED: *In Old Chicago* 20th Century-Fox Studio Music Dept.; Louis Silvers, head. (No composer credit.) *Make A Wish* (Lesser, RKO) Dr Hugo Riesenfeld, musical director. Score by Dr Hugo Riesenfeld. *Maytime* (MGM) M-G-M Studio Music Dept.; Nat W. Finston, head. Score by Herbert Stothart. *Snow White And The Seven Dwarfs* (Disney, RKO) Walt Disney Studio Music Dept.; Leigh Harline, head. Score by Frank Churchill, Leigh Harline and Paul J. Smith. *Something To Sing About* (Grand National) Grand National Studio Music Dept.; C. Bakaleinikoff, musical director. Score by Victor Schertzinger.

Dance Direction
(Award not given after this year.)
Hermes Pan for 'Fun House' number from *A Damsel In Distress*
NOMINATIONS INCLUDED: Busby Berkeley for 'The Finale' number from *Varsity Show* (WB). Bobby Connolly for 'Too Marvelous For Words' number from *Ready, Willing And Able* (WB). Dave Gould for 'All God's Chillun Got Rhythm' number from *A Day At The Races* (MGM). Sammy Lee for 'Swing Is Here To Stay' number from *Ali Baba Goes To Town* (20th Century-Fox). Harry Losee for 'Prince Igor Suite' number from *Thin Ice* (20th Century-Fox). LeRoy Prinz for 'Luau' number from *Waikiki Wedding*.

The Annual Top Moneymaking Films
INCLUDED: *Artists And Models. The Big Broadcast Of 1937* (Paramount). *Born to Dance* (MGM). *College Holiday* (Paramount). *Maytime, Mountain Music* (Paramount). *One In A Million* (20th Century-Fox). *On The Avenue* (20th Century-Fox). *Pigskin Parade* (20th Century-Fox). *Rainbow On The River* (Principal, RKO). *Shall We Dance. Swing Time* (RKO). *Wake Up And Live* (20th Century-Fox). *Waikiki Wedding. You Can't Have Everything* (20th Century-Fox).

Although Martha Raye received top billing for the first time in **Hideaway Girl** (Paramount), Joseph Moncure March's screenplay (story by David Garth) centred on co-star Shirley Ross and her unfortunate marriage to a phoney count (Monroe Owsley) who steals other people's jewels for a living. Miss Raye, in an attempt to repeat the success she had had with a Sam Coslow song called 'Mr Paganini' in *Rhythm On The Range* (Paramount, 1936) belted out a number called 'Beethoven, Mendelssohn and Liszt' (also by Mr Coslow), but the joke wasn't as amusing the second time around, and it was left to Shirley Ross (illustrated) to make something of the movie's only potential hit – 'You're Dancing Into My Heart' by Ralph Freed and Burton Lane. Robert Cummings (illustrated), Louis Da Pron, Wilma Francis and Elizabeth Russell were also in it; it was produced by A.M. Botsford and directed by George Archainbaud. Other songs: *What Is Love?* Ralph Rainger, Leo Robin, Victor Young; *Two Birdies Up A Tree* Ralph Freed, Burton Lane.
▽

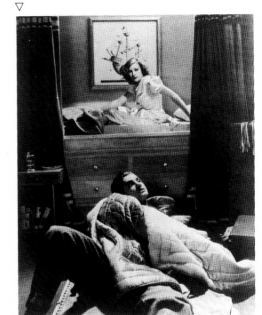

Though Lily Pons (right) sang 'Una Voce Poco Fa' from Rossini's *The Barber of Seville* in **That Girl From Paris** (RKO), the goings-on in her latest effort were decidedly low-brow. The story (by Jane Murfin, based on a magazine story by I. Carey Wonderly) required the *diva* to jilt a rather persistent suitor by masquerading as a peasant and joining up with a group of swing musicians collectively known as McLean's Wildcats. In no time at all she falls in love with the Wildcats' leader Windy (Géne Raymond, 2nd left) and – well, that, more or less, was it. As insubstantial as air, it existed only to show off its petite star's vocal prowess in a range of moods and styles, and, accordingly, the varied musical programme featured Johann Strauss II's 'The Blue Danube' in swing-time and Heinrich Panofka's 'Tarantella' – plus a handful of songs by Arthur Schwartz and Edward Heyman. P.J. Wolfson and Dorothy Yost's screenplay gave comic employment to Jack Oakie (centre), Herman Bing, Lucille Ball (left), Mischa Auer (2nd right), and Frank Jenks (3rd right); it was produced by Pandro S. Berman, and briskly directed by Leigh Jason. Andre Kostelanetz conducted the operatic sequences. Songs: *Seal It With A Kiss; My Nephew From Nice; Love and Learn; Moonface; The Call To Arms.* Remake of *Street Girl* (1929).

On The Avenue (20th Century-Fox) was a routine backstage musical, but with enough Irving Berlin numbers in it to lull audiences into forgetting the trivia which claimed their attention. Dick Powell (right) played a Broadway star-cum-producer whose current show contains a lampooning sketch of a society millionairess (Madeleine Carroll), and had Miss Carroll doing her damnedest to make Powell drop the sketch but succeeding only in falling in love with him – much to the chagrin of the show's star, Alice Faye. Although Faye (centre) was third-billed, she dominated the proceedings, singing such Berlin favourites as 'This Year's Kisses', 'I've Got My Love To Keep Me Warm' (with Dick Powell), 'He Ain't Got Rhythm', and 'Slumming On Park Avenue'. The Ritz Brothers, Alan Mowbray, George Barbier, Cora Witherspoon, Stepin Fetchit (left), Joan Davis, Sig Rumann and Billy Gilbert supported. Darryl F. Zanuck produced, Seymour Felix directed the dances and Roy Del Ruth the film, from a screenplay by Gene Markey and William Conselman. Reworked by 20th Century-Fox (1960) as Let's Make Love. Other songs: The Girl On The Police Gazette; You're Laughing At Me. Oddly, the title song was dropped prior to the film's release.

Darryl F. Zanuck paid Olympic ice-skating champion Sonja Henie $75,000 to make her screen debut in One In a Million (20th Century-Fox) and was not in the least bit surprised when, at the final accounting, the film netted a mammoth $2,000,000. Cleverly buttressed by a strong cast that included Adolphe Menjou, Jean Hersholt (right), and Don Ameche (centre), with the Ritz Brothers, Arline Judge and Dixie Dunbar there to supply the laughs – screen newcomer Henie (left) skated her way across a thin-ice plot which had her being trained for a future Olympics by her Swiss innkeeper father (Hersholt). Menjou appeared as the impresario of an all-girl band, with Borrah Minnevitch and his Harmonica Rascals, Leah Ray, Shirley Deane, Montagu Love and Albert Conti completing the cast. Miss Henie's fresh, wholesome personality, coupled with her unquestioned ability to set poetry in motion every time she slapped on her blades, made her an instant star and one of the studio's biggest money-makers. Leonard Praskins and Mark Kelly provided both the story and screenplay; Zanuck produced, and it was directed by Sidney Lanfield. Songs: One In A Million; We're Back In Circulation Again; Who's Afraid Of Love? Lovely Lady In White; The Moonlight Waltz Sidney Mitchell, Lew Pollack.

Little Jane Withers (centre) thwarted a spy plot in The Holy Terror (20th Century-Fox), though her sleuthing activities were not nearly as entertaining as the production's numerous musical and comical embellishments – such as the singing of Tony Martin and Leah Ray, the familiar clowning of El Brendel, ditto Joan Davis, and the rubber-legged antics of Joe Lewis (foreground left). John Eldredge, Andrew Tombes, Gavin Muir and Fred Kohler Jr were also in it, and it was written by Lou Breslow and John Patrick with James Tinling directing. Songs: There I Go Again; Don't Know Myself Since I Know You; Don't Sing; The Call Of The Siren; Everybody Swing Sidney Clare, Harry Akst.

In With Love And Kisses (Melody Pictures) Pinky Tomlin (2nd left, foreground) was a country-bumpkin songwriter who can only write when he is milking cows. Maybe scriptwriter Sherman Lowe (story by Lowe and Al Martin) should have indulged in a spot of milking as well, for there was no sign of inspiration anywhere in this 67-minute programmer. The far-fetched plot had a radio singer (Toby Wing, left) stealing one of Tomlin's songs, then being pursued by a racketeer (Russell Hopton) who has decided to go into the music publishing business hoping to make a mint out of Tomlin's cow-inspired compositions. The below par direction was by Leslie Goodwins whose cast included Arthur Houseman (foreground centre), Fuzzy Knight, and, as themselves, The Peters Sisters, Jerry Bergen and Billy Gray, and Chelito and Gabriel. Songs included: Don't Ever Lose It; I'm Right Back Where I Started Coy Poe, Pinky Tomlin; The Trouble With Me Is You Harry Tobias, Tomlin; Sweet Buddy LeRoux, Tomlin, Al Heath; With Love And Kisses Connie Lee; Sittin' On The Edge Of My Chair Paul Parks, Coy Poe, Tomlin.

What happens when an elegant Viennese waltz-palace loses its three-quarter-time patrons to the more energetic tempi of an American jazz band who have taken up residence next door, was the subject of Champagne Waltz (Paramount), a pleasant but by no means vintage musical that starred Gladys Swarthout (as the daughter of the ousted waltz maestro) and Fred MacMurray (as the jazz band's leader), with Jack Oakie, Veloz and Yolanda (illustrated), Herman Bing, Vivienne Osborne, Frank Forest, Benny Baker, Ernest Cossart and Fritz Leiber rounding off the cast. Basically a contest between 'serious' music and the more popular kind, it was climaxed by an elaborate production number featuring both forms, with neither emerging from the melée particularly well. Don Hartman and Frank Butler wrote it from a story by Billy Wilder and H.S. Kraft, it was produced by Harlan Thompson and directed, with only the occasional lightness of touch it required, by Edward Sutherland. Apart from 'The Blue Danube' by Strauss II and 'Champagne Waltz' by Milton Drake, Ben Oakland and Con Conrad (danced by Veloz and Yolanda), the score included: Could I Be In Love Leo Robin, William Daly; The Merry-Go-Round Ann Ronell; Paradise In Waltz Time Sam Coslow, Frederick Hollander; When Is A Kiss Not A Kiss Ralph Freed, Burton Lane.

THIRTIES MUSICALS

Only one song – 'Will You Remember?' – ▷ remained from Sigmund Romberg's original score in the film version of **Maytime** (MGM) – and it was reprised six times in various forms throughout this sumptuously mounted (by Hunt Stromberg) production for Jeanette Mac-Donald and Nelson Eddy (illustrated). The rest of the music comprised mainly operatic extracts, which was perfectly acceptable since the re-furbished story (by Noel Langley, who also wrote the screenplay) concerned a great opera singer and the tragic love affair she has with a young baritone. In one of his more jocular moods, Eddy sang 'Ham and Eggs', in which he codded several famous arias, but the film's big musical event was a specially composed opera called 'Czaritza', based on themes from Tchaikovsky's Fifth Symphony, during which its two principals (MacDonald and Eddy) realize, as they sing their hearts out to each other, that, after years apart, they are still passionately in love. If **Maytime** was pleasing to the ear, it was also a treat for the eye, being the best photographed (by Oliver T. Marsh) of all the MacDonald-Eddy black and white operettas. Director Robert Z. Leonard kept the proceedings tasteful despite the melodramatic plot, and imbued the film with a melancholy appropriate to the passing of time. The story, told in flashback by the aged soprano Marcia Mornay (MacDonald) to a young would-be singer (Lynne Carver), pointed the moral that a love once found must never be relinquished, no matter what. John Barrymore appeared as Mac-Donald's jealous mentor, dominating the screen in what was to be one of his last decent roles, with Herman Bing, Tom Brown, Sig Rumann, Rafaela Ottiano, Charles Judels, Paul Porcasi, Guy Bates Post and Billy Gilbert prominent in a large supporting cast. Other music included: *Now Is The Month Of Maying* traditional, with lyrics by Thomas Morley; *Summer Is A Cumin In* (trad); *Love's Old Sweet Song* J.L. Molloy, G. Clifton Bingham; *Vive L'Opera* folk song with lyrics by Bob Wright and Chet Forrest; *Le Regiment De Sambre Et Meuse* Robert Planquette; *Plantons La Vigne* (trad); *Carry Me Back To Old Virginny* James Bland; *Santa Lucia* Teodoro Cottrau; *Les Filles De Cadiz* Delibes, de Musset; an aria from *Les Huguenots* Meyerbeer.

Hollywood's exotic idea of Hawaii was splashed ▷ across the screen in **Waikiki Wedding** (Paramount), a hula-hula romance which starred Bing Crosby (centre) as a public relations man for a pineapple concern, and Shirley Ross (right) as a disillusioned Miss Pineapple Girl. The story had the former doing his persuasive best to convince the latter that Hawaii was the most love-kissed spot on earth – and, with some help from composers Ralph Rainger, Leo Robin and Harry Owens, and some hindrance from choreographer LeRoy Prinz, whose grass-skirted dances were enough to put the most ardent Hawaiian chauvinist off the place, he succeeded. Particularly winning was Owens's 'Sweet Leilani', crooned into immortality by Bing. Martha Raye (left) was in it too, so was comedian Bob Burns, as well as George Barbier, Leif Erickson, Grady Sutton, Granville Bates and Anthony Quinn. It was written by Frank Butler, Don Hartman and Walter DeLeon (from a story by Butler and Hartman), produced by Arthur Hornblow, and directed by Frank Tuttle. Other songs: *Sweet Is The Word For You*; *In A Little Hula Heaven*; *Blue Hawaii*; *Okolehao*; *Nani Ona Pua* Rainger, Robin.

Grace Moore (featured centre) played an Australian prima donna in **When You're In Love** (Columbia), with Cary Grant as the man she marries out of convenience in order to gain entrance to the United States from Mexico. The rest of Robert Riskin's screenplay (from an idea by Ethel Hill and Cedric Worth) predictably concerned itself – between songs – with turning the marriage of convenience into a genuine love match. Aline MacMahon played Miss Moore's manager, with Henry Stephenson, Thomas Mitchell, Catharine Doucet, Luis Alberni, Gerald Oliver Smith, Emma Dunn, George Pearce and Frank Puglia completing the cast. Jerome Kern and Dorothy Fields supplied Miss Moore with two new numbers: 'Our Song' and 'The Whistling Boy' – both pleasant enough; Leon Leonidoff (of Radio City Music Hall) staged the production ensembles. It was directed by Robert Riskin, with Everett Riskin as associate producer. Other songs: *Minnie The Moocher* Cab Calloway, Irving Mills, Clarence Gaskill (arranged for Grace Moore by Al Siegal); *In The Gloaming* Meta Orred, Annie F. Harrison; *Siboney* Dolly Morse, Ernest Lecuona; Schubert's *Serenade*; *The Waltz Song* ◁ (from 'Romeo and Juliet') Gounod.

In **Top Of The Town** (Universal) Gertrude Niesen sang four Harold Adamson–Jimmy McHugh songs: 'Blame It On The Rhumba', 'Where Are You?', 'Jamboree', and 'Top Of The Town', and Ella Logan sang three more: 'I Feel That Foolish Feeling Coming On', 'There's No Two Ways About It', and 'Fireman Save My Child'. The Three Sailors (alias Jason, Robson and Blue) did several imitations, including one of a giraffe; Mischa Auer turned his talents to *Hamlet* (for which he deserved no thanks) and a 12-year-old Jacqueline-of-all-trades called Peggy Ryan made her debut. Gregory Ratoff (as an agent) was also in it; so were George Murphy (left), Hugh Herbert, Henry Armetta, Claude Gillingwater, Ernest Cossart, The Californian Collegians and The Four Esquires. As for the plot, it had something to do with an heiress (Doris Nolan, right) who opens a fashionable Manhattan nightclub on top of a skyscraper. Brown Holmes and Charles Grayson wrote it (from a story by Lou Brock, who was also the associate producer) and the director was Ralph Murphy.

The story of **Swing While You're Able** (Melody Pictures) went something like this: Rich gal and her father have motor breakdown in the sticks, discover a hillbilly crooner and sign him to a radio contract. Business manager for the gal's old man sees the newcomer as a rival to romance and has him kidnapped on the eve of his first broadcast. Singer escapes, catches cold, and loses his voice. But he regains it – as well as the girl. End of story. Irredeemable in every way it featured Pinky Tomlin (right) as the hillbilly and Toby Wing (centre) as his girl. Marshall Neilan directed it (badly) from a story by Stanley Lowenstein and Charles Condon (screenplay by Condon and Sherman Lowe), with a cast that included H.C. Bradley, Monte Collins, Bert Roach, Suzanne Kaaren and 'Prince' Michael Romanoff, as well as Jimmy Newell and the Three Brian Sisters. Songs: *I'm Gonna Swing While I'm Able* Paul Parks, Connie Lee; *Swing, Brother, Swing* Al Heath, Buddy LeRoux; *Leave It Up To Uncle Jake* Parks, Lee, Heath, LeRoux; *You're My Strongest Weakness* Coy Poe, Heath, LeRoux; *One Girl In My Arms* Harry Tobias, Roy Ingraham; *I'm Just A Country Boy At Heart* Pinky Tomlin, Parks, Lee.

A lively little entry from Paramount, **Turn Off The Moon** satirized, to the accompaniment of several Sam Coslow songs, the astrology business. It starred Charles Ruggles as the owner of a furniture shop, and featured Marjorie Gateson as a secretary called Myrtle Tweep whom Ruggles has had every intention of marrying. Trouble is, their stars, so far, have never been right. They come right (according to astrologer Andrew Tombes) the night before the store's much trumpeted silver jubilee show (featuring Kenny Baker, several specialty acts, and Phil Harris and His Orchestra). All sorts of plot complications (courtesy of scenarists Marguerite Roberts, Harlan Ware and Paul Gerard Smith; story by Mildred Harrington) occurred – mainly involving Eleanore Whitney (illustrated) and Johnny Downs, a young couple whose own romance (according to the astrologer) has to be settled before Ruggles and Gateson get to say 'I do'. But it all came right in the end and, under Lewis Seiler's direction (choreography by LeRoy Prinz), the show twinkled brightly. It was edited by future director Edward Dmytryk. Also cast: Ben Blue, Romo Vincent – doing an impression of Charles Laughton in *Mutiny On The Bounty* (MGM, 1935) – Constance Bergen and Franklin Pangborn. Songs: *Turn Off The Moon*; *Easy On The Eyes*; *Jammin*; *That's Southern Hospitality*; *Little Wooden Soldier*.

Sing And Be Happy (20th Century-Fox) was the one about the irresponsible young blade who flouts the family business tradition (they run a successful ad. agency) to pursue a carefree existence of his own choosing. Anthony (Tony) Martin (right) finally made it to the top of the bill with this one, but the Ben Markson-Lew Breslow–John Patrick screenplay allowed him little opportunity to shine in anything but the songs (by Sidney Clare and Harry Akst). Leah Ray (left) provided the romantic interest, with other parts in it for stiff-necked Helen Westley, Joan Davis, Allan Lane, Dixie Dunbar (wasted), Chick Chandler and Berton Churchill. Milton H. Feld produced and the director was James Tinling. Songs included: *Sing And Be Happy*; *Travelin' Light*; *What A Beautiful Beginning*.

Nobody's Baby (MGM) was clearly intended to bring out the maternal instincts of the distaff members of the audience in telling the story of a ballroom dancer (Rosina Lawrence) who abandons her husband just as she is about to have a baby. She is cared for by Patsy Kelly (on bed) and Lyda Roberti (illustrated standing), as well as their respective boyfriends, Lynne Overman and Robert Armstrong. So much for the plot (by Harold Law, Hal Yates and Pat C. Flick, who also provided the screenplay). Director Gus Meins managed to chalk up a few hearty laughs, thanks to the comedic abilities of his two leading ladies, but by and large **Nobody's Baby** was nobody's triumph. Don Alvarado, Tom Dugan, Orrin Burke, and Dora Clement were also cast, and the producer was Hal Roach. Songs: *Quien Sabe*; *I Dreamed About This*; *All Dressed Up In Rhythm*; *Nobody's Baby* Walter Bullock, Marvin Hatley.

Another musical which found its inspiration in radio, **Wake Up And Live** (20th Century-Fox) top-billed Walter Winchell and Ben Bernie, capitalizing on the real-life radio 'feud' between them. Alice Faye, in third place as radio's 'wake up and live' advice-dispensing girl, got to sing one of her biggest hits – Mack Gordon and Harry Revel's 'There's A Lull In My Life', and Jack Haley (illustrated with Faye), as a crooner with mike fright, was a successful recipient of Miss Faye's good counselling who, with his microphone phobia finally conquered, becomes known on the air as 'The Phantom Troubadour'. The serviceable screenplay was by Harry Tugend and Jack Yellen (story by Curtis Kenyon from a novel by Dorothea Brande); it was directed by Sidney Lanfield for associate producer Kenneth MacGowan, and the cast included Patsy Kelly, Leah Ray – excellent singing Gordon and Revel's 'I Love You Much Too Much Muchacha', which number Joan Davis followed with a specialty dance – Ned Sparks, Walter Catlett, Grace Bradley and Douglas Fowley, as well as another two specialty acts, The Condos Brothers and The Brewster Twins. Jack Haley's singing voice was provided by the dubbing of Buddy Clark. Other songs: *Wake Up And Live*; *Never In A Million Years*; *Red Seal Malt*; *It's Swell Of You*; *Oh, But I'm Happy*; *I'm Bubbling Over* Mack Gordon, Harry Revel; *De Camptown Races* Stephen Foster.

THIRTIES MUSICALS

◁ **High Wide And Handsome** (Paramount), set in Pennsylvania in 1859, was one of the screen's few really worthwhile 'pioneer' musicals. Written by Oscar Hammerstein II, and with a beautiful and beautifully integrated score by Hammerstein and Jerome Kern, it depicted the bitter struggle between poor oil prospectors and the greedy railroad freight tycoons who set out to prevent them from building a pipe-line. A supremely good example of the Hollywood musical in advance of the stage musical (the epoch-making *Oklahoma!* arrived on Broadway six years later), it starred Irene Dunne (illustrated) – who had four songs in all, including the rousing title number and the lyrical 'Folks Who Live On The Hill',Randolph Scott (illustrated) as a farmer, and Dorothy Lamour as a singer, as well as Alan Hale and Akim Tamiroff as a pair of agreeable villains, Elizabeth Patterson, Charles Bickford, William Frawley and Raymond Walburn. Responsible for its striking unity of vision was director Rouben Mamoulian, again making a significant contribution to the evolution of the film musical. The choreographer was LeRoy Prinz. Other songs: *Can I Forget You?*; *The Things I Want*; *Allegheny Al*; *Will You Marry Me Tomorrow, Maria?*

After *A Night At The Opera* (MGM, 1935), the Marx Brothers kept their fans waiting two years for **A Day At The Races** while they went on the road to try out, before live audiences, many of the routines used in their second MGM film. The end product revealed their Marxmanship to be slightly off centre – but not disastrously so, and if the irreverent zaniness that dominated most of their work at Paramount was less conspicuous than it had been before, the film still had enough good things in it to keep the front office happy. Musically it was more elaborate than any of its predecessors, the most effective sequence being 'All God's Chillun Got Rhythm' composed, as was the rest of the score, by Gus Kahn, Walter Jurmann and Bronislau Kaper. A musical interlude dominated by negros (including a teenage Dorothy Dandridge), it blended spirituals with jitterbug, and featured Harpo (illustrated) as a really swinging Pied Piper. Less successful was a long and curious ballet sequence ('Blue Venetian Waters') that was pure kitsch and had not a single positive feature. Groucho played Dr Hugo Hackenbush, a horse doctor who takes over a sanitorium at the request of wealthy Mrs Upjohn (Margaret Dumont); Harpo was a jockey, Chico a Tootsie-Frootsie ice-cream vendor. The film's horse-race finale was in the best Marxian tradition and the funniest thing in the film. Sam Wood directed. Also cast: Allan Jones, Maureen O'Sullivan, Douglass Dumbrille, Sig Rumann, Robert Middlemass and The Crinoline Choir. Other songs: *Tomorrow Is Another Day*; *A Message From The Man In The Moon* (fragment).
▽

Described at the time as 'an amateur show put on by professionals', **The Hit Parade** (Republic) made an assiduous attempt to follow in the more illustrious footsteps of the *Big Broadcast* series, but lost its way round about reel two. Added to which, its roster of stars, including The Gentle Maniacs, The Toc Toc Girls, Eddy Duchin, Duke Ellington and Carl Hoff's Orchestras, Pick and Pat, Al Pearce (the Voice of Experience), Oscar and Elmer, ventriloquist Max Terhune (whose specialty was imitating trains) and Ed Thorgersen were no match for Bing Crosby, Kate Smith, Jack Oakie, Burns and Allen, Ethel Merman, Bill Robinson, Lyda Roberti, Cab Calloway and The Mills Brothers – all of them distinguished alumni of the Paramount series. The story (by Bradford Ropes, screenplay by Ropes and Samuel Ornitz), which would barely fill an eye-glass, concerned Phil Regan's attempts to find a new singing star for his radio show. He does, in the shape of Frances Langford (illustrated, with Phil Regan) who fits the bill on every count, except that she's being pursued by a parole officer – a fact that only comes to light on the eve of her big broadcast . . . Louise Henry, Pert Kelton, Edward Brophy, Inez Courtney, Monroe Owsley and William Demarest were in it too; it was produced by Nat Levine and directed by Gus Meins. Songs: *Sweet Heartache* Ned Washington, Sammy Stept; *Hail Alma Mater* Sammy Stept; *Last Night I Dreamed Of You*; *You'd Like It*; *I'll Reach For A Star*; *The Lady Wants To Dance*; *Was It Rain*; *Love Is Good For Anything That Ails You* Lou Handman, Walter Hirsch; *I've Got To Be A Rug Cutter* Duke Ellington.

△

Though called **New Faces Of 1937** (RKO), there weren't many of them about in this top-heavy revue into which everything, except flair, was thrown. It starred Joe Penner, Milton Berle, Parkyakarkas (radio comedian Harry Parks) and Harriet Hilliard, with Jerome Cowan, Thelma Leeds, Lorraine Krueger, Tommy Mack, Bert Gordon. The Three Chocolateers (illustrated), Patricia Wilder and, making her debut in a small way, Ann Miller. A backstage excuse for a series of songs, dances (staged by Sammy Lee) and sketches, it had very little to recommend it with the exception of several Sammy Fain–Lew Brown songs, the best of them being 'Our Penthouse On Third Avenue', 'Love Is Never Out Of Season', 'It Goes To Your Feet', and 'I Didn't Have You'. No fewer than six people had a hand in the screenplay (Nat Perrin, Philip G. Epstein, Irving Brecher, Harold Kussell, Harry Clork and Howard J. Green) which, in turn, was derived from a story by George Bradshaw appropriately called *Shoestring*. Edward Small produced, and the director was Leigh Jason. Other songs included: *Take The World Off Your Shoulders* Fain, Brown; *Widow In Lace* Walter Bullock, Harold Spina; *New Faces* Charles Henderson; *Peckin'* Ben Pollack, Harry James.

James Melton's three-picture contract with Warner Bros. was completed with **Melody For Two**. Unfortunately, it was not a case of third time lucky, and Melton (illustrated) left the movie business forever but for a brief appearance in the 'La Traviata' sequence in MGM's *Ziegfeld Follies* (1946), having signally failed to achieve anything resembling stardom. Granted, he hadn't exactly been helped by his material which, in this instance was no better than his first two attempts. This time, Richard Macaulay's story (screenplay by George Bricker, Luci Ward and Joe K. Watson) cast him as an unsympathetic, self-indulgent and querulous bandleader who is eventually taken out of his ill humour by Patricia Ellis, but alas, too late for audiences to care. Marie Wilson (illustrated), Eddie Anderson, Charles Foy, Fred Keating, Dick Purcell, Winifred Shaw, Craig Reynolds and Donald O'Connor were also in it for director Louis King and supervisor Brian Foy; and the musical numbers were staged by Bobby Connolly and Richard Vreeland. Songs included the Al Dubin-Harry Warren classic, 'September In The Rain', which had first been heard as background music in *Stars Over Broadway* (Warner Bros. 1935). Dubin and Warren also composed the title number. Other songs: *A Flat In Manhattan*; *An Excuse For Dancing*; *Jose O'Neill The Cuban Heel*; *Dangerous Rhythm* M.K. Jerome, Jack Scholl.
▽

△

△

Fred Astaire and Ginger Rogers's seventh feature in four years was **Shall We Dance** (RKO) in which Astaire was cast as a ballet dancer with a phoney Russian name (Petroff) and accent, and Rogers as an equally phoney broad who wishes to marry into society. They soon catch each other out and, after the inevitable complications and misunderstandings provided by Allan Scott and Ernest Pagano's screenplay (adapted by P.J. Wolfson from a story by Lee Loeb and Harold Buchman), end up as a dancing team. It was, alas, all rather infantile, with Edward Everett Horton and Eric Blore contributing to the general tedium of the plot. But who cared about plot when there were so many glorious George and Ira Gershwin numbers (eg 'Slap That Bass', 'They All Laughed', 'Let's Call The Whole Thing Off') to take one's mind off it? For 'Slap That Bass' (choreography by Hermes Pan and Harry Losee), Van Nest Polglase created a highly stylized ship's engine room in which Astaire (illustrated) imitated the movement of the machines to a jivey arrangement of the number accompanied by the ship's black engineers; while 'Let's Call The Whole Thing Off' was a sensational rollerskate routine and a sparkling highlight; as was the ironic and wistful presentation (by Astaire) of the classic 'They Can't Take That Away From Me'. Yet, in spite of the marvellous moments, the film remained curiously unsatisfying. Mark Sandrich again directed, with Pandro S. Berman producing. Completing the cast were Jerome Cowan, Ketti Gallian, William Brisbane, Frank Moran and Harriet Hoctor. Other numbers: *Beginner's Luck*; *Shall We Dance*; *Walking The Dog*.

▽

There was feudin', fightin', fussin' and fun a-plenty in **Mountain Music** (Paramount), a raucous romp through hillbilly territory, that starred Bob Burns and zippy Martha Raye as two of the dog-garndest sweethearts yew ever did see. Trouble is, he's suffering from bouts of schizophrenia, and only loves Miss Raye when he's aberrating. As it only takes a bucket of cold water poured over his head to bring him back to his senses, a determined Martha spends most of her time preventing him from being sluiced. Musical highlights to emerge from this good-natured nonsense were Raye's energetic handling of 'Good Morning', and Rufe Davis's one-man-band interpretation of 'Mama Don't 'Low No Bull Fiddle Playin' In Heah' – both by Sam Coslow, who supplied the entire score. John C. Moffitt, Duke Atterbury, Russel Crouse and Charles Lederer wrote it from a story by MacKinlay Kantor; it was produced by Benjamin Glazer, directed by Robert Florey and had a cast that also included John Howard, Terry Walker (left), George 'Gabby' Hayes (centre), Jan Duggan and Fuzzy Knight (right). Other songs: *If I Put My Heart In A Song*; *Can't you Hear That Mountain Music?*; *Thar She Comes*; *Hillbilly Wedding*.

For his first musical since Warner Bros. 'Footlight Parade' (1933), James Cagney (2nd right) moved to Grand National and, under Victor Schertzinger's direction, danced and sang his way through several numbers in **Something To Sing About**. He played a band leader who, after fame and fortune beckons in the shape of a Hollywood contract, marries his former band singer (Evelyn Daw, right) only to find the terms of his contract require his bachelorhood, which he then has to fake. William Frawley (left), Kathleen Lockhart (2nd left), James Newill, Mona Barrie and Harry Barris were also cast. Austin Parker wrote the lively screenplay, Harland Dixon staged the dance numbers, and the producer was Zion Myers. Songs: *Right Or Wrong*; *Any Old Love*; *Something To Sing About*; *Loving You*; *Out Of The Blue* Victor Schertzinger.

▽

First seen as a Paramount silent in 1919, **23½ Hours Leave**, a World War I comedy, resurfaced from Grand National with its story more or less intact (a rookie takes a bet that he will breakfast with his general – and wins), but with the addition of four sprightly songs by Ted Koehler and Sammy Stept. It was produced by Douglas MacLean who had played the lead in the first version; directed by John G. Blystone, and this time featured James Ellison (right), Terry Walker, Morgan Hill, Arthur Lake (centre) Paul Harvey, Pat Gleason (left), Wally Maher Andy, and Ward Bond. The screenplay was by Harry Ruskin and Henry McCarty (additional dialogue by Samuel J. Warshawsky) from a story by Mary Roberts Rinehart. Whatever significance its story, with its special emphasis on life in a training camp, may have had in 1919, had evaporated by 1937 and the film made no impression whatever. Songs: *Good Night My Lucky Day*; *Now You're Talking My Language*; *It Must Be Love*; *We Happen To Be In The Army*.

THIRTIES MUSICALS

Photographed in a sepia tint midway between rose and brown, MGM's **The Firefly** ran 138 minutes and was a lavishly produced bore, redeemed only by its Rudolf Friml score and by some splendid singing from its stars Jeanette MacDonald and Allan Jones (illustrated). Bearing absolutely no relation to its stage counterpart (in which a lady street singer from New York, disguised as a cabin boy follows her sweetheart to Bermuda on a yacht belonging to his fiancée), the screen version relocated itself in Spain at the time of the Napoleonic invasion and became the protracted story of a spy called Nina Maria (MacDonald) who charms information out of French officers. Jones played Don Diego, a counter-spy for the French and together he and Jeanette made beautiful music – most notably with 'The Donkey Serenade', which was specially arranged for the film by Herbert Stothart from Friml's 1920 solo piano piece 'Chanson', with lyrics by Bob Wright and Chet Forrest. Otto Harbach's original book was adapted by Ogden Nash, with Frances Goodrich and Albert Hackett responsible for the rather waterlogged screenplay. The musical numbers were staged by the ubiquitous Albertina Rasch, Hunt Stromberg produced and Robert Z. Leonard directed. Also in it were Warren William, Henry Daniell, Douglass Dumbrille, Leonard Penn, Tom Rutherford and George Zucco. Songs: *Giannina Mia* lyrics by Otto Harbach; *Love Is Like A Firefly*; *English March*; *A Woman's Kiss* new lyrics by Bob Wright, Chet Forrest; *He Who Loves And Runs Away* lyrics by Gus Kahn; *Sympathy* lyrics by Kahn, Otto Harbach; *When A Maid Comes Knocking At Your Heart* lyrics by Harbach, Wright, Forrest; *Danse Jeanette* Herbert Stothart; *Para La Salud* arranged by Stothart; *Ojos Rojos* Argentine folk song, arranged and played by Manuel Alvarez Maciste.

Bobby Breen's third feature, **Make A Wish** (Principal/RKO) was his best to date, thanks to its sugar-free screenplay by Gertrude Berg – who also provided the story – Bernard Schubert and Earle Snell (additional dialogue by William Hurlburt). A simple, uncluttered yarn in which young master Breen (right) helps to inspire Basil Rathbone (left), a composer suffering from composer's block, to finish his operetta, it also featured newcomer Marion Claire as Breen's widowed mother, a singer who soon finds herself romantically involved with the struggling Mr Rathbone. A pleasant Oscar Straus–Paul Francis Webster–Louis Alter score, including 'Music In My Heart' and 'My Campfire Dreams', both appealingly sung by Breen, kept audiences whistling for months. Henry Armetta, Ralph Forbes, Billy Lee, Donald Meek, Herbert Rawlinson and Leonid Kinskey completed the cast. It was produced by Sol Lesser and directed – extremely well – by Kurt Neumann. Other songs: *Make A Wish*; *Birch Lake Forever* Straus, Webster, Alter; *Old Man Rip* Webster, Alter; *Polly Wolly Doodle* (traditional).

In **The Life Of The Party** (RKO) Joe Penner (left) starred as the wealthy suitor chosen by Ann Shoemaker to wed her singing daughter Harriet Hilliard. But Miss Hilliard has other ideas – the best one being Gene Raymond, with whom she falls in love, and after a few rather tedious complications, marries. A cast that also included Parkyakarkus, Victor Moore (as a private detective hired specifically to see that Raymond remains free of woman trouble), Helen Broderick (as Miss Hilliard's agent), Billy Gilbert, Ann Miller, Franklin Pangborn and Margaret Dumont (right) promised more than they delivered; it was written by Bert Kalmar, Harry Ruby and Viola Brothers Shore (story by Joseph Santley), produced by Edward Kaufman and directed by William A. Seiter. The film's one production number – 'Yankee Doodle Band' (by Herb Magidson and Allie Wrubel) featured Ann Miller in a shameless emulation of Eleanor Powell (the vocal by Miss Hilliard), with choreography by Sammy Lee that was, at best, serviceable; while Hilliard and Raymond were handed the show's best tune, 'Let's Have Another Cigarette' by Magidson and Wrubel. Other songs: *The Life Of The Party*; *So You Won't Sing*; *Chirp A Little Ditty* Magidson, Wrubel; *Roses In December* George Jessel, Ben Oakland.

Talent Scout (GB: **Studio Romance**) was a Warner Bros./First National concoction which intended to glorify the scouts who went up and down the country seeking out new talent. The idea, apparently, had been inspired by the studio's own promotion campaign for *Gold Diggers Of 1937* which sent a bevy of chorus beauties across the continent by air. In the event, the movie had a young girl singer (Jeanne Madden centre) discovered and catapulted to fame, not by a Hollywood talent scout, but by a Hollywood matinée idol (Donald Woods right) who falls in love with her. The flaccid screenplay was by George Bilson and William Jacobs, William Clemens directed, and Bryan Foy supervised the production. Fred Lawrence, Rosalind Marquis, Joseph Crehan and Charles Halton (left) were also in it. Songs: *In The Silent Picture Days*; *I Am The Singer, You Are My Song*; *Born To Love*; *I Was Wrong* M.K. Jerome, Jack Scholl.

△ Four talented writers – Jerry Wald, Richard Macaulay, Sig Herzig and Warren Duff – dreamed up **Varsity Show** which, at 120 minutes, proved to be one of Warner Bros.' longest musicals, but, where plot was concerned, one of its shortest. Supervised by Lou Edelman and directed by William Keighley, the movie starred Dick Powell as a Broadway impresario and former Winfield College alumnus who steps in to save the day when the annual Winfield show is about to flounder for want of a producer. The show-within-the-show's finale was staged by Busby Berkeley who, working on a staircase fifty feet high and sixty feet wide, designed it as a tribute to halls of learning everywhere with a series of overhead shots in which a chorus of several hundred men and women (see illustration) spelled out the initals of several colleges across the country. Also featured were Fred Waring and His Pennsylvanians, Priscilla and Rosemary Lane (debut for all three), Walter Catlett and Ted Healy. Songs: *Love Is On The Air Tonight*; *Moonlight On The Campus*; *Old King Cole*; *Have You Got Any Castles, Baby?*; *We're Working Our Way Through College*; *On With The Dance*; *You've Got Something There*; *When Your College Days Are Gone* Johnny Mercer, R.A. Whiting. Remade in 1950 as *Fine And Dandy*.

Sonja Henie's (illustrated) second feature, **Thin** ▷ **Ice** (20th Century-Fox), had a more substantial screenplay (by Boris Ingster and Milton Sperling, from a play by Attila Orbok) and was marginally better than its predecessor. All about a skating instructress in a large Swiss hotel and the romance she has with a newspaper correspondent who, to Miss H.'s surprise, turns out not to be a newspaperman at all, but Prince Rudolph, it co-starred Tyrone Power as the Prince, with Arthur Treacher, Raymond Walburn, Joan Davis (who got to sing a marvellous Mack Gordon–Harry Revel number called 'I'm Olga From The Volga'), Sig Rumann, Alan Hale, Leah Ray and Melville Cooper, excellent in support. Harry Losee staged the eye catching ballet and dance sequences; Raymond Griffith produced and the director was Sidney Lanfield. Other songs: *My 'Secret Love Affair*; *Over Night*; *My Swiss Hillbilly* Sidney Mitchell, Lew Pollack.

One Hundred Men And A Girl (Universal) was a resounding hit for its young star Deanna Durbin, whose spontaneous charm and refreshing light soprano voice were more than adequate compensation for her lack of acting ability. Not that a strong dramatic performance would, in any way, have enhanced this delightful fairy-tale about a young girl's determination to form a symphony orchestra in order to give work to a hundred unemployed musicians; and, once having formed her orchestra, to beg, borrow, or steal the services of Leopold Stokowski (illustrated, with Durbin, orchestra) to help launch it on the public. Energetic enthusiasm was what was called for, and that, precisely, was what Miss Durbin delivered, leaving the acting to costar Adolphe Menjou (as her father), Eugene Pallette, Mischa Auer, and Alice Brady. The unsophisticated screenplay by Bruce Manning, Charles Kenyon, Hans Kraly and James Mulhauser was just the job for the occasion, and its climax in which the musicians, having inveigled themselves into Stokowski's residence, embark on Liszt's *Hungarian Rhapsody No. 2*, triggered off a chain reaction of excited delight in audiences everywhere. It was produced by Charles Rogers and Joe Pasternak (the latter returning again and again to this sort of subject, both at Universal and later at MGM), and directed with a beguiling ingenuousness by Henry Koster. Songs: *It's Raining Sunbeams* Sam Coslow, Frederick Hollander; *A Heart That's Free* Alfred G. Robyn, Thomas T. Railey; *Alleluia* Mozart (from Exultate, Jubilate K165); excerpts from *Lohengrin* Wagner; *La Traviata* Verdi; Tchai- ▷ kovsky's *Fifth Symphony*.

Though **Music For Madame** (RKO) was Jesse L. Lasky's third attempt to turn singer Nino Martini into a star (and his third failure to do so), its only point of interest lay in the fact that it marked the debut of Joan Fontaine (right), who received second billing. For the rest it told a rather melodramatic tale about a young Italian tenor (Martini, singing, left) who, after arriving in Hollywood in search of screen stardom, falls in with a bunch of thieves who use him as a front man. Thus, while Signor M. is singing his soul out in an impassioned interpretation of Leoncavallo's 'Vesti la Giubba' (from *Pagliacci*) at a wedding, the crooks are looting the gifts. Robert Harari and Gertrude Purcell's screenplay took advantage of its Hollywood background to make some satirical comments on the movie capital, but the film was basically too lightweight an affair to sustain this element which evaporated without trace. Alan Mowbray, Billy Gilbert, Alan Hale (centre right), Grant Mitchell, Erik Rhodes (centre), Lee Patrick, and Jack Carson in a brief appearance as an assistant director, were also in the cast. John Blystone directed. Songs: *Music For Madame* Herb Magidson, Allie Wrubel; *My Sweet Bambino*; *I Want The World To Know* Rudolf Friml, Gus Kahn; *King Of The Road* Nathaniel Shilkret, Eddie Cherkose. ▽

1938

Academy Awards

Best Picture
NOMINATIONS INCLUDED: *Alexander's Ragtime Band* (20th Century-Fox) produced by Darryl F. Zanuck with Harry Joe Brown

Supporting Actress
NOMINATIONS INCLUDED: Miliza Korjus *The Great Waltz* (MGM)

Writing (Original Story)
NOMINATIONS INCLUDED: *Alexander's Ragtime Band* Irving Berlin. *Mad About Music* (Universal) Marcella Burke and Frederick Kohner.

Cinematography
The Great Waltz Joseph Ruttenberg
NOMINATIONS INCLUDED: *Mad About Music* Joseph Valentine

Art Direction
NOMINATIONS INCLUDED: *Alexander's Ragtime Band* Bernard Herzbrun and Boris Leven. *Carefree* (RKO) Van Nest Polglase. *The Goldwyn Follies* (Goldwyn, UA) Richard Day. *Mad About Music* Jack Otterson.

Sound Recording
NOMINATIONS INCLUDED: *Sweethearts* (MGM) Douglas Shearer. *That Certain Age* (Universal) Bernard B. Brown.

Film Editing
NOMINATIONS INCLUDED: *Alexander's Ragtime Band* Barbara McLean. *The Great Waltz* Tom Held.

Music (New Classifications)
Song
'Thanks For The Memory' *Big Broadcast Of 1938* (Paramount) Ralph Rainger *cm*; Leo Robin *lyr*.
NOMINATIONS INCLUDED: 'Change Partners And Dance With Me' *Carefree* Irving Berlin. 'Jeepers Creepers' *Going Places* (WB) Harry Warren *cm*; Johnny Mercer *lyr*. 'My Own' *That Certain Age* Jimmy McHugh *cm*; Harold Adamson *lyr*. 'Now It Can Be Told' *Alexander's Ragtime Band* Irving Berlin. 'A Mist Over The Moon' *The Lady Objects* Ben Oakland *cm*; Oscar Hammerstein II *lyr*.

Scoring
Alexander's Ragtime Band Alfred Newman
NOMINATIONS INCLUDED: *Carefree* Victor Baravalle. *The Goldwyn Follies* Alfred Newman. *Mad About Music* Charles Previn and Frank Skinner. *Sweethearts* Herbert Stothart. *Tropic Holiday* Boris Morros.

Original Score
NOMINATIONS INCLUDED: *Breaking The Ice* (RKO) Victor Young

Special Awards
To Deanna Durbin and Mickey Rooney for their significant contribution in bringing to the screen the spirit and personification of youth and as juvenile players setting a high standard of ability and achievement. (miniature statuette trophies)
To Walt Disney for *Snow White And The Seven Dwarfs* (Disney, RKO), recognized as a significant screen innovation which has charmed millions and pioneered a great new entertainment field for the motion picture cartoon. (one statuette – seven miniatures)
Oliver Marsh and Allen Davey for colour cinematography on *Sweethearts* (MGM).

The New York Film Critics Awards
Special Award
Snow White And The Seven Dwarfs

The New York Times Annual 'Ten Best'
1st *Snow White And The Seven Dwarfs*

The Annual Top Moneymaking Films
INCLUDED: *Alexander's Ragtime Band*. *The Firefly* (MGM). *The Girl of The Golden West* (MGM). *The Goldwyn Follies*. *Happy Landing* (20th Century-Fox). *In Old Chicago* (20th Century-Fox). *Rosalie* (MGM). *Snow White And The Seven Dwarfs*.

The Great Chicago Fire of 1871 provided the climax to **In Old Chicago** (20th Century-Fox), a disaster musical whose roisterous tale of political chicanery was interspersed with seven songs and a jig. Alice Faye (right) was a music-hall singer torn between two brothers: bad guy Tyrone Power (centre), and good guy Don Ameche (left). Fate supplied the denouement and, as Chicago burned spectacularly in the background, all matters of the heart were satisfactorily resolved. The period detail was well attended to by director Henry King, with Faye's musical numbers helping to evoke the appropriate atmosphere of the era in which it all took place. Alice Brady, Andy Devine, Brian Donlevy and Berton Churchill offered reliable support; it was written by Lamar Trotti and Sonya Levien from an original story by Niven Busch, and produced by Darryl F. Zanuck with Kenneth MacGowan as his associate. Songs: *In Old Chicago* Mack Gordon, Harry Revel; *I'll Never Let You Cry*; *Take A Dip In The Sea* Sidney Mitchell, Lew Pollack; *Carry Me Back To Old Virginny* James A. Bland; *Sweet Genevieve* George Cooper, Henry Tucker; *How Many Miles To Dublin Town* (traditional); *The Irish Washerwoman* (traditional jig).
▽

Columnist Walter Winchell and orchestra leader Ben Bernie (left) found themselves locked in comic combat in **Love And Hisses** (20th Century-Fox), a snappily written (by Curtis Kenyon and Art Arthur) entertainment with a better-than-average plot and several specialty numbers. The storyline had Winchell publicly panning Bernie's latest singing discovery (Simone Simon). Determined not to let Mrs Winchell's little boy get away with it, Bernie makes his singer change her name to Yvette – the idea being to re-present her to Winchell, whom he feels sure will fall for the deception, and then expose him. Joan Davis and Bert Lahr (centre) provided musical as well as comic support. Also in it: Robert Kellard (right), and The Raymond Scott Quintet, specialty performers Ruth Terry, Chilton and Thomas, The Peters Sisters and The Brewster Twins. Sidney Lanfield directed for producer Kenneth MacGowan. Songs: *Sweet Someone*; *Broadway Gone Hawaiian*; *I Want To Be In Winchell's Column*; *Be A Good Sport*; *Lost In Your Eyes* Mack Gordon, Harry Revel; *Power House* Raymond Scott; *The Wolf Song* Norman Zeno; *Darling, Je Vous Aime Beaucoup* Anna Sosenko.

Humphrey Bogart, of all people, turned up in a musical for Warner Bros. and, clearly, wasn't at all happy about it. Hardly surprising, for the idiotic subject matter of **Swing Your Lady** was no more than a protracted, ill-conceived jape. The screenplay, by Joseph Schrank and Maurice Leo from the play by Kenyon Nicholson and Charles Robinson, had Bogey starring as an unsuccessful wrestling promoter who conceives the lunatic idea of matching a hulking thickhead against a lady blacksmith of Amazonian proportions. The two unfortunates called on to make something of these undignified roles were Nat Pendleton and Louise Fazenda, with Penny Singleton, Sammy White (illustrated), Frank McHugh, Allen Jenkins, Ronald Reagan, Leon Frank and Elviry Weaver also in it for director Ray Enright. The musical numbers, written by M.K. Jerome and Jack Scholl and staged by Bobby Connolly, comprised: *Mountain Swingaroo*; *Hillbilly From Tenth Avenue*; *The Old Apple Tree*; *Swing Your Lady*; *Dig Me A Grave In Missouri*.

Sonja Henie's third – and at 102 minutes, longest – feature, was also her sprightliest to date. Called **Happy Landing** (20th Century-Fox), it was a tasty casserole of a musical whose several and varied ingredients were kept nicely simmering under chef Darryl F. Zanuck's watchful and expert eye. Don Ameche (illustrated right) co-starred, and the original screenplay, devised by Milton Sperling and Boris Ingster, with parts as well for Cesar Romero (illustrated centre, as an orchestra leader who is managed by Mr Ameche) and Ethel Merman, had Miss Henie (illustrated) being conquered in love by the dashing Cesar. But when she realizes that underneath his smooth exterior beats the heart of a heel, she changes her romantic allegiance to the likeable Don. Several ballet-on-ice sequences, an energetic tap routine by the Condos Brothers (danced to Raymond Scott's 'War Dance of the Wooden Indians'), a clutch of songs from Merman, plus the comic contributions of funnymen Billy Gilbert, Wally Vernon and El Brendel, all contributed to a superior musical entertainment, expertly directed by Roy Del Ruth. Songs: *Hot And Happy*; *Yonny And His Oompah*; *You Are The Music To The Words In My Heart*; *A Gypsy Told Me* Jack Yellen, Samuel Pokrass; *You Appeal To Me* Walter Bullock, Harold Spina.

Mae West (right) wrote and starred in **Every Day's A Holiday** (her last film for Paramount), a turn-of-the-century tale that found its formidable star well below form. She played Peaches O'Day, a game gal who thinks nothing of selling Brooklyn bridge to any 'schnook' who's stupid enough to believe it's hers to sell; and who, to escape the police, pretends to be Mademoiselle Fifi, a Parisian musical comedy star. A trite story, with trite, laboured dialogue, **Every Day's A Holiday** disappointed West fans everywhere and was in no way comparable to her previous efforts. Edmund Lowe co-starred, with other roles going to Charles Butterworth, Walter Catlett (left), Lloyd Nolan, Roger Imhof, Charles Winninger, Herman Bing and Chester Conklin. Emanuel Cohen produced, and it was directed by Edward Sutherland. Songs: *Jubilee* Stanley Adams, Hoagy Carmichael; *Fifi*; *Flutter By, Little Butterfly* Sam Coslow; *Every Day's A Holiday*; *Along The Broadway Trail* Coslow, Barry Trivers.

The Goldwyn Follies (United Artists) was Sam Goldwyn's first all-Technicolor production and it cost him a couple of million dollars. A two-hour extravaganza with music and lyrics by George and Ira Gershwin, with Vernon Duke supplying the music for the ballet sequences – and utilizing the talents of George Balanchine and The American Ballet in a bid to bring culture to the masses – it was basically a variety show with a tenuous plot that unsuccessfully attempted to recreate, cinematically, some of the magic of the Ziegfeld Follies. The musical programme consisted of a 'Romeo and Juliet' ballet and a 'Water Nymph' ballet with Vera Zorina (illustrated centre), making her screen debut, 'Here, Pussy, Pussy' (by Ray Golden and Sid Kuller), 'Serenade To A Fish' performed by The Ritz Brothers, and Kenny Baker singing 'Love Walked In', 'Love Is Here To Stay' (by the Gershwins), and 'Spring Again' (by Vernon Duke and Ira Gershwin). In addition, Charles Kullman and Helen Jepson sang arias from Verdi's *La Traviata*, Ella Logan presented 'I Was Doing Alright' (the Gershwins), Jepson returned with 'La Serenata' (by Alfred Silvestri and Enrico Toselli), and 'I Love To Rhyme' (the Gershwins) featured Phil Baker, and Edgar Bergen and Charlie McCarthy (also making their screen debut). The mish-mash, while well-intentioned, demonstrated the maxim that one bad turn deserved another, and was directed by George Marshall with H.C. Potter (uncredited) from a screenplay credited to Ben Hecht (although, apparently, 10 other writers had been involved along the way). Also cast: Adolphe Menjou, Andrea Leeds (singing voice dubbed by Virginia Verrill), Jerome Cowan, Nydia Westman, and The Goldwyn Girls. On 11 July 1937, George Gershwin died, leaving Vernon Duke – with Oscar Levant's help – to polish up the final construction of his last four songs for the film. ▷

It took four years to make **Snow White And The Seven Dwarfs** (RKO), the first full-length animated film (illustrated), and despite the gloomy prognostications of the industry, the risk paid off and marked the beginning of the fabulous Walt Disney empire. It also established animation as a new and vital art form, although some of the film's detractors found many of the images too horrifying for children, while others thought much of it too twee for adults. Neither observation was entirely spurious, but it cannot be denied that its overall conception, and the superb invention in the animation itself, was breathtaking. Music played an important part in its success, and many of the show's songs became instant hits – most notably 'Some Day My Prince Will Come', 'Whistle While You Work' and 'Heigh-Ho' by Frank Churchill and Larry Morey, scored and arranged by Paul J. Smith and Leigh Harline. The latter two skilfully helped to characterize each of the seven dwarfs. The voices on the sound track belonged to Adriana Caselotti, Harry Stockwell, Lucille La Verne, Scotty Matraw, Roy Atwell, Pinto Colvig, Billy Gilbert, Moroni Olsen and Stuart Buchanan, and the supervising director was David Hand. Other songs: *I'm Wishing*; *With A Smile And A Song*; *The Washing Song*; *Isn't This A Silly Song?*; *One Song*; *Buddle-Uddle-Um-Dum*; *Music In Your Soup*; *You're Never Too Old To Be Young*.

THIRTIES MUSICALS

As Vernon and Irene Castle were the Fred Astaire and Ginger Rogers of their day, it seemed natural that Fred and Ginger (illustrated) should star in **The Story of Vernon and Irene Castle**, the last film they made for RKO. Financially, it was the least successful of their movies together and, artistically, it was very uneven, although their ballroom dancing was undeniably captivating and effortless, and there were some good individual moments – a montage depicting a whirlwind tour of the States by the Castles, with the couple dancing across a giant map of America was particularly effective. There was an infectious joy, too, in their routines to 'Waiting For The Robert E. Lee' (by L. Wolfe Gilbert and Abel Baer) and 'Too Much Mustard' (by Cecil Macklin). But, after eight light-hearted and jubilant musicals together, the public simply could not, and would not, accept the death of Fred (alias Vernon) in the last reel, and withdrew their support. The overweening presence of the real Irene Castle on the set had not helped matters, understandably causing both

Astaire and Rogers to feel somewhat restricted in approaching their roles. The film was produced by George Haight and Pandro S. Berman, directed by H.C. Potter and choreographed by Hermes Pan. The screenplay, based on the books *My Husband* and *My Memories of Vernon Castle* by Irene Castle, was by Richard Sherman, Oscar Hammerstein II and Dorothy Yost, and the supporting cast included Edna May Oliver (a splendid comic performance), Walter Brennan, Lew Fields, Etienne Girardot, Rolfe Sedan, Leonid Kinsky and Clarence Derwent. Though the only song to be specifically written for the film was 'Only When You're In My Arms' (by Con Conrad, Bert Kalmar and Harry Ruby), a large number of other songs germane to the period were featured. Excluding background tunes, these were: *Oh You Beautiful Doll* A. Seymour Brown, Nat D. Ayer; *Glow Little Glow Worm* Lillia Cayley Robinson, Paul Lincke; *By The Beautiful Sea* Harold Atteridge, Harry Carroll; *Row, Row, Row* William Jerome, James V. Monaco; *The Yama Yama Man* Collin Davis, Karl

Hoschna; *Come, Josephine In My Flying Machine* Alfred Bryan, Fred Fisher; *By The Light Of The Silvery Moon* Edward Madden, Gus Edwards; *Cuddle Up A Little Closer* Otto Harbach, Karl Hoschna; *King Chanticleer (Texas Tommy)* Nat D. Ayer; *While They Were Dancing Around* Joseph McCarthy, James V. Monaco; *The Darktown Strutters' Ball* Shelton Brooks, French lyrics by Elsie Janis; *Rose Room* Harry Williams, Art Hickman; *Très Jolie Waltz* Emil Waldteufel; *Syncopated Walk* Irving Berlin; *Maxixe Dengozo* Ernesto Nazareth; *Little Brown Jug* Joseph E. Winner; *You're Here And I'm Here* Harry B. Smith, Jerome Kern; *Chicago* Fred Fisher; *Hello, Frisco, Hello* Gene Buck, Louis A. Hirsch; *Way Down Yonder In New Orleans* Henry Creamer, Turner Layton; *Take Me Back To New York Town* Andrew B. Sterling, Harry von Tilzer; *It's A Long Way To Tipperary* Jack Judge, Harry Williams; *Hello, Hello, Who's Your Lady Friend* Worton David, Bert Lee, Harry Fragson; *Destiny Waltz* Sidney Baynes; *Nights Of Gladness* Charles Ancliffe; *Missouri Waltz* J.R. Shannon, Frederick Logan, John Eppell.

△

Children featured prominently in **They Shall Have Music** (GB: **Melody of Youth**), another attempt by producer Samuel Goldwyn (for United Artists) to bring culture to the masses. It was certainly more successful in every respect than the misguided *The Goldwyn Follies* (United Artists, 1938), and it top-billed Jascha Heifetz (illustrated, for whose services Goldwyn paid $120,000) as a violinist who is persuaded by a bunch of quasi-juvenile delinquents, led by Gene Reynolds (now the producer of TV's *M.A.S.H.*), to save their settlement home by giving a fund-raising concert. Heifetz's co-operation ensured a happy ending, but not before scriptwriter John Howard Lawson (story by Irmgard Von Cube) released a veritable Niagara of tears from audiences everywhere. The word 'heartwarming' could have been invented for the sole purpose of describing the feeling director Archie Mayo conveyed in his overtly sentimental approach to the story; but so adroit was his handling of the various elements in Goldwyn's prestigious production, only the flintiest cynic would disagree with that assessment of its quality. Walter Brennan, Andrea Leeds, Joel McCrea, Porter Hall, Terry Kilburn and the Peter Merembum California Junior Symphony Orchestra helped round out an excellent cast. Musical items included Heifetz performing *The Rondo Capriccioso* Saint-Saens; *Souvenir d'un Lieu Cher, opus 42, No 3* Tchaikovsky; *Hora Staccato* Dinicu-Heifetz; *Concerto in E Minor For Violin And Orchestra (3rd Movement)* Mendelssohn; *Waltz in D Flat, Opus 64, No 1 (The Minute Waltz)* Chopin (this last played by Dolly Loehr, later Diana Lynn, making her film debut).

Considered by Bob Hope (centre right) to be the low spot of his career, **Some Like It Hot** (Paramount) – not to be confused with Billy Wilder's 1959 masterpiece – cast the comedian as an amusement park barker who sets out to exploit the talents of Gene Krupa (background centre) as well as his sweetheart Shirley Ross (centre left) in an attempt to keep his dying sideshow alive. Weighing in at 64 minutes, it was a really puerile attempt to blend music with comedy, and buried alive the talents of its stars and supporting players Una Merkel, Rufe Davis, Bernard Nedell, Frank Sully and Bernadene Hayes. It was directed by George Archainbaud, and scripted by Lewis R. Foster and Wilkie C. Mahoney from a play by Ben Hecht and Gene Fowler, with William C. Thomas as associate producer. Songs included: *The Lady's In Love With You* Frank Loesser, Burton Lane; *Some Like It Hot* Loesser, Gene Krupa, Remo Biondi; *Heart And Soul* Loesser, Hoagy Carmichael.

▽

△

Though Al Jolson, virtually at the end of his screen career, was given third billing in **Rose of Washington Square** (20th Century-Fox), he almost stole the show with his electric interpretation of such golden oldies as 'California, Here I Come' (by B.G. De Sylva, Joseph Meyer and Jolson), 'My Mammy' (by Joe Young, Sam Lewis, Walter Donaldson), 'Pretty Baby' (by Gus Kahn, Tony Jackson and Egbert Van Alstyne), 'Toot Toot Tootsie Goodbye' (by Gus Kahn, Ernie Erdman and Dan Russo) and 'Rock-A-Bye Your Baby With A Dixie Melody' (by Jean Schwartz, Sam Lewis and Joe Young). Unfortunately, there wasn't nearly as much wattage in the plot, which had Alice Faye (illustrated centre) – an excellent performance – falling for no-goodnik Tyrone Power and sticking by him even when he ends up in Sing Sing. And sing sing she did through thick and thin, her big musical moment being 'My Man' by Channing Pollock and Maurice Yvain, a number generally associated with Fanny Brice. In fact, producer Nunnally Johnson's screenplay clung so closely to the facts of Miss Brice's life, that the celebrated comedienne sued the studio and received an out of court settlement. Also cast were William Frawley, Joyce Compton, Hobart Cavanaugh and Louis Prima (left). The dances were staged by Seymour Felix with Gregory Ratoff directing. Other songs: *I Never Knew Heaven Could Speak* Mack Gordon, Harry Revel; *Rose Of Washington Square* James Hanley, Ballard MacDonald, Joseph McCarthy; *The Curse Of An Aching Heart* Al Piantadosi, Henry Fink; *I'm Sorry I Made You Cry* N.J. Clesi; *The Vamp* Byron Gay; *Ja-da* Bob Carleton; *I'm Just Wild About Harry* Noble Sissle, Eubie Blake.

▽

△

Dick Powell (seated) who had served the Warner Bros. musicals so well for so long, ran out of steam as far as the studio was concerned towards the end of the decade, and was relegated to second billing below Ann Sheridan in his last film for the studio called **Naughty But Nice**. Powell played a composer attempting to get his symphony published, in the course of which attempts he gets involved with a bunch of Tin Pan Alley-ites, one of whom is conveniently Miss Sheridan (then at the height of the studio's 'oomph' girl campaign) who got to sing more songs than her leading man. The screenplay, by Richard Macaulay and Jerry Wald, set out to take a few satirical swipes at Tin Pan Alley and its endless 'borrowings' from the classics, but the satire didn't sit and, in spite of music from Johnny Mercer, Harry Warren, Wagner, Liszt, Mozart and Bach, it was a pretty tedious affair. Produced by Sam Bischoff and directed by Ray Enright, it also featured Gale Page (centre), Helen Broderick (centre right), Ronald Reagan (2nd left), William Davidson (left) and ZaSu Pitts (2nd right). Songs: *Corn Pickin*; *Hooray For Spinach*; *I'm Happy About The Whole Thing*; *In A Moment of Weakness*; *I Don't Believe In Signs*.

The **Wizard of Oz** (MGM) was an enchanting entertainment that really lived up to the blurb – 'for children of all ages'. Today, it still seems as fresh as it was in 1939, when it became an instant movie classic and made an international star of 17-year-old Judy Garland. Although Mervyn LeRoy's production was beset with problems in every department – not least that of the screenplay which went through numerous versions – the finished product was superb, more than compensating for the many difficulties encountered in its gruelling five-month shooting schedule, and the many months of pre-production preparation. In the end, everything worked – from the final screenplay adapted from L. Frank Baum's novel and credited to Noel Langley, Florence Ryerson and Edgar Allan Woolf – to the songs, by Harold Arlen and E.Y. Harburg, giving plenty of opportunity for excitement, spectacle, tenderness and comedy. Four noted directors were involved in the production: Richard Thorpe was fired after 12 days and his footage scrapped because it lacked fairy-tale feeling. George Cukor directed three days of tests in which he got rid of Judy's blonde wig and 'cute' doll-face make-up (a hang-over, perhaps, from the studio's unsuccessful attempt to obtain Shirley Temple), which made the point that restoring Dorothy's down-to-earth ingenuousness was the way to enhance the fairy-tale quality of her Technicolored adventure in the Land of Oz. Victor Fleming, who received sole director credit, spent four months getting these sequences on film before having to leave to take over *Gone With The Wind*. Fleming drew unsurpassed performances from Ray Bolger as the Scarecrow, Bert Lahr as the Cowardly Lion, Jack Haley (replacing Buddy Ebsen who fell ill with aluminium poisoning) as the Tin Man (all three illustrated, with Garland), and Margaret Hamilton as the Wicked Witch. Choreographer Bobby Connolly was in charge of the musical numbers and the daunting task of teaching 150 midget-Munchkins to sing and dance. (In all, 9,200 actors were employed on the film, and there were 3,210 costume designs, 8,428 separate make-ups and 68 sets!) Though it was a

brilliant idea to open the film in black and white for the Kansas scenes, directed by King Vidor in 10 days after Fleming departed, and then going into colour as Dorothy (Garland) enters the Land of Oz, it was not the eye-catching colour photography or Connolly's elaborately staged musical numbers that lingered in the memory, but Vidor's staging of Judy's simple and tender singing of 'Over The Rainbow' in her own backyard. Incredible as it now seems, anti-LeRoy politicking after the first sneak preview nearly succeeded in getting this classic sequence cut out of the picture. Billie Burke (dubbed by Lorraine Bridges) was cast as Glinda the Good Witch, and Frank Morgan played the Wonderful Wizard, with Charles Grapewin as Uncle Henry, Clara Blandick as Auntie Em, and Pat Walshe as Chief of the Wicked Witch's Winged Monkeys. Other songs: *Come Out, Come Out Wherever You*

Are (Burke); *It Really Was No Miracle* (Garland); *Ding Dong The Witch Is Dead* (Garland, Burke, Munchkins); *We Welcome You To Munchkinland* (Munchkins); *Follow The Yellow Brick Road* (Garland, Munchkins); *We're Off To See The Wizard* (Garland, Bolger, Lahr, Haley); *If I Only Had A Brain (A Heart, The Nerve)* (Bolger, Lahr, Haley); *Lions And Tigers And Bears* (Lahr); *You're Out Of The Woods* (chorus); *The Merry Old Land Of Oz* (chorus); *If I Were King Of The Forest* (Lahr); *Optimistic Voices* (chorus on soundtrack).

THIRTIES MUSICALS

Described by one contemporary critic as 'the Watteau shepherdess of Universal', Deanna Durbin was given her first screen kiss (amidst much newspaper ballyhooing of the fact) in **First Love**. A modern-day Cinderella story, it had Durbin (right), as an orphan, being rescued from unappreciative relatives by Robert Stack (left), the handsome bestower of that much publicized kiss. Helen Parrish played Deanna's attractive but sour glamour-girl cousin, Eugene Pallette her wealthy uncle (who, with justification hates every member of his family), and Leatrice Joy an astrology-obsessed aunt, with other parts going to Lewis Howard, June Storey and Charles Coleman. The serviceable, if crushingly unoriginal, screenplay was by Bruce Manning and Lionel Houser, Joe Pasternak produced, and the director was that reliable *schmaltz*-monger, Henry Koster. Songs and other musical numbers included: *Spring In My Heart* (from a melody by Johann Strauss adapted by Hans Salter, lyrics Ralph Freed); *Amapola* Albert Gamse, Joseph M. LaCalle; *Home Sweet Home* John Howard Payne, Sir Henry Bishop; *One Fine Day* from Puccini's 'Madame Butterfly'.

Suggested by the career of showman Gus Edwards – the man who discovered Eddie Cantor and Eleanor Powell – **The Star Maker** (Paramount) was curiously lacking in talent, with Bing Crosby (centre) the only name in its cast. As the singing showman, Crosby sets up a vaudeville act with a group of under-seventeens, until he gets into trouble with the law which rules that children of a certain age cannot work after eight at night. So he enters that sensational new medium – radio. Crosby sailed through it all with his usual charm and rich baritone (and had another hit with 'An Apple For The Teacher' by Johnny Burke and James V. Monaco); the kids were fine, and so were Linda Ware, Louise Campbell, Ned Sparks and Laura Hope Crews in support. Roy Del Ruth directed from a screenplay by Frank Butler, Don Hartman and Arthur Caesar (story by Caesar and William Pierce), and Charles R. Rogers produced. Other songs: *Go Fly A Kite*; *A Man And His Dream*; *Still The Bluebird Sings* Burke, Monaco; *School Days*; *If I Were A Millionaire* Will Cobb, Gus Edwards; *Jimmy Valentine* Edward Madden, Edwards; *Sunbonnet Sue* Robert B. Smith, Edwards.

On Your Toes (Warner Bros./First National) should, on paper, have been a blockbuster of a musical. It was based on a successful George Abbott stage play, had a Rodgers and Hart score, the great Balanchine was its choreographer, James Wong Howe and Sol Polito photographed it and Orry-Kelly designed the clothes. In the event, however, an awful screenplay by Jerry Wald and Richard Macaulay sabotaged the venture, and for a film that could so easily have danced its way to glory, it was, apart from the noteworthy 'Slaughter On Tenth Avenue' sequence, exceptionally dull. All about an American composer/dancer who is mistaken for a traitor by a visiting Russian ballet company, it starred Eddie Albert (left – Ray Bolger created the role on stage) and Vera Zorina (2nd left) with James Gleason, Alan Hale (centre), Frank McHugh (centre left), Leonid Kinskey (2nd right), Donald O'Connor, Gloria Dickson (right) and Queenie Smith in support. Ray Enright directed for associate producer Robert Lord. Songs and musical numbers (all heard as background only) included: *There's A Small Hotel*; *Quiet Night*; *On Your Toes*; *Princess Zenobia Ballet*.

A routine programmer to demonstrate the skating wizardry of six-year-old Irene Dare (centre foreground), **Everything's On Ice** (RKO) did just that and, in addition, threw in a plot about the kid being financially exploited by uncle Roscoe Karns in Florida. It was written by Adrian Landis and Sherman Lowe, directed by Erle C. Kenton and produced by the man in charge of Bobby Breen's cinematic adventures, Sol Lesser. Also cast: Edgar Kennedy, Lynne Roberts, Eric Linden, Mary Hart and Bobby Watson. Songs included: *Georgie Porgie*; *Everything's On Ice* Milton Drake, Fred Stryker.

Δ

▽

Δ **Hawaiian Nights** (Universal) was a tired programmer, set in the land of hula skirts, that starred Johnny Downs (featured right centre) as a bandleader whose occupation angers his father (Thurston Hall) to such an extent that he banishes the lad to the South Seas – the most inappropriate place imaginable, as Charles Grayson and Lee Loeb's screenplay (story by John Grey) made boringly clear. Mary Carlisle (centre), Constance Moore, Eddie Quillan (left) Etienne Girardot, Samuel S. Hinds and Princess Luana were in it for producer Max H. Golden, and it was directed by Albert S. Rogell. Come back Dorothy Lamour, all is forgiven! Songs: *Hawaii Sang Me To Sleep; Hey, Good Lookin!; I Found My Love; Then I Wrote The Minuet In G* (based on a melody by Beethoven) Frank Loesser, Matt Malneck.

Δ From Hawaii to **Honolulu** (MGM) where, despite the slight change in geography, the situation continued grim. Robert Young played two parts in it: a film star, and the pineapple farmer with whom he changes places, with Eleanor Powell (illustrated left on walkway) top-starred as a dancing lady Young (the film star) meets on board ship. Miss Powell at least, was given several opportunities to do what she did best, and on one occasion even did it with a skipping rope. Also in tow were George Burns and Gracie Allen (illustrated with Powell), Rita Johnson, Clarence Kolb and Sig Rumann (as a psychiatrist). Because there was so little musical activity at Warner Bros., musicals again having temporarily fallen out of favour by 1939, Harry Warren was loaned to MGM to write the score, which he did with Gus Kahn as lyricist. Best musical moments were 'The Leader Doesn't Like Music' which had Gracie Allen doing a Mae West, and The King's Men, led by Ken Darby spoofing the Marx Brothers. Herbert Fields and Frank Partos wrote the original screenplay, Edward Buzzell directed and the producer was Irving Cummings. Other songs included: *This Night Was Made For Dreaming; Honolulu* Warren, Kahn; *Hymn To The Sun* P.G. Wodehouse, Armand Versey.

Not nearly as inventive as Walt Disney's *Snow White And The Seven Dwarfs* (RKO, 1937), nor as well drawn, **Gulliver's Travels** (Paramount) was another full-length animated cartoon (see illustration) in Technicolor aimed at the pre-teenage market – and with very little in it to appeal to adults. Concentrating on the Lilliputian section of Swift's satire (the satirical tone on this occasion being totally eliminated), it had a screenplay by Edmond Seward, Dan Gordon, Cal Howard, Red Pierce and I. Sparber (Seward was credited with the adaptation), was produced by Max Fleischer (whose crowning artistic achievement was his creation of Betty Boop), and directed by his brother Dave. The voices of Jessica Dragonette and Lanny Ross were used in the musical sequences. Songs: *Bluebirds In The Moonlight; All's Well; We're All Together Again; Forever; Faithful; Faithful Forever* (the previous two numbers joined); *I Hear A Dream* Ralph Rainger, Leo Robin; *It's A Hap-Hap-Happy Day* Sammy Timberg, Winston Sharples, Al Neiburg.

The Great Victor Herbert (Paramount) was a largely fictionalized account of the life of the great Victor Herbert, with Walter Connolly as the eponymous maestro, and Allan Jones (featured foreground centre) and Mary Martin as a temperamental tenor and an actress who both played a large part in Russel Crouse and Robert Lively's lightweight screenplay (story by Lively and Andrew L. Stone, the latter also serving as producer and director). A quintessential Hollywood biopic, dedicated more to entertaining than enlightening, its *raison d'être* was to present Herbert's impressive catalogue of hits, and this it did unstintingly, with twenty-eight numbers in all being featured. Singing newcomer Susanna Foster (centre right) was also cast; so were Lee Bowman, Judith Barrett, Jerome Cowan, John Garrick (foreground centre left), Pierre Watkin and Richard Tucker. Songs (and their lyricists) included: *Someday* William Le Baron; *Al Fresco; Thine Alone; Punchinello; Kiss Me Again; All For You; Neapolitan Love Song* Henry Blossom; *Absinthe Frappé; Rose Of The World; March Of The Toys* Glen Macdonough; *There Once Was An Owl; To The Land Of Romance* Harry B. Smith; *Ah, Sweet Mystery Of Life; I'm Falling In Love With Someone* Rida Johnson Young; *Sweethearts* Robert B. Smith.

THIRTIES MUSICALS

Kay Kyser and his 'Kollege of Knowledge' – hitherto the exclusive property of radio – made their cinematic bow in **That's Right, You're Wrong** (RKO) whose trumped-up story (by David Butler and William Conselman, screenplay by Conselman and James V. Kern) had Kyser (right) and his mob being signed to do a film that was never made because its scriptwriters could not come up with a workable idea – a case of fiction mirroring fact. It was produced and directed by David Butler with a cast that also included Adolphe Menjou, May Robson, Lucille Ball, Dennis O'Keefe, Edward Everett Horton, Roscoe Karns, and Kyser regulars Ginny Simms (centre), Harry Babbitt (centre left), Sully Mason (left) and Ish Kabibble. Songs: *I'm Fit To Be Tied* Walter Donaldson; *Scatterbrain* Johnny Burke, Frankie Masters, Kahn Keene, Carl Bean; *Little Red Fox* James Kern, Hy Heath, Johnny Lange, Lew Porter; *The Answer Is Love* Charles Newman, Sammy Stept; *Chatterbox* Jerome Brainin, Allan Roberts; *Happy Birthday To Love* Dave Franklin.

A highly romanticized, largely fictitious account of the life, times and music of Stephen Foster. **Swanee River** (20th Century-Fox) in no way did justice to the memory of one of America's great songsmiths. The fact that the real-life Foster married a girl from Pittsburgh, whereas his celluloid counterpart (played by Don Ameche) becomes betrothed to a Southern lass (Andrea Leeds) was of no consequence to scenarists John Taintor Foote and Phillip Dunne who might arguably have been forgiven for twisting history had their fiction, at least, proved entertaining. But it didn't – rendering their unscrupulous manipulations inexcusable. Salvageable from the Technicolored detritus of Darryl F. Zanuck's production were a handful of Foster favourites, galvanically performed in blackface by Al Jolson as minstrel singer E.P. Christy (illustrated centre with Ameche). Felix Bressart, Chick Chandler, Russell Hicks, and George Reed were also cast; so were The Hall Johnson Choir. The musical items were staged by Nick Castle and Geneva Sawyer, and the film was directed by Sidney Lanfield. Songs: *Oh Susanna*; *De Camptown Races*; *My Old Kentucky Home*; *Ring Ring De Banjo*; *Jeannie With The Light Brown Hair*; *Old Black Joe*; *Swanee River*; *Suite For Small Orchestra* Foster; *Curry A Mule* Sidney Lanfield, Louis Silver; *Gwine Down The River* William O. Davis; *Mule Song* Hall Johnson.

There were very few set-pieces in **At the Circus** (MGM) to compare, for example, with the cabin scene in *A Night At The Opera* (MGM, 1935), but Groucho singing 'Lydia The Tattooed Lady' (by E.Y. Harburg and Harold Arlen) in his inimitable off-key voice and then attempting an accompanying dance, was a delight. Of course, any film with The Marx Brothers (illustration: Groucho, left, Chico, centre) was bound to contain comic gems, although in this instance they were as loosely strung together as the plot (circus owner Kenny Baker has to find $10,000 to save his show and gets Groucho, alias lawyer J. Cheever Loophole, to help him). Florence Rice, Eve Arden, Margaret Dumont and Fritz Feld were also cast. Edward Buzzell directed for producer Mervyn LeRoy and the screenplay was by Irving Brecher. Bobby Connolly directed the dances. Other songs: *Two Blind Loves*; *Step Up And Take A Bow*; *Swingali* Harburg, Arlen; *Blue Moon* (Harpo's harp solo) Richard Rodgers and Lorenz Hart.

Based on the 1936 English operetta with music by George Posford and Bernard Grun (book and lyrics by Eric Maschwitz), **Balalaika** (MGM) was about the struggle between the nobility and the revolutionaries in Russia. Reflecting Hollywood's revived interest in a potential ally against the growing Nazi threat, the film didn't really take sides, but made Russia in revolution seem more like Ruritania. In its own way an attempt at *detente*, it would have been about as welcome in the Kremlin as Hitler, but in America it was accepted as a splendid musical entertainment in the opulent MGM tradition. Nelson Eddy (illustrated centre) played Prince Peter Karagin, a Cossack who poses as a poor music student because of his love for Lydia, a revolutionary-minded singer played by Hungarian Ilona Massey in her first starring role and billed as 'the new Dietrich'. Unfortunately, her limited soprano voice and insipid acting proved hindrances throughout her brief career, and this occasion was no exception. Although one song, 'At The Balalaika' (by Posford and Maschwitz, with new lyrics by Bob Wright and Chet Forrest), was retained from the original London production, there were plenty of replacement numbers, all sung by Eddy and, as MGM thought befitting, a fulsome male chorus, Frank Morgan, Dalies Frantz, Lionel Atwill, C. Aubrey Smith (left) and the Russian Cossack Choir gave adequate support to the screenplay by Leon Gordon, Charles Bennett and Jacques Deval. Reinhold Schunzel directed it for producer Lawrence Weingarten. Other songs and musical numbers: *After Service* (traditional Russian religious chant, arranged by Herbert Stothart); *A Life For The Czar* Mikhail Glinka (lyricist uncertain); *Ride, Cossack Ride*; *Tanya*; *Wishing Episode* (*Mirror Mirror*) Stothart, Wright, Forrest; *Gorko* (traditional Russian drinking song, adapted by Stothart); *Polonaise In A Flat, Opus 53* Chopin; *Song Of The Volga Boatman* (traditional, arranged by Chaliapin and Koeneman); *Chanson Boheme*; *Chanson du Toreador*; *Si Tu M'Aimes* (all from 'Carmen') Bizet; *Shadows On The Sand* (from *Scheherazade*) Rimsky-Korsakov, arranged by Wright and Forrest; *God Save The Czar* Alexei Lvov; Vasili Zhukovsky; *Stille Nacht* (*Silent Night*) Franz Gruber, Joseph Mohr; *Otchichornya* (traditional); *Flow, Flow, White Wine* Stothart, Gus Kahn; *The Magic Of Your Love* Franz Lehar, new lyrics Kahn, Clifford Grey.

Babes In Arms (MGM), from the Broadway hit by Richard Rodgers and Lorenz Hart, was the first film Busby Berkeley directed in its entirety at MGM, and the first produced by lyricist Arthur Freed. Both debuts were auspicious: Berkeley redeemed himself from the failure of his kitschy finale for *Broadway Serenade* and began an important second phase in his extraordinary career; and Freed was to become one of Hollywood's greatest producers of musicals. Brilliantly adapting to the MGM house-style, Berkeley was able to bring out the best in his stars Mickey Rooney and Judy Garland (illustrated), both of whom were given ample opportunity to display their multiple talents in a large-scale minstrel show, as well as in several more intimate songs. Rooney even managed to squeeze in excellent impersonations of Clark Gable and Lionel Barrymore. Jack McGowan and Kay Van Riper's screenplay concerned a group of impecunious vaudevillians and their enterprising offspring who, in order to raise funds for their parents, stage a hit revue and, in the process, gave birth to a whole cycle of musicals in which someone or other (usually Rooney) would exclaim exuberantly: 'Hey kids,

∇

let's put on a show!' Charles Winninger, Guy Kibbee (a survivor from Berkeley's Warner Bros. days), June Preisser, Grace Hayes, Betty Jaynes, Ann Shoemaker and Margaret Hamilton were also cast. Of the original Rodgers and Hart score, only 'Babes In Arms' and 'Where Or When' remained. Other songs and musical numbers: *Broadway Rhythm* (Garland); *Good Morning* (Garland and Rooney); *You Are My Lucky Star* (Jaynes) Arthur Freed, Nacio Herb Brown; *I Cried For You* (Garland) Freed, Gus Arnheim, Abe Lyman; *God's Country* (Garland, Rooney, Jaynes and chorus) Harold Arlen, E.Y. Harburg, Roger Edens; *Ja-da* (Winninger) Bob Carleton; *Rock-A-Bye, Baby* (chorus) Effie I. Crockett; *Silent Night* (chorus) Franz Gruber, arranged Edens; *Darktown Strutters' Ball* (chorus) Shelton Brooks; *I Like Opera, I Like Swing* (Garland, Jaynes); *Figaro* (Garland); *My Daddy Was A Minstrel Man* (chorus) Roger Edens; *Oh! Susanna* (chorus) Stephen Foster; *Ida, Sweet As Apple Cider* (chorus) Eddie Leonard, Eddie Munson; *Moonlight Bay* (chorus) Edward Madden, Percy Wenrich; *I'm Just Wild About Harry* (Garland) Noble Sissle, Eubie Blake; *The Stars And Stripes Forever* (chorus) John Philip Sousa.

△

A 63-minute programmer featuring Cecil Cunningham (centre), Constance Moore, Johnny Downs, Janet Beecher (left), Marjorie Rambeau (centre left), Hedda Hopper (right), Edgar Kennedy, William Demarest, Horace McMahon and Paula Stone, Universal's **Laugh It Off** (GB: **Lady Be Gay**) was the saga of four down-and-out actresses who, in a last desperate attempt to salvage their careers, requisition a down-and-out nightclub to stage a floor show. Taking its title literally was easier said than done, for, as written by Harry Clork and Lee Loeb (from a story by Loeb and Mortimer Braus) and directed by Albert S. Rogell (who also produced), there wasn't much in it to laugh off. Songs: *My Dream And I*; *Doin' The 1940*; *Laugh It Off*; *Who's Gonna Keep Your Wigwam Warm?* Sam Lerner, Ben Oakland.

1940

Joseph Tierney and Harry McCarthy's 1919 stage musical **Irene** came to the screen via RKO with Herbert Wilcox in charge of the production and direction, and his future wife Anna Neagle (illustrated) as its star. A tuneful, if old-fashioned affair, it featured Miss Neagle as an Irish sales girl who, in the best Cinderella tradition, is introduced into Long Island's *haut monde* with two personable Prince Charmings hovering in the background for her attention. A glossy concoction whose visual highlight was a ball sequence photographed in Technicolor, at which Miss Neagle sang and danced to the durable 'Alice Blue Gown', it also starred Ray Milland and Alan Marshal as the two suitors, Roland Young as a couturier and Billie Burke as Marshall's mother, with May Robson, Arthur Treacher, Marsha Hunt, Isabel Jewell and Doris Nolan completing the cast. The screenplay was by Alice Duer Miller. Pleasant but dated, it was the sort of picture you could take or leave without noticing the difference. Songs: *Irene; Castle Of Dreams; You've Got Me Out On A Limb; There's Something In The Air; Worthy Of You; Sweet Vermosa Brown* Tierney, McCarthy. ▽

Walt Disney's second full-length animated feature was **Pinocchio** (RKO), a captivating re-telling of the famous Collodi fantasy about a puppet boy (see illustration) who can only become flesh and blood after he acquires the virtues of truth, courage and unselfishness. Considered by many to be superior even to *Snow White And The Seven Dwarfs* (RKO, 1937), it also combined music with animation in a glorious burst of inspiration, and has provided pleasure and wonderment for children of all ages during the forty years it has been on release. Ben Sharpsteen and Hamilton Luske were the supervising directors, it was photographed in Technicolor, and featured the voices of Dickie Jones as Pinocchio, Christian Rub as Gepetto the woodcarver, Cliff Edwards as Jiminy Cricket (Pinocchio's conscience), Evelyn Venable as the Blue Fairy, Walter Catlett as J. Worthington Foulfellow, Frankie Darro as Lampwick, and Charles Judels as Stromboli and the coachman. Songs: *When You Wish Upon A Star; Little Woodenhead; Hi-Diddle-Dee-Dee (An Actor's Life For Me); I've Got No Strings; Give A Little Whistle; As I Was Say'n' To The Duchess; Pinocchio; Three Cheers For Anything; Turn On The Old Box; Jiminy Cricket* Leigh Harline, Ned Washington.

Universal was at it again, stealing song titles to boost programmer musicals, with **Oh Johnny, How You Can Love!** in which Tom Brown starred as a travelling salesman who picks up a spoiled young heiress (Peggy Moran) after the car in which she is travelling to an elopement rendezvous is involved in a crash. After the usual plot complications, which included an encounter with escaping bank robbers, the salesman and the heiress decide they are made for each other, thus cueing in the end title with the inevitable clinch. A really sophomoronic effort, it was written by Edwin Rutt, produced by Ken Goldsmith, directed by Charles Lamont and featured Betty Jane Rhodes (who sang the catchy title number, by Abe Olman and Ed Rose, at an auto-camp jamboree), Allen Jenkins, Donald Meek (illustrated with Moran), Juanita Quigley and Isabel Jewell. They all deserved better. Other songs included: *Maybe I Like What You Like*; *Swing Chariot Swing*; *Make Up Your Mind* Paul Gerard Smith, Frank Skinner.
▽

Road to Singapore (Paramount) was the first of the long-running 'Road' series, and although one of the year's top-grossing films, wasn't all that good. Bing Crosby (centre) played a carefree millionaire's son who, to escape matrimony and the prospect of becoming actively involved in the family shipping business, takes off for exotic Singapore in tandem with his game-for-anything buddy, Bob Hope (right). There they meet sarong-girl Dorothy Lamour (left) whose idea of making a living is having cigarette ends whipped out of her mouth by mean-looking Anthony Quinn. Messrs Hope and Crosby take her away from all that and – well, you know the rest. Charles Coburn played Crosby's wealthy father, Judith Barrett was the fiancée Crosby deserts, with other parts in Don Hartman and Frank Butler's less-than-scintillating screenplay (story by Harry Hervey) being filled by Jerry Colonna, Pierre Watkin and Gaylord Pendleton, It was produced by Harlan Thompson and the director was Victor Schertzinger. The musical numbers were staged by LeRoy Prinz. Songs: *Sweet Potato Piper*; *Too Romantic*; *Kaigoon* Johnny Burke, James V. Monaco; *Captain Custard*; *The Moon And The Willow Tree* Burke, Victor Schertzinger. Interesting sideline: George Burns and Fred MacMurray were originally offered the male leads, but on reading the script gave it the thumbs down.

It's A Date was the annually prescribed dose of Deanna Durbin (left) from Universal Studios, and although it underwent a change in its customary director – from Henry Koster to William A. Seiter – the ineffable and always very popular Durbin persona remained unchanged in this story of a famous actress's daughter whose rise to fame is in direct proportion to her illustrious mother's decline. Kay Francis co-starred as the mother, with other parts in this entertaining if slightly far-fetched tale going to Walter Pidgeon, Eugene Pallette, Lewis Howard (right), Samuel S. Hinds, S.Z. Sakall, Henry Stephenson, Virginia
▽

Brissac, and Harry Owens and His Royal Hawaiians. It was written by Norman Krasna from a story by Jane Hall, Frederick Kohner and Ralph Block and, musically, offered Miss Durbin a pot-pourri of numbers which included Schubert's 'Ave Maria'. Other songs: *Love Is All* Pinky Tomlin, Harry Tobias; *It Happened In Kaloha* Ralph Freed, Frank Skinner; *Rhythm Of The Islands* Eddie Cherkose, Leon Belasco, Jacques Press; *Hawaiian War Chant* Ralph Freed, Johnny Noble, Prince Leleiohaku of Hawaii; *Quando M'en Vo (Musetta's Waltz)* from Puccini's 'La Boheme'; *Loch Lomond* (traditional).

Forties Musicals

A low-budget programmer running a mere 69 minutes, **Music In My Heart** (Columbia) starred Tony Martin (foreground) as a foreign singer who, in order to avoid deportation, appears in a musical comedy with Rita Hayworth (second-billed), a girl of the tenements and the object of newspaper publisher Alan Mowbray's affections. Miss Hayworth looked stunning throughout, and some of the songs by Bob Wright and Chet Forrest were more than serviceable in the flimsy context of James Edward Grant's screenplay. And that, in the final accounting, was that. Also cast: Edith Fellows, Eric Blore, George Tobias, Joseph Crehan, George Humbert and Andre Kostelanetz and His Orchestra (illustrated). Irving Starr produced and the director was Joseph Santley. Songs: *No Other Love*; *Punchinello*; *Oh What A Lovely Dream*; *Prelude To Love*; *I've Got Music In My Heart*; *It's A Blue World* Wright, Forrest.

A reworking of their 1929 movie, *The Broadway Melody*, MGM's **Two Girls On Broadway** (GB: **Choose Your Partners**) starred curvaceous Lana Turner (left), and Joan Blondell (right, making her MGM debut), as sisters in the roles originally played by Anita Page and Bessie Love, with George Murphy (centre) as the hoofer they both fall for. The rest of the non-stellar cast included Kent Taylor, Richard Lane, Wallace Ford and Otto Hahn. A production number in which Turner and Murphy demonstrated their terpsichorean skills was the musical highlight in this otherwise modest and moderately entertaining remake. It was written by Joseph Fields and Jerome Chodorov from the story by Edmund Goulding, produced by Jack Cummings and directed by S. Sylvan Simon. Songs: *Rancho Santa Fe*; *True Love* Gus Kahn, Walter Donaldson; *My Wonderful One Let's Dance* Arthur Freed, Nacio Herb Brown, Roger Edens; *Maybe It's The Moon* Bob Wright, Chet Forrest, Donaldson; *Broadway's Still Broadway* Ted Fetter, Jimmy McHugh.

A limp-wristed programmer about a press agent who cultivates a model by pronouncing her Miss Manhattan in order to promote a line of inexpensive clothes, **Ma, He's Making Eyes At Me** (Universal) starred Tom Brown as the press agent and Constance Moore as the model (illustrated with Brown), with Anne Nagel, Richard Carle, Fritz Feld, Jerome Cowan and Elisabeth Risdon in support. Charles Grayson and Edmund L. Hartmann wrote it from a story by Ed Sullivan, and it was directed by Harold Schuster. Songs included: *Ma, He's Making Eyes At Me* Sidney Clare, Con Conrad; *Unfair To Love* Sam Lerner, Frank Skinner; *A Lemon In The Garden Of Love* M.E. Rourke, Richard Carle.

Jack Benny (illustrated) as Buck Benny in **Buck Benny Rides Again** was aided and abetted by his comic sidekick Andy Devine, as well as Eddie (Rochester) Anderson, Phil Harris, Virginia Dale, Lillian Cornell and Kay Linaker as he attempted to convince Ellen Drew, the love interest, that looks deceive and that underneath his unlikely exterior beats the heart of a pure cowboy. Inspired by Benny's radio programme, it was amiable nonsense that attracted the customers and notched up a box-office hit for Paramount. William Morrow and Edmund Beloin wrote it from an adaptation by Zion Myers of a story by Arthur Stringer, and it was produced and directed by Mark Sandrich. Songs: *Drums In The Night*; *My My*; *Say It (Over And Over Again)*; *My Kind Of Country* Frank Loesser, Jimmy McHugh.

Bing Crosby and 12-year-old songstress Gloria Jean (illustrated) were teamed for **If I Had My Way** (Universal) but failed to make box-office music together. Bing played a construction worker who takes charge of Gloria after her father is killed in an accident, and together they journey to New York in search of Gloria's great-uncle (Charles Winninger), an erstwhile vaudevillian. Aided by travelling companion El Brendel, they turn a neighbourhood restaurant into a nightclub, calling on old-time entertainers like Blanche Ring and Eddie Leonard to get the place going with their inimitable renditions of 'Ida, Sweet As Apple Cider' (by Eddie Leonard and Eddie Munson) and 'I've Got Rings On My Fingers' (by Maurice Scott, R.P. Western and F.J. Barnes). It was a fifth carbon copy of a well-worn plot, hacked out by William Conselman and James V. Kern, with David Butler producing and directing a cast that also included Allyn Joslyn, Donald Woods, Claire Dodd, Nana Bryant and Moroni Olsen as well as Trixie Friganza and Julian Eltinge. Other songs: *I Haven't Time To Be A Millionaire*; *Meet The Sun Halfway*; *April Played The Fiddle*; *The Pessimistic Character (With The Crab Apple Face)* Johnny Burke, James V. Monaco; *If I Had My Way* Lew Klein, James Kendis.

The highlight of **Broadway Melody of 1940** (MGM) was undoubtedly Fred Astaire and Eleanor Powell dancing to Cole Porter's 'Begin the Beguine' (see illustration). It was a sequence so magical that it made one regret that this was their only film together. The number, photographed in sharply contrasting black and white, and danced on a glittering mirrored floor against a starry background, contained two separate duos by the stars, both routines triumphantly surviving the rather kitschy stage-dressing provided for the occasion by choreographer Bobby Connolly. Porter wrote the rest of the score as well, which included Astaire's 'I've Got My Eyes On You', and another excellent ship-board production number for Eleanor Powell called 'I Am The Captain'. Astaire and co-star George Murphy did a simple but effective vaudeville routine in 'Please Don't Monkey With Broadway', and Murphy and Powell danced well together in the lyrical 'Between You And Me'. The only miscalculation was the arty, pierrot-like ballet version of 'I Concentrate On You' for Powell, Astaire and Douglas MacPhail, which suited none of their personalities. The film also contained one of the funniest sequences ever committed to celluloid: Charlotte Arren's screwy version (*à la* Beatrice Lillie and Fanny Brice) of the song 'Il Bacio' (by Luigi Arditi). In a terrible miscarriage of justice, the lady received no billing at all for her hilarious effort. The screenplay by Leon Gordon and George Oppenheimer (from a story by Jack McGowan and Dore Schary, the latter to become the head of MGM in the fifties), in no way matched the incomparable dazzle of its two stars, and told the trivial tale of a pair of hoofers (Astaire and Murphy) who split when one of them (Murphy) mistakenly gets a contract to dance on Broadway without the other. In the interests of the plot Murphy (who made his reputation as a hoofer) had the ego-deflating role of being the lesser of the two dancers – which, of course, he was. Frank Morgan, Ian Hunter, Florence Rice and Lynne Carver supported. Jack Cummings produced, and Norman Taurog directed. There was one other musical number, 'Juke Box Dance', for Powell and Astaire.

Forties Musicals

20th Century-Fox's **Lillian Russell** was set in the gay nineties, an era to which studio head Darryl F. Zanuck would return again and again throughout the forties. Though handsomely mounted, with meticulous attention to period detail lavished on Travis Banton's sumptuous costumes and Thomas Little's elegant settings, William Anthony McGuire's screenplay was a slow-moving encumberance which gave moviegoers only the merest whiff of Miss Russell's extraordinary life and career. The fact that McGuire shed two of Russell's four marriages from the scenario didn't prevent it from being a bit of a bore – with performances from Don Ameche as her first husband, and Henry Fonda (a reporter) as her second, that contributed to the all-pervading *ennui*. Alice Faye (illustrated) was top-cast as Lillian Russell and, although she was beautifully photographed throughout and sang some of Miss Russell's golden oldies with deep-throated verve, the few opportunities provided by the screenplay to be anything more than a walking cliché, coupled with her own limited abilities as a dramatic actress, left audiences with very little for their money. The film was far better served by Helen Westley and comedians Weber and Fields, who came out of retirement to lend an air of authenticity to an otherwise synthetic occasion. Others in the cast were Edward Arnold (as Diamond Jim Brady, a role he had played once before, in *Diamond Jim* Universal, 1935), Leo Carillo as Tony Pastor, the first man to give Russell a break in show business, as well as Dorothy Peterson, Ernest Truex, Lynn Bari, Eddie Foy Jr, and Nigel Bruce and Claude Allister as a bickering Gilbert and Sullivan. It was produced by Darryl F. Zanuck and directed by Irving Cummings with Seymour Felix in charge of the musical numbers. Songs: *Blue Lovebird* Gus Kahn, Bronislau Kaper; *Adored One* Mack Gordon, Alfred Newman; *Waltz Is King* Gordon, Charles Henderson; *Back In The Old Days Of Broadway* Henderson, Newman; *Come Down Ma Evenin' Star*; *Ma Blushin' Rosie* John Stromberg, Robert B. Smith; *After The Ball* Charles K. Harris; *The Band Played On* John E. Palmer. Charles B. Ward.

▽

△

Richard Rodgers and Lorenz Hart's superbly melodic score for their hit **The Boys From Syracuse** (Universal), first presented on Broadway in 1938, received short shrift from producer Jules Levey, whose filmed version of this quintessential tale of mistaken identity (based on Shakespeare's *The Comedy Of Errors*) fell just this side of disaster. Numbers like 'Sing For Your Supper', 'Falling In Love With Love', 'He And She' and 'This Can't Be Love' – classics every one of them – were only included by default, or in truncated versions that failed to do them justice, while new ones (such as 'Who Are You' and 'The Greeks Have No Word For It'), were added. Leonard Spigelgass and Charles Grayson's screenplay (based on the George Abbott stage version) traded in anachronisms at the expense of the satire originally intended, with cigar-smoking Greeks and checkered chariot-cabs typical of the humour on offer. All about two pairs of twins – one pair married, the other not – and the confusion that is wrought when the married pair and the unmarried pair become mixed up, it starred Allan Jones (left) and Joe Penner in the dual roles of the twins with Martha Raye (right), Rosemary Lane (centre), Charles Butterworth, Irene Hervey, Alan Mowbray, Eric Blore and Samuel S. Hinds also cast. Dave Gould choreographed and the director was Edward Sutherland.

Universal continued to borrow titles for programmer musicals from popular tunes with **Margie** – a marginally better effort than *Ma, He's Making Eyes At Me* – about the marital difficulties encountered by would-be songwriter Tom Brown, and his would-be radio scriptwriter wife Nan Grey. The accent was more on comedy than music, with Allen Jenkins, Eddie Quillan (right), Wally Vernon (left), Edgar Kennedy and Mischa Auer providing most of the laughs. It was written by Erna Lazarus, W. Scott Darling and Paul Gerard Smith (story by Lazarus and Darling), produced by Joseph G. Sandford and directed by Otis Garrett and Paul Gerard Smith. Songs included: *Margie* Benny Davis, J. Russell Robinson, Con Conrad; *When Banana Blossoms Bloom* Sam Lerner, Charles Previn; *Oh Fly With Me* Paul Gerard Smith. Previn.

▽

△

One of Bing Crosby's better musicals, **Rhythm on the River** (Paramount) cast Bing (illustrated) as an easy-going songwriter who'd much rather own a catboat than write music but who, to keep the wolf from the door, becomes a ghost composer for a played-out tunesmith (Basil Rathbone). Working as Rathbone's ghost lyricist is Mary Martin and, after an uneasy courtship and unwitting collaboration, the young couple finally get each other – and the recognition they deserve. Charmingly directed by Victor Schertzinger, with pleasing, relaxed performances from its principal players, the film benefited from a better-than-average screenplay by Dwight Taylor (story by Billy Wilder and Jacques Thery) as well as the supporting performances of Oscar Levant, as Rathbone's deliciously cynical assistant, Charles Grapewin, Lillian Cornell and William Frawley. The producer was William Le Baron. Songs: *Rhythm On The River*; *Only Forever*; *That's For Me*; *Ain't It A Shame About Mame?*; *When The Moon Comes Over Madison Square*; *What Would Shakespeare Have Said?* Johnny Burke, James V. Monaco.

Judy Canova (left) received star billing for **Scatterbrain** (Republic), a musical with a country-and-western flavour to it – especially in the Ozarkian twang perpetrated by its leading lady. A mistaken-identity tale, in which Miss C. finds herself being packed off to Hollywood as the star of a forthcoming movie, it was a modest effort that yielded modest returns, both financially and artistically. Alan Mowbray co-starred as the harassed film director whose unenviable task it is to off-load·an unwilling Miss Canova as best he can, with Joseph Cawthorn in support as the producer and Ruth Donnelly as his quick-witted secretary. Also cast: Billy Gilbert (right), Luis Alberni, Eddie Foy Jr and Isabel Jewell. Gus Meins produced and directed; Jack Townley and Val Burton scripted, with additional dialogue by Paul Conlan. The film contained one production number, 'Scatterbrain' (by Johnny Burke, Frankie Masters, Kahn Keene and Carl Bean), and other songs included *Benny The Beaver* by Johnny Lange and Lew Porter.

Bearing in mind that *Naughty Marietta* (1935) was one of MGM's biggest hits, scenarists Jacques Deval and Robert Arthur came up with an almost identical story line for the same studio with **New Moon** (based on the operetta by Oscar Hammerstein II, Laurence Schwab and Frank Mandel). Jeanette MacDonald (right) again played a French aristocrat forced to flee to Louisiana, and Nelson Eddy (left) the pirate chief she falls for. Five years had added a bit to Eddy's girth and, in other ways too, the film was heavier than its predecessor. But it did have some bewitching Sigmund Romberg melodies to recommend it, the MGM sheen germane to such occasions, and stalwart support from Mary Boland, George Zucco, Richard Purcell, H.B. Warner, Grant Mitchell and, in a very small role, Buster Keaton. The musical sequences were staged by Val Raset, with Robert Z. Leonard as both producer and director. Songs: *Lover Come Back To Me*; *Softly As In A Morning Sunrise*; *Stout-Hearted Men*; *Dance Your Cares Away*; *The Way They Do It In Paris*; *Shoes*; *One Kiss*; *Wanting You*; *Marianne*; *Ombra Mai Fu* (*Handel's Largo*); *La Marseillaise* Claude Rouget de Lisle.

◁ Shirley Temple's last film for 20th Century-Fox for nine years was **Young People** in which the ageing twelve-year-old (centre) played an orphan who is given a home by old-time vaudevillians Jack Oakie (left) and Charlotte Greenwood (right). A formula Temple movie, utilizing clips from some of her earlier films, its screenplay by Edwin Blum and Don Ettlinger peddled the usual *schmaltz* – but, as she had done on so many previous occasions, Temple somehow managed to make it all quite palatable. Arleen Whelan, George Montgomery, Kathleen Howard, Minor Watson, Mae Marsh and Frank Sully had roles in it too; it was produced by Harry Joe Brown, and directed by Allan Dwan. The score was by Mack Gordon and Harry Warren, the latter having left Warner Bros. after seven brilliantly prolific years as their number one songsmith. Songs: *Tra-la-la*; *Fifth Avenue*; *I Wouldn't Take A Million*; *The Mason-Dixon Line*; *Young People*.

Hugh Herbert (centre) played no fewer than six characters in **La Conga Nights** (Universal), all of them in desperate search of an author. For the story, devised by scenarists Jay Dratler, Harry Clork and Paul Smith, comprised more shadow than substance, involving, as it did, a cab driver-cum-amateur-vaudevillian (Dennis O'Keefe), the small-town singer (Constance Moore, centre right) he meets, and the show they put on in a boarding house. Herbert – playing himself, his four sisters and his mother – turns out to be the owner of the boarding house, and is thus able to quash the eviction order slapped on tenant O'Keefe (far left) for non-payment of rent. Mindless to a degree, it also featured Ferike Boros (2nd right), Armida (who sang the traditional 'La Cucaracha', arranged by Harold Potter), Eddie Quillan and Joe Brown Jr. Ken Goldsmith produced and the direction was by Lew Landers. Songs included: *Carmenita McCoy*; *Havana*; *Chance Of A Lifetime* Frank Skinner, Sam Lerner.

Forties Musicals

The Ritz Brothers, having left 20th Century-Fox for Universal, continued to pilfer scenes that weren't worth stealing in the first place in **Argentine Nights**, a musical whose Latin American background provided the inspiration for a tale about a trio of destitute girl singers who, in cahoots with their managers (the brothers Ritz) flee their creditors by heading for the Argentine. The only good thing that came out of it was The Andrews Sisters (illustrated), though it was a shame that their movie debut couldn't have been more auspicious. Constance Moore, George Reeves, Peggy Moran and Anne Nagel were also cast; it was written by Arthur T. Horman, Ray Golden and Sid Kuller (from a story by J. Robert Bren and Gladys Atwater), produced by Ken Goldsmith, and directed by Albert S. Rogell. Songs included: *Hit The Road*; *Oh, He Loves Me* Don Raye, Hughie Prince, Vic Schoen *Rhumboogie* Raye, Prince; *Brooklynonga*; *The Spirit of 77B* Hal Borne, Sid Kuller, Ray Golden; *Amigo We Go Riding Tonight*; *The Dowry Song* Sammy Cahn, Saul Chaplin.

Another B-picture musical romance from the ▷ Universal stable, **I'm Nobody's Sweetheart Now** was a simple, moderately entertaining tale about a couple of youngsters, Dennis O'Keefe and Helen Parrish (illustrated), who thwart their politically-minded parents by refusing to marry other people for political expediency and settling, instead, for each other. Lewis Howard and Constance Moore played the rejected pair, with twittery Laura Hope Crews, Samuel S. Hinds, Berton Churchill, Margaret Hamilton, Marjorie Gateson and The Dancing Cansinos also featured in Scott Darling, Erna Lazarus and Hal Block's 64-minute screenplay. Arthur Lubin directed and the associate producer was Joseph Sandford. Songs included: *I'm Nobody's Sweetheart Now* Gus Kahn, Ernie Erdman, Billy Meyers, Elmer Schoebel; *There Goes My Love*; *Got Romance* Everett Carter, Milton Rosen.

A bargain-basement musical, with newcomer Jane Frazee resembling a marked-down Lana Turner and diminutive Mary Lee a junior, cut-price Judy Garland, **Melody and Moonlight** (Republic) was a radio-inspired yarn with Johnny Downs top-cast as a bell-boy with ambitions to become a hoofer; and Miss Frazee a deb whose show-biz aspirations are vetoed by her millionaire father (Jonathan Hale) who, in the final reel, becomes the radio sponsor for his daughter's (and Downs's) tap-dancing radio show. Every bit as silly as it sounds, it was efficiently directed by Joseph Santley from a screenplay by Bradford Ropes (story by David Silverstein) and featured Jerry Colonna (left), Barbara Jo Allen (radio's Vera Vague, right), Mary Lee and Frank Jenks. Robert North produced. Songs: *Rooftop Serenade*; *Tahiti Honey*; *Top O'The Mornin*; *I Close My Eyes*; *Melody And Moonlight* Jule Styne, Sol Meyer, George Brown. ▽

◁ Republic paid $500 to *Collier's* magazine for a story they published called **Sing Dance Plenty Hot** (GB: **Melody Girl**) then discarded the content, retaining only the title. The new plot by Vera Caspary and Bradford Ropes (screenplay by Ropes) was an anaemic contrivance about a phoney promoter of charity shows (Lester Matthews) who absconds with the money he is allegedly engaged in raising for clients Barbara Jo Allen, Elisabeth Risdon and Ruth Terry – three prospective purchasers of a children's home. Miss Terry and Johnny Downs were top-cast as the romantic interest, with Billy Gilbert (doing an abbreviated version of his oft-performed sneezing act), Claire Carleton, Mary Lee and Leonard Carey completing the cast. It was produced by Robert North and directed by Lew Landers. Illustration shows a production number. Songs: *Tequila*; *When A Fella's Got A Girl*; *What Fools These Mortals Be*; *I'm just A Weakie* Jule Styne, George Brown, Sol Meyer.

A backstage musical with a vengeance (as well as with Maureen O'Hara, Louis Hayward, Lucille Ball (illustrated), Ralph Bellamy, Virginia Field and Maria Ouspenskaya), **Dance Girl Dance** (RKO) charted the tribulations that befall chorus girls in their journey from anonymity to stardom, with a mis-cast O'Hara and a bouncing Ball as members of Ouspenskaya's dancing troupe. Maureen has cultural aspirations and wishes to be a ballet dancer; Lucille is more realistic and settles for fame as a stripper. Both fall for attractive Mr Hayward. So much for the plot. Ball, third-billed, ran away with the film (not that there was anywhere special to take it to) as well as the notices, and with her number 'Oh Mother, What Do I Do Now?' (by Bob Wright and Chet Forrest) proved once and for all, that she was no mere chorine. (Several years later she proved her business acumen as well by buying the studio!) Mary Carlisle, Katherine Alexander, Edward Brophy, Walter Abel, Harold Huber and Ernest Truex completed the cast. It was written by Tess Slesinger and Frank Davis from a story by Vicki Baum, produced by Erich Pommer and directed by Dorothy Arzner. Other songs: *Morning Star* Wright, Forrest; *The Jitterbug Bit* Wright, Forrest, Ed Ward; *Urban Ballet* Ward. ▽

Again using a hit tune as a title, **I Can't Give You Anything But Love** (Universal) offered audiences 61 ludicrous minutes of non-entertainment as Broderick Crawford, a gangster with a passion for lyric writing, kidnaps Johnny Downs (right), a young composer with whom he works in a collaborative effort to get a message in song to a long-lost sweetheart. Peggy Moran (left), Warren Hymer, John Sutton, Gertrude Michael and Jessie Ralph also appeared for director Albert S. Rogell; it was written by Arthur T. Horman (adaptation by Paul Gerard Smith) and produced by Ken Goldsmith. Songs included: *I Can't Give You Anything But Love* Dorothy Fields, Jimmy McHugh; *Sweetheart Of School* 59; *Day By Day* Paul Gerard Smith, Frank Skinner.

▽

△

Another in the 'let's put on a show' mould, **Strike Up the Band** (MGM) was an exuberant paean to youth, with Mickey Rooney, now the nation's number one box-office attraction (as he had been in 1939 and would be again in 1941), on the very top of his form. There was nothing the kid could not do – and under maestro Busby Berkeley's watchful eye, he did it all. Whether singing, dancing, playing the drums, the xylophone, or the hapless hero in a turn-of-the-century melodrama, Mickey reigned supreme. His confidence and energy were positively awesome and although John Monks Jr and Fred Finkelhoffe's scenario (about the attempts of a high-school orchestra to enter a coast-to-coast band contest) landed him with some blush-making sentimental dialogue – particularly to his mother (Ann Shoemaker) Rooney pulled it off magnificently, turning what could, in less capable hands, have been an embarrassment, into a triumph. His perfect foil was Judy Garland whose natural, unassuming performance was in such marked contrast to his own larger-than-life, bull-dozing effort, that it was easy to underestimate her overall contribution to the film. If Rooney (right) had versatility and vitality, Garland (left) had charm, and it was nowhere better demonstrated than in her wistful rendition of Roger Eden's song 'Nobody', sung in the college library, in which she bemoans the fact that though Romeo has Juliet and Metro-Goldwyn has Mayer, she has nobody at all. The film's finale, to the Gershwins' rousing 'Strike Up The Band' was another military-type extravaganza of which Berkeley was so fond and an excellent example of what could be achieved with imaginative camera set-ups (and superb editing) rather than lavish sets. The film also featured Paul Whiteman (as himself) as well as June Preisser, William Tracy, Larry Nunn, Margaret Early, and Virginia Brissac. The producer, not surprisingly, was Arthur Freed, whose song 'Our Love Affair', written with Roger Edens, and in which a bowl of fruit miraculously turns into a symphony orchestra (thanks to Vincente Minnelli who supplied the idea, and animator George Pal who executed it) was one of the musical highlights of the film. Other songs and musical numbers: *Drummer Boy; Do The Conga; Nell of New Rochelle* Roger Edens; *Sing, Sing, Sing* Louis Prima; *I Just Can't Make My Eyes Behave* Will Cobb, Gus Edwards; *Heaven Will Protect The Working Girl* Edgar Smith, A. Baldwin Sloane; *The Curse Of An Aching Heart* Henry Fink, Al Piantadosi; *The Sidewalks Of New York* James W. Blake, Charles B. Lawlor; *Light Cavalry Overture* Franz von Suppé; *Over The Waves* Juventino Rosas.

177

Forties Musicals

While an appendectomy prevented Betty Grable from playing the lead in Paramount's *Man About Town* (1939), ironically, it was an appendectomy that clinched her star-billing in **Down Argentine Way** (20th Century-Fox). This time it was Alice Faye who was rushed to hospital, with Betty being summoned from Broadway by producer Darryl F. Zanuck to take her place. And, although it made a star of her, a Brazilian bombshell called Carmen Miranda (illustrated centre) was the real hit of the show – despite the fact (or maybe because of it) that she had nothing whatsoever to do with the plot. She sang three songs (including the catchy 'South American Way' by Al Dubin and Jimmy McHugh) and took the country by storm. For the rest, it was a brightly Technicolored concoction, all about an American heiress (Grable) who falls in love with an Argentinian horse-breeder (Don Ameche). Betty's legs looked a treat, so did co-star Charlotte Greenwood's. The Nicholas Brothers and Thomas and Catherine Dowling featured as specialty items, with J. Carrol Naish, Henry Stephenson, Katherine Aldridge, Leonid Kinskey, Chris Pin Martin and Robert Conway in support. The musical numbers were staged by Nick Castle and Geneva Sawyer, 'Down Argentine Way' being the choreographic hit of the show. Another was the Greenwood-Kinskey ditty, 'Sing To Your Senorita' (both numbers by Mack Gordon and Harry Warren). The director was Irving Cummings. Other songs: *Two Dreams Met*; *Nenita* Gordon, Warren; *Mama Yo Quiero* Al Stillman, Jaraca and Vincente Paiva; *Doin' The Conga* Gene Rose; *Bambu.*

▽

Spring Parade (Universal) was the cinematic equivalent of a liberal helping of *Sacher torte mit schlag*. A free 'n easy, Viennesey tale of love and romance, it starred Deanna Durbin (illustrated) – prettily perched on the brink of womanhood – as a baker's assistant who falls in love with a dashing young corporal (Robert Cummings, illustrated conducting orchestra) right under Emperor Franz Joseph's (Henry Stephenson) very nose. Insubstantial but delightful was the general consensus of opinion, and with S.Z. Sakall (as the baker), Walter Catlett, Allyn Joslyn, Reginald Denny, Franklin Pangborn and a couple of engaging youngsters called Butch and Buddy in support, producer Joe Pasternak delivered another hit to Universal. Bruce Manning and Felix Jackson wrote it (from a story by Ernst Marischka), and Henry Koster directed. Songs and musical numbers: *Blue Danube Dream* Johann Strauss II, lyrics by Gus Kahn; *Waltzing In The Clouds*; *It's Foolish But It's Fun*; *When April Sings* Kahn, Robert Stolz; *In A Spring Parade* Kahn, Charles Previn.

▽

△

With no other purpose than to provide an opportunity for some of Paramount's younger contract artists to peddle their wares, **Dancing on a Dime** was a routine backstage yarn about a stranded theatrical troupe who, despite insufficient finances, stage a successful show. Robert Paige (3rd right), Grace McDonald, Peter Hayes (right), Eddie Quillan (centre), Frank Jenks (left), Virginia Dale, Carol Adams, Lillian Cornell and William Frawley appeared, it was directed by Joseph Santley from a screenplay by Maurice Rapf, Anne Morrison Chapin, and Allen Rivkin (story by Jean Lustig and Max Kolpe) and was produced by A.M. Botsford. Songs: *I Hear Music*; *Manana*; *Dancing On A Dime* Frank Loesser, Burton Lane; *Lovable Sort Of Person*; *Debutante Of The Year* Loesser, Victor Young.

Originally intended as a follow-up to their successful *Alexander's Ragtime Band* (1938), 20th Century-Fox's **Tin-Pan-Alley** was written for Alice Faye, Tyrone Power and Don Ameche. But it didn't work out that way, and instead John Payne and Jack Oakie were given the male leads. And, while in the process of changing the original conception, Zanuck shrewdly had scenarists Robert Ellis and Helen Logan (story by Pamela Harris) write in a part for Betty Grable, who had recently scored such a success in *Down Argentine Way*. Although Grable (right) received second billing to Faye (left) and played her dancing partner sister, she didn't have a great deal to do with the plot, lending, in the main, a decorative quality to the show's several musical numbers – most notably 'The Sheik Of Araby' (by Harry B. Smith, Francis Wheeler and Ted Snyder). As originally staged by dance director Seymour Felix, the number – which also featured Faye and Billy Gilbert – revealed too much flesh for the Hays Office and had to be trimmed accordingly. All about the frustrating attempts of a pair of songwriters (Payne and Oakie) to establish a music publishing firm, the film spanned 24 years (from 1915 to 1939) but you'd never have known it from the enviable agelessness of the leading players. The score offered only one new number: 'You Say The Sweetest Things, Baby' (by Mack Gordon and Harry Warren), the rest being 'oldies'. Allen Jenkins, Esther Ralston, John Loder and Elisha Cook Jr were also in it, together with The Nicholas Brothers, Princess Vanessa Ammon, The Brian Sisters and The Robert Brothers.

Kenneth MacGowan was the associate producer and the director was Walter Lang. It was remade by 20th Century-Fox in 1950 as *I'll Get By*. Other songs: *America I Love You* Edgar Leslie, Archie Gottler; *Goodbye Broadway, Hello France* Francis Riesner, Benny Davis, Billy Baskette; *K-K-K-Katy* Geoffrey O'Hara; *Moonlight Bay* Edward Madden, Percy Wenrich; *Honeysuckle Rose* Andy Razaf, Thomas 'Fats' Waller; *Moonlight And Roses* Ben Black, Neil Moret, Edwin H. Lemare.

The Trade Descriptions Act was emphatically contravened by the title of **A Little Bit of Heaven** (Universal) which, while not exactly a little bit of the other place either, was certainly no musical paradise. A predictable story about an East Side kid whose singing triumph on radio causes all sorts of domestic upheavals in her suddenly wealthy family, it was another vehicle for 12-year-old Gloria Jean (centre), who brought no particular distinction to Daniel Taradash, Gertrude Purcell, and Harold Goldman's pedestrian screenplay (story by Grover Jones). A strong supporting cast which included Robert Stack, Hugh Herbert, C. Aubrey Smith, Charles Previn (left), Stuart Erwin, Nan Grey, Eugene Pallette, Billy Gilbert, Butch and Buddy, Frank Jenks, Sig Arno (right), Noah Beery Jr and Monte Blue, made no impact whatsoever on Joe Pasternak's production; neither did Andrew Marston's ho-hum direction. Songs: *A Little Bit Of Heaven* J. Keirn Brennan, Ernest Ball; *What Did We Learn At School?* Vivian Ellis; *Dawn Of Love* Ralph Freed, Charles Previn; *After Every Rain Storm* Sam Lerner, Frank Skinner.

Forties Musicals

Any film that boasted the combined talents of Peter Lorre (right), Boris Karloff and Bela Lugosi surely couldn't be all that bad, but **You'll Find Out** (RKO), defying common sense and the law of averages, was a wholesale stinker that top-starred Kay Kyser and his Kollege of Knowledge in a woebegone musical chiller whose plot pivoted on whether or not the aforementioned trio of ghouls will succeed in bumping off a certain person at a house party being given in her honour. Kyser (left) and his team are signed up to provide the party with its entertainment, and although they soon become involved in the strange goings-on, find the time, every fifteen minutes or so, to fulfil their part of the contract. Helen Parrish, Alma Kruger, Joseph Eggenton and Kyser regulars Ish Kabibble, Ginny Simms, Harry Babbitt and Sully Mason completed the cast. It was written by James V. Kern from a story by Kern and David Butler, with Butler also producing and directing. Songs: *You've Got Me This Way*; *Like The Fella Once Said*; *The Bad Humour Man*; *I'd Know You Anywhere*; *I've Got A One Track Mind*; *Don't Think It Ain't Been Charming* Johnny Mercer, Jimmy McHugh. ▷

Fantasia (RKO), the third full-length Walt Disney feature, was the most daring cinematic experiment since Warner Bros.' *The Jazz Singer* 13 years earlier. Filmed in dazzling Multiplane Technicolor and 'Fantasound', it was introduced by Deems Taylor with Leopold Stokowski and the Philadelphia Orchestra in charge of the music, and offered a once-in-a-lifetime experience that, if anything, has gained in stature over the last forty years to become one of the cinema's undisputed works of art. Setting out to marry images to three kinds of music (music that tells a story, music that paints a picture, and 'absolute' music for music's sake) the film, which opened with a brilliant abstract realization of Bach's Toccata and Fugue in D Minor, was a miraculous blending of animation and musical sound. The item that perhaps best illustrated Disney's achievement in synchronizing the two, was the sequence to 'The Sorcerer's Apprentice' (Dukas) in which Mickey Mouse was featured as the apprentice (illustrated) who, after his master retires for the night, invokes some magic of his own. The spell, involving a broom which comes to life, goes completely out of control, and it is only after the sorcerer's lair has been flooded that order is finally restored. Less programmatic was 'The Nutcracker Suite' (Tchaikovsky), whose lilting melodies conjured up an enchanted forest, illuminated by fairies of light and inhabited by mushroom Chinamen and dancing flower Cossacks. A feast for eye and ear, it was matched in its invention and graphic detail by Disney's vision of the 'Pastoral Symphony' (Beethoven) set in an idyllic mythological kingdom of nymphs and satyrs, and in whose best moment the Goddess of Night skims across the sky with her cloak of black. **Fantasia**'s comic highspot was a spirited interpretation of 'The Dance Of The Hours' (from Ponchielli's *La Gioconda*), performed by prancing hippopotami, undulating crocodiles, ostriches engaging in *entrechats*, and light-footed elephants. Stravinsky's 'Rite Of Spring' graphically evoked the Creation, with belching craters of fire and warring prehistoric monsters, while the powers of Good and Evil were strikingly contrasted by 'Night On The Bare Mountain' (Mussorgsky) – with grotesque and frightening images of floating skeletons and satanic cauldrons – and Schubert's sublime 'Ave Maria' with its cleansing vision of light-infused landscapes. Joe Grant and Dick Huemer were in charge of the story direction, and the production was supervised by Ben Sharpsteen.

◁ Judy Garland played a dual role in **Little Nellie Kelly** (MGM): grown-up Nellie Kelly who dies in childbirth, then (for the rest of the film's running time) Nellie's daughter. Though Judy (left) sang her way through Jack McGowan's screenplay with her usual charm and sparkle, the 18-year-old George M. Cohan play on which it was based emerged as an over-brogued bit of burdensome blarney in which grandad Charles Winninger, having done his best to put the kibosh on his daughter's romance, is after doin' the very same t'ing to his granddaughter. George Murphy (right) was in it too; so were Douglas MacPhail, Arthur Shields, Rita Page and Forrester Harvey. Norman Taurog directed, Arthur Freed produced. Songs: *Nellie Kelly I Love You* George M. Cohan; *Nellie Is A Darlin'*; *It's A Great Day For The Irish* Roger Edens; *A Pretty Girl Milking Her Cow* (adapted by Edens); *Singin' In The Rain* Arthur Freed, Nacio Herb Brown; *Danny Boy* (traditional, arranged by Frederick Weatherly).

1941

Academy Awards

Writing (Original Screenplay)
NOMINATIONS INCLUDED: *Tall, Dark And Handsome* (20th Century-Fox) Karl Tunberg and Darrell Ware

Cinematography
(black and white)
NOMINATIONS INCLUDED: *The Chocolate Soldier* (MGM) Karl Freund. *Sun Valley Serenade* (20th Century-Fox) Edward Cronjager.
(colour)
NOMINATIONS INCLUDED: *Louisiana Purchase* (Paramount) Harry Hallenberger and Ray Rennahan

Art Direction (Interior Decoration)
(For the first time Set Designers are given plaques, while Art Directors continue to receive Oscars)
(colour)
NOMINATIONS INCLUDED: *Louisiana Purchase* Raoul Pene du Bois and Stephen A. Seymour

Sound Recording
NOMINATIONS INCLUDED: *The Chocolate Soldier* Douglas Shearer

Music
Best Song
'The Last Time I Saw Paris' *Lady Be Good* (MGM) Jerome Kern *cm*; Oscar Hammerstein II *lyr*.
NOMINATIONS INCLUDED: 'Baby Mine' *Dumbo* (Disney, RKO) Frank Churchill *cm*; Ned Washington *lyr*. 'Blues In The Night' *Blues In The Night* (WB) Harold Arlen *cm*; Johnny Mercer *lyr*. 'Boogie Woogie Bugle Boy Of Company B' *Buck Privates* (Universal) Hugh Prince *cm*; Don Raye *lyr*. 'Chattanooga Choo Choo' *Sun Valley Serenade* Harry Warren *cm*; Mack Gordon *lyr*. 'Dolores' *Las Vegas Nights* (Paramount) Lou Alter *cm*; Frank Loesser

lyr. 'Out Of The Silence' *All American Co-Ed* (Roach, UA) Lloyd B. Norlind. 'Since I Kissed My Baby Goodbye' *You'll Never Get Rich* (Columbia) Cole Porter.

Scoring of a Musical Picture
(New classification)
Dumbo Frank Churchill and Oliver Wallace
NOMINATIONS INCLUDED: *All American Co-Ed* Edward Ward. *Birth Of The Blues* (Paramount) Robert Emmett Dolan. *Buck Privates* Charles Previn. *The Chocolate Soldier* Herbert Stothart and Bronislau Kaper. *Ice Capades* (Republic) Cy Feuer. *Sun Valley Serenade* Emil Newman. *Sunny* (RKO) Anthony Collins. *You'll Never Get Rich* Morris Stolof.

Special Awards
To Leopold Stokowski and his associates for their unique achievement in the creation of a new form of visualized music in Walt Disney's production of *Fantasia*, thereby widening the scope of the motion picture as entertainment and as an art form.
(certificate)
To Walt Disney, William Garity, John N.A. Hawkins and the RCA Manufacturing Company for their outstanding contribution to the advancement of the use of sound in motion pictures through the production of *Fantasia*. (certificates)

1941 Irving G. Thalberg Award
Walt Disney

The New York Times Annual 'Ten Best'
8th *Dumbo*

The Annual Top Moneymaking Films
INCLUDED: *Hold That Ghost* (Universal). *Road to Zanzibar* (Paramount) *Ziegfeld Girl* (MGM) *Buck Privates*.

Singer 'Wee' Bonnie Baker and the band leader Orrin Tucker (centre) made indifferent movie debuts in **You're The One** (Paramount), a lower case musical whose narrative centred on agent Edward Everett Horton's attempts to book his client, Baker, as a singer in Tucker's band. After much unfunny horseplay, he succeeded. It was produced by Gene Markey (who also scripted), and featured Albert Dekker, Jerry Colonna (right), Lillian Cornell (left) and Walter Catlett. Ralph Murphy directed, and musical numbers were staged by LeRoy Prinz. Songs: *Strawberry Lane*; *I Could Kiss You For That*; *My Resistance Is Low*; *The Yogi Who Lost His Will Power*; *Gee I Wish I'd Listened To My Mother* Johnny Mercer, Jimmy McHugh; *Oh, Johnny, Oh* Abe Olman, Ed Rose.

A musical more flat than sharp and rarely natural, **Let's Make Music** (RKO) starred Bob Crosby in a musty old tale about a music teacher (class of students illustrated) who, while on holiday in New York, comes to realize that Bach, Beethoven and Brahms are all very well, but that Boogie hath charms too. It was written by Nathanael West, directed by Leslie Goodwins for producer Howard Benedict, and also featured Jean Rogers (as the teacher), Elisabeth Risdon, Joseph Buloff, Joyce Compton, Bennie Bartlett and Louis Jean Heydt. Songs: *Fight On Newton High* Dave Dreyer; *You Forgot About Me* Dick Robertson, Sammy Mysels, James Hanley; *Big Noise From Winnetka* Gil Rodin, Bob Haggart, Ray Bauduc, Bob Crosby; *Central Park* Johnny Mercer, Matt Malneck.

A Night At Earl Carroll's (Paramount) was precisely that, with showman Carroll relying on the most anaemic of plot excuses to present a nightclub act (chorus number illustrated) of varying quality. The story had a gangster kidnapping Carroll's floor-show principals as part of a feud he (the gangster) is having with a fictitious Hollywood mayor (not to be confused with the factual Hollywood Mayer) thereby forcing the master showman to improvise a scratch entertainment – utilizing the talents of a singing cigarette vendor, the boys and girls of the chorus, and a couple of the paying customers. The film had little marquee value, with Ken Murray, Rose Hobart, Elvia Allman, Blanche Stewart, Russell Hicks (as the mayor) and Mr Carroll himself the prime attractions. It was written by Lynn Starling and directed by Kurt Neumann. Songs: *Li'l Boy Love* Frank Loesser, Frederick Hollander; *I Wanna Make With The Happy Times* Loesser, Gertrude Niesen; *Cali-Con-Ga* Earl Carroll, Dorcas Cochran, Nilo Menendez; *One Look At You* Carroll, Ned Washington, Victor Young.

Both Bud Abbott and Lou Costello, as well as Universal Pictures, struck it lucky with **Buck Privates**. The comedy team found stardom and a place (third) in the nation's popularity polls (Mickey Rooney and Clark Gable were occupying spots one and two); while the studio, who invested a mere $90,000 in the movie's production, recouped its cost 10 times over. **Buck Privates** was a runaway hit, and Universal's top grossing film in 1941. Bud and Lou played street-corner tie salesmen who, while fleeing the police, take cover in a movie theatre. Except that it isn't a movie theatre any longer but an army induction centre. In no time at all they find themselves enlisted, whereupon reality gives way to fantasy, with life in the army revealed as one long laugh from start to finish. The War Office couldn't have wished for a better 84 minutes of recruitment propaganda than this, especially with The Andrews Sisters (illustrated) as a trio of Pied Pipers doing their close-harmony best for the war effort with such numbers as 'Boogie Woogie Bugle Boy From Company B', and 'Bounce Me Brother With A Solid Four' (both by Don Raye and Hughie Prince). Lee Bowman and Alan Curtis (who were billed above Abbott and Costello) also appeared as recruits (Bowman as a wealthy socialite, Curtis as his bodyguard), with Jane Frazee, Nat Pendleton, Samuel S. Hinds, Harry Strang, Nella Walker, Leonard Elliott and Shemp Howard completing the cast. It was written by Arthur T. Horman and directed by Arthur Lubin. Other songs: *When Private Brown Meets A Sergeant*; *Wish You Were Here* Raye, Prince; *You're A Lucky Fellow Mr Smith* Raye, Prince, Sonny Burke; *I'll Be With You In Apple Blossom Time* Neville Fleeson, Albert von Tilzer.

△

Another wad of army propaganda, but not nearly as amusing as *Buck Privates*, **Cadet Girl** (20th Century-Fox) focussed on the dilemma of George Montgomery (left) as to whether to marry Carole Landis (right) and embark on a life of unruffled domesticity; or whether he should enter West Point and study for a commission. It hardly mattered one way or another, for Stanley Rauh and H.W. Hanemann's screenplay, from a story by Jack Andrews and Richard English, was so under-written and under-characterized that it precluded involvement. John Shepperd, William Tracy, Janis Carter, Robert Lowery, Basil Walker, Charles Tannen and Chick Chandler were also featured, and the director was Ray McCarey. Songs: *My Old Man Was An Army Man*; *She's A Good Neighbour*; *I'll Settle For You*; *It Happened, It's Over, Let's Forget It*; *It Won't Be Fun (But It's Got To Be Done)*; *Making A Play For You*; *Uncle Sam Gets Around* Ralph Rainger, Leo Robin.

△

Lupe Velez, as Madame La Zonga (centre), the star of a niterie of the same name, was the only reason for wasting time on **Six Lessons From Madame La Zonga** (Universal). Leon Errol co-starred as a phoney Latin, with other roles in this ineffectual little programmer going to Charles Lang as the leader of an Oklahoma band trying desperately to land a café date in Cuba, Helen Parrish as the girl of his dreams, and Eddie Quillan as his pal. Cast in support were Guinn Williams and Shemp Howard. Its quartet of scenarists were Stanley C. Rubin, Marion Orth, Larry Rhine and Ben Chapman, the director was John Rawlings, and it was produced by Joseph G. Sandford. Songs and musical numbers included: *Six Lessons From Madame La Zonga* Charles Newman, James V. Monaco; *The Matador's Wife*; *Jitterumba* Everett Carter, Milton Rosen.

The eighth film to feature cartoonist Chic Young's Blondie and Dagwood, **Blondie Goes Latin** (GB: **Conga Swing**) from Columbia, relied this time as much on music as it did on comedy. Richard Flournoy and Karen DeWolf's entertaining account of what happened when the Bumsteads joined ailing boss J.C. Dithers on a Latin American cruise again had Penny Singleton (right) and Arthur Lake impersonating Young's immortal Mr and Mrs, with Larry Simms as Baby Dumpling, and other parts shared out between Ruth Terry, Tito Guizar (left), Jonathan Hale, Danny Mummert and Irving Bacon. The original story was by Quinn Martin, it was produced by Robert Sparks and directed by Frank R. Strayer. Songs: *You Don't Play A Drum (You Beat It)*; *I Hate Music Lessons*; *Querida*; *You Can't Cry On My Shoulder*; *Castillian Cotillion* Bob Wright, Chet Forrest.

▽

Forties Musicals

Leon Errol, Helen Parrish (centre right) and Charles Lang starred in **Where Did You Get That Girl?** an off-the-cuff programmer from Universal in which a struggling singer (Parrish) and songwriter (Lang), after meeting by chance and falling in love, team up with a dance band led by Eddie Quillan (centre left) and, during a rehearsal in a recording studio, are inadvertently involved in a hold-up. The ensuing publicity lands them a recording contract and the film ends with the love-birds about to be married. Jay Dratler, Paul Franklin and Stanley Crea Rubin wrote it (story by Dratler), Arthur Lubin directed a cast that also included Franklin Pangborn, Stanley Fields and Tom Dugan; and the producer was Joseph G. Sandford. Songs included: *Where Did You Get That Girl?* Harry Puck, Bert Kalmar; *Sergeant Swing*; *Rug-Cuttin' Romeo* Milton Rosen, Everett Carter.

▽

One of the glories of the Fox musical was its colour: gaudily bright, unashamedly splashy, and just the job for taking audiences' minds off the similarities of the plots it embellished. **That Night in Rio** was *the* quintessential Fox war-time musical – an over-blown, over-dressed, over-produced and thoroughly irresistible cornucopia of escapist ingredients whose sheer professionalism was as dazzling as the colour, the sets, the costumes and the girls (see illustration) that had been poured into it. A remake of *Folies Bergère* (20th Century/United Artists, 1935) it gave Alice Faye lead billing, though when Carmen Miranda wasn't scene-stealing everytime *she* appeared, the film was very much Don Ameche's. In the role originally played by Maurice Chevalier, Ameche (illustrated, at desk) was called upon to prove he wasn't just a pretty face by playing a dual role: an American singer in a Rio nightclub, and a well-known local banker with a quite uncanny resemblance to the entertainer. George Seaton, Bess Meredyth and Hal Long's screenplay (additional dialogue by Samuel Hoffenstein, based on a play by Rudolph Lothar and Hans Adler, and adapted by Jessie Ernst) stuck very closely to the earlier version, with Miranda in the Ann Sothern role, and Faye in the part originally played by Merle Oberon. Mack Gordon and Harry Warren provided the film with an infectiously bouncy score, and Carmen Miranda with two of her biggest hits – 'Chica Chica Boom Chic' (an exuberantly staged production number by Hermes Pan) and 'I Yi Yi Yi Yi (I Like You Very Much)'. The supporting cast included S.Z. Sakall, J. Carrol Naish, Curt Bois, Leonid Kinskey and Frank Puglia. Miranda's orchestra The Banda Da Lua, were also on hand to make music; so were a specialty trio called The Flores Brothers. Maria Montez also appeared in a bit part. Fred Kohlmar was the associate producer and it was directed by Irving Cummings. Other songs: *Boa Noite (Good Night)*; *They Met In Rio*; *The Baron Is In Conference* Gordon, Warren; *Cae Cae* (Portuguese) Roberto Martins.

In *That Certain Age* (Universal, 1938), Deanna Durbin had slipped painlessly, and with the minimum amount of fuss, into puberty. Three years later in **Nice Girl?** (seated centre), having at last reached womanhood, she flexed her seductive muscles at Franchot Tone (seated left) who, as a New York representative of a Scientific Foundation on a visit to her professor father, reacts to the flirtation with acute embarrassment. After a few more unsuccessful flirtations Durbin decides to keep her blossoming womanhood in check, and sensibly returns to her long-standing, home-grown sweetheart (Robert Stack, standing left). Richard Connell and Gladys Lehman's screenplay (from a story by Phyllis Duganne) kept it all very proper, indeed, almost innocent, and, as performed by the ingenuous Miss Durbin as well as a first-rate cast including Walter Brennan (as a lovesick postman), Robert Benchley (seated right, as the *paterfamilias*) and Ann Gillis (standing, as Deanna's man-hungry younger sister), as well as Helen Broderick, Anne Gwynne (seated right), Elizabeth Risdon and Nana Bryant, it was as refreshing as a breeze in a heatwave. Joe Pasternak produced, and calling the shots was William A. Seiter. Songs: *Love At Last* Eddie Cherkose, Jacques Press; *Perhaps* Aldo Franchetti, Andreas De Segurola; *Beneath The Lights Of Home*; *Thank You America* Bernie Grossman, Walter Jurmann; *The Old Folks At Home* Stephen Foster.

▽

△

Nevada's gambling haven was put to no good use at all in **Las Vegas Nights** (Paramount), a musical whose paltry excuse for existing at all was Tommy Dorsey and His Orchestra. Vaguely concerned with a group of impecunious entertainers at loose in the city, it featured Phil Regan, an unfunny Bert Wheeler (foreground centre), without Woolsey, Constance Moore, Lillian Cornell, Virginia Dale, Hank Ladd, and a trio of Mexicans collectively known as Mexican Trio. It was written by Ernest Pagano and Harry Clork with additional dialogue by Eddie Welch, and was directed by Ralph Murphy for producer William Le Baron. The most notable feature of this nothing film was that a young singer called Frank Sinatra made his screen debut, singing 'Dolores' (by Frank Loesser and Louis Alter) with Dorsey's band. Songs: *Song Of India* Rimsky-Korsakov, arranged by 'Red' Bone; *On Miami Shore* William Le Baron, Victor Jacobi; *I'll Never Smile Again* Ruth Lowe; *I've Gotta Ride*; *Mary, Mary, Quite Contrary* Frank Loesser, Burton Lane.

Flung together in an obvious attempt to capitalize on the success of Universal's *Buck Privates*, Republic's **Rookies On Parade** (GB: **Jamboree**) was a dispiriting effort written by Karl Brown, Jack Townley and Milt Gross from a story by Sammy Cahn and Saul Chaplin. The plot pivoted around the attempts of Bob Crosby and Eddie Foy Jr, two songwriters who are drafted into the army, to put on a show, and it buried them in the hole it made. Ruth Terry, Gertrude Niesen (centre), Marie Wilson (2nd left), Cliff Nazarro, William Demarest and Sidney Blackmer (right) were also in it for producer Albert J. Cohen. Nick Castle staged the dances, and the director was Joseph Santley. Songs: *The Army Builds Men*; *I Love You More*; *Mother Never Told Me Why*; *My Kinda Love*; *You'll Never Get Rich*; *What More Do You Want* Sammy Cahn, Saul Chaplin; *Rookies On Parade* Eddie Cherkose, Jule Styne.

Pot O' Gold (GB: **The Golden Horn**) was a hit-and-miss affair from United Artists which scored more misses than hits in a radio-orientated tale of a music-hating sponsor's battle with a group of down-and-out entertainers. Charles Winninger was the crusty old sponsor, with personable James Stewart (illustrated) and beautiful Paulette Goddard heading the cast. Mary Gordon, Frank Melton, Jed Prouty, Dick Hogan, James Burke, and Horace Heidt and His Orchestra also appeared; it was written by Walter DeLeon from a story by Andrew Bennison, Monte Brice and Harry Tugend (idea by Haydn Roth Evans and Robert Brilmayer), produced by James Roosevelt (son of the President) and directed by George Martin. Songs: *Do You Believe In Fairy Tales?* Mack David, Vee Lawnhurst; *When Johnny Toots His Horn* Hy Heath, Fred Rose; *A Knife, A Fork And A Spoon* Dave Franklin; *Broadway Caballero*; *Pete The Piper*; *Hi Cy, What's Cookin?*; *Slap Happy Band* Lou Forbes, Henry Sullivan.

Suffering from the law of diminishing returns, The Marx Brothers's (left) MGM efforts contained fewer laughs with each new film, **Go West** being their least funny to date. It did, however, have a chase sequence on a train that was a comic gem. For the rest, it was a routine tale about three guys from the East who become involved with all sorts of unsavoury characters in the West. Irving Brecher wrote it, it was directed by Edward Buzzell for producer Jack Cummings, and in supporting roles featured John Carroll (far right), Diana Lewis (right), Walter Woolf King and Robert Barrat. Songs: *Ridin' The Range* Gus Kahn, Roger Edens; *You Can't Argue With Love*; *As If I Don't Know* Kahn, Bronislau Kaper; *Land Of The Sky Blue Water* (in a rendition by Harpo) Charles Wakefield Cadman; *Beautiful Dreamer*; *Oh Susanna* Stephen Foster.

A wacky, slightly demented Adolphe Menjou (left) joined forces with millionaire playboy John Hubbard in **Road Show** (United Artists), an off-beat, off-balance effort which also starred Carole Landis (right) as a beautiful but bankrupt carnival owner. Supporting players Charles Butterworth (centre), Patsy Kelly, George E. Stone, Margaret Roach, Willie Best, and The Charioteers did their best to keep it buoyant, but the dead weight of Arnold Belgard, Harry Langdon and Mickell Novak's screenplay (from a novel by Eric Hatch) was more than mere flesh and blood could carry. It was produced and directed by Hal Roach with a decided air of desperation infiltrating every scene. Songs: *I Should Have Known You Years Ago* Hoagy Carmichael; *Slav Annie*; *Yum Yum*; *Calliope Jane* Carmichael, Stanley Adams.

After the surprise success of *Road To Singapore* (Paramount, 1940), the studio teamed Bing Crosby (centre right), Dorothy Lamour and Bob Hope (centre) in **Road To Zanzibar** which, in every way, was superior to their first faltering, albeit financially successful effort. This time Bing and Bob played a couple of carnival performers and conmen who, after selling a phoney diamond mine to the kind of murderous heavy it isn't wise to sell phoney diamond mines to, leave the country as fast as they can and make for exotic Zanzibar. There, in a parody of every jungle epic that ever featured a restless native or a throbbing tom-tom, the intrepid duo link up with two con-women – a sarong-free Miss Lamour and her sidekick Una Merkel – and together they set out on a cross-country safari that left audiences limp with laughter. The rib-tickling screenplay (always allowing for the Crosby–Hope ad libs *en route*) was by Frank Butler and Don Hartman (story by Hartman and Sy Bartlett), it was produced by Paul Jones, and directed by Victor Schertzinger. Songs: *You Lucky People, You*; *It's Always You*; *You're Dangerous*; *On The Road To Zanzibar*; *Birds Of A Feather* Johnny Burke, Jimmy Van Heusen.

MGM pulled out all the stops for **Ziegfeld Girl**, an eye-filling spectacle that traced the lives and loves of three Ziegfeld girls: vaudeville singer Judy Garland (left), elevator girl Lana Turner (right), and wife of a penniless violinist, Hedy Lamarr (centre). Garland makes it; Turner doesn't; and Lamarr swaps her place in the chorus for married bliss. With Busby Berkeley in charge of the production numbers, Cedric Gibbons the sumptuous sets and Adrian the mind-boggling costumes, the visual aspect of the film was, in every respect, splendiferous. Where it let itself down was in its soap-opera plot (by William Anthony McGuire, screenplay by Marguerite Roberts and Sonya Levien), an endless parade of sob-story clichés that held not a single surprise. Viewed today through the jaundiced eyes of the eighties, the film emerges as a camp wallow from start to finish; a highly-charged dose of forties sentimentality that also happens to be quite preposterously entertaining. All the same, apart from Busby Berkeley's brilliantly inventive staging of a Spanish dance by Antonio and Rosario, where the lighting and the camera movements create an excitement equal to that provided by the performers, the two big set pieces – 'Minnie From Trinidad' by Roger Edens (performed by Garland) and 'You Stepped Out Of A Dream' (sung by Tony Martin) by Gus Kahn and Nacio Herb Brown relied on opulence rather than on invention for their effects. Pandro S. Berman's production borrowed several sequences from *The Great Ziegfeld* (MGM, 1936), including the famous 'wedding cake set' but, instead of Virginia Bruce being the cherry on the top of the giant edifice (as she was in the earlier film), part of the set was reconstructed to allow Judy Garland to take her place which, in a skilful piece of editing, she did most tellingly. The men in **Ziegfeld Girl** were James Stewart (top-billed) as Miss Turner's truckdriver sweetheart, Tony Martin, who has a brief dalliance with the beauteous Hedy Lamarr, together with Jackie Cooper, Ian Hunter, Charles Winninger (as Mr Gallagher), Al Shean (as himself), Edward Everett Horton, Philip Dorn, Paul Kelly and Dan Dailey. The cast was completed by Eve Arden, Felix Bressart and Rose Hobart. It was directed very stylishly by Robert Z. Leonard. Other songs and musical numbers included: *Laugh? I Thought I'd Split My Sides* (Garland, Winninger) Roger Edens; *Caribbean Love Song* (Martin) Edens, Ralph Freed; *I'm Always Chasing Rainbows* (Garland) Joseph McCarthy, Harry Carroll; *Whispering* (unidentified male vocal trio) John Schonberger, Richard Coburn, Vincent Rose; *Mr Gallagher And Mr Shean* (Winninger, Shean) Ed Gallagher and Al Shean; *You Never Looked So Beautiful Before* (Garland, chorus) Walter Donaldson, Harold Adamson.

△

Too Many Blondes (Universal) was minor league entertainment that starred Rudy Vallee (right) and Helen Parrish (centre) as a newlywed radio team. and Iris Adrian as the blonde siren who comes between them. Sixty minutes and four songs later. it all ended happily for the couple. Audiences. however. were less fortunate. Lon Chaney Jr. Jerome Cowan (left), Shemp Howard, Eddie Quillan and Humberto Herpera and His Orchestra were also in it; it was directed by Thornton Freeland from a screenplay by Maxwell Shane and Louis S. Kaye (story by Shane) and produced by Joseph G. Sandford. Songs: *Whistle Your Blues To A Bluebird; Don't Mind If I Do; Let's Love Again* Everett Carter, Milton Rosen; *The Man On The Flying Trapeze* George Leybourne, Alfred Lee, adapted by Walter O'Keefe.

△

Hollywood's wooing of Latin America continued with **They Met in Argentina** (RKO), though it is doubtful whether this minor offering did anything to further the cause of hemispheric solidarity. Producer Lou Brock was clearly unable to decide whether the film was primarily for the USA or the South American market. with the result that it found favour in neither place – despite a score by no less a team than Richard Rodgers and Lorenz Hart. All about a Texas oil millionaire (Robert Middlemass) – who, after failing to secure oil lands in Argentina, seeks out a famous race horse in Buenos Aires and orders his representative (James Ellison) to buy the nag at any price – it centred on the love affair Ellison has with Maureen O'Hara (featured centre), the beautiful daughter of the prize horse's owner. One production number, called 'The Chaco', brightened proceedings momentarily. but it was 76 minutes of tedium just the same, with co-stars Alberto Vila (featured left) and Buddy Ebsen, as well as Robert Barrat. Diosa Costello, Victoria Cordova and Antonio Moreno hopelessly at sea in Jerry Cady's silly screenplay (story by Lou Brock and Harold Daniels). It was directed by Leslie Goodwins and Jack Hively proving, indisputably, that two heads are not necessarily better than one. Songs: *You've Got The Best Of Me; Amarillo; Cutting The Cane; Never Go To Argentina; Lolita; North America Meets South America; Simpatica.*

A splashy, big-budget Technicolor merry-go-round of a musical, **Moon Over Miami** (20th Century-Fox) starred Betty Grable (illustrated) as a waitress in an open-air hamburger joint who, after coming into a legacy, takes off with her aunt and sister (Carole Landis) for Miami – the millionaires' playground. A remake of *Three Blind Mice* (20th Century-Fox, 1938), which featured Loretta Young in the Grable role, it wrapped up its slender story in several opulently staged production numbers and several more bouncy Ralph Rainger-Leo Robin songs and, one way and another, was a most delightfully packaged assortment of goodies. Don Ameche (top-starred) and Robert Cummings provided the romantic interest, and Charlotte Greenwood and Jack Haley the comedy, with Jack Cole and Company, as well as the dancing Condos Brothers (foreground left) punctuating the narrative with some specialty turns. The cast was completed by Cobina Wright Jr, Lynne Roberts, Robert Conway, George Lessey, Robert Greig and Minor Watson. It was written by Vincent Lawrence and Brown Holmes from a play by Stephen Powys, and adapted by George Seaton and Lynn Starling, Hermes Pan staged the musical numbers and the breezy direction was by Walter Lang. Songs and musical numbers: *What Can I Do For You?*; *You Started Something*; *Kindergarten Conga*; *Oh Me Oh Mi-A-Mi*; *Is That Good*; *Solitary Seminole*; *Loveliness And Love*; *I've Got You All To Myself* Rainger, Robin; *Moon Over Miami* Edgar Leslie, Joe Burke (played behind main titles only). It was remade in 1946 as *Three Little Girls in Blue* (20th Century-Fox).

Melody Lane (Universal) offered an ineffectual hour in which The Merry Macs played a quartet of entertainers from Iowa who are signed to appear in a radio show in New York. But the show is sponsored by a breakfast food magnate whose interference in the radio programme he pays for is a one-way ticket to trouble. Leon Errol (left) was the meddlesome magnate, with other roles going to Anne Gwynne, Robert Paige, Billy Lenhart, Kenneth Brown, Louis Da Pron, Butch and Buddy (illustrated), and Little Sandy. Hugh Wedlock Jr, Howard Snyder and Morton Grant wrote it from a story by Bernard Feins (adaptation by George Rony), and it was directed for producer Ken Goldsmith by Charles Lamont. Songs and musical numbers: *Listen To The Mocking Bird*; *Septimus Winner*; *Peaceful Ends The Day*; *Cherokee Charlie*; *Let's Go To Calicabu*; *Swing-A-Bye My Baby*; *Changeable Heart*; *If It's A Dream Don't Wake Me*; *Since The Farmer In The Dell* Norman Berens, Jack Brooks.

Radio came to the rescue of **Swing It Soldier**, a 'B' from Universal whose cast (Ken Murray, Frances Langford (centre), Don Wilson, Blanche Stewart, Elvia Allman, Susan Miller, Iris Adrian, Hanley Stafford and Thurston Hall) – not to mention its plot about a pregnant soldier's wife and the twin sister who agrees to stand in for her in a radio show – was augmented by such airwave favourites as Skinnay Ennis and His Orchestra, Kenny Stevens, Stop, Look and Listen and Three Cheers. Louis Da Pron appeared in a snappy solo devised by choreographer Reginald Le Borg, Susan Miller scored in a jazzed-up version of 'Annie Laurie'; while Langford's big moment found her singing 'I'm Gonna Swing My Way To Heaven' (Eddie Cherkose, Jacques press). Dorcas Cochran and Arthur V. Jones wrote it, the producer was Joseph G. Sandford, and Harold Young directed. Other songs and musical numbers included: *Rug-Cuttin' Romeo* Everett Carter, Milton Rosen; *My Melancholy Baby* George Norton, Ernie Burnett.

With a cast that included Ann Miller (illustrated), Rudy Vallee, Rosemary Lane and Allen Jenkins, plus several specialty acts such as Six Hits and A Miss, Glen Gray and His Casa Loma Orchestra, Eddie Durant's Rhumba Orchestra, as well as The Three Stooges, **Time Out For Rhythm** (Columbia) promised to deliver the goods. But it was dull, dull, dull, with the unstoppable Miss Miller valiantly tapping away in a hopeless attempt to infuse vitality into a plot about two quarrelling theatrical agents. It was based on a play by Alex Ruben and a story by Bert Granet, with a screenplay by Edmund L. Hartmann and Bert Lawrence. Irving Starr produced and his director was Sidney Salkow. Songs and musical numbers: *Boogie Woogie Man; Time Out For Rhythm; Twiddlin' My Thumbs; Obviously The Gentleman Prefers To Dance; As If You Didn't Know; The Rio De Janeiro; Shows How Wrong A Gal Can Be* Sammy Cahn, Saul Chaplin.

As originally written for the stage by Clare Booth, **Kiss The Boys Goodbye** (Paramount) was a caustic satire on Hollywood and its eternal search for new talent, especially someone to play Scarlett O'Hara in *Gone With The Wind*. The film version, with a score by Frank Loesser and Victor Schertzinger (Schertzinger also directed), removed its sting and watered down its pungent content, substituting, instead, a familiar tale about a Southern chorus girl who makes good. Mary Martin (illustrated) was Cindy Lou, and her singing of 'That's How I Got My Start' was the bright spot in a film sadly lacking in them. Don Ameche, who received top billing, played a movie director unable to resist Miss Martin's charms, with Oscar Levant (illustrated left), tossing around gags and harpsichord toccatas with equal abandon. Connee Boswell (who scored a personal hit singing the film's best song 'Sand In My Shoes', which became an enduring standard), Eddie (Rochester) Anderson, Virginia Dale, Barbara Jo Allen, Raymond Walburn, Elizabeth Patterson and Jerome Cowan rounding off the cast. Harry Tugend and Dwight Taylor scripted it. Other songs: *Find Yourself A Melody; I'll Never Let A Day Pass By; Kiss The Boys Goodbye;* and several negro spirituals.

Jane Frazee (left), Johnny Downs, Iris Adrian and The Peters Bros lent vocal support to a Universal quickie called **Sing Another Chorus**, with Sunnie O'Dea (right) featuring in a dance routine staged by Larry Ceballos. Best musical item, however, was a Spanish specialty by Rosario and Antonio. For the rest, it was formula film-making with a screenplay by Marion Orth, Paul Gerard Smith and Brenda Weisberg (story by Sam Robins) in which a college graduate, after being tricked by a producer into persuading his dress-manufacturing father to put up the coin for a show, finds that the producer has absconded with the money. A happy ending, however, is provided by the manufacturer's employees, who resourcefully stage a fashion show to everyone's satisfaction, turning imminent disaster into triumph. Director Charles Lamont, alas, was unable to do the same for his film, nor could a cast that included Mischa Auer (centre), George Barbier, Joe Brown Jr, Walter Catlett and Charles Lane. Ken Goldsmith produced. Songs: *Boogie Woogie Boogie Man; Dancing On Air; Walk With Me; Two Weeks Vacation With Pay; Mr Yankee Doodle; We Too Can Sing* Everett Carter, Milton Rosen.

Four musical numbers, two by Ted Lewis (left) and two by The Andrews Sisters, tended to reduce the lickety-split pace set by director Arthur Lubin in **Hold That Ghost** (Universal), another successful Abbott and Costello (illustrated) vehicle which took place for most of its running time in the allegedly haunted house the duo inherit after the murder of a gangster. Costello, as usual, was the chief victim of the strange goings on that bedevil the manse, and one of the funniest sequences involved an airborne candle that stubbornly refuses to perform when Costello's shrieks bring Abbott racing into the room. Joan Davis played a professional radio screamer whose voice fails her at a crucial moment in Robert Lees and Fred Rinaldo's plot (screenplay by Lees, Rinaldo and John Grant), with Richard Carlson, Mischa Auer, Evelyn Ankers (another well-known screamer), Marc Lawrence, Shemp Howard and Russell Hicks also contributing to the fun. The associate producers were Bert Kelly and Glenn Tryon. Songs: *Sleepy Serenade* Mort Greene, Lou Singer; *Aurora* Harold Adamson, Mario Lago, Roberto Roberti; *When My Baby Smiles At Me* Harry von Tilzer, Andrew B. Sterling; *Me And My Shadow* Billy Rose, Al Jolson, Dave Dreyer.

As World War II continued, audiences looked for escapist entertainment and musical movies continued to abound – or, as in the case of **Navy Blues** (Warner Bros.), to rebound. This particular offering attached some songs by Arthur Schwartz and Johnny Mercer to a really pathetic story which did no more than follow a noisy crew on a frenzied journey to Honolulu. Lloyd Bacon directed a cast that included Ann Sheridan, Jack Oakie (right), Martha Raye, Jack Haley (left), Herbert Anderson, Jack Carson and Jackie Gleason, none of whom could rescue the drivel written by Sam Perrin, Jerry Wald, Richard Macaulay and Arthur T. Horman, and produced by Hal B. Wallis and Jerry Wald, with choreography by Seymour Felix. Songs: *In Waikiki; You're A Natural; Navy Blues; When Are We Going To Land Abroad?*

Forties Musicals

Columbia's classiest, most expensive musical to date, **You'll Never Get Rich**, had a score by Cole Porter and starred Fred Astaire and Rita Hayworth (illustrated) – together for the first time. Yet, despite the 'triumphant teaming of beauty and rhythm' as the ads put it, the film came to life only in flashes and hardly lived up to the promise of its attractive ingredients. The story of a Broadway dance director who finds himself drafted into the army, its only surprise lay in Hayworth's extraordinary abilities as a dancer. The equal of her illustrious partner in grace and precision, she danced her way through several numbers – most notably the 'Boogie Barcarolle', and 'So Near And Yet So Far', revealing herself, in the opinion of many, to be one of the best partners Astaire ever had – notwithstanding Ginger Rogers. Certainly she was a better dancer than Rogers, but whether or not she was a better partner, remains open to debate. Other musical highlights included 'The A-stairable Rag' danced by Astaire and backed by the Delta Rhythm Boys (Buddy Colette on clarinet, A. Grant on guitar, Chico Hamilton on drums, Red Mack on trumpet, Joe Comfort on a jug); 'Shootin' The Works For Uncle Sam' (Astaire and a bevy of pretty chorus girls), and the 'Wedding Cake Walk', a production number (staged by Robert Alton) featuring a chorus line of fifty, in a set comprising a giant wedding cake with a tank on top of it. The film also starred Robert Benchley as a producer up to his neck in romantic entanglements, with John Hubbard, Osa Massen, Frieda Inescort, Guinn Williams, Donald MacBride, Cliff Nazarro, Ann Shoemaker and Marjorie Gateson in support. The direction was by Sidney Lanfield for producer Samuel Bischoff. Other songs and musical numbers: *Since I Kissed My Baby Goodbye*; *Dream Dancing*.

In its modest way **Zis Boom Bah** (Monogram), a college caper, was a triumph of professionalism over poor material, with featured performers Grace Hayes, Peter Lind Hayes (her real-life son), Mary Healy (left) and Benny Rubin refusing to be floored by Connie Lee and Harvey Gates's hoary old screenplay, or the conspicuous lack of anything resembling an adequate budget. Miss Hayes played a successful musical comedy star who is reunited with her college-student son after twenty years. Grace buys her boy a café which she then transforms into a fashionable theatre restaurant, and the film ends with a floor show staged by local students – the best of the bunch being a young dancer called Roland Dupree. Skeets Gallagher, Huntz Hall, Jan Wiley (right), Frank Elliott, Eddie Kane and Leonard Sues completed the cast, and the director was veteran William Nigh. Songs: *Annabella*; *It Makes No Difference When You're In The Army* Johnny Lange, Lew Porter; *Put Your Trust In The Moon* June Baldwin, Charles Callender; *Zis Boom Bah* Elaine Cannon; *Good News Tomorrow*; *I've Learned To Smile Again* Neville Fleeson.

Having neatly tucked the army and the navy under their comic belts, Abbott and Costello did the inevitable and, in **Keep 'em Flying** (Universal), their fourth film in 1941, joined the airforce. They, in turn, were joined by Martha Raye (illustrated) playing twin sisters, one of whom adores Costello (illustrated) while the other does not. The usual A. and C. 'shtick' permeated the proceedings, with plot once again taking second place to it. The new songs were by Don Raye and Gene De Paul, best of which was the very popular 'Pig Foot Pete' sung by Miss Raye, and 'You Don't Know What Love Is'. Dick Foran was in it too, as a stunt flyer, and the cast was completed by Carol Bruce, William Gargan, Charles Lang, Truman Bradley, William Davidson and Loring Smith. It was written by True Boardman, Nat Perrin and John Grant from a story by Edmund Hartmann and directed by Arthur Lubin. Other songs included: *Together*; *I'm Looking For The Boy With The Wistful Eyes*; *Let's Keep 'Em Flying* Raye, De Paul; *I'm Getting Sentimental Over You* Ned Washington, George Bassman.

A tribute of sorts to the Original Dixieland Jazz Band, a quintet of musicians who helped introduce jazz to the white folk, **Birth of the Blues** (Paramount) was an entertaining, if somewhat simplistic, account of the rough passage had by jazz when it first infiltrated the consciousness of a generation more at home with the staid rhythms of the waltz. Bing Crosby (in one of his favourite roles) played an itinerant clarinettist who fetches up in New Orleans and, together with a rag-bag collection of musicians, including a hot trumpet player (Brian Donlevy) whose services he acquires after bailing him out of jail, sets up shop in a posh Bourbon Street niterie and, after a couple of initial set-backs, becomes the hottest thing in the Vieux Carré. Mary Martin (illustrated) co-starred as a singer who joins his group and, in a snappy performance of 'Wait Till The Sun Shines Nellie' (by Andrew Sterling and Harry von Tilzer) came as near to movie greatness as she ever would. Other musical highlights included 'The Waiter And The Porter And The Upstairs Maid' (by Johnny Mercer), sung by Crosby, Martin and Jack Teagarden, and an impassioned account of W.C. Handy's classic 'St Louis Blues' by Ruby Elzy. Harry Tugend and Walter DeLeon wrote it (story by Tugend) with parts for Eddie (Rochester) Anderson (illustrated left), Jack Teagarden (and his orchestra), J. Carrol Naish, Warren Hymer, Horace MacMahon, and a monstrous moppet called Carolyn Lee. It was directed by Victor Schertzinger, who died shortly after its completion. Other songs: *Gotta Go To The Jailhouse*

Robert E. Dolan, Harry Tugend; *Memphis Blues* W.C. Handy; *By The Light Of The Silvery Moon* Edward Madden, Gus Edwards; *Tiger Rag* The Original Dixieland Jazz Band; *Waiting At The Church* Henry Pether, F.W. Leigh; *Cuddle Up A Little Closer* Otto Harbach, Karl Hoschna; *Shine* Lew Brown, Cecil Mack, Ford Dabney; *My Melancholy Baby* George Norton, Ernie Burnett; *St James Infirmary* Joe Primrose; *Birth Of The Blues* Buddy De Sylva, Lew Brown, Ray Henderson; *At A Georgia Camp Meeting* Kerry Mills.

Strictly for hinterland audiences, Republic's **Puddin' Head** (GB: **Judy Goes to Town**) was a corny-copia of hayseed gags dispensed, in the main, by Judy Canova (right), who played a country gal (what else?) living on a farm in the middle of Fifth Avenue, New York. Her property is encroached upon by a neighbouring skyscraper, and her privacy by a couple of city slickers (Raymond Walburn and Eddie Foy Jr) who do their best to get her to sell. Slim Summerville was also cast, and so were Francis Lederer (illustrated left), Astrid Allwyn, Alma Kruger, Hugh O'Connell, Chick Chandler, Paul Harvey, and The Sportsmen. Jack Townley and Milton Gross wrote it (original story by Townley), with additional dialogue by Howard Snyder and Hugh Wedlock Jr. Albert J. Cohen produced and the flaccid direction was by Joseph Santley. Songs and musical numbers included: *Hey Junior; You're Telling I; Manhattan Holiday; Puddin' Head* Eddie Cherkose, Sol Meyer, Jule Styne.

Forties Musicals

Having previously been down Argentine Way, and spent a night in Rio, audiences were invited to take time off for a **Week-End in Havana** (20th Century-Fox), another tuneful and colourful excursion into Latin America – Hollywood style – with Alice Faye and Carmen Miranda (illustrated) joined, this time, by John Payne. Story had Faye (as a Macy's shop girl) being given a free weekend in Havana after her cruise ship runs aground in a storm, and falling head over heels for shipping executive Payne. Miranda (now earning $5,000 a week) played a night-club entertainer (her usual role on such occasions) who has a crush on co-star Cesar Romero, and she was a knockout in the climactic 'The Nango' (by Mack Gordon and Harry Warren), excitingly staged by Hermes Pan. Cobina Wright Jr, George Barbier, Sheldon Leonard, Leonid Kinskey and Billy Gilbert also appeared, it was written by Karl Tunberg and Darrell Ware, produced by William Le Baron, and breezily directed for the mindless escapism it was, by Walter Lang. Other songs: *Tropical Magic; A Weekend In Havana; When I Love I Love* Gordon, Warren; *Romance And Rhumba* Gordon, James V. Monaco; *Mama Inez* L. Wolfe Gilbert, Eliseo Grenet; *Rebola A Bola* Oliveira, Almaro.
▽

◁ **The Chocolate Soldier** (MGM) was something of a curiosity. Plot-wise it had nothing whatsoever to do with the Oscar Straus operetta (based on Shaw's *Arms And The Man*) from which it took its title, although it retained several of the score's more popular numbers such as 'My Hero', 'Sympathy' and 'The Flower Presentation'. It was, in fact, a modest remake of Ferenc Molnar's *The Guardsman*, which first reached the screen via MGM in 1931 as a vehicle for the distinguished husband-and-wife team, Alfred Lunt and Lynn Fontanne. In the remake, Nelson Eddy had the Lunt role, with opera star Rise Stevens as his wife. Instead of their being actors, the new version (with a screenplay by Leonard Leigh and Keith Winter) cast them (illustrated) as opera stars currently appearing in Straus's 'The Chocolate Soldier' and, as was the case with *Sweethearts* (MGM 1938), the operetta extracts heard in the film were featured as part of a show-within-a-show. The story of a husband so jealously in love with his wife that he appears to her in disguise in order to test her fidelity, it gave Eddy his best-ever opportunity to shine. And although his 'straight' moments as the jealous spouse were lamentably unconvincing, his performance while masquerading as a flamboyant Cossack, was a revelation, and the most effective piece of acting he ever committed to film. Nigel Bruce, Florence Bates, Dorothy Gilmore, Nydia Westman, Max Barwyn and Charles Judels completed the cast; it was directed by Roy Del Ruth for producer Victor Saville, with Ernst Matray in charge of the musical staging. Other songs and musical numbers: *Thank The Lord The War Is Over; Ti-ra-la-la; Seek The Spy* Straus, Stanislaus Stange; *While My Lady Sleeps* Bronislau Kaper, Gus Kahn; *Mephistopheles' Song Of The Flea* Mussorgsky; *Mon Coeur S'Ouvre A Ta Voix* (from 'Samson and Delilah') Saint-Saens.

An insubstantial jape, **Rise and Shine** (20th Century-Fox) starred Jack Oakie (illustrated) as Boley Bolenciecwcz, a brainless footballer placed in the charge of a screwy professor (Donald Meek) and his family, and whose well-being is a major concern of a big-time gambler from New York called Jimmy M'Gonigle (Sheldon Leonard). Just why, didn't really matter. What did was Oakie's engaging central performance (one of his best ever), plus the excellent support offered by George Murphy as Leonard's undercover man, Linda Darnell (illustrated centre) as the love interest, Walter Brennan, Milton Berle, Ruth Donnelly, Raymond Walburn and Donald MacBride. Based on James Thurber's *My Life And Hard Times*, its genuinely wacky screenplay was by Herman J. Mankiewicz and it was produced by Mark Hellinger, with Allan Dwan directing at an exuberant pace. Songs: *I'm Making A Play For You; Central Two Two Oh Oh; I Want To Be The Guy; Hail To Bolenciecwcz; Get Thee Behind Me Clayton; Men Of Clayton* Ralph Rainger, Leo Robin.
▽

△

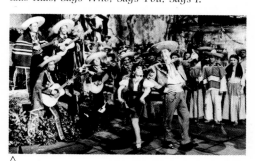

△

Blues in the Night (Warner Bros.) was a compact little musical with a serious flavour that, despite an intermittent tendency to melodrama, made for above average entertainment. A pretty accurate account of the milieu inhabited by itinerant jazz musicians as they drift through a series of one-night engagements and involve themselves with a variety of women, Robert Rossen's screenplay (from a play by Edwin Gilbert) was given strong support by his principal actor, Richard Whorf (later to become a well-known director) with a cast that included Priscilla Lane, Betty Field (centre), Lloyd Nolan (right), Jack Carson (left), Wallace Ford (background) and Billy Halop. Jimmy Lunceford and Will Osborne, with their orchestras, were also featured, and Elia Kazan appeared as a clarinettist. Director Anatole Litvak kept a perceptive grip on the proceedings for producer Henry Blanke, and Johnny Mercer and Harold Arlen wrote the songs, two of which were notable: the great title standard, which was introduced in the film by William Gillespie with the Lunceford orchestra, and 'This Time The Dream's On Me' (sung by Priscilla Lane). Other songs: Hang On To Your Lids Kids; Says Who, Says You, Says I.

With their filming of Olson and Johnson's **Hellzapoppin'**, Universal were clearly not prepared to emulate the risks taken with the stage version, and their reticence was spelled out at the beginning of the movie when Richard Lane (playing the director) quite categorically told Messrs O. and J. (illustrated centre) that there has to be more to a film than just a rag-bag collection of gags. After all, he exclaims, 'This is Hollywood, we change everything here. We've *got* to.' And they did, adding a routine love triangle between Robert Paige (who is endeavouring to stage a show at his palatial Long Island estate), Jane Frazee, and Lewis Howard. Martha Raye was also in it, her chief contribution to the unorthodox proceedings being to pursue Mischa Auer (as a moneyed count), and to sing the zany 'Watch The Birdie' (by Don Raye and Gene De Paul). A hit and miss affair with lots of good sight gags and an equal amount of laboured ones, **Hellzapoppin**'s chief fault was that it went only so far when it should have gone further. The result was a curious hybrid that left audiences more baffled than entertained. Hugh Herbert popped in and out of the film as a private detective; Shemp Howard surfaced briefly as a cinema projectionist, and Clarence Kolb, Nella Walker, Katherine Johnson, Elisha Cook Jr, and a specialty act called Slim and Sam were also featured. It was written by Nat Perrin and Warren Wilson (story by Perrin) with H.C. Potter directing for producer Jules Levey. Other songs: *What Kind Of Love Is This?*; *You Were There*; *Heaven For Two*; *Hellzapoppin'*; *Putting On The Dog*; *Congeroo*; *Conga Beso* Raye, De Paul; *Waiting For The Robert E. Lee* L. Wolfe Gilbert, Lewis F. Muir.

Playmates (RKO) offered audiences the sad and sorry spectacle of John Barrymore at the end of his professional tether. Giving a wildly undisciplined performance, he masochistically caricatured and parodied himself, playing a much-married, out-of-work actor who, in order to land a radio contract and rid himself of his creditors, agrees to give Kay Kyser (right) a crash course in Shakespeare. The result? A ghastly finale in which Mr K. and his Kollege of Knowledge put a beat to the bard's iambic pentameters and did some terrible things to *Romeo and Juliet*. Lupe Velez was in it too (as a lady bull-fighter); so were May Robson, Patsy Kelly, Peter Lind Hayes, and Kyser regulars Ginny Simms (centre), Harry Babbitt (left), Ish Kabibble and Sully Mason. James V. Kern wrote it from a story he devised with M.M. Musselman (additional dialogue by Arthur Phillips) and it was produced and directed by David Butler. Songs: *Humpty Dumpty Heart*; *How Long Did I Dream?*; *Que Chica*; *Thank Your Lucky Stars And Stripes*; *Romeo Smith And Juliet Jones* Johnny Burke, Jimmy Van Heusen.
▽

If brevity is the soul of wit, it can also do wonders for a slender story, as demonstrated in **Fiesta** (United Artists), another of producer Hal Roach's 'streamlined' quickies which ran only 43 minutes. Brilliantly photographed in Technicolor and featuring five numbers, it told the simple story of a suitor's successful attempts to win back the love of his fiancée after she switches her affections. Ann Ayars was topbilled as the fickle lass at the heart of the tale, with George Negrete and George Givot (right) as the men in her life. It all took place during a fiesta on a Mexican ranch owned by Antonio Moreno, with Miss Ayars and Negrete, as well as Armida (illustrated centre), Jose Arias and His Mexican Tipica Orchestra and the Guadalajara Trio supplying the music. Courtland Fitzsimmons supplied the dialogue from an adaptation by Kenneth Higgins, and the director was LeRoy Prinz (who also co-produced). Songs: *El Ralajo* Lamberto Layva, Jesus Castillion, Oscar Felix; *I'll Never Forget Fiesta* Bob Wright, Chet Forrest, Nilo Menendez; *Never Trust A Jumping Bean*; *Quien Sabe* Wright, Forrest, Ed Ward; *La Golondrina* Narciso Serradell.

1942

Academy Awards

Best Picture
NOMINATIONS INCLUDED: *Yankee Doodle Dandy* (WB) produced by Jack Warner and Hal B. Wallis, with William Cagney

Best Actor
James Cagney *Yankee Doodle Dandy*

Best Supporting Actor
NOMINATIONS INCLUDED: Walter Huston *Yankee Doodle Dandy*

Direction
NOMINATIONS INCLUDED: Michael Curtiz *Yankee Doodle Dandy*

Writing (Original Story)
NOMINATIONS INCLUDED: *Holiday Inn* (Paramount) Irving Berlin. *Yankee Doodle Dandy* Robert Buckner.
(Original Screenplay)
NOMINATIONS INCLUDED: *The Road To Morocco* (Paramount) Frank Butler and Don Hartman

Art Direction (Interior Decoration) (colour)
My Gal Sal (20th Century-Fox) Richard Day and Joseph Wright; Thomas Little

Sound Recording
Yankee Doodle Dandy Nathan Levinson
NOMINATIONS INCLUDED: *Bambi* (Disney, RKO) Sam Slyfield. *The Road To Morocco* Loren Ryder. *You Were Never Lovelier* (Columbia) John Livadary.

Film Editing
NOMINATIONS INCLUDED: *Yankee Doodle Dandy* George Amy

Music
Song
'White Christmas' *Holiday Inn* Irving Berlin
NOMINATIONS INCLUDED: 'Always In My Heart' *Always In My Heart* (WB) Ernesto Lecuona

cm: Kim Gannon *lyr*. 'Dearly Beloved' *You Were Never Lovelier* Jerome Kern *cm*: Johnny Mercer *lyr*. 'How About You?' *Babes on Broadway* (MGM) Burton Lane *cm*: Ralph Freed *lyr*. 'It Seems I Heard That Song Before' *Youth on Parade* (Republic) Jule Styne *cm*: Sammy Cahn *lyr*. 'I've Got A Gal In Kalamazoo' *Orchestra Wives* (20th Century-Fox) Harry Warren *cm*: Mack Gordon *lyr*. 'Love Is A Song' *Bambi* Frank Churchill *cm*: Larry Morey *lyr*. 'Pennies For Peppino' *Flying With Music* (Roach, UA) Edward Ward *cm*: Chet Forrest and Bob Wright *lyr*. 'Pig Foot Pete' *Hellzapoppin'* (Universal) Gene de Paul *cm*: Don Raye *lyr*. 'There's A Breeze On The Lake Louise' *The Mayor Of 44th Street* (RKO) Harry Revel *cm*: Mort Greene *lyr*.

Scoring Of A Dramatic Or Comedy Picture (Slight alteration of classification)
NOMINATIONS INCLUDED: *Bambi* Frank Churchill and Edward Plumb

Scoring Of A Musical Picture
Yankee Doodle Dandy Ray Heindorf and Heinz Roemheld
NOMINATIONS INCLUDED: *Flying With Music* Edward Ward. *For Me And My Girl* (MGM) Roger Edens and George Stoll. *Holiday Inn* Robert Emmett Dolan. *It Started With Eve* (Universal) Charles Previn and Walter Scharf. *My Gal Sal* Alfred Newman. *You Were Never Lovelier* Leigh Harline.

The New York Film Critics Awards
Best Actor
James Cagney *Yankee Doodle Dandy*

The New York Times Annual 'Ten Best'
7th *Yankee Doodle Dandy*

The Annual Top Moneymaking Films
INCLUDED: *Holiday Inn. Louisiana Purchase* (Paramount). *My Gal Sal. Yankee Doodle Dandy*.

The young 'uns were at it again in **Get Hep to Love** (GB: **It Comes Up Love**) whose faintly ludicrous story (by M.M. Musselman, screenplay by Jay Dratler) was little more than a funnel into which Universal poured all of its teenage talent. It starred Gloria Jean (left) now a ripe old 14, as a talented soprano who, to escape the greedy clutches of an exploiting aunt (Edith Barrett) runs away and gets herself adopted by a young married couple (Jane Frazee and Robert Paige). Miss Jean sang 'Sempre Libera' from Verdi's *La Traviata*, 'Villanelle' (by Eva Dell Acqua and Ralph Freed) and 'Drink To Me Only With Thine Eyes', in a manner that failed to bring the opera houses of the world clamouring to secure her services; and was supported by Donald O'Connor (right), Peggy Ryan, Cora Sue Collins, Nana Bryant, Irving Bacon and The Jivin' Jacks and Jills. The director was Charles Lamont. Other songs: *Siboney* Dolly Morse, Ernesto Lecuona; *Those Endearing Young Charms* Thomas Moore, Matthew Locke; *Let's Hitch A Horsie To The Automobile* Al Hoffman, Mann Curtis, Jerry Livingston; *Heaven For Two* Don Raye, Gene De Paul.
▽

Louisiana Purchase (Paramount), a Broadway musical with music and lyrics by Irving Berlin and a book by Morrie Ryskind from a story by Buddy De Sylva, reached the screen in glorious Technicolor with Bob Hope (illustrated centre) in the role originally created by William Gaxton. A sharp-witted satire on political corruption, the film had Hope being framed by his crooked associates and becoming the target of an investigation by US Senator Oliver P. Loganberry (Victor Moore, in the role he played in the Broadway production). Vera Zorina (also from the Broadway production) was cast as a dancer employed by the grafters to compromise Loganberry, with other roles going to Irene Bordoni (also from Broadway), Dona Drake, Andrew Tombes (2nd left), Donald McBride (left), Raymond Walburn (2nd right), Maxie Rosenbloom and Frank Albertson (right). Hope's big moment comes near the end when 'through courtesy of Jimmy Stewart' (who did the same thing in *Mr Smith Goes To Washington*, Columbia, 1939) he conducts a filibuster on the legislature, reciting *The Face On The Bar-room Floor* and reading from *Gone With The Wind*! The film, written for the screen by Jerome Chodorov and Herbert Fields, featured only four Berlin songs, and a ballet for Zorina. Buddy De Sylva produced, and the director was Irving Cummings. Songs: *Prologue: Take A Letter To Paramount Pictures* and *Before The Picture Starts*; *You're Lonely And I'm Lonely*; *Louisiana Purchase*; *It's A Lovely Day Tomorrow*; *Dance With Me (At the Mardi Gras)*.
◁

Those curious enough to find out **What's Cookin'** (Universal) (GB: **Wake Up and Dream**), left the cinema with very little on their plates. Really a jam session by The Andrews Sisters (Patti and Maxene, illustrated), Woody Herman and His Orchestra, Jane Frazee and The Jivin' Jacks and Jills, about a group of youngsters (Grace McDonald, Donald O'Connor, Gloria Jean, Peggy Ryan) determined to make it into show business. Robert Paige was the male lead with other parts going to Leo Carillo (centre right), Charles Butterworth (left), Billie Burke, Franklin Pangborn and little Susan Levine (right). Jerry Cady and Stanley Roberts wrote it and it was adapted by Haworth Bromley from a story by Edgar Allan Woolf. Edward F. Cline directed. Songs and musical numbers included: *What To Do* (Andrews Sisters) Sid Robin; *Blue Flame* (Herman) James Noble; *Woodchopper's Ball* (Herman) Joe Bishop, Herman; *I'll Pray For You* (Frazee, Andrews Sisters, Jean) Arthur Altman, Kim Gannon; *Amen (Yea-Man)* (Herman) Roger Segure, Bill Hardy, Vic Schoen; *You Can't Hold A Memory In Your Arms* (Frazee, Herman and orchestra) Hy Zaret, Arthur Altman; *If; Love Laughs At Anything* Don Raye, Gene De Paul.

Juke Box Jenny (Universal) offered 61 minutes of swing and jitterbug via the orchestras of Charles Barnet (left) and Wingy Manone, as well as The Milt Herth Trio and The King's Men. It had a story – a harebrained effort in which Harriet Hilliard (centre), through some manipulative exploitation by record salesman Ken Murray, becomes the Juke Box Jenny of the title – but it was just a thread on which to hang the musical numbers. Don Douglas, Iris Adrian, Marjorie Gateson, Sig Arno and Joe Brown Jr were also cast. Robert Lees, Fred Rinaldo, Arthur V. Jones and Dorcas Cochran wrote it; the associate producer was Joseph G. Sandford, and the director was Harold Young. Songs included: *Swing It Mother Goose; Give Out; Macumba* Everett Carter, Milton Rosen; *Fifty Million Nickels* Charles Barnet; *Sweet Genevieve* George Cooper, Henry Tucker; *Then You'll Remember Me* Alfred Bunn, Michael Balfe.

If you took your cue from screenwriters Fred Finkelhoffe and Elaine Ryan and paid little attention to the plot of **Babes on Broadway** (MGM), it was possible to have a pretty good time. For the show was generously larded with songs, all of them expertly staged by Busby Berkeley, who also directed for producer Arthur Freed. Its narrative was little more than a formula contrivance (a bunch of kids get together to put on a settlement-house show in order to raise enough money to send some underprivileged children to the country), but its marquee value was enormous, with Mickey Rooney (right, voted the world's most popular star three years in a row) and Judy Garland (left) heading a cast that also included youngsters Ray McDonald, Virginia Weidler and Richard Quine, as well as Fay Bainter, Donald Meek, James Gleason, Luis Alberni and, playing himself, Alexander Woollcott. Though the film ended with a spectacular minstrel show featuring its two young stars in blackface, there were other pleasures along the way, such as the delightful 'How About You' (by Ralph Freed and Burton Lane), sung and danced by Rooney and Garland and staged in a modest living-room by Berkeley at his most resourceful and inventive; and the infectious 'Hoe Down' (by Freed and Roger Edens) performed by the younger members of the cast whose combined energy output was enough to light up Broadway. Also effective was the shamelessly sentimental 'Chin Up, Cheerio, Carry on' (by E.Y. Harburg and Burton Lane) sung by Garland against a backdrop of the Houses of Parliament and other London landmarks, for English children everywhere; and a lengthy production number set in a derelict theatre, memories of whose past successes are conjured up in Mickey and Judy's imagination, as, in turn, they impersonate Scotland's very well known entertainer, Sir Harry Lauder, Walter Hampden (as Cyrano de Bergerac), Fay Templeton, George M. Cohan, Blanche Ring and Sarah Bernhardt. Mickey also did an impersonation of Carmen Miranda as she appeared in *Down Argentine Way* (20th Century-Fox, 1940) that was quite breathtakingly accurate. Other songs and musical numbers: *Babes On Broadway* Freed, Lane; *Bombshell From Brazil; Blackout Over Broadway* Edens; *Mama, Yo Quiero* Al Stillman, Jaraca and Vincente Paiva; *Franklin D. Roosevelt Jones* Harold Rome; *Anything Can Happen In New York* Harburg, Lane; *By The Light Of The Silvery Moon* Edward Madden, Gus Edwards; *Alabamy Bound* Buddy De Sylva, Bud Green, Ray Henderson; *Old Folks At Home (Swanee River)* Stephen Foster; *Waiting For The Robert E. Lee* L. Wolfe Gilbert, Lewis F. Muir; *Mary's A Grand Old Name; Yankee Doodle Boy* George M. Cohan; *She Is Ma Daisy* Sir Harry Lauder, J.D. Harper; *I've Got Rings On My Fingers* F.J. Barnes, R.P. Weston, Maurice Scott.

Bambi (RKO) was Walt Disney's most naturalistic film. Based on the famous story by Felix Salten, it was low-keyed and the gentlest of all the Disney animated cartoons, and in its total commitment to its protrayal of the seasons and elements of nature, set a pattern that Disney would follow years later in his True-Life Adventure series. As in all past Disney cartoon features, colour and music played an important part in helping to create mood and atmosphere, the brilliantly detailed 'April Shower' sequence – revealing the forest at its most mysterious and beautiful – exemplifying the superb craftsmanship that went into every frame. In **Bambi** (illustrated) the world was introduced to the character of Thumper who, along with the seven dwarfs, Dumbo, and Jiminy Cricket, became a favourite with children everywhere. The film's supervising director was David D. Hand; the story was adapted by Larry Morey with Perce Pearce in charge of the story direction. No vocal credits were given. Songs: *Love Is A Song; Let's Sing A Gay Little Spring Song; Little April Shower; I Bring You A Song* Frank Churchill, Larry Morey.

A backstage musical starring John Payne, Betty Grable and Victor Mature, **Footlight Serenade** (20th Century-Fox) was the story of an egotistical prizefighter (Mature) who, after finding himself in the cast of a Broadway show, makes a play for chorus girl Grable (illustrated left). Trouble is, Betty's married to Payne, who is not at all amused by the flirtation and who, by the long arm of coincidence, has a scene in the show with Mature in which he spars with him. Now read on . . . Jane Wyman (right), James Gleason, Phil Silvers, Cobina Wright Jr and June Lang were also in it. Robert Ellis, Helen Logan and Lynn Starling wrote the screenplay from a story by Fidel La Barba and Kenneth Earl, it was efficiently directed by Gregory Ratoff, and the producer was William Le Baron. Somewhat surprisingly, the film was shot in black and white. Songs: *Are You Kidding?; I'm Still Crazy For You; I Heard The Birdies Sing; Living High; I'll Be Marching To A Love Song; Land On Your Feet* Ralph Rainger, Leo Robin; *I'm Stepping Out With A Memory Tonight* Herb Magidson, Allie Wrubel.

▽

As ridiculous as a zoot suit and just as shapeless, **Private Buckaroo** (Universal) was a 68-minute contribution (or hindrance) to the war effort that showed what happened when the Andrews Sisters joined forces with Harry James and His Music Makers to stage a show for servicemen. One good song emerged: 'Don't Sit Under The Apple Tree With Anyone Else But Me' by Lew Brown, Sammy Stept and Charles Tobias, splendidly harmonized by the trio. For the rest, it was little more than a jam session which utilized the talents of Dick Foran, Joe E. Lewis, Jennifer Holt, Shemp Howard (illustrated, with the Andrews Sisters), Richard Davies, Mary Wickes, Donald O'Connor, Peggy Ryan, Huntz Hall and The Jivin' Jacks and Jills. It was stencilled by Edmund Kelso and Edward James from a dozen or so previous Universal efforts (story by Paul Gerard Smith) and directed by Edward F. Cline. Songs: *Three Little Sisters* Irving Taylor, Vic Mizzy; *Private Buckaroo* Charles Newman, Allie Wrubel; *Johnny Get Your Gun Again* Don Raye, Gene De Paul; *We've Got A Job To Do* Vickie Knight; *You Made Me Love You* Joseph McCarthy, James V. Monaco; *Six Jerks In A Jeep* Sid Robin; *That's The Moon My Son* Art Kassel, Sammy Gallop.

Another Bud Abbott and Lou Costello caper, **Pardon My Sarong** (Universal) cast them as Chicago bus drivers whose involvement with a wealthy playboy yacht racer (Robert Paige, illustrated) leads to all sorts of unlikely adventures, including a skirmish with jewel thief Lionel Atwill and a chase through an island volcano and a Tarzan-like jungle. Native islander Nan Wynn (whose major contribution to the film industry was as Rita Hayworth's singing voice) was in charge of the musical side of things, with other parts going to Virginia Bruce as yachtsman Paige's sister, William Demarest, Leif Erickson, Samuel S. Hinds, and The Ink Spots who did a turn in a West Coast nightclub before the frantic events in True Boardman, Nat Perrin and John Grant's screenplay got underway. Also involved: The Sarango Girls, Jack La Rue, Tip, Tap And Toe, The Katherine Dunham Dancers and Charley The Seal. Katherine Dunham staged the dances and the director was Erle C. Kenton. Songs: *Island Of The Moon; Lovely Luana; Vingo Jingo* Don Raye, Gene De Paul; *Do I Worry?* Bobby Worth, Stanley Cowan; *Shout Brother Shout* Clarence Williams.

They should have handed out magnifying glasses to every customer attending **Priorities on Parade** (Paramount), so hard was it to find its plot. Those with 20-20 vision, however, might barely have discerned a piece of patriotism in the guise of entertainment, as a group of swing musicians took up employment in an aeroplane factory – including shapely Ann Miller (left), who looked a treat in overalls and, together with welder Betty Rhodes (centre), helped convey the message to American womanhood that their services in the war effort would be greatly appreciated. The film also featured Johnnie Johnston (right), Vera Vague (Barbara Allen), Harry Barris, Eddie Quillan, Dave Willock and an act called The Debonairs. A rag-bag of songs, dances, sketches, gags and anything else scriptwriters Art Arthur and Frank Loesser could think up as they went along, comprised the content of the film which Albert S. Rogell directed with as much subtlety as a pratfall. Songs: *I'd Love To Know You Better; Here Comes Katrinka; Co-Operate With Your Air-Raid Warden; Concita Marquita Lolita Pepita Rosetta Juanita Lopez; Payday* Herb Magidson, Jule Styne; *You're In Love With Someone Else But I'm In Love With You* Frank Loesser, Styne.

There was plot-a-plenty in Republic's **Joan of Ozark** (GB: **Queen of Spies**), a Judy Canova starrer, with Joe E. Brown (centre) and Eddie Foy Jr as the male leads. Canova was an Ozark hillbilly who, while quail-potting one day, lands a pigeon. The pigeon turns out to be a carrier for a bunch of Nazi spies, chief of whom is Jerome Cowan. Canova hands the message to the FBI and becomes 'public patriot number one', while Cowan (left), who runs a night club in New York as a front to his activities, orders Canova's immediate execution. Enter theatrical agent Joe E. Brown. He goes to the Ozarks and signs Canova for Cowan's niterie – with mind-boggling results. Best musical moment was 'The Lady From Lockheed' number (by Mort Greene and Harry Revel) nicely staged by Nick Castle. Alexander Granach, Anne Jeffreys, Otto Reichow, Wolfgang Zilzer and Donald Curtis completed the cast. It was written by Monte Brice and Bradford Ropes from a story by Robert Harari and Eve Greene (additional dialogue by Jack Townley), produced by Harriet Parsons, and directed by Joseph Santley. Other songs: *Backwoods Barbecue* Greene, Revel; *Wabash Blues* Dave Ringle, Fred Meinken.

▽

Though the Andrews Sisters received top billing in Universal's 65-minute programmer **Give Out Sisters**, it was co-star Grace McDonald (centre) around whom Paul Gerard Smith and Warren Wilson's screenplay (story by Lee Sands) revolved. McDonald played an heiress whose successful attempts to break into show business as a dancer result, among other things, in the Andrews Sisters having to masquerade as her three elderly, disapproving aunts. It was utter drivel, of course, but directed by Edward F. Cline with enough flair to make it watchable. There were five songs in all, four of them harmonized by the Sisters Andrews; a few dance routines (staged by John Mattison) and a fair amount of comedy by Charles Butterworth. Walter Catlett and William Frawley. Also cast for producer Bernard W. Burton were Dan Dailey (centre with McDonald), Donald O'Connor (centre right), Peggy Ryan (centre left), Edith Barrett, Marie Blake, Fay Helm, Emmett Vogan and The Jivin' Jacks and Jills. Songs and musical numbers: *Pennsylvania Polka* Lester Lee, Zeke Manners; *The New Generation* Walter Donaldson; *Who Do You Think You're Fooling?* Ray Stillwell, Ray Gold; *Jiggers, The Beat* Al Lerner, Sid Robin; *You're Just A Flower From An Old Bouquet.*

▽

Clearly there was something special about Eleanor Powell and ships. At least as far as MGM was concerned. After her battleship finale in *Born To Dance* (1936) they put her to sea in *Honolulu* (1939), gave her a shipboard production number in *Broadway Melody of 1940*, and in **Ship Ahoy** starred her as the unwitting carrier, while on a cruise to Puerto Rico, of a magnetic device coveted by enemy agents. The film was unmitigated nonsense from start to finish, but Powell (illustrated centre) interrupted the narrative doldrums with her dancing – particularly effective in a number called 'I'll Take Tallulah' (by E.Y. Harburg and Burton Lane). On board for a few easy laughs and to complicate the simple-minded plot, were Red Skelton (centre left), Bert Lahr and Virginia O'Brien, with Tommy Dorsey (right foreground) and His Orchestra (plus Frank Sinatra, Connie Haines, The Pied Pipers and Jo Stafford), momentarily blowing life into the proceedings with a ditty called 'Last Call For Love' (by Harburg, Lane and Margery Cummings). Harry Clork, Harry Kurnitz and Irving Brecher wrote it from a story by Matt Brooks, Bradford Ropes and Bert Kalmar; the dance numbers were staged by Bobby Connolly, Jack Cummings produced it, and the director was Edward Buzzell. Other songs and musical numbers: *Poor You* (Skelton, O'Brien, Dorsey, Sinatra) Lane, Harburg; *Tampico* (Powell) Walter Ruick; *On Moonlight Bay* (Dorsey, Sinatra, Pied Pipers) Percy Wenrich, Edward Madden.

▷

Despite a really cockle-brained story, absurd even by musical programmer standards, **Youth on Parade** (Republic), against all the odds and thanks largely to an excellent performance by Ruth Terry, emerged as an entertaining trifle and one of the better campus romps of the year. All about a bunch of students who 'invent' a model pupil then, to avoid expulsion, have to produce her to satisfy their psychology professor, the film starred John Hubbard (right, as the Professor), Martha O'Driscoll (left, vocals dubbed by Margaret Whiting), Tom Brown, Yvonne De Carlo, Charles Smith, Lynn Merrick, Chick Chandler and Nana Bryant. The aforementioned Miss Terry was the model pupil – a New York actress hired by the students to carry off the deception. It was written by George Carleton Brown with additional dialogue by Frank Gill Jr, produced by Albert J. Cohen, and directed by Albert S. Rogell. It was also the first time that the famous songwriting team of Jule Styne and Sammy Cahn were paired, their big hit in this instance being 'I've Heard That Song Before', introduced here by Bob Crosby and His Orchestra, although it was Harry James's recorded version that went on to sell over a million copies. Other songs: *You're So Good To Me; If It's Love; Man; Cotcha Too Ta Mee; You Got To Study Buddy.*

▽

Composers Mack Gordon and Harry Warren who provided the score for **Orchestra Wives** (20th Century-Fox) had two more walloping hits with 'I've Got A Gal In Kalamazoo' and 'At Last' and – as performed by Glenn Miller (left) and His Orchestra, with special emphasis on Tex Beneke, Marion Hutton and The Modernaires – captured to perfection America's musical tastes in the early forties. The rest of the film was nowhere as good, with George Montgomery, Ann Rutherford, Lynn Bari (vocals dubbed by Pat Friday), Carole Landis, Cesar Romero, Virginia Gilmore, Mary Beth Hughes, Tamara Geva, Frank Orth, Henry Morgan, Grant Mitchell and The Nicholas Brothers trying valiantly to pep up a story involving the antagonism shown by several orchestra-members' wives to Miss Rutherford, the new spouse of one of the players. It was written with neither wit nor verve by Karl Tunberg and Darrell Ware from a story by James Prindle, and directed for producer William Le Baron by Archie Mayo. Other songs: *Serenade In Blue; People Like You and Me; That's Sabotage.*

△

That old musical standby, the campus caper, surfaced again in **Sweater Girl** (Paramount) which elevated Eddie Bracken (illustrated) to star status, and co-starred him with June Preisser, whose pretty face and way with a cartwheel were about the sum total of what she had to offer. A tale that any self-respecting professor of creative literature would have jettisoned with an 'F', it involved a group of college kids in the preparation of a musical revue but with a spot of murder (the victim being campus editor Kenneth Howell) thrown in for no good measure at all. Frieda Inescort, Betty Rhodes, Nils Asther, Ella Neal and Johnnie Johnston (another murder victim) were also cast for producer Sol C. Siegel, it was written by Eve Greene (additional dialogue by Robert Blees) from a story by Beulah Marie Dix and Bertram Milhauser; and directed by William Clemens. Songs included: *I Don't Want To Walk Without You; I Said No; Sweater Girl; What Gives Out Now* Frank Loesser, Jule Styne. Interesting sideline: according to Styne, it was 'I Don't Want To Walk Without You' (and the slightly risqué 'I Said No') that made him and Loesser 'hot properties' in the Hollywood composer stakes. Introduced by Johnnie Johnston in the film, it was a huge wartime hit. Remake of *College Scandal* (1935).

209

Even its star, Leon Errol (illustrated), looked unhappy throughout **Gals Incorporated** (Universal). Fortunately, his suffering (and ours) was over in a mere 61 minutes – the time it took director Leslie Goodwins to unfurl Edward Dein's screenplay (from a story by Dave Gould and Charles Marion) about a millionaire (Errol) who plays sugar daddy to a nightclubful of gold diggers, much to the consternation of his sister (Minna Phillips) and his son (David Bacon). Harriet Hilliard, Grace McDonald, Betty Kean, Maureen Cannon and Lillian Cornell completed the cast, with Glen Gray and His Casa Loma Orchestra, plus The Pied Pipers, supplying the music. Songs included: *Here's Your Kiss; Hep Hep Hooray; All The Time It's You* Everett Carter, Milton Rosen.

Mary Lee (illustrated, centre left foreground) emerged as the star of the Annual Pennington Revue (Pennington being a school for the kids of show folk) in **Nobody's Darling** (Republic), an unassuming 'B' whose whisper of a story was little more than a pedestal on which its young star was prettily perched. Gladys George appeared as Mary's mum, Louis Calhern was her dad, with other roles in Olive Cooper's screenplay (original story by F. Hugh Herbert) going to Jackie Moran (as Mary's youthful inamorata), Lee Patrick, Bennie Bartlett, Marcia Mae Jones and Lloyd Corrigan. Anthony Mann directed and the producer was Harry Grey. Songs and musical numbers included: *It Had To Be You* Gus Kahn, Isham Jones; *Blow, Gabriel, Blow* Cole Porter; *I'm Always Chasing Rainbows* Joseph McCarthy, Harry Carroll; *On The Sunny Side Of The Street* Dorothy Fields, Jimmy McHugh; *Row, Row Your Boat.*

▽

There were lots of topical gags about war-time rationing in **Let's Face It** (Paramount), a musical farce based on the stage show by Cole Porter and Herbert and Dorothy Fields (and a play by Norma Mitchell and Russell G. Medcraft). The film version starred Bob Hope (illustrated centre) in the role created on Broadway by Danny Kaye and, let's face it, with three philandering businessmen, their justifiably suspicious wives, the three soldiers hired by the put-upon wives to make their spouses jealous, as well as the three legitimate girlfriends of the soldiers and the three floozies being dated by the husbands all showing up at the same time, confusion reigned supreme. With fifteen people to juggle around in the finale, director Sidney Lanfield had his hands full, but coped with it all as if it were a military manoeuvre. And just to add to the plot's density, scenarist Harry Tugend had Hope heroically capturing an enemy submarine by holding a mirror to the periscope and sending it aground off Long Island Sound. Betty Hutton (centre left) co-starred as Hope's fiancée – a woman who runs a health farm for overweight ladies – and the trio of aggrieved wives were Eve Arden, ZaSu Pitts and Phyllis Povah. Other roles in Fred Kohlmar's production went to Dave Willock, Cully Richards, Marjorie Weaver, Dona Drake, Raymond Walburn, Andrew Tombes and Arthur Loft. Songs and musical numbers included: *Let's Not Talk About Love* (Hutton); *Let's Face It* (Willock, Richards, chorus) Cole Porter; *Who Did? I Did* (Hope, Hutton) Jule Styne, Sammy Cahn.

◁ **Du Barry was a Lady** (MGM) was, to say the least, a disappointment. Although its basic story was similar to Cole Porter's Broadway original (by Buddy De Sylva and Herbert Fields) in which a nightclub employee wins a sweepstake, drinks a Mickey Finn, and dreams that he is Louis XV, and that his Du Barry is the nightclub's singer with whom he happens to be hopelessly in love, practically everything else that made the Broadway show such a hit was changed or discarded. Though three of Porter's songs survived the transition, the majority of the numbers were written by Ralph Freed and Burton Lane, E.Y. Harburg, Lew Brown and Roger Edens, and although there was nothing fundamentally wrong with them, they weren't as good as the Porter songs, neither were they as *risqué*. Lucille Ball (centre left) and Red Skelton (centre) played the roles created on Broadway by Ethel Merman and Bert Lahr, with Rags Ragland and Zero Mostel in support. Gene Kelly (left) was in it too, as a dancer in love with Miss Ball, and who, in the dream sequence, is reincarnated as a dashing revolutionary known as The Black Arrow. His best moment came near the beginning in a routine called 'Do I Love You' (by Porter) which choreographer Charles Walters staged with an imaginative and exciting fusion of music and movement. Virginia O'Brien (centre right) appeared in the role created on Broadway by Betty Grable, and devoured a rather sexy number Roger Edens wrote for her called 'No Matter How You Slice It, It's Still Salome'. Tommy Dorsey (right) and his boys (including Dick Haymes, and with female vocalist Jo Stafford) gave a good account of 'Katie Went To Haiti' (Porter), as well as an instrumental rendition of 'I'm Getting Sentimental Over You' (by Ned Washington and George Bassman), and the entire company ended the film with Porter's rousing 'Friendship'. If only the screenplay (by Irving Brecher) had matched the quality of some of the aforementioned musical sequences, Du Barry would indeed have been a lady – as it turned out, she was a bit of a tramp and – worse still – a bit of a bore. Arthur Freed produced in Technicolor, and the director was Roy Del Ruth. Other songs and musical numbers: *Du Barry Was A Lady* Ralph Freed, Burton Lane; *I Love An Esquire Girl* Freed, Roger Edens, Lew Brown; *Ladies Of The Bath* Edens; *Madame, I Love Your Crepes Suzettes* Freed, Lane, Brown.

On learning that her employees can't stand her, Esther Dale, president of Bird Dairies, sets out to discover why, by posing as a labourer, in **Swing Your Partner** (Republic). The screenplay, written by Dorrell and Stuart McGowan provided roles for Lulubelle and Scotty, Richard Lane (centre left), Vera Vague (centre right), Roger Clark and Judy Clark as well as for radio entertainers Ransom Sherman, Harry 'Pappy' Cheshire,
▽

George 'Shug' Fisher and The Tennessee Ramblers. Armand Schaefer produced and it was directed by Frank McDonald. Songs included: *Cheese Cake*; *Swing Your Partner* Charles Henderson; *Cracker Barrel County* Frank Loesser, Jule Styne; *Everybody Kiss Your Pardner* Dick Sanford, John Redmond, Frank Weldon; *Shug Shug Yodel* George 'Shug' Fisher; *In The Cool Of The Evening* Walter Bullock, Jule Styne.

△

The oft-quoted remark about there being nothing wrong with a bad musical that a new book, new music, new lyrics, new sets and new performances wouldn't improve, applied to **Follies Girl** (PRC), a no-no effort whose marquee value was limited to the very limited Wendy Barrie, Gordon Oliver and Doris Nolan (centre), plus several of radio's currently popular band-
▽

Is Everybody Happy? (Columbia) opened with ▷ clarinettist Ted Lewis (illustrated foreground centre) playing an engagement in San Francisco. At an army camp there, he meets the son of an old vaudeville partner of his and learns that the lad (Larry Parks) refuses to marry the girl he loves (Nan Wynn) because he fears returning home from the war an invalid. So Ted tells him a story (in flashback) about a pianist who, in World War I, had his hand blown off in the trenches, but returned home to marry the girl he left behind and, with piano playing no longer possible, took up the trumpet instead. Convinced, the young man decides he'll marry his girl after all, and does so in a military ceremony. And was everybody happy? Not according to the indifferent box-office returns. Michael Duane, Lynn Merrick, Bob Haymes and Dick Winslow were also in it; it was written by Monte Brice and directed by Charles Burton. Musical numbers: *It Had To Be You* Gus Kahn, Isham Jones; *More Than Anyone Else In The World* Charles Kenny, Ruth Lowe; *This Old High Hat of Mine* Ted Lewis; *Cuddle Up A Little Closer* Otto Harbach, Karl Hoschna; *I'm Just Wild About Harry* Eubie Blake, Noble Sissle; *Way Down Yonder In New Orleans* Henry Creamer, Turner Layton; *On The Sunny Side Of The Street* Dorothy Fields, Jimmy McHugh; *St Louis Blues* W.C. Handy; *Pretty Baby* Kahn, Tony Jackson, Egbert Van Alstyne; *Am I Blue?* Grant Clarke, H. Akst.

leaders including Johnny Long, Bobby Byrne, Ray Heatherton and Ernie Holst. Realizing that this line-up might not be enough, producer-director William Rowland hired the services of The Charles Weidman Dance Group, Lazara and Castellanos, The Song Spinners, The Heat Waves, Gil Thompson, and Claire and Arena. The story – a convoluted and highly implausible yarn featuring a burlesque singer, a dress designer, a private in the army, and several whiskery ploys such as mistaken identity, was by Marcy Klauber and Charles Robinson. Songs: *Keep The Flag A-Flying* Mary Schaefer; *No Man In The House* Nick and Charles Kenny, Sonny Burke; *Someone To Love* Robert Warren; *I Told A Lie* Nick Kenny, Kim Gannon, Ken Lane; *Shall We Gather At The Rhythm?* Kenny, Burke, John Murphy; *Fascination*; *I Knew Your Father's Son*; *Thoity Poiple Boids* Fred Wise, Buddy Kaye, Sidney Lippman.

Allan Jones (centre in tuxedo), Kitty Carlisle ▷ (centre) and Leo Carillo starred in **Larceny with Music** (Universal), with Carillo as the owner of a nightspot who, believing that Jones is about to inherit a fortune, hires the singer for his club. The most striking aspect of the film was the extraordinary number of complications that scenarist Robert Harari managed to work into 64 minutes of screen time. Lee Patrick, William Frawley, Gus Schilling, Samuel S. Hinds and Sig Arno were in it, together with The King Sisters (illustrated, foreground left and right), and Alvino Rey and His Orchestra. Howard Benedict produced and the director was Edward Lilley. Songs and musical numbers included: *When You Wore A Tulip* Jack Mahoney, Percy Wenrich; *For The Want Of You* Jule Styne, Eddie Cherkose; *They Died With Their Boots Laced*; *Do You Hear Music*; *Please Louise* Don Raye, Gene De Paul; *Only In Dreams* Sam Lerner, Charles Previn.

The most distinctive thing about **The Sky's The Limit** (RKO) – apart, that is, from the Johnny Mercer-Harold Arlen evergreen it yielded in 'One For My Baby (And One More For The Road)' – was the fact that it was the only Fred Astaire film to date in which he was not once called upon to wear white tie and tails. For the rest it was a lustreless musical that featured Astaire (illustrated) as a Flying Tiger war hero who, rather than spend time on a coast-to-coast glory tour, assumes a false name and takes himself to New York where he meets and falls for Joan Leslie. The usual misunderstandings helped pad out Frank Fenton and Lynn Root's flaccid screenplay; so did three so-so dance routines, staged by Astaire. Miss Leslie's singing voice was dubbed by Sally Sweetland (though she did all her own dancing – and not too badly at that), and the cast was completed by Robert Benchley, Robert Ryan, Elizabeth Patterson, Marjorie Gateson, Eric Blore, Clarence Kolb, Richard Davies, Paul Hurst, Ed McNamara, Olin Howlin, and Freddie Slack and His Orchestra. David Hempstead produced and the director was Edward H. Griffith. Other musical numbers: *My Shining Hour*; *A Lot In Common With You* Mercer, Arlen.

Sonja Henie's last film for her *alma mater*, 20th ▷
Century-Fox, was **Wintertime**, and it was the
least good of the series: an ice-capade that
melted long before the final fade. Plot with a
small 'p' had Sonja (illustrated centre) as a
Norwegian skating star, saving a run-down
winter resort in Canada simply by being there.
Appearing opposite Miss Henie were Jack Oakie
(as the owner of the resort), S.Z Sakall as her
uncle, and Cornel Wilde as the romantic inter-
est. Also: Cesar Romero, Carole Landis, Helene
Reynolds, Don Douglas, Geary Steffen, Dick
Elliott, and Woody Herman and His Orchestra.
E. Edwin Moran, Jack Jevne and Lynn Starling
wrote it from a story by Arthur Kober, John
Brahm directed, and the producer was William
Le Baron. Musical numbers: *Wintertime*; *Later
Tonight*; *Dancing In The Dawn*; *I'm All A-Twitter
Over You*; *We Always Get Our Girl*; *I Like It Here*;
Ice Ballet (arranged by David Raksin) Nacio Herb
Brown, Leo Robin.

MGM's big-budget contribution to Uncle Sam's
war effort was the roaringly successful
Thousands Cheer, not to be confused with Irving
Berlin's 1933 Broadway revue *As Thousands
Cheer*. What originally started life as a small-
scale romance between a colonel's daughter and
a circus aerialist-turned-soldier, became a full-
scale musical crowned with a jewelled tiara of
guest stars, all of whom appeared in a lengthy
▽

showcase finale. Gene Kelly played the army
private and former aerialist, Kathryn Grayson
(illustrated), was the colonel's daughter, John
Boles the colonel, and Mary Astor his estranged
wife. The finale, set in a servicemen's camp, had
Mickey Rooney as MC, again giving his imitations of Clark Gable and Lionel Barrymore (in
MGM's *Test Pilot*, 1938), just as he had done four
years earlier in *Babes In Arms* (MGM). If the

studio's proud boast was that it had more stars
than there were in heaven, they were all in
Thousands Cheer. Eleanor Powell, no longer as
youthful or as agile as she had been in her
Broadway Melody series, still managed to dance
up a storm; Red Skelton did an item with child
star Margaret O'Brien in which they had a
competition to see who could eat the most ice
cream; Frank Morgan as a phoney medic leer-
ingly examined three WAVES (one of whom was
Lucille Ball); deadpan Virginia O'Brien sang 'In
A Little Spanish Town' (by Sam M. Lewis, Joe
Young, Mabel Wayne) flanked by Gloria De
Haven and June Allyson; Lena Horne gave a
memorable account of 'Honeysuckle Rose' (by
Andy Razaf and Fats Waller); Kay Kyser, Bob
Crosby and Benny Carter appeared with their
respective bands; Maxine Barrett and Don Loper
danced beautifully together to 'Tico Tico' (by
Zequinha Abreu), while Judy Garland – snap-
pily accompanied by Jose Iturbi – belted out a
number called 'The Joint Is Really Jumpin' in
Carnegie Hall' (by Ralph Blane, Hugh Martin
and Roger Edens), Kathryn Grayson sang 'Day-
break' (by Harold Adamson and Ferde Grofé),
'Three Letters In The Mailbox' (by Paul Francis
Webster and Walter Jurmann), 'Let There Be
Music' (by E.Y. Harburg and Earl Brent), 'The
United Nations On The March' (by Dimitri
Shostakovitch, Harburg, Harold Rome and Herbert Stothart), and 'Sempre Libera' from Verdi's
La Traviata. The only chance Gene Kelly got to
dance was when, confined to quarters for in-
subordination and made to clean the local PX,
he did what was called 'The Mop Dance' – the
freshest, most inventive few minutes in the
show, to music comprising 'I Dug A Ditch' (by
Lew Brown, Ralph Freed and Burton Lane) and
'Let Me Call You Sweetheart' (by Beth Slater
Whitson and Leo Friedman). The rest of the cast
was completed by Ben Blue, Frances Rafferty,
Mary Elliott, Frank Jenks, Frank Sully, Dick
Simmons and Ben Lessy, with guest appearances
also from Ann Sothern, Marsha Hunt, Marilyn
Maxwell, John Conte and Sara Haden. The film
was written by Paul Jarrico and Richard Collins,
the director was George Sidney, and it was produced by Joseph L. Pasternak, who, with this
one, presented MGM with one of the top money-
making musical movies of the year. Other songs
and musical numbers: *Should I?* Arthur Freed,
Nacio Herb Brown; Medley: *American Patrol*
E.H. Meacham; *Columbia, The Gem of The
Ocean* (authorship disputed); *Yankee Doodle*
(anonymous).

△

Another star-studded variety show from Warner Bros. tailored to the war-torn times, **This is the Army** was Irving Berlin's glowing musical homage to the American soldier. A film version of the stage success that had raised the astronomical sum of $1,951,045.11 for Army Emergency Relief, it succeeded in earning a great deal more than that for producer Hal B. Wallis who took back only his production costs from the profits. Michael Curtiz directed with a patriotic flavour that was faithful to the original, and which featured the 350 soldiers who had appeared in the Broadway production, as well as Joan Leslie, George Murphy, Ronald Reagan, George Tobias, Alan Hale, Charles Butterworth, Dolores Costello, Frances Langford, Gertrude Niesen, Kate Smith, and Sergeant Joe Louis. The screenplay was by Casey Robinson and Captain Claude Binyon; LeRoy Prinz and Robert Sidney took charge of the musical numbers, and composer-lyricist Berlin appeared in one of them – 'Oh How I Hate To Get Up In The Morning'. Most of the principals contributed their services free, while the soldiers worked for their regular army pay. Other songs and musical numbers: *This Is The Army Mr Jones* (Full company); *The Army's Made A Man Out Of Me* (M/Sgt Ezra Stone, Sgt Julie Oshins, Sgt Philip Truex); *God Bless America* (Kate Smith); *I'm Getting Tired So I Can Sleep* (Sgt James Burell); *What The Well-Dressed Man In Harlem Will Wear* (Pvt James Cross); *I Left My Heart At The Stagedoor Canteen* (Adjt Earl Oxford); *How About A Cheer For The Navy* (Company, illustrated); *Poor Little Me, I'm On K.P.* (Tobias, chorus); *With My Head In The Clouds* (Sgt Robert Shanley); *Your Country And My Country* (Gertrude Niesen); *My Sweetie* (Murphy); *We're On Our Way To France* (Murphy, Tobias, Hale, company); *What Does He Look Like* (Frances Langford); *Mandy* (Cpl Ralph Magelssen, company); *Ladies Of The Chorus* (Hale, company); *This Time Is The Last Time* (Sgt Shanley, company); *American Eagles* (Shanley, company).

Never a Dull Moment (Universal) was The Ritz Brothers' last film, and the best of the three they made for Universal. Running exactly an hour, it was true to its title, with the brothers posing as Chicago mobsters as part of their nightclub act. When, however, they discover that what they've really been hired for is to receive stolen jewels pick-pocketed from the club's patrons by Mary Beth Hughes, they want out. Which was easier said than done. Frances Langford (illustrated seated) co-starred as the club's resident nightingale, with Stuart Crawford, Elisabeth Risdon, George Zucco, Jack La Rue, Ruby Dandridge (standing right) and Franklin Pangborn (left) also featured. Apart from Miss Langford, who sang 'My Blue Heaven' (by George Whiting and Walter Donaldson), and 'Sleepytime Gal' (by Richard Whiting, Joseph Alden, Ray Egan and Ange Lorenzo), there were appearances by The Rogers Dancers, and ballroom dancers Grace and Igor Poggi. Mel Ronson and Stanley Roberts wrote it (story by Roberts), it was produced by Howard Benedict, and directed by Edward Lilley. Other songs and musical numbers included: *Hello; Yakimboomba* Eddie Cherkose, David Rose, Jacques Press; *Once You Find Your Guy* Cherkose, Rose.

▽

Thank Your Lucky Stars (Warner Bros.) typified a certain kind of movie musical which only a major studio could afford to turn out during the war: one which presented a bumper pack of stars (not all of them necessarily equipped as musical performers) to bring entertainment into the lives of the soldiers overseas as well as the families they left behind. With a screenplay by Norman Panama, Melvin Frank and James V. Kern (from a flimsy story by Everett Freeman and Arthur Schwartz) about two producers – S.Z. Sakall and Edward Everett Horton – who get involved with an unknown female songwriter (Joan Leslie, centre), a singer (Dennis Morgan, left), and Eddie Cantor (right) in a dual role. **Thank Your Lucky Stars** boasted a line-up of talent which had Dinah Shore, Ann Sheridan, Alexis Smith, Joyce Reynolds, Hattie McDaniel, Willie Best, Spike Jones and His City Slickers, Jack Carson, Alan Hale, Errol Flynn, Olivia De Havilland, Jesse Lee Brooks, and Ida Lupino all appearing in the charity show which formed the movie's grand finale. Even John Garfield turned up – with a really excruciating rendition of 'Blues In The Night', by Johnny Mercer and Harold Arlen – but the cherry on the top was the now legendary appearance of Bette Davis singing the Arthur Schwartz-Frank Loesser war-time lament, 'They're Either Too Young Or Too Old'. LeRoy Prinz choreographed, David Butler directed and Mark Hellinger produced. Other songs and musical numbers: *How Sweet You Are* (Shore); *I'm Riding For A Fall* (Morgan, Leslie); *Goodnight Good Neighbour* (Morgan, chorus, Alexis Smith); *Love Isn't Born, It's Made* (Sheridan, Reynolds); *Thank Your Lucky Stars* (Shore); *We're Staying Home Tonight* (Cantor); *No You, No Me* (Morgan, Leslie); *The Dreamer* (Shore, reprised by De Havilland, Lupino, Tobias); *Ice-Cold Katy* (McDaniel, Best, Brooks, Rita Christina); *I'm Going North* (Carson, Hale); *That's What You Jolly Well Get* (Flynn, chorus) Schwartz, Loesser; *Hotcha Cornia* (Jones), a madcap version of 'Otchichornya'.

▽

Forties Musicals

More routine programmer fare from Universal with **You're a Lucky Fellow Mr Smith**. Story this time showed how Evelyn Ankers, *en route* to Chicago to marry David Bruce so as to clinch an inheritance, is tricked into marriage with Allan Jones (left) before her arrival in the windy city. Patsy O'Connor (right, cousin to Donald) was responsible for promoting the romance between them, with other parts going to Stanley Clements (centre), Billie Burke, Luis Alberni, Mantan Moreland and Francis Pierlot. The King's Men were in it too, and sang five songs. It was written by Lawrence Riley, Ben Barzman and Louis Lantz (story by Oscar Brodney), with Felix Feist directing for producer Edward Lilley. Songs and musical numbers: *Your Eyes Have Told Me So* Gus Kahn, Walter Blaufuss, Egbert Van Alstyne; *When You're Smiling* Joe Goodwin, Mark Fisher, Larry Shay; *What Is This Thing Called Love?* Cole Porter; *On The Crest Of A Rainbow* Al Sherman, Harry Tobias; *You're A Lucky Fellow Mr Smith* Don Raye, Hughie Prince, Sonny Burke; *Soldier Specialty* Inez James, Buddy Pepper.

Around the World (RKO) was a mish-mash thrown together with a little bit of this (Kay Kyser and His Band, illustrated), and a little bit of that (Joan Davis, Mischa Auer) – the former involved in a touring camp show, the latter with Nazi agents. They all worked so hard to be entertaining, you could almost see the perspiration beading their brows. For the record (and the record-buying public), there were seven songs by Harold Adamson and Jimmy McHugh in it, the best being 'Roodle-Ee-Doo', and 'Don't Believe Everything You Dream'. Marcy McGuire, Wally Brown, Alan Carney, and Kyser regulars Georgia Carroll, Harry Babbitt, Ish Kabibble and Sully Mason, completed the cast. Ralph Spence wrote it, and there was special material by Carl Herzinger. It was produced and directed by Allan Dwan. Other songs: *Candlelight And Wine*; *He's Got A Secret Weapon*; *They Chopped Down The Old Apple Tree*; *Great News In The Making*; *A Moke From Shamokin*.

Always a Bridesmaid (Universal) was another Andrews Sisters programmer which hardly involved them in the plot at all – a responsibility that fell, instead, to Patric Knowles (centre left) as a detective who joins a lonely hearts club to uncover a swindler who is using the club as a front for his nefarious activities. In the end, Knowles gets his man, and, as it turns out, his woman too, a detective played by Grace McDonald (centre). The Andrews Sisters starred as the club hostesses – three lonely gals who can hold a tune better than they can hold a man. Also cast: Charles Butterworth, Billy Gilbert, Edith Barrett, Addison Richards, Walter Baldwin, and The Jivin' Jacks and Jills. It was written by Mel Ronson from a story by Oscar Brodney, and directed by Erle C. Kenton for producer Ken Goldsmith. Songs included: *Thanks For The Buggy Ride* Jules Buffano; *Yoo-Hoo* Vic Schoen, Ray Jacobs, John Wilforth; *As Long As I Have You* Earl Hanbrich, Al Lewis, Howard Simon; *That's My Affair* Hy Zaret, Irving Weiser; *Mr Five By Five* Don Raye, Gene De Paul; *Ride On* Harold Adamson, Jimmy McHugh.

Romance was the key-note of **She's For Me** (Universal), an hour-long filler whose plot (by scenarist Henry Blankfort) centred around the niece (Lois Collier, centre) of an attorney (David Bruce, centre left), her resentment at his continual curbing of her extravagant ways, and her setting out to woo his playboy buddy (George Dolenz, centre right), Bruce disapproves of this situation, so he solicits the help of a singer (Grace McDonald) to break up the romance, but falls in love with her himself. Helen Brown, Mantan Moreland, Charles Dingle, Douglas Wood, Leon Belasco, Frank Faylen, Eddie Le Baron's Rhumba Orchestra and The Rogers Trio were also in it. Frank Gross produced, the dances were staged by Louis Da Pron, and it was directed by Reginald Le Borg. Songs and musical numbers included: *Cae Cae* John Latouche, Pedro Barrios, Roberto Martins; *Do I Know What I'm Doing?*; *Closer And Closer*; *Ain't You Got No Time For Love?*.

In **Swingtime Johnny** (Universal), The Andrews Sisters (illustrated standing) did their bit for the war effort by donning overalls in a munitions factory and making shell casings. In a rather depressing 61 minutes, they made more music than munitions, none particularly memorable – unless you included 'Boogie Woogie Bugle Boy' (by Don Raye and Hughie Prince) which they first sang in Universal's *Buck Privates* in 1941. Harriet Hilliard (right), Peter Cookson, Tim Ryan, Matt Willis, Bill Phillips, Tom Dugan, Ray Walker, and Mitchell Ayres and His Orchestra also appeared for producer Warren Wilson (who also provided the story); it was scripted by Clyde Bruckman and directed by Edward Cline. Other songs and musical numbers: *Sweet And Low*; *Poor Nell* Everett Carter, Milton Rosen; *You Better Give Me Lots Of Loving* Kermit Goell, Fred Spielman; *I May Be Wrong But I Think You're Wonderful* Henry Sullivan, Harry Ruskin; *Boogie Woogie Choo Choo* Johnny Murphy, Roy Jordan; *When You And I Were Young Maggie* J.A. Butterfield, George W. Johnson.

The top man in Universal's **Top Man** (GB: **Man Of The Family**) was Donald O'Connor (left) who, in the best Andy Hardy tradition, takes over the running of the Warren household when Papa Warren (Richard Dix, right) is called up for active service. Without wasting a second, energetic O'Connor organizes a morale-boosting show in an airplane factory, and is even commended for his efforts by the Navy Department. O'Connor worked industriously to keep it on the boil, and despite the film's obvious Hardy family derivations, succeeded. Susanna Foster was the romantic interest (the type of role usually played by Judy Garland), with other parts going to Lillian Gish (as Mrs Warren), Peggy Ryan, Anne Gwynne, David Holt, Noah Beery Jr, Marcia Mae Jones, Louise Beavers (centre) and Samuel S. Hinds. Count Basie and His Orchestra were in it; so were Borrah Minnevitch and His Harmonica Rascals. It was written by Zachary Gold from a story by Ken Goldsmith, produced by Milton Schwarzwald, and directed by Charles Lamont. Songs and musical numbers included: *Wrap Your Troubles In Dreams* Ted Koehler, Harry Barris, Billy Moll; *Basie Boogie* Count Basie; *Dark Eyes*.

A remake of Buster Keaton's silent comedy *Spite Marriage* (MGM, 1929), the same studio's **I Dood It** (GB: **By Hook or by Crook**) was slightly reshaped by Sig Herzig and Fred Saidy to suit the antic humour of Red Skelton (illustrated). In his most energy-consuming performance to date, Skelton played a pants presser besotted with an actress (Eleanor Powell) currently appearing in a Civil War melodrama. Powell marries him on the rebound when her sweetheart ups and leaves her for another but, after foiling a saboteurs' plot (the film's only topical war-time reference) and making a hilarious appearance in the Civil War melodrama, Skelton discovers to his delight that his wife really loves him after all. A frantic potboiler, with the star working over-time to keep it buoyant, it wasted Powell in a couple of indifferent Bobby Connolly-staged dance routines, both of which were shot before director Vincente Minnelli began work on the film, and which, contrary to his wishes, were retained by producer Jack Cummings. One of these routines, danced to Cole Porter's 'Swinging The Jinx Away', was first seen in MGM's *Born To Dance* in 1936, and had Miss Powell on a battleship yet again! Lena Horne, playing herself, was in it too, and sang the enchanting Vernon Duke-Ted Fetter-John Latouche standard 'Taking A Chance On Love', as well as Leo Robin and Richard Myers's 'Jericho', which also featured Hazel Scott. Jimmy Dorsey and His Orchestra, plus Helen O'Connell and Bob Eberly, were also featured, Dorsey's big moments being 'Star Eyes' by Don Raye and Gene De Paul, and 'One O'Clock Jump' by Count Basie. The rest of the cast included Richard Ainley, Patricia Dane, Sam Levene, Thurston Hall, John Hodiak, Butterfly McQueen and Andrew Tombes. Other musical numbers: *Hola E Pae* Johnny Noble; *So Long Sarah Jane* Lew Brown, Ralph Freed, Sammy Fain.

Originally intended for Alice Faye but given to Betty Grable when Miss Faye decided to opt for domesticity, **Sweet Rosie O'Grady** was just one more 20th Century-Fox formula musical, set in the 1880s and drenched in sumptuous Technicolor. In this production Grable (illustrated) played Madeleine Marlowe, a Brooklyn-born musical comedy star who, after a triumphant tour of England, returns to America where a reporter (Robert Young) from *The Police Gazette* tarnishes her refined image by exposing her origins. Miss Marlowe is, in fact, Rosie O'Grady, an erstwhile singer at *Flugelman's Beer Garden* in the Bowery. Grable retaliates by exposing Young as a former suitor out to further his own career in the ensuing glare of the publicity his 'revelations' create. Of course, they're both really crazy about each other – even though it takes them 74 minutes to realize it. Meantime, their squabbling was sandwiched between several songs by, among others, Mack Gordon and Harry Warren, of which the most durable was 'My Heart Tells Me', sung by Grable – at her most attractive – in a bath tub. The production numbers were staged by Hermes Pan and included 'Get Your Police Gazette', 'The Wishing Waltz' (in which Pan was featured), and 'Going To The County Fair' (all by Gordon and Warren). Unlike John Payne, Don Ameche or Cesar Romero, Robert Young was no singer and, apart from joining in a couple of choruses of four of the songs, including the title number, left the bulk of the vocalizing to his leading lady. Adolphe Menjou co-starred with characteristic aplomb as the editor of *The Police Gazette*, with other roles in William Perlberg's pleasant (and profitable) production going to Phil Regan, Lilyan Irene, Frank Orth, Virginia Grey, Reginald Gardiner, Sig Rumann, Alan Dinehart, Hobart Cavanaugh, The Leo Diamond Solidaires, and St Brendan's Choir. It was scripted by Ken Englund from a story by William R. Lipman, Frank Stephani and Edward Van Every, and directed by Irving Cummings. Other songs and musical numbers: *Waiting At The Church* (Grable, chorus) Fred W. Leigh, Henry E. Pether; *Battle Cry* (Irene) Maude Nugent; *Sidewalks Of New York* (orch) Charles Lawlor, James Blake; *Two Little Girls In Blue* (Grable, Young) Charles Graham; *Little Annie Rooney* (Grable, Young, Orth) Michael Nolan; *My Sam* (Grable); *Where, Oh Where Is The Groom?* (Grable, chorus) Gordon, Warren; *Heaven Will Protect The Working Girl* (Grable, Young) Edgar Smith, A. Baldwin Sloane.

Though Deanna Durbin (illustrated) was now over twenty-one, her girlish charms had by no means evaporated, and her role in **His Butler's Sister** (Universal) brought out the same qualities that had made her a star in the mid-thirties. She played an ingenuous young singer who arrives in New York hoping to find fame and fortune as the protégée of composer Franchot Tone (illustrated). It just so happens that Mr Tone has in his employ a butler (Pat O'Brien) who turns out to be none other than Miss Durbin's half-brother and, in no time at all, she is put to work as a maid. But a love affair blossoms between employer and employee and, after several misunderstandings, the situation is satisfactorily resolved. A delightfully inconsequential romance, it provided Deanna with several occasions on which to burst into song, most notably in a number by Bernie Grossman and Walter Jurmann called 'In The Spirit Of The Moment'. She also sang an aria from Puccini's *Turandot*, Victor Herbert's 'When You're Away' (lyrics Henry Blossom Jr), and a medley of popular Russian songs. The original screenplay was by Samuel Hoffenstein and Betty Rheinhardt, with roles in it for Akim Tamiroff, Alan Mowbray, Frank Jenks, Hans Conried and Sig Arno as a quintet of middle-aged suitors. Iris Adrian and Robin Raymond were also in it and sang 'Is It True What They Say About Dixie?' (by Irving Caesar, Sammy Lerner and Gerald Marks). Frank Borzage directed the confection sweetly, and the producer was Felix Jackson.

A prefabricated programmer about a girl (Gloria Jean) who leaves her rural existence in Vermont to attend a drama school in New York, but returns home when she runs out of money, **Moonlight In Vermont** (Universal) was about as low key as they came. It ended with a barnyard revue (production number illustrated) staged by some of Miss Jean's fellow students who arrive in Vermont to help out with the harvest and, apart from focussing on the promising song and dance talents of newcomer Ray Malone, offered very little in the way of solid entertainment. George Dolenz, Fay Helm, Betty McCabe and Sidney Miller were also in it for director Edward Lilley, it was scripted by Eugene Conrad, choreographed by Louis Da Pron, and produced by Bernard Burton. Songs and musical numbers: *In The Middle Of Things*; *Something Tells Me*; *Dobbin And A Wagon Full Of Hay*; *Be A Good Girl*; *After The Beat*; *Pickin' The Beets* Inez James, Sidney Miller; *Lover* Richard Rodgers, Lorenz Hart.

Forties Musicals

Despite its title, there was no attempt in **Dough-boys in Ireland** (Columbia) to portray the life of Yankee soldiers in Northern Ireland. Most of the characters were American rangers whose only skirmish was a brief raid on an unidentified coast. The film was really a showcase for the pleasant tenor of Kenny Baker (left) who, in the midst of romancing pretty colleen Jeff Donnell (right), sang a clutch of well known Irish ballads. Lynn Merrick appeared as Miss Donnell's romantic competition, with other parts going to Guy Bonham, Wamp Carlson, Buddy Yarus, Dorothy Vaughan, Harry Shannon and The Jesters and, making his tenth screen appearance, Bob (Robert) Mitchum. Howard J. Green scripted it (additional dialogue by Monta Bell), Lew Landers directed, and the producer was Jack Fier. Songs included: *Mother Machree* Rida Johnson Young, Chauncey Olcott, Ernest R. Ball; *When Irish Eyes Are Smiling* Ball, Olcott, George Graff Jr; *My Wild Irish Rose* Olcott; *All Or Nothing At All* Jack Lawrence, Arthur Altman; *I Have Faith*; *I Knew*; *Little American Boy*; *McNamara's Band* Shamus O'Connor, John J. Stanford; *There Must Be An Easier Way To Make A Living*.

The Gang's All Here (GB: **The Girl He Left Behind**) was Alice Faye's last musical before retiring into motherhood, and the first film that Busby Berkeley directed in colour. It was also the only occasion on which star and director worked together. A no-expense-spared production (by William Le Baron for 20th Century-Fox) that took as much as seven months to shoot, it was probably the costliest of Fox's war-time musicals, with Berkeley indulging himself in a couple of large-scale production numbers that echoed his pre-war work at Warner Bros. 'The Lady With The Tutti-Frutti Hat' was one of them. 'The Polka Dot Polka' (both by Leo Robin and Harry Warren) the other. In the first, Carmen Miranda (shown left) – second billed – made an entrance in a golden cart pulled by two gold painted oxen and wearing a mammoth headdress of fruit. The number featured 60 girls carrying giant bananas which they formed into various patterns, and was so suggestive in its phallic overtones that it was banned in Brazil! The film's finale offered audiences another of Berkeley's extravagant flights of fancy, and involved two 50ft high by 15ft wide mirrors brought together in a 'V' shape, the centre of which contained a revolving platform, 18 ft in diameter, on which he placed his dancers, thus enabling them to form an endless variety of characteristic Berkeley patterns. The sequence also featured 60 neon-lit hoops which the girls used to stunning effect throughout the rest of the number. In the film's less flashy moments, Alice Faye sang two enchanting Robin-Warren ballads, 'A Journey To A Star', and 'No Love, No Nothin'', both of which became enormous hits. The plot? A bubble about a soldier (James Elli-

son) who has to choose between showgirl Faye (right) and his fiancée, Sheila Ryan (centre). Charlotte Greenwood, Edward Everett Horton, Phil Baker, Eugene Pallette and Dave Willock were also cast; so were Tony De Marco and Benny Goodman, who even shared a vocal with Miranda. June Haver made her debut as a hat-check girl, and Jeanne Crain was seen for the first time too, in a one-line part. It was written by Walter Bullock from a story by Nancy Wintner, George Root Jr and Tom Bridges. Other songs and musical numbers: *Paducah* (Miranda, Goodman); *Minnie's In The Money* (Goodman, orchestra); *You Discover You're In New York* (Miranda, Baker) Robin, Warren; *Brazil* (Miranda, tenor, chorus) Ary Barroso, S.K. Russell; and the rather elaborate finale, *Polka Dot Ballet*, by David Raksin.

Ole Olsen (left) and Chic Johnson's (right) first film since *Hellzapoppin'* (Universal, 1941) was the moderately diverting **Crazy House** (Universal), in which they starred as a pair of zany movie makers. Director Edward Cline kept it going at an appropriately brisk pace, only putting the brakes on in the romantic interludes between Patric Knowles and Martha O'Driscoll, and in the film's two production numbers – 'Pocketful Of Pennies' (by Eddie Cherkose and Franz Steininger), and 'Tropicana' (by Don Raye and Gene De Paul). Cass Daley (centre) who with each new film came to resemble Martha Raye more, played a dual role, with Percy Kilbride, Leighton Noble. Thomas Gomez, Edgar Kennedy and Franklin Pangborn also cast. There were cameo appearances from Alan Curtis, Allan Jones, Billy Gilbert, Hans Conried, Shemp Howard, Lon Chaney Jr, Andy Devine, Robert Paige, The Glenn Miller Singers with Marion Hutton, Count Basie and His Band, Tony and Sally De Marco, The Chandra Kaly Dancers, The Laison Brothers, The Five Hertzogs, The Delta Rhythm Boys, Basil Rathbone and Nigel Bruce as Sherlock Holmes and Dr Watson, The Bobby Brooks Quartet, Andrew Tombes – and Uncle Tom Cobleigh and all. It was written by Robert Lees and Frederick Rinaldo. Other songs and musical numbers included: *Get On Board, Little Children* Raye, De Paul; *Lament Of A Laundry Girl* Jerry Seelen, Lester Lee, Ted Shapiro; *Donkey Serenade* Rudolf Friml, Bob Wright, Chet Forrest; *My Rainbow Song* Mitchell Parish, Matt Malneck, Frank Signorelli; *My Song Without Words* John Latouche, Vernon Duke; *I Ought To Dance* Sammy Cahn, Saul Chaplin; *Crazy House* Cherkose, Rosen.

△
Girl Crazy (MGM) was one of the year's best musicals and a much more beguiling entertainment than the earlier version of it made in 1932 by RKO. Realizing that there was simply no way in which they could improve upon the George and Ira Gershwin score, the studio wisely decided to retain the numbers, as well as the story (by Guy Bolton and Jack McGowan) in which a young, girl-crazy playboy is sent to an all-male college in Arizona, and discovers that six o'clock in the morning is the time people get up – and not the other way round. He also discovers the dean's granddaughter and, together, they stage a bumper rodeo to raise much needed funds for the college. It was the perfect vehicle for Mickey Rooney (centre) and Judy Garland (right) who, in this, their eighth film together, were perfect in it. Busby Berkeley was originally signed to direct the entire film, but his disagreements with Roger Edens, the show's musical arranger, as well as with Judy Garland (with whom he had not seen eye-to-eye on *For Me And My Gal* at MGM in 1942), led to his dismissal by producer Arthur Freed, though his services were retained for the finale, a typical Berkeley-esque whirlabout to the tune of 'I've Got Rhythm'. The other dance numbers were staged by Charles Walters. Garland sang 'Embraceable You', 'Bidin' My Time' and 'But Not For Me', and, it must be said, Gershwin never had it so good. 'Could You Use Me', her duet with Rooney, was just one more musical highlight in a show full of them. Rooney teamed up with June Allyson for 'Treat Me Rough', and Tommy Dorsey and His Orchestra were featured in 'I Got Rhythm', 'Bronco Busters', 'Fascinatin' Rhythm', and 'Cactus Time In Arizona'. There was one new song, 'Happy Birthday Ginger', by Roger Edens. The cast also included Gil Stratton, Robert E. Strickland, Rags Ragland (left), Nancy Walker, Guy Kibbee and Frances Rafferty. The screenplay was by Fred Finkelhoffe, and the director who replaced Berkeley was Norman Taurog. The film was remade for a third time in 1965 as *When The Boys Meet The Girls* (MGM).

Mae West returned to the screen, after a three year absence, in a luke-warm entertainment from Columbia called **The Heat's On** (GB: **Tropicana**). Apart from a seduction scene involving the hapless Victor Moore which recalled some of her more distinctive moments way back in the thirties, the film – about a musical comedy star (West) and her association with two crooked producers (Moore, and William Gaxton) – failed to pack a knockout punch. By 1943, what was left of the celebrated West innuendo was decidedly *passé*. Xavier Cugat and His Orchestra (illustrated), vocalist Lina Romay, and pianist Hazel Scott helped buttress Fitzroy Davis, George S. George and Fred Schiller's original screenplay; so did a series of production numbers by David Lichine. But whichever way you looked at it, it was West one always came back to and, for once in her life, she failed to deliver the goods. Also cast: Alan Dinehart, Mary Roche, Almira Sessions and Lloyd Bridges. Milton Carter produced and the director was Gregory Ratoff. Songs and musical numbers: *Just A Stranger In Town; Hello, Mi Amigo; The White Keys And The Black Keys; There Goes That Guitar* Henry Meyers, Edward Eliscu, Jay Gorney; *Antonio* Leo Huntley, John Blackburn, Fabian Andre; *The Caissons Go Rolling Along* Edmund L. Gruber; *There Goes My Heart* Benny Davis, Abner Silver; *Thinking About The Wabash* Jule Styne. ◁

Sigmund Romberg's gloriously tuneful operetta, **The Desert Song**, which Warner Bros. had originally filmed in 1929, got new treatment from the same studio – treatment which was in keeping with Warner's dedication to contemporary issues. Thus audiences found the Riffs being oppressed by the Nazis in French Morocco in 1939. The Nazis are attempting to have a railway built between Dakar and the North African coast, but what they don't know is that the downtrodden Riff labourers are in fact led by an American who fought in the Spanish Civil War, and who naturally sees to it that the job is never completed. This genial heroic twaddle was given considerable help by the score, as well as by the star, Dennis Morgan (left) and his leading lady Irene Manning (right), who, between them, sang most of it. Robert Buckner wrote the screenplay from Lawrence Schwab, Frank Mandel, Oscar Hammerstein II and Otto Harbach's original musical play. LeRoy Prinz staged the dance numbers, and Robert Florey directed (in Technicolor). Also cast were Bruce Cabot, Gene Lockhart, Lynne Overman, Faye Emerson, Victor Francen, Curt Bois and Jack La Rue. Songs and musical numbers: *The Riff Song; Desert Song; One Alone; Romance; French Military Marching Song; One Flower* Harbach, Hammerstein, Romberg; *Fifi's Song* Jack Scholl, Romberg; *Gay Parisienne* Scholl, Serge Walters; *Long Live The Night* Scholl, Mario Silva, Romberg. ◁

Dorothy Lamour (right) wiggled her shapely body to little effect in **Riding High** (GB: **Melody Inn**), an insipid musical from Paramount in which she played an ex-burlesque queen who returns to her Arizona home to find papa Victor Moore's (left) silver mine on the skids. Dick Powell (centre) co-starred as a mining engineer (and Dorothy's male interest), with other parts going to Cass Daley (as the owner of a dude ranch), Gil Lamb, Bill Goodwin, Rod Cameron and Glenn Langan, Milt Britton's Orchestra and dancer Cy Landry supplied the rhythm, while scenarists Walter DeLeon, Arthur Phillips and Art Arthur (working from a play by James Montgomery) supplied the blues. Miss Daley and Mr Lamb, in an attempt to lift some of those blues, worked well beyond the call of duty with a few energetic routines; so did Victor Moore, but in the end they were defeated by the poor material. Danny Dare staged the dances, Fred Kohlmar produced, and the director was George Marshall. Songs and musical numbers: *You're The Rainbow; Get Your Man; Whistling In The Light* Ralph Rainger, Leo Robin; *I'm The Secretary To The Sultan* Robin; *Injun Gal Heap Hep* Rainger, Robin, Joseph Lilley; *Willie The Wolf Of The West* Johnny Mercer, Lilley; *He Loved Me Till The All-Clear Came* Mercer, Harold Arlen.
▽

1944

Academy Awards

Best Picture
Going My Way (Paramount) produced by Leo McCarey

Best Actor
Bing Crosby *Going My Way*
NOMINATIONS INCLUDED: Barry Fitzgerald *Going My Way*

Supporting Actor
Barry Fitzgerald *Going My Way*

Direction
Leo McCarey *Going My Way*

Writing (Original Story)
Going My Way Leo McCarey
(Original Screenplay)
NOMINATIONS INCLUDED: *Two Girls And A Sailor* (MGM) Richard Connell and Gladys Lehman
(Screenplay)
Going My Way Frank Butler and Frank Cavett
NOMINATIONS INCLUDED: *Meet Me In St Louis* (MGM) Irving Brecher and Fred F. Finklehoffe.

Cinematography (black and white)
NOMINATIONS INCLUDED: *Going My Way* Lionel Lindon
(colour)
NOMINATIONS INCLUDED: *Cover Girl* (Columbia) Rudy Mate and Allen Davey. *Lady In The Dark* (Paramount) Ray Rennahan. *Meet Me In St Louis* George Folsey

Art Direction (Set Decoration) (black and white)
NOMINATIONS INCLUDED: *Step Lively* (RKO) Albert S. D'Agostino and Carroll Clark; Darrell Silvera and Claude Carpenter.
(colour)
NOMINATIONS INCLUDED: *Cover Girl* Lionel Banks and Cary Odell; Fay Babcock. *The Desert Song* (WB) Charles Novi; Jack McConaghy. *Lady In The Dark* Hans Dreier and Raoul Pene du Bois; Ray Moyer.

Sound Recording
NOMINATIONS INCLUDED: *Brazil* (Republic) Daniel J. Bloomberg. *Cover Girl* John Livadary. *His Butler's Sister* (Universal) Bernard B. Brown. *Hollywood Canteen* (WB) Nathan Levinson. *Music In Manhattan* (RKO) Stephen Dunn.

Film Editing
NOMINATIONS INCLUDED: *Going My Way* Leroy Stone

Music
Song
'Swinging On A Star' *Going My Way* Jimmy Van Heusen *cm*; Johnny Burke *lyr*.
NOMINATIONS INCLUDED: 'I Couldn't Sleep A Wink Last Night' *Higher And Higher* (RKO) Jimmy McHugh *cm*; Harold Adamson *lyr*. 'I'll Walk Alone' *Follow The Boys* (Feldman, Universal) Jule Styne *cm*; Sammy Cahn *lyr*. 'I'm Making Believe' *Sweet And Lowdown* (20th Century-Fox) James V. Monaco *cm*; Mack Gordon *lyr*. 'Long Ago And Far Away' *Cover Girl* Jerome Kern *cm*; Ira Gershwin *lyr*. 'Now I Know' *Up In Arms* (RKO) Harold Arlen *cm*; Ted Koehler *lyr*. 'Remember Me To Carolina' *Minstrel Man* (PRC) Harry Revel *cm*; Paul Webster *lyr*. 'Rio de Janeiro' *Brazil* Ary Barroso *cm*; Ned Washington *lyr*. 'Silver Shadows And Golden Dreams' *Lady Let's Dance* (Monogram) Lew Pollack *cm*; Charles Newman *lyr*. 'Sweet Dreams Sweetheart' *Hollywood Canteen* M.K. Jerome *cm*; Ted Koehler *lyr*. 'Too Much In Love' *Song Of The Open Road* (Rogers, UA) Walter Kent *cm*; Kim Gannon *lyr*. 'The Trolley Song' *Meet Me In St Louis* music and lyrics by Ralph Blane and Hugh Martin.

Scoring Of A Musical Picture
Cover Girl Carmen Dragon and Morris Stoloff
NOMINATIONS INCLUDED: *Brazil* Walter Scharf. *Higher And Higher* (RKO) C. Bakaleinikoff. *Hollywood Canteen* Ray Heindorf. *Irish Eyes Are Smiling* (20th Century-Fox) Alfred Newman. *Knickerbocker Holiday* (RCA, UA) Werner R. Heymann and Kurt Weill. *Lady In The Dark* Robert Emmett Dolan. *Lady Let's Dance* Edward Kay. *Meet Me In St. Louis* George Stoll. *The Merry Monahans* (Universal) H.J. Salter. *Minstrel Man* Leo Erdody and Ferde Grofé. *Sensations Of 1945* (Stone, UA) Mahlon Merrick. *Song Of The Open Road* Charles Previn. *Up In Arms* (Avalon, RKO) Louis Forbes and Ray Heindorf.

Special Awards
To Margaret O'Brien, outstanding child actress of 1944. (miniature statuette)
To Bob Hope, for his many services to the Academy, a Life Membership in the Academy of Motion Picture Arts and Sciences.

The New York Film Critics Awards
Best Motion Picture
Going My Way

Best Actor
Barry Fitzgerald *Going My Way*

Best Direction
Leo McCarey *Going My Way*

The New York Times Annual 'Ten Best'
4th *Going My Way*. 9th *Meet Me In St Louis*.

The Annual Top Moneymaking Films
INCLUDED: *Cover Girl*. *The Gang's All Here* (20th Century-Fox). *Girl Crazy* (MGM). *Going My Way*. *Lady In The Dark*. *Let's Face It* (Paramount). *Sweet Rosie O'Grady* (20th Century-Fox). *Thank Your Lucky Stars* (WB). *Thousands Cheer* (MGM).

△

All about a runaway socialite (Martha O'Driscoll, illustrated left) who yearns to join the WACS, and the adventures she has with a shipyard worker (Noah Beery Jr, standing centre) on a weekend's leave, **Weekend Pass** (Universal), with a mere tendril of a plot by its producer Warren Wilson (screenplay by Clyde Bruckman), needed a stronger cast than the one working for director Jean Yarbrough to keep it buoyant. Several specialty acts, including The Delta Rhythm Boys (singing 'All Or Nothing At All' by Jack Lawrence and Arthur Altman), ballroom dancer Mayris Chaney and partner, Leo Diamond and his harmonica trio, and The Sportsmen, were roped in for added diversion, but it was no use. **Weekend Pass** was a perfunctory non-starter whose supporting cast included George Barbier, Andrew Tombes, Irving Bacon and Dennis Moore (seated right). Other musical numbers included: *I Am, Are You?*; *I Like To Be Loved*; *She's A Girl A Man Can Dream Of*; *We Build 'Em, You Sail 'Em* Everett Carter, Milton Rosen; *We're In The Navy* Don Raye, Gene De Paul.

Allan Jones's full-throated singing was the chief attraction of Universal's **Sing a Jingle** (GB: **Lucky Days**), a 'home-front' B-musical whose tiny plot concerned the complications that arise when famous tenor Jones (illustrated) enrols for war work in a mid-west defence plant. June Vincent (left) was his attractive romantic foil, with other parts in John Grey, Eugene Conrad, Lee Sands and Fred Rath's churned-out screenplay going to Edward Norris, the comedy team of Betty Kean and Gus Schilling, Samuel S. Hinds, Jerome Cowan, and an acrobatic tap dancer called Dicky Love. It was produced and directed by Edward C. Lilley. Songs and musical numbers included: *Sing A Jingle*; *We're The Janes That Make The Planes*; *Mademoiselle* Inez James, Sidney Mitchell; *The Night We Called It A Day* Tom Adair, Matt Dennis; *Beautiful Love* Haven Gillespie, Wayne King, Victor Young, Egbert Van Alstyne; *Love You Are My Music* Dan Twohig, Gustave Klemm.

▽

A showcase to display the skating wizardry of Belita (illustrated), **Lady Let's Dance** (Monogram) actually had some money spent on it, and featured five full-scale production numbers staged by Dave Gould. However, it still couldn't actually boast a story, although one was credited to Bradbury Scott and producer Scott R. Dunlap. The screenplay (by Peter Milne and Paul Gerard Smith) also gave employment to James Ellison, Walter Catlett (centre), Lucien Littlefield, Maurice St Clair (left) and ice comedians Frick and Frack. The direction was by Frank Woodruff. Songs and musical numbers: *Dream Of Dreams*; *Rio*; *In The Days Of Beau Brummel*; *Lady Let's Dance*; *Happy Hearts*; *Ten Million Men And A Girl* Dave Oppenheim, Ted Grouya; *Silver Shadows And Golden Dreams* Charles Newman, Lew Pollack.

▽

Though **Swing Out The Blues** (Columbia) starred Bob Haymes, the narrative, fashioned by Dorcas Cochran from a story by Doris Malloy, mainly concerned the efforts of a quartet of singing instrumentalists called The Vagabonds (illustrated), to hang on to their professional meal-ticket (Haymes) after he weds socialite Lynn Merrick. Considering the overall slimness of the material and the lack of star names, it was a better than average quickie, adroitly directed by Mal St Clair, whose cast also included Janis Carter, Tim Ryan, Joyce Compton, Arthur Q. Bryan and Kathleen Howard. Sam White produced. Songs included: *Prelude To Love* Chet Forrest, Bob Wright; *Rockabye Baby* Effie I. Crockett; *Dark Eyes* (English version of 'Otchichornya', lyric by A. Salami); *It Can't Be Love*; *We Should Be Ever So Quiet*.

▷

△

Set in a mythical college called Adams, **You Can't Ration Love** (Paramount) found a group of college girls in a co-ed institution doing just that: rationing dates, due to the war-time unavailability of eligible men. The story showed how one of the non-draftees (Johnnie Johnston), a hitherto insipid chemistry student, suddenly becomes a swoon crooner and the school's very own celebrity. Betty Rhodes (right) played the girl responsible for Johnston's unexpected stardom, with other roles in Val Burton's screenplay (from a story by Muriel Roy Bolton) going to Bill Edwards, Marjorie Weaver, Marie Wilson (left), Johnnie 'Scat' Davis, The Artega All-Girl Orchestra and Mabel Paige. Acrobats Roland Dupree and Christine Forsythe were there too. Walter McEwen produced, and the director was Lester Fuller. Songs and musical numbers: *Love Is This*; *Ooh-A-Oh*; *Look What You Did To Me*; *How Did It Happen?* Jerry Seelen, Lester Lee; *I Don't Want To Walk Without You* Frank Loesser, Jule Styne; *Oodles of Noodles* Jimmy Dorsey; *One O'Clock Jump* Count Basie, Harry James; *Louise* Leo Robin, Richard A. Whiting.

△

In **She's a Sweetheart**, a passable low-budget filler from Columbia, Jane Darwell (left) was featured as the proprietor of a boarding house who turns her establishment into a canteen for servicemen with short-time passes. Jane Frazee (top-billed) played an entertainer with Larry Parks (centre) as her co-star and romantic interest. Nina Foch, Jimmy Lloyd (right), Ross Hunter and Carole Mathews were also in it for producer Ted Richmond. The original screenplay was by Muriel Roy Bolton, and the director was Del Lord. Songs and musical numbers: *Who Said Dreams Don't Come True?* Benny Davis, Al Jolson, Harry Akst; *I've Waited A Lifetime* Edward Brandt; *I Can't Remember When* Robert Schermann, Jack Krakeur; *What The Sergeant Said* Jackie Camp; *My Other Love* Bob Wright, Chet Forrest; *Mom* Saul Chaplin; *American Prayer* Lawrence Stock, Vincent Rose, Al Stillman.

Higher and Higher was a stage musical by Richard Rodgers and Lorenz Hart, with a book by Joshua Logan and Gladys Hurlbut, that had a moderate run on Broadway in 1940 – the star turn of the evening being a performing seal. The property was bought by RKO, underwent several changes, and resurfaced with a new score and a cast that included Michele Morgan, Jack Haley (who appeared in it on Broadway), Frank Sinatra (illustrated centre), Leon Errol (3rd left), Victor Borge, Marcy McGuire, Mary Wickes (2nd right), Elisabeth Risdon, Barbara Hale (centre with Sinatra), Mel Torme (right), Paul and Grace Hartman and Dooley Wilson. About a pretty scullery maid (Morgan) transformed, through the connivance of a group of servants, into a debutante, in which guise she catches the attention of the personable young man next door (Sinatra), it was a variation on the usual Cinderella theme in that Miss Morgan spurns the love of the story's Prince Charming, preferring, instead, butler Jack Haley. Of the eight featured songs by Harold Adamson and Jimmy McHugh, Sinatra sang five, soloing on 'A Lovely Way To Spend An Evening', 'The Music Stopped', and 'I Couldn't Sleep A Wink Last Night'. And although he didn't get the girl in the end, he got the bobby-soxers shrieking hysterically every time he opened his mouth. It was written by Jay Dratler and Ralph Spence (additional dialogue by William Bowers and Howard Harris), choreographed by Ernest Matray and produced and directed by Tim Whelan. Other songs and musical numbers: *Disgustingly Rich* Rodgers, Hart; *I Saw You First*; *Boccherini's Minuet In Boogie*; *It's A Most Important Affair*; *Today I'm A Debutante*; *You're On Your Own*.

▽

Though **Lady in the Dark** (Paramount) lit up box offices throughout the land, it was, despite its glorious Technicolor, only a pale imitation of the Moss Hart-Kurt Weill stage musical on which it was based, with star Ginger Rogers (paid a generous $122,500 for participating in her first colour film) no substitute in the show's more dramatic moments, for Gertrude Lawrence who created the role on Broadway. Rogers (illustrated) played the editor of a chic fashion magazine who, on the verge of a nervous breakdown, consults a psychiatrist (Barry Sullivan) in an attempt to clarify her thoughts on three men (Ray Milland, Warner Baxter, Jon Hall) in her life. In her sessions with analyst Sullivan, she relates her decidedly Freudian dreams to him – the final dream, set in a circus, becoming the film's main production number, and featuring Weill's 'The Saga of Jenny', its renowned lyric by Ira Gershwin. Regrettably, executive producer Buddy De Sylva eliminated much of the show's original score, including the marvellous 'My Ship', only a few bars of which remained, thus rendering nonsensical a major 'psychological' plot point with which the song was concerned. Also gone was the brilliant patter number 'Tchaikovsky', sung on Broadway by Danny Kaye, whose role as a photographer was now played by Mischa Auer. Frances Goodrich and Albert Hackett wrote the rather confused screenplay, it was produced by Dick Blumenthal, stunningly costumed by Raoul Pene Du Bois, and directed as best as he was able to in the interfering circumstances by Mitchell Leisen. Other songs and musical numbers: *Suddenly It's Spring* Johnny Burke, Jimmy Van Heusen; *Girl of The Moment; One Life To Live; It Looks Like Liza; This is New* Ira Gershwin, Kurt Weill; *Artist's Waltz* Robert Emmett Dolan; *Dream Lover* Clifford Grey, Victor Schertzinger. ▷

△

In **Swing Fever** (MGM) Kay Kyser (left) played a somewhat retiring musician with an uncanny gift for hypnosis. He should have used it on screenwriters Nat Perrin and Warren Wilson (story by Matt Brooks and Joseph Hoffman), for the *mélange* of music and comedy they offered (involving Kyser and his 'gift' to help win a prizefight) needed all the outside help it could get. There was nothing at all hypnotic about the show, and director Tim Whelan, and a cast that included Marilyn Maxwell (right), William Gargan, Lena Horne, Nat Pendleton, Curt Bois, Morris Ankrum, Maxie Rosenbloom and the Meriel Abbot Dancers, were powerless to make it appear otherwise. Two 'gag' appearances by Harry James and Tommy Dorsey didn't help much either. Meriel Abbott choreographed, and the producer was Irving Starr. Songs and musical numbers: *Mississippi Dream Boat* Lew Brown, Ralph Freed, Sammy Fain; *I Planted A Rose; One Girl And Two Boys* Freed, Brown, Nacio Herb Brown; *You're So Different* Fain; *Sh! Don't Make A Sound* Sunny Skylar.

In **Ghost Catchers** (Universal), a formula musical farce, Messrs Olsen and Johnson (centre and right) play a pair of nightclub owners who find themselves involved with a Southern colonel (Walter Catlett), his two daughters (Gloria Jean, left, and Martha O'Driscoll) and a haunted mansion. Leo Carrillo, Henry Armetta and Lon Chaney were in it too; so were music makers Morton Downey, Ella Mae Morse and Kirby Grant and his orchestra. Louis Da Pron staged the dances, it was written and produced by Edmund T. Hartmann and directed by Edward F. Cline. Songs and other musical numbers included: *Blue Candlelight; Three Cheers For The Customer* Paul Francis Webster, Harry Revel; *Quoth The Raven* Webster, Revel, Edward Ward; *I'm Old Enough To Dream* Ward, Everett Carter; *These Foolish Things* Harry Link, Holt Marvell, Jack Strachey; *After You've Gone* Henry Creamer, Turner Layton.

▽

△

Pre-dating *Kiss Me Kate* (MGM) by nine years, **Casanova in Burlesque** took Shakespeare's *The Taming of the Shrew* and, utilizing the okay-for-some talents of comedian Joe E. Brown, as well as his attractive co-star June Havoc, gave it the hepcat works. Brown (featured left) played a college professor, Miss Havoc a burlesque actress with Shakespearian ambitions. A surprisingly lively entry from Republic, it also featured Dale Evans, Marjorie Gateson, Lucien Littlefield, Ian Keith and Roger Imhof. Albert J. Cohen produced and it was directed from an excellent screenplay by Frank Gill Jr (story by John Wales) by Leslie Goodwins, with choreography by Dave Gould. Songs and musical numbers: *Who Took Me Home Last Night?* Harold Adamson, Jule Styne; *Mess Me Up; Casanova Joe; Five-A-Day Fatima; Willie The Shake; Taming Of The Shrew* Walter Kent, Kim Gannon.

When defence worker Una Merkel knocks herself out while demonstrating to her foreman what she thinks is wrong with the particular machine she is working on, she has a dream, and in **Sweethearts of the USA** (GB: **Sweethearts on Parade**) – an inept programmer from Monogram – we share her dream with her. Parkyakarkus featured prominently in it as an addlepated, music-loving detective on the lookout for a bunch of bank robbers, with other figments of Miss Merkel's far-fetched subconscious materializing in the shape of Donald Novis, Lillian Cornell, Judith Gibson, Joel Friend, Cobina Wright Sr, Marion Martin, Vince Barnett and Ralph Sanford. The orchestras of Jan Garber, Henry King and Phil Ohman provided what little entertainment value there was in the film's 63-minute running time. Lester Cutler produced, it was scripted by Arthur St Clare, Jane Keith and Richard Long (story by Keith) and directed by Lew Collins. (Musical number illustrated). Songs and musical numbers: *Sweethearts Of The USA; All The Latins Know Is Si Si; You Can't Brush Off A Russian; We're The Ones; Hold On To Your Hat; That Reminds Me* Charles Newman, Lew Pollack.

Frances Langford (featured left) sang four songs in **Career Girl** (PRC), none of them very distinguished. She starred as a Kansas City hopeful who arrives in New York, takes up residence (just as others had done before her in Edna Ferber's *Stage Door*) at a theatrical boarding house and, after the usual disappointments, lands a make-or-break job singing in a revue. Audiences were left in suspense as to the outcome of the job, for the film ended while the show was still in rehearsal. A programmer with no redeeming qualities, it was written by Sam Neuman from a story by Dave Silverstein and Stanley Rauh, produced by Jack Schwartz and directed by Walter W. Fox whose cast included Edward Norris, Iris Adrian, Craig Woods, Linda Brent, Ariel Heath and Lorraine Krueger. Songs and musical numbers included: *Blue In Love Again; Dream Come True* Tony Romano, Morey Amsterdam; *That's How The Rhumba Began; Some Day* Sam Neuman, Michael Brown.

▽

Hammered together with a couple of rusty nails and with little sense of shape, **Beautiful But Broke** (Columbia) was very much in the 'B' league. It starred Joan Davis (left foreground), whose chief function in Monte Brice's screenplay (story by Arthur Housman, adaptation by Manny Seff), apart from pulling funny faces, was to take over a theatrical agency specializing in big bands when the boss goes off to war. The current shortage of male combos forces her to form an all-girl troupe, which she does, but which she then leaves stranded in a Nevada warplant community. In an attempt to give the haphazard narrative even a modicum of entertainment value, producer Irving Briskin

Donald O'Connor (illustrated) without whom no Universal musical would be complete, starred in **Chip Off The Old Block**. He played a naval school cadet who falls in love with the pretty and talented daughter of a musical comedy star, and, needless to say, finds himself in show business. Ann Blyth (her first lead role) was the daughter, with other parts in this juvenile farrago by Eugene Conrad and Leo Townsend (story by Robert Arthur) taken by Peggy Ryan (illustrated), Helen Vinson, Helen Broderick, Arthur Treacher, Patric Knowles, J. Edward Bromberg, Ernest Truex, Minna Gombell, Dean Manning and quiz-kid Joel Kupperman. Bernard W. Burton produced, with Louis Da Pron in charge of the dances, and Charles Lamont the direction. Songs and musical numbers: *Is It Good Or Is It Bad?* Charles Tobias; *Mighty Nice To Have Met You; Spelling Prep* Bill Grage, Grace Shannon; *I Gotta Give My Feet A Break* Inez James, Sidney Miller; *Love Is Like Music* Milton Schwarzwald; *My Song* Lew Brown, Ray Henderson, *Sailor Song* Eugene Conrad.

▽

called on the talents of Jane Frazee (centre foreground), Bob Haymes, Judy Clark (right foreground), and Willie West and McGinty – but it was no use. As directed by Charles Barton, it stubbornly refused to play. Also cast: John Hubbard, Danny Mummert, Byron Foulger and George McKay. Songs and musical numbers: *Pistol Packin' Mama* Al Dexter; *Just Another Blues* Jimmy Paul, Dick Charles, Larry Marks; *Shoo-Shoo Baby* Phil Moore; *Take The Door To The Left* James Cavanaugh, Walter G. Samuels; *Mama, I Want To Make Rhythm* Walter Kent, Richard Byron, Richard Jerome; *Mr Jive Has Gone To War* L. Wolfe Gilbert, Ben Oakland; *We're Keeping It Private* Mort Greene, Walter Donaldson.

Harriet Hilliard starred in **Hi Good Lookin'** (Universal), a superior programmer in which she played a singer from the midwest who arrives in Hollywood – not to break into pictures, but to make it as a radio vocalist. With a little bit of help from newcomer Kirby Grant, she succeeds. Grant and Hilliard sang several songs, separately and together; Ozzie Nelson's orchestra contributed a few up-tempo arrangements; Jack Teagarden and His Orchestra made one brief appearance; The Delta Rhythm Boys launched into 'Paper Doll' (by Johnny Black) and Tip, Tap and Toe (illustrated) delivered one dance routine. Eddie Quillan co-starred, and was joined in the comedy bits by Betty Kean and Fuzzy Knight. Also in it were Roscoe Karns, Vivian Austin, Marjorie Gateson and Milburn Stone. It was written by Bradford Ropes, Eugene Conrad and Paul Gerard Smith from a story by Smith, produced by Frank Gross and directed by Edward Lilley. Other songs and musical numbers included: *You're Just The Sweetest Thing* Buzz Adlam, Walter Bishop; *Deacon Jones* Johnny Lange, Hy Heath, Richard Loring; *Aunt Hagar's Blues* W.C. Handy; *Just A Stowaway On A Ship Of Dreams* Vic Knight; *A Slight Case Of Love* Buzz Adlam; *By Mistake* Inez James, Sidney Miller; *I Won't Forget The Dawn* Don Raye, Gene De Paul.

▽

Forties Musicals

Cover Girl (Columbia), written by Virginia Van Upp, and adapted by Marion Parsonnet and Paul Gangelin from a play by Erwin Gelsey, was the conventional story of a Brooklyn nightclub dancer (Rita Hayworth, left) who deserts her lover (Gene Kelly, right) and becomes a cover girl. But she soon learns that money and fame are no substitute for love, and returns to the simple life and the man she cares for. The story was told against a series of flashbacks, set at the turn of the century, in which Hayworth's grandmother (also played by Hayworth) is shown to have followed exactly the same course. Lee Bowman and Otto Kruger were the two wealthy men who lured Hayworth away from Kelly; Phil Silvers was Kelly's faithful side-kick, while Eve Arden was cast as a wise cracking, high-powered executive on the look-out for the ideal cover girl. Apart from its hackneyed plot, the film groaned under the weight of much that was trite and unoriginal, not least of which was the main production number (staged by Seymour Felix) glorifying the American cover girl through giant 'blow-ups' of the country's most famous magazines. (MGM would do it better in *Easter Parade* 1947, to the accompaniment of Irving Berlin's 'The Girl On The Magazine Cover'). Yet, for all its blemishes, **Cover Girl** was important in that it marked Kelly's transition from hoofer to dancer, his famous 'alter ego' sequence being remarkably advanced for its time. The dance began in a mood of tranquillity, with Kelly walking alone through Brooklyn late one night and suddenly seeing his reflection in a shop window. The reflection turns to flesh and blood, and steps down from the window into the street. At first Kelly and his 'doppelganger' dance in unison. Then they begin to challenge each other until in the end, the ego image is destroyed and the dance ends quietly – as so many of Kelly's dances tended to do. The rest of the numbers – all but one by Jerome Kern and Ira Gershwin – were far less innovative, the two best staged being the haunting 'Long Ago and Far Away' sung by Kelly and Hayworth (the latter dubbed by Martha Mears) and set in a dingy Brooklyn nightclub against a back-drop of chairs piled on tables (illustrated). **Cover Girl** was important to Gene Kelly's career in that it contained several elements which he would later refine, rework and enlarge in some of his musicals at MGM. Who, for example, would deny that the street setting of the 'alter ego' dance influenced the title number in *Singin' In The Rain* (1952)? Or that the 'Make Way For Tomorrow' (co-lyricist E.Y. Harburg) routine, which he performed together with Phil Silvers and Hayworth, contained exactly the kind of exuberance that permeated the whole of *On The Town* (1949)? **Cover Girl** was produced (in Technicolor) by Arthur Schwartz, choreographed by Felix, Val Raset and Kelly, and also featured Jinx Falkenburg, Leslie Brooks, Jess Barker, Curt Bois, Ed Brophy, Thurston Hall and The Cover Girls. Other songs and musical numbers: *Put Me To The Test* (Kelly, Hayworth); *Sure Thing* (Hayworth); *That's The Best Of All*; *The Show Must Go On* (Hayworth, chorus); *Who's Complaining* (Silvers) Kern, Gershwin; *Poor John* (Hayworth) Fred W. Leigh, Harry E. Pether.

Pardon My Rhythm (Universal) was formula entertainment which starred Gloria Jean (left), whose adolescent romance with a drummer (Mel Torme, centre) comes in for some rough patches when Bob Crosby, in order to sign Torme to a contract, gets Marjorie Weaver to flirt with him. Gloria, in turn, points her playwright father (Patric Knowles) in Miss Weaver's direction, thus generating sufficient confusion to pad out Val Burton and Eugene Conrad's routine screenplay (story by Hurd Barrett). The Misses Jean and Weaver were each given two songs to sing, while Bob Crosby took time off from the plot to croon the Gus Kahn-Isham Jones standard, 'I'll See You In My Dreams'. Also in it: Walter Catlett, Evelyn Ankers, Patsy O'Connor (right) and Ethel Griffies. Jack Slattery and The Mel Torme Trio also appeared. It was produced by Bernard Burton and directed by Felix Feist. Other songs: *Do You Believe In Dreams?* Don George, Irving Bibo, Al Piantadosi; *Spell Of The Moon*; *Shame On Me*; *Drummer Boy*; *You've Got To Hand It To The Band*.

▽

Ann Sheridan and Dennis Morgan (illustrated) made a pleasing star team in **Shine on Harvest Moon** (Warner Bros.), a run-of-the-mill back-stage musical with far too weak a script to fill out its long (111 minutes) running time. Though it set out to tell the real life stories of Nora Bayes (Miss Sheridan), a honky-tonk girl in vaudeville, and songwriter Jack Norworth (Morgan) with whom she went into partnership and then married, there were so many fictional embellishments in it that real life gave way to reel-life in an avalanche of clichés. Among the redeeming features were several pleasant songs, particularly the enduring title number attractively photographed in Technicolor (the rest of the film was in black and white) and the splendid singing of co-star Irene Manning. Jack Carson and Marie Wilson were also in it and at their best in a comedy number called 'So Dumb But So Beautiful' by M.K. Jerome and Kim Gannon; and the supporting players included S.Z. Sakall, Robert Shayne, William Davidson and Bob Murphy. It was directed in a pedestrian fashion by David Butler from a pedestrian screenplay by Sam Hellman, Richard Weil, Francis Swann and James V. Kern, choreographed by LeRoy Prinz and produced by William Jacobs. Other songs included: *Shine On Harvest Moon* Jack Norworth, Nora Bayes; *When It's Apple Blossom Time In Normandy* Harry Gifford, Huntley Trevor, Tom Mellor; *What's The Matter With Father?* Harry Williams, Egbert Van Alstyne; *Pretty Baby* Gus Kahn, Tony Jackson, Van Alstyne; *Time Waits For No One* Cliff Friend, Charles Tobias; *I Go For You* M.K. Jerome, Kim Gannon; *Every Little Movement Has A Meaning Of Its Own* Otto Harbach, Karl Hoschna; *Just Like A Gypsy* Seymour B. Simons, Bayes; *Take Me Out To The Ball Game* Norworth, Albert von Tilzer; *Breezin' Along With The Breeze* Haven Gillespie, Seymour B. Simons, Richard A. Whiting.

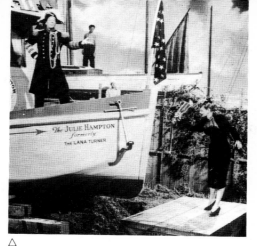

△ **Meet the People** started life as a small-scale revue in Los Angeles in 1940, failed to make the grade on Broadway, and finished its days as an undistinguished musical for MGM starring Lucille Ball (right) and Dick Powell. Ball played a Broadway luminary who accepts a job as a welder in a Delaware shipyard in order to 'meet the people' and to prove to playwright Powell, who has dismissed her from his show as being a snooty bitch, that she isn't too proud to undertake some of life's more menial tasks. Point made and duly taken, she becomes queen of the yard, and wins Powell's undying love. Bert Lahr (left) also appeared, so did Virginia O'Brien (who was in the original show in Los Angeles, and as a result of her work in it was signed by MGM). Miss O'Brien sang 'Say That We're Sweethearts Again' (by Earl Brent) and ran away with the notices. June Allyson had a small part in it too, and the cast was completed by Rags Ragland, Steve Geray, Howard Freeman, Paul Regan and Betty Jaynes. Specialty items included a couple of Oriental dancers called Mata and Hari, Vaughn Monroe and His Orchestra, The King Sisters, and Spike Jones and His City Slickers. It was scripted by S.M. Herzig and Fred Saidy from a story by Sol and Ben Barzman and Louis Lantz. produced by E.Y. Harburg, directed by Charles F. Riesner, and choreographed by Sammy Lee, Charles Walters and Jack Donohue. Other songs and musical numbers included: *Meet The People*; *In Times Like These*; *Schickelgruber* Ralph Freed, Sammy Fain; *I Like To Recognize The Tune* Richard Rodgers, Lorenz Hart; *It's Smart To Be People* E.Y. Harburg, Burton Lane.

△ **Hot Rhythm** (Monogram) set out to be a gentle spoof on radio commercials but finished up, 79 minutes later, as a conventional love story between a jingle writer (Robert Lowery) and a singer (Dona Drake, far right). Standard B-picture fare, it also featured Tim Ryan, Irene Ryan (centre), Sidney Miller, Jerry Cooper, Robert Kent, and Harry Langdon (centre left). William Beaudine directed it from a story and screenplay by Tim Ryan and Charles Marion, and the producer was Lindsley Parsons. Songs and musical numbers included: *Where Were You?*; *Talk Me Into It*; *Happiest Girl In Town*; *Right Under My Nose*; *Say It With Your Heart* Edward J. Kay, N. Brown, Virginia Wicks, Lou Herscher.

△ Not exactly a programmer, but unable to stand up on its own without double-bill support, **Hey Rookie** (Columbia) was a so-so effort which involved Larry Parks – as an enlisted musical comedy producer – in staging a show for his fellow soldiers, despite the hindering antics of comedians Joe Besser (featured centre left) and Jimmy Little. Ann Miller (centre) provided the glamour, with other parts going to Joe Sawyer, Selmer Jackson, Larry Thompson, Barbara Brown, Charles Trowbridge and Charles Wilson, as well as Hi-Lo-Jack and a Dame, The Condos Brothers, Jack Gilford, Bob Evans and his dummy, The Vagabonds, and the Johnson Brothers. Based on a musical staged in Los Angeles' Belasco Theatre where it had a 36-week run, it was written by Henry Myers, Edward Eliscu and Jay Gorney who, together with Sergeant J.C. Lewis also wrote the songs. Val Raset and Stanley Donen choreographed, Irving Briskin produced, Charles Barton directed. Musical numbers included: *There Goes Taps*; *When The Yardbirds Come To Town*; *So What Serenade*; *Hey Rookie*; *Take A Chance*; *You're Good For My Morale*; *It's Great To Be In Uniform*; *Streamlined Sheik*; *It's A Swelluva Life In The Army*.

△ A romantic musical of no consequence whatsoever, **Moon Over Las Vegas** (Universal) featured Anne Gwynne (right) and David Bruce as a young married couple who cannot make a go of their relationship, and Vera Vague (centre) as a well-meaning relative who advises Miss Gwynne that the only way to salvage the situation is to make her hubby jealous. Most of it took place in Las Vegas, and betting on the happy-ever-after outcome (after a few obligatory complications) was no gamble at all. Vivian Austin, Alan Dinehart (2nd right), Lee Patrick, Joe Sawyer, Milburn Stone (centre right), Addison Richards, Mantan Moreland, Gene Austin and The Sherill Sisters, Connie Haines, Capella and Patricia, Lillian Cornell, Anne Triola, Jimmy Dodd, and The Sportsmen completed the cast. George Jeske and Clyde Bruckman wrote it (original story by Jeske) and it was produced and directed by Jean Yarbrough. Songs and musical numbers: *A Dream Ago*; *Faithful Flo*; *Moon Over Las Vegas*; *So Goodnight* Everett Carter, Milton Rosen; *A Touch Of Texas* Frank Loesser, Jimmy McHugh; *You Marvellous You* Gene Austin; *Oklahoma's One With Me* Jimmy Dodd; *My Blue Heaven* George Whiting, Walter Donaldson.

Forties Musicals

△

Two Girls and a Sailor (MGM), one of the year's better musicals, was about two girls (June Allyson, 2nd left, and Gloria De Haven) and the sailor (Van Johnson, left) they meet in a canteen they run for servicemen. Both are smitten by his charm and good looks. In the end he reveals himself to be a millionaire whose money, unbeknown to the girls, has made their 'canteen' possible; and, after being faced with a choice between Allyson and De Haven, he chooses the former. So much for the plot (story and screenplay by Richard Connell and Gladys Lehman), a sturdy enough chassis on which producer Joe Pasternak, director Richard Thorpe and choreographer Sammy Lee mounted several well-staged numbers and showcased the talents of its stars, as well as those of Lena Horne (singing 'Paper Doll' by Johnny Black), Virginia O'Brien (singing 'Take It Easy' by Albert De Bru, Irving Taylor, Vic Mizzy) and Jose and Amparo Iturbi playing De Falla's 'Ritual Fire Dance'. Jimmy Durante (centre) was also in it, as an old-time vaudevillian, and sang one of his best and most famous songs: 'Inka Dinka Doo' (by Durante and Ben Ryan). The rest of the cast was completed by Tom Drake, Henry Stephenson, Henry O'Neill, Ben Blue (right), Carlos Ramirez, Frank Sully, Donald Meek and Frank Jenks, with guest stars Gracie Allen (performing a 'Concerto for Index Finger,' conducted by Albert Coates, which included scales and 'chopsticks'!), The Wilde Twins, Harry James and His Band (with Helen Forrest) and Xavier Cugat and His Orchestra (with Lina Romay) contributing substantially to the general air of merriment that pervaded it all. Other songs and musical numbers: *My Mother Told Me* (De Haven, reprised Johnson, Drake, Sully) Ralph Freed, Jimmy McHugh; *A Love Like Ours* (Allyson, De Haven) Mann Holiner, Alberta Nichols; *In A Moment Of Madness* (James, Forrest) Freed, McHugh; *Young Man With A Horn* (Allyson, James) Freed, George Stoll; *Sweet And Lovely* (Allyson, De Haven, James) Gus Arnheim, Jules Lemare, Harry Tobias; *Granada* (Ramirez, James) Dorothy Dodd, Augustin Lara; *Estrellita* (James) Manuel Ponce, adapted Frank La Forge; *A-Tisket-A-Tasket* (Allyson, De Haven) Al Feldman, Ella Fitzgerald; *Did You Ever Have The Feeling?* (Durante) Durante; *Flash* (James) James; *Charmaine* (James) Erno Rapee, Lew Pollack; *Babalu* (Cugat) Bob Russell, Marguerita Lecuona; *The Thrill Of A New Romance* (Cugat) Harold Adamson, Xavier Cugat; *You Dear* (James) Freed, Sammy Fain; *Castles In The Air* (James); *Who Will Be With You When I'm Far Away?* (Durante) Durante; *Dardanella* (orchestral) Fred Fisher, Felix Bernard, Johnny S. Black; *My Wonderful One Let's Dance* (orchestral) Roger Edens, Arthur Freed, Nacio Herb Brown.

Kurt Weill and Maxwell Anderson's 1938 Broadway flop **Knickerbocker Holiday** was a heavy-handed anti-fascist tract that also criticized governmental interference from Washington. It came to the screen via the Producers Corporation of America and United Artists, with its political content watered down and with only three of the original Weill-Anderson songs in the score. What emerged in this trite screen reincarnation was a tedious period piece set in New York during the time of Peter Stuyvesant and involving a romance between a printer of subversive literature (Nelson Eddy, right) and the pretty daughter (Constance Dowling, left) of a Dutch councillor. Charles Coburn (in the role created on stage by Walter Huston) played Stuyvesant, and got to sing the show's one undisputed hit, 'September Song' (by Weill and Anderson). Ernest Cossart, Johnnie 'Scat' Davis, Richard Hale, Shelley Winter (later Winters), Glenn Strange, Fritz Feld, Otto Kruger, Chester Conklin, Percival Vivian and Charles Judels were also in it, and David Boehm, Roland Leigh and Harold Goldman, working from an adaptation by Thomas Lennon, wrote the screenplay. It was produced and directed by Harry Joe Brown. Other songs and musical numbers: *The One Indispensable Man* (Coburn, Cossart); *There's Nowhere To Go But Up* (Eddy, male chorus) Weill, Anderson; *Hear Ye* (Conklin, chorus); *Love Has Made This Such A Lovely Day* (Eddy, Dowling, Winters); *Zuyder Zee* (male quartet); *One More Smile* (Eddy, Dowling) Jule Styne, Sammy Cahn; *Holiday* (Davis, chorus) Theodore Paxton, Nelson Eddy; *Jail Song* (Eddy) Weill, Furman Brown, Eddy; *Sing Out* (Eddy, chorus) Franz Steininger, Furman Brown.

▽

A slightly subdued Donald O'Connor (illustrated right) starred with Susanna Foster in **This is the Life**, a better-than-average 'B' from Universal which even managed, at times, to be quite charming. All about the crush young Miss Foster develops for an older army officer, and the efforts of O'Connor (her boyfriend) to keep the two of them apart, it featured Patric Knowles (as the officer), Louise Allbritton, Dorothy Peterson, Peggy Ryan (left), Jonathan Hale, Eddie Quillan and Frank Jenks, as well as Ray Eberle and His Orchestra and the Bobby Brooks Quartet, in a neat little screenplay by Wanda Tuchock (from a play by Sinclair Lewis and Fay Wray). Louis Da Pron choreographed, and it was directed by producer Bernard W. Burton by Felix Feist. Songs and musical numbers: *Gremlin Walk*; *It's The Girl*; *Yippee-I-Vot* Inez James, Sidney Miller; *With A Song In My Heart* Richard Rodgers, Lorenz Hart; *All Or Nothing At All* Jack Lawrence, Arthur Altman; *You're A Lallapalooza* Bill Grage, Grace Shannon; *At Sundown* Walter Donaldson; *L'Amour Toujours L'Amour* Rudolph Friml, Catherine Chisholm Cushing.

Based on an actual USO Camp Tour of England and North Africa, undertaken in 1943 by Kay Francis (left), Carole Landis (centre), Martha Raye (right) and Mitzi Mayfair (2nd right), **Four Jills in a Jeep** (20th Century-Fox) starred the same quartet of travellers in a decidedly tepid entertainment, hastily flung together by producer Irving Starr to capitalize on that much publicized tour. Music and romance were the main items on the girls' agenda (in real life Miss Landis met a pilot on the tour and married him; in the film she does the same), the musical aspect being augmented for the occasion by the guest appearances of Alice Faye, Betty Grable and Carmen Miranda. George Jessel was Master of Ceremonies. Grable sang 'Cuddle Up A Little Closer' (by Karl Hoschna and Otto Harbach from *Coney Island*, 20th Century-Fox, 1943), Faye reprised 'You'll Never Know' (by Mack Gordon and Harry Warren, from *Hello, Frisco, Hello*, 20th Century-Fox, 1943), while Miranda again launched into 'I Yi Yi Yi Yi, I Like You Very Much' (by Gordon and Warren, from *That Night In Rio*, 20th Century-Fox, 1941). John Harvey, Phil Silvers, Dick Haymes, Lester Matthews, Paul Harvey and Miles Mander were also in it, and so were Jimmy Dorsey and His Orchestra. Robert Ellis, Helen Logan, and Snag Werris wrote it from a story by Froma Sand and Fred Niblo Jr, Don Loper staged the dances, and it was directed by William A. Seiter. Other songs and musical numbers: *Crazy Me*; *You Send Me*; *How Blue The Night*; *How Many Times Do I Have To Tell You?* Harold Adamson, Jimmy McHugh; *Mr Paganini* Sam Coslow; *No Love, No Nothing* Leo Robin, Harry Warren; *Over There* George M. Cohan; *When The Caissons Go Rolling Along* Edmund L. Gruber.

▽

▷

Bob Crosby (illustrated) was worth his weight in prairie dust in **The Singing Sheriff**, a 60-minute Western spoof from Universal in which he appeared as a Broadway star who, through a series of unlikely circumstances, finds himself playing sheriff in a small mid-western town and rounding up a murderous gang of bandits. Crosby's performance (a collection of double and treble takes) was about as convincing as Henry Blankfort and Eugene Conrad's cornball screenplay (story by John Grey), and it was left to Fay McKenzie, Fuzzy Knight, Iris Adrian, Samuel S. Hinds, Edward Norris, Andrew Tombes, Joe Sawyer and the Spade Cooley Orchestra to salvage what they could of Bernard W. Burton's slapdash production. Leslie Goodwins directed. Crosby sang five of the songs, which included: *Beside The Rio Tonto* Don Raye, Gene De Paul; *Reach For The Sky*; *You Look Good To Me* Inez James, Sidney Miller; *Another Night* Don George, Irving Bibo; *Who's Next* Virginia Wicks, Bill Lava; *When A Cowboy Sings* Dave Franklin.

Rosemary Lane and Johnny Downs (left) starred in **Trocadero** (Republic) as a couple of youngsters who inherit a nightclub, but only make a success of it when they hire a swing band. The rest of the plot was taken care of when romance entered their lives. But the story (by Charles F. Chaplin and Garret Holmes, screenplay by Allen Gale) was secondary to the musical programme, with several big bands (led by Bob Chester, Matt Malneck, Gus Arnheim, Wingy Manone and, the real-life owner of the Trocadero, Eddie Le Baron) contributing strongly to the film's box-office potential. Ida James was also in it (singing Phil Moore's 'Shoo-Shoo Baby'); so were The Radio Rogues, doing a few more of their celebrated imitations. Cartoonist Dave Fleischer did some drawings, and Cliff Nazarro entertained with his double-talk. The cast was completed by Dick Purcell, Ralph Morgan, Sheldon Leonard, Marjorie Manners (right) and Emmett Vogan. It was directed for producer Walter Colmes by old-timer William Nigh. Other songs and musical numbers included: *The Music Goes 'Round And Around* Red Hodgson, Ed Farley, Mike Riley; *Roundabout Way* Sidney Clare, Lew Porter; *Bullfrog Jump*; *How Could You Do That To Me* Porter; *The King Was Doing The Rhumba* Jay Chernis, Porter; *Trying To Forget* Tony Romano; *Can't Take The Place Of You* Walter Colmes, Porter.

Eddie Cantor celebrated thirty-five years in show business by producing and starring in **Show Business** (RKO), an entertaining if familiar backstage yarn in which he played a character called Eddie Martin. The route taken by Joseph Quillan and Dorothy Bennett's screenplay (story by Bert Garnet) ended at the Ziegfeld Follies (by way of Miner's Bowery), and was a conventional rags-to-riches cliché which contained a romantic sub-plot for co-stars George Murphy (left, as a burlesque hoofer) and Constance Moore. Cantor (centre) and Joan Davis supplied the comedy – such as it was – and the cast was completed by attractive Nancy Kelly (right), Don Douglas and Pat Rooney. Nick Castle choreographed and Edwin L. Marin directed. Songs and musical numbers included: *It Had To Be You* (Murphy,

Moore) Gus Kahn, Isham Jones; *I Don't Want To Get Well* (Murphy, Cantor) Howard Johnson, Harry Pease, Harry Jentes; *I Want A Girl* (Murphy, Moore, Cantor, Davis) Harry von Tilzer, William Dillon; *They're Wearing 'Em Higher In Hawaii* (Cantor, Murphy) Joe Goodwin, Halsey K. Mohr; *Alabamy Bound* (Cantor) Buddy De Sylva, Bud Green, Ray Henderson; *The Curse Of An Aching Heart* (Cantor) Harry Fink, Al Piantadosi; *While Strolling Through The Park One Day* (Murphy, Moore, Cantor, Davis) Robert A. King; *Making Whoopee* (Cantor) Walter Donaldson, Gus Kahn; *Dinah* (Murphy, Moore, Cantor, Davis) Sam M. Lewis, Joe Young, Harry Akst; *You May Not Remember* (Kelly) George Jessel, Ben Oakland; *The Daughter Of Rosie O'Grady* (Rooney) Monte Brice, Donaldson.

Leon Errol played twin brothers in **Slightly Terrific** (Universal): an impresario who promises a group of youngsters he will stage their show, and the impresario's manufacturer brother. The two men are mistaken for each other, and the ensuing confusion provided scenarists Edward Dein and Stanley Davis (story by Edith Watkins and Florence McEnany) with barely enough material to spread across the film's 61-minute running time. The younger brigade included Anne Rooney (left), Eddie Quillan, Ray Malone (right) and Betty Kean, with Lillian Cornell. The Stardusters, The Maritza Dancers, The Eight Rhythmeers, Donald Novis, Jayne Forrest and Lorraine Krueger also in it for producer Alexis Thurn-Taxis and director Edward F. Cline. Songs and musical numbers included: *Hold That Line*; *Me And My Whistle*; *A Dream Said Hello*; *Rhythm's What You Need*; *The Happy Polka*; *Stars And Violins* Everett Carter, Milton Rosen; *The Blue Danube* Johann Strauss (melody adapted and lyric written by Katherine Bellamann); *Put Your Arms Around Me Honey* Junie McCree, Albert von Tilzer.

What happened to a Merchant Marine crew during their seven days shore leave in San Francisco, was chronicled without much panache or originality in **Seven Days Ashore** (RKO). Wally Brown, Alan Carney, Alan Dinehart, Marcy McGuire (centre), Gordon Oliver, Margaret Dumont, Dooley Wilson, Virginia Mayo, Marjorie Gateson, as well as Freddie Slack and Freddie Fisher and their bands were featured in Edward Verdier, Irving Phillips and Lawrence Kimble's screenplay (story by Jacques Deval); Charles O'Curran was in charge of the dances and it was produced and directed by John H. Auer. Songs and musical numbers included: *Apple Blossoms In The Rain*; *Hail And Farewell*; *Jive Samba*; *Ready, Aim, Kiss*; *Sioux City Sue* Mort Greene, Lew Pollack.

Jam Session (Columbia) was a tuneful miscellany aimed specifically at hepcats and with only one purpose in mind: to unleash on them a set of swinging musical numbers. Hence Charlie Barnet and His Band gave out with 'Cherokee' (by Ray Noble); Louis Armstrong was seen and heard in 'I Can't Give You Anything But Love' (by Dorothy Fields and Jimmy McHugh); Teddy Powell and His Orchestra were on hand for 'Murder He Says' (by Frank Loesser and Jimmy McHugh); Glen Gray and his boys delivered a Gray original called 'No Name Jive'; Jan Garber and Orchestra played 'I Lost My Sugar In Salt Lake City' (by Leon René and Johnny Lange), while Nan Wynn sang 'Brazil' (by S.K. Russell and Ary Barroso) and The Pied Pipers gave out 'It Started All Over Again' (by Bill Carey and Carl Fischer). Ann Miller (illustrated centre), who top-starred, wound up the proceedings with Sammy Cahn and Jule Styne's 'Victory Polka'. Manny Seff's screenplay (story by Harlan Ware and Patterson McNutt) featured Miller as the winner of a dance contest, her prize being a round-trip ticket to Hollywood. The plot, such as it was, involved Miss Miller in a romance with a screenwriter (Jess Barker) whose career she almost ruins through a series of unintentional mishaps. Stanley Donen staged the numbers, Irving Briskin produced, Charles Barton directed and the supporting cast included Charles D. Brown, Eddie Kane, George Eldredge, Renie Riano and Clarence Muse. Other songs and musical numbers: *Teddy Bear Boogie* (Powell and Orch) Teddy Powell; *St Louis Blues* (Armstrong) W.C. Handy; *Jive Bomber* (Powell and Orch) Lyle 'Spud' Murphy; *C-Jam Blues* Duke Ellington.

Considering its total absence of star names, **Stars on Parade** (Columbia) was something of a misnomer, but quite entertaining just the same. Another 'let's-put-on-a-show' effort (this time to demonstrate to the talent-seeking producers of Los Angeles that there is an abundance of saleable young performers in their very own back yard), it featured Larry Parks (left), Lynn Merrick (seated centre), Ray Walker (centre), Jeff Donnell, Judy Clark (2nd right), Robert Williams (right) and Selmer Jackson as well as Frank and Jean Hubert (doing their popular drunk act), The Chords doing their musical instrument imitations, The Ben Carter Choir in a selection of negro spirituals, The King Cole Trio, and tenor Danny O'Neill. Monte Brice wrote it, Wallace MacDonald produced and the director was Lew Landers. Songs and musical numbers included: *My Heart Isn't In It* Jack Lawrence; *It's Love Love Love* Mack David, Joan Whitney, Alex Kramer; *Ezekiel Saw The Wheel* negro spiritual; *When They Ask About You* Sammy Stept; *Jumpin' At The Jubilee* Ben Carter, Mayes Marshall; *Taking Care Of You* Lew Brown, Harry Akst; *Where Am I Without You?* Don Raye, Gene De Paul; *Two Hearts In The Dark* Dave Franklin; *Somewhere This Side of Heaven*.

MGM threw a great deal of talent but not much ▷ craftsmanship into **Broadway Rhythm**. Garishly photographed in Technicolor, it was inspired by the Jerome Kern-Oscar Hammerstein II stage show *Very Warm For May*, but retained only the great Kern ballad 'All The Things You Are' sung by Ginny Simms – a Louis B. Mayer favourite who failed to achieve stardom – preceded by a perfunctory medley of 'That Lucky Fellow,' 'In Other Words' 'Seventeen' and 'All In Fun' sung by George Murphy. All about a Broadway producer (Murphy) and the problems that beset his latest show, the film served as a showcase for several talented young people, most notably Lena Horne who, hideously costumed and against a strikingly awful set, did her best with 'Brazilian Boogie' by Hugh Martin and Ralph Blane (see illustration). She was better served in the more simply staged 'Somebody Loves Me' (by Buddy De Sylva, Ballard MacDonald and George Gershwin). Nancy Walker and Ben Blue were terrific in the delightfully eccentric 'Milkman Keep Those Bottles Quiet' (by Don Raye and Gene De Paul), and the three Ross Sisters, contortionists *extraordinaire*, twisted their bodies into some really weird shapes to the tune of 'Solid Potato Salad' (by Raye and De Paul), and 'Manhattan Serenade' (by Louis Alter). Gloria De Haven and Charles Winninger as Murphy's sister and father sang and danced 'Pretty Baby' (by Gus Kahn, Tony Jackson and Egbert Van Alstyne) with Kenny Bowers and, from Dean Murphy, there were several impersonations – the one of Bette Davis coming off best. The cast was completed by Eddie (Rochester) Anderson, Hazel Scott, and Tommy Dorsey and His Orchestra. Scenarists Dorothy Kingsley and Harry Clork had the unenviable task of concocting a screenplay from a story by Jack McGowan that would accommodate the various talents on hand while still making sense of the narrative, and it was directed (without any visual flair at all) by Roy Del Ruth for producer Jack Cummings. Other songs and musical numbers: *Oh You Beautiful Doll* (Winninger) A. Seymour Brown, Nat D. Ayer; *Amor* (Simms) Sunny Skylar, Gabriel Ruiz, Ricardo Lopez Mendez; *I Love Corny Music* (Winninger, Dorsey); *Irresistible You* (Murphy, Simms, Dorsey); *Who's Who In Your Love Life?* (Ensemble) Raye, De Paul; *National Emblem March* (Dorsey) E.E. Bagley; *What Do You Think I Am?* (De Haven, Bowers) Hugh Martin, Ralph Blane; *Waltz in D Flat, Opus 64, No 1* ('Minute Waltz') (Hazel Scott) Chopin; *Ida, Sweet As Apple Cider* (Bowers) Eddie Leonard, Eddie Munson; *A Frangesa* (orchestral) P.M. Costa.

Bathing Beauty (MGM) covered a peanut of a plot (songwriter enrols as a student at a women's college to be near his swimming-instructress wife) with lashings of Technicolored icing, and the result was a lavish piece of escapist entertainment on a par with 20th Century-Fox's *The Gang's All Here* (1943). It starred Red Skelton as the songwriter and Esther Williams as his instructress wife, with Basil Rathbone, Janis Paige, Bill Goodwin, Jean Porter, Carlos Ramirez, Donald Meek, Margaret Dumont, and Jacqueline Daly also in it for producer Jack Cummings and director George Sidney. Skelton drew attention away from Kenneth Earl, M.M. Musselman and Curtis Kenyon's story (adaptation by Joseph Schrank, screenplay by Dorothy Kingsley, Allen Boretz and Frank Waldman) in a series of comic routines, the best being his participation (complete with tutu) in a ballet class; and there was diversion too, from Harry James and His Orchestra (with Helen Forrest singing 'I Cried For You' by Arthur Freed, Gus Arnheim and Abe Lyman); Xavier Cugat and His Orchestra (with Lina Romay singing 'Bim Bam Boom' by J. Camacho and Noro Morales); and organist Ethel Smith with her electrifying version of 'Tico-Tico' (by Zequinha Abreu). But nothing topped the spectacular water ballet (illustrated) that climaxed the film. Staged by John Murray Anderson, it featured Esther Williams (centre) and several dozen aquatic chorines in a deliciously kitschy rendition of Strauss's 'Blue Danube Waltz' with alternate jets of water and flame bursting out of an Olympic-sized swimming pool to the rhythms of the music. The rest of the show was choreographed by Robert Alton and Jack Donohue. Other songs and musical numbers: *By The Waters of Minnetonka* (Smith) Thurlow Lieurance, J.M. Cavanass; *Hora Staccato* (James) Grigoras Dinicu, Jascha Heifetz; *Te Quiero Dijiste* (*Magic Is The Moonlight*) (Ramirez) Maria Grever, Charles Pasquale; *I'll Take The High Note* (Skelton, James, Porter, Smith, Janis Paige, Ramirez, Forrest, Buddy Moreno) Harold Adamson, Johnny Green; *Trumpet Blues and Cantabile* (James); James, Jack Mathias; *Loch Lomond* (girls' chorus) traditional.

Another war-time parade of talent for the especial delight of the lads at the front, **Follow The Boys** ransacked Universal's list of contract artists (and added several free-lancers) to come up with a star-studded tribute to the many artists who brought entertainment to the troops via the Hollywood Victory Committee. Lou Breslow and Gertrude Purcell's screenplay contained the merest smidgin of a plot (about hoofer George Raft's neglect of his wife Vera Zorina – both illustrated – and his involvement with the effort), but it was nothing more than a shaky clothes line on which to peg the contributions of the guest stars. Using footage of celebrities doing actual wartime entertainment duty, producer Charles K. Feldman concocted a film whose historic interest today far outweighs its achievement as a piece of film-making. Charles Grapewin, Grace McDonald, Charles Butterworth, George Macready, Elizabeth Patterson Theodore von Eltz and Regis Toomey completed the cast, as far as the 'plot' was concerned, though it was the guest artists audiences really came to see. They included Dinah Shore singing 'I'll Get By' (by Roy Turk and Fred Ahlert), 'I'll Walk Alone' (by Jule Styne and Sammy Cahn) and 'Mad About Him, Sad About Him, How Can I Be Glad Without Him Blues' (by Larry Marks and Dick Charles); Sophie Tucker, who sang 'Some Of These Days' (by Shelton Brooks) and 'The Bigger The Army And The Navy' (by Jack Yellen); Jeanette MacDonald reprising 'Beyond The Blue Horizon' (by Richard A. Whiting, W. Franke Harling and Leo Robin), as well as Gus Kahn and Isham Jones's 'I'll See You In My

Dreams'; the Andrews Sisters performing a ▷ medley of past and present hits including 'Bei Mir Bist Du Schoen' (by Sammy Cahn, Saul Chaplin, Jacob Jacobs, Sholom Secunda); 'Beer Barrel Polka' (by Lew Brown and Jaromir Vejvoda) and 'Shoo Shoo Baby' (by Phil Moore); Artur Rubinstein playing Chopin's 'Polonaise in A Flat', and – from the sublime to the ridiculous – The Delta Rhythm Boys doing 'The House I Live In' (by Earl Robinson and Lewis Allan). Also featured were Orson Welles and Marlene Dietrich (in a magic act), Donald O'Connor and Peggy Ryan, W.C. Fields, Carmen Amaya, Leo and Gautier's Dog Act, The Bricklayers, Ted Lewis, Freddie Slack, Charlie Spivak and Louis Jordan and their orchestras and, in the Hollywood Victory Committee sequence, Maria Montez, Susanna Foster, Louise Allbritton, Robert Paige, Alan Curtis, Lon Chaney Jr, Gloria Jean, Andy Devine, Turhan Bey, Evelyn Ankers, Noah Beery Jr, Samuel S. Hinds, Louise Beavers, Clarence Muse, Gale Sondergaard, Peter Coe, Nigel Bruce, Thomas Gomez, Martha O'Driscoll, Maxie Rosenbloom, Lois Collier, Elyse Knox, and Randolph Scott. The choreographers were George Hale and Joe Schoenfeld, and the film was directed by Edward Sutherland. Other songs and musical numbers included: *A Better Day Is Coming* Cahn, Styne; *Tonight* Kermit Goell, Walter Donaldson; *Is You Is Or Is You Ain't My Baby?* Billy Austin, Louis Jordan; *I Feel A Song Coming On* Dorothy Fields, Jimmy McHugh, George Oppenheimer; *Kittens With Their Mittens Laced* Inez James, Buddy Pepper; *Liebestraum* Liszt.

△

Jack Haley (illustrated left), the star of **Take It Big** (Paramount), spent much of the film's 76 minutes bemoaning his lot as the rear section of Pansy the horse in an act he shares with Richard Lane (the horse's front), singer Harriet Hilliard, and band leader Ozzie Nelson. Then one day he inherits a dude ranch and believes his troubles are over. But they're just beginning – for the swanky establishment he takes possession of belongs to someone else, *his* ranch being a dilapidated old property on the verge of collapse. The drivel was partially rescued by Miss Hilliard's pleasant vocalizing, the singing of Frank Forest (who, at one point, launched into an aria from Rossini's 'The Barber of Seville') and several good tunes by Jerry Seelen and Lester Lee; but the best tune was 'Sunday, Monday Or Always', an established hit by Johnny Burke and Jimmy Van Heusen, which Crosby had introduced in *Dixie* (Paramount, 1943). The film also featured Arline Judge, Mary Beth Hughes, Fritz Feld, Fuzzy Knight, Lucille Gleason and Nils T. Granlund. It was written by Howard J. Green, with Frank McDonald directing for producers William Pine and William Thomas. Other songs and musical numbers included: *Love And Learn*; *Life Can Be Beautiful*; *Take It Big*; *I'm A Big Success With You*.

With over two million copies of her famous pin-up girl pose (i.e. the one in which she wears a white bathing suit and looks seductively over her shoulder) adorning the lockers of servicemen everywhere, it was only a matter of time before 20th Century-Fox featured their blonde star Betty Grable (illustrated centre) in a musical called, quite simply, **Pin-Up Girl**. The results, however, were far from favourable, due, in the main, to an asinine screenplay by Robert Ellis, Helen Logan and Earl Baldwin (story by Libbie Block) that cast Grable as a stenographer in Washington who, after meeting Navy hero John Harvey, pretends to be a Broadway star. Joe E. Brown and Martha Raye were drafted into the sliver of a plot to provide humour, and for audiences who found it difficult enough taking them on their own, the combination was decidedly deadly. For spectacle there was The Skating Vanities in an interminable number called 'Red Robins, Bob Whites and Blue Birds' ▽

(by Mack Gordon and James V. Monaco, who provided the film with all its music and lyrics); while the energetic Condos Brothers tapped themselves into quite a frenzy on two breathless occasions. Grable and choreographer Hermes Pan danced together in a production number called 'Once Too Often'; and Martha Raye did exactly what was expected of her in 'Yankee Doodle Hayride'. The film ended with a military-style finale (led by Grable) that was a stultifying bore. Eugene Pallette, Dorothea Kent, Dave Willock, Robert Homans, Marcel Dalio, Roger Clark and Charles Spivak and His Orchestra completed the cast. Bruce Humberstone directed, and it was produced (in Technicolor) by William Le Baron. Grable was seven months pregnant when the film was completed. Other songs and musical numbers: *You're My Little Pin-Up Girl*; *Time Alone Will Tell*; *Don't Carry Tales Out of School*; *Story Of The Very Merry Widow*.

Forties Musicals

The cast list of **Sensations of 1945** (United Artists) included Eleanor Powell (as a lady with a penchant for getting her name in the papers), W.C. Fields, Sophie Tucker (doing one of her standards called 'You Can't Sew A Button On A Heart'), Cab Calloway and Woody Herman and their bands, The Lew Paul Trio, The Pallenberg Bears, David Lichine, Gene Rodgers, The Coplands, Mel Hall, 'Uncle Willie', The Johnson Brothers, Hubert Castle, Dorothy Donegan and The Cristianis, as well as Dennis O'Keefe, C. Aubrey Smith, Eugene Pallette, Mimi Forsythe, Lyle Talbot and Bert Roach. That they were quite unable to give producer-director Andrew Stone's casserole a distinctive flavour was due to the anything-goes manner of its presentation and a storyline by Frederick Jackson (screenplay by Dorothy Bennett and Andrew Stone) that was so tenuous – involving, as it did, Miss Powell (illustrated) in a series of promotional stunts, one of which lands her in jail – it might just as easily have been dispensed with altogether. It was choreographed by Lichine and Charles O'Curran. Songs and musical numbers included: *Mister Hepster's Dictionary; Wake Up Man You're Slippin'; One Love; Kiss Serenade; No Never; Spin Little Pin Ball* Harry Tobias, Al Sherman.

Martha Tilton (left), best known as a swing singer with Benny Goodman's band, starred in **Swing Hostess** (PRC), a really hackneyed effort about a singer's frustrated attempts to find employment with a band. Iris Adrian (centre), Cliff Nazarro, Harry Holman (right), Emmet Lynn, Betty Brodel, and Charles Collins and His Band were also in it; Louise Rousseau and Gail Davenport wrote it and Sam Neufeld produced and directed. Songs and musical numbers included: *I'll Eat My Hat; Let's Capture This Moment; Say It With Love; Music To My Ears; Highway Polka; Got An Invitation* Ray Evans, Jay Livingston, Lewis Bellin.

Frank Sinatra, at the height of his popularity, received top billing in **Step Lively** (RKO), a musical remake of the Marx Brothers comedy *Room Service* (RKO, 1938). He played a playwright and his co-star was George Murphy as a small-time revue producer holed up in a hotel with a cast of twenty, and no money to pay the bill. Gloria De Haven (in bath) appeared as a curvaceous showgirl who takes Sinatra's fancy, with Adolphe Menjou, Walter Slezak, Eugene Pallette, Wally Brown, Alan Carney, Anne Jeffreys and Grant Mitchell completing the cast. If a singing playwright wasn't exactly true to the frenzied spirit of the John Murray-Allen Boretz play on which it was based, Sinatra's legion of screaming fans certainly didn't complain, and with his vocalizing of such Jule Styne-Sammy Cahn numbers as 'Come Out, Come Out Wherever You Are', 'As Long As There's Music' and 'Some Other Time', he had them swooning in the aisles. The musical numbers were staged by Ernest Matray; Warren Duff and Peter Milne wrote it; Tim Whelan directed with a jolly sense of pace, and the producer was Robert Fellows. Other songs: *Where Does Love Begin; Ask The Madame; Why Must There Be An Opening Song?* Styne, Cahn.

Betty Hutton (right), now earning $5,000 a week, was again teamed with Dorothy Lamour (centre left) in **And The Angels Sing** (Paramount). They in turn were joined by Diana Lynn (centre right) and Mimi Chandler (left) to form a quartet of sisters (called Angel) whose vocal talents are 'discovered' by Fred MacMurray, a conniving bandleader who fleeces them of $190 but nonetheless finishes up in the arms of Miss Lamour. A rather slapdash affair, knocked together by Melvin Frank and Norman Panama from the fragments of story provided by Claude Binyon, it did at least allow the frenetic Miss Hutton to shine in several Johnny Burke-Jimmy Van Heusen songs, the best being 'Bluebirds In My Belfry' and 'His Rocking Horse Ran Away'. For the rest, it was pretty witless stuff, with Raymond Walburn as the girls' easy-going father, Eddie Foy Jr, Frank Albertson, Mikhail Rasumny and Frank Faylen also cast. Danny Dare choreographed, the producer was E.D. Leshin and it was directed with little sparkle by George Marshall. Other songs and musical numbers: *For The First Hundred Years; It Could Happen To You; Knocking On Your Own Front Door; How Does Your Garden Grow; My Heart's Wrapped Up In Gingham; When Stanislaus Got Married* Burke, Van Heusen.

Gloria Jean starred in **Reckless Age** (Universal), a 63-minute quickie which found her rebelling against the rules of her home life as laid down by her wealthy grandfather (Henry Stephenson), running away and, unbeknown to Grandpa, joining one of his many dime stores as a clerk. She sang three songs, 'Il Bacio' (by Luigi Arditi), 'The Cradle Song' (by Irving Bibo, based on Brahms's *Wiegenlied*), and 'Santa Lucia' (by Teodoro Cottrau), with other musical numbers going to Harold Nicholas of the pre-war Nicholas Brothers, who did a song-and-dance version of 'Mama Yo Quiero' (by Al Stillman and Jaraca and Vincente Paiva), and The Delta Rhythm Boys. Kathleen Howard was also in it, so were Jane Darwell, Franklin Pangborn (centre foreground), Andrew Tombes, Marshall Thompson (centre), Lloyd Corrigan, and nightclub comedian Jack Gilford, whose contribution to producer-director Felix F. Feist's workaday programmer was a sketch about an employee trying to keep awake during a pep talk from the boss, first introduced by Gilford in the 1940 stage revue *Meet The People*. Gertrude Purcell and Henry Blankfort wrote the screenplay from an original story by Al Martin. Other songs and musical numbers included: *Get On Board Little Children* Don Raye, Gene De Paul; *Very Often On My Face* Bill Grage, Grace Shannon.

An oater with music, starring Jane Frazee and such radio favourites as The Hoosier Hotshots, Cousin Emmy (illustrated centre), Jimmy Wakely and His Oklahoma Cowboys, Red River Dave and, from Harlem, The King Cole Trio, Columbia's **Swing in the Saddle** (GB: **Swing and Sway**) designed for backward (or, at best, back-wood) audiences, told the story of a couple of actresses (Frazee and Sally Bliss) in the west who find themselves mistaken for kitchen help. Elizabeth Beecher, Morton Grant and Bradford Ropes's screenplay (from a story by Maurice Leo) had them going along with the idea in order to discover the identity of a 'lonely hearts' correspondent who has proposed marriage to them. Guinn Williams, Slim Summerville, Mary Treen, Carole Mathews and Byron Foulger also appeared for producer Jack Fier, and the director was Lew Landers. Songs and musical numbers included: *Amor* Sunny Skylar, Gabriel Ruiz; *Hey Mabel* Fred Stryker; *By The River Sainte Marie* Edgar Leslie, Harry Warren; *She Broke My Heart In Three Places* Oliver Drake; *When It's Harvest Time In Peaceful Valley* Robert Martin, Raymond McKee; *There'll Be A Jubilee* Phil Moore.
▽

Crooner Benny Fields (illustrated right) was the *raison d'être* for **Minstrel Man** (PRC), a senti-mental weepie, about a minstrel headliner (Fields) who allows his daughter to be reared by Gladys George and Alan Dinehart after his wife (Molly Lamont) dies in childbirth. Meanwhile Fields continues to pursue his career wherever he can. Years later, with his daughter (Judy Clark, illustrated in blackface) now grown up and a per-former herself, he returns in time to catch the opening night of her show, and, in the best Holly-wood tradition, joins her on stage in a chorus of his hit song 'Remember Me To Carolina' (by Paul Francis Webster and Harry Revel). Apart from Fields's easy-going personality, the film was notable for its musical arrangements by Ferde Grofé. Roscoe Karns, Jerome Cowan, John Raitt, Eddie Kane and The Ernestos completed the cast for producer Leo Fromkess. Irwin Franklin and Pierre Gendron wrote it from a story by Martin Mooney and Raymond L. Schrock, and the director was Joseph H. Lewis. Other songs: *My Melancholy Baby* George A. Norton, Ernie Bur-nett; *Cindy*; *I Don't Care If The World Knows About It*; *Shakin' Hands With The Sun*; *The Bamboo Cane* Webster, Revel.
▽

It took 61 minutes for **South Of Dixie** (Universal) ▷ to tell the lightweight, far-fetched tale of a phoney writer of Southern pop tunes (David Bruce, on bed) who, after being promoted as a subject for a film biography, has to go South to whip up a suitable family background for him-self. He takes Southerner Anne Gwynne along to tutor him in the proper accent, and also finds himself involved in a romance with the daugh-ter (Ella Mae Morse) of a Southern colonel (Samuel S. Hinds). Jerome Cowan (kneeling), Joe Sawyer, Eddie Acuff, Marie Harmon, Oscar O'Shea and Louise Beavers were also cast; Clyde Bruckman wrote it from a story by Sam Coslow, and it was produced and directed by Jean Yarbrough. Songs and musical numbers in-cluded: *Shoo Shoo Baby* Phil Moore; *Never Again*; *I'm A-Headin' South*; *Loo-Loo-Louisiana*; *Cross My Heart* Everett Carter, Milton Rosen; *When It's Darkness On The Delta* Marty Symes, A.J. Neiberg, Jerry Livingston; *Weep No More My Lady* Joan Whitney, Alex Cramer.

One of Bing Crosby's best, and best-loved, films, **Going My Way** was a heart-warming hit from Paramount that revealed the popular crooner (right) to be the possessor of more than just a melting voice. He played Father Chuck O'Malley, a young Catholic priest sent to Saint Dominic's Church to take over the day-to-day running of it from Father Fitzgibbon (Barry Fitzgerald), the last of whose 45 years as pastor has resulted in a general decline (through old age and old-fashioned ideas) in the premises and in the number of people attending services. The film's mainstay was the relationship between the two men, which producer-director Leo McCarey never allowed to topple over into sentimentality, even though he came pretty close to it every now and then. A first-rate screenplay by Frank Butler and Frank Cavett (original story by McCarey) also contributed substantially to the film's overall success; as did its pleasing score, especially the tender 'Too-ra-loo-ra-loo-ra' (by J.R. Shannon) sung by Crosby to Fitzgerald, and 'Swingin' On A Star' (by Johnny Burke and Jimmy Van Heusen) per-formed by Crosby and a group of kids. Frank McHugh, *diva* Rise Stevens, Gene Lockhart, William Frawley, James Brown (left), Jean Hea-ther (centre), Porter Hall, Fortunio Bonanova and Eily Malyon made up the excellent support-ing cast. Also featured were the Robert Mitchell Boys' Choir. Other songs included: *The Day After Forever* (Crosby, Heather); *Going My Way* (Crosby, Stevens) Burke, Van Heusen; *Silent Night* (Crosby, Robert Mitchell Boys' Choir) Franz Gruber, Joseph Mohr; *Habanera* (Stevens) from Bizet's 'Carmen'; *Ave Maria* Schubert.
▽

△

Carmen Miranda (illustrated centre) was top-starred for the first time in **Greenwich Village** (20th Century-Fox), one of the studio's few financially unsuccessful Technicolor musicals of the period, and was unable to carry the entire production (as she was expected to do) on her slender shoulders. Her co-stars, Don Ameche and William Bendix, weren't much help either, their names not being strong enough to light up the marquees of the world with promise and expectation. All about a composer (Ameche) who, in the 1920s arrives in Greenwich Village, falls in love with a singer and finds his concerto turned into a smash hit song thanks to nightclub proprietor Bendix presenting it in a flashy show uptown, it also featured Vivian Blaine (as the singer Ameche falls for), with other roles in scenarists Earl Baldwin and Walter Bullock's fabrication (based on a story by Frederick Hazlitt Brennan, adapted by Michael Fessier and Ernest S. Pagano) going to Felix Bressart, B.S. Pully, Emil Rameau and Frank Orth. Padding out the slender material were dancers Tony and Sally de Marco, a group called The Revuers – Judy Holliday, Betty Comden and Adolph Green (whose act was cut from the release print) and The Four Step Brothers. The surviving specialties were all far more entertaining than the top-billed performers. William Le Baron produced, and the director was Walter Lang. Songs and musical numbers included: *I Like To Be Loved By You* Vermelho, Silva; *I'm Down To My Last Dream*; *It Goes To Your Toes*; *Give Me A Band And A Bandana*; *Oh Brother*; *It's All For Art's Sake*; *I Have To See You Privately*; *This Is Our Lucky Day*; *You Make Me So Mad*; *Never Before*; *I've Been Smiling In My Sleep*; *Tell Me It's You*; *That Thing They Talk About* Leo Robin, Nacio Herb Brown; *Whispering* John Schonberger, Richard Coburn, Vincent Rose; *Swinging' Down The Lane* Gus Kahn, Isham Jones; *When You Wore A Tulip* Jack Mahoney, Percy Wenrich; *I'm Just Wild About Harry* Eubie Blake, Noble Sissle.

A modest, and modestly enjoyable, excursion into nostalgia, **Atlantic City** (Republic) chronicled the attempts of a young impresario (Brad Taylor) to turn Atlantic City into an international playground. The problems he encountered, both in his private and professional life, formed the basis of Doris Gilbert, Frank Gill Jr and George Carleton Brown's screenplay (story by Arthur Caesar), but by the final fade they were resolved to everyone's satisfaction. Constance Moore (kneeling right) was top-cast as the neglected wife who walks out on Taylor (but returns after his amusement pier is reduced to ashes in a fire), with other roles going to Charles Grapewin, Jerry Colonna (centre, appearing in various guises as a general factotum) and Robert E. Castaine, plus Al Shean and Jack Kenny (as Gallagher and Shean), Gus Van and Charles Marsh (as Van and Schenck), Belle Baker, Jose Frisco, Buck and Bubbles, and Paul Whiteman and Louis Armstrong with their orchestras. Seymour Felix choreographed ('Kiddyland Revue' sequence illustrated), Albert J. Cohen produced, and it was directed by Ray McCarey. Songs and musical numbers included: *Nobody's Sweetheart* Gus Kahn, Ernie Erdman, Billy Meyers, Elmer Schoebel; *Mister Gallagher And Mister Shean* Gallagher, Shean; *On A Sunday Afternoon* Andrew B. Sterling, Harry von Tilzer; *Ain't Misbehavin'* Andy Razaf, Fats Waller, Harry Brooks; *After You've Gone* Henry Creamer, Turner Layton; *I Ain't Got Nobody* Roger Graham, Dave Peyton, Spencer Williams; *By The Beautiful Sea* Harry Carroll, Harold Atteridge; *The Bird On Nellie's Hat* Arthur J. Lamb, Alfred Solman; *Darktown Strutters' Ball* Shelton Brooks.

Anne Shirley (2nd right), Dennis Day (centre) and Philip Terry (centre right) proved no draw at all for **Music in Manhattan** (RKO), a rather mindless programmer which found Miss Shirley, much to her discomfort, being pursued by an air force hero (Terry) whom, a short while before, she had pretended she was married to. The story, devised by Maurice Tombragel, Hal Smith and Jack Scholl (screenplay by Lawrence Kimble), made no sense at all, and at best, was an excuse for the film's musical numbers which Charles O'Curran staged without flair, and which featured the orchestras of Charlie Barnet and Nilo Menendez as well as Bob Mascagno and Italia De Nubila. Raymond Walburn (left), Jane Darwell (right) and Patti Brill completed the cast for producer-director John H. Auer. Songs and musical numbers included: *Did You Happen To Find A Heart?*; *One Night In Acapulco*; *When Romance Comes Along*; *Mexico*; *I Can See You Now* Herb Magidson, Lew Pollack.

246

Very much a *Road To . . .* film at heart, but with Eddie Bracken and Gil Lamb substituting for Crosby and Hope, **Rainbow Island** (Paramount) did at least have Dorothy Lamour (illustrated, top starred) giving audiences a taste of what it might have been had her two regular travellers been on hand to dispense the mirth and the music. All about a trio of sailors (Bracken, Lamb and Barry Sullivan) who find themselves cast away on a Pacific Island, the story (by Seena Owen, screenplay by Walter DeLeon and Arthur Phillips) was mainly concerned with the trio's attempts to keep themselves from being taken as sacrificial victims by the island's resident natives. They succeed, of course, in this case thanks solely to Bracken's resemblance to one of their local gods. A moderately entertaining spoof which had Lamour sending herself up in a sarong (and singing 'Beloved' by Ted Koehler and Burton Lane), it could have done with a slightly more inventive script than the one it had but, on the credit side, it allowed Bracken to give his most effective comic performance to date. Forrest Orr, Anne Revere, Reed Hadley, Marc Lawrence (left), Adia Kuznetzoff, Olga San Juan and Elena Verdugo were also cast; it was produced (in Technicolor) by Sol C. Siegel, choreographed by Danny Dare and directed by Ralph Murphy. Other songs and musical numbers: *What A Day Tomorrow*; *We Have So Little Time*; *The Boogie Woogie Man Will Get You If You Don't Watch Out* Koehler, Lane.

Danny Kaye (centre) made a spectacularly successful bid for screen stardom in his first film, **Up In Arms**, produced in Technicolor by Sam Goldwyn and released by RKO. Arriving in Hollywood via vaudeville, the 'Borscht Circuit', Broadway, and the nightclubs, Kaye's cinematic debut was described by one critic at the time as the most exciting since Garbo's, and watching him work in **Up In Arms** it is not difficult to see why he inspired such extravagant plaudits. As Danny Weems, a hypochondriac employed as an elevator boy in a building full of doctors, his performance offered a whacky blend of inspired clowning and madcap exuberance (as well as some excellent singing) that had the added distinction of being totally original. A drastic reworking of Eddie Cantor's 1930 vehicle *Whoopee* (United Artists), **Up In Arms**'s screenplay (by Don Hartman, Allan Boretz and Robert Pirosh) made good use of Kaye's unique talents, involving him in a plot in which he, his room-mate (Dana Andrews, left) and their respective

Bob Crosby (left) starred in a woebegone filler from Columbia called **Meet Miss Bobby Socks**. He played a war veteran who finds fame as a crooner, as well as romance in the shape of Lynn Merrick (right). All that audiences found was 68 minutes of *ennui*. Ina Ray Hutton co-starred, and the rest of the cast included Louis Jordan, Louise Erickson (2nd left), the Kim Loo Sisters, Pat Parrish, Mary Currier (centre), and Howard Freeman (2nd right). It was written by Muriel Roy Bolton, produced by Ted Richmond, and directed by Glenn Tryon. Songs and musical numbers included: *Fellow On A Furlough* Bobby Worth; *I'm Not Afraid* Kim Gannon, Walter Kent; *Come With Me My Honey* Mack David, Joan Whitney, Alex Kramer; *Two Heavens* Don George, Ted Grouya; *Deacon Jones* Johnny Lange, Hy Heath, Richard Loring.

girlfriends (Dinah Shore, right, and Constance Dowling) find themselves drafted to the Pacific. In between the resultant confusion, there were several well staged (by Danny Dare) production numbers, the most memorable being Kaye's 'Manic-Depressive Pictures Presents' (by Sylvia Fine, soon to become Mrs Kaye, and Max Liebman), a paean to movie credits which took place in the lobby of a cinema. Another Fine and Liebman contribution was 'Melody In 4F' – a typical Kaye scat song first performed by him in Cole Porter's 1941 Broadway hit, *Let's Face It*. Also in the cast for director Elliott Nugent were Louis Calhern, George Mathews, Benny Baker, Elisha Cook Jr, Lyle Talbot, June Lang, Walter Catlett, Donald Dickson, Margaret Dumont and Richard Powers, and The Goldwyn Girls (including Virginia Mayo who would soon be appearing in several more Kaye vehicles as a star in her own right). Other songs and musical numbers: *Now I Know*; *All Out For Freedom*; *Tess's Torch Song*; *Jive Number* Ted Koehler, Harold Arlen.

Twelve musical numbers were spread over 62 minutes in **Twilight on the Prairie** (Universal), leaving very little time for scenarist Clyde Bruckman to develop his plot (from an original story by Warren Wilson) about a buckaroo radio band (illustrated) who, after finding themselves marooned in Texas while on their way to Hollywood to make a picture, are given employment in a ranch owned by Vivian Austin, and run by a dyspeptic Leon Errol. Eddie Quillan received top billing and the rest of the cast included Johnny Downs, Connie Haines, Dennis Moore, and Jack Teagarden and His Band. A routine filler aimed at the lower half of a double bill, it was produced by Warren Wilson and directed by Jean Yarbrough. Songs and musical numbers included: *Let's Love Again*; *Where The Prairie Meets The Sky*; *Don't You Ever Be A Cowboy* Everett Carter, Milton Rosen; *Texas Polka* Oakley Haldeman, Vic Knight, Lew Porter; *No Letter Today* Frankie Brown; *I Got Mellow In The Yellow Of The Moon* Jimmy Dodd; *Sip Nip Song* Don George, Brenda Weisberg; *Salt-Water Cowboy* Redd Evans; *The Blues* Jack Teagarden; *Little Brown Jug* Joseph E. Winner; *And Then* Sidney Mitchell, Sammy Stept.

The music publishing business formed the background of **Kansas City Kitty** (Columbia), a programmer in which Joan Davis (illustrated at piano) starred as a song plugger who is tricked into buying a publishing house, only to have a plagiarism suit flung at her by an irate composer claiming that 'Kansas City Kitty', the hit song published by the firm, wasn't written by the cowboy who has put his name to it but by himself. Matt Willis was the outraged songsmith, with other roles in Ted Richmond's indifferent little production going to Jane Frazee (centre left) and Bob Crosby (who had little to do in Manny Seff's trifling screenplay), Erik Rolf, Tim Ryan, Robert Emmett Keane, John Bond, and The Williams Brothers (all four illustrated, Andy right). Stanley Donen staged the dances, Del Lord directed. Songs included: *Kansas City Kitty* Walter Donaldson, Edgar Leslie; *Tico Tico* Zequinha Abreu, Ervin Drake; *Nothing Boogie From Nowhere* Saul Chaplin; *Pretty Kitty Blue Eyes* Mann Curtis, Vic Mizzy.

The backstage trials and tribulations that befall a vaudeville family called the Monahans was the hackneyed subject of Universal's **The Merry Monahans** which – apart from Donald O'Connor, Peggy Ryan and Jack Oakie (featured centre) playing the family in question – offered cinema audiences a nostalgic trip down memory lane to the musical accompaniment of at least twenty old favourites from way back when. Ann Blyth was also among the cast and sang 'Isle d'Amour' by Earl Carroll and Leo Edwards and 'When You Wore A Tulip' by Jack Mahoney and Percy Wenrich, with other parts in Michael Fessier and Ernest Pagano's how-many-times-have-we-seen-it-before? screenplay going to Rosemary De Camp, John Miljan, Gavin Muir, Isabel Jewell, Robert Homans and Marion Martin, Louis Da Pron and Carlos Romero were in charge of the musical staging, Fessier and Pagano produced, and it was directed by Charles Lamont. Songs and musical numbers included: *Lovely*; *Beautiful To Look At*; *We're Having A Wonderful Time*; *Impersonations*; *Stop Foolin'* Don George, Irving Bibo; *What Do You Want To Make Those Eyes At Me For?* Howard Johnson, Joseph McCarthy, James V. Monaco; *Rock-A-Bye Your Baby With A Dixie Melody* Sam Lewis, Joe Young, Jean Schwartz; *Rose Room* Harry Williams, Art Hickman; *I'm Always Chasing Rainbows* Joseph McCarthy, Harry Carroll; *In My Merry Oldsmobile* Vincent Bryan, Gus Edwards; *I Hate To Lose You* Grant Clarke, Archie Gottler.

Adapted by Edward Dein from a story by Patricia Harper, and scripted by Eugene Conrad, **My Gal Loves Music** (Universal) was an hour-long filler that starred Grace McDonald (left) who, thanks to a brainstorm by medicine-man Walter Catlett, poses as a 14-year-old prodigy and wins a trip to New York with a radio appearance on a show sponsored by a vitamin pill manufacturer (Alan Mowbray). Best song was 'Over and Over' (by Everett Carter and Milton Rosen) attractively sung by Miss McDonald. Producer-director Edward Lilley kept it light and frothy, drawing the best from a cast that also included Bob Crosby (right) as a piano-playing band leader, Betty Kean, a young tenor called Freddie Mercer, Tom Daly, and Chinita and Trixie. Other songs and musical numbers included: *I Need Vitamin U* Clarence Gaskill; *Somebody's Rockin' My Rainbow*; *Give Out, Pepita*; Carter, Rosen.

The best thing about **Song of the Open Road** (United Artists) was that it introduced screen audiences to a fresh new talent called Jane Powell (left). For the rest it was an adolescent (in every sense) yarn about a juvenile film star (Powell) who runs away to join a youth hostel, every last one of whose members can either sing, dance or play a musical instrument. They included Bonita Granville, Jack Moran, Peggy O'Neill and Bill Christy. Also cast were Reginald Denny, Regis Toomey, Rose Hobart, Sig Arno and, as themselves, Edgar Bergen and Charlie McCarthy, W.C. Fields (right), Pat Starling, The Condos Brothers, The Lipham Four, The Hollywood Canteen Kids, Catron and Popp, and Sammy Kaye and His Orchestra. It was scripted by Albert Mannheimer from a story by Irving Phillips and Edward Verdier, choreographed by George Dobbs and directed by S. Sylvan Simon for producer Charles R. Rogers. Songs and musical numbers included: *Here It Is Monday*; *Rollin' Down The Road*; *Too Much In Love* Kim Gannon, Walter Kent; *Marche Militaire* Schubert; *Hawaiian War Chant* Johnny Noble, Ralph Freed, Prince Leleiohaku of Hawaii; *Notre Dame*; *Carmona*.

Benny Goodman and His Band (illustrated) featured prominently in **Sweet and Low Down**, a pot-boiler from 20th Century-Fox whose narrative (screenplay by Richard English) concerned the romances and overriding ambition of a swollen-headed trombone player (James Caldwell) attached to the Goodman outfit. It was dull, predictable, and indifferently acted by a cast that included Linda Darnell and Lynn Bari (as the girls in Caldwell's life), Jack Oakie as his faithful buddy, as well as Allyn Joslyn, John Campbell, Dickie Moore, Buddy Swan, Beverly Hudson and The Pied Pipers. Archie Mayo directed for producer William Le Baron. Joe Harris played the trombone for Caldwell, and Lynn Bari's vocals were dubbed by Lorraine Elliott. Best sequence: a gig at the senior prom of a boys' military school whose 15-year-old 'generals' all appear to have the aplomb of an Eisenhower. Songs and musical numbers: *I'm Making Believe*; *Chuch-Chug-Choo-Choo-Chug*; *Hey Bub, Let's Have A Ball*; *Ten Days With Baby* Mack Gordon, James V. Monaco; *I Found A New Baby* Jack Palmer, Spencer Williams; *Jersey Bounce* Robert B. Wright, Bobby Plater, Tiny Bradshaw, Edward Johnson; *Let's Dance* Fanny Baldridge, Gregory Stone, Joseph Bonine; *The World Is Waiting For The Sunrise* Gene Lockhart, Ernest Seitz; *Mozart's Clarinet Quintet* (performed by Goodman and strings); *No Love No Nothing* Leo Robin, Harry Warren; *Rachel's Dream* Benny Goodman; *I Yi Yi Yi Yi, I Like You Very Much* Gordon, Warren.

247

Forties Musicals

△

Meet Me in St Louis (MGM) was a tender and loving account of a year in the life of a prosperous St Louis family called Smith (see illustration). Nothing earth-shattering actually happened to them between 1902 and 1903 apart from romance entering the lives of two of the four Smith sisters, and father's decision (to the delight of his brood) not to move to New York. But, as lovingly scripted by Irving Brecher and Fred Finkelhoffe from a series of *New Yorker* stories by Sally Benson, the domestic trivia that surrounded the day-to-day activities of the Smith family was the very stuff of life itself. Apart from the fact that the film lacks a knock-out finale, ending as it does, with a shot of the family attending the opening of the St Louis Exposition, but showing practically nothing of the Fair itself, it remains 113 minutes of unalloyed delight. Directed by Vincente Minnelli with a lingering eye for period detail and a marvellous sense of nostalgia for the good old days and the good old sense of values that informed them, its basically sentimental content was never allowed to cloy, thanks to a complete absence of cuteness throughout. Even child star Margaret O'Brien as Tootie, the baby of the family, gave a performance which had a hard centre to it. Falling into four distinct sections, the film not only reflected a way of life (slightly romanticized, to be sure) but also the changing moods in the household as dictated by each season. Technicolor (employed by Minnelli for the first time) was brilliantly used to enhance these seasonal changes and was one of the film's chief sources of pleasure. But then almost everything about **Meet Me in St Louis**

gave pleasure, not least Judy Garland's (centre) glowing performance as Esther, the Smith sister who develops a crush on the boy next door (Tom Drake, 2nd left, standing) and expresses it in two songs: 'The Boy Next Door' and, in five of the most magical minutes ever proffered in a musical, the brilliantly orchestrated (by Conrad Salinger) 'Trolley Song' (both numbers by Hugh Martin and Ralph Blane). Another musical highlight was Garland's singing of 'Under The Bamboo Tree' (by Bob Cole and J. Rosamond Johnson), in which she was joined vocally, and in a brief cake-walk, by Margaret O'Brien. The choreography was by Charles Walters, and the exquisite photography by George Folsey. Lucille Bremer (3rd left, standing) and Joan Carroll (centre right on floor) were the other Smith sisters, Henry Daniels Jr the Smiths' (Leon Ames and Mary Astor) only son (seated with Margaret O'Brien on lap), Harry Davenport grandpa, and Marjorie Main their stentorian maid Katie, as much a part of the family as if she were born into it. The film's meticulous production carried the unmistakable imprint of its producer, Arthur Freed. Other songs and musical numbers: *Have Yourself a Merry Little Christmas* (Garland) Blane, Martin; *Meet Me In St Louis* (Garland, Bremer, Carroll, Davenport) Andrew B. Sterling, Kerry Mills; *Skip To My Lou* (Garland, Bremer, Daniels Jr, Drake) traditional, revised by Martin and Blane; *You And I* (Ames, dubbed by Arthur Freed, and Astor, dubbed by D. Markas) Freed, Nacio Herb Brown; *I Was Drunk Last Night* (O'Brien) traditional; *Over The Bannister* (Drake, Garland) traditional, arranged Salinger.

△

Kay Kyser starred in **Carolina Blues** (Columbia), as a bandleader out to raise money for a cruiser through a series of war bond rallies featuring himself and his well-known band. Ann Miller co-starred as an entertainer who looks to Mr K for a job; and Victor Moore was in it too, playing six elderly members (both male and female) of a family called Carver. Kyser regulars Georgia Carroll, Harry Babbitt, and the relentlessly un-funny Ish Kabibble were also featured in Joseph Hoffman and Al Martin's silly screenplay (story by M.M. Musselman and Kenneth Earl); so were Harold Nicholas (centre), The Cristianis, The Layson Brothers, and The Four Step Brothers. Sammy Cahn and Jule Styne provided the score. Sam Bischoff produced, Sammy Lee choreographed, and the director was Leigh Jason. Songs and musical numbers included: *Poor Little Rhode Island*; *There Goes That Song Again*; *Thinking About The Wabash*; *You Make Me Dream Too Much*; *Thanks A Lot*; *Mr Beebe*.

△ Dorothy and Herbert Fields and Cole Porter's successful 1943 Broadway musical, **Something for the Boys**, came to the screen from 20th Century-Fox in glorious Technicolor, but with only one contribution to the film's score by Porter (the title song). All about a trio of fancy-free cousins who inherit a rambling mansion in Kentucky near an army camp, and turn it into a home for soldiers' wives, it top-starred Carmen Miranda (illustrated 2nd left) – now one of the highest paid women in America at a salary in excess of $200,000 a year – featured Vivian Blaine (left) and Phil Silvers as the proprietors, and introduced Perry Como to movie audiences. Also in it were Michael O'Shea, Sheila Ryan (centre right), Glenn Langan (right), Roger Clark, Thurston Hall and, in a small part, Judy Holliday. Humorous, tuneful, and always attractive to look at, it was snappily directed by Lewis Seiler from a screenplay by Robert Ellis, Helen Logan and Frank Gabrielson, vigorously choreographed by Nick Castle, and produced in characteristically splashy Fox style by Irving Starr. The musical numbers were by Harold Adamson and Jimmy McHugh and they included: *I'm In The Middle Of Nowhere* (Como); *Wouldn't It Be Nice* (Blaine, O'Shea); *Samba Boogie* (Miranda); *I Wish We Didn't Have To Say Goodnight* (Blaine, Como); *Boom Brachee* (Miranda).

A follow up to Universal's musical chiller, *The Phantom of the Opera* (1943), **The Climax** starred that vintage ghoul, Boris Karloff, as the resident physician of a European opera house who labours under a chronic disability: madness. Years before, his unrequited passion for a soprano ended in his murdering her and storing her body in his attic. Twenty years later he meets a girl (Susanna Foster, illustrated) with a similar voice to that of his former love, and is determined to see that she, too, goes the way of all flesh . . . Enjoyable hokum and stylishly directed by George Waggner (who produced, and also wrote the film's lyrics to Edward Ward's music), it featured Turhan Bey, Gale Sondergaard, Thomas Gomez, June Vincent, George Dolenz and Ludwig Stossel. It was written by Curt Siodmak and Lynn Starling from a play by Edward Locke, with Siodmak in charge of the adaptation. The operetta sequences were staged by Lester Horton. Songs and musical numbers included: *Now At Last*; *Someday I Know*; *The Magic Voice*; *The Boulevardier* Waggner, Ward; themes from the music of Schubert and Chopin.

▽

Mexico's popular singing star Tito Guizar (illustrated) starred in **Brazil**, a big-budget musical from Republic that utilized middle-of-the-road talents in a small story about a Brazilian composer (Guizar) and his successful efforts to tame an American authoress (Virginia Bruce, illustrated) who has just written an unflattering book called *Why Marry A Latin?* Needless to say, by the end of the film Miss Bruce, with Señor Guizar, is in a far better position to answer her own question. Pleasant but unexceptional entertainment, it also featured Edward Everett Horton, Robert Livingston, Veloz and Yolanda, Fortunio Bonanova, Richard Lane, Frank Puglia and specialty dancer Aurora Miranda (Carmen's sister). Roy Rogers made a guest appearance singing 'Hands Across The Border' (by Ned Washington and Phil Ohman), which he first introduced in Republic's western of the same name the previous year. **Brazil**'s screenplay was by Frank Gill Jr and Laura Kerr (story by Richard English), and it was directed for producer Robert North by Joseph Santley. Other songs and musical numbers included: *Brazil*; *Rio de Janeiro*; *Upa Upa* Ary Barroso, Bob Russell; *Moonlight Fiesta* Harry Tobias, Al Sherman.

Night Club Girl (Universal) was a rags-to-riches yarn about a couple of kids (Vivian Austin, left, and Billy Dunn) who, thanks to the help of columnist Edward Norris, are given a chance to try out their act at a Hollywood niterie run by Maxie Rosenbloom. Unfortunately, they overeat on hot dogs and, when it comes to the crunch, are too sick to do themselves justice. As written by Henry Blankfort and Dick L. Hyland from a story by Adele Commandini, there was no excuse for it at all – except, possibly, as a springboard for the appearances of several well-established nightclub and specialty acts, including The Delta Rhythm Boys, The Mulcays and Paula Drake. Also cast were Judy Clark (right), Leon Belasco, Andrew Tombes, Fred Sanborn, Virginia Brissac, Minna Gombell (centre), and Clem Bevans. Frank Gross produced, Louis Da Pron choreographed and Edward F. Cline directed. Songs and musical numbers included: *Wo-Ho* Jimmy Nolan, Jim Kennedy; *One O'Clock Jump* Count Basie; *The Peanut Song* Nate Wexler, Red Maddock, Al Trace; *Vingo Jingo* Don Raye, Gene De Paul; *I Need Love* Milton Pascal, Edgar Fairchild; *What A Wonderful Day* Harry Tobias, Al Sherman; *Pagan Love Song* Arthur Freed, Nacio Herb Brown.

◁ Just as Betty Grable was once groomed to replace Alice Faye, so June Haver waited in the wings to take over from Betty – and, in **Irish Eyes Are Smiling**, another in 20th Century-Fox's series of turn-of-the-century song *fests*, her bid for stardom finally arrived. Haver played Mary 'Irish' O'Brien, a blonde lass who falls in love with Ernest R. Ball, the real-life composer (with Chauncey Olcott and Rida Johnson Young) of 'Mother Machree' (sung by a boy soprano in the film), 'Dear Little Boy Of Mine' (with J. Keirn Brennan), and 'When Irish Eyes Are Smiling' (with Olcott and George Graff), sung by Dick Haymes. A largely fictitious biopic, with Haymes as Ball, the film top-starred Monty Woolley as a Broadway impresario and, in secondary roles, featured Anthony Quinn, Beverly Whitney, Maxie Rosenbloom, Veda Ann Borg, Clarence Kolb and Chick Chandler. Specialty dancer Kenny Williams also appeared; so did operatic stars Leonard Warren and Blanche Thebom. Familiar to a degree, its backstage intrigues and boy-meets-loses-gets-girl plot (screenplay by Earl Baldwin and John Tucker Battle from a story by E.A. Wellington) were pretty tedious, requiring more personality than Haver and Haymes (both illustrated) possessed to give it the fillip it pitifully lacked. Best song was a 'newie' by Mack Gordon and James V. Monaco called 'Bessie With A Bustle' which was brightly staged by Hermes Pan, and looked good in Technicolor. Damon Runyon produced, and the formula direction was by Gregory Ratoff. Other songs and musical numbers: *Let The Rest Of The World Go By*; *A Little Bit Of Heaven* Ball, J. Keirn Brennan; *Strut Miss Lizzie* Henry Creamer, Turner Layton; *I'll Forget You* Ball, Annalu Burns; *Love Me And The World Is Mine* Ball, Dave Reed Jr; *I Don't Want A Million Dollars* Gordon, Monaco; *Be My Little Baby Bumble Bee* Stanley Murphy, Henry I. Marshall.

▷

▷

Forties Musicals

In **Here Come The Waves** (Paramount), Bing Crosby took a few satirical swipes at the bobby-soxers of the nation whose swooning over crooners like himself and Sinatra (the latter deliciously parodied in a dreamy version of 'That Old Black Magic' by Harold Arlen and Johnny Mercer) was, by the mid-forties, reaching epidemic proportions. He played Johnny Cabot, a singing idol who, together with his buddy Sonny Tufts, meets a singing sister act, both girls being played by the volatile Betty Hutton (illustrated). One of the sisters (Sue) falls for Crosby's charm at first sight; the other (Allison) is totally unimpressed. Needless to say it is in the latter guise that Miss Hutton succeeds in winning her man, but not before a plethora of plot complications (screenplay by Allan Scott, Ken Englund, and Zion Myers) sabotages the progress of their romance. As the story unfurls, Crosby (illustrated) joins the navy hoping to be assigned to destroyer duty, but finds himself instead – thanks to the connivance of Hutton (as Sue) – in charge of the benefit shows being presented by the Waves. An undemanding *mélange* of comedy and music, it was choreographed by Danny Dare, boasted several good numbers by Arlen and Mercer (the best being 'Accentuate The Positive' performed by Crosby and Tufts) and was spiritedly directed by Mark Sandrich, who also produced. The rest of the cast included Ann Doran, Gwen Crawford, Noel Neill, Catherine Craig and Marjorie Henshaw. Other songs and musical numbers: *I Promise You; Let's Take The Long Way Home; There's A Fella Waiting In Poughkeepsie; Here Come The Waves; Join The Navy.*

▽

△

One of Universal's rare 'A' sized musicals in that it ran over an hour (94 minutes in fact) and had some money spent on it, **Bowery to Broadway** did not, however, rate an 'A' for achievement. A period piece set in an era which seemed to be the exclusive property of 20th Century-Fox, it featured Jack Oakie and Donald Cook as a couple of Irishmen who both run beer gardens under the El railroad tracks of New York. In time, they put their friendly rivalry to one side, join forces, move uptown to bustling 42nd Street, and become the toast of Broadway with a series of no-expense-spared shows. What such familiar material needed was a stronger, more exciting line-up of talent than the one assembled by producer John Grant, and which included Maria Montez (top starred), Susanna Foster, Turhan Bey, Ann Blyth, Louise Allbritton (as Lillian Russell), Frank McHugh, Rosemary De Camp, Leo Carillo, Andy Devine and, doing a specialty called 'He Took Her For A Sleigh Ride', Donald P'Connor and Peggy Ryan (both illustrated in carriage). It was written by Edmund Joseph, Bart Lytton and Arthur T. Horman (story by Joseph and Horman), choreographed by Louis Da Pron, Carlos Romero and Johnny Boyle, and directed by Charles Lamont. Other songs and musical numbers included: *The Love Waltz; There'll Always Be A Moon* Everett Carter, Edward Ward; *Montevideo; Coney Island Waltz* Kim Gannon, Walter Kent; *My Song Of Romance* Don George, Dave Franklin; *Under The Bamboo Tree* Bob Cole, J. Rosamond Johnson; *Daisy Bell* Harry Dacre; *Yip-I-Addy-I-Ay* Will Cobb, John H. Flynn; *Wait Till The Sun Shines Nellie* Andrew B. Sterling, Harry von Tilzer; *Just Because You Made Dem Goo Goo Eyes At Me* Hughie Cannon, John Queen.

▽

One of the most successful of all the war effort musicals was **Hollywood Canteen**, which grossed an absolute fortune for Warner Bros. while serving the purpose of keeping the boys at the front, and the public back home, happy. The screenplay, by Delmer Daves who also directed the film, had even less plot than was usual for entertainments of this nature: Robert Hutton and Dane Clark, two soldiers on sick leave from the South Pacific, spend a couple of memorable nights at the Hollywood Canteen before returning to active duty. Hutton finds himself the lucky winner of the prize for the millionth guest at the Canteen and gets a luxury suite and a car for the weekend, as well as a date with his dream girl, Joan Leslie, who played herself. However, it wasn't its story which brought queues to the box office, but the guest artists who embroidered it. In alphabetical order, they included The Andrews Sisters, Jack Benny (centre), Joe E. Brown, Eddie Cantor, Kitty Carlisle, Jack Carson, Joan Crawford, Helmut Dantine, Bette Davis (right), Faye Emerson, Victor Francen, John Garfield, Sydney Greenstreet, Alan Hale, Paul Henreid, Andrea King, Peter Lorre, Ida Lupino, Irene Manning, Nora Martin, Joan McCracken, Dolores Moran, Dennis Morgan, Eleanor Parker, William Prince, Joyce Reynolds, John Ridgely, Roy Rogers and Trigger, S.Z. Sakall, Alexis Smith, Zachary Scott, Barbara Stanwyck, Craig Stevens, Joseph Szigeti (left), Donald Woods, Jane Wyman, and Efrem Zimbalist, as well as Jimmy Dorsey and Carmen Cavallaro and their orchestras. It was produced by Alex Gottlieb, with choreography by LeRoy Prinz. Songs and musical numbers: *Don't Fence Me In* (Andrews Sisters, Roy Rogers) Cole Porter; *You Can Always Tell A Yank* (Morgan, Brown) E.Y. Harburg, Burton Lane; *What Are You Doing The Rest Of Your Life?* (Wyman, Carson) Ted Koehler, Burton Lane; *We're Having A Baby (My Baby And Me)* (Cantor, Martin) Harold Adamson, Vernon Duke; *Sweet Dreams Sweetheart* (Carlisle, Leslie); *Hollywood Canteen* Ted Koehler, M.K. Jerome, Ray Heindorf; *I'm Gettin' Corns For My Country* (Andrews Sisters) Jean Barry, Dick Charles; *Once To Every Heart* (Carlisle) Dorothy Donnelly, Sigmund Romberg; *Tumbling Tumbleweeds* (Sons of the Pioneers) Bob Nolan; *King Porter Stomp* (Dorsey Band) Jelly Roll Morton; *The General Jumped At Dawn* (Dorsey, Golden Gate Quartet) Larry Neal, Jimmy Mundy; *Ballet In Jive* (McCracken) Ray Heindorf; *Slavonic Dance* (Szigeti) Dvorak; *Voodoo Moon* (Cavallaro, Rosario and Antonio) Marion Sunshine, Julio Blanco, Obdulio Morales.

A boy-meets-girl-on-ice story, **Lake Placid Serenade** (Republic) allowed Czechoslovakian figure-skating star Vera Hruba Ralston (illustrated) to don her blades on several occasions and, in the end, to find herself in the arms of Robert Livingston. There was little more to it than that, with Walter Catlett (a high-pressure producer), Lloyd Corrigan (a genial Czechoslovakian godfather), Eugene Pallette (a paternal American uncle), and Stephanie Bachelor (Miss Ralston's predatory rival in love) doing their best to flesh out Dick Irving Hyland and Doris Gilbert's insubstantial screenplay (story by Frederick Kohner). Also cast, and playing themselves, were Ray Noble and His Orchestra, Harry Owens and His Royal Hawaiians, Roy Rogers, and ice specialty acts McGowan and Mack, Twinkle Watts, and The Merry Messiters. Steve Sekely directed. Musical numbers included: *Deep Purple* Mitchell Parish, Peter De Rose; *My Isle Of Golden Dreams* Gus Kahn, Walter Blaufuss; *National Emblem March* E.E. Bagley; *Winter Wonderland* Dick Smith, Felix Bernard; *Intermezzo* Robert Henning, Heinz Provost; *Waiting For The Robert E. Lee* L. Wolfe Gilbert, Lewis F. Muir; *When Citrus Is In Bloom*; *Drigo's Serenade* Ricardo Drigo; *While Strolling In The Park* Robert A. King.

Patty, Maxene and LaVerne Andrews starred in **Moonlight and Cactus** (Universal), a short (60 minutes) but tuneful programmer whose plot (by scenarists Eugene Conrad and Paul Gerard Smith) told the uncomplicated story of a rancher who returns to his ranch after active service with the merchant marines to find that, in his absence, all the cowhands have been replaced by women. Believing that a woman's place is in the home, and not on his land, he resents their invasion of his property, but soon changes his tune when his lady foreman proves to him that women can be as efficient as men. The Andrews Sisters (illustrated, with Shemp Howard) served little purpose other than to sing, with the main burden of the plot falling on Tom Seidel as the returning rancher and Elyse Knox as his female foreman. Best song was a novelty item performed by the Andrews girls called 'Send Me A Man, Amen' (by Ray Gilbert and Sidney Miller). Leo Carillo played a cattle thief, with other parts going to Eddie Quillan, Murray Alper, Tom Kennedy and Minerva Urecal. Mitchell Ayres and His Orchestra were also featured. Edward F. Cline directed, the dances were staged by Charles O'Curran and the producer was Frank Gross. Other songs and musical numbers: *Wa Hoo* Cliff Friend; *Home* Harry and Jeff Clarkson, Peter Van Steeden; *C'Mere Baby* Lanny Gray, Roy Jordan; *Heave Ho My Lads, Heave Ho* Jack Lawrence; *Down In The Valley* Frank Luther; *Sing* Harold Mooney, Hughie Prince.

Bearing a decided resemblance in mood and atmosphere to the Rodgers and Hammerstein Broadway smash, *Oklahoma!*, Universal's **Can't Help Singing** (it even had a song in it called 'Cal-i-for-ni-ay') sashayed onto the screen in abundant Technicolor, and told the outdoor story (set in 1847) of a sprightly young girl who ignores her father's wishes and journeys west in order to marry an army lieutenant. But she changes her mind *en route* when she meets a gentleman who appeals to her more. Deanna Durbin (illustrated), looking enchanting in Technicolor, was the girl. Robert Paige (illustrated) the fellow she settles for, and Ray Collins her disapproving father. With a charming score by Jerome Kern and E.Y. Harburg, some really dazzling outdoor photography (by Woody Bredell and W. Howard Greene), and a spirited performance by its leading lady, Lewis R. Foster and Frank Ryan's screenplay (from a story by John Klorer and Leo Townsend, based, in turn, on *Girl of the Overland Trail* by Samuel J. and Curtis B. Warshawsky) stood up remarkably well considering its operetta-like machinations. Akim Tamiroff and Leonid Kinskey as a pair of Slavic fortune hunters new to the foreign customs of the country, were excellent in comic support, and the rest of producer Felix Jackson's cast included Clara Blandick, David Bruce, Olin Howlin, June Vincent, Thomas Gomez, Andrew Tombes and George Cleveland. The capable direction was by Frank Ryan. Songs and musical numbers: *Can't Help Singing*; *More And More*; *Cal-i-for-ni-ay*; *Elbow Room*; *Swing Your Sweetheart*; *Any Moment Now*.

Babes on Swing Street (Universal) was, as its title suggested, another excuse to allow a group of industrious kids to put on a show. This time they do so in order to raise enough money to further their education at music school. A sub-plot involving the timid uncle (Leon Errol) of one of the youngsters who lives in fear and trembling of his maiden aunt, Errol's sister (Alma Kruger), helped pad out Howard Dimsdale and Eugene Conrad's workaday screenplay (story by Brenda Weisberg). Ann Blyth (left), top-billed, sang 'Peg O'My Heart' (by Alfred Bryan and Fred Fisher); Peggy Ryan (centre) co-starred. Also cast: Andy Devine (right), Anne Gwynne, June Preisser, Kirby Grant, Billy Dunn, Freddie Slack and His Orchestra, The Rubenettes, and Marion Hutton, who sang the catchy 'Take It Easy' (by Albert De Bru, Irving Taylor and Vic Mizzy). Louis Da Pron choreographed, and it was directed by Edward Lilley for associate producer Bernard W. Burton. As programmers go, this one went. Other songs and musical numbers: *Just Being With You*; *Hotcha Sonja*; *I've Got A Way With The Boys*; *Wrong Thing At The Right Time*; *Musical Chairs*; *Music And You* Inez James, Sidney Miller; *Youth Is On The March* Everett Carter, Milton Rosen; *Siboney* Dolly Morse, Ernesto Lecuona; *Loch Lomond* (traditional).

Producer Joe Pasternak and director Henry Koster were united for the first time since their Universal days in **Music for Millions** (MGM), an irresistible weepie that combined a soppy story with dollops of classical music. It told of cellist June Allyson (right) who is about to have a baby, but is suffering because she has had no word from her serviceman husband away on active duty in the Pacific. Margaret O'Brien (left), who received top billing, was cast as Allyson's comforting younger sister, with Jimmy Durante on hand as maestro Jose Iturbi's manager (!) to dispense a couple of characteristic Durante-type ditties in characteristic Durante-type style, most notably 'Umbriago' which he wrote with Irving Caesar. Also from Durante came 'Toscanini, Iturbi and Me' (by Walter Bullock and Harold Spina) and it brought the house down. Marsha Hunt, Hugh Herbert, Harry Davenport, Marie Wilson, Larry Adler, Ben Lessy and Ethel Griffies completed the cast. The screenplay was an original, written by Myles Connolly. Other songs and musical numbers included: *At Sundown* Walter Donaldson; *Summer Holidays* Helen Deutsch, Herbert Stothart; Debussy's *Clair de Lune*, and a selection of various pieces by Tchaikovsky, Dvorak and Grieg.

1945

A well-mounted production did little for **A Song For Miss Julie**, routine programmer fare from Republic about a couple of playwrights (Barton Hepburn and Roger Clark) who have great difficulty in persuading the oldest living relative of the subject of their new operetta to give her permission for the project to go ahead. Shirley Ross received top billing as the fan-dancing wife of playwright Hepburn, with other roles in Rowland Leigh's screenplay (story by Michael Foster) going to Cheryl Walker, Elisabeth Risdon (as the troublesome elderly relative), and Jane Farrar (illustrated left, with Roger Clark), with appearances, too, from the famous ballet dancers Alicia Markova and Anton Dolin. Larry Ceballos choreographed it, the producers were William Rowland and Carley Harriman, with Rowland also in charge of the direction. Songs and musical numbers included: *It All Could Have Happened Before; That's What I Like About You; The Country Ain't The Country Anymore; I Love To Remember; Sweet Sunday* Marla Shelton, Louis Herscher.
▽

There was not much fun in **Dixie Jamboree**, a filler from PRC, which was as slow-moving as the Mississippi on which most of the 'action' took place. Story (by Lawrence E. Taylor, screenplay by Sam Neuman) concerned a show boat called the *Ellabella* and all who sailed in her. Guy Kibbee, for example, sells patent medicines to its passengers; Lyle Talbot (2nd right) and Frank Jenks are on board posing as holidaymakers when in fact they're a couple of fugitive conmen; Eddie Quillan (left), as a trumpeter, comes along for the ride in the company of a pair of Indians he's adopted and, providing them all with entertainment, are Frances Langford (right), Fifi D'Orsay (centre) and Charles Butterworth, as well as the Ben Carter Negro Choir. Jack Schwarz produced and the director was Christy Cabanne. Songs and musical numbers included: *Dixie Show Boat; No, No, No; If It's A Dream; You Ain't Right With The Lord; Big Stuff* ◁ Michael Breen, Sam Neuman.

A sort of animated *Hellzapoppin*, **The Three ▷ Caballeros** (RKO) was a visual humdinger from Walt Disney that showered the screen with a wealth of shapes, forms, sounds, colour and images. What little structure it had revolved around a birthday package received by Donald Duck. The first gift he opens is a movie projector, and the film accompanying it is all about a penguin who sails for the South Seas because he hasn't been able to acclimatize himself to the Antarctic. After that we are introduced to Little Gauchito, who wins a local donkey race but is disqualified when the spectators realize that the donkey he has entered has wings. The next gift Donald unwraps is a pop-up book on Brazil, inside of which is his old pal Joe Carioca. In no time at all, the two of them insinuate themselves into the pages and embark on a wild musical adventure in the course of which they meet Aurora Miranda (illustrated) with whom Donald falls hopelessly in love. The last gift is Mexico, where Donald and Joe Carioca are joined by a rooster called Panchito for a magic carpet tour of the country, culminating in a fiesta and a bull-fight. Brilliantly inventive throughout, and with some exhilarating live-action sequences combined with animation, **The Three Caballeros** remains one of Disney's most dazzling achievements. The production supervisor and director was Norman Ferguson and, apart from Miss Miranda, the numerous performers seen or heard included Carmen Molina, Dora Luz, Nestor Amarale, Almirante, Trio Calaveras, Ascensio Del Rio Trio, The Padua Hill Players and the voices of Clarence Nash (Donald Duck), Sterling Holloway, Jose Olivera (Joe Carioca), Joaquin Garay (Panchito), Fred Shield, Frank Graham, and Carlos Ramirez. Songs and musical numbers: *The Three Caballeros* Manuel Esperon, Ray Gilbert, Ernesto Cortazar; *Baia* Ary Barroso, Gilbert; *Os Quindins De Yaya (Angel-May-Care)* Barroso, Ervin Drake; *You Belong To My Heart* Augustin Lara, Gilbert; *Mexico* Charles Wolcott, Gilbert.

As a piece of accurate screen biography, **A Song To Remember** (Columbia) was a film to forget. As a solid, if somewhat fanciful, piece of commercial story-telling, embellished by some great music, and lushly packaged in exquisite Technicolor, it was more than acceptable. Purporting to be the life story of the great Polish composer Frederic Chopin, it starred Cornel Wilde (right) as the tubercular young pianist (Jose Iturbi dubbed the actual piano playing) and beautiful Merle Oberon (left) as George Sand (Mademoiselle Dudevant). Paul Muni, however, received billing above them both as Professor Joseph Elsner – and, under Charles Vidor's unrestraining direction, gave one of the wildest, most undisciplined performances of his distinguished career. Stephen Bekassy played Franz Liszt, Nina Foch was Constantia and George Coulouris Louis Pleyel. As scripted by Sidney Buchman (from a story by Ernst Marischka) they emerged as caricatured stereotypes, allowing audiences not a single glimpse into their souls – a criticism applied even more strenuously to Chopin and Sand, the latter being made to appear as the villain of the piece. ('Discontinue that so-called Polonaise jumble you've been playing for days,' she says to Chopin in one of the great bad lines of all time). Still, it looked good, and made an absolute fortune for the studio. Louis F. Edelman produced. Also cast: Sig Arno, Howard Freeman, George Macready, Claire DuBrey and Frank Puglia. The music: *Valse in D Flat (Minute Waltz) Op 64 No 1* (about half was played); *Mazurka in B Flat Op 7 No 1* (complete); *Impromptu No 4 in C Sharp Minor (Fantasie Impromptu) Op 66* (complete); *Etude in A Flat Op 25 No 1* (first ten bars only); *Polonaise in A Flat Op 53* (only half was played); *Scherzo in B Flat Minor Op 31* (complete); *Etude in E Op 10 No 3* (theme of film); *Nocturne in E Flat Op 9 No 2* (almost complete); *Berceuse in D Flat Op 57* (complete); *Waltz in C Sharp Minor Op 64 No 2* (almost complete); *Nocturne in C Minor Op 48 No 1* (almost complete); a montage consisting of *Etude in A Minor Opus 25 No 11*; *Ballade in A Flat Opus 47*; *Valse in A Flat Op 42*; *Valse in A Flat Op 34 No 1*; *Etude in C Minor Op 10 No 12 (Revolutionary Etude)*.

Designed for the lower half of a double bill, **Blonde Ransom** (Universal) was a par-for-the-course filler that starred Donald Cook (left) as a New York nightclub owner in danger of losing his club through gambling debts, and Virginia Grey (right) as a wealthy socialite who fakes a kidnapping in order to raise the $63,000 Cook needs to save his club from bankruptcy. Pinky Lee and Collette Lyons were also featured, so were George Barbier, Jerome Cowan and George Meeker. M. Coates Webster wrote it from a story by Robert T. Shannon, and William Beaudine directed. Songs: *Musical Wedding*; *The Life Of The Party*; *A Million Dollars Worth Of Dreams*; *Hinky Dinky Pinky* Jack Brooks, Norman Berens, Al Sherman.

Bud Abbott (right) and Lou Costello (left) starred in **Here Come The Co-Eds** (Universal), one of the better of their more recent efforts. They played a pair of caretakers who come to the rescue of a girls' school which is due to close through lack of funds. Also in it was Lon Chaney Jr who, for reasons of his own, *wants* the school to close, and, in the guise of a wrestler called The Masked Marvel, meets dumpy Lou in the ring. Their bout together was the best thing in a film that also included some energetic tapping from Peggy Ryan (2nd left), and some spirited playing from Phil Spitalny and His All-Girl Orchestra featuring Evelyn Kaye (Mrs Spitalny) and Her Magic Violin! Martha O'Driscoll (centre), June Vincent (2nd right), Donald Cook, Charles Dingle, Richard Lane, Joe Kirk and Bill Stern completed the cast. Arthur T. Horman and John Grant wrote it from a story by Edmund L. Hartmann (Grant also producing) and it was directed by Jean Yarbrough. Songs and musical numbers included: *Hooray For Our Side*; *I Don't Care If I Never Dream Again*; *Jumping On Saturday Night*; *Someday We Will Remember*; *Let's Play House* Edgar Fairchild, Jack Brooks. ▽

Forties Musicals

Tonight and Every Night (Columbia) was a wartime musical about war-torn London, which took place in the intimate Music Box Theatre (supposedly the Windmill Theatre) whose proud boast was that it never closed. Its English setting was reflected in the studio's choice of producer-director Victor Saville, but not in its cast, all of whom were American. Rita Hayworth and Janet Blair starred as a couple of dancers who find romance when a pilot (Lee Bowman) enters Rita's life, and a young dancer (Marc Platt) falls for Janet. Drama intrudes when Platt and Blair are killed in an air-raid and the film ends with Hayworth (illustrated centre) reluctantly rejecting marriage to Bowman in order to continue entertaining the troops at the Music Box. Though Saville's skilful handling of Lesser Samuels and Abem Finkel's screenplay (based on the play *Heart Of A City* by Lesley Storm) kept the narrative well clear of bathos, the chief architects of the film's success were choreographers Jack Cole and Val Raset, without whose lusciously staged production numbers, particularly Hayworth's exotic 'You Excite Me' (all the songs were written by Sammy Cahn and Jule Styne), and 'Tonight And Every Night'– an intriguing and imaginative item in which the characters in a newsreel actually step out from the edges of the screen to form part of the number itself – the film would not have been nearly as entertaining as it was. Marc Platt indulged in a rather bizarre dance number which called on him to mime to one of Hitler's speeches; and Janet Blair, apart from her singing of the attractive title number and a pretty ballad called 'Anywhere', was also seen (and heard) to excellent effect in a comic duet with Hayworth called 'The Boy I Left Behind'. Completing the cast were Leslie Brooks, Professor Lamberti, Dusty Anderson, Florence Bates (as the Music Box's owner), Stephen Crane, Jim Bannon, Ernest Cossart, Patrick O'Brien and Gavin Muir. The stunning Technicolor photography was by Rudolph Mate and it was beautifully costumed by Jean Louis and Marcel Vertes. Hayworth's vocals were dubbed by Martha Mears. Other songs and musical numbers: *Cry And You Cry Alone* (Hayworth, Platt) *What Does An English Girl Think Of A Yank?* (Hayworth).

A showcase for some of the younger talent under contract to Columbia, **Let's Go Steady** was an hour-long programmer about a group of out-of-town youngsters who, having been conned out of fifty dollars by a phoney New York publisher, decide to promote themselves by persuading bandleaders and radio stations to give their efforts an airing. The film featured crooners Jackie Moran and Mel Torme, singer-dancer June Preisser (left), mimic Jimmy Lloyd, Arnold Stang (right), Pat Parrish, and Skinnay Ennis and His Band. It was written by Erna Lazarus from a story by William R. Sackheim, and directed by Del Lord for producer Ted Richmond. Songs and musical numbers included: *Tantza Babele*; *Sioux Falls S.D.*; *Baby Boogie* Mel Torme.

Though Maxene, Patty and La Verne Andrews received top billing in **Her Lucky Night** (Universal), the undernourished screenplay which Clyde Bruckman badgered out of a story by producer Warren Wilson, revolved around the efforts of Martha O'Driscoll to nab herself a beau after a fortune teller predicts that the man in her life will be found sitting next to her in a movie house. With this in mind, she buys two cinema tickets, tosses one out of the window and hopes for the best. Noah Beery Jr co-starred, with other parts going to George Barbier, Maurice Cass, Olin Howlin and Robert Emmett Keane. The Andrews gals (illustrated) played nightclub entertainers as well as cupids in Miss O'Driscoll's romance, and sang five songs in all, including the popular 'Dance With A Dolly With A Hole In Her Stocking' by Terry Shand, Mickey Leader and Jimmy Eaton. Edward Lilley directed. Other songs and musical numbers: *Sing A Tropical Song* Frank Loesser, Jimmy McHugh; *Is You Is Or Is You Ain't My Baby?* Billy Austin, Louis Jordan; *Straighten Up And Fly Right* Nat King Cole, Irving Mills; *The Polka Polka* Maxine Manners.

Bring on the Girls (Paramount), filmed in Technicolor, was the one about the millionaire who is bugged by the thought that women find his money more attractive than they do him. So he decides to join the navy on the assumption that girls never think of sailors as being wealthy. Eddie Bracken was the man with the problem; Veronica Lake a sexy, gold-digging cigarette girl who, despite Bracken's subterfuge, sets out to nab him. Marjorie Reynolds was the secondary romantic interest and, apart from falling for Bracken's buddy Sonny Tufts, got to sing most of the songs. Alan Mowbray appeared as a butler, with other roles going to dancer Johnny Coy, Grant Mitchell, Peter Whitney, Porter Hall, Thurston Hall, Lloyd Corrigan, Sig Arno, Andrew Tombes and, as a hat-check girl, Yvonne De Carlo. Spike Jones and His Orchestra were also in it, contributing a characteristically unorthodox interpretation of 'Chloe' by Gus Kahn and Neil Moret. Danny Dare choreographed, Sidney Lanfield directed – without making an attempt to give the well-worn material (screenplay by Karl Tunberg and Darrell Ware) anything other than the faintest re-tread – and the producer was Fred Kohlmar. (Production number illustrated). Other songs and musical numbers: *How Would You Like To Take My Picture?*; *Uncle Sammy Hit Miami*; *Bring On The Girls*; *You Moved Right In*; *I'm Gonna Hate Myself In The Morning* Harold Adamson, Jimmy McHugh; *Egyptian Ella* Walter Doyle.

Eadie was a Lady (Columbia) was a lively, if somewhat implausible, concoction about a vivacious student from a strait-laced girls' school who leads a life of impeccable respectability by day, but spends her nights as the chief attraction of a burlesque show. Ann Miller (left) was the lady with a double life, with Joe Besser, her co-star, playing a burlesque comedian turned school teacher. William Wright (centre) was Miss Miller's sweetheart (and manager of the burlesque house at which she is employed), with other parts in Monte Brice's screenplay going to Jeff Donnell, Jimmy Little, Marion Martin (right), Kathleen Howard, Tom Dugan and Douglas Wood. Hal McIntyre and His Orchestra were also in it. Michael Kraike produced, Jack Cole was in charge of the dances, and the director was Arthur Dreifuss. Songs and musical numbers included: *Tabby The Cat* Harold Dickinson, Howard Gibeling; *She's A Gypsy From Brooklyn* L. Wolfe Gilbert, Ben Oakland; *Next Victory Day*; *I'm Gonna See My Baby* Phil Moore; *Eadie Was A Lady* Nacio Herb Brown, Buddy De Sylva, Richard A. Whiting.

Part adventure, part musical, part comedy and wholly unsatisfactory, Song of the Sarong (Universal), made for the bottom half of a twin bill, recounted the escapades of intrepid William Gargan who, in return for $1,000,000, agrees to journey to a remote island in order to seek out a fortune in pearls – the catch being that the gems are heavily guarded by savages. Sarong-clad Nancy Kelly (illustrated) played the white queen of the island, with Eddie Quillan and Fuzzy Knight on hand to give slapstick support to producer-scenarist Gene Lewis's creaking plot. Also in it: George Dolenz, George Cleveland, Mariska Aldrich, Morgan Wallace and Larry Keating. The dances were staged by Charles Romero and the director was Harold Young. Songs and musical numbers included: *Ridin' On The Crest Of A Cloud*; *Pied Pipers From Swingtown* Jack Brooks; *Island Of The Moon*; *Lovely Luana* Don Raye, Gene De Paul; *De Camptown Races* Stephen Foster.

Will pretty Audrey Long, a feature writer for a glossy American magazine, marry photographer Phillip Terry? Or will she marry her fiancée (Marc Cramer), an American businessman in Rio? That was the question posed in Pan-Americana (RKO), as good (or as bad) an excuse as any for an avalanche of Latin-American song and dance numbers provided by such exotic talents as Rosario and Antonio, Miguelito Valdes (foreground left), Harold and Lola, Chinita Marin, Chuy Castillon, The Padilla Sisters, Chuy Reyes and His Orchestra and the Nestor Amaral Samba Band. Eve Arden as the magazine's managing editor and Robert Benchley (its foreign editor) were in it to garner the odd laugh or two, but Lawrence Kimble's screenplay (story by Frederick Kohner and John H. Auer, who also produced and directed) didn't make it easy for them. Ernest Truex and Isabelita (illustrated) completed the cast. The choreographer was Charles O'Curran. Songs and musical numbers included: *Stars In Your Eyes*; *Rhumba Matumba*; *Guadalajara*; *Negra Leona*; *La Morine De Mi Copla*; *Baramba* Mort Green, Gabriel Ruiz; *Ba-Ba-Lu* Bob Russell, Marguerita Lecuona.

Running exactly an hour, Honeymoon Ahead (Universal) was a briskly paced programmer which starred Allan Jones (right) as a crooning convict whose unexpected release from jail causes havoc in the prison choir. So much so, that certain influential members of the choir immediately hatch a plot involving their singing star in a bank robbery in order to get him back. Jones's love interest was Grace McDonald (centre) whose father was Raymond Walburn, with other roles in Ellwood Ullman and Val Burton's screenplay (story by Burton) going to Vivian Austin, Jack Overman, Murray Alper, Eddie Acuff (left) and John Abbott. William Cowan produced and the director was Reginald Le Borg. Songs and musical numbers included: *Time Will Tell*; *Now And Always*; *Round The Bend*; *How Lovely* Everett Carter, Milton Rosen.

The youthful team of Donald O'Connor and Peggy Ryan (both illustrated) lent their considerable energies to Patrick the Great (Universal), a pleasant, but in no way exceptional, show-biz story about the conflict that arises between O'Connor and his actor father (Donald Cook) when the former is offered a part in a Broadway show that the latter wanted for himself. It's partly resolved, though, when Frances Dee accepts Cook's proposal of marriage. Miss Dee wasn't given a chance to be anything other than just personable in the Bertram Milhauser-Dorothy Bennett screenplay (story by Jane Hall, Frederick Kohner and Ralph Block); and Eve Arden, as a wise-cracking secretary, was wasted too. Completing the cast for producer Howard Benedict were Thomas Gomez, Gavin Muir, Andrew Tombes and Irving Bacon. It was directed by Frank Ryan with Louis Da Pron in charge of the dances. The songs and musical numbers were by Charles Tobias, David Kapp, Sidney Miller, Inez James and Charles Previn, and they included: *Song Of Love*; *For The First Time*; *Don't Move*; *Ask Madam Zan*; *The Cubacha*; *When You Bump Into Someone You Know*.

Too familiar in content even to support its one-hour running time, Penthouse Rhythm (Universal) was about three brothers and a sister and the difficulties they encounter in their bid for musical recognition. Jimmy Dodd, Bobby Worth, Louis Da Pron and Judy Clark were the kids on the make, with other roles in Stanley Roberts and Howard Dimsdale's screenplay (from a story by Roberts and Min Selvin) going to Kirby Grant, Lois Collier, Edward Norris, Maxie Rosenbloom, Eric Blore, Minna Gombell, Edward S. Brophy, Marion Martin, Donald MacBride, Velasco and Lenee (illustrated centre) and Harry Barris. Edward Cline directed and the producer was Frank Gross. Songs and musical numbers included: *Society Numbers*; *Let's Go American*; *When I Think Of Heaven*; *Up Comes Love*; *Peter Had A Wife And Couldn't Keep Her*.

Forties Musicals

Prettily dolled up in eye-catching Technicolor, **Belle of the Yukon** (International/RKO) had no place to go but down, due, in the main, to a screenplay that choked on its relentless diet of clichés. All about Randolph Scott's attempt to become a law-abiding citizen of Malamute (whose notorious dance hall is his favourite haunt), it also starred Gypsy Rose Lee (illustrated foreground centre), the Belle of the title with whom Scott is romantically involved, and Dinah Shore as a singer in love with a piano player (William Marshall). Sub-plots abounded, and there were several musical interludes, most notably Dinah Shore's singing of 'Sleigh Ride in July', and 'Like Someone In Love' (by Johnny Burke and Jimmy Van Heusen). But when the screenplay, by James Edward Grant from a story by Houston Branch, wasn't tying itself up into complicated knots, it was traversing territory too familiar for comfort. William Seiter directed, it was choreographed by Don Loper, and also featured Bob Burns, Charles Winninger, William Marshall, Guinn Williams, Robert Armstrong, Florence Bates, Victor Kilian and Edward Fielding. Other songs and musical numbers included: *Every Girl Is Different; Belle Of The Yukon* Burke, Van Heusen; *I Can't Tell Why I Love You But I Do, Do, Do* Will Cobb, Gus Edwards.

In **I'll Tell The World** (Universal), a crisply scripted (by Henry Blankfort) quickie, Lee Tracy played an announcer who puts a fair-to-middling radio station on the map by establishing a popular lonely hearts programme. Several specialties – from tap dancers to cowboy crooners – provided the musical accompaniment, with Brenda Joyce, Raymond Walburn (centre), June Preisser (right), Thomas Gomez (left), Howard Freeman and Lorin Raker also cast for producer Frank Gross and director Leslie Goodwins. Songs and musical numbers included: *Slap Polka* Harry Revel, Paul Francis Webster; *Walk A Little Faster* Dave Franklin; *Moonlight Fiesta* Harry Tobias, Al Sherman; *Where The Prairie Meets The Sky* Everett Carter, Milton Rosen.

Swing Out Sister, an adequate hour-long programmer from Universal, followed the romantic complications of a young singer (Frances Raeburn, centre) who is trilling away at a nightclub when she should be pursuing her operatic studies. The two men in her life are the club's proprietor (Milburn Stone) and a symphony conductor with boogie-woogie tendencies (Rod Cameron, right). Both men in turn are accepted and rejected while Little Miss Indecision makes up her mind whether it is the highbrows or the lowbrows to whom she should appeal. Miss Raeburn, incidentally, was Kathryn Grayson's sister in real life. The screenplay by Henry Blankfort was teased out of a story by Eugene Conrad and Edward Dein; Bernard W. Burton produced, and the director was Edward Dein. Others cast were Billie Burke in another of her bird-brained characterizations, and Arthur Treacher (2nd left) as Cameron's British-accented, bass-playing sidekick, as well as Jacqueline De Wit (left), Samuel S. Hinds, Fuzzy Knight, Edgar Dearing and The Leo Diamond Quintet. Songs and musical numbers: *Emperor Waltz* Johann Strauss II; *Only In Dreams; Love Is A Bluebird On The Wing; All I Want To Do Is Swing; Happy-Go-Lucky-Lady; Swing It Mr Chumbly.*

The Naughty Nineties (Universal), starring Bud Abbott, and Lou Costello (illustrated), almost went that far back in time for its material. The comedians played a couple of interfering employees on a Mississippi river boat, and repeated in their desperation for a laugh, their oft-performed 'Who's On First?' routine. Alan Curtis, Rita Johnson, Henry Travers, Lois Collier, Joe Sawyer, and Joe Kirk were also involved; it was written by Edmund L. Hartmann (who also produced), John Grant, Edmund Joseph and Hal Fimberg, John Boyles staged the dances, and the director was Jean Yarbrough. Songs and musical numbers: *Rolling Down The River; Uncle Tom's Cabin; I Can't Get You Out Of My Mind* Jack Brooks, Edgar Fairchild; *On A Sunday Afternoon* Andrew B. Sterling, Harry von Tilzer; *I'd Leave My Happy Home For You* Will Heelan, Von Tilzer; *Nora Malone* Junie McCree, Albert von Tilzer; *Ma Blushin' Rosie* John Stromberg, Edgar Smith.

In their desperation to find a new plot that would encompass all the old backstage clichés, Republic came up with **Earl Carroll Vanities** which told the unlikely tale of a mythological princess (known as Drinia of Turania, and played by Constance Moore) who, while on a fund-raising trip to New York with her mother (Mary Forbes), becomes the leading lady in one of Mr Carroll's Broadway extravaganzas (production number illustrated). Dennis O'Keefe was the romantic interest, Alan Mowbray appeared as a Grand Duke, with other roles in Frank Gill Jr's silly screenplay (from a silly story by Cortland Fitzsimmons) going to Stephanie Bachelor, Eve Arden, Otto Kruger, Pinky Lee, Parkyakarkus and Leon Belasco. Woody Herman and His Orchestra were also in it for producer Albert J. Cohen; Sammy Lee choreographed, and the director was Joseph Santley. Best song: 'Endlessly', by Kim Gannon and Walter Kent, sung by Miss Moore. Other songs and musical numbers: *Apple Honey* Woody Herman; *Who Dat Up Dere?* Gannon, Kent; *Riverside Jive* Alfred Newman; *Rockabye Boogie; You Beautiful Thing, You.*

A programmer from Columbia, **Blonde From Brooklyn** was a thoroughly inconsequential entertainment that starred Robert Stanton (illustrated – formerly Bob Haymes, brother of Dick) as a song-and-dance man newly released from the army, and Lynn Merrick (illustrated) as the jukebox singer he meets and with whom he plans a radio career as a musical duo. Erna Lazarus's screenplay made sure that a lot of things went wrong before they finally went right, and gave employment to Thurston Hall (as a rascally pseudo-Southern colonel), Mary Treen, Walter Soderling, Arthur Loft and Regina Wallace. Ted Richmond produced and the director was Del Lord. Songs included: *My Baby Said Yes* Sid Robin, Ted Walters.

Olsen and Johnson made an unhappy exit from movies with **See My Lawyer** (Universal), playing a couple of comedians who attempt to worm their way out of a nightclub contract by insulting the guests when club owner Franklin Pangborn refuses to release them. In the process, they bring several law suits upon themselves, giving much needed employment to three clientless attorneys. Producer Edmund L. Hartmann, and Stanley Davis's screenplay (from a play by Richard Maibaum and Harry Clork) gave employment to a host of specialty acts including Carmen Amaya and her dance company, The King Cole Trio (with Nat King Cole), The Cristianos Troupe, The Rogers Adagio Trio, The Six Willys, The Hudson Wonders and The Four Teens, as well as Alan Curtis, Grace McDonald, Noah Beery Jr, Edward S. Brophy, Richard Benedict, Lee Patrick and Gus Schilling. Which didn't leave much time or room for Messrs O. and J. whose only good scene was the one in which they insulted the guests at Pangborn's niterie by squirting soda in their faces and flinging mud in their eyes. Director Edward Cline bravely attempted to give it some cohesion, but failed (production number illustrated). Songs and musical numbers included: *Fuzzy Wuzzy* Bob Bell, Roy Branker; *Penny Arcade* Dave Franklin; *We're Making A Million*; *Take It Away*; *It's Circus Time* Everett Carter, Milton Rosen; *Man On The Little White Keys* Joe Greene, Nat King Cole.

A Technicolored commercial for showman Billy Rose, **Billy Rose's Diamond Horseshoe** was assembly-line entertainment from 20th Century-Fox. Betty Grable (illustrated centre) starred as a showgirl with a 'mink coat complex', and her co-star was up-and-coming Dick Haymes, playing a young doctor with greasepaint in his veins. It all took place in and around Rose's opulent niterie, and together the two attractive stars made beautiful music, courtesy of Mack Gordon and Harry Warren, particularly in their duets 'I Wish I Knew' and 'The More I See You'. Phil Silvers (as a stage manager) breezed in and out of director George Seaton's conventional screenplay (suggested from a play by John Kenyon Nicholson), making the most of the gags provided for him, with William Gaxton (as Haymes's hoofer father) bringing to his role the authority and experience of a lifetime on the Broadway boards. Beatrice Kay, Margaret Dumont and Roy Benson completed the cast, with Carmen Cavallaro and Willie Solar featured as specialties. Resident choreographer Hermes Pan was given several opportunities to interrupt the narrative with some well-staged dance routines, especially 'Cooking Up A Show'. William Perlberg produced. **Billy Rose's Diamond Horseshoe** was the last score Harry Warren wrote for Fox before moving to MGM. Other songs and musical numbers: *Welcome To The Diamond Horseshoe* (Grable, chorus); *In Acapulco* (Grable, Cavallaro); *You'll Never Know* (Grable); *Play Me An Old-Fashioned Melody* (Grable, Gaxton, Kay); *A Nickle's Worth Of Jive* (Grable) Gordon, Warren; *Carrie Marry Harry* (Kay, Gaxton) Junie McCree, Albert von Tilzer; *Let Me Call You Sweetheart* (Kay) Beth Slater Whitson, Leo Friedman; *Sleep Baby Sleep* (Kay) S.A. Emery; *Shoo Shoo Baby* (Grable) Phil Moore; *Aba Daba Honeymoon* (Solar) Arthur Fields, Walter Donovan; *I'd Climb The Highest Mountain* (Haymes) Lew Brown, Sidney Clare; *My Melancholy Baby* (Haymes) George A. Norton, Ernie Burnett.

That's The Spirit (Universal) was a musical fantasy that starred Jack Oakie (left) as a long-deceased hoofer who returns to earth in order to help his daughter (Peggy Ryan) make a career for herself on the stage – much to the disapproval of her grandfather (Gene Lockhart). Unfortunately, whimsy of this nature needed a more skilful screenplay than the producer-writer team of Michael Fessier and Ernest Pagano provided, and much tighter direction than it got from Charles Lamont. June Vincent (illustrated) played Oakie's widow, with other parts going to tap-dancer Johnny Coy, Andy Devine, Arthur Treacher, Irene Ryan, and Buster Keaton. Songs and musical numbers: *Oh, Oh, Oh*; *Fellow With A Flute* Inez James, Sidney Miller; *Evenin' Star*; *No Matter Where You Are* Jack Brooks, H.J. Salter; *Nola* Felix Arndt; *How Come You Do Me Like You Do?* Roy Bergere, Gene Austin; *Baby, Won't You Please Come Home?* Clarence Williams, Charles Warfield; *Bugle Call Rag* J. Hubert Blake, Carey Morgan; *Ja-Da* Bob Carleton; *Do You Ever Think Of Me?* Earl Burnett, John Cooper, Harry D. Kerr.

Forties Musicals

Sam Goldwyn followed his successful screen ▷
launch of Danny Kaye in *Up In Arms* (RKO,
1944) with **Wonder Man** (RKO), and offered
audiences a package they couldn't and didn't
refuse: two Danny Kayes for the price of one,
with Technicolor, the inevitable Goldwyn
Girls, and the debut of another promising newcomer – Vera-Ellen – thrown in as added
attractions. The result was one of the top
money-making films of the year. Another
musical fantasy, it told the story of two brothers
(both played by Kaye), one of whom is a devil-
may-care nightclub performer, the other a
rather ascetic scholar who spends most of his
time in public libraries because he loves the
smell of leather bindings. The plot pivoted on the
confusion caused when the extrovert brother is
murdered by gangsters, and his soul mischiev-
ously enters the body of the introvert, demand-
ing vengeance. Virginia Mayo (illustrated right),
an ex-Goldwyn Girl now elevated to star status,
co-starred (as a librarian) with Kaye (left) in
what was to be the first of four films they made
together; with Vera-Ellen third-billed as the
murdered brother's fiancée and dance partner.
Donald Woods, Allen Jenkins, Edward S.
Brophy, Steve Cochran (his debut), Otto Kruger,
Richard Lane, Natalie Schafer and Huntz Hall
also appeared. Sylvia Fine provided Kaye with
two specialty songs – 'Orchi Tchornya', in
which he gave a hilarious impression of a
Russian baritone beset by a sneezing fit; and
'Opera Number' – a frenetic opera parody that
also happened to further the plot for, in it, Kaye
was able to sing the whole story of his brother's
murder (and reveal whodunnit) to the district
attorney in the audience. There were two other
numbers: 'Bali Boogie' (by Sylvia Fine), performed by Kaye, Vera-Ellen, Jack Norton and
The Goldwyn Girls, and 'So In Love' by Leo
Robin and David Rose, sung by Vera-Ellen
(whose vocals were dubbed by June Hutton),
with Cecil Cunningham and The Goldwyn Girls.
John Wray choreographed. The screenplay was
by Don Hartman, Melville Shavelson and Phillip
Rapp, based on an adaptation of an Arthur
Sheekman story by Jack Jevne and Eddie Moran;
it was produced by Goldwyn (in Technicolor)
and directed with an appropriate sense of the
ridiculous by Bruce Humberstone.

Hitchhike To Happiness (Republic) featured ▷
radio's Al Pearce (left) as a would-be playwright
who, while waiting for his big break, takes
employment as a waiter in a small New York
restaurant frequented largely by show folk. His
customers, aware of his theatrical yearnings,
decide to perpetrate a hoax on an irritating
Hungarian producer (Willy Trenk) by leading
him to believe that Pearce has written a masterpiece that will make all concerned with it rich.
Complications proliferate, with Dale Evans (as a
famous radio singer), Brad Taylor (as a songwriter), William Frawley (a producer), Irving
Bacon (a playwright), Joyce Compton (centre),
Robert Strong (right) and Jerome Cowan (a faded
star) all contributing to the fun. Jack Townley
wrote it (story by Manny Seff and Jerry Horwin);
Joseph Santley directed for producer Donald H.
Brown. Songs included: *Hitchhike To Happiness*;
For You And Me; *Sentimental*; *My Pushover Heart*
Kim Gannon, Walter Kent.

◁ Jane Powell (left) starred in **Delightfully Dangerous**, a ponderous offering from United Artists in
which she appeared as a charming Miss Fixit
who, after learning that her big sister (Constance
Moore, right) isn't a famous Broadway star at
all, but a burlesque queen, sets out to rectify
matters – in the course of which she also
manages to marry her off to a good-looking
Broadway producer (Ralph Bellamy). Fifteen-
year-old Miss Powell warbled a collection of old
and new songs in her pretty coloratura, providing Walter DeLeon and Arthur Phillips's screenplay, from a story by Irving Phillips, Edward
Verdier and Frank Tashlin, with its only genuine
freshness. Arthur Treacher played a butler
(that's how original it all was!), with Louise
Beavers, Ruth Tobey, Ruth Robinson, Andre
Charlot, Shirley Hunter Williams, and Morton
Gould and His Orchestra completing the cast for
producer Charles R. Rogers and director Arthur
Lubin. Songs and musical numbers included: *In
A Shower Of Stars*; *Mynah Bird*; *I'm Only Teasin'*;
Through Your Eyes To Your Heart; *Once Upon A
Song* John Jacob Loeb, Redd Evans; and, to
showcase Miss Powell's range of vocal abilities, a
medley of songs by Johann Strauss.

Charles Coburn played a professional card sharp
in the moderately entertaining **Shady Lady**
(Universal), with Ginny Simms (illustrated) as
his nightclub singer niece and Robert Paige as
the deputy State Attorney in charge of gambling. Alan Curtis was cast as Simms's racketeer
boss, with other roles going to Martha O'Driscoll, Kathleen Howard, James Burke, John Gallaudet, Joe Frisco and Thomas E. Jackson. It was
produced and directed by George Waggner,
scripted by Curt Siodmak, Gerald Geraghty and
M.M. Musselman (additional dialogue by Monty
Collins) and choreographed by Lester Horton.
Songs and musical numbers: *In Love With Love*;
Mam'selle Is On Her Way George Waggner,
Milton Rosen; *Tango* Edgar Fairchild; *Cuddle Up A
Little Closer* Karl Hoschna, Otto Harbach.

Where Do We Go From Here? (20th Century-Fox), which had a pleasing score by Kurt Weill and Ira Gershwin, was an ambitious musical fantasy that starred Fred MacMurray (right) as a disappointed 4-F yearning to get into the army. Instead he is confined to a salvage depot where, while polishing an old lamp one day, he releases a genie (Gene Sheldon) who gratefully grants him three wishes. Naturally, MacMurray says he wants to be drafted – and, indeed he is. Except that genie Sheldon's magic is as rusty as the lamp from which he sprang – and MacMurray finds himself spirited off to Valley Forge in the days of Washington. His trip through history continues when he finds himself aboard Columbus's Santa Maria, (the best sequence in the film, staged as an opera) and, on yet another occasion, purchases Manhattan Island from a Red Indian for twenty-four dollars. The two women he meets in the course of his travels are Joan Leslie and June Haver (left), with other parts in Morrie Ryskind's original screenplay (based on a story by himself and Sig Herzig) going to Anthony Quinn (centre, as an Indian chief), Alan Mowbray (as Washington) and Fortunio Bonanova (as Columbus) as well as Herman Bing, Howard Freeman and John Davidson. In general Gregory Ratoff's direction lacked the requisite lightness of touch the material demanded, but it had its moments. The dances were staged by Fanchon, and the producer was William Perlberg. Songs and musical numbers: All At Once; Song Of The Rhineland; The Nina, The Pinta and The Santa Maria; Christopher Columbus; If Love Remains; Morale.

George Gershwin's rise to fame from his humble East-side origins provided scenarists Howard Koch and Elliot Paul (story by Sonya Levien) with a springboard from which to launch their platitudinous and overworked screenplay for **Rhapsody in Blue**, Warner Bros.' largely fictitious account of the great composer's life and times. With no more than a passing nod at verisimilitude, producer Jesse L. Lasky cast Robert Alda (at piano) as Gershwin, and allowed his team of writers to put words into his subject's mouth that were, at times, frankly embarrassing. But with the complete Gershwin catalogue at the studio's disposal, music spoke louder than words – especially the performances (by Oscar Levant) of the celebrated 'Rhapsody In Blue', first heard by movie audiences in Universal's 1930 Technicolor revue King of Jazz, and the Concerto in F. Joan Leslie played ingenue Julie Adams, with Alexis Smith cast as the moneyed 'other' woman. Charles Coburn appeared as music publisher Max Dreyfus, Albert Basserman was Gershwin's benevolent music professor and mentor, Julie Bishop (centre) was Lee Gershwin, Herbert Rudley (2nd left), Ira Gershwin, and Rosemary De Camp and Morris Carnovsky Ma and Pa Gershwin. Oscar Levant (right – who had the best lines in the film), Paul Whiteman, Al Jolson, George White, Hazel Scott and Anne Brown played themselves. Mickey Roth and Darryl Hickman were the young George and Ira. Other roles: Stephen Richards (left, later Mark Stevens), Martin Noble (as Jascha Heifetz), Will Wright (as Rachmaninov), Ernest Golm (as Otto Kahn), Eddie Marr (as Buddy De Sylva) and Oscar Loraine (Ravel). The excellent orchestral arrangements were by Ray Heindorf. LeRoy Prinz choreographed, and the direction was by Irving Rapper. Ray Turner played the piano for Alda, and Louanne Hogan dubbed the vocals for Joan Leslie. It was beautifully photographed in black and white by Sol Polito. Other songs and musical numbers (lyrics by Ira Gershwin unless otherwise indicated): Somebody Loves Me Buddy De Sylva, Ballard MacDonald; Fascinating Rhythm; Summertime Du Bose Heyward; Delishious; The Man I Love; Mine; Yankee Doodle Blues De Sylva, Irving Caesar; Liza Ira Gershwin, Gus Kahn; Oh Lady Be Good; Clap Yo' Hands; Bidin' My Time; Love Walked In; Do It Again De Sylva; I'll Build A Stairway To Paradise De Sylva, Arthur Francis (pseudonym of Gershwin); Blue Monday Blues Buddy De Sylva; Swanee by Irving Caesar; Someone To Watch Over Me; Cuban Overture; An American In Paris; 'Swonderful; I Got Rhythm; Variations on I Got Rhythm; My One And Only; Embraceable You.

Instead of Jose Iturbi adorning a trite tale with a few popular classics, producer Joe Pasternak persuaded Wagnerian tenor Lauritz Melchior to handle the long-haired stuff in **Thrill Of A Romance**, a glossy entertainment from MGM with lots of spit and polish, but not much else by way of solid musical entertainment. Mrs Johnson's boy Van (right) topped the cast list as an air force hero on vacation at a Sierra Nevada mountain lodge, with Esther Williams (left) as the girl he woos (between her dips in the resident swimming pool). Except that she's a newlywed whose prosaic businessman husband has had to leave suddenly for Washington. Johnson's romance with water-sprite Williams was the raison d'être of Richard Connell and Gladys Lehman's uneventful screenplay, and pretty predictable it turned out to be. Two hit songs emerged: 'Please Don't Say No, Say Maybe' by Ralph Freed and Sammy Fain, boomingly sung by Mr Melchior, and 'I Should Care' by Sammy Cahn, Axel Stordahl and Paul Weston, sung by Robert Allen. The direction was by Richard Thorpe, who relied on additional musical support from Tommy Dorsey and Xavier Cugat and their orchestras, as well as The King Sisters. Other songs and musical numbers included: Lonely Night George Stoll, Richard Connell; Vive L'Amour Stoll, Ralph Blane, Kay Thompson; Schubert's Serenade; The Thrill Of A Romance.

Forties Musicals

△

The last, and most stylish, of the year's four musical fairy tales was **Yolanda And The Thief** (MGM), set in Latin America and starring Fred Astaire (centre) as a conman-cum-thief, and Lucille Bremer as a wealthy, gullible young heiress he plans to fleece by pretending to be the earthly incarnation of her guardian angel. But love intrudes and his plans go awry. Directed with immense sophistication by Vincente Minnelli, the finished product was a triumph of style over content, with Irving Brecher's mundane screenplay (from a story by Ludwig Bemelmans and Jacques Thery) uncomfortably at variance with the elegant visual flair imposed on the narrative by Minnelli, his cameraman Charles Rosher, art directors Cedric Gibbons and Jack Martin Smith, and costume designer Irene Sharaff. Photographed in superb Technicolor, it looked a dream and, indeed, the best sequence in it was a dream ballet in which Astaire, torn between his love for Bremer and his love of money, agonizes over which to choose. Very surreal and very exotic, it lasted for sixteen ravishing minutes, its only blemish being a regrettable lyric (by Arthur Freed) which interrupted Eugene Loring's choreography and Harry Warren's music with lines like 'Let The Band Begin, Playing Lohengrin . . .' In complete contrast was the film's joyous finale – a conventional 'big finish', set against a roisterous carnival background to the accompaniment of the show's most accessible tune, 'Coffee Time', also by Freed and Warren, who wrote all of the film's five songs. The cast was completed by Frank Morgan, Mildred Natwick, Mary Nash and Leon Ames – all of them hampered by the inanities of Brecher's screenplay. Too whimsical for mass audience appeal, the film lost over $1,600,00 on its initial release and, of all Astaire's MGM musicals, is the least seen and the least known. Other songs: *This Is The Day For Love* (Bremer); *Angel* (Bremer); *Yolanda* (Astaire); *Will You Marry Me* (dream ballet).

Gloria Jean sang four of the songs in **Easy To Look At**, a small-budget programmer from Universal which offered minimal entertainment. She was cast as an ambitious costume designer who comes to New York to make a name for herself in her chosen field, never for a moment thinking that the name she would make would be a bad one. For, as scripted by Henry Blankfort (who also produced), she is unjustly accused of being a design thief. It all came right in the last reel, though, with Kirby Grant having designs of his own on Miss Jean (right), and J. Edward Bromberg (left), a once famous couturier now reduced to foreman of a clothes emporium, being recognized all over again for the genius he is. George Dolenz, Eric Blore, Leon Belasco, Mildred Law, Dick French (centre), and The Delta Rhythm Boys were also featured. The director was Ford Beebe. Songs and musical numbers included: *Come Along My Heart*; *Just For the Devil Of It*; *That Does It*; *Umbrella With A Silver Lining*; *Swing Low Sweet Lariat* Charles Newman, Arthur Altman; *Is You Is Or Is You Ain't My Baby?* Billy Austin, Louis Jordan.

▽

Just as Bing Crosby took the mickey out of Frank Sinatra in Paramount's *Here Come The Waves* (1944), so Eddie Bracken did the same to Crosby in **Out Of This World** (Paramount) – and with Crosby's voice too. For every time Bracken opened his mouth to croon, out popped Crosby. A gentle spoof on the type of mellifluous warbling guaranteed to elicit squeals of joy from bobby-soxers everywhere, **Out Of This World** was the story of a crooning telegram boy (Bracken, right) whose life becomes needlessly complicated when he hitches up with a stranded all-girl orchestra led by Diana Lynn, who played Chopin's 'Minute Waltz' as part of a Sam Coslow number called 'The Ghost of Mr Chopin'. Bracken's particular brand of clowning helped plug the cracks in Walter DeLeon and Arthur Phillips's screenplay (based on stories by Elizabeth Mehan and Sam Coslow), and there was energetic support from Cass Daley, who gave a fair imitation of a whirling dervish while delivering a number called 'A Sailor With An Eight Hour Pass' (by Ben Raleigh and Bernie Wayne). Veronica Lake (left) received second billing, but was wasted in the role of a theatrical booking agent secretary who helps turn Bracken from singing messenger into singing sensation. The cast was completed by Parkyakarkus, Donald MacBride, Florence Bates, Don Wilson, Mabel Paige, Olga San Juan and Irving Bacon. Also joining in the fun were the four Crosby sons, Carmen Cavallaro, Ray Noble, Ted Fiorito, Henry King and Joe Reichman. Sammy Lee choreographed it, Sam Coslow produced and the director was Hal Walker. Songs and musical numbers included: *June Comes Around Every Year*; *Out Of This World* Johnny Mercer, Harold Arlen; *I'd Rather Be Me* Eddie Cherkose, Felix Bernard, Sam Coslow; *All I Do Is Beat That Golden Drum*; *It Takes A Little Bit More* Coslow.

▽

Anchors Aweigh (MGM), produced in Technicolor by Joe Pasternak, was an archetypal Gene Kelly musical, many of whose ideas would be repeated in future Kelly offerings, most notably in *On The Town* (MGM, 1949). The story (by Natalie Marcin, screenplay by Isobel Lennart) concerned a couple of sailors on leave in Hollywood and the romantic adventures they have, particularly between Kelly and would-be singer Kathryn Grayson, whose ambition it is to audition for Jose Iturbi. In order to impress her, Kelly lies to her that his buddy (Frank Sinatra) and Iturbi are good friends and that with a word in the maestro's ear from Frank, the audition is as good as fixed. Grayson believes him and for the rest of the film (which ran 140 minutes) Kelly and Sinatra rush around Hollywood trying to find Iturbi, in the course of which Sinatra meets a girl (Pamela Britton) from Flatbush, his hometown, and pairs off with her, leaving the way clear for his buddy to pursue Miss Grayson and Iturbi (whom he never manages to find, but who finds Grayson instead), thus ensuring a happy ending. So much for the plot – a typical Pasternakian trifle in which audiences were offered equal quantities of popular music and light classics. Though Pasternak's particular brand of middle-European *schmaltz* was thickly spread over the storyline, Kelly's energetic presence gave the narrative a freshness and a vigour it lacked both in synopsis and in director George Sidney's rather pedestrian handling of it, its best sequences being the three major dances Kelly devised for himself. In one of them (a fantasy in which he woos Grayson on a sound-stage at MGM) the set became a romantic Spanish courtyard with Kelly, dressed in a dazzling gold shirt, red and black cape and black trousers, giving full expression to his characteristic athletic prowess in a fandango-style routine (to the accompaniment of *La Cumparsita* by G.H. Matos Rodriguez) that had him scaling battlements, leaping over parapets and making a 45ft vine-swinging jump from a rooftop to the balcony of his señorita in the most romantic Fairbanks style. In the traditional 'Mexican Hat Dance', performed in a studio reconstruction of Olvera Street (the Mexican section of Los Angeles), with its colourful market place, he partnered little Sharon McManus in a routine which, although self-consciously cute, contained some delightful moments. The third and best sequence (illustrated) was a dance that combined live action and cartoon in which sailor Kelly teaches a grumpy mouse (Jerry from the Tom and Jerry cartoons) how to dance 'The Worry Song' by Ralph Freed and Sammy Fain. Apart from Kelly's contribution to the film (he also choreographed it together with Stanley Donen), there were several songs from Grayson and Sinatra and a fair amount of serious music making from Jose Iturbi, including a snatch of Tchaikovsky's Piano Concerto No. 1 in B Flat Minor, and a complete performance of Liszt's Second Hungarian Rhapsody, played by Iturbi and a veritable battalion of young pianists at the Hollywood Bowl. The cast also included Dean Stockwell (as Miss Grayson's small nephew), Rags Ragland, Billy Gilbert, Carlos Ramirez, James Flavin and Edgar Kennedy. Other songs and musical numbers: *Jealousy* (Grayson) Vera Bloom, Jacob Gade; *Donkey Serenade* (Iturbi) Bob Wright, Chet Forrest, Rudolf Friml; *My Heart Sings* (Grayson) Harold Rome, Herpin; *If You Knew Susie* (Kelly, Sinatra) Joseph Meyer, Buddy De Sylva, new lyrics by Sammy Cahn; *What Makes The Sunset?* (Sinatra); *I Begged Her* (Sinatra, Kelly); *We Hate To Leave* (Sinatra, Kelly); *The Charm Of You* (Sinatra); *I Fall In Love Too Easily* (Sinatra) Cahn, Jule Styne; *Cradle Song (Wiegenlied, Opus 49, No 4)* (Sinatra) Brahms; *Waltz (from Serenade in C, Opus 48)* (Grayson) Tchaikovsky; *Largo Al Factotum* (from the opera 'The Barber of Seville') (Ramirez) Rossini; *Anchors Aweigh* (orchestra, conducted by Iturbi) Alfred H. Miles, Royal Lovell, Charles A. Zimmerman.

Forties Musicals

Often similar to *Hello, Frisco, Hello* (20th Century-Fox, 1943), **Nob Hill** was another Technicolored period piece from the Fox lot set in San Francisco during the heyday of the Barbary Coast. It starred George Raft (standing right) as the proprietor of a café, Vivian Blaine (centre) as his singing sweetheart and Joan Bennett as the rich society girl he temporarily deserts her for. Pasted together from bits and pieces of past Fox successes by Wanda Tuchock and Norman Reilly Raine (story by Eleanore Griffin), and directed by Henry Hathaway with no sense of occasion at all, it also featured Peggy Ann Garner, Alan Reed (standing left), B.S. Pully, Emil Coleman, The Three Swifts and Rory Calhoun. Nick Castle choreographed it, and the producer was Andre Daven. Songs and musical numbers included: *I Don't Care Who Knows It; I Walked In; Touring San Francisco; Paris Of The USA* Harold Adamson, Jimmy McHugh; *What Do You Want To Make Those Eyes At Me For?* Howard Johnson, Joseph McCarthy, James V. Monaco; *San Francisco* Gus Kahn, Bronislau Kaper, Walter Jurmann; *On San Francisco Bay* Vincent Bryan, Gertrude Hoffman; *King Chanticleer (Texas Tommy)* Nat D. Ayer; *Chinatown, My Chinatown* William Jerome, Jean Schwartz; *Too-ra-loo-ra-loo-ra* James Royce Shannon.

There was nothing much to tell in **Tell It To A Star** (Republic), a 67-minute double feature support which starred Ruth Terry as a cigarette girl who'd rather be a singer, Alan Mowbray as a financier who happens to be stone broke but whose gift of the gab helps Miss Terry realize her ambitions, and Robert Livingston as the bandleader she falls for. Aurora Miranda (illustrated centre) was also featured. It was written by John K. Butler from an original story by Gerald Drayson Adams and John Kraft, and directed by Frank McDonald for producers Armand L. Schafer and Walter Goetz. Songs and musical numbers included: *Tell It To A Star* Shirley Botwin; *Love Me Or Leave Me* Gus Kahn, Walter Donaldson; *You're So Good To Me* Sammy Cahn, Jule Styne; *A Batucada Corazon* Ary Barroso.

Jack Oakie and Peggy Ryan (both illustrated) were teamed as a father and daughter vaudeville partnership in **On Stage Everybody** (Universal), a programmer loosely inspired by the radio show of the same name, and telling a story in which Oakie, having at first rejected radio and everything it stood for, finds himself auditioning a talented group of youngsters for the very medium he once so despised. The slender story and screenplay by Warren Wilson and Oscar Brodney was given a modicum of substance by several specialty acts including The King Sisters, and a fair amount of time was devoted to the winners of the Radio Show Contest, all of whom appeared as themselves. Johnny Coy (a replacement for Donald O'Connor who had enlisted) received second billing to Peggy Ryan, with Julie London (her debut), Otto Kruger, Esther Dale, Wallace Ford, Milburn Stone, Stephen Wayne and Jimmy Clark also in it for producer Warren Wilson and associate producer Lou Goldberg, and director Jean Yarbrough. Songs and musical numbers included: *For Him No Love; It'll All Come Out In The Wash; I'm So At Home With You* Inez James, Sidney Miller; *Stuff Like That There* Ray Evans, Jay Livingston; *Put Put Put Your Arms Around Me* Mann Curtis, Al Hoffman, Jerry Livingston; *Take Me In Your Arms* Mitchell Parish, Fred Markush, Fritz Rotter; *What Do I Have To Do To Be A Star?* Bobby Kroll; *Dance With A Dolly With A Hole In Her Stocking* Terry Shand, Jimmy Eaton, Mickey Leader.

Columbia struck another blow for good neighbourliness between America and Latin America with **The Gay Senorita**, 69 minutes of cheerful propaganda in which Jim Bannon set out to convert the Mexican section of a Californian town into a factory site, but changed his plans after falling madly in love with Jinx Falkenburg, the happy senorita of the title. Also cast: Corinna Mura, Steve Cochran, Thurston Hall, Isabel Withers, Marguerite Sylva, Tommy Cook and Lita Baron (Isabelita – illustrated). It was written by Edward Eliscu from a story by J. Robert Bren, produced by Jay Gorney and directed by Arthur Dreifuss. Songs included: *Buenos Noches* Don George, Serge Walters.

Betty Hutton's most important role to date was as Texas Guinan in **Incendiary Blonde** (Paramount), a typical Hollywood biopic that skittered uneasily between fact and fantasy but was never less than entertaining – if one didn't mind Hutton (illustrated) hurling herself head first into the part. Always an energetic worker, she made a frontal attack on the role of Texas with such determined gusto there was hardly time for her to catch her breath between her heavy belting of the numbers, and her heavy emoting in the more dramatic bits. Audiences were left hoarse just watching her! Claude Binyon and Frank Butler's screenplay began in 1909, with Texas winning fifty dollars for riding a bucking bronco. Her days as a Broadway chorine and as a silent screen heroine were also charted, but the film's main concern was with the years between 1923 and her untimely death ten years later after she had become a legend as Broadway's most famous nightclub hostess with her phrase 'Hello Suckers!'. Though no mention was made of her brushes with government prohibition agents, the film dwelt on her association with an assorted collection of bootleggers in several hugely enjoyable, if wildly overplayed scenes. Barry Fitzgerald was cast as Texas's father, a schemer whose numerous ventures always ended in ash, Arturo De Cordova played her gangster lover, with other roles going to Charles Ruggles, Albert Dekker, Mary Philips, Bill Goodwin and Eduardo Ciannelli. Also cast were The Maxellos and Maurice Rocco as themselves. The musical numbers were staged by Danny Dare, Joseph Sistrom produced (in Technicolor), and the numerous switches of mood in the narrative were well handled by director George Marshall. Songs and musical numbers included: *It Had To Be You* (Hutton) Gus Kahn, Isham Jones; *Ragtime Cowboy Joe* (Hutton) Maurice Abrahams, Lewis F. Muir, Grant Clarke; *Oh By Jingo* (Hutton, chorus) Lew Brown, Albert von Tilzer; *Sweet Genevieve* (Fitzgerald, chorus) Henry Tucker, George Cooper; *Row Row Row* (Hutton) William Jerome, James V. Monaco; *Darktown Strutters' Ball* (Rocco) Shelton Brooks; *What Do You Want To Make Those Eyes At Me For?* (Hutton) Howard Johnson, Joseph McCarthy, James V. Monaco; *Ida, Sweet As Apple Cider* (performer unidentified) Eddie Leonard, Eddie Munson.

State Fair (20th Century-Fox), a musical remake of Will Rogers's 1933 film of the same name, brought Jeanne Crain (in the role originally played by Janet Gaynor) to prominence as Margy Frake, the brunette heroine of Phil Stong's cosy, homespun novel. Apart from Crain accompanying her parents Charles Winninger (in the Rogers role) and Fay Bainter to Iowa's big state fair, where she meets and falls in love with reporter Dana Andrews (right), not a great deal happened in Oscar Hammerstein II's screenplay (adapted from the novel by Sonya Levien and Paul Green) – unless you considered Winninger's obsession with his prize hog, and his wife's concern over her pickles as happenings. Instead, the pleasures were mainly to be derived from the marvellous score (by Richard Rodgers and Hammerstein II), from the gentle, bucolic atmosphere conveyed in Walter Lang's direction, and from the delightfully fresh and invigorating central performance by Miss Crain (centre). Dick Haymes (left) played her crooning brother Wayne and Vivian Blaine appeared as a dance-band singer, with other roles in William Perlberg's delightful Technicolor production going to Donald Meek, Frank McHugh, Henry Morgan, Percy Kilbride and William Marshall. Jeanne Crain's vocals were dubbed by Louanne Hogan. It was remade again in 1962. Songs and musical numbers: *It's A Grand Night For Singing*; *It Might As Well Be Spring*; *That's For Me*; *Isn't It Kinda Fun?*; *All I Owe I-O-Way*; *Our State Fair*.

The title told it all: Radio Stars on Parade (RKO) was little more than a collection of radio celebrities in a 69-minute free-for-all that top-starred Wally Brown and Alan Carney as the managers of a Hollywood talent agency who find themselves caught up in Ralph Edwards's popular show *Truth or Consequences*. Others appearing were Frances Langford (illustrated) as a nightclub singer aspiring to radio work, Rufe Davis, Robert Clarke, Sheldon Leonard, Ralph Peters, Don Wilson, Tony Romano, The Town Criers, The Cappy Barra Boys, and Skinnay Ennis and His Band. Robert E. Kent and Monte Brice wrote it and it was directed by Leslie Goodwins for producer Ben Stoloff. Songs and musical numbers included: *I Couldn't Sleep A Wink Last Night* Jimmy McHugh, Harold Adamson; *That Old Black Magic* Harold Arlen, Johnny Mercer.

One of the songs in Columbia's I Love A Bandleader (GB: Memory For Two) was called 'Good, Good, Good' (by Allan Roberts and Doris Fisher) – not an accurate appraisal of the film to which it was attached, but a jive-orientated ditty sung by star Phil Harris (foreground left) as a duet with Leslie Brooks (foreground centre). Harris played a nightclub painter who, after literally falling head over heels for Miss Brooks, winds up with amnesia, in which state of mind he becomes a successful bandleader. Taking advantage of Harris's loss of memory, Brooks poses as his fiancée in order to land herself a job as a singer, and when a second blow on the head restores Harris's memory to him, complications proliferate. Paul Yawitz scripted it from a story by John Grey, Del Lord directed, Michael Kraike produced and the cast included Walter Catlett, Frank Sully and the Four V's.

A *pot-pourri* from Paramount, Duffy's Tavern (loosely inspired by the radio show of the same name) involved the bar's polygot keeper Archie (Ed Gardner, left) and an inebriated patron of the establishment (Victor Moore, right) in an effort to revive the flagging fortunes of a recording studio. Anyone familiar with plots like this, could tell at a glance that the film was little more than a contrivance to display the variegated talents of the studio's contract artists in a series of musical numbers and sketches of fluctuating quality. Best of the offerings were Betty Hutton's (centre) maniacal rendition of 'Doin' It The Hard Way' (by Johnny Burke and Jimmy Van Heusen), Cass Daley's equally frenetic handling of 'You Can't Blame A Gal For Trying' (by Ben Raleigh and Bernie Wayne), and an amusing parody on Burke and Van Heusen's 'Swinging On A Star' by Bing Crosby, Betty Hutton, Dorothy Lamour, Diana Lynn and Arturo De Cordova. Alan Ladd and Veronica Lake rehearsed a radio murder script, much to the consternation of Victor Moore who thought it was all for real, with other bits and pieces falling to Paulette Goddard, Eddie Bracken, Brian Donlevy, Sonny Tufts, Barry Fitzgerald, Robert Benchley, William Demarest, Walter Abel, Billy De Wolfe, Johnny Coy, Howard Da Silva, and Gary, Phillip, Dennis and Lin Crosby. Melvin Frank and Norman Panama's screenplay also utilized the talents of Marjorie Reynolds and Barry Sullivan (as the love interest), Charles Cantor, Eddie Green and Ann Thomas. Billy Daniels was in charge of the choreography; Joseph Sistrom produced with Danny Dare as his associate, and the director was Hal Walker. Other songs and musical numbers included: *Leave Us Face It* (Frank Loesser, Abe Burrows).

A public relations job for the folks down Mexico way, Mexicana (Republic) was a musical travelogue of sorts that featured Tito Guizar (Mexico's answer to Frank Sinatra) as a singing idol who, to discourage his fans from ripping the shirt off his back everytime he appears in public, persuades a visiting sporano (Constance Moore, illustrated lying down) to pose as his wife. And before you could say caramba! – well, you know the rest. Estelita Rodriguez as a long standing admirer of Señor Guizar didn't approve at all, and who could blame her? Frank Gill Jr's screenplay also found parts for Leo Carillo, Jean Stevens (illustrated), Howard Freeman and Steve Geray, as well as The St Luke Choristers and The Peter Meremblum Junior Orchestra. The choreographer was Nick Castle and it was produced and directed by Alfred Santell. Songs and musical numbers: *Mexicana*; *Lupita*; *See Mexico*; *Heartlessness*; *Time out For Dreaming*; *De Corazon A Corazon* Ned Washington, Gabriel Ruiz; *Somewhere There's A Rainbow* Washington, Walter Scharf.

Forties Musicals

△

Nothing was scandalous about **George White's Scandals of 1945** (RKO) except, possibly, its woeful lack of originality. A backstage musical, relying for interest on the hazards attendant on putting on a show, its screenplay written in committee by Hugh Wedlock, Howard Snyder, Parke Levy and Howard Green, from a story by Wedlock and Snyder – also involved audiences in a couple of perfunctory romances between stars Joan Davis and Jack Haley and featured players Phillip Terry and Martha Holliday: the former encountering resistance from Haley's spinster aunt (Margaret Hamilton); the latter fraught with misunderstandings. Davis and Haley scored in a number from the 1931 stage edition of the *Scandals* called 'Life Is Just A Bowl Of Cherries' by Lew Brown and Ray Henderson; and from guest star Ethel Smith there was a pyrotechnical display on the organ of 'Liza' by George and Ira Gershwin. And that was about it. George White produced, Ernest Matray choreographed (production number illustrated), and the director was Felix Feist. Other songs and musical numbers included: *I Wake Up In The Morning* (Davis, Haley); *I Want To Be A Drummer* (Gene Krupa and His Band); *Who Killed Vaudeville?* (Davis, Haley) Jack Yellen, Sammy Fain; *Bolero In The Jungle* (Gene Krupa) Tommy Peterson, Krupa; *Wishing* (Smith) Buddy De Sylva.

Susanna Foster (illustrated centre) was so irredeemably stage-struck in **That Night With You** (Universal) that, in order to land herself a part in a Broadway show, she tells producer Franchot Tone she's his daughter – the result of a one-day marriage undertaken in his youth. Miss Foster wasn't the sort of actress to get away with foolishness of this ilk, and had to rely on her pleasant singing voice to see her through the contrivances of producers Michael Fessier and Ernest Pagano's witless screenplay (story by Arnold Belgard). David Bruce, Louise Allbritton, Jacqueline De Wit, Irene Ryan, Barbara Sears, Anthony Caruso and Buster Keaton (seen briefly as a short-order cook) completed the cast. The dances were staged by Lester Horton and Louis Da Pron and the film was directed by William A. Seiter. Songs and musical numbers included: *Once Upon A Dream* Jack Brooks, Hans J. Salter; *Market Place*; *Shadows*; *Largo Al Factotum* from Rossini's 'The Barber of Seville' (a female version performed in a beauty parlour).

Studio head Darryl F. Zanuck purchased John Kenyon Nicholson's story, **The Dolly Sisters**, as a vehicle for Betty Grable (left) and Alice Faye. But, unable to coax Miss Faye out of retirement, Zanuck finally agreed to producer George Jessel's casting of June Haver (right) instead. The result was a typical Fox musical, monotonous in its fidelity to the genre's form, but handled with such pazazz and showmanship that it proved an irresistible (and financially rewarding) splash of Technicolored, turn-of-the-century escapism. Its fictionalized account of the two Hungarian brunettes (not blondes, as the film would have us believe) who achieved stardom after Oscar Hammerstein engaged them to appear at his Music Hall, was the perfect excuse for several old (and several new) numbers, plus a couple of romances to pad out its fragile plot. John Payne as a composer called Harry Fox was Grable's choice, while Haver settled for a far less turbulent relationship with Frank Latimore. The two hit songs to emerge were 'I Can't Begin To Tell You' by Mack Gordon and James V. Monaco, sung by Grable, Payne and Haver; and 'I'm Always Chasing Rainbows' by Joseph McCarthy and Harry Carroll (based on a Chopin melody), sung by Grable. The musical numbers were staged by Seymour Felix with such kitschy vulgarity (especially a gaudy item glorifying a woman's make-up kit called 'Powder, Lipstick and Rouge' by Mack Gordon and Harry Revel) that, viewed today, they

▽

cannot be considered as anything other than monuments to bad taste. At the same time, what cannot be denied is just how compulsively enjoyable they are. The film was stunningly costumed by Orry-Kelly and directed by Irving Cummings with a cheerful disregard for period accuracy. The rest of the capable cast included S.Z. Sakall as the sisters' genial uncle Latsie, Reginald Gardiner, Gene Sheldon, Sig Rumann, Trudy Marshall, Collette Lyons and Frank Middlemass (playing Oscar Hammerstein). Other songs and musical numbers: *Give Me The Moonlight* (Grable, Payne) Lew Brown, Albert von Tilzer; *On The Mississippi* (Male quartet) Ballard MacDonald, Arthur Fields, Harry Carroll; *We Have Been Around* (Grable, Haver) Mack Gordon, Charles Henderson; *Carolina In The Morning* (Grable, Haver) Gus Kahn, Walter Donaldson; *Arrah Go On I'm Gonna Go Back To Oregon* (Payne) Joe Young, Sam Lewis, Bert Grant; *Darktown Strutters' Ball* (Grable, Haver) Shelton Brooks; *The Vamp* (Grable, Haver) Byron Gay; *Hungarian Dance No 5 in F Sharp Minor* (danced by Evon Thomas and Donna Jo Gribble playing the sisters as children, then by Grable and Haver) Brahms; *Smiles* (Soldiers' chorus) J. Will Callahan, Lee S. Roberts; *Oh Frenchie* (Soldiers' chorus) Sam Ehrlich, Con Conrad; *Pack Up Your Troubles* (Soldiers' chorus) Felix Powell, George Asaf; *Mademoiselle From Armentières* (Soldiers' chorus); *The Sidewalks Of New York* (Grable, Haver) James Blake, Charles B. Lawlor.

▷

A big grosser for Paramount, **The Stork Club** was an inexpensively produced (by Buddy De Sylva; associate producer Harold Wilson) starring vehicle for Betty Hutton (centre). She played a hat-check girl at the famous nightspot who, on one of her afternoons off, saves an elderly bum (Barry Fitzgerald, right) from drowning. Except that he isn't a bum at all but a millionaire, who rewards her by setting her up in a penthouse complete with limousine, charge account and chauffeur. When her bandleader boyfriend (Don Defore) returns from active service, he isn't at all happy at the set-up, incorrectly suspecting Hutton of paying in kind for the services rendered her. But scriptwriters De Sylva and John McGowan waved their magic pencil over it all, and in the end everyone lived happily ever after – as was usually the way with fairy tales. Musical highlight was Hutton's wildcat performance of 'Doctor, Lawyer, Indian Chief' by Paul Francis Webster and Hoagy Carmichael. She had another solo called 'I'm A Square In The Social Circle' (by Ray Evans and Jay Livingston) and was joined by wishy-washy Andy Russell in an indifferent duet called 'If I Had A Dozen Hearts' by Webster and Harry Revel. Robert Benchley (left) appeared as a counsellor, with Bill Goodwin, Iris Adrian, Mary Young, Charles Coleman, Perce Launders and Mikhail Rasumny completing the cast. The choreography was by Billy Daniels and the direction by Hal Walker. Other songs and musical numbers included: *Love Me* Sammy Cahn, Jule Styne; *China Boy* Dick Winfree, Phil Boutelje; *Baltimore Oriole* Webster, Carmichael; *In The Shade Of The Old Apple Tree* Harry H. Williams, Egbert Van Alstyne.

The sort of musical one expected to see coming from 20th Century-Fox rather than from Monogram, **Sunbonnet Sue**, set in the colourful Bowery era *circa* 1902, was a nostalgic trip down memory lane to the accompaniment of several popular tunes of the period, and a mere *soupçon* of a plot involving the fortunes of a saloon owner (George Cleveland) who allows his daughter (Gale Storm, centre) to sing and dance to the delight of his customers, but to the disapproval of her socially-minded aunt (Minna Gombell). Miss Storm managed to bring a charm and freshness to the role despite its conventionality, with the rest of the cast (Phil Regan, Edna M. Holland (right), Raymond Hatton, Alan Mowbray (left) and Charles Judels) also responding well to Ralph Murphy's thoroughly professional direction. Murphy also scripted it, together with Richard A. Carroll, from a story by Paul Gerard Smith and Bradford Ropes and the dances were staged by Jack Boyle. Edward J. Kay's musical scoring was particularly good. Songs and musical numbers: *School Days*; *Sunbonnet Sue* Gus Edwards, Will D. Cobb; *The Bowery* Charles H. Hoyt, Percy Gaunt; *Yip-I-Addy-I-Ay* Cobb, John H. Flynn; *Yoo Hoo, Ain't You Comin Out Tonight?* Carson Robison; *By The Light Of The Silvery Moon* Ed Madden, Edwards; *If I Had My Way* Lou Klein, James Kendis; *While Strolling Through The Park One Day* Ed Haley; *Donegal*; *Roll Dem Bones*; *Look For The Rainbow* Ralph Murphy, C. Harold Lewis.

Universal's **Senorita From The West** embellished the oft-told tale of the ambitious youngster who arrives in the big city fresh from the backwoods, with a couple of plot twists that were more contrived than ingenious. The youngster, played by Bonita Granville (centre) is a gold-mine heiress, except that her guardians haven't informed her of the fact lest she should fall prey to some fortune-hunting city slicker. The man she does eventually choose is a bashful singer (Allan Jones) who ghosts for 'crooner' Jess Barker, a con artist who learns of Miss Granville's wealth and immediately sets out to ensnare her. George Cleveland, Fuzzy Knight, Oscar O'Shea, Renny McEvoy, Olin Howlin and Bob Merrill were also in it, with Spade Cooley (centre right foreground) and His Orchestra supplying much of the music. The makeshift direction was by Frank Strayer, the equally makeshift script by Howard Dimsdale, and the producer was Phil Cahn. Songs and musical numbers included: *Lonely Love* Everett Carter, Ray Sinatra; *Lou Lou Louisiana* Everett Carter, Milton Rosen; *What A Change In The Weather* Kim Gannon, Walter Kent; *These Hazy, Lazy Old Hills*; *All The Things I Wanna Say*.

Sing Your Way Home was an unintelligent, wretchedly plotted programmer from RKO which starred Jack Haley (illustrated centre) as a war correspondent *en route* to New York from Europe after V-J Day, and in whose care are a group of hepcat American teenagers hitherto trapped in Europe by the war. The main plot complication – involving a coded message sent by Haley to his editor – defied belief; but then so did everything else about this fabricated yarn (screenplay by William Bowers, story by Edmund Joseph and Bart Lytton), including Haley's shipboard romance with singer Anne Jeffreys. Marcy McGuire (centre left, leg up) showed zest as one of the homeward-bound teenagers, and was the only bright spot in a cast that also included Glenn Vernon, Donna Lee, Patti Brill and James Jordan Jr. Herb Magidson and Allie Wrubel's score was better than producer Bert Granet's film deserved, especially 'I'll Buy That Dream', sung by Anne Jeffreys, which became a standard. Anthony Mann directed. Other songs and musical numbers included: *Heaven Is A Place Called Home*; *Seven O'Clock In The Morning (Waking Up Boogie)*; *Somebody Stole My Poor Little Heart* Magidson, Wrubel; *The Lord's Prayer* arranged by Albert Hay Malotte.

1946

Academy Awards

Best Actor
NOMINATIONS INCLUDED: Larry Parks *The Jolson Story* (Columbia)

Supporting Actor
NOMINATIONS INCLUDED: William Demarest *The Jolson Story*

Writing (Original Screenplay)
NOMINATIONS INCLUDED: *The Road To Utopia* (Paramount) Norman Panama and Melvin Frank

Cinematography (colour)
NOMINATIONS INCLUDED: *The Jolson Story* Joseph Walker

Sound Recording
NOMINATIONS INCLUDED: *The Jolson Story* John Livadary

Film Editing
NOMINATIONS INCLUDED: *The Jolson Story* William Lyon

Music
Song
'On The Atchison, Topeka And The Santa Fe' *The Harvey Girls* (MGM) Harry Warren *cm*; Johnny Mercer *lyr*.
NOMINATIONS INCLUDED: 'All Through The Day' *Centennial Summer* (20th Century-Fox) Jerome Kern *cm*; Oscar Hammerstein II *lyr*. 'I Can't Begin To Tell You' *The Dolly Sisters* (20th Century-Fox) James V. Monaco *cm*; Mack Gordon *lyr*. 'You Keep Coming Back Like A Song' *Blue Skies* (Paramount) Irving Berlin.

Scoring Of A Musical Picture
The Jolson Story Morris Stoloff
NOMINATIONS INCLUDED: *Blue Skies* Robert Emmett Dolan. *Centennial Summer* Alfred Newman. *The Harvey Girls* Lennie Hayton. *Night And Day* (WB) Ray Heindorf and Max Steiner.

The New York Times Annual 'Ten Best'
2nd *The Road To Utopia*

The Annual Top Moneymaking Films
INCLUDED: *The Dolly Sisters. Easy To Wed* (MGM). *The Harvey Girls. The Kid From Brooklyn.* (Goldwyn, RKO). *Night And Day. The Road To Utopia. The Stork Club* (Paramount). *Ziegfeld Follies* (MGM).

Meet Me On Broadway (Columbia) needed a stronger cast than the one assembled for it by producer Burt Kelly. Fred Brady played an arrogant young director whose know-it-all attitude ruins his chances of Broadway success and reduces him to staging a country club show with amateurs; Jinx Falkenburg was the rich gal whose dad owns the country club and Marjorie Reynolds (top billed) was his faithful long-standing sweetheart. Also cast: Loren Tindall, Allen Jenkins, Spring Byington and Gene Lockhart. Several production numbers (staged by Billy Daniels, see illustration) helped pass **Meet Me On Broadway's** 77 minutes painlessly enough but, in the end, the rendezvous was hardly worth keeping. George Bricker, who thought it all up, wrote the screenplay with Jack Henley, and it was directed by Leigh Jason. Songs and musical numbers included: *I Never Had A Chance; Fifth Avenue; Is It Worth It; Only For Me* Saul Chaplin, Edgar De Lange; *She Was A Good Girl* Allan Roberts, Doris Fisher.

Composer Harry Warren (together with lyricist Johnny Mercer) scored his first really big hit at MGM with George Sidney's **The Harvey Girls**, a glorious 'frontier' musical (in Technicolor) whose plot followed a group of ultra-refined waitresses employed by restaurateur Fred Harvey into the wild and woolly West. A veritable army of scenarists (Edmund Beloin, Nathaniel Curtis, Harry Crane, James O'Hanlon, Samson Raphaelson, Kay Van Riper, from a story by Samuel Hopkins Adams, Eleanore Griffin and William Rankin) gave the film its narrative thrust by generally focussing on the conflict between the decorous waitresses and the somewhat less proper women of the town; and in particular on one rather straitlaced lass (Judy Garland, illustrated) and her private war with the proprietor (John Hodiak) of a local bawdy house, with whom she soon falls in love. Garland was enchanting in the role, and there was good work too from Ray Bolger, Virginia O'Brien (marvellous in 'The Wild Wild West') and Angela Lansbury. Cyd Charisse was in it too (vocals dubbed by Betty Russell); so were Marjorie Main, Preston Foster, Kenny Baker, Chill Wills, Selena Royle and Ruth Brady. Warren and Mercer composed eleven songs for the film, eight of which were finally used, the undoubted and most durable hit being the legendary 'On The Atchison, Topeka And The Santa Fe', choreographed by Robert Alton and performed by Garland, Bolger and a train load of Harvey girls. Arthur Freed produced, Conrad Salinger did the memorable orchestrations, Kay Thompson was in charge of the vocal arrangements and Lennie Hayton the musical direction. The associate producer, and one of the most influential and invaluable members of the celebrated 'Freed unit' was Roger Edens. The film grossed over $5,000,000 on its initial release. Other songs and musical numbers: *In The Valley* (Garland); *Wait And See* (Baker, Charisse, Lansbury); *The Train Must Be Fed* (ensemble); *Swing Your Partner Round And Round* (Garland, Bolger, Main, ensemble); *It's A Great Big World* (Garland, Charisse, O'Brien); *Oh You Kid* (Lansbury).

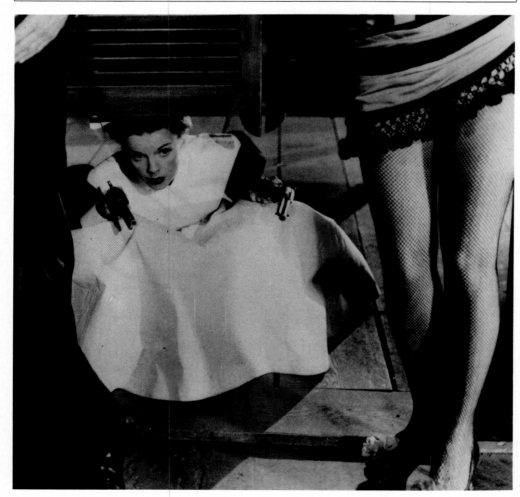

Though most of the youngsters cast by producer Sam Katzman in his youth-orientated **Junior Prom** (Monogram) seemed a trifle too old for their school-kid roles, the film emerged as an exuberant little programmer whose all but invisible plot concerned a campus election campaign and the battle among several contenders for presidency. Freddie Stewart (right) topped the bill, with acrobatic June Preisser (centre) as his co-star, and other roles going to Judy Clark, Noel Neill, Jackie Moran, Frankie Darro, Warren Mills (left) and Murray Davis. Helping to put a beat in it were Abe Lyman and Eddie Heywood with their orchestras, Harry (The Hipster) Gibson, and The Airliners. Erna Lazarus and Hal Collins wrote it and Arthur Dreifuss directed. Songs and Musical numbers included: *Keep The Beat*; *Teen Canteen* Sid Robin; *Trimball For President* Stanley Cowan; *(All Of A Sudden) My Heart Sings* Herpin, Harold Rome (English lyrics), Jamblan (French lyrics); *Loch Lomond* (traditional); *It's Me Oh Lawd* (negro spiritual).
▽

Music and slapstick were the main ingredients of **People are Funny** (Paramount), a spin-off of the popular radio show of the same name. Written by Maxwell Shane and David Lang (story by Lang), it concerned the attempts of a radio producer (Phillip Reed) to find a replacement show when sponsor Rudy Vallee expresses dissatisfaction with the one currently on the air. What, of course, he comes up with, is 'People Are Funny' – and just how he does so – in the company of Helen Walker (illustrated right), Ozzie Nelson, Bob Graham, Barbara Roche, Art Linkletter, Clara Blandick, and Roy Atwell and The Vagabonds – was what producer-director Sam White's pleasant little film was all about. Frances Langford was prominently billed as guest star, with Jack Haley (left) heading the cast as a small-town radio announcer and the originator of the radio programme in question. Songs included: *I'm In The Mood For Love* Dorothy Fields, Jimmy McHugh; *Angelina* Doris Fisher, Allan Roberts; *The Old Square Dance Is Back Again* Don Reid, Henry Tobias; *Alouette* (traditional French Canadian); *Every Hour On The Hour* Don George, Duke Ellington.
▽

A Coast Guard romance involving Janet Blair and Alfred Drake, **Tars And Spars** (Columbia) relied solely on the comic antics of newcomer Sid Caesar (seen at his best in an hilarious parody of a bad war film) to keep it alive and kicking. Otherwise it was just another routine musical with a wartime background, desperately in need of a few fresh ideas and a couple of good tunes. John Jacoby, Sarett Tobias and Decla Dunning hammered it out from a story by Barry Trivers, the lustreless score was by Jule Styne and Sammy Cahn, Alfred E. Green directed, Jack Cole choreographed, Milton H. Bren produced, and the cast was completed by dancers Anita Alvarez and Marc Platt (illustrated), Jeff Donnell, Ray Walker and James Flavin. Only Caesar came, saw, and conquered. Songs and musical numbers; *I'm Glad I Waited For You*; *Love Is A Merry-Go-Round*; *Kiss Me Hello, Baby*; *I Always Meant To Tell You*; *He's A Hero*; *Don't Call On Me*; *After The War Baby*; *When I Get To Town*; *I Love Eggs*; *I Have A Love In Every Port*.
▽

△

Adequate programmer fare with more music (production number illustrated) than plot, **Swing Parade of 1946** (Monogram) starred Gale Storm as a young lady with a burning desire to become a nightclub entertainer, and Phil Regan as a nightclub owner whose club she finds herself singing in. Russell Hicks played Regan's wealthy father who, after mistakenly believing Miss Storm to be a summons server, employs her to serve a summons on his son's club, with other roles going to Ed Brophy, Mary Treen and Leon Belasco. Also in it were The Three Stooges, Connee Boswell (singing Harold Arlen and Ted Koehler's 'Stormy Weather'), and the bands of Louis Jordan and Will Osborne. It was produced by Lindsley Parsons and Harry A. Romm, written by Tim Ryan from a story by Edmund Kelso, and directed by Phil Karlson. Other songs and musical numbers included: *On The Sunny Side of The Street* Dorothy Fields, Jimmy McHugh; *Oh Brother* Matt Malneck, Allie Wrubel; *Don't Worry About That Mule* William Davis, Duke Groner, Charles Stewart; *A Tender Word Will Mend It All* Doris Fisher, Allan Roberts; *After All This Time* Paul DeFur, Ken Thompson; *Caldonia* Fleecie Moore; *Just A Little Fond Affection* Elton Box, Desmond Cox, Lewis Ilda.

One of the best of all the *Road* pictures, **Road To Utopia** (Paramount), made in 1944 but released two years later, benefitted from a wonderfully zany screenplay (provided by Norman Panama and Melvin Frank) that was as anarchic and as anachronistic as it was funny, and which cast Bing Crosby (left) and Bob Hope (right) as a pair of vaudevillians who, in cahoots with singer Dorothy Lamour (as a soloist in an Alaskan dance hall), set out to locate an old Alaskan goldmine, in the course of which they are hotly pursued by villains Robert Barrat, Nestor Paiva, Douglass Dumbrille and Jack La Rue. Hal Walker's direction was totally in accord with the outrageous antics perpetrated by all concerned, and the songs – by Jimmy Van Heusen and Johnny Burke – most notably 'Personality' sung by Lamour, were first rate. Most of the story was told in flashback and, for once, it was Hope who got the girl, Crosby having been abandoned on an ice-floe and presumed dead. In the film's final scene, however, many years after the events described, he arrives unexpectedly at Hope's residence only to discover that the child Hope and Lamour have had, is the spittin' image of himself. It was an inspired joke on which to end an often inspired piece of screen lunacy. Robert Benchley lent his services as narrator, with other parts going to Hillary Brooke, Will Wright, Jimmy Dundee, Billy Benedict and Arthur Loft. Danny Dare choreographed, and the producer was Paul Jones. Other songs and musical numbers: *Welcome To My Dream* (Crosby); *Put It There Pal* (Crosby, Hope); *It's Anybody's Spring* (Crosby); *Would You* (Lamour); *Good-time Charley* (Crosby, Hope).
▽

William Powell appeared briefly in **Ziegfeld Follies**, again playing the role of Florenz Ziegfeld. He reminisces (in heaven) about his tenure on earth when, as showman *extraordinaire*, he presented a series of revues unparallelled in their opulence. If only, he muses, he could produce just one more show, utilizing all the fabulous talent available at MGM – now that *really* would be something. It would open with Fred Astaire, Lucille Ball and Cyd Charisse in a typical Ziegfeld paean to pulchritude called 'Bring on the Beautiful Girls' (by Earl Brent and Roger Edens). Virginia O'Brien would then reprise the number, this time, however, singing the praises of men ('Bring On Those Wonderful Men'). Next, opera stars James Melton and Marion Bell would be seen and heard in 'The Drinking Song' from Verdi's *La Traviata*. After that Keenan Wynn would appear in a sketch called 'Number Please', to be followed by a cooling water ballet performed by Esther Williams to a musical arrangement by Roger Edens. Another couple of sketches would quickly follow: 'Pay The Two Dollars' with Victor Moore, Edward Arnold, Ray Teal and Joseph Crehan, and 'The Sweepstakes Ticket' with Fanny Brice, Hume Cronyn and William Frawley. Next would come one of the highlights of the entire show – Fred Astaire and Lucille Bremer in a superb Arthur Freed–Harry Warren number called 'This Heart Of Mine'. After that, a scorching performance from Lena Horne, singing 'Love' by Ralph Blane and Hugh Martin. Red Skelton would then appear in

'When Television Comes', doing his famous vaudeville routine, 'Guzzler's Gin', as a TV announcer who gets progressively drunker with each mouthful he takes of the product he is advertising. Another highlight, 'Limehouse Blues' (by Philip Braham and Douglas Furber) about a Chinese coolie and his infatuation with a beautiful Oriental woman would again feature Fred Astaire and Lucille Bremer (illustrated), to be followed by Judy Garland doing a wicked impersonation of Greer Garson in 'The Great Lady Gives An Interview' ('Madame Crematon') by Roger Edens and Kay Thompson. Fred Astaire and Gene Kelly would then make the first of only two appearances together in a little-known number by the Gershwin brothers called 'The Babbitt And The Bromide'. Finally, the revue would end with Kathryn Grayson (surrounded by foam) singing 'There's Beauty Everywhere' by Arthur Freed and Harry Warren. Thus thought the Great Ziegfeld, and thus it came to pass. Vincente Minnelli received sole directorial credit, though several other directors, including Charles Walters, Roy Del Ruth and George Sidney, were also involved. Robert Alton was given dance director credit, Roger Edens was in charge of the musical adaptation; Lennie Hayton conducted, and the brilliant orchestrations were by Conrad Salinger and Wally Hegelin, two indispensable members of producer Arthur Freed's celebrated production team. Though inconsistent in quality, **Ziegfeld Follies** was awesomely professional and never dull.

Based on an indifferent play by Louise (Gypsy Rose Lee) Hovick, **Doll Face** (GB: **Come Back To Me**), scripted by Leonard Praskins, was just another 20th Century-Fox backstage musical about a burlesque star with Broadway aspirations. It did, however, give the vivacious Vivian Blaine top billing and the leading role. The men in her life were played by Dennis O'Keefe (right) and Michael Dunne, with other parts in this inexpensively produced (in black and white by Bryan Foy) effort going to Carmen Miranda (illustrated left), Perry Como (whose big moment came in a song called 'Dig You Later' by Harold Adamson and Jimmy McHugh), Martha Stewart, Reed Hadley, Frank Orth and Donald MacBride. The invigorating direction was by Lewis Seiler. Other songs and musical numbers: *Here Comes Heaven Again; Chico Chico; Somebody's Walking In My Dreams; Red Hot And Beautiful* Adamson. McHugh.

268

△

Robert Alda starred in a small-scale musical called **Cinderella Jones** (Warner Bros.), directed by Busby Berkeley with a score by Sammy Cahn and Jule Styne. Despite its credentials, it was a tepid non-starter. Charles Hoffman's screenplay from a rather mundane story by Philip Wylie told of a young lady who, in order to inherit $10,000,000, has to marry a man of exceptional intelligence by a given date. Made in 1944, it was full of wartime references which might have added to its appeal, but these were edited out when the release of the film was delayed for two years. Reason for the delay was that the studio was hoping to capitalize on Alda's success in the Gershwin biopic *Rhapsody in Blue*. Unfortunately for all concerned, Mr Alda (illustrated 2nd left) never quite made it, and the studio's gamble misfired. Also, director Berkeley was going through an unhappy period in his private life and the film was totally bereft of his characteristic flair. Joan Leslie (left) was cast as the girl at the centre of the plot, and the rest of the cast included Julie Bishop (right foreground), William Prince (centre), S.Z. Sakall (2nd right), Edward Everett Horton, Elisha Cook Jr, Ruth Donnelly (centre left) and Hobart Cavanaugh. The producer was Alex Gottlieb. Songs: *If You're Waitin' I'm Waitin' Too*; *Cinderella Jones*; *You Never Know Where You're Goin' Till You Get There*; *When The One You Love Simply Won't Love Back*.

Moderate programme entertainment, **Talk About A Lady** (Columbia) starred Jinx Falkenburg as an unspoiled country girl who inherits assets worth several million dollars, as well as a nightclub, and finds herself doing battle with socialite Trudy Marshall, who feels the booty should have gone to her. Forrest Tucker and Joe Besser (illustrated) co-starred, and the supporting cast included Richard Lane, Jimmy Little, Frank Sully, Jack Davis, Robert Regent and Mira McKinney. Stan Kenton and His Orchestra also appeared. Richard Weil and Ted Thomas wrote it from a story by Robert D. Andrews and Barry Trivers, it was produced by Michael Kraike and directed by George Sherman. Songs and musical numbers included: *You Gotta Do Watcha Gotta Do*; *Avocado*; *I Never Had A Dream Come True* Allan Roberts, Doris Fisher; *A Mist Is Over The Moon* Oscar Hammerstein II, Ben Oakland.

▽

Freddie Stewart played a dual role in **Freddie Steps Out** (Monogram): a swoon crooner and a young student called Freddie – his physical double. When the crooner disappears, Freddie's chums decide to play a joke on their schoolmate by giving out the news that he is none other than the missing singer. Things get out of hand with the arrival of the real crooner's wife (Julie Gibson) and baby; and much of Hal Collins's screenplay was involved in returning order to the lives of all concerned. Warren Mills, June Preisser (left, as Freddie's girl-friend), Ann Rooney (centre), Noel Neill (right), Jackie Moran and Frankie Darro were also in it for producer Sam Katzman, and director Arthur Dreifuss (who co-scripted). It was a livelier-than-average, low-budget programmer. Songs and musical numbers included: *Patience And Fortitude* Billy Moore Jr, Blackie Warren; *Let's Drop The Subject* Hal Collins, Joe Sanns; *Don't Blame Me* Dorothy Fields, Jimmy McHugh.

▽

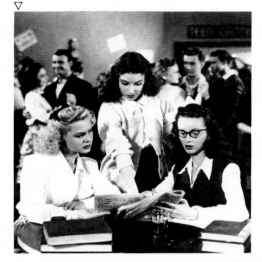

Danny Kaye was **The Kid From Brooklyn** (RKO), the best and highest grossing of his three movies to date. In the role first created on screen by Harold Lloyd in Paramount's *The Milky Way* (1936), he played Burleigh, a milkman who inadvertently becomes involved with a prize-fighter and his dim-witted trainer, and finds himself middleweight champion of the world. Don Hartman and Melville Shavelson's screenplay, based on the earlier screenplay by Grover Jones, Frank Butler and Richard Connell which, in turn, was adapted from a Broadway flop by Lynn Root and Harry Clork, gave Kaye every opportunity to demonstrate his versatility, and the result was a knockout. Skilfully negotiating the dramatic change in character Burleigh undergoes when he has his first taste of success in the ring (all his initial fights have been rigged, though he does not realize this), Kaye proved for the first time that he was as good an actor as he was a set-piece performer. Though the bulk of the musical numbers (by Jule Styne and Sammy Cahn) were shared between co-stars Virginia Mayo as Kaye's *vis-à-vis*, and Vera-Ellen (illustrated centre) as his sister, as well as the 18 Goldwyn Girls, Kaye had a specialty of his own – a Martha Graham parody called *Pavlova*, written years earlier for one of his nightclub acts by Sylvia Fine and Max Liebman. Lionel Stander as the trainer repeated the role he originally played in the 1936 version, with other parts going to Walter Abel, Eve Arden, Fay Bainter, and Steve Cochran as prizefighter Speed McFarlane. It was filmed in Technicolor, choreographed by Bernard Pearce and directed by Norman Z. McLeod. Virginia Mayo and Vera-Ellen's vocals were dubbed by Dorothy Ellers and Betty Russell respectively. Songs and musical numbers: *I Love An Old-Fashioned Song*; *You're The Cause Of It All*; *Josie*; *Sunflower Song*; *Hey, What's Your Name?*; *Welcome Burleigh*.

▽

Forties Musicals

Producer Joe Pasternak made the perfect choice ▷ when he signed Henry Koster to direct **Two Sisters From Boston** (MGM), an enjoyable black and white musical not dissimilar in mood to some of the team's Deanna Durbin offerings at Universal in the mid-thirties. Set at the turn of the century, it starred Kathryn Grayson (right) and June Allyson (left) as sisters from Boston, one of whom (Grayson) arrives in New York where she is cared for by pianist Jimmy Durante, in whose saloon she sings. She fancies herself as an opera singer and tries to push herself in the direction of the Met, while Miss Allyson who follows her sister to New York, settles for the son (Peter Lawford) of an opera sponsor. Lauritz Melchior was in it, sharing some of the vocals with Miss Grayson, and performing on his own (most memorably) 'The Prize Song' from Wagner's *Die Meistersinger*. Grayson joined Durante for 'The Fire Chief's Daughter', 'There Are Two Sides To Every Girl' and 'Down By The Ocean' (by Ralph Freed and Sammy Fain) while, on his own, Durante made a meal of 'Gwan, Your Mudder's Callin'' (also by Freed and Fain). Ben Blue, Isobel Elsom, Harry Hayden, Thurston Hall and Nella Walker completed the cast. Myles Connolly wrote the sympathetic screenplay, with additional dialogue by James O'Hanlon. Other songs and musical numbers: *Nellie Martin*; *After The Show* Freed, Fain, *Hello, Hello, Hello* Durante; sequences from an opera especially contrived for the occasion, utilizing melodies by Mendelssohn and Liszt.

△

Some doubling up (but not, alas, with laughter) in **Hit The Hay** (Columbia), with Judy Canova (illustrated centre) starring as a backwoods opera *diva* whose agile coloratura belies an ability to act. She is discovered (by Ross Hunter) singing operatic arias while milking a cow, and immediately groomed for a career in grand opera. When it is realized she cannot act her way out of a paper bag let alone a convoluted operatic plot, an actress who looks like her (also played by Canova) is hired to go on in her place and mime to the music, while coloratura Canova stands by singing in the wings. Tiring of this dishonest ploy, Canova decides to re-vamp Rossini's *William Tell* as a burlesque calling it 'Tillie Tell', which she does with great success, thus saving the impecunious opera house which mounts it and, at the same time, finding herself a husband (Fortunio Bonanova, left). Two Canovas for the price of one was more than most audiences could be expected to take, and although her vocalizing was surprisingly good, her rubber-faced antics were irritatingly unstoppable. The result was that **Hit The Hay** bit the dust. Doris Merrick, Gloria Holden, Francis Pierlot, Grady Sutton and Louis Mason were also in it; Richard Weil and Charles R. Marion wrote it, Del Lord directed and the producer was Ted Richmond. The musical items included extracts from Flotow's *Martha* and a jazz version of Rossini's *William Tell*.

Frances Langford (illustrated) starred as **The** ▷ **Bamboo Blonde** (RKO), a nightclub singer who has a brief romance with a B-29 pilot (Russell Wade, right) the night before he departs for active service in the Pacific. The bomber crew steal the picture of herself Langford has given him, paint her portrait on their plane, and christen her the Bamboo Blonde. Back in New York, the nightclub manager for whom Langford works capitalizes on the fact when the 'Bamboo Blonde' crew (as they become known) turn out to be the hottest in the force. Romantic complications occur with Wade's return to New York (he happens to be engaged to Jane Greer) but all ends happily, as audiences, after the first seven minutes running time, predicted it would. Ralph Edwards, Iris Adrian, Richard Martin, Glenn Vernon and Paul Harvey were also in it; it was written by Olive Cooper and Lawrence Kimble from a story by Wayne Whittaker; had one of the shortest and silliest 'production' numbers ever devised (choreography by Charles O'Curran) and was directed for executive producer Sid Rogell by Anthony Mann. Songs: *I'm Good For Nothing But Love*; *Dreaming Out Loud*; *Moonlight Over The Islands*; *Right Along About Evening* Mort Greene, Lew Pollack.

In order to achieve her ambition and become a successful Tin Pan Alley song-plugger, Ellen Drew (right), the heroine of **Sing While You Dance** (Columbia), embarks on a course of far-fetched behaviour which includes inducing the widow (Ethel Griffies) of a deceased millionaire composer to allow her late husband's music to undergo certain commercial changes. Too silly for words (as well as music), it was the brainchild of Robert Stephen Brode, whose screenplay (from a story by Lorraine Edwards) gave employment to Robert Stanton (left, as an amateur composer), Andrew Tombes, Edwin Cooper, Robert Stevens, and Amanda Lane (centre). Leon Barsha produced and the director was D. Ross Lederman. Songs included: *Oh What A Lovely Dream* Milton Drake, Ben Oakland; *It's A Blue World* Bob Wright, Chet Forrest; *I Don't Know How You Did It* Doris Fisher, Allan Roberts. ◁

△

Cole Porter deserved a better tribute to his life and work than **Night And Day** (Warner Bros.), a shoddy Technicolored biopic in the worst Hollywood tradition that even contained the cliché 'Wait a minute, I think I've got it!' uttered by Porter as his muse finally descends to help him complete his most famous song, 'Night And Day'. With the miscasting of Cary Grant (illustrated left) as Porter, the film perpetrated the most serious of its many errors, at the same time setting the tone of fantasy that permeated everything about Arthur Schwartz's misconceived production. Apart from the horse-riding accident in Central Park that crippled Porter for the remainder of his life, his story was hardly one that burst its seams with narrative incident, and it emerged, in its screen incarnation, as little more than a riches-to-riches yarn, devoid of anything remotely resembling the man's true personality or his nature. His homosexuality, for example, was not even hinted at. The result was a story wretchedly thin on incident and offering, instead, a succession of Porter standards. Which would have been fine had they not been so indifferently staged by LeRoy Prinz, or so woefully under-powered in performance. Ginny Simms sang several of the songs first introduced by Ethel Merman ('You're The Top', 'I Get A Kick Out Of You') but with none of Merman's vivacity, leaving the vocal honours to Mary Martin (illustrated centre) whose rendering of 'My Heart Belongs To Daddy', which she introduced to audiences in the 1938 Broadway musical *Leave It To Me*, was by far the best single item in the show. Alexis Smith was cast as Porter's wife Linda, with other roles going to Monty Woolley (playing himself as a bombastic ex-Yale actor-professor), Jane Wyman (illustrated right), Eve Arden, Alan Hale, Victor Francen, Dorothy Malone, Tom D'Andrea, Selena Royle, Donald Woods, Henry Stephenson, Sig Rumann, and Herman Bing. Carlos Ramirez was featured in 'Begin the Beguine', Milada Mladova and George Zoritch did a dance specialty, and from Estelle Sloan came an energetic tap routine. The film was scripted by Charles Hoffman, Leo Townsend and William Bowers (adaptation by Jack Moffitt) and directed without distinction by Michael Curtiz. Ray Heindorf's orchestrations were, Miss Martin notably excepted, the film's one saving excellence. Other musical numbers: *I've Got You Under My Skin; What Is This Thing Called Love? Miss Otis Regrets; Just One Of Those Things; Do I Love You; An Old-Fashioned Garden; Bullfrog; In The Still Of The Night; Love For Sale; Let's Do It; You Do Something To Me; Easy to Love; You've Got That Thing; Don't Fence Me In; I'm Unlucky At Gambling; I'm In Love Again; Rosalie; Anything Goes* Porter; *I Wonder What's Become Of Sally* Jack Yellen, Milton Ager.

Do You Love Me? (20th Century-Fox), a pleasing Cinderella story shot in Technicolor, starred Maureen O'Hara as a sedate and bespectacled music student whose involvement with a band-leader-cum-trumpeter (Harry James, illustrated centre) and a crooner (Dick Haymes, right) radically alters her outlook on life. Reginald Gardiner (left), who first got to conduct an orchestra (albeit an imaginery one) in *Born To Dance* (MGM, 1936), was given another chance to wield the baton in this one, with other parts in Robert Ellis and Helen Logan's screenplay (story by Bert Granet) in the capable hands of Richard Gaines, Stanley Prager, B.S. Pully, Chick Chandler and Alma Kruger. Also featured was the dance team of Jack Scordi and Diane Ascher. If the story was meagre even by musical comedy standards, there was always Haymes's dreamy crooning, James's wizardry on the trumpet, and O'Hara's stunning red hair to claim one's attention – plus a surprise appearance by Betty Grable at the climax. It was produced (opulently) by George Jessel, and the slick and efficient direction was by Gregory Ratoff. The choreographer was Seymour Felix. Songs and musical numbers included: *As If I Didn't Have Enough On My Mind* Charles Henderson, Lionel Newman, Harry James; *I Didn't Mean A Word I Said* Harold Adamson, Jimmy McHugh; *Moonlight Propaganda* Herb Magidson, Matt Malneck; *Do You Love Me?* Harry Ruby.

▽

In **Cuban Pete** (GB: **Down Cuba Way**), Universal Studios manacled Desi Arnaz (right) to a bottom-rung programmer as a popular Cuban bandleader lured to New York by advertising agent Joan Fulton (centre) in order to star in a commercial radio show whose sponsor (Jacqueline De Wit) has threatened to cancel Fulton's contract unless she can secure Arnaz. The script (by Robert Presnell Sr and M. Coates Webster from a story by Bernard Feins) was as trite as its plot, and relied for support on the musical numbers offered, which included an organ solo from Ethel Smith called 'The Breeze And I' (by Al Stillman and Ernesto Lecuona).

▽

△

A Technicolor remake of *Libelled Lady* (MGM, 1936), **Easy to Wed** (MGM) was an engaging attraction which featured Keenan Wynn and Lucille Ball (right) in the roles originally taken by Spencer Tracy and Jean Harlow; and starred Van Johnson (centre) and Esther Williams (left) in the parts that were created by William Powell and Myrna Loy. Wynn played a harassed newspaper editor in the midst of a libel suit brought by a millionaire's daughter, with Ball as his helpful fiancée; Williams was the pretty plaintiff, and Johnson an ex-reporter employed by Wynn to persuade Williams to withdraw her charges. Aided and abetted by several musical numbers (staged by Jack Donohue), it emerged as pleasant lightweight entertainment, nicely scripted by Dorothy Kingsley (from the original screenplay by Maurice Watkins, Howard Emmett Rogers and George Oppenheimer) and competently directed by journeyman Edward Buzzell for producer Jack Cummings. Also in the cast were Cecil Kellaway, Carlos Ramirez, Ben Blue, Ethel Smith, June Lockhart, Grant Mitchell, Josephine Whittell and Paul Harvey. Songs and musical numbers included: *Easy To Wed* Ted Duncan, Johnny Green; *Goosey-Lucy; It Shouldn't Happen To A Duck* Robert Franklin, Green; *Continental Polka; Gonna Fall In Love With You* Ralph Blane, Green; *Come Closer To Me* Osvaldo Farres, Al Stewart.

Arnaz had four songs in all, including the title number (by José Norman) which he sang twice; and there was additional vocalizing from the King Sisters. Completing the cast were Don Porter, Pedro de Cordoba, and little Beverly Simmons (left), with Igor de Navrotzki and Yvette von Koris featured as specialty dancers. Will Cowan produced and the director was Jean Yarbrough. Other songs and musical numbers included: *El Cumbanchero* Rafael Hernandez; *Lullaby* (adapted from the traditional Mexican folk song *Cielito Lindo*) Bill Driggs; *After Tonight* Jack Brooks, Milton Schwartzwald; *Rhumba Matumba* Bobby Collaza.

Forties Musicals

Two years after *Meet Me In St Louis* (MGM) came **Centennial Summer**, an unsuccessful attempt on behalf of 20th Century-Fox and producer-director Otto Preminger to recapture some of the family nostalgia and fireside cosiness of the earlier film. Instead of St Louis, 1904, **Centennial**'s setting was Philadelphia, 1876, the time of the big Exposition and, as in the MGM film, the family in question was female-dominated – this time by Jeanne Crain and Linda Darnell (illustrated centre). Dorothy Gish and Walter Brennan were their decent, middle-class parents and Cornel Wilde (left) the handsome Frenchman on a visit to Philadelphia who causes rivalry in romance between the two sisters. The best thing about the film was the music composed for it by Jerome Kern (who died shortly after completing it), but it too often received lacklustre vocal performances, Miss Crain's singing being indifferently dubbed by Louanne Hogan. Nor did Dorothy Fox's tepid choreography do justice to a score bursting with possibilities. Constance Bennett appeared as Gish's Paris-based sister, with other featured roles going to William Eythe (right), Barbara Whiting, Larry Stevens, Kathleen Howard, Buddy Swan and dancer Avon Long. It was written by Michael Kanin from the novel by Albert E. Idell and photographed in Technicolor. Songs and musical numbers: *All Through The Day* (lyrics by Oscar Hammerstein II); *In Love In Vain*; *The Right Romance* (lyrics by Leo Robin); *Cinderella Sue* (lyrics by E.Y. Harburg); *Centennial*; *Up With The Lark*; *Railroad Song* (lyrics for all three by Leo Robin).

A musical remake of *Thanks A Million* (20th Century-Fox, 1937), **If I'm Lucky** (20th Century-Fox) was a colourless piece of arrant nonsense, entirely bereft of convincing performances and without a single good tune. All about a crooner who decides to enter politics and run for State Governor, hoping that his impecunious musical colleagues will, as a result of his switch in careers, find radio employment a bit easier, it starred singer Perry Como (illustrated centre) who, as an actor, displayed limited ability. Vivian Blaine (top-billed), Harry James and His Music Makers, Carmen Miranda, Phil Silvers and Edgar Buchanan were in it too, all floundering hopelessly in the mire of mediocrity provided by scenarists Snag Werris, Robert Ellis, Helen Logan and George Bricker. Kenny Williams choreographed it, Bryan Foy was the producer and it was directed by Lewis Seiler with both eyes closed. Songs and musical numbers: *If I'm Lucky*; *One More Kiss*; *Publicity*; *Bet Your Bottom Dollar*; *Follow The Band*; *That American Look* Josef Myrow, Edgar De Lange.

The thrill of Brazil was absent from **The Thrill Of Brazil** (Columbia), a vacuous remake of *His Girl Friday* (Columbia, 1940) whose story concerned itself with producer Keenan Wynn's attempts to prevent the marriage of his ex-wife Evelyn Keyes to Allyn Joslyn, the vice-president of a toothpaste concern. Bolstering this flimsy tale were Latin-American singing star Tito Guizar, Enric Madriguera and His Orchestra, the dancing team of Veloz and Yolanda, and the terpsichorean skills of Ann Miller (illustrated) whose vivacity had never been more welcome! Completing the cast were Felix Bressart, Sid Tomack and Eugene Borden. The choreographic chores were shared between Nick Castle and Jack Cole, and the production chores between Sidney Bidell and Alan Rivkin. S. Sylvan Simon directed, substituting speed for energy. Songs and musical numbers included: *Thrill Of Brazil*; *Copa-Cabana*; *Custom House*; *A Man Is Brother To A Mule*; *That's Good Enough For Me*; *My Sleepy Guitar* Doris Fisher, Allan Roberts.

Fred Brady (left) played twin brothers in **Slightly Scandalous** (Universal), and wasn't much good in either role. One of the brothers has three girl friends and is trying to sell a television show to a fountain pen manufacturer; the other has no girl friend at all, and is a humble insurance man. The quiet one invests money in his twin's TV show and, in the process of protecting his investment, becomes involved with his brother's romances. So much for the plot by Erna Lazarus and David Mathews (who also scripted, with additional dialogue by Joel Malone and Jerry Warner). Partially rescuing it from total tedium were the musical contributions of Isabelita, The Guadalajara Trio, Nico Moro, Frank Yaconelli and specialty dancers Dorese Midgley and Georgann Smith. Paula Drew and Sheila Ryan (right) provided the soporific love interest, with Walter Catlett and Louis Da Pron completing the cast. Stanley Rubin and Marshall Grant produced, and the director was Will Jason. Songs and musical numbers: *I Couldn't Love You Anymore*; *When I Fall In Love*; *Negra Leona*; *Same Old Routine*; *The Mad Hatter*; *Baa Baa To You* Jack Brooks.

Running 127 minutes and out-staying its welcome by a good half-an-hour, **Holiday In Mexico** was Jane Powell's first film for MGM and, although better than her previous efforts for United Artists, was no masterpiece. She played the teenage daughter of a widowed American Ambassador in Mexico (Walter Pidgeon) who, in between running his home for him, finds time to develop a king-sized crush on Jose Iturbi (illustrated right), much to the disapproval of her resident boyfriend Roddy McDowall. Produced by Joe Pasternak in rather garish Technicolor and with a characteristically Pasternakian mixture of popular classics and contemporary music, it appealed to a large cross-section of audiences and registered a healthy box-office gross. The film also featured Hungarian beauty Ilona Massey, as well as Xavier Cugat, Amparo Iturbi (illustrated left), Tonia and Teresa Hero, Hugo Haas, Mikhail Rasumny, Helene Stanley, William 'Bill' Phillips and Linda Christian. Isobel Lennart wrote it from a story by William Kozlenko and it was directed by George Sidney – whose handling of Iturbi's piano solos (with the camera literally placed behind the strings inside the instrument so that one was able to see the hammers pounding away as Iturbi's fingers danced up and down the keyboard) was both bizarre and inventive. The indifferent choreography was by Stanley Donen. Songs and musical numbers: *I Think Of You* (based on 2nd theme of 1st movement of Rachmaninov's Piano Concerto No 2) Jack Elliott, Don Marcotte; *Walter Winchell Rhumba* Carl Sigman, Noro Morales; *Yo Te Amo Mucho (And That's That)* Sammy Stept, Ervin Drake, Cugat, Morales; *You, So It's You* Earl Brent, Nacio Herb Brown; *And Dreams Remain* Ralph Freed, Raoul Soler; *Holiday In Mexico* Freed, Sammy Fain; *Ave Maria* Schubert; *Les Filles De Cadiz* Leo Delibes, Alfred De Musset; *Italian Street Song* Victor Herbert, Rida Johnson Young; *Rachmaninov's Piano Concerto No 2 in C Minor* (abbreviated); *Polonaise in A Flat Major* Chopin; *Goodnight Sweetheart* Ray Noble, James Campbell, Reg Connelly; *Three Blind Mice* (arranged by Andre Previn); *The Music Goes 'Round And Around* Red Hodgson, Ed Farley, Mike Riley; *Liebestod* (from 'Tristan and Isolde') Wagner, arranged for two pianos.

▽

A disastrous flop for all concerned, **No Leave, No Love** (MGM) was indeed a no-no that combined romance with music as a couple of Marine buddies (Van Johnson, left, and Keenan Wynn, right) spent time and money living it up in the big city. Pat Kirkwood, imported from England to play a radio singer and the object of Johnson's affection, made no impact at all in her first (and last) Hollywood film, but with a script as tenuous as the one provided by Charles Martin and Leslie Kardos, the fault was not entirely hers. Also floundering were Edward Arnold, Marie Wilson, Leon Ames and Selena Royle. Musical diversion was provided by Xavier Cugat and Guy Lombardo with their respective orchestras, a specialty dance team called The Garcias, and Marina Koshetz, as well as Sugarchile Robinson and Joey Preston, the former a boy pianist, the latter a child drummer. It was directed by Charles Martin, choreographed by Stanley Donen and produced by Joe Pasternak. Songs and musical numbers: *All The Time* Ralph Freed, Sammy Fain; *Love On A Greyhound Bus* Kay Thompson, Ralph Blane, George Stoll; *Isn't It Wonderful?* Thompson; *It'll Be Great To Be Back Home* Charles Martin; *Old Sad Eyes* Irving Kahal, Fain; *When It's Love* Edgar De Lange, Nicholas Kharito.

▽

△

In **Make Mine Music** (RKO), Walt Disney attempted, with varying degrees of success, to do for popular music what *Fantasia* (RKO, 1940) had done for the classics. 'A Music Fantasy In Ten Parts', it opened with The King's Men singing 'The Martins And The Coys' (by Al Cameron and Ted Weems), using the hillybilly hit to depict a feud between two mountain families. Next came the Ken Darby Chorus singing 'Blue Bayou' (by Bobby Worth and Ray Gilbert), a piece involving the moon and a flamingo. This was followed by 'A Jazz Interlude' featuring Benny Goodman and His Orchestra in a number called 'All The Cats Join In' (by Alec Wilder, Ray Gilbert and Eddie Sauter) about a couple of bobby-soxers in a jitterbug session at the local malt shop. 'Without You' (by Osvaldo Farres and Ray Gilbert) was sung by Andy Russell in an atmospheric item called 'A Ballad In Blue'; while Jerry Colonna appeared next in 'A Musical Recitation', telling the story of 'Casey At The Bat' (by Ray Gilbert, Ken Darby and Eliot Daniel). Ballet dancers Tatiana Riabouchinska and David Lichine of the Ballet Russe performed in 'Ballade Ballet' to a vocal by Charles Wolcott and Ray Gilbert called 'Two Silhouettes' sung by Dinah Shore. Prokofiev's 'Peter and the Wolf' followed, narrated by Sterling Holloway, then The Benny Goodman Quartet (clarinet, drums, bass and piano) offered a wildly surreal version of 'After You've Gone' (by Henry Creamer and Turner Layton). The Andrews Sisters lent their voices to 'Johnny Fedora and Alice Blue Bonnet' (by Allie Wrubel and Ray Gilbert), a story about two hats who fall in love in the window of a department store; and the grand finale was 'Opera Pathetique', the best of the items on offer, featuring the voice of Nelson Eddy in the touching fantasy of Willie, an opera-singing whale (see illustration) whose one ambition in life is to sing at the Met. The music for the entire sequence comprised 'Shortnin' Bread' a traditional song arranged by Jacques Wolfe, and operatic excerpts from Rossini's 'The Barber of Seville', Donizetti's 'Lucia di Lammermoor', Leocavallo's 'I Pagliacci', Wagner's 'Tristan and Isolde', Boito's 'Mefistofele' and Flotow's 'Martha'. All the parts in these excerpts – soprano, tenor, baritone, bass and chorus – were sung by Eddy! **Make Mine Music** was filmed in Technicolor with Joe Grant in charge of the production. The film received a disappointing press on its initial release and was not particularly successful at the box office.

Forties Musicals

If one had to kick the truth around in the service of a commercial biopic, the way to do it was the way producer Sidney Skolsky did it in **The Jolson Story**. A blockbuster from Columbia, it had the distinction of containing practically every known cliché in the musical genre yet, at the same time, was cobbled with such expertise that it emerged as an unashamedly entertaining wallow from its opening scene to its compulsively watchable finale in which Jolson, after a period of self-imposed vocal celibacy, rediscovers the joy of singing and, at the same time, loses his wife who walks out on him. Of course it wasn't like that at all in real life. What audiences were really getting was a retread of *The Jazz Singer* (Warner Bros. 1927) in which a stage-struck Jewish boy defies his Cantor father for a career in show business. In his first major screen assignment, Larry Parks was cast as Jolson (though Jolson's own, somewhat frayed voice was used in the majority of the numbers) and came as close as possible to conveying the dynamism of the man many considered to be the greatest entertainer of them all (see illustration). Jolson himself was seen only once in the film, performing in long shot. Evelyn Keyes was Julie Benson, the show girl he marries (in reality Ruby Keeler, but Miss Keeler refused to allow her name to be used), her best moment being the spirited imitation she gave of Jolson singing 'California Here

I Come' (by Buddy De Sylva, Jolson and Joseph Meyer). Jolson's parents were played by Ludwig Donath and Tamara Shayne in performances that, at times, came perilously close to caricature, with William Demarest filling the key role of Steve Martin, the man who discovers young Ase Joelson (Scotty Beckett) in a vaudeville theatre before the lad's voice breaks and thereafter becomes his lifelong friend and mentor. Stephen Longstreet's screenplay (adapted by Harry Chandler and Andrew Solt) attempted to show something of Jolson's arrogance and general unlikeability, but in the main his scenario was a valentine to a man so in love with show business (and himself) that nothing else in life mattered an iota. Jack Cole and Joseph H. Lewis staged the dance numbers, Morris Stoloff and Saul Chaplin were in charge of the musical direction and the director was Alfred E. Green, a veteran who knew exactly how to turn a cliché to enormous profit. It was no surprise to anyone that the film grossed a mammoth $8,000,000 making it the third biggest moneymaker of the year (the other two were Sam Goldwyn's *The Best Years Of Our Lives* at $11,600,000 and David O. Selznick's *Duel In The Sun* at $10,750,000), and the biggest moneymaker in Columbia's history up to that time. Songs and musical numbers: *Swanee* Irving Caesar, George Gershwin; *You Made Me Love You* Joseph

McCarthy, James V. Monaco; *By The Light Of The Silvery Moon* Edward Madden, Gus Edwards; *I'm Sitting On Top Of The World* Sam Lewis, Joe Young, Ray Henderson; *There's A Rainbow Round My Shoulder* Jolson, Billy Rose, Dave Dreyer; *My Mammy* Lewis, Young, Walter Donaldson; *Rock-A-Bye Your Baby With A Dixie Melody* Lewis, Young, Jean Schwartz; *Liza* Gus Kahn, George and Ira Gershwin; *Waiting For The Robert E. Lee* L. Wolfe Gilbert, Lewis F. Muir; *April Showers* Buddy De Sylva, Louis Silvers; *About A Quarter To Nine* Al Dubin, Harry Warren; *I Want A Girl Just Like The Girl That Married Dear Old Dad* Will Dillon, Harry von Tilzer; *The Anniversary Song* Jolson, Saul Chaplin, J. Ivanovici; *The Spaniard Who Blighted My Life* Billy Merson; *Let Me Sing And I'm Happy* Irving Berlin; *When You Were Sweet Sixteen* James Thornton; *Toot Toot Tootsie Goodbye* Gus Kahn, Ernie Erdman, Dan Russo; *Eli Eli* (traditional); *On The Banks Of The Wabash* Paul Dresser; *Ma Blushin' Rosie* Edgar Smith, John Stromberg; *Ave Maria* Schubert; *After The Ball* Charles K. Harris; *Blue Bell* Edward Madden, Theodore F. Morse; *Every Little Movement Has A Meaning Of Its Own* Otto Harbach, Karl Hoschna. A short medley comprising: *Lullaby of Broadway*; *42nd Street*; *A Latin From Manhattan*; *We're In The Money* Al Dubin, Harry Warren; *Avalon* Jolson, Vincent Rose.

◁ **Three Little Girls In Blue** (20th Century-Fox), first seen as *Three Blind Mice* (1938), then as *Moon Over Miami* (1941), was a breezy Technicolor romp set in 1902 and starring June Haver, Vivian Blaine and Vera-Ellen (dubbed by Carol Stewart) as the damsels of the title. Pretending to be wealthy, they set out to ensnare millionaire husbands in Atlantic City, only to find that love and a healthy bank balance do not always go arm-in-arm. In the end Haver gets penniless George Montgomery (dubbed by Ben Gage); Vera-Ellen (illustrated left) finishes up with wine waiter Charles Smith (right) – inexplicably uncredited – and Vivian Blaine with wealthy aristocrat Frank Latimore. Josef Myrow and Mack Gordon provided a cheerful score, one of its highlights being a dream ballet danced by Vera-Ellen and Charles Smith (dubbed by Del Porter) called 'You Make Me Feel So Young' (later popularized by Frank Sinatra) and delightfully staged by Babe Pearce. Celeste Holm, fresh from her Broadway triumph as Ado Annie in *Oklahoma*, made her film debut in it and injected a vibrant sense of humour into her number 'Always A Lady'. It was adapted by Brown Holmes, Lynn Starling, Robert Ellis and Helen Logan from a play by Stephen Powys, and scripted by Valentine Davies. Mack Gordon produced and the exuberant direction was by Bruce Humberstone. Other songs and musical numbers (staged by Seymour Felix): *On The Boardwalk In Atlantic City; Somewhere In The Night; I Like Mike; A Farmer's Life Is A Very Merry Life; Oh My Love; Three Little Girls In Blue; Always A Lady* Myrow, Gordon; *If You Can't Get A Girl In The Summertime* Bert Kalmar, Harry Tierney.

Songwriters Jule Styne, Sammy Cahn, Byron Stokes, F. Dudleigh Vernon, Slim Gaillard, Lee Ricks, Merle Maddern, Lanier Darwin, Will Jason, Val Burton, Eddie Seiler, Sol Marcus and Al Kaufman gave generously of their talents to ensure that the remake of **Sweetheart Of Sigma Chi** (Monogram) remained buoyant for most of its 76 minutes, the best of the numbers being Styne and Cahn's 'Five Minutes More'. With a campus-full of youngsters – including Anne Gillis (left), Fred Colby, Alan Hale Jr. David Holt, Marjorie Hoerner, William Beaudine Jr, Emmett Vogan Jr and Fred Datig Jr – ready, willing and able to breathe life into a tired old plot about a couple of crooks who set about rigging a rowing race in order to cash in on a large bet, the show had more bounce in it than a bad cheque, proving that when it tried hard, even Monogram could deliver the goods. Ross Hunter as a rowing star lately returned to college after doing war duty was also in it, so were Elyse Knox (right), Phil Regan (centre), Phil Brito, Tom Harmon, Virginia Grey, Paul Guilfoyle and Edward Brophy. Also featured were The Slim Gaillard Trio, and Frankie Carle and His Orchestra. It was written by Frank L. Moss from a story by George Waggner and directed by Jack Bernhard for producer Jeffrey Bernard. Other songs and musical numbers included: *Sweetheart of Sigma Chi* F. Dudleigh Vernon, Byron D. Stokes; *Penthouse Serenade* Will Jason, Val Burton; *It's Not I'm Such A Wolf, It's Just You're Such A Lamb* Merle Maddern, Lanier Darwin; *And Then It's Heaven* Edward Seiler, Sol Marcus, Al Kaufman; *Cement Mixer* Slim Gaillard, Lee Ricks; *Yeproc-Heresi* Gaillard; *Bach Meets Carle* (a Bach pastiche by Frankie Carle).

▽

△
A routine backstage musical from Republic, whose whiff of a plot concerned itself with a romantic misunderstanding between singing star Constance Moore (illustrated left) and her songwriter beau William Marshall, **Earl Carroll Sketchbook** (GB: **Hats Off To Rhythm**) was a sketchy excuse for a musical whose handful of songs by Sammy Cahn and Jule Styne yielded but one worthwhile tune – 'I've Never Forgotten' – unexcitingly sung by Miss Moore, who did better with 'I've Got A Right To Sing The Blues' (by Harold Arlen and Ted Koehler), first heard in one of Carroll's stage revues. For the rest it was formula film-making, with a screenplay by Frank Gill Jr and Parke Levy (original story by Gill) with Bill Goodwin, tap-dancer Johnny Coy, Vera Vague (right) and Edward Everett Horton (centre) also cast for producer Robert North and director Albert S. Rogell. The choreographer was Nick Castle. Other songs and musical numbers included *I Was Silly; Lady With A Mop; Oh Henry; What Makes You Beautiful, Beautiful?*

△
Monogram's **High School Hero** went back to the thirties for its subject matter, and to somewhere just this side of the Dark Ages for its method of presentation. A typical campus carry-on, it involved two high school football teams – one good, one lousy. The problem posed by scenarists Hal Collins and Arthur Dreifuss (who also directed) was how to bring the inferior team up to scratch. It starred Freddie Stewart and June Preisser with Noel Neill. Anne Rooney, Jackie Moran, Frankie Darro, Warren Mills (foreground centre), Milt Kibbee and Douglas Fowley in support. The orchestras of Freddie Slack and Jan Savitt (with Isabelita) were also featured. Sam Katzman produced, and the dances were staged by Jack Boyle. Songs and musical numbers: *You're For Me; Come To My Arms; Whitney High; Night Time And You* Edward J. Kay; *You're Just What I Crave* Arthur Alexander; *Fairview High* Phil Grayson; *Southpaw Serenade* Freddie Slack.

Forties Musicals

Period specialists 20th Century-Fox went back to the not-too-distant Twenties for **Margie**, an enchanting piece of nostalgic Americana helmed by veteran director Henry King with a great deal of affection. Told in flashback as the grown Margie (Jeanne Crain) recalls her youth to her bobbysoxer daughter (Ann Todd Jr) it evoked the era of racoon coats, flagpole sitting, ragtime and charleston, while telling with warmth and humour of Margie's adolescent adventures – her unspoken rivalry with her flighty friend (Barbara Lawrence), her problems with boys and with the elastic in her bloomers (the latter a running gag that came close to being overworked), her impassioned participation in the debating society and her infatuation (along with the rest of the school females) for the handsome new French teacher (Glenn Langan). All very slight, but utterly charming, and punctuated with over a dozen songs woven throughout the narrative with unobtrusive skill by King and musical director Alfred Newman. The nearest to a production number was a skating sequence in which the camera glided and swirled with the skaters, at one point executing a 360-degree pan as the orchestra played 'Three O'Clock In The Morning' (by Dorothy Terriss and Julian Robledo). Equally captivating was Lawrence's rendition of 'A Cup Of Coffee, A Sandwich And You' (by Billy Rose, Al Dubin and Joseph Meyer) on a twilit porch, the song being

taken up by Crain in her bedroom. Later, while preparing for bed and rehearsing her debating speech, Crain hears the strains of 'I'll See You In My Dreams' (by Gus Kahn and Isham Jones) from a gramophone record outside. She hums a few bars, the song continues and, with supreme confidence in his material and his creation of atmosphere, King allows his camera to linger after Margie is snug beneath her counterpane with the song coming to its close – the mating of music and image a wistful and beguiling paean to youth and innocence, photographed with a soft glow by Charles G. Clarke. Crain (right) was perfection, leading a cast that included Esther Dale (left, as Margie's grandmother), Hobart Cavanaugh (as her father), Lynn Bari, Alan Young, Conrad Janis, Hattie McDaniel and Vanessa Brown. The screenplay was by F. Hugh Herbert from stories by Ruth McKenny and Richard Bransten, and it was produced by Walter Morosco. Other songs: *Margie* Benny Davis, Con Conrad, J. Russel Robinson; *At Sundown* Walter Donaldson; *My Time Is Your Time* Eric Little, Leo Dance; *Avalon* Al Jolson, Vincent Rose; *Collegiate* Mo Jaffe, Nat Bonx; *Charmaine*; *Diane* Erno Rapee, Lew Pollack; *April Showers* Buddy De Sylva, Louis Silvers; *Charleston* Cecil Mack, James P. Johnson; *Wonderful One* Dorothy Terriss, Paul Whiteman, Ferde Grofé, from a theme by Marshall Neilan; *Ain't She Sweet?* Jack Yellen, Milton Ager.

Walt Disney's **Song Of The South** (RKO) was partially redeemed by the cartoon sequences illustrating Uncle Remus's stories about Br'er Fox, Br'er Rabbit and Br'er Bear. For the rest it was a syrupy tale about an unhappy youngster (Bobby Driscoll, illustrated), and his friendship with the aforementioned Uncle Remus (James Baskett), as well as with a poor but pretty little moppet (Luana Patten, illustrated) who is equally unhappy because her brothers want to drown her puppy. Scenarists Dalton Raymond, Morton Grant and Maurice Rapf (working from stories by Joel Chandler Harris) reduced them all to caricatures, a fault compounded in Wilfred Jackson's direction (the more successful cartoon sequences were directed by Harve Foster). It was photographed in Technicolor and the associate producer was Perce Pearce. The rest of the cast included Ruth Warrick, Hattie McDaniel, Lucile Watson, Glenn Leedy, George Nokes and Gene Holland. Songs and musical numbers: *How Do You Do* Robert McGimsey; *Song Of The South* Sam Coslow, Arthur Johnston; *Uncle Remus Said* Eliot Daniel, Hy Heath, Johnny Lange; *Sooner Or Later* Charles Wolcott, Ray Gilbert; *Everybody Has A Laughing Place*; *Zip-a-dee-doo-dah* Allie Wrubel, Gilbert; *You'll Always Be The One I Love* Sunny Skylar, Ticker Freeman; *Let The Rain Pour Down*; *Who Wants To Live Like That?* Foster Carling.

Familiarity was the keynote struck by **It's Great To Be Young** (Columbia), with Leslie Brooks (left), Jimmy Lloyd (centre), Jeff Donnell, Robert Stanton, Jack Williams, Jack Fina, Frank Orth, Ann Codee (right) and Milton DeLugg and His Swing Wing featuring in an all too familiar yarn about a group of ex-GIs with greasepaint in their veins who, after landing a Borscht Circuit engagement and suffering the usual heartbreaks endemic to show-biz, stage a show at a summer resort, and finish up on Broadway. Jack Henley wrote it from a story by Karen DeWolfe (as well as an inordinate number of uncredited writers), Ted Richmond produced, and it was directed for the platitude it was by Del Lord. Not one of the performances made any impression. Songs and musical numbers: *It's Great To Be Young*; *A Thousand And One Sweet Dreams*; *Five Of The Best*; *That Went Out With High-Button Shoes*; *Frankie Boogie* Doris Fisher, Allan Roberts; *Bumble Boogie* (based on Rimsky-Korsakov's 'Flight of the Bumble Bee') Jack Fina.

◁ **Susie Steps Out** (United Artists) moved away from the familiar world of radio and into the up-and-coming medium of television, with Cleatus Caldwell (left) second-billed to crooner David Bruce as an employee in an advertising agency. When she loses her job as a result of a mix-up with the boss's wife, her little sister comes to the financial aid of their ailing father (Percival Vivian) by successfully posing as a nightclub singer and, in the final reel, makes the grade as a TV star. A compendium of clichés compiled by Elwood Ullman from an original story by director Reginald Le Borg, and Kurt Neuman, the Buddy Rogers-Ralph Cohn production also featured Howard Freeman, Grady Sutton Ann Hunter (right), Margaret Dumont, John Berkes and Joseph J. Greene. Songs and musical numbers included: *When You're Near*; *For The Right Guy*; *I'm So Lonely*; *When Does Love Begin* Hal Borne; *Bob-Bob That Did It* Borne, Eddie Cherkose.

An inept remake of Carole Lombard's screwball farce *True Confession* (Paramount, 1937), **Cross My Heart** (Paramount) had larger-than-life Betty Hutton (left) confessing to a murder she was totally innocent of in order to give her attorney boyfriend (Sonny Tufts, right) the chance of a lifetime to establish his reputation in the legal profession by defending her. It was hardly surprising that audiences didn't swallow it. Rhys Williams played the prosecuting attorney, Alan Bridge was a detective, Ruth Donnelly was Betty's mother and Michael Chekhov a hammy Russian actor and the murderer in question. He should have done away with scenarists Harry Tugend and Claude Binyon whose screenplay (based on a play by Louis Verneuil and Georges Berr, additional dialogue by Charles Schnee), was equally criminal. Tugend also produced and the director was John Berry. Songs and musical numbers included: *Love Is The Darndest Thing*; *That Little Dream Got Nowhere*; *How Do You Do It?*; *Does Baby Feel Alright?*; *It Hasn't Been Chilly In Chile* Johnny Burke, Jimmy Van Heusen; *Cross My Heart* Robert Emmett Dolan, Larry Neill (all sung by Hutton).

Judy Canova (illustrated) did neither herself nor her radio fans any good by appearing in **Singin' in the Corn** (Columbia), a staggeringly poor filler in which she played a carnival mind reader who inherits her uncle's estate on the proviso that, before receiving a cent, she has to return a local ghost town to the Indians. The blame for the screenplay rested with Isabel Dawn and Monte Brice, who wrote it from an equally culpable story by Richard Weil. Allen Jenkins (illustrated) co-starred as Canova's partner, and the cast was completed by Guinn Williams, Alan Bridge, Charles Halton, Robert Dudley and Nick Thompson. Also appearing were The Singing Indian Braves, who had to be just that in order to lend themselves to twaddle of this sort. Ted Richmond produced and the director was Del Lord. Songs and musical numbers included: *I'm A Gal Of Property*; *Pepita Chequita*; *An Old Love Is A True Love* Doris Fisher, Allan Roberts; *Ma, He's Making Eyes At Me* Sidney Clare, Con Conrad.

Weighing in at $3,000,000, **Blue Skies** was an efficient entertainment and an almighty smash from Paramount that reunited Bing Crosby and Fred Astaire (first seen together in *Holiday Inn*, Paramount, 1942) in a musical spectacle that echoed, in several instances, their earlier collaboration. Both movies had scores by Irving Berlin, both featured Crosby and Astaire as erstwhile partners in a song-and-dance-team, both had them falling for the same girl and, in both, Crosby got her. As was the case in *Holiday Inn*, the plot of **Blue Skies** (adapted by Allan Scott from an idea by Berlin, and scripted by Arthur Sheekman) was little more than a serviceable framework constructed to support a clutch of Berlin songs, 20 of them featured, and of the 20, four written especially for the film. Recounted in flashback, the story began in 1919 and followed the private and professional lives of the two men for the next 27 years, focussing particularly on Crosby's up and down marriage (which ended in divorce) to Joan Caulfield. Musically, the film was drenched in nostalgia, the choreographic high point being Hermes Pan's staging of 'Puttin On The Ritz', and Astaire's galvanic interpretation of it. With its two male stars (Crosby left, Astaire right) occupying centre stage for most of the remaining time, there weren't many opportunities available for the rest of the cast to register anything other than adequate support, though Billy De Wolfe was allowed to intrude every now and then with some resistible bits of clowning. Also cast: Olga San Juan, Jimmy Conlin, Cliff Nazarro, Frank Faylen, Jack Norton,

Will Wright, Victoria Horne, Karolyn Grimes and Roy Gordon. Sol C. Siegel produced (in Technicolor) and the director was Stuart Heisler. Other songs and musical numbers: *A Pretty Girl Is Like A Melody* (Astaire, male chorus); *I've Got My Captain Working For Me Now* (Crosby, De Wolfe); *You'd Be Surprised* (San Juan); *Serenade To An Old-Fashioned Girl* (Caulfield, male quartet); *I'll See You In C-U-B-A* (Crosby, San Juan); *A Couple Of Song And Dance Men* (Astaire, Crosby, Nazarro on piano); *Always* (chorus); *You Keep Coming Back Like A Song* (Crosby, male chorus); *Blue Skies* (Crosby); *The Little Things In Life* (Crosby); *Not For All The Rice In China* (Crosby); *Everybody Step* (Crosby, danced by chorus); *How Deep Is The Ocean?* (Crosby, female chorus); *Getting Nowhere* (Crosby); *Heat Wave* (San Juan, chorus; danced by Astaire and San Juan); *Any Bonds Today?* (Crosby); *This Is The Army Mr Jones* (Crosby); *White Christmas* (Crosby); *Russian Lullaby* (Crosby). Background music: *Nobody Knows*; *Tell Me Little Gypsy*; *Some Sunny Day*; *Mandy*; *When You Walked Out*; *Because I Love You*; *How Many Times*; *The Song Is Ended*; *Lazy*. Interesting sideline: The film was originally scheduled to be produced by Mark Sandrich, who cast Paul Draper in the Astaire role. Nine days into shooting, however, Sandrich suffered a fatal heart attack. The production was taken over by Sol C. Siegel who replaced Draper with Astaire, the latter announcing that it would be his last film. Happily this was not the case, though no musical he made before or after **Blue Skies** was as successful.

Forties Musicals

◁ The usual clichés attendant on the musical ▷ biopic came cascading forth in glorious Technicolor in **Till The Clouds Roll By**, MGM's star-studded salute to the greatest ever melodist of the American musical theatre – Jerome Kern. And with so many of their contract artists on hand to bring his immortal music to life, what did it matter if the accompanying story hardly shook the world? The fact was that Kern's songs spoke louder than actions; the fiction was – well, whatever scenarists Myles Connolly and Jean Holloway (working from a loose adaptation by George Wells of a story by Guy Bolton) cared to dream up. Beginning on 27 December 1927 with the opening night of Kern's masterpiece *Show Boat* (written with Oscar Hammerstein II), the film flashes back in time to the 'early days' with Kern (Robert Walker) a struggling young songwriter, receiving platitudinous counsel from earnest Van Heflin who implores him not to waste his time on 'little tunes' but to 'think big'. Which is exactly what the aspiring composer does, going from one success to another, marrying along the way and, at one point, offering advice of his own to Heflin's stage-struck daughter (Lucille Bremer, vocals dubbed by Trudy Erwin) who throws a tantrum when a number he has written for her is given to Marilyn Miller (Judy Garland) instead. The finale (directed by George Sidney) was a massive production number featuring several Kern ever-greens, and climaxed by Frank Sinatra singing 'Ol' Man River' from *Show Boat*. The film ran 137 minutes, featured nearly two dozen Kern classics and almost the same number of stars. With its vocal arrangements by Kay Thompson, musical direction by Lennie Hayton, superb orchestrations by Conrad Salinger, and the attractive staging of the numbers by Robert Alton (at his best in the title number) and Vincente Minnelli (the latter in charge of Judy Garland's three sequences), the musical side of the show was in the hands of the most capable team of experts in the business. Arthur Freed produced, Richard Whorf directed. Also cast: Dorothy Patrick (as Mrs Kern), Joan Wells, Paul Langton, Mary Nash and Harry Hayden. Songs, musical numbers, performers and lyricists: *Cotton Blossom* (chorus); *Make Believe* (Kathryn Grayson, Tony Martin); *Can't Help Lovin' Dat Man* (Lena Horne); *Ol' Man River* (Caleb Peterson); *Life Upon The Wicked Stage* (Virginia O'Brien); *Who Cares If My Boat Goes Upstream?* (Martin) Oscar Hammerstein II; *Till The Clouds Roll By* (June Allyson, Ray McDonald, illustrated right) P.G. Wodehouse; *How D'You Like To Spoon With Me?* (Angela Lansbury) Edward Laska; *They Didn't Believe Me* (Dinah Shore) Herbert Reynolds; *The Last Time I Saw Paris* (Shore) Hammerstein II; *I Won't Dance* (Van Johnson, Bremer) Otto Harbach, Hammerstein II; *Why Was I Born?* (Horne) Hammerstein II; *Smoke Gets In Your Eyes* (Cyd Charisse, Gower Champion) Harbach; *Who?* (Garland) Harbach, Hammerstein II; *Look For The Silver Lining* (Garland) Buddy De Sylva; *Sunny* (chorus), danced by Garland, illustrated left) Harbach, Hammerstein II; *Cleopatterer* (Allyson); *Leave It To Jane* (Allyson) Wodehouse; *One More Dance* (Bremer) Hammerstein II; *The Land Where The Good Songs Go* (Bremer); *Kalua* (orchestra); *Polka From Mark Twain Suite* (orchestra); *Yesterdays* (chorus) Harbach; *Long Ago And Far Away* (Grayson) Ira Gershwin; *A Fine Romance* (O'Brien) Dorothy Fields; *All The Things You Are* (Martin) Hammerstein II; *She Didn't Say Yes* (Wilde Twins) Harbach.

Warner Bros.' last musical in 1946 was **The Time, The Place And The Girl** (not to be confused with their 1929 pic of the same name). Written by Francis Swann, Agnes Christine Johnston and Lynn Starling (story by Leonard Lee), it involved Jack Carson (left) and Dennis Morgan (right) in an attempt to put on a show against the wishes of a retired opera singer (Florence Bates), but with the assistance of Miss Bates's husband (S.Z. Sakall) and her glamorous grand-daughter (Martha Vickers, centre right). An air of stale familiarity pervaded the movie, but with a solid score by Arthur Schwartz and Leo Robin that included 'A Gal In Calico' and 'A Rainy Night in Rio', some imaginative dance sequences by LeRoy Prinz, and a decent quota of laughs, the movie was a smash. Engaging performances came from Carson, Morgan, Vickers, Janis Paige (centre left), and a supporting cast that included Alan Hale, Donald Woods, and Angela Greene. Carmen Cavallaro and His Orchestra, The Condos Brothers and Chandra Kaly were in it too. It was produced, in Technicolor, by Alex Gottlieb, and directed by David Butler. Other songs: *Oh But I Do*; *Through A Thousand Dreams*; *A Solid Citizen Of The Solid South*; *I Happened To Walk Down First Street*.
▽

1947

Academic Awards

Cinematography (colour)
NOMINATIONS INCLUDED: *Mother Wore Tights* (20th Century-Fox) Harry Jackson

Music
Song
'Zip-A-Dee-Doo-Dah' *Song Of The South* (Disney, RKO) Allie Wrubel *cm*; Ray Gilbert *lyr*.
NOMINATIONS INCLUDED: 'A Gal In Calico' *The Time, The Place And The Girl* (WB) Arthur Schwartz *cm*; Leo Robin *lyr*. 'I Wish I Didn't Love You So' *The Perils Of Pauline* (Paramount) Frank Loesser, 'Pass That Peace Pipe' *Good News* (MGM) Ralph Blane *cm*; Hugh Martin and Roger Edens *lyr*. 'You Do' *Mother Wore Tights* Josef Myrow *cm*; Mack Gordon *lyr*.

Scoring Of A Musical Picture
Mother Wore Tights Alfred Newman
NOMINATIONS INCLUDED: *Fiesta* (MGM) Johnny Green. *My Wild Irish Rose* (WB) Ray Heindorf and Max Steiner. *Road To Rio* (Paramount) Robert Emmett Dolan. *Song Of The South* Daniele Amfitheatrof, Paul J. Smith and Charles Wolcott.

The Annual Top Moneymaking Films
INCLUDED: *Blue Skies* (Paramount). *California* (Paramount). *This Time For Keeps* (MGM). *I Wonder Who's Kissing Her Now* (20th Century-Fox). *The Jolson Story* (Columbia). *Margie* (20th Century-Fox). *Mother Wore Tights*. *No Leave, No Love* (MGM). *The Perils Of Pauline*. *Till The Clouds Roll By* (MGM). *Variety Girl* (Paramount). *Welcome Stranger* (Paramount).

Eddie Bracken should have sued scenarists Edmund Beloin, Jack Rose and Lewis Meltzer (story by William Bowers and Robinson Holbert) for letting him down so badly in **Ladies' Man** (Paramount). Considering the feebleness of the plot (country bumpkin strikes oil, comes to the big city to celebrate, and becomes involved with a radio programme as well as with some gold-digging females), he needed all the assistance he could get, his innocent, village-idiot mien not being a sturdy enough prop on this sorry occasion. Desperately trying to pummel it into life were co-star Cass Daley, tap-dancer Johnny Coy, and Spike Jones and His City Slickers. They were spasmodically successful, but it was uphill for most of the way, with an unusually dull score by the usually reliable Jule Styne and Sammy Cahn, and a few 'oldies', contributing to the pervading mediocrity of it all. Completing the cast were The Virginias, Welles and Field, Lewis Russell, Georges Renavent and Roberta Jonay. Daniel Dare produced, the dances were staged by Billy Daniels, and it was directed by William D. Russell (production number illustrated). Songs and musical numbers: *I Gotta Girl I Love In North And South Dakota*; *What Am I Gonna Do About You?*; *I'm As Ready As I'll Ever Be*; *Away Out West* Styne, Cahn; *Cocktails For Two* Sam Coslow, Arthur Johnston; *Holiday For Strings* David Rose; *Mama Yo Quiero* Al Stillman, Jaraca and Vincente Paiva.

As **The Shocking Miss Pilgrim** (20th Century-Fox) was set in stuffy Boston of 1874, and featured its star, Betty Grable (illustrated) as a woman typist fighting for suffrage in the male-dominated world of big business, there was little chance of her showing off her celebrated legs. Still, despite the lack of flesh, and a really stultifying screenplay by George Seaton (from a story by Ernest and Fredericka Maas), it was a box-office success that proved its star's enormous drawing power regardless of the quality of her scripts. Dick Haymes was her co-star and boss, with other roles going to Anne Revere (as Haymes's progressive aunt), Allyn Joslyn, Gene Lockhart, Elisabeth Risdon, Arthur Shields, Charles Kemper, Roy Roberts, Stanley Prager and 'The Outcasts'. Some hitherto unpublished manuscripts by George Gershwin, collated and adapted by Kay Swift and Ira Gershwin, with new lyrics by the latter, comprised the score, the most durable number being 'For You, For Me, For Evermore' sung as a duet by Grable and Haymes. Scenarist Seaton also directed (flatly) and the dances were staged by Hermes Pan. William Perlberg produced (in Technicolor). Other songs and musical numbers: *Aren't You Kinda Glad We Did*; *Changing My Tune*; *Back Bay Polka*; *One Two Three*; *But Not In Boston*; *Sweet Packard*; *Stand Up And Fight*; *Waltzing Is Better Sitting Down*; *Waltz Me No Waltzes*; *Demon Rum*.

Deanna Durbin sang four songs in **I'll Be Yours** (Universal International), a moderately diverting remake of Ferenc Molnar's *The Good Fairy*, first produced by Universal in 1935 with William Wyler directing from a script by Preston Sturges. In the new version, also with a script by Sturges (adapted from the Hungarian by Jane Hinton), the fantasy inherent in the original was nowhere in evidence, and instead of Margaret Sullavan in the central role of a young woman who helps a struggling young lawyer to find employment with a meat packer by passing him off as her jealous spouse, there was Miss Durbin (illustrated). Adolphe Menjou, in the role originally played by Frank Morgan was somewhat miscast as the meat packer, and there wasn't much sparkle, either, from Tom Drake as the lawyer. Still, director William A. Seiter, aided by a passable performance from his leading lady kept it simmering amiably along its innocuous way. Also cast: Walter Catlett, Franklin Pangborn, William Trenk, Joan Fulton, Patricia Alphin and William Brooks. Felix Jackson produced. Songs: *It's Dreamtime*; *Cobbleskill School Song* Jack Brooks, Walter Schumann; *Granada* Augustin Lara, English lyrics Dorothy Dodd; *Sari Waltz* C.C.S. Cushman, E.P. Heath, Emmerich Kalman; *Lullaby* Brahms.

Two veterans, producer-director Allan Dwan and silent star Irene Rich, surfaced in **Calendar Girl**, a turn of the century tale from Republic in which Miss Rich was cast as the kindly landlady of a boarding house peopled by the usual motley collection of young hopefuls – including Jane Frazee (top-starred) as a singer, William Marshall as a struggling young composer, and James Ellison (left) as a painter whose calendar portrait of Frazee (illustrated) causes a rift between her and her beau Marshall (centre). Victor McLaglen played an Irish fireman, and Gail Patrick made a token appearance as a wealthy Bostonian. More prominently featured were Kenny Baker and Janet Martin who, together with Frazee and Marshall, handled the bulk of the film's seven songs (by Harold Adamson and Jimmy McHugh). Franklin Pangborn, Gus Schilling and Charles Arnt completed the cast. The script was by Mary Loos, Richard Sale and Lee Loeb from a story by Loeb, and the choreography was by Fanchon. Songs and musical numbers: *Have I Told You Lately?*; *Calendar Girl*; *A Lovely Night To Go Dreaming*; *At The Fireman's Ball*; *New York's A Nice Place To Visit*; *Let's Have Some Pretzels And Beer*; *A Bluebird Is Singing To Me*.

A 67-minute programmer from RKO, **Beat The Band** wrapped several musical numbers around a flimsy box of clichés whose contents contained a second-hand yarn about a gal from the sticks (Frances Langford, right) who comes to the big city to take opera lessons, and falls into the clutches of unscrupulous Phillip Terry (centre right), a bandleader pretending to be a singing teacher. Ralph Edwards (left) was cast as Terry's comic manager, with other parts in Lawrence Kimble's screenplay (adapted by Kimble and Arthur Ross from a play by George Abbott) going to June Clayworth (centre), Mabel Paige, Andrew Tombes and Donald MacBride. Miss Langford did most of the singing, and there was additional musical support from Gene Krupa and His Band. Michael Kraike produced and the director was John H. Auer. Songs and musical numbers included: *Kissin' Well*; *I'm In Love*; *I've Got My Fingers Crossed*; *Beat The Band* Mort Greene, Leigh Harline; *Shadow Rhapsody*.
▽

Russ Morgan and His Orchestra supplied most of the pleasant music for **Cigarette Girl** (Republic). In between the musical numbers, however, was the decidedly bankrupt business of the plot by Edward Huebach (screenplay by Henry K. Moritz). A story-book romance, it had Leslie Brooks (illustrated) and Jimmy Lloyd wooing each other; he in the guise of an oil company president, she as a famous nightclub singer. In fact, they're nothing of the sort, but, as the story unfurls, he does become a business tycoon and she, in the best Cinderella-like fashion, a Broadway star. Ludwig Donath, Doris Colleen, Howard Freeman, Joan Barton, Mary Forbes, Francis Pierlot, and Eugene Borden were also cast, William Bloom produced and the director was Gunther V. Fritsch. Songs and musical numbers included: *It's All In The Mind*; *The More We Get Together*; *How Can You Tell?*; *They Won't Let Me Sing*; *Honeymoon On A Dime* Doris Fisher, Allan Roberts.
▽

When 20th Century-Fox wasn't dispensing dollops of period nostalgia it was acting as a tour agent for Latin America: viz *That Night In Rio* (1941), *A Weekend In Havana* (1941), and *Down Argentine Way* (1940). The studio's latest excursion into the travel business was **Carnival In Costa Rica**, a Technicolored cliché that filled the eye but not the mind. The story of a young couple (Dick Haymes – at the height of his popularity – and second-billed Vera-Ellen, illustrated centre) who, against their bickering parents' wishes, refuse to marry, it starred Cesar Romero as well as Celeste Holm (who was far too talented a lady to waste her time on junk like this), ditto Anne Revere, as well as J. Carrol Naish (who generally wasted his time on junk like this), Pedro de Cordoba, Barbara Whiting, Nestor Paiva and Fritz Feld. It was choreographed by the distinguished Russian choreographer Leonide Massine, scripted by John Larkin, Samuel Hoffenstein and Elizabeth Reinhardt, and directed for producer William A. Bacher by Gregory Ratoff. Songs and musical numbers: *I'll Know It's Love*; *Another Night Like This*; *Mi Vida*; *Costa Rica*; *Rhumba Bomba*; *Maracas* Harry Ruby, Ernesto Lecuona; *Qui Pi Pia* Al Stillman, Sunny Skylar.

△

With the war over, audiences found **Wake Up And Dream** (20th Century-Fox), a Technicolored wadge of whimsy with a wartime background, not at all to their liking. John Payne, though top-starred, only appeared briefly at the beginning of the film – and again at the end – as a soldier believed lost in battle. June Haver (illustrated left) was his waitress girlfriend, and Connie Marshall (sitting left) his kid sister who sets out, in company with Miss Haver and elderly Clem Bevans (right) on the latter's boat, to find him. Based on Robert Nathan's novel *The Enchanted Voyage*, there was nothing enchanted about director Lloyd Bacon's tepid musical voyage of discovery, though one good song 'Give Me The Simple Life' by Harry Ruby and Rube Bloom did emerge. John Ireland (standing right), as a would-be dentist, went along for the ride, with Charlotte Greenwood, George Cleveland, Oliver Blake, Charles Russell, Charles D. Brown and Irving Bacon completing the cast for producer Walter Morosco. The script was by Elick Moll. Other songs and musical numbers included: *I Wish I Could Tell You*; *Into The Sun* Ruby, Bloom; *Who Knows?* Don Raye, Gene De Paul.

△

What happened in **It Happened In Brooklyn** (MGM) was that Frank Sinatra, returning home from the war, met and fell in love with pretty music teacher Kathryn Grayson, but lost her to Peter Lawford. And all to the accompaniment of several passable Jule Styne-Sammy Cahn songs, the best being 'Time After Time' which went on to become a Sinatra standard. Jimmy Durante was in it too (as a school janitor), and his duet with Sinatra, 'The Song's Gotta Come From The Heart' (illustrated) was the best novelty item in the show, though Sinatra's charmingly ill-conceived rendering (with Miss Grayson) of 'La Ci Darem La Mano' from Mozart's *Don Giovanni* might equally be con-

sidered the comic highspot – albeit unintentionally. Jack Cummings' modest black and white production also featured Gloria Grahame, Marcy McGuire, Aubrey Mather, Tamara Shayne, Bobby Long, tap-dancer Billy Roy and, heard but not seen, the piano playing of 17-year-old Andre Previn who had recently joined the studio's music department. The dances were staged by Jack Donohue, and the serviceable direction was by Richard Thorpe. Modest it may have been, but it made a box-office killing. Other songs *Brooklyn Bridge*; *It's The Same Old Dream*; *I Believe*; *Whose Baby Are You*; *Otchichornya* (traditional); *The Bell Song* (from 'Lakme') Delibes.

Forties Musicals

According to scenarists Richard English, Art Arthur and Curtis Kenyon – in their screen biography of the Dorsey Brothers called **The Fabulous Dorseys** (United Artists) – Tommy (on trombone) and Jimmy (on saxophone) spent the greater part of their youth bickering with each other: a state of affairs they carried through into manhood. But a happy ending was imposed on their uneasy relationship when a family bereavement reunites them. With most musical biopics, it was the subject's work rather than his life story that people paid to see, and **The Fabulous Dorseys** was no exception. Tommy and Jimmy played themselves (Bobby Ward, left, and Buz Buckley, centre, were the brothers as children), and Sara Allgood and Arthur Shields (right) were their parents. Also cast were Janet Blair, William Lundigan, James Flavin, William Bakewell, Dave Willock and (as himself) Paul Whiteman. There were guest appearances too, from Henry Busse, Bob Eberly, Charlie Barnet, Mike Pingatore, Ziggy Elman, Art Tatum, Helen O'Connell, Ray Bauduc and Stuart Foster. Charles R. Rogers produced and Alfred E. Green directed. Musical numbers included: *At Sundown* (Dorseys, Whiteman) Walter Donaldson; *I'll Never Say Never Again, Again* (Dorseys band) Harry Woods; *To Me* (Tommy Dorsey, Blair, Lundigan) Allie Wrubel, Don George; *Green Eyes* (Jimmy Dorsey, Eberly, O'Connell) Nilo Menendez, Adolfo Utrera, English lyrics E. Rivera, Eddie Woods; *Dorsey Concerto* (Dorseys, Whiteman) Leo Shuken, Ray Bauduc; *Art's Blues* (Dorseys, Tatum, Barnet, Busse, Elman, Bauduc) Tatum; *Everybody's Doin' It* (local band) Irving Berlin; *Marie* (Tommy Dorsey, Blair, Foster, Dorsey Band) Berlin; *The Object Of My Affection* (Dorsey Brothers Band) Pinky Tomlin, Coy Poe, Jimmie Grier; *Runnin' Wild* (Dorsey Brothers Band) Joe Grey, Leo Wood, A. Harrington Gibbs; *When You And I Were Young Maggie* (Dorseys band) James Austin Butterfield, George W. Johnson; *Waitin' At The Gate For Katy* Richard Whiting, Gus Kahn.

Set during the roistering years of the motion picture's infancy, **The Perils of Pauline** (Paramount) gave Betty Hutton (illustrated) her best role to date as serial queen Pearl White. And although the screenplay by P.J. Wolfson and Frank Butler was in many instances sheer fabrication, it made for unbridled, high-spirited entertainment. Several old-timers, including Paul Panzer, Hank Mann, James Finlayson, Creighton Hale, Bert Roach and Chester Conklin were on hand to provide the touch of verisimilitude so conspicuously absent from the scenario; and there were a few amusing scenes depicting the haphazard way movies were shot before they found their voice. John Lund costarred as Hutton's romantic involvement and contributed very little to the boy-meets-girl romance that developed between them, with other roles going to Billy De Wolfe as a Shakespearean ham, William Demarest as a movie director, and Constance Collier as an ageing trouper. Hutton sang several Frank Loesser songs in that inimitable way of hers, the best being 'Poppa Don't Preach To Me', one of her biggest commercial hits. Billy Daniels choreographed, George Marshall directed with little sense of period but with a compensating flair for humour, and the Technicolor production was in the hands of Sol C. Siegel. Other songs and musical numbers: *I Wish I Didn't Love You So; Rumble Rumble Rumble; The Sewing Machine* Loesser; *Poor Pauline* Raymond Walker, Charles McCarron.

New Orleans from United Artists, wasted a lot of hot jazz on a cold plot (by Elliot Paul and Herbert J. Biberman, screenplay by Paul and Dick Irving Hyland). With such musicians as Louis Armstrong, Billie Holiday, Woody Herman, Kid Ory, Zutty Singleton, Barney Bigard, Bud Scott, Charle Beale, Red Callender and Meade Lux Lewis on hand, it was criminal that its scenarists couldn't have come up with anything stronger than a story about a young girl (Dorothy Patrick) who has to make a choice between the worlds of classical music and jazz. Basically a potted history of jazz, spanning forty years, it was limply directed by Arthur Lubin for producer Jules Levey, the best thing in it being 'Do You Know What It Means To Miss New Orleans' (by Edgar De Lange and Louis Alter) marvellously performed by Armstrong (illustrated centre) and His All Stars, Billie Holiday, Woody Herman and Dorothy Patrick. Arturo de Cordova was the male lead (and the object of Miss Patrick's

affections) and Shelley Winters was seen briefly as his secretary, with other roles going to Irene Rich as Patrick's society-orientated mother, John Alexander, Richard Hageman and Marjorie Lord. Other musical numbers included: *Endie* (Armstrong, Herman); *The Blues Are Brewin'* (Armstrong Holiday, Herman) Alter, De Lange; *Where The Blues Were Born In New Orleans* (Armstrong) Bob Carleton, Cliff Dixon; *New Orleans Stomp* (Patrick) Joe 'King' Oliver; *West End Blues* (Armstrong) 'King' Oliver, Clarence Williams; *Buddy Bolden's Blues* (Armstrong) Jelly Roll Morton; *Dippermouth Blues* (Armstrong) 'King' Oliver; *Shim-Me-Sha-Wabble* (Armstrong) Spencer Williams; *Honky Tonk Train Blues* Meade Lux Lewis; *Basin Street Blues* (Armstrong); Spencer Williams; *Mahogany Hall Stomp* (Armstrong) Spencer Williams; *Farewell To Storyville* (Armstrong, Holiday) Spencer Williams; *Maryland, My Maryland* (Armstrong) James Ryder Randall, Walter de Mapes.

Choreographer Jack Cole made the biggest contribution to **Down To Earth** (Columbia), a lush fantasy in gorgeous Technicolor which reintroduced the character of Mr Jordan (Roland Culver), first seen in the delightful 1941 comedy *Here Comes Mr Jordan* (Columbia) in which he was played by Claude Rains. Jordan, who operates from on high, is capable of manipulating mere mortals to satisfy his own caprices and, on this occasion, sends Terpsichore (Rita Hayworth, illustrated) down to earth as the star of a musical comedy. Enter Jack Cole, whose production numbers gave a basically insubstantial tale what little substance it had. A Greek ballet with music by Mario Castelnuovo-Tedesco, was especially effective, with Hayworth looking breathtakingly beautiful throughout. Larry Parks costarred as the show's director – a philistine who'd rather have his star perform in swingtime than indulge in classical lyricism, and their very mortal romance padded out much of the plot. Marc Platt was the featured male dancer, with Edward Everett Horton (as Messenger 7013) and James Gleason as fight-manager-turned-agent Max Corkle repeating the roles they had created in the earlier film. Edwin Blum and Don Hartman's screenplay also found parts for Adele Jergens, George Macready, William Frawley, Jean Donahue, Kathleen O'Malley and William Haade. It was produced by Hartman, and the director was Alexander Hall (who had also directed *Here Comes Mr Jordan*). Miss Hayworth's vocals were dubbed by Anita Ellis and Adele Jergens's by Kay Starr. Other songs and musical numbers included: *The Nine Muses; They Can't Convince Me; This Can't Be Legal; People Have More Fun Than Anyone; Let's Stay Young Forever* Doris Fisher, Allan Roberts.

Forties Musicals

△

Like so many musical biopics of the period, **My Wild Irish Rose** (Warner Bros.) chose to inflict on audiences an account of the life of a composer in which it was difficult to tell fact from fantasy. In this case, the subject was Chauncey Olcott, whose claim to fame was a couple of well-known tunes such as 'Mother Machree' (which he wrote with Ernest R. Ball and Rida Johnson Young) and 'When Irish Eyes Are Smiling' (with Ball and George Graff Jr). Dennis Morgan (centre), with a curious Irish brogue, played Olcott, whose existence, if the screenplay (by Peter Milne, story by Rita Olcott) was anything to judge by, must have been extremely dull and depressing. Doing their best to penetrate the clichés were Andrea King as Lillian Russell, George O'Brien as Iron Duke Muldoon and, by way of a cheering bonus, beautiful newcomer Arlene Dahl (right) as the girl Olcott marries. There was an attempt to pep the whole thing up with some interminable specialty dances performed by Igor Dega, Pierre Andre, The Three Dunhills, and Louis Willis Jr, and the rest of the cast included Ben Blue, Sara Allgood, William Frawley and Don McGuire (left). David Butler directed for producer William Jacobs who, in spite of the mediocre quality of the piece, turned in a box-office hit. Other songs and musical numbers: *Wee Rose Of Killarney*; *Miss Lindy Lou*; *There's Room In My Heart For Them All*; *The Natchez And The Robert E. Lee* M.K. Jerome, Ted Koehler; *One Little, Sweet Little Girl* Dan Sullivan; *My Wild Irish Rose* Olcott; *A Little Bit Of Heaven* J. Keirn Brennan, Ball; *My Nellie's Blue Eyes* William J. Scanlan; *Come Down Ma' Evenin' Star* Edgar Smith, John Stromberg.

Undeniably good-looking, but bereft of a single original idea, **This Time For Keeps** (MGM) was a glossy and trivial boy-meets-girl story embroidered with a mixture of pop and classical music in producer Joe Pasternak's corny old way. Esther Williams (as the star of a spectacular 'aquacaper') was the girl, Johnnie Johnston (the wealthy son of an operatic tenor) the boy, and Mackinac Island the setting for their on-off-on romance. Jimmy Durante (illustrated – as Williams's faithful bodyguard-cum-pianist) was in it too, and brightened up the proceedings whenever he was allowed to – most memorably in an attempt to find the lost chord. Lauritz Melchior (as Johnston's tenor-father) received second billing, and redressed the light-hearted musical balance by singing 'M'Appari' from Flotow's *Martha* and 'La Donna E Mobile' from Verdi's *Rigoletto*. He also sang Cole Porter's 'Easy To Love'. Other musical highlights were a water ballet designed to display the aquatic ▽

◁ A programmer from PRC, **Linda Be Good** starred Elyse Knox as an authoress who, while her husband (John Hubbard, centre) is out of town, joins a burlesque show in order to absorb local colour for a new novel she is writing. Complications set in when Miss Knox (centre left), in the company of dumb blonde Marie Wilson (centre right, a strip queen) is dated by her husband's married boss (Gordon Richards). Finale has Knox blackmailing Richards into giving her husband a vice-presidency. It came and went without anyone noticing the difference. Jack Norton, Ralph Sandford, Joyce Compton, Frank Scannell, Sir Lancelot, Lenny Breman and Byron Foulger were also cast, and a guest spot featured Professor Lamberti. The screenplay was by Leslie Vale and George Halasz (original story by Richard Irving Hyland and Howard Harris), Matty Kemp produced, and Frank McDonald directed. Songs and musical numbers included: *Old Woman With The Rolling Pin*; *Young Girls Of Today* Sir Lancelot; *My Mother Says I Mustn't* Jack Mason, Sy Miller; *Linda Be Good* Mason, Charles Herbert.

talents of Miss Williams, and Durante's singing of his own and Ben Ryan's 'Inka Dinka Doo'. Completing the cast were Dame May Whitty, Sharon McManus, Dick Simmons, Mary Stuart, Ludwig Stossel, Dorothy Porter, Nella Walker, Holmes Herbert and, playing themselves, Tommy Wonder and Xavier Cugat (and his orchestra). The screenplay was by Gladys Lehman from a story by Erwin Gelsey and Lorraine Fielding, it was choreographed by Stanley Donen, and directed with little sense of rhythm or pace by Richard Thorpe. Other musical numbers: *Chiquita Banana* Leonard Mackenzie, Garth Montgomery, William Wirges; *No Wonder They Fall In Love*; *Ten Per Cent Off* Ralph Freed, Sammy Fain; *The Man Who Found The Lost Chord*; *A Little Bit Of This And A Little Bit Of That* Durante; *Why Don't They Let Me Sing A Love Song?*; *Little Big Shot* Benny Davis, Harry Akst; *I Love To Dance* Freed, Burton Lane; *When It's Lilac Time On Mackinac Island* Leslie Kirk.

△

Though purists might argue that **Living In A Big Way** (MGM) was not, strictly speaking, a musical, it did contain three numbers which its star Gene Kelly choreographed (assisted by Stanley Donen) and performed. In the first, Kelly and his co-star Marie McDonald danced in an Astaire-Rogers-like fashion to 'It Had To Be You' (by Gus Kahn and Isham Jones); the second, a number called 'Fido And Me' (by Louis Alter and Edward Heyman), was danced by Kelly and a little dog around a statue in a garden, and was all about rejection (both the dog and Kelly having been rejected by Miss McDonald); while the third took place in, under and over the skeletal frame of an incomplete apartment block and made effective use of metal rings, step-ladders and planks of wood. The number, performed with children, to the accompaniment of 'Ring Around The Rosy', 'In And Out The Windows', 'Loo By Loo' and 'Yankee Doodle', was quintessential Kelly in its athleticism and in the easy, spontaneous way the youngsters in it were involved. Stylishly directed by Gregory La Cava, the film cast Kelly (illustrated) as a soldier who meets and marries a girl (McDonald) the night before he is drafted, only to discover, once the war is over, that she is a millionairess and always has been. He bitterly regrets the marriage and wants a divorce. A box-office catastrophe and rarely seen today, its theme – that of the proletariat versus the good life – was a favourite of its director who, although working in familiar territory, was able to eschew stereotype characterizations and avoid sentimentality. It deserved a better fate than it received. Also cast: Charles Winninger, Phyllis Thaxter, Spring Byington, Jean Adair, Shelley Winters and Clinton Sundberg. It was written by La Cava and Irving Ravetch; Pandro S. Berman produced.

Two Blondes And A Redhead (Columbia) starred Jean Porter (foreground left) as a society girl who plays hookey from her exclusive girls' school and appears in the chorus of a musical. When the show closes, she invites two of her chorine friends to her hometown, whereupon all sorts of complications filled out the 69-minute running time. June Preisser (foreground right) and Judy Clark (centre) were Miss Porter's chums, with other roles in Sam Katzman's routine production going to Jimmy Lloyd (as a rich lad pretending to be a servant), Rick Vallin, Charles Smith, Douglas Wood and Regina Wallace. Also featured: Tony Pastor (foreground centre) and His Orchestra. It was written by Victor McLeod and Jameson Brewer from a story by Harry Rebuas, and directed by Arthur Dreifuss. Songs: *It's So Easy*; *All I Know Is Si Si* Doris Fisher, Allan Roberts; *Boogie Woogie From Nowhere* Saul Chaplin; *On The Sunny Side Of The Street* Dorothy Fields, Jimmy McHugh.
▽

Yet another backwoods-to-Broadway yarn, **Glamour Girl** (Columbia) starred Gene Krupa, whose main contribution to the M. Coates Webster-Lee Gold screenplay was an all-out performance on drums of Segar Ellis and George Williams's 'Gene's Boogie'. Otherwise the plot revolved around a zither-plucking singer (Susan Reed, centre) who's discovered in the sticks by a record talent scout (Virginia Grey, right) and brought to New York, where she finds instant anonymity. Undaunted, Grey and partner Michael Duane (left) start a company of their own and, in no time at all (68 minutes), Miss Reed is the talk of the town. Jack Leonard, singer Carolyn Grey, Jimmy Lloyd, Pierre Watkin and Eugene Borden were adequate in support. Sam Katzman produced and Arthur Dreifuss directed. Other songs and musical numbers included: *Anywhere* Jule Styne, Sammy Cahn; *Without Imagination* Allan Roberts, Doris Fisher.
▽

△

June Allyson was not the greatest singer on MGM's roster, and Peter Lawford's song-and-dance efforts would give Astaire no sleepless nights, but that didn't stop **Good News** (MGM), a colourful remake of the campest of all campus comedies, from being knockout entertainment. The plot was pretty similar to the original 1930 version, but this time it was Patricia Marshall who set her sights on the football hero (Lawford) and demure little June who finally got him. With Charles Walters and Robert Alton in charge of the dances, the film rated an 'A' for ebullience, from its rousingly vigorous opening ensemble performance of the title tune to its spirited finale 'The Varsity Drag' (illustrated, with Allyson and Lawford foreground), both numbers by Buddy De Sylva, Lew Brown and Ray Henderson, the latter engagingly performed by Allyson and Lawford as they led the company in a complex, but fluently controlled *mélange* of high-stepping dance patterns. Zesty Joan McCracken, fresh from Broadway's *Bloomer Girl* and *Billion Dollar Baby*, contributed some wry comedy and led the chorus in another choreographic highlight 'Pass That Peace Pipe' (by Roger Edens, Ralph Blane and Hugh Martin) which for *élan* and inventiveness ranks with the Hollywood musical's best. But every number was a gem: Allyson and Lawford's 'The French Lesson', written especially for the film by Roger Edens, with lyrics by Betty Comden and Adolph Green, who also contributed the screenplay (their first), and the other De Sylva, Brown and Henderson numbers from the original score: 'Just Imagine', plaintively warbled by Allyson, 'Lucky In Love' sung by all the principals in turn in another expertly staged ensemble sequence, 'He's A Ladies' Man', buoyantly performed by Lawford, Ray McDonald and Mel Torme and the durable ballad 'The Best Things In Life Are Free', sung first by Allyson, and later reprised by Mel Torme and (in French) by Lawford. Robert Strickland, Donald MacBride, Tom Dugan, Clinton Sundberg, Loren Tindall and Connie Gilchrist were also cast. Arthur Freed produced (in Technicolor) and Charles Walters made an impressive directorial debut. **Good News** originally started life as a Broadway musical by Lawrence Schwab, Frank Mandel, De Sylva, Brown and Henderson in 1927 and ran 557 performances.

1948

Academy Awards

Best Actor
NOMINATIONS INCLUDED: Dan Dailey *When My Baby Smiles At Me* (20th Century-Fox)

Costume Design (New Category) (colour)
NOMINATIONS INCLUDED: *The Emperor Waltz* (Paramount) Edith Head and Gile Steele

Music
Song
NOMINATIONS INCLUDED: 'For Every Man There's A Woman' *Casbah* (Marston. U-I) Harold Arlen *cm*; Leo Robin *lyr*. 'It's Magic' *Romance On The High Seas* (WB) Jule Styne *cm*; Sammy Cahn *lyr*. 'This Is The Moment' *That Lady In Ermine* (20th Century-Fox) Frederick Hollander *cm*; Leo Robin *lyr*.

Scoring Of A Musical Picture
Easter Parade (MGM) Johnny Green and Roger Edens
NOMINATIONS INCLUDED: *The Emperor Waltz* Victor Young. *The Pirate* (MGM) Lennie Hayton. *Romance On The High Seas* Ray Heindorf. *When My Baby Smiles At Me* Alfred Newman.

The Annual Top Moneymaking Films
INCLUDED: *Road To Rio* (Paramount). *Easter Parade*. *The Emperor Waltz*. *A Date With Judy* (MGM). *Sitting Pretty* (Paramount). *My Wild Irish Rose* (WB). *When My Baby Smiles At Me*. *On An Island With You* (MGM).

△

Heavy on musical numbers, light on plot (air hostess becomes a bandsinger), **Mary Lou** (Columbia) starred Joan Barton (right), Robert Lowery (as her boyfriend), Glenda Farrell, Abigail Adams, Frank Jenks, Emmett Vogan, Thelma White, Pierre Watkin, Chester Clute, and Frankie Carle and His Orchestra. Passable double-bill support, it was written by M. Coates Webster, choreographed by Jack Doyle, produced by Sam Katzman and directed by Arthur Dreifuss. Songs and musical numbers: *Mary Lou* J.R. Robinson, Abe Lyman, George Waggner; *Don't Mind My Troubles*; *I'm Sorry I Didn't Say I'm Sorry* Allan Roberts, Lester Lee; *That's Good Enough For Me*; *Wasn't It Swell Last Night?* Roberts, Doris Fisher; *Carle's Boogie* Frankie Carle; *Learning To Speak English* Facundo Rivero, Ben Blossner.

▽

A quickie from Republic, **Campus Honeymoon** concerned a marriage of convenience between two young war veterans (Richard Crane, 2nd left, and Hal Hackett, left) and a couple of sisters (the Wilde twins, Lyn and Lee, illustrated). Unmarried, the men are not eligible for a pair of houses in a special veteran's housing project, hence the 'arrangement'. But in no time at all the ex-GIs find they really *are* in love with the girls, and vice versa, the assumption at the end of 61 minutes of lightweight joviality being that they all live happily ever after. It was produced by Fanchon with a cast that also included Adele Mara, Wilson Wood and Stephanie Bachelor, and directed by Richard Sale who also scripted it, with Jerry Gruskin, from a story by Thomas R. St George. Songs included: *How Does It Feel to Fall In Love?*; *Who's Got A Tent For Rent?*; *Are You Happening To Me?* Sale, Gruskin; *Rocked In The Cradle Of The Deep* J.P. Knight, Emma Willard; *It's So Nice To Have A Man About The House* Jack Elliott, Harold Spina; *Opalooka Song* Sale, Nathan Scott.

△

The fifth, and most conventional of the 'Road' films, **Road To Rio** (Paramount) relied more on its storyline than on the anachronistic 'sight' gags that had hitherto dominated the series and, compared to *Road To Utopia* (Paramount, 1946) was a sober effort indeed. Compared to most other comedies, though, it was a riot. Crosby (left foreground) and Hope (centre) played a pair of musicians who, after accidentally setting fire to a carnival, sail for Rio. On board ship they meet Dorothy Lamour (right) a mysterious beauty whose mercurial changes in temperament baffle them – until they realize that she is being hypnotized by her aunt (Gale Sondergaard) into marrying a man in Brazil she does not love. With its attractive score by Johnny Burke and Jimmy Van Heusen, whose three best numbers were 'You Don't Have To Know The Language' sung by Crosby and The Andrews Sisters (appearing as themselves), 'But Beautiful', which became a Crosby standard, and 'Experience', sung by Lamour, plus a laugh-laden screenplay by Edmund Beloin and Jack Rose, **Road To Rio** was an appealing package of fun that outgrossed every other film in 1948. Frank Faylen and Joseph Vitale were the obligatory heavies, with other roles going to the Wiere Brothers as a trio of whacky Brazilian entertainers, Nestor Paiva, Robert Barrat, Frank Puglia, Jerry Colonna, Charles Middleton and Stanley Andrews. The dances were staged by Bernard Pearce and Billy Daniels, Daniel Dare produced and the director was Norman Z. McLeod. Other songs and musical numbers: *Apalachicola Fla*; *Cavaquinho* Burke, Van Heusen; *Brazil* Ary Barroso, English lyrics Bob Russell.

Though not dissimilar in plot to producer Joe Pasternak's *Three Smart Girls* (Universal, 1937), MGM's **Three Daring Daughters** (GB: **The Birds And The Bees**), also produced by Pasternak, had the advantage of Technicolor and, instead of Miss Durbin dominating the proceedings, top-starred Jeanette MacDonald (in her penultimate film). As a magazine editor, and divorced mother of three self-consciously cute daughters, Miss M. (2nd right) brought a welcome dollop of sophistication to the narrative. Jose Iturbi (playing himself, 2nd left) received second billing and, in his most substantial screen role to date, was required by the Albert Mannheimer-Frederick Kohner-Sonya Levien-John Meehan screenplay, to become Miss MacDonald's husband! Plot pivoted on the objections to the relationship lodged by MacDonald's three young daughters (Jane Powell, centre, Mary Eleanor Donahue, right, Ann E. Todd, left), who are under the much mistaken impression that their divorced father (a newspaperman) is a paragon of virtue. The girls are eventually won over by Iturbi who proves to them that he is just as much at home playing Bobby Troup's 'Route 66', as he is with Liszt's 'Liebestraum'. The film's one durable hit was 'The Dickey Bird Song' by Sammy Fain and Howard Dietz, charmingly sung by MacDonald and her three offspring, and reprised with Iturbi at the piano. The Iturbis – Amparo joined her brother – on twin pianos played Enesco's Rumanian Rhapsody in A, Opus 11, No I, with Larry Adler on the harmonica, and full orchestra. Edward Arnold was cast as the 'thirteenth richest man in the world' and the boss of MacDonald's (unseen) ex-husband, with other parts under the *schmaltzy* eye of director Fred Wilcox going to Harry Davenport, Moyna McGill, Kathryn Card, Richard Simmons, Thurston Hall, and Virginia Brissac. Dorothy Porter also appeared as herself and the Misses Donahue and Todd's singing was dubbed by Beverly Jean Garbo and Pat Hyatt respectively. Interesting sideline: The film was considered 'morally objectionable in part for all' by the Catholic League of Decency as it 'tended to justify as well as accept the respectability of divorce'. Other songs and musical numbers: *Alma Mater* Georgie Stoll, Billy Katz; *Fleurette* Victor Herbert, Ralph Freed; *Passepied* Leo Delibes, Princess Anna Eristoff; *Where There's Love* (based on a waltz from 'Der Rosenkavalier') Richard Strauss, Earl Brent; *Ritual Fire Dance* (El Amor Brujo) Manuel de Falla; *You Made Me Love You* Joseph McCarthy, James V. Monaco; *Happy Birthday* Patty Smith Hill, Mildred J. Hill; *Je Veux Vivre* (Juliet's Waltz from 'Romeo et Juliette') Gounod; *Hungarian Fantasy* Liszt; *Sweethearts* Victor Herbert, Bob Wright, Chet Forrest; *Allegro Appassionato, Opus 10* Saint-Saens; *Springtide* (*An den Fruhling*) *Opus 43, No 6* Edward Grieg, Earl Brent; *Coda of the fourth movement of Tchaikovsky's Fourth Symphony*; *Piano Sonata No 11 in A, K331* Mozart.
▽

△

That exhausted, if not entirely dead, horse, the backstage musical, was flogged again in **April Showers** (Warner Bros.), a damp excursion into the ups and downs of vaudeville. On this occasion, Jack Carson (left) played Joe Thyme (known as Big Thyme), the head of a family act called 'The Three Happy Thymes'. Joe hits the bottle and causes the disintegration of the act, whose members each go their sad and separate ways. But, as written by Peter Milne from a story by Joe Laurie Jr, an opportunity on Broadway reunites the little band who, unlike the film – become a smash hit. Carson's unfortunate wife and his extrovert son were played by Ann Sothern (right) and Robert Alda, with the ubiquitous S.Z. Sakall (foreground), Richard Rober and Joseph Crehan in support. James Kern directed for producer William Jacobs. Songs and musical numbers included: *Little Trouper* Kim Gannon, Walter Kent; *World's Most Beautiful Girl* Gannon, Ted Fetter; *It's Tulip Time In Holland* Dave Radford, Richard A. Whiting; *April Showers* Buddy De Sylva, Louis Silvers; *Carolina In The Morning* Gus Kahn, Walter Donaldson.

△

Eddie Cantor produced and starred in **If You Knew Susie** (RKO), a nebulous brew of songs and gags mixed in with an idiot plot about a retired vaudevillian (Cantor, 2nd left) who discovers that the US government, as a result of a financial transaction undertaken with his ancestors, owes him a fortune in back interest. Joan Davis (left) co-starred as his wife, with other parts in Warren Wilson and Oscar Brodney's laboured screenplay (additional dialogue by Bud Peterson and Lester A. White) going to Bobby Driscoll (right) and Margaret Kelly (as Cantor's offspring), Allyn Joslyn, Charles Dingle, Sheldon Leonard, Joe Sawyer, Dick Humphreys (centre) and Peggy Lynch (2nd right). Charles O'Curran choreographed, Gordon M. Douglas directed. Songs and musical numbers included: *If You Knew Susie* Buddy De Sylva, Joseph Meyer; *My How The Time Goes By*; *My Brooklyn Love Song*; *What Do I Want With Money?*; *Living The Life I Love* Harold Adamson, Jimmy McHugh.

Tony Martin (left) was cast as Pepe Le Moko in **Casbah** (Universal International), the third version of the story which bears its hero's name (the other two being the French *Pepe Le Moko* with Jean Gabin; and *Algiers* United Artists, 1938, starring Charles Boyer). Though not ideal casting, his handling of the interpolated songs was more than adequate, underlining the impression that he was better at singing than he was at crime. Marta Toren was the woman whose love he dies for, with other featured roles in Ladislaus Bus-Fekete and Arnold Manoff's screenplay (based on the novel by Detective Ashelbe, and a 'musical' adaptation by Erik Charell) going to Hugo Haas as a Casbah guide, Peter Lorre (excellent) as Inspector Slimane and Yvonne De Carlo (centre). Also cast: Thomas Gomez, Douglas Dick (right), Herbert Rudley, Virginia Gregg, and Katherine Dunham and her dancers. It was produced by Nat G. Goldstone, choreographed by Bernard Pearce, and directed by John Berry. Songs and musical numbers: *For Every Man There's A Woman*; *It Was Written In The Stars*; *Hooray For Love*; *What's Good About Goodbye?* Harold Arlen, Leo Robin.
▽

Campus Sleuth (GB: **Smart Politics**) a musical whodunnit, was a time-waster from Monogram that involved Freddie Stewart and June Preisser (both illustrated) in a campus murder. In this instance it was difficult to tell who the victim was: a dead magazine photographer or the paying customers out front. Warren Mills, Noel Neill, Donald MacBride, Monte Collins and Stan Ross were also in it; so were Bobby Sherwood and His Orchestra and Gerri Gallian and his piano. Hal Collins wrote it from a story by himself and Max Wilson. Will Jason produced and directed. It was thankfully all over in 57 minutes. Songs: *Baby You Can Count On Me*; *What Happened?*; *Neither Could I*; *Jungle Rhumba*; *Sherwood's Forest* Will Jason, Sid Robin.
▽

△

Donald O'Connor did one excellent number in **Are You With It?** (Universal International) – a really bravura piece of hoofing – and it took place in a restaurant. Most of the film, however, was set in a Carnival, and nothing its young star perpetrated there matched his energetic dancing in the earlier sequence. In fact a boringly, albeit elaborately, staged ballet which climaxed the film was, frankly, an embarrassment (choreography by Louis Da Pron). Top-billed O'Connor (left) played a mathematical genius who joins a carnival when he is fired for misplacing a decimal point. Olga San Juan was his romantic object, and Lew Parker (in the role he originally played in the Broadway show of the same name), a carnival pitch man. Also cast: Martha Stewart, George O'Hanlon (right), Walter Catlett, Pat Dane, Ransom Sherman, Louis Da Pron, Noel Neill and Julie Gibson. O'Connor mugged his way through most of Oscar Brodney's undemanding screenplay (based on the Sam Perrin-George Balzer stageshow), his rubber face working overtime in a routine called 'Down At Baba's Alley' (by Sidney Miller and Inez James, who contributed all of the music). Robert Arthur produced and it was directed by Jack Hively. Other songs and musical numbers were: *It Only Takes A Little Imagination*; *What Do I Have To Do To Make You Love Me?*; *Daddy Surprise Me*; *I'm Looking For A Prince Of A Fellow*; *Are You With It?*.

First seen on Broadway in 1945, with a score by Sigmund Romberg and a book by Herbert and Dorothy Fields, **Up In Central Park** (Universal International) came to the screen shorn of most of its songs – a considerable miscalculation from which the film never recovered, especially as its star, Deanna Durbin (illustrated) was a far better singer than she was an actress. Set in New York when Tammany Hall was in its heyday, it featured Durbin as the immigrant daughter of a park superintendent (Albert Sharpe) who, together with *New York Times* reporter John Matthews (Dick Haymes) manages to uncover the crooked political activities of Boss Tweed (Vincent Price) and his organization. As both Haymes and Price were miscast and Miss Durbin misused, there wasn't much value for money in Karl Tunberg's production (Tunberg also scripted it) and, not surprisingly, it repeated its disappointing Broadway history by failing to find mass audience support. Completing the cast were Tom Powers, Hobart Cavanaugh, Thurston Hall, Howard Freeman, Mary Field, Tom Pedi and Moroni Olsen. The director was William A. Seiter. Songs: *Oh Say, Do You See What I See?*; *When She Walks In The Room*; *Carousel In The Park* Romberg, Fields; *Pace, Pace Mio Dio* (from 'La Forza Del Destino') Verdi.

Scripted by Whitfield Cook and Anne Morrison Chapin (additional dialogue by Aben Kandel) from a story by Miklos Laszlo as adapted by Nanette Kutner, **Big City** (MGM) was the sentimental story of an orphan who finds herself adopted by a Jewish cantor (Danny Thomas), a Protestant minister (Robert Preston) and an Irish-Catholic cop (George Murphy). As the orphan was played by top-starred Margaret O'Brien (illustrated) a dewy-eyed time was had by all. Conflict intruded when cop Murphy marries saloon singer Betty Garrett (her debut) and has the unpopular notion of supplying Miss O'Brien with a *bona fide* mother. But it all worked out satisfactorily, as produced by Joe Pasternak in whose particular make-believe world everything had to be sweetness and light. And musical. Hence little Margaret (dubbed by Marni Nixon) trilled away in company with opera star Lotte Lehmann who (as Thomas's mother) sang 'God Bless America' (by Irving Berlin), Brahms's 'Lullaby', and 'The Kerry Dance' (by James Lyman Molloy). Berlin was also represented by 'What'll I Do?' (sung by Danny Thomas); and from Miss Garrett, fresh from her triumph on Broadway in *Call Me Mister*, came 'Ok'l Baby Dok'l' (by Inez James and Sidney Miller). Also cast: Karin Booth, Edward Arnold, Butch Jenkins, Connie Gilchrist and The Page Cavanaugh Trio. The caring, if over sentimental, direction was by Norman Taurog. Other songs and musical numbers: *Shoo Shoo Baby* Phil Moore; *I'm Gonna See A Lot Of You* Janice Torre, Fred Spielman; *Don't Blame Me* Dorothy Fields, Jimmy McHugh; *Yippee-O-Yippee-Ay Ay* Jerry Seelen, Walter Pepp.

◁

Another *pot-pourri* of animated musical numbers from the Disney studios, **Melody Time** (RKO) was the last of the series and qualitatively on a par with *Make Mine Music* (RKO, 1945). There were seven segments in all, the two best being 'The Story Of Johnny Appleseed' (with Dennis Day's voice as Appleseed), and 'Pecos Bill' which featured Roy Rogers (left), the Sons Of The Pioneers, Bobby Driscoll and Luana Patten (right) in a tale about a youngster raised by coyotes who finds his equal in a wonderhorse called Widowmaker. The film opened with a sequence called 'Once Upon A Wintertime' by Bobby Worth and Ray Gilbert (sung by Frances Langford). This was followed by 'Bumble Boogie', a jazzy version of Rimsky-Korsakov's 'The Flight Of The Bumble Bee' arranged by Jack Fina, and performed by Freddy Martin and His Orchestra, with Fina on piano. 'Johnny Appleseed' came next, and after that The Andrews Sisters sang the story of a young tugboat called 'Little Toot' (by Allie Wrubel). Fred Waring and His Pennsylvanians featured in a rather self-consciously 'arty' sequence called 'Trees' (from the poem by Joyce Kilmer with music by Oscar Rasbach); followed by Ethel Smith and The Dinning Sisters performing 'Blame It On The Samba' (by Ernesto Nazareth and Ray Gilbert) in an item which reunited Donald Duck with Joe Carioca. The finale was the aforementioned 'Pecos Bill'. The production supervisor was Ben Sharpsteen and the cartoon directors Clyde Geronimi, Wilfred Jackson, Hamilton Luske and Jack Kinney. Other songs and musical numbers: *Melody Time* George Weiss, Bennie Benjamin; *The Lord Is Good To Me*; *The Pioneer Song*; *The Apple Song* Kim Gannon, Walter Kent; *Blue Shadows On The Trail*; *Pecos Bill* Eliot Daniel, Johnny Lange.
▽

Three songs, two of which developed into full-scale tap numbers for star Donald O'Connor, helped considerably to enliven **Feudin', Fussin' And A-Fightin'** (Universal International), a slaphappy hunk of hokum in which O'Connor (left) starred as a travelling salesman who, after being kidnapped by the townsfolk of Rimrock, finds himself taking part in their annual foot-race against a rival village. O'Connor's taps were tops, and there was some boisterous over-acting from Marjorie Main as Rimrock's stentorian mayor and from Percy Kilbride as a local livery stable owner. Also doing their bit for the backwoods: Joe Besser, Harry Shannon, Fred Kohler Jr, Howland Chamberlin and, for romantic interest, Penny Edwards (right). D.D. Beauchamp scripted it from a story he wrote for *Colliers Magazine*, Leonard Goldstein produced, Louis Da Pron choreographed and the director was George Sherman. Songs and musical numbers included: *S'posin'* Andy Razaf, Paul Denniker; *Me And My Shadow* Al Jolson, Billy Rose, Dave Dreyer; *Feudin' And Fightin'* Al Dubin, Burton Lane.

The Pirate (MGM) produced by Arthur Freed and directed by Vincente Minnelli was, if possible, even more artificial in its 'look' and in the stagey atmosphere it created than the same team's *Yolanda And The Thief* (MGM, 1945). And, like *Yolanda*, it was not a box-office success. The story (with music by Cole Porter) of a strolling player called Serafin who pretends to be the notorious Caribbean pirate, Macoco, in order to win the love of wealthy Manuela, it was pitched at an airless, stifling temperature of 95° in the shade so that the very water in the quay at San Sebastian (the Caribbean Island on which it all takes place) seemed sizzling to the touch. Judy Garland (right) was cast as Manuela and Gene Kelly (left) as Serafin. Giving performances as stylized and as theatrical as Jack Martin Smith's sets, they played all their non-musical scenes in capital letters, and punctuated every gesture with an exclamation mark. The overall results were 'arty' rather than artistic, which explains why the film failed, on its initial release, to find a willing audience for its excesses. The passage of time, however, has allowed for a reassessment of its qualities, and although neither the claustrophobia nor the frenzied quality of the performances has lessened with time, there can be no denying Minnelli's brilliant use of colour throughout. And if the rather tiresome screen-play (by Albert Hackett and Frances Goodrich, from a play by S.N. Behrman) remains instantly forgettable, what seems to have improved with the years is the dazzling dance direction by Kelly and Robert Alton, 'Nina' being the choreographic highlight of the film. In a routine of sustained inventive brilliance, danced to a catchy bolero rhythm, Kelly, dressed in black trousers, colourful waistcoat and dashing hat, curls himself around decorative poles and clambers over rooftops as he courts every girl in San Sebastian in that overtly masculine manner which is his stylistic trade-mark. It is not only Kelly's *braggadocio* approach to the dance which makes it so appealing, but the editing of the sequence (by Blanche Sewell), the Technicolor photography (by Harry Stradling), the colours chosen by Minnelli to offset it all and, of course, the wizardry of Porter's song. Less inventive, but also visually exciting, is the 'Pirate' ballet, in which Kelly, as Serafin, dances out his fantasy as Macoco, cavorting boisterously up, down and across a screen of billowing mauve clouds and belching smoke. Choreographically it is of much less consequence than 'Nina', and also excrutiatingly noisy. The film's quieter moments arrived in the shape of two Porter ballads, 'You Can Do No Wrong', which followed a wild knock-about scene in which Garland hurled words as well as objects at Kelly; and 'Love Of My Life', following Kelly and The Nicholas Brothers' energetic 'Be A Clown'. Both ballads were sung, quite marvellously, by Garland, whose other big song was the rousing 'Mack The Black'. Walter Slezak, Gladys Cooper, Reginald Owen and George Zucco all gave supporting performances bordering on caricature. On balance, a memorable failure.

Just as old timer Charles Winninger (right) refused to admit that vaudeville was a thing of the past, and that he and his juggling son and partner, Dan Dailey (left), had missed the boat, so 20th Century-Fox's **Give My Regards To Broadway** refused to admit that backstage sagas of this particular ilk were by now just as *passé*, especially when regurgitated in so makeshift and familiar a fashion as this one was. Fay Bainter played wife and mother to her fretting husband and son, and her two non-show business daughters, Barbara Lawrence (centre) and Jane Nigh. Also cast: Nancy Guild, Charles Russell, Sig Rumann, Howard Freeman, Herbert Anderson and Harry Seymour. Walter Morosco produced, the director was Lloyd Bacon, Seymour Felix staged the routines and it was scripted by Samuel Hoffenstein and Elizabeth Reinhardt from a story by John Klempner. (Technicolor). Songs and musical numbers: *Give My Regards To Broadway* George M. Cohan; *When Frances Dances With Me* Benny Ryan, Sol Violinsky; *Let A Smile Be Your Umbrella* Sammy Fain, Irving Kahal, Francis Wheeler; *Whispering* John Schonberger, Richard Coburn, Vincent Rose; *Where Did You Get That Hat?* J.W. Kelly; *Linger Awhile* Harry Owens, Rose.

293

Forties Musicals

'There was something about the way she looked at a man that rang bells', claimed the ads for **Lulu Belle**. They were referring to star Dorothy Lamour (illustrated right) as the titular heroine of Charles MacArthur and Edward Sheldon's 1926 Broadway play which came to the screen, via Columbia, in a whitewash job that changed Lulu's profession from prostitute to saloon *chanteuse*, and her face from black to white. Unfortunately, there was nothing about the film that rang bells and nothing about Miss Lamour's underpowered performance to justify the publicity blurb. Set in 1900 and told in flashback, the film catalogued the various romantic dalliances enjoyed by its heroine – from her marriage to attorney George Montgomery, to her liaison with prizefighter Greg McClure, his manager Albert Dekker, and railroad tycoon Otto Kruger who transports her from New Orleans to Broadway where she becomes a star. Not surprisingly, she stops a bullet, at which point the film became something of a whodunnit. Addison Richards, Glenda Farrell (left), Charlotte Wynters, William Haade and Clancy Cooper were also cast by producer Benedict Bogeaus, Everett Freeman scripted it (additional dialogue by Karl Kamb), Nick Castle choreographed, and it was directed by Leslie Fenton. Songs and musical numbes: *Lulu Belle* Edgar De Lange, Henry Russell; *Sweetie Pie* John Lehman, Russell; *I'd Be Lost Without You* Russell; *Ace In The Hole* George Mitchell, James Dempsey; *Sweetheart Of The Blues* Lester Lee, Allan Roberts.

Director Billy Wilder's characteristic cynicism was nowhere in evidence in **The Emperor Waltz** (Paramount), a charming fantasy for grown-ups which he both directed and scripted (with producer Charles Brackett). Set against a Technicolored Tyrolean backdrop, in the time of Emperor Franz Joseph, it starred Bing Crosby (right) as a phonograph salesman whose particular assignment is to sell the contraption to a thoroughly uninterested, not to say suspicious, Emperor (Richard Haydn). After being ejected from the royal presence, Crosby attempts to reach the unyielding Emperor through his pretty niece, Johanna Franziska Von Stultzenberg (Joan Fontaine, left). But she, too, will have nothing to do with the travelling salesman, and it is left to their respective pet dogs (his fox terrier, her poodle) to bring them together. Considering the cornball nature of the material, Wilder and Brackett's screenplay was a miracle of invention and resourcefulness that kept it all deliciously palatable. The central performances were completely charming, and there was good work as well from Roland Culver, Lucile Watson, Harold Vermilyea and Sig Rumann. Billy Daniels choreographed. Songs and musical numbers: *Get Yourself A Phonograph* Johnny Burke, Jimmy Van Heusen; *I Kiss Your Hand, Madame* Ralph Erwin, Sam M. Lewis, Joe Young, German lyrics Fritz Rotter; *The Kiss In Your Eyes* Burke (an adaptation, with English lyrics, of 'Im Chambre Separée' from Richard Heuberger's 'Der Opernball'); *Friendly Mountains* (based on traditional Swiss songs) Burke; *The Emperor Waltz* Burke, Johann Strauss (all sung by Crosby).

◁ A former singer with Les Brown's band, Doris Von Kappelhof, better known as Doris Day, achieved international stardom via the Warner Bros. studio in her first film **Romance On The High Seas** (GB: **It's Magic**) much of which, as the title suggested, took place on board a luxury liner. One of those convoluted mistaken identity yarns, the film featured Miss Day (illustrated) as a singer who is hired by a wealthy socialite (Janis Paige) to take her place on an ocean voyage to Rio so that she (Paige) can remain in New York and secretly spy on her husband (Don DeFore) whom she believes is being unfaithful to her. DeFore, meanwhile, suspicious that his wife wants to take a trip without him, hires a detective (Jack Carson, left – top starred) to watch over her! Julius J. and Philip G. Epstein's screenplay (from a story by S. Pondal Rios and Carlos A. Olivari; additional dialogue I.A.L. Diamond) pepped up a basically tired series of situations with several well-written scenes, as did the score by Sammy Cahn and Jule Styne, whose 'It's Magic' and 'Put Em In A Box, Tie 'Em With A Ribbon, And Throw 'Em In The Deep Blue Sea' (both sung by Day) became king-sized hits. Though the star was given fourth billing (the part was originally offered to Judy Garland, then Betty Hutton), she was the undoubted hit of a show whose cast also included Oscar Levant, S.Z. Sakall, Fortunio Bonanova, Eric Blore and Franklin Pangborn, plus specialties Avon Long, Sir Lancelot, The Samba Kings and The Page Cavanaugh Trio. Busby Berkeley returned to Warner Bros. to create and stage the dance sequences (surprisingly he was not credited). Alex Gottlieb produced, and Michael Curtiz directed. Other songs and musical numbers: *It's You Or No One* (Day); *I'm in Love* (Day); *The Tourist Trade* (Sir Lancelot); *Run, Run, Run* (Carson) Cahn, Styne; *Cuban Rhapsody* (Levant) Ray Heindorf, Oscar Levant.

Two Guys From Texas (Warner Bros.) was a lightweight spoof of musical westerns which again teamed Jack Carson (centre) and Dennis Morgan (left) – this time as a couple of not-too-successful song and dance men who end up on a dude ranch where they encounter a series of misadventures and a dose of romance. The screenplay, by I.A.L. Diamond and Allen Boretz (from a play by Louis Pelletier Jr and Robert Sloane), provided a lot of opportunity for comedy which Carson embraced with gusto. Some slick musical numbers, and suitably pacey direction from David Butler, kept the mild diversion going, with adequate support from Dorothy Malone, Penny Edwards (2nd right), Fred Clark, Forrest Tucker, Gerald Mohr and John Alvin. Monte Blue also turned up; so did The Philharmonic Trio. Alex Gottlieb produced. Songs: *Every Day I Love You Just A Little Bit More*; *Hankerin'*; *I Don't Care If It Rains All Night*; *There's Music In The Land*; *I Wanna Be A Cowboy In The Movies* Jule Styne, Sammy Cahn.

It was really Gene Kelly who was responsible for Fred Astaire's return to pictures. A few weeks before shooting on Irving Berlin's **Easter Parade** (MGM) was due to commence, Kelly, who was scheduled to appear in it with Judy Garland, sprained his ankle in a volleyball game and suggested to producer Arthur Freed that Astaire replace him. Freed did not need much persuading; neither, as it turned out, did Astaire. Tired of his period of relative inactivity since his 'retirement' two years earlier, he jumped at the chance of working with Judy Garland and immediately began reworking some of the routines that had been planned for Kelly. The result was the year's best musical. It grossed $4,200,000, making it the second biggest money maker in 1948 (the first was Paramount's *Road To Rio*). Astaire played Don Hewes, a dancer who, at the beginning of the film, is ditched by his partner (Ann Miller) when Ziegfeld beckons her for a part in his new show. Bent on revenge, he determines to prove that he can make a star out of anyone he chooses, selects Garland from a chorus line, and sets about grooming her. At first it isn't easy, the situation being aggravated by the fact that he is still in love with Miller. But time heals everything, makes a thorough pro of Garland and, in the end, she and Astaire find themselves in love with one another – the happy realization coming just in time for them to be seen arm-in-arm in the Fifth Avenue Easter Parade. As backstage romances go, it was no world-beater, but the perfect cue for a casket of Berlin evergreens which its attractive cast (including Peter Lawford as Astaire's best friend) sang and danced with immense *élan*. Of the 17 Berlin standards on offer, the most memorable were Astaire's 'Drum Crazy' solo performed in a toy

shop at the start of the film; 'Stepping Out With My Baby', another Astaire routine which innovatively combined slow motion with normal motion at one and the same time; and the joyous 'A Couple Of Swells' sung and danced by Garland and Astaire as tramps (illustrated). Ann Miller's 'The Girl On The Magazine Cover' (sung by Richard Beavers) was the show's big production number, and it was elegantly staged by Robert Alton who was in charge of the dance direction throughout. 'Shaking The Blues Away' was another Miller item (visually stunning in grey and yellow) and, like every other number in this catalogue of delights, was a knockout. Garland's 'Better Luck Next Time' was touchingly delivered to a sympathetic bartender (Clinton Sundberg) and provided a striking contrast to her more energetic numbers, the most exuberant being the catchy title song, and the quartet of oldies ('When the Midnight Choo-Choo Leaves For Alabam', 'Snooky Ookums', 'Ragtime Violin' and 'I Love A Piano') she shared with Astaire. **Easter Parade** was scripted by Sidney Sheldon, Frances Goodrich and Albert Hackett from a story by Hackett and Miss Goodrich, and its cast was completed by Jules Munshin, Jeni Le Gon, Dick Simmons, and specialty dancers Pat Jackson, Dee Turnell and Bobbie Priest. The appropriately bright and breezy direction was by the reliable Charles Walters. Other songs and musical numbers: *Happy Easter* (Astaire); *It Only Happens When I Dance With You* (Astaire, danced by Astaire and Miller, reprised by Garland); *Everybody's Doin' It* (Garland, chorus); *I Want To Go Back To Michigan* (Garland); *Beautiful Faces Need Beautiful Clothes* (Astaire, Garland); *A Fella With An Umbrella* (Lawford, Garland).

A low-budget programmer from Columbia, also low on entertainment, **I Surrender Dear** revolved around a feud between Gloria Jean's (left) orchestra-leader boyfriend (David Street) and her father (Robert Emmett Keane, right) after the former ousts the latter from his radio station job by becoming a disc jockey. All the requisite complications came tumbling out of scenarist M. Coates Webster's screenplay (additional dialogue by Hal Collins) with roles in it for Don McGuire, Alice Tyrrell, Douglas Wood, Byron Foulger, Regina Wallace, and, in brief appearances, disc jockeys Jack Eigen, Dave Garroway and Peter Potter, as well as The Novelties. Sam Katzman produced and it was directed by Arthur Dreifuss. Best song was Allan Roberts and Doris Fisher's 'Amado Mio', first heard in *Gilda* (Columbia 1946). Other songs and musical numbers: *I Surrender Dear* Harry Barris, Gordon Clifford; *How Can You Tell?* Roberts, Fisher; *When You Are In The Room* Oscar Hammerstein II, Ben Oakland; *Nobody Else But Elsie* Allie Wrubel.

MGM's big-hearted (though small-scale) Technicolor musical, **A Date With Judy**, was dominated by adolescents, but it was Carmen Miranda (fourth billed) who, with her delicious performance of 'Cuanto La Gusta' (by Ray Gilbert and Gabriel Ruiz), made the greatest impact in Joe Pasternak's jolly little production. And the scene in which she teaches top-billed Wallace Beery how to rhumba was, unquestionably, the best in the show. For the rest it was a bright, formula entertainment, whose main concern hinged on the rivalry between Jane Powell (illustrated) and Elizabeth Taylor for the attentions of handsome Robert Stack. Young Scotty Beckett (illustrated) played Miss Taylor's brother, and the cast was completed by Selena Royle, Leon Ames, Clinton Sundberg, George Cleveland, Lloyd Corrigan, Jerry Hunter, Jean McLaren and, playing himself, Xavier Cugat. Dorothy Kingsley and Dorothy Cooper concocted a cheerful screenplay from characters originally created by Aleen Leslie, and it was directed with the right spirit by Richard Thorpe. The dances were staged by Stanley Donen, notably a lively duet for Powell and Beckett, 'Strictly On The Corny Side' (by Stella Unger and Alec Templeton). Other songs and musical numbers: *It's A Most Unusual Day* Harold Adamson, Jimmy McHugh; *Judaline* Don Raye, Gene De Paul; *I've Got A Date With Judy*; *I'm Gonna Meet My Mary* Bill Katz, Calvin Jackson; *Temptation* Arthur Freed, Nacio Herb Brown; *Mulligatawny*.

Forties Musicals

◁ The problem with Esther Williams was finding storylines that would allow her to interrupt the scenario every now and then to take to the nearest swimming pool for demonstrations of the combination crawl and backstroke that helped make her one of the most bankable stars on the MGM lot. The problem wasn't particularly licked in **On An Island With You**, a water-logged romance about a film crew in Honolulu and the romance its star, Williams, has with aviator Peter Lawford (both illustrated). Ricardo Montalban was also in it; so was Jimmy Durante who sang the best number in the film – a ditty he wrote called 'I Can Do Without Broadway, But Can Broadway Do Without Me'. Also there: Cyd Charisse, Leon Ames, Kathryn Beaumont, Dick Simmons, and giving it that Latin *quelque chose*, Xavier Cugat and His Orchestra. Jack Donohue staged the numbers, Joe Pasternak produced, and it was breezily directed from a screenplay by Dorothy Kingsley, Dorothy Cooper, Charles Martin and Hans Wilhelm (story by Martin and Wilhelm), for the piece of fluff it was by Richard Thorpe. It made a fortune and became one of the top grossing films of the year. Songs and musical numbers: *On An Island With You*; *If I Were You*; *Taking Miss Mary To The Ball*; *Dog Song*; *Buenas Noches, Buenos Aires* Nacio Herb Brown, Edward Heyman; *Wedding Samba* Abraham Ellstein, Allan Small, Joseph Liebowitz.

Ernst Lubitsch began, but did not live to complete, **That Lady In Ermine** (20th Century-Fox). On his death, Otto Preminger stepped in to finish off the job – and finish it off he certainly did. For what should have been a light, airy, operetta-like romance between a beautiful countess and a dashing hussar, was ruined by Preminger, who pounded the fragile life out of it (it was a remake of *Bride Of The Regiment*, 1st National, 1930). The whimsy inherent in Rudolph Schanzer and Ernest Welisch's story from which Samson Raphaelson wrote his screenplay (the plot jumped backwards and forwards between 1561 and 1861, with the romance initially all taking place in the hussar's dreams), cried out for the celebrated Lubitsch 'touch' – what it got, instead, was the Preminger boot, which was of no help to Betty Grable (right), its star who, in a
▽

dual role, needed all the assistance she could get as far as her acting was concerned. Vocally she was fine, though, and did well by the two best songs: 'OOOh What I'll Do To That Wild Hungarian' and 'This Is The Moment' by Leo Robin and Frederick Hollander. Douglas Fairbanks Jr (left, also in a dual role) played the hussar, with Cesar Romero (centre) mildly amusing as Grable's meek husband of one day's duration. Also cast: Walter Abel, Reginald Gardiner, Harry Davenport, Virginia Campbell, Whit Bissell, Edmund McDonald and David Bond. It was choreographed by Hermes Pan, and Lubitsch received credit for both the production and the direction. (Technicolor). Other songs and musical numbers included: *There's Something About Midnight*; *The Melody Has To Be Right*; *Jester's Song* Robin, Hollander.

Marilyn Monroe's second film was **Ladies Of The Chorus** (Columbia), a 59-minute also-ran in which she played a burlesque chorus girl in love with a wealthy socialite (Rand Brooks). The story had Monroe's mother (Adele Jergens, left), who features in the same burlesque show as her daughter, opposing the match on the grounds that years ago, she herself loved beyond her station, and it didn't work out. In time, however, the conflict was solved to everyone's satisfaction, and the film ended with a double wedding: Monroe (second left) to Brooks, and Jergens to a former burlesque comic (Eddie Carr). Nana Bryant, Steve Geray, Bill Edwards and Marjorie Hoshelle also appeared; Henry Sauber and Joseph Carole wrote it from a story by Sauber; Jack Boyle choreographed, Harry A. Romm produced and Phil Karlson directed. Monroe coped adequately with the inferior material, and did well by Lester Lee and Allan Roberts's 'Everybody Needs A Da-Da-Daddy'. Other songs and musical numbers included: *Ladies Of The Chorus*; *Anyone Can Tell I Love You*; *Crazy For You*; *You're Never Too Old* Lee, Roberts.
▽

Tireless Joe Pasternak was at it again, blending the light with the heavy in **Luxury Liner** (MGM), a musical ocean voyage whose passenger list included Metro's youngest thrush (Jane Powell, just turned twenty), her widowed middle-aged dad (George Brent), tenor Lauritz Melchior (illustrated), soprano Marina Koshetz, bandleader Xavier Cugat, The Pied Pipers, and Frances Gifford as a widow whom interfering Miss Powell is determined shall marry her pa. So much for the plot (by Gladys Lehman and Richard Connell who also scripted). The romantic shipboard setting, with the help of Technicolor and all the handsome production values the studio could accord it, gave the film a glossy veneer that more than compensated for its lack of substance. Contributing to its success, too, was the music, and there was lots of it, from Miss Powell's rendition of the French-Canadian folk song 'Alouette' which she sang with various members of the crew, to Melchior and Powell's dramatic reading of the Act II duet from Verdi's *Aida*. Richard Whorf's direction was competent, and his cast was completed by John Ridgely, Thomas E. Breen and Richard Derr. Other songs and musical numbers: *Spring Came Back To Vienna* (Powell) Janice Torre, Fred Spielman, Fritz Rotter; *The Peanut Vendor* (Powell) L. Wolfe Gilbert, Marion Sunshine, Moisés Simons; *Yes We Have No Bananas* (The Pied Pipers) Frank Silver, Irving Cohn; *Come Back To Sorrento* (Melchior) Ernesto De Curtis, Claude Aveling; *Gavotte* (from Massenet's 'Manon') Massenet (Powell); *Cugat's Nougat* (Cugat) Cugat; *I've Got You Under My Skin* (Koshetz) Cole Porter; *Con Maracas* Cugat, Candido Dimanlig.

The answer to the question in the title of Paramount's **Isn't It Romantic?** was an emphatic no. Nor was it entertaining. A luke-warm period musical set in Indiana and recounting the activities of a trio of sisters (Veronica Lake, right, Mona Freeman, left, and Mary Hatcher), it was charmless, colourless (being photographed in black and white) and, with the notable exception of Pearl Bailey as the household maid, deficient in talent. Bailey sang a number called 'I Shoulda Quit When I Was Ahead' (by Jay Livingston and Ray Evans who wrote most of the score), but failed to heed the advice. Other roles went to Roland Culver as the three sisters' civil war veteran father, Billy De Wolfe (centre) as Miss Lake's beau, and Patric Knowles as a fake oil stock peddler who woos Miss Lake away from De Wolfe without too much difficulty. De Wolfe scored with a send-up of silent screen clichés ('At The Nickleodeon'), and there was a passable tune called 'Miss Julie July'. The rest, however, was tedium. Theodore Strauss, Josef Mischel and Richard L. Breen wrote it from a story by Jeanette Covert Nolan, Josephine Earl staged the dances, Daniel Dare produced and the direction was by Norman Z. McLeod. Other musical numbers: *Wondering When*; *Indiana Dinner* Livingston, Evans; *Isn't It Romantic?* Richard Rodgers, Lorenz Hart.

A frightful bowdlerization of the S.J. Perelman-Ogden Nash-Kurt Weill stage musical on which it was based, **One Touch Of Venus** was a stinker from Universal International which starred Ava Gardner (in the role created by Mary Martin) as a statue of Venus who springs miraculously to life after being kissed by a window dresser in a department store. The man doing the kissing was Robert Walker (illustrated), and it is to be regretted that he did not bring his osculatory skills to bear on Harry Kurnitz and Frank Tashlin's screenplay, on William A. Seiter's dreary direction and on his own and Miss Gardner's lustreless performances. Of the sixteen Weill songs originally featured in the show, only a mere handful were retained, and were indifferently sung. Dick Haymes was also in it, and the cast was completed by Eve Arden, Olga San Juan, Tom Conway, James Flavin and Sara Allgood. The dance routines (such as they were) were staged by Billy Daniels. Lester Cowan produced and Miss Gardner's vocals were dubbed by Eileen Wilson. Songs and musical numbers: *My Week*; *Don't Look Now But My Heart Is Showing*; *That's Him* (lyrics by Ann Ronell); *The Trouble With Women*; *Speak Low* Ogden Nash, Weill.

Danny Kaye's fifth and last film for Samuel Goldwyn was **A Song Is Born** (RKO), a remake in Technicolor by director Howard Hawks of *Ball Of Fire* (RKO, 1941), which Hawks also directed, and which starred Gary Cooper and Barbara Stanwyck. Based on a story by Thomas Monroe and Billy Wilder, and with a screenplay (uncredited) by Harry Tugend, it was the tale of a group of musicologists in general and Kaye in particular who, while in the midst of writing a mammoth history of music in the imposing and monastic confines of The Totten Foundation, have their studies interrupted by a singer called Honey Swanson (Virginia Mayo). Mayo is on the run from the district attorney as well as from her gangster boyfriend and, in seeking sanctuary with the musicologists, unleashed the chain of events which formed the basis of the storyline. The participation of several eminent jazz musicians – including Benny Goodman (as one of the professors), Tommy Dorsey, Louis Armstrong, Lionel Hampton and Charlie Barnet, with their orchestras, as well as Mel Powell, The Golden Gate Quartet, The Page Cavanaugh Trio, Buck and Bubbles, and Russo and The Samba Kings, helped take the edge off the air of desperation that permeated the entire project, but not completely. **A Song Is Born**, despite the talent invested in it, was a walloping bore which denied Kaye (illustrated) the chance to do the sort of things he did best, and in which Mayo was dull and undercast but superbly dubbed by Jerri Sullivan. Appearing as the other professors were Hugh Herbert, J. Edward Bromberg, Felix Bressart, Ludwig Stossel and O.Z. Whitehead, with Steve Cochran, Esther Dale, Mary Field and Howland Chamberlin also cast. Songs and musical numbers: *Stealin' Apples* (Hampton, Goodman, Powell, Harry Babsin, Alton Hendrickson) Andy Razaf, Fats Waller; *Flyin' Home* (Armstrong, Goodman, Dorsey, Barnet, Powell) Hampton, Goodman, Sid Robin; *Bach Boogie* (Buck on piano); *I'm Getting Sentimental Over You* (Dorsey, Orch) George Bassman; *Anitra's Dance* from incidental music to 'Peer Gynt' (Buck on piano, Goodman on clarinet) Grieg; *Blind Barnabas* (Golden Gate Quartet); *Redskin Rhumba* (Barnet, Orch) Barnet; *The Goldwyn Stomp* (Armstrong, with Hampton, Orch); *Mockin' Bird* (Golden Gate Quartet) traditional; *Sweet Genevieve* (Kaye) George Cooper, Henry Tucker; *Gaudeamus Igitur* (Professors) traditional; *Joshua Fit De Battle* (Golden Gate Quartet) traditional spiritual; *A Song Was Born* (Mayo, Armstrong, Goodman, Dorsey, Hampton, Barnet, Powell, Louis Bellson) Don Raye, Gene De Paul; *Daddy-O* (Mayo, Cavanaugh Trio); *Longhair Jam Session* (Mayo, Professors, Bubbles) a medley comprising Act IV Quartet from Verdi's 'Rigoletto'; Rossini's 'William Tell' overture; *Anvil Chorus* from Verdi's 'Il Trovatore' and *Song Of The Volga Boatmen* (traditional).

Falling midway between *Meet Me In St Louis* (MGM, 1944) and a typical Andy Hardy comedy, **Summer Holiday** (MGM) was a palatable slice of Americana which owed more to producer Arthur Freed and his adroit production team than it did to Eugene O'Neill, on whose gentle comedy *Ah Wilderness* it was based. Whereas O'Neill's play was a subtle delineation of a young lad's first faltering steps into manhood, Freed, and his able director Rouben Mamoulian (whose *Love Me Tonight*, Paramount, 1932, was one of the key musicals in the entire genre), while retaining much of the play's basic story-line, opened out the piece to accommodate the prerequisites of musical comedy but, at the same time, blurred the carefully articulated sensibilities of the original, and coarsened most of the characterizations. Yet, for all their tampering (the simplistic screenplay by Frances Goodrich and Albert Hackett, from the adaptation of the play by Irving Brecher and Jean Holloway, was partially written in rhyming couplets), the film succeeded on its own terms thanks, in the main, to Mamoulian's superb visual flair (his use of Technicolor was striking, especially in the bar-room encounter between Mickey Rooney and singer Marilyn Maxwell); and a first-rate score by Harry Warren and Ralph Blane. As the young protagonist at the film's centre, Rooney (illustrated foreground) bulldozed his way through the role with his usual air of super-confidence, and was prettily partnered by Gloria De Haven (foreground right) who was adequate as the girl in his life. Walter Huston (centre) was the *paterfamilias* and Selena Royle (right) his wife, with other parts going to Frank Morgan, Agnes Moorehead (left), Jackie 'Butch' Jenkins, Shirley Johns, Anne Francis and Hal Hackett. The film was gorgeously costumed by Walter Plunkett, and zestfully choreographed by Charles Walters, with Cedric Gibbons and Jack Martin Smith's sets also contributing to its well-evoked period atmosphere. Songs and musical numbers: *Afraid To Fall In Love* (Rooney, De Haven); *It's Our Home Town* (ensemble); *Independence Day* (Moorehead, Royle, Huston, Morgan); *Weary Blues* (Maxwell); *All Hail Danville High* (chorus); *I Think You're The Sweetest Kid I've Ever Known* (Rooney, Maxwell); *The Stanley Steamer* (De Haven, Rooney, Moorehead, Royle, Huston, Jenkins).

Numbingly familiar, **When My Baby Smiles At Me** (20th Century-Fox), adapted by Elizabeth Reinhardt and scripted by Lamar Trotti from George Manker Watters and Arthur Hopkins's Broadway play *Burlesque*, was a remake of two earlier Paramount films: *The Dance Of Life* (1929) with Nancy Carroll, and *Swing High Swing Low* (1937) with Carole Lombard. This time the star was Betty Grable who, though competent and professional in everything she did, was out-distanced by co-star Dan Dailey (illustrated) as a putty-nosed burlesque comedian who winds up in Bellevue Hospital after his successful career hits the skids. A performance of distinction, combining charm, pathos, and vitality, it was the freshest thing in a show turned stale by its reliance on past successes. June Havoc and Jack Oakie purveyed some low comedy; Jean Wallace, Richard Arlen, James Gleason, Vanita Wade, Robert Emmett Keane, Jerry Maren and George Lewis completed the cast. The dance routines were staged by Seymour Felix; Josef Myrow and Mack Gordon provided the film with its two new songs, 'By The Way' and 'What Did I Do?', George Jessel produced (in Technicolor), and the uninspired direction was by Walter Lang. Other musical numbers: *Oui Oui Marie* Alfred Bryan, Joseph McCarthy, Fred Fisher; *Don't Bring Lulu* Billy Rose, Lew Brown, Ray Henderson; *Shoe Shine Blues* (introductory routine to *Birth Of The Blues*); *Birth Of The Blues* Buddy De Sylva, Brown, Henderson; *When My Baby Smiles At Me* Andrew B. Sterling, Ted Lewis, Bill Munro; *The Daughter Of Rosie O'Grady* M.C. Brice, Walter Donaldson; *Say Si-Si* Al Stillman, Ernesto Lecuona.

Frank Sinatra (illustrated) came a cropper in **The Kissing Bandit** (MGM), a musical romance whose vivid colour by Technicolor in no way compensated for the dullness of Isobel Lennart and John Briard Harding's screenplay. Sinatra, at his scrawniest, seemed ill at ease throughout as a meek young fellow who finds himself having to step into his father's *braggadocio* role as a womanizing desperado. Kathryn Grayson, his co-star and romantic *vis-a-vis* fared somewhat better and got to sing the best song in the film, 'Love Is Where You Find It' (by Nacio Herb Brown and Earl Brent who, with Edward Heyman, provided the rest of the score as well); and from Ann Miller, Ricardo Montalban and Cyd Charisse there was a frenetic show-stopper called 'Dance Of Fury', excitingly staged by Stanley Donen (added after the film's completion). J. Carrol Naish, Mildred Natwick, Mikhail Rasumny, Billy Gilbert, Clinton Sundberg, Carleton E. Young and dancer Sono Osato were also in it for producer Joe Pasternak, and director Laszlo Benedek. Other songs and musical numbers: *If I Steal A Kiss*; *Señorita*; *Siesta*; *What's Wrong With Me?*; *Tomorrow Means Romance*; *I Like You* (Whip Dance).

Set in the twenties, **You Were Meant For Me** (20th Century-Fox) – a loose remake of the same studio's *Orchestra Wives* (1941) – strung a series of familiar old songs on to a thread of a plot involving a bandleader and his girl. Dan Dailey (right) was the bandleader; Jeanne Crain (left) the girl. They marry, and all goes well until Crain tires of following her husband and his band from one small town to another. Matters reach a head with the advent of the Depression, at which point true love happily reasserts itself, saving them from bankruptcy and a trip to the divorce courts. Elick Moll and Valentine Davies's screenplay gave it all a lot more credibility than the plot summary might suggest was possible, and there was solid support from Oscar Levant (who played Dailey's business manager, as well as George Gershwin's 'Concerto in F'), Barbara Lawrence, Selena Royle, Bob McCord, Harry Barris, Percy Kilbride and Herbert Anderson. Lee Clark and Kenny Williams staged the dance routines, Fred Kohlmar produced and the director was Lloyd Bacon. Songs and musical numbers: *Crazy Rhythm* Irving Caesar, Roger Wolfe Kahn, Joseph Meyer; *You Were Meant For Me* Arthur Freed, Nacio Herb Brown; *Goodnight Sweetheart* James Campbell, Reginald Connolly, Ray Noble; *If I Had You* Campbell, Connolly, Ted Shapiro; *Ain't She Sweet* Jack Yellen, Milton Ager; *Ain't Misbehavin'* Andy Razaf, Fats Waller; *I'll Get By* Roy Turk, Fred Ahlert.

A featherweight *mélange* of comedy and songs from Columbia, **Manhattan Angel** took 61 minutes to show how Gloria Jean (centre), the linchpin of a Youth Centre, manages to raise $25,000 to save the premises from demolition. A passable programmer which Arthur Dreifuss directed from a screenplay by Albert Deer (story by Deer and George H. Plympton), it was produced by Sam Katzman with a cast that included singer Toni Harper, Ross Ford, Patricia White, Thurston Hall, Alice Tyrrell, Benny Baker, Russell Hicks and Fay Baker. Songs included: *I'll Take Romance* Oscar Hammerstein II, Ben Oakland; *Candy Store Blues* Nick Castle, Herb Jeffries, Eddie Beal; *Naughty Aloysius* Robert Wilder; *It's A Wonderful, Wonderful Feeling* Jack Segal, Dewey Bergman.

△

Producer Arthur Freed should never have bothered to attach a largely fictitious story to **Words And Music** (MGM), his Technicolor biopic of the lives and careers of Richard Rodgers and Lorenz Hart. Far greater justice to the incomparable songwriting team would have been done had the studio simply paid tribute to their talents by stringing together, in a revue-type format, a collection of their songs. As Rodgers's life wasn't particularly exciting (he simply went from one success to another) and Hart, the more complex and interesting of the two, was homosexual (a taboo cinematic subject in 1948), it would surely have been kinder to let their words and music speak for themselves, rather than to allow the pack of half-truths and downright lies perpetrated in Fred Finklehoffe's anachronistic screenplay (from a story by Guy Bolton and Jean Holloway) to be passed off as fact. Mickey Rooney starred as Lorenz Hart and, although he made some sort of attempt to capture the mercurial nature of the man, it was basically a hammy and superficial performance as broad as Rooney was short. As for Tom Drake as Rodgers, the less said the better. Which left the musical numbers, most of which were staged by Robert Alton with his characteristic panache. Best sequences were Lena Horne's renditions of 'The Lady Is A Tramp' and 'Where or When'; Judy Garland's powerhouse performance of 'Johnny One Note'; June Allyson and The Blackburn Twins in 'Thou Swell' and, best of all, Gene Kelly and Vera-Ellen's 'Slaughter On Tenth Avenue' (illustrated) from *On Your Toes* (choreographed by Kelly). Also on hand: Cyd Charisse, Ann Sothern, Mel Torme, Dee Turnell, Allyn McLerie, Perry Como, Betty Garrett, Marshall Thompson, Janet Leigh, Jeanette Nolan, Harry Antrim, Richard Quine, Clinton Sundberg, Ilka Gruning, Emory Parnell, Helen Spring and Edward Earle. The musical direction was by Lennie Hayton and the superb orchestrations by Conrad Salinger. Norman Taurog directed. Other songs and musical numbers: *Lover* (orchestra over titles); *I Wish I Were In Love Again* (Garland, Rooney); *The Girl Friend* (instrumental); *This Can't Be Love* (Charisse, Turnell); *Blue Room* (Como, Charisse); *With A Song In My Heart* (Como); *Manhattan* (Rooney); *There's A Small Hotel* (Garrett); *Where's That Rainbow* (Sothern); *On Your Toes* (instrumental); *Way Out West* (Garrett); *Blue Moon* (Torme); *Mountain Greenery* (Como, McLerie); *Spring Is Here* (Rooney).

One Sunday Afternoon (Warner Bros.), a Technicolor musical starring Dennis Morgan (2nd left), Don De Fore (centre), Janis Paige (right) and Dorothy Malone, was the third screen version of James Hagan's play, first made by Paramount in 1933 as *One Sunday Afternoon*, and remade by Warner's in 1941 as *The Strawberry Blonde*. The bitter-sweet tale of a dentist (Morgan) who loses his strawberry blonde love (Paige) to his smoothie, man-about-town, not to mention crooked, friend (De Fore), and marries a more reliable girl (Malone) on the rebound, it suffered from a lack of pace which left audiences uninvolved. The culprit was director Raoul Walsh who, having directed the 1941 version with James Cagney, Olivia De Havilland, Jack Carson and Rita Hayworth, seemed unable to raise any enthusiasm the second time around. In fact, sad to relate, it was all a bore. Ralph Blane composed a set of songs which, while not unpleasant, failed to capture the period lilt of the piece (the sets and costumes, however, were admirable in this respect). Robert L. Richards pounded out the screenplay, LeRoy Prinz staged the dances, Jerry Wald produced, and the supporting cast included Ben Blue (left), Dorothy Ford, Oscar O'Shea, Alan Hale Jr (centre right) and George Neise. Songs: *Girls Were Made To Take Care Of Boys*; *Some Day*; *Johnny And Lucille*; *Sweet Corner Girl*; *One Sunday Afternoon* Blane; *Amy, You're A Little Bit Old-Fashioned* Marion Sunshine, Henry I. Marshall; *In My Merry Oldsmobile* Vincent Bryan, Gus Edwards; *Daisy Bell* Harry Dacre; *Deck The Halls With Boughs Of Holly* (traditional carol); *Auld Lang Syne* (traditional melody, words by Robert Burns).

▽

A Walt Disney live-action feature with three short animated sequences, **So Dear To My Heart** (RKO) was specifically aimed at the kids with its simple story of a young, rural lad (Bobby Driscoll, illustrated right) and his endeavours to enter his pet ram at the county fair. His efforts are successful, and he wins first prize. Set in Indiana in 1903, its charming rustic atmosphere permeated every frame, with Beulah Bondi as Master Driscoll's kindly old granny and Burl Ives as Uncle Hiram, the local handyman-cum-blacksmith, thickly laying on the nostalgia in convincing 'backwoods' performances that were a credit to John Tucker Battle's screenplay (adapted by Maurice Rapf and Ted Sears from the story by Sterling North). Particularly enjoyable was Ives's singing of such folk songs as 'Sourwood Mountain' and 'Billy Boy'. Completing the cast were Harry Carey, Luana Patten (illustrated left), Raymond Bond, Walter Soderling, Mat Willis and Spelman B. Collins, plus the voices of John Beal, Ken Carson, Bob Stanton and The Rhythmaires. It was photographed in Technicolor, and the director was Harold Schuster. Other songs: *So Dear To My Heart* Ticker Freeman, Irving Taylor; *Ol' Dan Patch*; *Lavender Blue (Dilly Dilly)*; *Stick-to-it-ivity* Elliot Daniel, Larry Morey; *It's Whatcha Do With Whatcha Got* Don Raye, Gene De Paul; *County Fair* Robert Wells, Mel Torme.

▽

△

After an absence of almost four years, Sonja Henie (illustrated) returned to the screen in **The Countess Of Monte Cristo** (Universal International). It was to be her last American film and, in terms of quality and box-office appeal, her least successful. Olga San Juan co-starred, and together they played a pair of Norwegian barmaids who, after landing jobs at a film studio in Oslo, utilize certain props in the prop department to help them masquerade as a countess (Henie) and her servant in an elegant resort hotel. Six ice-skating sequences and three songs comprised the musical programme – but the magic was missing and the film bombed. Also in it were Dorothy Hart, Michael Kirby, Arthur Treacher, Hugh French, Freddie Trenkler and Arthur O'Connell. Frederick De Cordova directed from a tired screenplay by William Bowers (story by Walter Reisch), and the producer was John Beck. Songs: *Friendly Polka*; *Count Your Blessings*; *Who Believes In Santa Claus?* (all sung by San Juan) Jack Brooks, Saul Chaplin.

1949

Warner Bros.' **My Dream Is Yours** (a remake in Technicolor of their *20 Million Sweethearts*, 1934) was an agreeable if utterly undistinguished movie about the struggles of a young hopeful to become a radio star. It starred Doris Day (centre) as a girl-next-door who just happens to have talent, co-starred Jack Carson (right) as a radio talent scout, and boasted, in its supporting cast, such stalwarts as Eve Arden (left), S.Z. Sakall, Adolphe Menjou, Lee Bowman (as a conceited crooner), and in one of its best sequences, the very welcome Bugs Bunny. Also: Selena Royle, Edgar Kennedy, Sheldon Leonard, Franklin Pangborn and Frankie Carle and His Orchestra. The dull script was by Harry Kurnitz and Dane Lussier (adapted by Allen Rivkin and Laura Kerr), and Michael Curtiz produced and directed. Songs and musical numbers: *My Dream Is Yours*; *Someone Like You*; *Tic Tic Tic*; *Love Finds A Way* Harry Warren, Ralph Blane; *I'll String Along With You* Warren, Al Dubin; *Canadian Capers* Gus Chandler, Bert White, Henry Cohen; *You Must Have Been A Beautiful Baby* Johnny Mercer, Harry Warren; *Nagasaki* Mort Dixon, Warren; *Jeepers Creepers* Mercer, Warren; *With Plenty Of Money And You* Dubin, Warren.

◁ Betty Grable was **The Beautiful Blonde From Bashful Bend** (20th Century-Fox), and her performance in this knockabout musical satire on the wild West (written, produced and directed by Preston Sturges from a story by Erle Felton) was tentative, to say the least. Miss Grable (right) played a pistol-packin' saloon gal mistaken by a pince-nez'd Rudy Vallee (left, as a Sunday school organist) for a mild-mannered school marm. The whole production (photographed in Technicolor) suffered from the makeshift, anything-goes air of improvisation that underlined it, and the finished result was emphatically unfunny, unappetising and unsuccessful. Also caught up in the circumlocutions of the plot were Cesar Romero, Olga San Juan (as an Indian half-breed), Sterling Holloway and Danny Jackson (as a pair of village idiots), Hugh Herbert, El Brendel, Porter Hall, Pati Behrs, Margaret Hamilton and Emory Parnell. Songs and musical numbers included: *Beautiful Blonde From Bashful Bend* Don George, Lionel Newman; *Everytime I Meet You* Mack Gordon, Josef Myrow; *In The Gloaming* Meta Orred, Annie F. Harrison.

MGM's **Take Me Out To The Ball Game** (GB: **Everybody's Cheering**), set at the turn of the century, centred around the amorous exploits of Gene Kelly (left foreground) and Frank Sinatra (foreground centre right) as baseball players-cum-vaudevillians. As in *Anchors Aweigh* (MGM 1945), Sinatra (top cast) was the more shy and retiring of the two men with, this time, Esther Williams (left), who also happens to be the manager of his baseball team, as the object of his affections. Williams, however, only has eyes for Kelly, which leaves Sinatra open to the advances of a determined Betty Garrett. Plot complications insinuated themselves in the form of a gang of crooks who want Kelly and his team to lose a vitally important game, but the narrative shenanigans were speedily disposed of and the film ended with a patriotic flag-waving finale called 'Strictly USA' written by Roger Edens, Betty Comden and Adolph Green who, apart from the title number (by Albert von Tilzer and Jack Norworth) and one other, wrote all the songs. Though **Ball Game** set out to glorify the all-American male, and was basically a Kelly-Sinatra vehicle, MGM gave Esther Williams second billing, and it was the unenviable task of scenarists Harry Tugend and George Wells (working from a story by Kelly and Stanley Donen who were paid $25,000 for the outline they handed to producer Arthur Freed) to devise situations in which she could take to the water. They only came up with one. Jules Munshin (left of Sinatra) was cast as a baseball-playing buddy of Kelly and Sinatra's, and the chemistry of the trio pleased the studio sufficiently to bring them together again in *On The Town* (1950). Also cast: Edward Arnold, Richard Lane (2nd right), Tom Dugan (far right), Murray Alper, William Graff. Though the film, directed in Technicolor by Busby Berkeley (his last as overall director), was by no means epoch-making, it had the sort of vitality that would characterize the three great Kelly musicals (*On The Town*, 1949, *An American In Paris*, 1951 and *Singin' In The Rain*, 1952) that would follow it. On the evidence of **Ball Game**'s story, Kelly and Donen were grossly overpaid for their efforts. The musical numbers, however, were delightful, and although Kelly clearly danced down to Sinatra in the simple but effective soft-shoe treatment of the title number, and mugged somewhat over enthusiastically with him and Munshin in 'O'Brien To Ryan To Goldberg', he came into his own in an exciting solo called 'The Hat My Father Wore On St Patrick's Day' (by William Jerome and Jean Schwartz) in which he executed a series of 'barrel rolls', akin to the backbend pirouette of ballet, which were breathtaking. Other musical numbers: *The Right Girl For Me* (Sinatra); *It's Fate, Baby It's Fate* (Garrett, Sinatra); *Yes Indeedy* (Kelly, Sinatra).

Bing Crosby (right) starred as New England blacksmith Hank Martin in the third and most elaborate screen version of Mark Twain's **A Connecticut Yankee In King Arthur's Court** (Harry C. Meyers was top-cast in the first version which William Fox made in 1921; and Will Rogers in Fox's remake of it in 1931). This version, from Paramount, was lavishly mounted by producer Robert Fellows and dazzlingly photographed in Technicolor by Ray Rennahan, with sets by Hans Dreier that were sumptuous and spectacular. The film was not only lovely to look at, but pretty good to listen to, with its catchy score by Johnny Burke and Jimmy Van Heusen. All about a blacksmith who, after being knocked unconscious in an accident during a rainstorm, wakes up and finds himself in Camelot at the time of King Arthur, Twain's story benefited from the addition of music and colour, and if Crosby's performance didn't quite carry the same conviction as Will Rogers's, it wasn't short on charm. Technicolor did wonders for his co-star Rhonda Fleming (as Lady Alesande) whose attractive red hair was far more striking than her performance; and as Sir Sagrimore, one of King Arthur's Knights, William Bendix (left) was, well, William Bendix. King Arthur himself was played by Sir Cedric Hardwicke, and the cast was completed by Henry Wilcoxon, Murvyn Vye, Joseph Vitale, Richard Webb, Alan Napier, Virginia Field and Julia Faye. It was written by Edmund Beloin, and directed with a pleasing sense of fantasy by Tay Garnett. Songs and musical numbers: *Once And For Always* (Crosby, Fleming); *Busy Doing Nothing* (Crosby, Hardwicke, Bendix); *If You Stub Your Toe On The Moon* (Crosby); *When Is Sometime?* (Fleming).

▽

◁

As with most showbiz biopics, William Jacobs's Technicolor production **Look For The Silver Lining** (Warner Bros.) reduced the life of Marilyn Miller, whose story it was purportedly telling (in flashback), to the usual vaudeville-to-Broadway format, with all its ups and downs. Although nominally the star of the proceedings, the anaemic June Haver (illustrated centre) was consistently upscreened by Ray Bolger, who played Miss Miller's mentor Jack Donohue, and gave this cloud of a musical its only silver lining with his tap rendition of Jerome Kern's immortal 'Who' (lyrics by Otto Harbach and Oscar Hammerstein II). Otherwise, it was boringly routine, with a routine cast that included Gordon MacRae as the star's first husband, Charles Ruggles (right), Rosemary De Camp (left), S.Z. Sakall and Walter Catlett. The sluggish dance numbers were by LeRoy Prinz and the dull direction by David Butler. The Ephrons, Phoebe and Henry, wrote it with Marian Spitzer from a story by Bert Kalmar and Harry Ruby. Songs and musical numbers: *Sunny* Kern, Harbach, Hammerstein II; *Look For The Silver Lining*; *Whip-Poor-Will* Buddy De Sylva, Jerome Kern; *A Kiss In The Dark* De Sylva, Victor Herbert; *Pirouette* Herman Finck; *Just A Memory* De Sylva, Lew Brown, Ray Henderson; *Time On My Hands* Mack Gordon, Harold Adamson, Vincent Youmans; *Wild Rose* Clifford Grey, Kern; *Shine On Harvest Moon* Nora Bayes, Jack Norworth; *Back, Back, Back To Baltimore* Harry Williams, Egbert Van Alstyne; *Jingle Bells* J.S. Pierpont; *Can't You Hear Me Callin', Caroline?* William H. Gardner, Caro Roma; *Carolina In The Morning* Gus Kahn, Walter Donaldson; *Yama Yama Man* George Collin Davis, Karl Hoschna; *Dengozo* Ernesto Nazareth; *Oh Gee! Oh Joy!* P.G. Wodehouse, the Gershwins.

Dorothy Lamour (illustrated) was the star of **Slightly French** (Columbia), a remake of *Let's Fall In Love* (Columbia, 1934) which starred Ann Sothern. A nothing-to-get-excited-about programmer, it featured Lamour as an Irish cooch dancer who, through the Professor Higgins-like determination of a fallen film producer (Don Ameche), is transformed from Irish Mary O'Leary into famous French actress Rochelle Olivia, in which guise she successfully attempts the Can-Can in a number (by Lester Lee and Allan Roberts) called 'Fifi From The Folies Bergère'. Her accent wasn't bad either. Others flitting in and out of Karen De Wolfe's screenplay (from a story by Herbert Fields) were Janis Carter, Willard Parker, Adele Jergens, Jeanne Manet and Frank Ferguson. Irving Starr produced and the solid direction was by Douglas Sirk. Other songs: *I Want To Learn About Love; Night; I Keep Telling Myself* Lee, Roberts; *Let's Fall In Love* Harold Arlen, Ted Koehler.

△

Make Believe Ballroom (Columbia) starred Jerome Courtland (left) and Virginia Welles (right) as a couple of collegiate carhops who enter a musical quiz show, fall in love, and win the top prize. The prize in producer Ted Richmond's low-budgeter wasn't its eye-glass full of plot nor its featured players (who included Ruth Warrick, Ron Randell, Al Jarvis, Adele Jergens, Paul Harvey and Louis Jean Heydt) but its roster of guest artists: Frankie Laine, The King Cole Trio, Toni Harper, Jack Smith, Kay Starr, The Sportsmen, Charlie Barnet, Jimmy Dorsey, Jan Garber, Gene Krupa and Ray McKinley. With so much musical talent on offer, there was nothing for Albert Duffy and Karen De Wolfe's screenplay (based on the radio programmes of Al Jarvis and Martin Block) to do but take a back seat, which it frequently did. The director was Joseph Santley. Songs and musical numbers: *Miss In Between Blues* Allan Roberts, Lester Lee; *The Way The Twig Is Bent* Roberts, Doris Fisher; *Make Believe Ballroom* Leon Rene, Johnny Mercer, Al Jarvis; *I'm The Lonesomest Gal In Town* Lew Brown, Albert von Tilzer; *On The Sunny Side Of The Street* Dorothy Fields, Jimmy McHugh; *It's A Blue World* Bob Wright, Chet Forrest; *The Trouble With You Is Me* Jack Segal, George Handy; *Hello Goodbye* Alex Sullivan, Lew Pollack; *Disc Jockey Jump* Gene Krupa, Gerry Mulligan; *Coming Out* M. Christiance, Harry J. Cole.

After the enormous success of *Easter Parade* (MGM, 1948), producer Arthur Freed planned a follow-up for its two stars, Fred Astaire and Judy Garland, called **The Barkleys Of Broadway**. Garland, however, cried off the assignment (or rather, she simply didn't show up for work) and was replaced by Ginger Rogers, whose last film with Astaire had been *The Story Of Vernon And Irene Castle* (RKO) ten years earlier. Thus, at a stroke, the world was deprived of a Garland musical, but enriched by one more Astaire-Rogers (both illustrated) offering. In it, the famous team seemed, almost, to parody themselves by playing a husband-and-wife dance team who temporarily go their separate ways when the wife decides she'd rather be a straight actress than a musical comedy star. They're finally reunited to the haunting strains of 'They Can't Take That Away From Me' by George and Ira Gershwin (reprised from Astaire and Rogers's 1937 success, *Shall We Dance*, RKO). The rest of the new songs were by Harry Warren with lyrics by Ira Gershwin, the highlight being Astaire's memorable and imaginative 'Shoes With Wings On' choreographed by himself and Hermes Pan, in which the star, as a repair man in a shoe shop, puts on a pair of white shoes after they miraculously begin to dance on their own. The other shoes in the shop suddenly spring to life as well, and only stop when Astaire shoots at them with a couple of pistols. Best of the rest was 'My One And Only Highland Fling' sung by Fred and Ginger in a thick Scots brogue, and Harry Warren's 'Bouncin' The Blues', a rapid rehearsal tap routine. Plot-wise, scenarists Betty Comden and Adolph Green made the most of the least, their screenplay skilfully negotiating the inherent clichés, and providing parts for Oscar Levant (as the team's jaundiced composer-cum-wet nurse), Billie Burke, Gale Robbins, Jacques Francois (as a French Playwright convinced that Miss Rogers is capable of playing Sarah Bernhardt), George Zucco and Clinton Sundberg. Robert Alton directed the dance sequences and Charles Walters the film. Other songs and musical numbers: *You'd Be Hard To Replace* (Astaire); *Manhattan Downbeat* (Astaire, Rogers); *A Weekend In The Country* (Astaire, Rogers, Levant) Warren, Gershwin; *Swing Trot* (credit sequence, danced by Astaire and Rogers) Warren, Gershwin; *Piano Concerto No 1* (Levant) Tchaikovsky; *Sabre Dance* (Levant) Khatchaturian; *This Heart Of Mine* (orchestral) Warren, Arthur Freed.

Set in the last years of the 'silent film' era, and continuing into the thirties, **You're My Everything** (20th Century-Fox) was a pleasant, well-written backstage story which starred Dan Dailey (illustrated centre in blackface) as a vaudeville hoofer and Anne Baxter as his wife, a one-time silent screen actress (known as the Hotcha Girl) who becomes a major film star with the arrival of talkies. Shari Robinson (illustrated) played their daughter and, encouraged by Dailey, lands a part in a movie. Her mother is furious, insisting that Shari lead a 'normal' non-showbiz life on the farm Dailey has bought for them. Dailey mollifies her by promising not to allow the child to make more than one film. But Shari turns out to be a sensation and is immediately put under contract by the studio. Baxter ups and leaves in a huff, taking Shari with her. A reconciliation is contrived by Baxter's wise Aunt Jane (Anne Revere) and all ends happily. A serviceable enough plot on which to mount several well-staged numbers (by Nick Castle), it also brought out the best in Dailey and Miss Baxter, but over-extended little Miss Robinson, whose success in the movies was clearly intended to mirror Shirley Temple's (she even sang

'On The Good Ship Lollipop', by Sidney Clare and Richard Whiting, from 20th Century-Fox's 1934 production *Bright Eyes*). Alas, the only thing Shari appeared to have in common with Shirley was the first two letters of her name – and watching the former work, it was hard to see what all the fuss was about. Still, that detail apart, **You're My Everything**, photographed in Technicolor, with a cast that also included Stanley Ridges, Henry O'Neill, Selena Royle, Alan Mowbray (as a director of silent movies), Robert Arthur, and, in two small scenes, Buster Keaton and lyricist Mack Gordon, was good, solid entertainment. Lamar Trotti (who also wrote it, with Will H. Hayes Jr, from a story by George Jessel) produced. Alfred Newman was in charge of the music, and it was most efficiently directed by Walter Lang. Songs and musical numbers included: *You're My Everything* Harry Warren, Mort Dixon, Joe Young; *Varsity Drag* De Sylva, Brown, Henderson; *'I May Be Wrong* Harry Ruskin, Henry Sullivan; *Chattanooga-Choo-Choo*; *Serenade In Blue* Warren, Mack Gordon; *I Can't Begin To Tell You* James V. Monaco, Gordon; *Would You Like To Take A Walk?* Warren, Mort Dixon, Billy Rose.

Red Hot And Blue (Paramount), a musical comedy thriller and a starring vehicle for Betty Hutton, had nothing in common with Cole Porter's 1936 Broadway show. Miss Hutton played a would-be actress whose romance with stage director Victor Mature is temporarily fouled up when a gangster-turned-backer is murdered while she is in his apartment. From this point on Hagar Wilde and John Farrow's screenplay (from a story by Charles Lederer) becomes a backstage whodunnit, with both the police and the dead man's cronies anxious to nail the killer, and with suspicion of course, falling on none other than Miss Hutton (illustrated centre). An ineffectually staged chase towards the end robbed the film of much of its potential, leaving Hutton with four Frank Loesser songs to justify the price of admission, the most effective being a parody on Shakespearean acting technique called 'Hamlet'. Loesser himself appeared, as a piano-playing hood. As an actor he was a pretty good tunesmith! Also cast: William Demarest (2nd left), June Havoc (left), Jane Nigh (right), William Talman, Raymond Walburn, Onslow Stevens and Joseph Vitale. Produced by Robert Fellows and directed unevenly by John Farrow. Other songs: *That's Loyalty; I Wake Up In The Morning Feeling Fine; (Where Are You) Now That I Need You.*

An amiable and mildly amusing spoof on Hollywood, **It's A Great Feeling** (Warner Bros.) starred Jack Carson (right) as an egotistical ham attempting, with the help of his buddy Dennis Morgan (left), to direct himself in a movie. The screenplay, by Jack Rose and Melville Shavelson from an original story by I.A.L. Diamond, took place for much of the time on the Warner lot, with such studio luminaries as Gary Cooper, Joan Crawford, Errol Flynn, Sydney Greenstreet, Danny Kaye, Patricia Neal, Eleanor Parker, Ronald Reagan, Edward G. Robinson and Jane Wyman on hand for token guest-star appearances. Also featured were directors Michael Curtiz, Raoul Walsh, King Vidor, and David Butler (who actually directed the film). Doris Day was second-billed as a waitress waiting for her big break, and one number in the pleasant Jule Styne-Sammy Cahn score, 'At The Cafe Rendezvous', had her singing in a strong French accent. It was produced, in Technicolor, by Alex Gottlieb, and choreographed by LeRoy Prinz whose big dream sequence was as uninspired as it was unnecessary. Also cast: Irving Bacon, Claire Carleton, Harlan Warde, Jacqueline De Wit. Other songs and musical numbers: *It's A Great Feeling; There's Nothing Rougher Than Love; That Was A Big Fat Lie; Give Me A Song With A Beautiful Melody; Blame My Absent-Minded Heart; Fiddle-dee-dee.*

Make Mine Laughs (RKO) was an enjoyable and varied compilation of celluloid clips from the RKO vaults; some of the material was new, most of it familiar. The show ran 63 minutes and featured Gil Lamb as master of ceremonies, Ray Bolger, Dennis Day (right), Frances Langford, Anne Shirley (left), Joan Davis, Jack Haley, Leon Errol, Robert Lamouret and his dummy duck in a ventriloquist routine, Manuel and Marita Viera with their monkey orchestra, Freddie Fisher and His Schnickelfritzers, Spanish dancers Rosario and Antonio, a muscle act called The Titans, Frankie Carle at the piano, a 1920 Pathe newsreel showing bathing beauties, and a tear-jerker of silent vintage. George Bilson produced, the Leon Errol sequence was scripted and directed by Hal Yates, while Richard Fleischer was in charge of the overall direction. Songs and musical numbers included: *You Go Your Way And I'll Go Crazy* (Bolger) Mack Gordon, Harry Revel; *Poor Little Fly On The Wall* (Fisher) Fisher; *If You Happen To Find My Heart* (Day, Shirley) Herb Magidson, Lew Pollack; *Carle Meets Mozart (Turkish Rondo from Mozart's Piano Sonata in A, K311)* (Carle) Carle, Frank De Vol; *Who Killed Vaudeville?* (Davis, Haley) Jack Yellen, Sammy Fain; *Moonlight Over The Islands* (Langford) Mort Greene, Pollack; *Send Back My Love To Me* (Langford).

Neptune's Daughter (MGM) starred Esther Williams, Ricardo Montalban, Betty Garrett and Red Skelton, all of whom sang the disarmingly catchy 'Baby, It's Cold Outside'. Garrett belted out 'I Love Those Men', and Montalban crooned 'My Heart Beats Faster' (all by Frank Loesser). Plot-wise it had Williams, as a chic manufacturer of chic swimwear, spending a great deal of time rejecting the persistent advances of Latin-American polo star Montalban. Far more entertaining, though, was its sub-plot which involved Garrett (right) in a mistaken identity romance with Skelton (left), a polo club masseur whom she believes to be millionaire Montalban. Dorothy Kingsley's racy screenplay was full of fun and skilfully accommodated the musical interpolations, including an elaborate voodoo dance number, and an eye-filling water ballet (staged by Jack Donohue). There were parts in it too for Keenan Wynn, Ted De Corsia, Mike Mazurki and Mel Blanc. Also: Xavier Cugat and His Orchestra. The Technicolor production was under the supervision of Jack Cummings, and the director was Edward Buzzell.

The blarney concocted by Edmund Beloin and Richard Breen to reunite Bing Crosby (left) and Barry Fitzgerald (centre left) for the third (and final) time, was called **Top O' The Morning** (Paramount), a bottom of the barrel entertainment, drenched in sentimentality, and overrun by a regiment of clichés to which Irish stories such as this one are prone. All about an American insurance investigator (Crosby) who arrives in the land of the shamrock to investigate the looting of the famous Blarney Stone, it featured Fitzgerald as a cantankerous, but lovable, old member of the Civil Guard and Ann Blyth as his pretty daughter who, in no time at all, captures Crosby's affections. Miss Blyth's fresh and engaging personality helped neutralize some of the film's more treacly passages; ditto a handful of new songs by Johnny Burke and Jimmy Van Heusen. Nor was there much wrong with the performances. It was the below-par quality of the story and screenplay that sabotaged the stars' efforts and made for 100 minutes of indigestible whimsy. Also cast: Hume Cronyn (centre right), Eileen Crowe, John McIntire, John Eldredge and John Costello. David Miller directed, Robert L. Welch produced. Songs: *Top O' The Morning; Oh 'Tis Sweet To Think; The Donovans; You Are In Love With Someone?* Burke, Van Heusen; *When Irish Eyes Are Smiling* Chauncey Olcott, George Graff Jr, Ernest R. Ball.

Forties Musicals

Judy Garland (illustrated right) was given ample opportunity to exploit her infectious sense of comedy in **In The Good Old Summertime** (MGM), a small-scale treat from producer Joe Pasternak that concerned the tender and touching romance between two pen pals, both of whom are unaware that they work in the same music shop. Not only do they see each other practically every day of their lives, but to spice the situation, a certain animosity exists between them. Based on Miklos Laszlo's play *The Shop Around The Corner* (filmed by MGM in 1940 with James Stewart and Margaret Sullavan) and scripted by Albert Hackett, Frances Goodrich and Ivan Tors from an extant screenplay by Samson Raphaelson, it also gave co-star Van Johnson (left) a marvellous chance to flex his comedic muscles and reveal himself as a lightweight performer of immense charm and a ▽

certain amount of style. S.Z. Sakall (as Otto Oberkugen, the owner of the emporium in which Garland and Johnson are employed) actually gave a performance rather than a caricature of himself, with Spring Byington (the secretary he has secretly loved for twenty years), Clinton Sundberg, Marcia Van Dyke and Lillian Bronson fine in support. Completing the cast was Buster Keaton who, as another employee of Sakall's, had one side-splitting moment when he steps on to a dance floor, slips, and crushes under his weight what he believes to be a priceless Stradivarius. The musical numbers were simply but effectively staged by Robert Alton, whose creative gifts could always be relied upon, the two best being 'I Don't Care' (by Jean Lenox and Harry Sutton) and 'Play That Barber Shop Chord' (by Ballard MacDonald, William Tracey and Lewis Muir), both sung by

Garland, with the latter backed by a splendid barber-shop quartet. One of the sweetest, most unpretentious entertainments of the year, it was subtly photographed in Technicolor, looked a dream in Cedric Gibbons and Randall Duell's period settings, and was directed with just the right lightness of touch by Robert Z. Leonard. Other songs and musical numbers: *In The Good Old Summertime* George Evans, Ren Shields; *Put Your Arms Around Me Honey* Junie McCree, Harry von Tilzer; *Meet Me Tonight In Dreamland* Beth Slater Whitson, Lee Friedman; *Merry Christmas* Janice Torre, Fred Spielman; *Chicago* (title music) Fred Fisher; *Wait Till The Sun Shines Nellie* Harry von Tilzer, Andrew B. Sterling. Interesting sideline: Liza Minnelli – aged 18 months – made her screen debut in the very last scene, as the child of Garland and Johnson who, in the plot, marry.

△
The first Walt Disney feature in seven years that didn't combine cartoon characters with live action was **The Adventures Of Ichabod And Mr Toad** (RKO). Taken from Kenneth Grahame's *The Wind In The Willows* and Washington Irving's *The Legend Of Sleepy Hollow*, the film told two separate stories. The first was about Mr Toad (illustrated) whose love of anything on wheels causes his downfall; the second was about Ichabod Crane, a superstitious school master, and his encounter with the Headless Horseman. Beautifully drawn and bristling with imaginative touches, it marked a return to form for Disney and his band of animators and was appreciatively welcomed by the press, though commercially it hardly matched the success of *Snow White And The Seven Dwarfs* (1937) or even *Bambi* (1942). Ichabod was narrated by Bing Crosby and Mr Toad by Basil Rathbone, with the voices of Eric Blore as Mr Toad, Pat O'Malley as Cyril, Claude Allister as Water Rat, John Ployardt as the prosecutor, Colin Campbell as Mole, Campbell Grant as Angus MacBadger and Ollie Wallace as Winky. The production supervisor was Ben Sharpsteen and the directors Jack Kinney, Clyde Geronimi and James Algar (Technicolor). Songs: *Ichabod*; *Katrina*; *The Headless Horseman* Don Raye, Gene De Paul; *Merrily On Our Way* Frank Churchill, Charles Wolcott, Larry Morey, Ray Gilbert.

S.Z. Sakall, having acquitted himself so favourably in *In The Good Old Summertime*, received third billing in **Oh You Beautiful Doll** (20th Century-Fox), a George Jessel-produced saunter down Nostalgia Lane in which he was given the most substantial role of his career. He gave a most effective performance as real-life composer Fred Fisher, a serious musician who found success, not in the concert hall or the opera houses of the world, but in Tin Pan Alley. According to Albert and Arthur Lewis's well-turned screenplay, Fisher (real name Alfred Breitenbach) was a struggling composer until a song plugger, spotting the commercial potential in some of his operatic arias, up-tempo'd some of the tunes and added popular lyrics. So ashamed was Breitenbach of his new found success, that he changed his name to Fisher, in which deception he continued to flourish as a songsmith-cum-publisher for forty years. As audiences were hardly aware of Fisher's existence, it hardly mattered that certain liberties were taken with his life. It was his tunes that counted, and as staged by Seymour Felix and performed by June Haver (illustrated), top-starred as Fisher's daughter, and leading man Mark Stevens (vocals dubbed by Bill Shirley), they sprang pleasingly to life. Charlotte Greenwood did some high kicking as Fisher's wife Anna, with other roles under John M. Stahl's direction going to Gale Robbins, Jay C. Flippen, Andrew Tombes, Eduard Franz, Eula Morgan and Nestor Paiva. (Technicolor). Songs (and lyricists) included: *Oh You Beautiful Doll* (Nat D. Ayer, A. Seymour Brown only); *There's A Broken Heart For Every Light On Broadway* (Howard Johnson); *Peg O' My Heart* (Alfred Bryan); *Chicago*; *I Want You To Want Me To Want You* (Bob Schafer, Bryan); *Come Josephine In My Flying Machine* (Bryan); *Who Paid The Rent For Mrs Rip Van Winkle?* (Bryan); *Daddy, You've Been More Than A Mother To Me*; *When I Get You Alone Tonight* (Joseph McCarthy, Joe Goodwin); *Dardanella* (Felix Bernard, Johnny S. Black, lyrics Fisher); *Ireland Must Be Heaven For My Mother Came From There* (McCarthy, Johnson).

△

Jolson Sings Again (Columbia) literally began where *The Jolson Story* (1946) left off (i.e. in a nightclub with Jolie giving an impromptu performance to the disapproval of his first wife, who walks out on him) and continued the story through the War when, after a period of despondency and dissipation, he regains his spirit by undertaking a series of USO camp shows. The strain of these shows proves detrimental to his health, resulting in the removal of a lung. It is while convalescing in hospital (according to Sidney Buchman's screenplay) that he meets and falls in love with Nurse Ellen Clark (Barbara Hale) from Arkansas, and marries her. From then on the film concerned itself with Jolson's recuperation and the making of *The Jolson Story*, offering some interesting insights into the way Jolson's voice was dubbed on to the soundtrack. Jolson himself never appeared, and in one curious scene audiences saw a double-exposure Larry Parks (illustrated) playing himself as well as Jolson. Barbara Hale did the best she could in a role that was never substantially scripted, and, of the principals, was the only newcomer to the cast. The rest were hold-overs from the earlier film, and included William Demarest as Steve Martin, Jolson's faithful friend and companion, Ludwig Donath and Tamara Shayne as Mama and Papa Joelson (Mama dying early on in the story) and Bill Goodwin as playwright Tom Baron. As was the case in *The Jolson Story*, it was Jolson's singing that proved the main attraction, and there were almost as many songs in the sequel as in the original, many of them repeats. Though **Jolson Sings Again** (produced in Technicolor by Buchman, and directed by Henry

Levin) wasn't nearly as good as its predecessor, it was the biggest grossing film of 1949 with a box-office take of over $5,500,000. Songs: *After You've Gone* Harry Creamer, Turner Layton; *Chinatown, My Chinatown* Joe Young, Sam Lewis, Jean Schwartz; *Give My Regards To Broadway* George M. Cohan; *I Only Have Eyes For You* Al Dubin, Harry Warren; *I'm Just Wild About Harry* Noble Sissle, Eubie Blake; *You Made Me Love You* Joseph McCarthy, James V. Monaco; *I'm Looking Over A Four Leaf Clover* Mort Dixon, Harry M. Woods; *Is It True What They Say About Dixie?* Sammy Lerner, Irving Caesar, Gerald Marks; *Ma Blushin' Rosie* Edgar Smith, John Stromberg; *Let Me Sing And I'm Happy* Irving Berlin; *Baby Face* Benny Davis, Harry Akst; *Sonny Boy* Buddy De Sylva, Lew Brown, Ray Henderson; *About A Quarter To Nine* Al Dubin, Harry Warren; *Anniversary Song* Saul Chaplin, Al Jolson, J. Ivanovici; *For Me And My Gal* Edgar Leslie, E. Ray Goetz; *California Here I Come* De Sylva, Jolson, Joseph Meyer; *Rockabye Your Baby* Sam Lewis, Joe Young, Jean Schwartz; *Carolina In The Morning* Gus Kahn, Walter Donaldson; *Toot Toot Tootsie Goodbye* Gus Kahn, Ernie Erdman, Dan Russo; *April Showers* De Sylva, Louis Silvers; *Swanee* George Gershwin, Irving Caesar; *My Mammy* Sam Lewis, Joe Young, Walter Donaldson (all sung by Jolson); *I'll Take Romance* (orchestral) Oscar Hammerstein II, Ben Oakland; *It's A Blue World* (orchestral) Bob Wright, Chet Forrest; *Learn To Croon* (Bing Crosby) Sam Coslow, Arthur Johnston; *Back In Your Own Backyard* Jolson, Billy Rose, Dave Dreyer; *When The Red Red Robin Comes Bob, Bob, Bobbin' Along* Harry Woods.

▽

Forties Musicals

△
Mario Lanza, hailed by MGM as the new Caruso, made an auspicious debut in **That Midnight Kiss**, produced (in glowing Technicolor) by producer Joe Pasternak with all the quintessential Pasternakian ingredients in ample evidence to ensure many happy box-office returns for the studio. With its full-to-overflowing mixture of classical music and popular standards, an easy-going, undemanding screenplay (by Bruce Manning and Tamara Hovey), plus a cast that top-starred Kathryn Grayson and included Jose Iturbi (as Jose Iturbi), Ethel Barrymore, Keenan Wynn, J. Carrol Naish, Jules Munshin, Thomas Gomez, Marjorie Reynolds and Arthur Treacher, it had the sweet smell of success stamped on

to every frame. Grayson played a Philadelphia heiress determined to become an opera star, and Lanza (illustrated right) a singing truck driver whose virile good looks and powerful high C's sweep her off her feet. Several misunderstandings helped thicken a very thin plot. In the end, however, music rather than words proved to be the food of love, with the warring couple singing their way into each other's hearts (and ours). It was high-grade *schmaltz*, quite irresistible in its shameless disregard for the mundane realities of life. Norman Taurog's sure-footed direction didn't miss a trick. Musical programme: *I Know, I Know, I Know* (Grayson) Bronislau Kaper, Bob Russell; *Three O'Clock In The Morning* (Naish)

Dorothy Terriss, Julian Robledo; *They Didn't Believe Me* (Grayson, Lanza) Jerome Kern, Herbert Reynolds; *Santa Lucia* (Naish) Teodoro Cottrau; *Down Among The Sheltering Palms* (Wynn, and quartet) James Brockman, Abe Olman; *Revolutionary Etude* (Jose and Amparo Iturbi) Chopin; *Caro Nome* (Grayson, Iturbi) from Verdi's 'Rigoletto'; *Celeste Aida* (Lanza) from Verdi's 'Aida'; *Una Furtiva Lacrima* (Lanza, Iturbi) from Donizetti's 'L'Elisir d'Amore'; *Piano Concerto In E Flat* Liszt; *Piano Concerto No 1* Tchaikovsky (segments only, Iturbi); *Mama Mia Che Vo Sape* (Lanza) from Mascagni's 'Cavalleria Rusticana'; *Finale: themes from Tchaikovsky's 5th Symphony* (Lanza, Grayson): *Russian Nightmare* (Grayson).

Coming four years before MGM's celebrated hit, *The Bandwagon*, **Dancing In The Dark** was a minor entry in Technicolor (from 20th Century-Fox) whose silly storyline concerned the efforts of the studio's production head, a man named Crossman (Darryl F. Zanuck, Fox's boss, wrote screenplays under the pseudonym Melville Crossman), to mount a film version of the Arthur Schwartz-Howard Dietz Broadway revue *Bandwagon*. The first thing Crossman (played by Adolphe Menjou) does, is to send a conceited has-been actor to New York in order to sign up a star to play the lead role in the impending film. William Powell (left) was top-starred as the disdainful erstwhile thespian, and the girl he chose was Betsy Drake (right), an unknown young actress – rather than the star Crossman wants – who throws all sorts of tantrums when she discovers that Powell is none other than the father who deserted her mother before she was born. Miss Drake's performance was on a par with Mary C. McCall Jr's fair-to-middling screenplay (adaptation by Marion Turk), but was no match for the Schwartz-Dietz evergreens she was expected to sing. Mark Stevens (centre) was second-billed as a press agent, with other roles going to Randy Stuart, Lloyd Corrigan, Hope Emerson, Walter Catlett, Don Beddoe, Jean Hersholt, Sid Grauman and Byron Foulger. George Jessel produced and the director was Irving Reis. Songs and musical numbers included: *Dancing In The Dark*; *I Love Louisa*; *New Sun In The Sky*; *Something To Remember You By.*

△ Warner Bros.' **The Inspector General** might have been termed 'suggested by' rather than 'based on' Gogol's classic, for, as played by Danny Kaye, Gogol's illiterate buffoon (who is mistaken for an important visiting dignitary in a small town) owed more to the spirit of burlesque than to European comic theatre. Kaye (illustrated centre) played the part of Georgi, a medicine show helper, to the hilt, unrestrainedly relishing the farcical confusion provided by Phillip Rapp and Harry Kurnitz's script and the witty patter songs written for him by his wife, Sylvia Fine, and Johnny Mercer. Although the supporting cast was long and, by the studio's standards, relatively distinguished, with Gene Lockhart (as a crooked mayor), Elsa Lanchester (as the mayor's flighty wife), Walter Slezak, Alan Hale, Walter Catlett, Rhys Williams and Benny Baker, director Henry Koster understood exactly where the film's appeal lay and resigned himself to recording, in Technicolor, a very funny one-man-show. The producer was Jerry Wald. Songs and musical numbers: *Onward Onward*; *The Medicine Show*; *The Inspector General*; *Lonely Heart*; *Gypsy Drinking Song*; *Soliloquy For Three Heads*; *Happy Times*; *Brodny*.

△ One of the rare feature films to star Milton Berle (illustrated), **Always Leave Them Laughing** (Warner Bros.), about the progression of a comedian from acting as master of ceremonies at a mosquito-plagued resort to becoming top banana on television, admirably geared its cliché-ridden plot to Berle's particular talents, allowing him to perform as many sketches as possible. There was a score of sorts, mixing some dispensable new songs with a couple of golden oldies, but it was the jokes that audiences came out humming. Adding to the general good humour was Bert Lahr proving all over again just how stunning and original a comedian he was; Virginia Mayo played his scheming wife, and Ruth Roman was Berle's romantic interest. Jack Rose and Melville Shavelson wrote the screenplay (from a story by Max Shulman and Richard Mealand), Roy Del Ruth directed and Jerry Wald produced. Songs and musical numbers included: *You're Too Intense*; *Always Leave Them Laughing* Milton Berle, Sammy Cahn; *Say Farewell* Cahn, Ray Heindorf; *Clink Your Glasses* Cahn, Johnny Mercer; *Embraceable You* George and Ira Gershwin; *By The Light Of The Silvery Moon* Edward Madden, Gus Edwards.

◁ More campus shenanigans in **Yes Sir That's My Baby** (Universal), a low-voltage offering whose one bid for originality lay in the fact that the college kids on parade weren't kids at all but war veterans completing their education. Problems arise when biology professor Charles Coburn tries to form a football team against the wishes of the students' wives (who'd rather their spouses stayed at home and helped bring up baby). But the women relent in the last reel when they learn that Coburn will lose his job if the local team fails to come through in an important match. Donald O'Connor (illustrated) and Gloria De Haven were the main husband-and-wife embroiled in the so-called conflict, with other parts in Oscar Brodney's laugh-sparse screenplay going to Barbara Brown (as a psychology professor), Joshua Shelley, Jack Lambert, Jack Overman, George Spaulding, Michael Dugan and June Fulton. George Sherman directed and the producer was Leonard Goldstein, (Technicolor). Songs and musical numbers: *Men Are Little Children*; *They've Never Figured Out A Woman*; *Look At Me* Jack Brooks, Walter Scharf; *Yes Sir, That's My Baby* Gus Kahn, Walter Donaldson.

△ A love affair between Desi Arnaz (illustrated centre) and his co-star Mary Hatcher (as a couple of wooing Cubans) formed the meagre content of **Holiday In Havana** (Columbia), a low-budget filler whose screenplay by Robert Lees, Frederick I. Rinaldo and Karen De Wolfe (from a story by Morton Grant) was as undistinguished as its score. Ann Doran, Steve Geray, Minerva Urecal and Sig Arno were also in it; Ted Richmond produced, and the director was Jean Yarbrough. Songs and musical numbers included: *Straw Hat Song* Fred Karger, Allan Roberts; *Rhumba Rumbero* Albert Gamse, Miguelito Valdez; *Copacabana* Doris Fisher, Allan Roberts; *Made For Each Other* Ervin Drake, Jimmy Shirl, Rene Touzet; *Holiday In Havana* Desi Arnaz; *I'll Take Romance* Oscar Hammerstein II, Ben Oakland.

On The Town (MGM) started life as a Jerome Robbins ballet called *Fancy Free*. The material was reworked by composer Leonard Bernstein with a book and lyrics by Betty Comden and Adolph Green, and surfaced as a hit Broadway musical in 1944. Producer Arthur Freed prevailed on Louis B. Mayer to purchase the property – which he reluctantly did while, at the same time, condemning the show as 'smutty' and 'Communistic' because of a scene in it in which a black girl danced with a white man. Five years later, Freed, now securely entrenched as the studio's top producer of musicals, was finally given the green light by Mayer to proceed with the project. The result was the freshest, most invigorating and innovative screen musical of the decade, and the perfect vehicle for Gene Kelly who not only starred in it, but directed and choreographed it together with Stanley Donen. The story of **On The Town** was not nearly as innovative as its production. Three sailors disembark from their battleship in the Brooklyn Navy Yard at six o'clock one morning and spend the next 24 hours in search of women and fun. Kelly falls in love with a poster of the subway's Miss Turnstiles (Vera-Ellen, illustrated with Kelly in main picture) and spends half the film searching for its model whom he finally tracks down at Symphonic Hall where she is receiving ballet instruction from an inebriated Maria Ouspenskaya-type ballet mistress (Florence Bates). Sinatra, again cast as the timid butter-wouldn't-melt-in-the-mouth innocent, is chased with relentless zeal by a lady cab driver called Brunnhilde Esterhazy (Betty Garrett), while the third (Jules Munshin) makes quite a hit with an anthropologist (Ann Miller) he happens to meet at the Anthropological Museum. Which more or less took care of the story, except that Kelly and Donen invested it with so much that was new and exciting – from the expressive 'Miss Turnstiles' Ballet (Bernstein) to the scintillating sequence atop the Empire State building where the three couples rendezvous – that they changed the entire concept of the film musical, opening it out (some of it was actually filmed on location in New York and its environs) and relying on the dance for its chief mode of musical expression. The underlying feeling of the film was essentially balletic, and even when its cast were standing still (which wasn't very often) you felt they were about to take off any second. In fact, so concerned was Kelly that **On The Town** should retain its balletic flavour, that in the 'Day In New York' ballet (Bernstein) he substituted four trained ballet dancers (Alex Romero, Gene Scott, Carol Haney and Marie Grosscup) for Sinatra, Munshin, Betty Garrett and Ann Miller. Agnes de Mille had done this six years earlier on stage in the Dream Ballet for *Oklahoma!*, but it had never been attempted on the screen before. The less overtly balletic numbers were equally successful, such as Roger Edens, Betty Comden and Adolph Green's 'Prehistoric Man', danced by Miller in the anthropology museum with support from the rest of the principals; and the rousing 'New York, New York' (by Leonard Bernstein, Comden and Green) exuberantly performed by Kelly, Sinatra and Munshin. It wasn't until the last 20 minutes or so that the high standard the film set for itself flagged and became bogged down in plot. And if, while watching the movie today, a slight feeling of *déjà vu* insinuates itself, it is because films such as *Hit The Deck* (MGM, 1955), *Skirts Ahoy* (MGM,

1952), *It's Always Fair Weather* (MGM, 1955), *All Ashore* (Columbia, 1953), *So This Is Paris* (Universal International, 1955), and *Three Sailors And A Girl* (Warner Bros, 1953), all of which contained similar ingredients to **On The Town**, have, over the years, blunted one's appetite for this kind of simple-minded yarn. Also, it is to be regretted that most of Leonard Bernstein's original Broadway score was jettisoned in favour of a more 'commercial' one by Roger Edens, a particularly unfortunate loss being 'Lonely Town', one of Bernstein's most poignant songs. All the same, **On The Town**, which cost $2,111,250 to make (and grossed over $4,500,000 on its initial release) pushed the Hollywood musical out of its claustrophobic confines in search of new ideas, and was a landmark of its time. Edens, Conrad Salinger and Lennie Hayton scored it, it was photographed by Harold Rosson, costumed by Helen Rose and designed by Cedric Gibbons and Jack Martin Smith. Completing the cast were Alice Pearce as ugly-duckling Lucy Schmeeler, George Meader, Bea Benedaret, Hans Conried and, making a brief appearance, singer Bern Hoffman. It was filmed in Technicolor. The inset picture shows (from left) Sinatra, Garrett, Munshin, Miller, Kelly and Vera-Ellen. Other songs and musical numbers: *I Feel Like I'm Not Out Of Bed Yet* (Hoffman); *Come Up To My Place* (Sinatra, Garrett) Bernstein, Comden, Green; *Miss Turnstiles Ballet* (Vera-Ellen) Bernstein; *Main Street* (Kelly, Vera-Ellen); *You're Awful* (Sinatra, Garrett); *On The Town* (Kelly, Sinatra, Munshin, Miller, Garrett, Vera-Ellen); *You Can Count On Me* (Kelly, Sinatra, Munshin, Miller, Garrett, Pearce); *Pearl Of The Persian Sea*; *That's All There Is, Folks* Edens, Comden, Green.

The Fifties The Fifties The Fifties The Fifties The Fifties The Fifties The Fifties The Fifties The Fifties The Fifties The Fifties The Fifties The Fifties The Fifties The Fifties The Fifties

1950

Cinematography (colour)
NOMINATIONS INCLUDED: *Annie Get Your Gun* (MGM) Charles Rosher

Art Direction (Set Decoration) (colour)
NOMINATIONS INCLUDED: *Annie Get Your Gun* Cedric Gibbons and Paul Groesse; Edwin B. Willis and Richard A. Pefferle

Sound Recording
NOMINATIONS INCLUDED: *Cinderella* (Disney, RKO) Disney Sound Department

Film Editing
Annie Get Your Gun James E. Newcom

Music
Song
NOMINATIONS INCLUDED: 'Be My Love' *The Toast Of New Orleans* (MGM) Nicholas Brodszky *cm*: Sammy Cahn *lyr*. 'Bibbidi-Bobbidi-Boo' *Cinderella* music and lyrics by Mack David, Al Hoffman and Jerry Livingston. 'Wilhelmina' *Wabash Avenue* (20th Century-Fox) Josef Myrow *cm*: Mack Gordon *lyr*.

Scoring Of A Musical Picture
Annie Get Your Gun Adolph Deutsch and Roger Edens
NOMINATIONS INCLUDED: *Cinderella* Oliver Wallace and Paul J. Smith. *I'll Get By* (20th Century-Fox) Lionel Newman. *Three Little Words* (MGM) Andre Previn. *The West Point Story* (WB) Ray Heindorf.

The Annual Top Moneymaking Films
INCLUDED: *Annie Get Your Gun. Cinderella. On The Town* (MGM). *Three Little Words. The Duchess Of Idaho* (MGM)

Producer William Jacobs invaded 20th Century-Fox territory with David Butler's Technicolor musical **The Daughter Of Rosie O'Grady** (Warner Bros.) in which the eponymous heroine (inoffensively played by June Haver, centre right) falls in love with the great Tony Pastor himself (Gordon MacRae, centre), to the disapproval of her tediously alcoholic father (James Barton, centre left). The script by Jack Rose, Melville Shavelson and Peter Milne was pure formula fare trading in turn-of-the-century nostalgia – though not nearly as effectively or with the panache of the Fox counterpart. Also in it: S.Z. Sakall, Gene Nelson (on Haver's right), Jane Darwell and a very young Debbie Reynolds. The sluggish dance direction was by LeRoy Prinz. Songs and musical numbers: *My Own True Love And I* M.K. Jerome, Jack Scholl; *As We Are Today* Ernesto Lecuona, Charles Tobias; *Ma Blushin' Rosie* Edgar Smith, John Stromberg; *The Rose Of Tralee* Charles Glover, C. Mordaunt Spencer; *A Farm Off Old Broadway; A Picture Turned To The Wall; Winter, Winter* A. Bryan-Gumble; *Winter Serenade; The Daughter Of Rosie O'Grady* Monty C. Brice, Walter Donaldson.

Michael Curtiz's **Young Man With A Horn** (GB: **Young Man Of Music**) involved a jazz trumpeter (Kirk Douglas, left) who, through a fanatical devotion to his art, wrecks his private life and almost forfeits the love of a long-suffering young singer (Doris Day). One of the less embarrassing biopics (the screenplay by Carl Foreman and Edmund H. North was inspired by a Dorothy Baker novel based on the legendary Bix Beiderbecke), it benefited from the customary intensity of Douglas's playing (both of the role itself and, via Harry James dubbed on the soundtrack, the trumpet) and the potent evocation, chiefly through music, of the '20s and '30s. Lauren Bacall (right) featured as a rich bitch who helps drive the musician to drink, with other roles going to Juano Hernandez, Jerome Cowan, Nestor Paiva and Mary Beth Hughes. It was narrated by Hoagy Carmichael, who also played a prominent supporting role, and produced for Warner Bros. by Jerry Wald. Songs: *The Very Thought Of You* Ray Noble; *I May Be Wrong* Henry Sullivan, Harry Ruskin; *The Man I Love* George and Ira Gershwin; *Too Marvellous For Words* Johnny Mercer, Richard A. Whiting; *Get Happy* Harold Arlen, Ted Koehler; *I Only Have Eyes For You* Al Dubin, Harry Warren; *Lullaby Of Broadway* Dubin, Warren; *With A Song In My Heart* Richard Rodgers, Lorenz Hart; *Can't We Be Friends* Paul James, Kay Swift; *Blue Room* Rodgers, Hart; *Chinatown* William Jerome, Jean Schwartz; *Manhattan Rhapsody* Ray Heindorf.

Romance, Music and Laughter were, according to the blurb circulated by Allied Artists, the chief ingredients of **There's A Girl In My Heart**. What the publicity boys failed to mention was its plot, whose chief ingredient was cobwebs. The story of a property developer who attempts (unsuccessfully) to acquire a valuable piece of property from an attractive widow and falls in love with her instead, it starred Lee Bowman as the developer and Elyse Knox as the widow, with Iris Adrian (illustrated centre), Gloria Jean, Peggy Ryan and Ray McDonald roped in for musical support. Lon Chaney (as Bowman's pal), Ludwig Donath, Joel Marston and Irene Ryan were also featured in Arthur Hoerl and the aptly named John Eugene Hasty's screenplay, and it was produced and directed by Arthur Dreifuss. Songs and musical numbers: *There's A Girl In My Heart* Arthur Dreifuss, Robert Bilder; *The Roller Skating Song; Be Careful Of The Tidal Wave; We Are The Main Attraction; Any Old Street* Robert Bilder; *A Bicycle Built For Two (Daisy Bell)* Harry Dacre; *After The Ball* Charles K. Harris.

Monogram's Bowery Boys made their only musical in **Blues Busters**, a pleasant programmer in which Huntz Hall (right), playing a character called Satch Debussy Jones suddenly finds himself the proud possessor of a marvellous crooning voice after undergoing a tonsillectomy. Bowery mastermind Leo Gorcey capitalizes on the discovery by remodelling a sweet shop owned by Louis Dumbrowsky (Bernard Gorcey) and turning it into a nightclub with Hall the stellar attraction. Adele Jergens appeared as rival club owner Craig Stevens's resident thrush, with other roles in Jan Grippo's production going to Gabriel Dell (left), Phyllis Coates, William Benedict, David Gorcey and Marty King. Charles R. Marion wrote it (additional dialogue by Bert Lawrence) and the director was William Beaudine. Songs included: *Wasn't It You; You Walk By* Ben Raleigh, Bernie Wayne; *Bluebirds Keep Singin' In The Rain* Johnny Lange, Eliot Daniel.

Walt Disney's version of **Cinderella** (RKO) was warmly welcomed by the press, but in no way showered with the kind of superlatives that greeted the same studio's *Snow White And The Seven Dwarfs* (1938) or *Pinocchio* (1940). Viewed today, it is every bit the equal of the two earlier films, matching them both in the skill of its animation (see illustration) and the scope of its invention. Based on the famous Charles Perrault fairy tale, the story was boldly reshaped by scenarists William Peed, Ted Sears, Erdman Penner, Winston Hibler and Harry Reeves to accommodate a host of Disneyesque characters, the most lovable being two household mice called Jacques and Gus-Gus who, in one of the film's most memorable sequences, join forces with several bluebirds to create a dress for Cinderella so that she might go to the ball after all. The more familiar *Cinderella* characters were traditionally realized in terms of good or evil, the ugly stepmother being almost too frightening for the comfort of the very young. Anastasia and Drusilla, the stepsisters, were, however, just right. Apart from the brilliance of its animation, **Cinderella** benefited, too, from a marvellous set of songs and, of course, from its vivid Technicolor. The production supervisor was again Ben Sharpsteen, and the voices on the soundtrack belonged to Ilene Woods (Cinderella), William Phipps (Prince Charming), Eleanor Audley (stepmother), Rhoda Williams and Lucille Bliss (Anastasia and Drusilla), Verna Felton (fairy godmother), Luis Van Rooten (King and Grand Duke) and James McDonald (Gus-Gus and Jacques). Songs: *Bibbidi-Bobbidi-Boo*; *So This Is Love*; *A Dream Is A Wish Your Heart Makes*; *Cinderella*; *The Work Song*; *Sing Sweet Nightingale* Mack David, Jerry Livingston, Al Hoffman.
▽

A minor entry from Columbia, **The Petty Girl** (GB: **Girl Of The Year**), photographed in Technicolor, starred Robert Cummings as a painter called George Petty and Joan Caulfield (illustrated foreground) as the prudish burlesque stripper who poses for him, then becomes his bride. Third-billed Elsa Lanchester committed grand larceny in every scene she was in, with other roles in producer Nat Perrin's screenplay (from a story by Mary McCarthy) going to Melville Cooper, Audrey Long, Mary Wickes, Frank Orth, John Ridgely, Raymond Largay, Ian Wolfe, Frank Jenks and Tim Ryan. Musical highlight: a production number featuring a dozen other 'Petty' girls in various stages of *deshabille* as each represents a different month of the year. The director of this lively little show was Henry Levin. Songs and musical numbers included: *Petty Girl*; *Fancy Free*; *Calypso Song*; *Ah Loves You* Harold Arlen, Johnny Mercer.
▽

Two lavish production numbers (staged by Jack Donohue), guest-star Lena Horne's singing of 'Baby Come Out Of The Clouds' (by Lee Pearl and Henry Nemo), and a lively routine by Mrs Glenn Ford (better known as Eleanor Powell, who tapped her way out of retirement for the occasion), were among the musical highlights in **The Duchess Of Idaho** (MGM), a Joe Pasternak-produced trifle, dazzlingly photographed in Technicolor, and starring Esther Williams and Van Johnson (both illustrated foreground). When not demonstrating the crawl and the backstroke, Miss Williams (playing a well-known swimming star) was helping her rather forlorn room-mate (Paula Raymond) to lead her wealthy playboy boss (John Lund) to the altar, in the process of which she and bandleader Van Johnson realize that they're mutually attracted. Scenarists Dorothy Cooper and Jerry Davis ensured a happy ending to their predictable story (the only surprise was an unbilled guest appearance by Red Skelton), and the director was Robert Z. Leonard. Also in it: Mel Torme, Clinton Sundberg, Connie Haines, Amanda Blake, Tommy Farrell, Sig Arno and Dick Simmons. Other songs and musical numbers: *You Can't Do Wrong Doin' Right*; *Let's Choo Choo Choo To Idaho*; *Of All Things*; *Or Was It Spring*; *Warm Hands, Cold Heart* Al Rinker, Floyd Huddleston; *Singlefoot Serenade* G.M. Beilenson, M. Beelby; *You Won't Forget Me* Kermit Goell, Fred Spielman.
▽

▷

△

A remake of Frank Capra's *Broadway Bill* (Columbia, 1934), **Riding High** (Paramount) starred Bing Crosby (in the role originally played by Warner Baxter) as a horse-trainer whose devotion to a faithful horse, at the expense of a romance with a millionairess, pays off with a handsome win. Unfortunately though, the horse dies in the process. Written by Robert Riskin, with additional dialogue by Melville Shavelson and Jack Rose, and again directed by Capra with a sureness of touch and a real feeling for its racing milieu, it was a perfect vehicle for Crosby (centre) who was marvellous in it. Four songs by Johnny Burke and Jimmy Van Heusen were neatly interspersed into the narrative and were a pleasing bonus to a screenplay that didn't really need musical embellishment. Coleen Gray (right) was the leading lady, with other roles going to Charles Bickford, William Demarest, and, repeating the roles they originally played, Clarence Muse (left, as Crosby's stableboy), Raymond Walburn, Douglass Dumbrille, Ward Bond, Paul Harvey. Also: Frankie Darro, Gene Lockhart, Charles Lane, Percy Kilbride, Frances Gifford and Margaret Hamilton. Capra produced. Songs: *The Horse Told Me*; *Sunshine Cake*; *We've Got A Sure Thing*; *Someplace On Anywhere Road* Burke, Van Heusen; *De Camptown Races* Stephen Foster; *Whiffenpoof Song* Meade Minnigerode, George S. Pomeroy, Tod B. Galloway.

◁ Producer Joe Pasternak dusted off one of Deanna Durbin's old scripts (*It's A Date*, Universal, 1940) and hired Sidney Sheldon to refurbish it (from the story by Jane Hall, Frederick Kohner and Ralph Block) as a starring vehicle for petite and pretty Jane Powell (centre left) and, in the role played a decade earlier by Kay Francis, Ann Sothern. The story of a mother and daughter who, while on an ocean voyage to Rio, both covet the same parts in a play, as well as the same man (Barry Sullivan), the slender narrative of **Nancy Goes To Rio** was padded out by a misunderstanding that arises when Miss Powell is thought to be pregnant. The musical programme accompanying the plot was a typical Pasternakian lucky-dip of the old and the new and the classical, the best of the middle category being 'Time And Time Again' by Earl Brent and Fred Spielman, pleasantly sung by Miss Powell. Pleasing too was Nick Castle's staging of 'Shine On Harvest Moon' (by Jack Norworth and Nora Bayes), delightfully rendered in song and dance by Powell, Sothern and Louis Calhern. Carmen Miranda was also in it (doing a number called 'Cha Bomm Pa Pa' by Ray Gilbert) with other parts going to Scotty Beckett (centre right with Powell), Fortunio Bonanova, Glenn Anders, Nella Walker, Hans Conried and Frank Fontaine. The glossy direction (in Technicolor) was by Robert Z. Leonard. Other songs and musical numbers: *Magic Is The Moonlight* Charles Pasquale, Maria Grever; *Love Is Like This* Ray Gilbert, Vianna; *Nancy Goes To Rio* George Stoll, Earl Brent; *Yipsee-I-O* Gilbert; *Musetta's Waltz* (from 'La Boheme') Puccini.

Despite the generous selection of operatic extracts in producer Joe Pasternak's **The Toast of New Orleans** (MGM), the song that made the biggest impression on audiences was 'Be My Love', composed by Nicholas Brodszky and Sammy Cahn, and sung by Kathryn Grayson and Mario Lanza, at the tops of their ample voices. Lanza (right), in a role not dissimilar to the one he played in *That Midnight Kiss* (MGM), was cast as a singing fisherman in a Louisiana bayou, Kathryn Grayson (left) was a famous soprano, David Niven was third-billed as Grayson's urbane manager who decides to groom Lanza for an operatic career. Cy Gomberg and George Wells's exiguous plot focused largely on Lanza's rough-and-ready behaviour as Niven's protègè, and his stormy romance with Grayson which only narrowly averts blows during the tender love duet from Act I of Puccini's *Madam Butterfly*. Though the narrative traded mainly in clichés, director Norman Taurog, aided by Technicolor, some glorious music and the volatile personality of his two stars, managed to impart to it a veneer of sophistication that went some way to disguise its basic lack of originality. Brodszky and Cahn contributed several other numbers to the jolly proceedings, most notably 'The Tina Lina' and 'Boom Biddy Boom Boom', and the supporting cast was completed by J. Carrol Naish as Lanza's doting, fisherman uncle, dancer James Mitchell (underused), Richard Hageman (centre), Clinton Sundberg, Sig Arno, Rita Moreno and Romo Vincent. The choreography was by Eugene Loring, and the musical direction by George Stoll and Johnny Green. Other songs, musical numbers, and operatic extracts: *Brindisi* (from 'La Traviata') Verdi; *O Paradiso* (from 'La Gioconda') Ponchielli; *The Toast Of New Orleans*; *I'll Never Love You*; *Song Of The Bayou* Brodszky. Cahn; *Flower Song* (from 'Carmen') Bizet; *Je Suis Titania* (from 'Mignon') Thomas; *M'Appari* (from 'Martha') Flotow.

◁ Ethel Merman belted it out on stage for 1,159 performances; Judy Garland was signed for the screen version, and Betty Hutton finally got to play it. The role was Annie Oakley, the show was Irving Berlin's **Annie Get Your Gun**, which George Sidney directed (replacing Busby Berkeley and Charles Walters) to give MGM its top money-making musical of 1950. Sidney Sheldon's adaptation and screenplay from Herbert and Dorothy Fields's original book stuck as closely to the Broadway version of the show as was considered decent by Hollywood's meddlesome standards – and although the score lost a few numbers between Times Square and Culver City (most notably 'Moonshine Lullaby' and 'Who Do You Love, I Hope') the spirit of the piece was left intact. The simple story of an unorthodox love affair between two prize sharpshooters who are attached to different Wild West shows, the film co-starred Howard Keel in the role played on stage by Ray Middleton, with Louis Calhern (who replaced Frank Morgan after the latter's death) as Buffalo Bill, J. Carrol Naish as Sitting Bull, and Edward Arnold as Pawnee Bill. Keenan Wynn. Benay Venuta and Clinton Sundberg completed the cast. It was photographed in Technicolor, and was another triumph for producer Arthur Freed, and for Robert Alton, whose staging of the musical numbers (Hutton in 'I'm An Indian Too' illustrated) did Berlin's magnificent score proud. All the performances were spot-on, especially Hutton's, which, after a slightly frenetic start, settled down to become the highwater mark of her career. The musical director was Adolph Deutsch. Songs and musical numbers: *Colonel Buffalo Bill* (chorus); *I've Got The Sun In The Morning* (Hutton); *You Can't Get A Man With A Gun* (Hutton); *They Say That Falling In Love Is Wonderful* (Hutton, Keel); *My Defences Are Down* (Keel); *There's No Business Like Show Business* (Hutton, Keel, Wynn, Calhern); *Doin' What Comes Naturally* (Hutton,and children); *The Girl That I Marry* (Keel); *Anything You Can Do* (Hutton, Keel).

Tea For Two, competently directed by David Butler, proved to be among the most delightful and successful of Warner Bros.' cycle of Doris Day musicals. Very loosely based on the Otto Harbach-Frank Mandel Broadway hit of 1924 *No, No, Nanette* (and its subsequent revivals), Harry Clork's screenplay concerned Doris's attempts to say 'no' to every offer or proposition not, as in her later Universal-International comedies, to preserve her virginity, but to win a bet whose stake would allow her to finance (and, naturally, star in) a Broadway show. The movie, told in flashback, was absolutely without pretensions, benefited from a collection of watertight standards and, ably supported by Gordon MacRae, Gene Nelson (illustrated), Patrice Wymore, Eve Arden, Billy De Wolfe, dancer Virginia Gibson, and the inevitable S.Z. Sakall, Miss Day's bright, scrubbed, American-as-apple-pie energy, especially in LeRoy Prinz's better than usual dance numbers, charmed even the most curmudgeonly spectator. It was produced, in Technicolor by William Jacobs. Songs and musical numbers: *I Want To Be Happy*; *Tea For Two* Vincent Youmans, Irving Caesar; *No, No Nanette* Youmans, Otto Harbach; *Oh Me, Oh My!* Youmans, Ira Gershwin; *I Know That You Know* Youmans, Anne Caldwell; *Do Do Do* George and Ira Gershwin; *Crazy Rhythm* Irving Caesar, Joseph Meyer, Roger Wolfe Kahn; *Charleston* Cecil Mack, Jimmie Johnson; *I Only Have Eyes For You* Al Dubin, Harry Warren; *The Call Of The Sea* Youmans, Caesar, Harbach.
▽

◁ After the beautiful music they made together in Fox's *When My Baby Smiles At Me* (1948), Betty Grable (left) and Dan Dailey (right) were again teamed for **My Blue Heaven** (20th Century-Fox) – but this one was a black mark for both their careers. The banal story of a husband-and-wife TV team who, after adopting a child, discover they're about to have one of their own, it was notable only in that it introduced movie audiences to Mitzi Gaynor. Apart from the title song, sung by Grable and Dailey and written by George Whiting and Walter Donaldson, the rest of the score was by Ralph Blane and Harold Arlen, the best of the batch being Gaynor's 'Live Hard, Work Hard, Love Hard'. David Wayne co-starred, and the cast was completed by Una Merkel, Louise Beavers and Laura Pierpont. Sol C. Siegel produced (in Technicolor), the *schmaltzy* direction was by Henry Koster, and it was written by Lamar Trotti and Claude Binyon from a story by S.K. Lauren. Other songs and musical numbers: *Don't Rock The Boat Dear*; *Friendly Islands*; *Halloween*; *I Love A New Yorker*; *It's Deductible*; *What A Man*.

314

Popular music stars Frankie Laine, Billy Daniels, The Mills Brothers, Bob Crosby, Kay Starr, and The Modernaires were the chief attractions of **When You're Smiling**, a low-budget entertainment from Columbia with a plot of sorts involving the unscrupulous activities of a recording-company boss (Jerome Cowan) who happens to be heavily in debt to a bookmaker. In order to alleviate his financial situation, he attempts to marry off his daughter (Margo Woode) to a supposedly wealthy Texas cowhand (Jerome Courtland, left). The cowhand, however, has a mind of his own, preferring Cowan's pretty secretary (Lola Albright, right). Miss Albright reciprocates his affections, and helps turn him into a star. Karen De Wolf and John R. Roberts were responsible for writing the clap-trap, Jonie Taps produced, and the director was Joseph Santley. Songs and musical numbers included: *When You're Smiling* Mark Fisher, Joe Goodwin, Larry Shay; *That Old Black Magic* Harold Arlen, Johnny Mercer; *When The Wind Was Green* Don Hunt.

After Betty Hutton's enormous personal success in MGM's *Annie Get Your Gun*, Paramount wasted no time in putting their top female star to work. Unfortunately, **Let's Dance** was an inferior little item in spite of the presence of Fred Astaire (second billed). It cast them as wartime entertainers whose act splits up when Betty's flyer husband is killed in action. She returns to Boston, her home town, and spends the next five years raising her child; meanwhile, Astaire becomes a business man. Tired of domesticity, Hutton (right) decides to make a show-biz comeback, persuades Astaire (left) to rejoin the act and, before you can say 'I told you so', the couple fall in love. Apart from its indifferent screenplay by Allan Scott and Dane Lussier (from a story by Maurice Zolotow), the thing that was really wrong with **Let's Dance** was the uneasy melding of the personalities of its two stars who never really seemed right together. A couple of lively dance routines – notably 'Can't Stop Talking' and 'Oh Them Dudes' (by Frank Loesser, who supplied all the lyrics and music) – were passingly enjoyable, but the sparkle wasn't there. Lucille Watson played a hissable mother-in-law out to gain custody of Miss Hutton's child, and Roland Young and Melville Cooper provided comic relief as her two attorneys, with other roles under Norman Z. McLeod's direction going to Ruth Warrick, Gregory Moffett, Barton MacLane, Shepherd Strudwick, Harold Huber and George Zucco. It was choreographed by Hermes Pan and the producer was Robert Fellows. Other songs and musical numbers: *Piano Dance* (interpolating *Tiger Rag*); *Jack And The Beanstalk*; *Why Fight The Feeling?*; *The Hyacinth*; *Tunnel Of Love*.

Three Little Words (MGM), a biopic of composers Bert Kalmar and Harry Ruby, was one of the better musicals of 1950. Relying more on plot than on a series of elaborately staged production numbers (though there were a few of those as well) it was an entertaining account of two showbiz careers, with Fred Astaire top-billed as lyricist Kalmar and a subdued Red Skelton as composer Ruby. George Wells's scenario took in the main points of the two men's lives, showing Kalmar to have been a vaudeville song-and-dance man (with a hankering to be a magician) who turns to lyric writing when a knee injury ends his career as a dancer; and Ruby to have been a honky-tonk pianist with a yearning to play baseball. The two men get together to form a songwriting team, take Broadway and Hollywood by storm, then split up over a misunderstanding. It is their wives (according to Wells's fanciful screenplay) who bring them together again. Vera-Ellen (whose vocals were dubbed by Anita Ellis) played Mrs Kalmar, Arlene Dahl was Mrs Ruby, with other parts going to Keenan Wynn, Gale Robbins, Phil Regan (as himself), Harry Shannon, Paul Harvey, Carleton Carpenter, George Metkovich and The Great Mendoza (as himself). In her third film, Debbie Reynolds

was seen as 'Boop-Boop-a-Doop' girl Helen Kane, with Miss Kane herself dubbing the vocals in Kalmar, Ruby and Herbert Stothart's 'I Wanna Be Loved By You'; while Gloria De Haven played her mother, Mrs Carter De Haven, and sang 'Who's Sorry Now' (Kalmar, Ruby and Ted Snyder). Other highlights were 'Mr And Mrs Hoofer At Home' danced by Astaire and Vera-Ellen (both illustrated) and the same team's 'Thinking Of You'. The choreography was by Hermes Pan, Andre Previn was the musical director, it was produced (in Technicolor) by Jack Cummings, and directed by Richard Thorpe. Other songs and musical numbers: *Three Little Words* (Astaire, Skelton, Vera-Ellen); *I Love You So Much* (Dahl, male chorus); *She's Mine, All Mine* (Barber Shop Quartet); *So Long Oo-Long* (Astaire, Skelton); *Hooray For Captain Spaulding* (incomplete) (Skelton, Astaire); *Up In The Clouds* (chorus); *All Alone Monday* (Robbins) Kalmar, Ruby; *Nevertheless* (Astaire, Vera-Ellen); *Where Did You Get That Girl?* (Astaire, Vera-Ellen) Kalmar, Ruby, Harry Puck; *My Sunny Tennessee* (Astaire, Skelton) Kalmar, Ruby, Herman Ruby; *Come On Papa* (Vera-Ellen, chorus) Harry Ruby, Edgar Leslie; *You Are My Lucky Star* (Regan) Arthur Freed, Nacio Herb Brown.

Fifties Musicals

John Carroll played a dual role in **Hit Parade of 1951** (Republic): a reckless Las Vegas gambler and a rather effeminate crooner. That old standby, mistaken identity, loomed large in Elizabeth Reinhardt, Aubrey Wisberg and Lawrence Kimble's screenplay (story by Wisberg), causing chaos and confusion when the gambler loses $200,000 and the crooner loses his dissatisfied girlfriend (Marie McDonald, illustrated). Euphemistically speaking, it was a routine affair, with several songs and production numbers included as garnishing. Estelita Rodriguez, Frank (John L.C. Sevony) Fontaine, Grant Withers, Mikhail Rasumny and Steve Flagg also appeared for producer-director John H. Auer, and the dances were staged by Val Raset. Songs and musical numbers included: *Square Dance Samba*; *You're So Nice*; *How Would I Know?*; *Wishes Come True*; *You Don't Know The Other Side Of Me* Al Rinker, Floyd Huddleston.

▽

△

Bing Crosby hardly extended his range in **Mr Music** (Paramount), a genial, albeit insubstantial effort that benefited from an agreeable score by Johnny Burke and Jimmy Van Heusen, the best number being the oft-reprised 'Life Is So Peculiar' – sung by Crosby and guest stars Peggy Lee and The Merry Macs. Marge (illustrated) and Gower Champion (as themselves) did it as a dance; and Groucho Marx (another guest star) joined Crosby to do it in a sketch. Also guesting was Dorothy Kirsten, who sang a duet with Crosby called 'Accidents Will Happen'. As for the plot, it was all about a songwriter who'd rather play golf than write songs . . . Nancy Olson as Bing's faithful secretary and Charles Coburn as a Broadway producer co-starred, with other parts in Arthur Sheekman's screenplay ('suggested' by Samson Raphaelson's play *Accent On Youth*) going to Ruth Hussey, Robert Stack, Tom Ewell, Ida Moore, Charles Kemper, Donald Woods and Richard Haydn. Haydn also directed, and the producer was Robert L. Welch. Other songs: *Mr Music*; *And You'll Be Home*; *High On The List*; *Wouldn't It Be Funny*; *Wasn't I There?*

Judy Garland's last film for MGM was **Summer Stock** (GB: **If You Feel Like Singing**) an old-fashioned 'let's put on a show in a barn' yarn, but with adults rather than adolescents in the star parts. Gene Kelly was cast opposite Garland, with other roles in George Wells and Cy Gomberg's screenplay going to Phil Silvers, Gloria De Haven, Eddie Bracken, Marjorie Main, Ray Collins, Nita Bieber, Carleton Carpenter and Hans Conried. Its simple story ran thus: Jane, New England farm girl (Garland), has her peaceful, bucolic existence interrupted when her sister Abigail (De Haven) invites a troupe of show folk to use their barn as a summer theatre. Garland is furious at this invasion of her privacy, and insists that the actors help out on the farm to pay for the use of the barn and the food they eat. In time, however, she falls in love with Ross (Kelly), the show's author, and, on opening night becomes a star when she has to step into De Haven's shoes. This juvenile scenario, unworthy of the talents of its two leading players, was redeemed by a series of splendidly staged musical numbers, the two most outstanding being Kelly's solo dance with a piece of newspaper and a squeaking floorboard (which he choreographed and devised himself to 'You Wonderful You' by Harry Warren, Jack Brooks and Saul Chaplin) and Garland's 'Get Happy' (by Harold Arlen and Ted Koehler), filmed three months after the movie's completion by Charles Walters. The sequence featured a slimline Garland – she was decidedly over-weight in the rest of the footage – sexily dressed in a man's tuxedo jacket and wearing a natty hat whose brim covered her right eye (see illustration). It was the classiest thing in the show and one of the best numbers Garland ever committed to film. **Summer Stock** was produced in Technicolor by Joe Pasternak and directed by Charles Walters. Other songs and musical numbers: *If You Feel Like Singing*; *Happy Harvest*; *Friendly Star*; *Blue Jean Polka*; *Mem'ry Island*; *Dig-Dig-Dig For Your Dinner* Harry Warren, Mack Gordon; *Heavenly Music* Saul Chaplin.

▷

△

Eight years after his triumph in Warner Bros.' *Yankee Doodle Dandy*, James Cagney returned to musicals in the same studio's **The West Point Story** (GB: **Fine And Dandy**). The Louis F. Edelman production told the lack-lustre story of a failed Broadway producer (Cagney, right) making his comeback with a spectacular show at the famous military academy and becoming, in the process, a cadet himself. In spite of Cagney's zestful and cocky central performance, and the efforts of a cast that included Doris Day, Gordon MacRae, Virginia Mayo (left), Gene Nelson, Alan Hale Jr, Jerome Cowan and Roland

Winters, the film's rather mindless endorsement of military life hardly met the requirements of musical comedy, and the score by Jule Styne and Sammy Cahn was one of the team's weakest. The credits (or debits) included John Monks Jr, Charles Hoffman and Irving Wallace for the longueur-filled script, Roy Del Ruth for the flabby direction, and LeRoy Prinz for the indifferent choreography. Songs and musical numbers: *Ten Thousand Four Hundred And Thirty Two Sheep*; *By The Kissing Rock*; *You Love Me*; *Military Polka*; *Long Before I Knew You*; *It Could Only Happen In Brooklyn*; *The Corps*; *Brooklyn*.

Though Jane Powell (left), Ricardo Montalban (right), Louis Calhern and Ann Harding were all billed above her, it was cute little Debbie Reynolds who hogged most of the notices for **Two Weeks With Love** (MGM), a nostalgic, turn of the century musical, set in the Catskills and all about the romantic adventures of Patti and Melba Robinson (Powell and Reynolds) who are spending a two-week vacation in the famous mountain resort with their parents (Calhern and Harding), and younger brothers (Gary Gray and Tommy Rettig). Powell, the elder of the two sisters (but still too young to wear corsets), falls for handsome Montalban (and has to compete for his affections with a more experienced Phyllis Kirk); while Reynolds makes a successful bee-line for gangly Carleton Carpenter. Together Reynolds and Carpenter performed 'Aba Daba Honeymoon' (by Arthur Fields and Walter Donovan) which was the highlight of producer Jack Cummings's entrancing little film. Less successful was a somewhat Freudian dream sequence, which combined Powell's fervent wish to be clothed in a corset with her equally fervent desire to be swept off her feet by Montalban. The number was staged by Busby Berkeley, who was in charge of the dance direction throughout and who, in 'The Oceana Roll' (by Roger Lewis and Lucien Denni), performed by Powell and a group of kids in the lounge of a hotel, again proved how effective a number could be without recourse to elaborate overhead shots or armies of extras. The director was Roy Rowland, and the cast was completed by Clinton Sundberg and Charles Smith. (Technicolor). Other songs and musical numbers: *A Heart That's Free* Thomas T. Railey, Alfred G. Robyn; *By The Light Of The Silvery Moon* Gus Edwards, Edward Madden; *My Hero* Stanislaus Stange, Oscar Straus; *Row Row Row* William Jerome, James V. Monaco; *That's How I Need You* Joe McCarthy, Joe Goodwin; *Beautiful Lady* Ivan Caryll, C.H.S. McClellan.

◁ A remake of *Tin Pan Alley* (20th Century-Fox, 1940), **I'll Get By**, also from the Fox factory, starred June Haver (2nd right) as a vocalist, William Lundigan (right) as a struggling music publisher whose career she helps to promote, and Dennis Day (centre) as a composer who becomes Lundigan's partner in a publishing business. Though no fewer than five (count 'em) writers were credited with the story (Robert Ellis, Helen Logan, Pamela Harris) and screenplay (Mary Loos, Richard Sale), the narrative was washed away in a tidal wave of music, leaving Haver and Lundigan very little to do in the way of acting. The same applied to co-stars Gloria De Haven (2nd left, as Haver's sister), Harry James (as himself, left) and Thelma Ritter. The story was updated from World War I to World War II, and the musical highlights included Haver and De Haven singing 'Taking A Chance On Love' (by John Latouche, Ted Fetter and Vernon Duke), as well as Haver's pleasant account of the title number (by Roy Turk and Fred Ahlert). Jeanne Crain, Victor Mature, Reginald Gardiner and Dan Dailey (who did a brief dance with Haver and De Haven) made guest appearances, it was directed by Richard Sale, choreographed by Larry Ceballos, and produced (in Technicolor) by William Perlberg. Other songs and musical numbers included: *Deep In The Heart Of Texas* June Hershey, Don Swander; *You Make Me Feel So Young* Mack Gordon, Josef Myrow; *I've Got The World On A String* Ted Koehler, Harold Arlen; *Once In A While* Bud Green, Michael Edwards; *Yankee Doodle Blues* Buddy De Sylva, Irving Caesar, George Gershwin; *Fifth Avenue*; *There Will Never Be Another You* Mack Gordon, Harry Warren; *McNamara's Band* Shamus O'Connor, J.J. Stamford; *It's Been A Long, Long Time* Sammy Cahn, Jule Styne; *No Love, No Nothin'* Leo Robin, Harry Warren; *Auld Lang Syne* music traditional, lyrics Robert Burns.

Despite its colourful Tahitian settings, the attractive presences of Esther Williams and Howard Keel, and a passable score, largely provided by Harry Warren and producer Arthur Freed, **Pagan Love Song** (MGM) was, artistically, the least successful of Freed's films, even though it grossed over $3,200,000 on the marquee value of Williams's name. The fault lay in Robert Nathan and Jerry Davis's amorphous screenplay (from the book *Tahiti Landfall* by William S. Stone), a mere bagatelle which had Keel as a schoolteacher arriving in Tahiti to take over his late uncle's coconut plantation and mistaking American-born Williams (illustrated foreground centre) for a *bona fide* island native. How he successfully woos her, and learns that when in Tahiti one does as the Tahitians do, provided the film with its dreary content. Freed and Nacio Herb Brown's famous 'Pagan Love Song' (first sung by Ramon Novarro in MGM's *The Pagan*, 1929) was given due prominence in the musical programme, and from Roger Edens came a number called 'Mata'. One lavish water ballet helped brighten the proceedings, and Williams sang 'The Sea Of The Moon' (by Warren and Freed) most pleasingly. Rita Moreno was in it too, so were Minna Gombell, Charles Mau, Philip Costa, Dione Leilani and Charles Freund. It was photographed in Technicolor, and directed and choreographed by Robert Alton, who replaced Freed's original choice, Stanley Donen, after Williams refused to work with him. Other songs and musical numbers: *The House Of Singing Bamboo*; *Singing In The Sun*; *Tahiti*; *Why Is Love So Crazy?*; *Etiquette* Warren, Freed.

Wabash Avenue (20th Century-Fox), a colourful remake of the same studio's *Coney Island* (1943), was set at the time of the 1892 Chicago World Fair, and starred 34-year-old Betty Grable (centre left), and Victor Mature (right foreground) and Phil Harris (seated 2nd left) as a couple of con-men artists who are both in love with her. Grable played a shimmy dancer in a gas-lit saloon and apart from bringing the house down with 'I Wish I Could Shimmy Like My Sister Kate' (by Armand J. Piron and Peter Bocage) was given ample opportunity to reveal that she still had the greatest pair of legs in the business. Mack Gordon and Josef Myrow provided her with several excellent new songs, the two best being a little item called 'Walking Along With Billy' and 'Baby Won't You Say You Love Me'. Though the storyline couldn't have been more hackneyed, scenarists Harry Tugend and Charles Lederer somehow managed to doll it up, imparting to it the kind of zest that had characterized the best of Fox's period musicals in the forties. The supporting cast included Reginald Gardiner (back left), James Barton, Barry Kelley (seated centre), Margaret Hamilton, Jacqueline Dalya, Robin Raymond, Hal K. Dawson and Irving Bacon. Henry Koster directed and it was produced by William Perlberg. Other songs and musical numbers: *Wilhelmina*; *May I Tempt You With A Big Red Rosy Apple?*; *Clean Up Chicago*; *Down On Wabash Avenue* Gordon, Myrow; *I've Been Floating Down The Old Green River* Bert Kalmar, Joe Cooper.

1951

Academy Awards

Best Picture
An American In Paris (MGM) produced by Arthur Freed

Direction
NOMINATIONS INCLUDED: Vincente Minnelli *An American In Paris*

Writing (Story and Screenplay)
An American In Paris Alan Jay Lerner

Cinematography (colour)
An American In Paris Alfred Gilks and John Alton
NOMINATIONS INCLUDED: *Show Boat* (MGM) Charles Rosher

Art Direction (Set Decoration) (colour)
An American In Paris Cedric Gibbons and Preston Ames; Edwin B. Willis and Keogh Gleason.

Music
Song
'In The Cool, Cool, Cool Of The Evening' *Here Comes The Groom* (Paramount) Hoagy Carmichael *cm*; Johnny Mercer *lyr*.
NOMINATIONS INCLUDED: 'A Kiss To Build A Dream On' *The Strip* (MGM) music and lyrics by Bert Kalmar, Harry Ruby and Oscar Hammerstein II. 'Never' *Golden Girl* (20th Century-Fox) Lionel Newman *cm*; Eliot Daniel *lyr*. 'Too Late Now' *Royal Wedding* (MGM) Burton Lane *cm*; Alan Jay Lerner *lyr*. 'Wonder Why' *Rich, Young And Pretty* (MGM) Nicholas Brodszky *cm*; Sammy Cahn *lyr*.

Scoring Of A Musical Picture
An American In Paris Johnny Green and Saul Chaplin
NOMINATIONS INCLUDED: *Alice In Wonderland* (Disney, RKO) Oliver Wallace. *The Great Caruso* (MGM) Peter Herman Adler and Johnny Green. *On The Riviera* (20th Century-Fox) Alfred Newman. *Show Boat* Adolph Deutsch and Conrad Salinger.

Costume Design (colour)
An American In Paris Orry-Kelly, Walter Plunkett and Irene Sharaff
NOMINATIONS INCLUDED: *The Great Caruso* Helen Rose and Gile Steele

Sound Recording
The Great Caruso Douglas Shearer, sound director.
NOMINATIONS INCLUDED: *Two Tickets To Broadway* (RKO) John Aalberg, sound director.

Honorary Award
To Gene Kelly, in appreciation of his versatility as an actor, singer, director and dancer and specifically for his brilliant achievements in the art of choreography of film. (statuette)

The New York Times Annual 'Ten Best'
7th *An American In Paris*

The Annual Top Moneymaking Films
INCLUDED: *Show Boat. An American in Paris. The Great Caruso* (Paramount). *At War With The Army* (Paramount). *Royal Wedding. Here Comes The Groom. On Moonlight Bay* (WB). *On The Riviera*.

Rhythm Inn, a programmer from Monogram, involved some pawned musical instruments belonging to a Dixieland band having to be smuggled out of the pawnshop every night so that the group can fulfil a contractual obligation. It also involved a music store clerk with a yen to be a songsmith, as well as his girlfriend whose dream it is to become a successful vocalist. What it failed to involve was audiences. Charles Smith was the would-be writer, Lois Collier the would-be singer, and Kirby Grant the bandleader. Jane Frazee (illustrated) also appeared as a band singer, so did Fritz Feld, Ralph Sanford, and specialties Armida, Anson Weeks and His Orchestra, skater Jean Ritchie, Ames and Arno, and Ramon Ros. Bill Raynor wrote it, Paul Landres directed and the producer was Lindsley Parsons. Songs and musical numbers included: *It's A Big Wide Wonderful World* John Rox; *Chi Chi* Armida; *Love* Bill Raynor, Edward J. Kay; *B Flat Blues*; *Return Trip*; *What Does It Matter?* Kay; *With A Twist Of The Wrist* Irvin Graham.
▽

△

On The Riviera (20th Century-Fox), first seen as a Broadway play (by Rudolph Lothar and Hans Adler) in 1934, then, a year later, as a showcase for Maurice Chevalier (*Folies Bergère*) and, in 1941 as a starring vehicle for Don Ameche (*That Night In Rio*) was the story of a nightclub entertainer whose striking physical resemblance to a well-known financier deceives even the financier's wife. This version starred Danny Kaye in the double lead, with Gene Tierney as the deceived wife and Corinne Calvet as the entertainer's girlfriend. Also: Marcel Dalio, Henri Letondal, Clinton Sundberg, Sig Rumann, Joyce MacKenzie, Marina Koshetz, Ann Codee and dancer Gwen Verdon. The familiar story was given a slight overhaul by Valentine Davies and Phoebe and Henry Ephron, its glamorous Riviera setting this time taking the place of Paris and Rio. Sylvia Fine provided a quartet of songs, best of which was 'Popo The Puppet' (illustrated, with Kaye) staged, as were the rest of the numbers, by Jack Cole. It was produced (in Technicolor) by Sol C. Siegel, and the pedestrian direction was by Walter Lang. Other songs and musical numbers: *On The Riviera*; *Rhythm Of A New Romance*; *Happy Ending* Fine; *Ballin' The Jack* Jim Burris, Chris Smith.

Of Men And Music (20th Century-Fox) was a showcase for the extraordinary talents of pianist Arthur Rubinstein, tenor Jan Peerce, soprano Nadine Connor, violinist Jascha Heifetz and conductor Dimitri Mitropoulos. In four unrelated sequences, and via four embarrassingly contrived little scenarios, they were put to work, with musical results that were more satisfactory than the flimsy narrative content. Rubinstein opened the programme with performances of Mendelssohn's 'Spinning Song', Liszt's 'Liebestraum', and Chopin's Waltz in C Sharp Minor and Polonaise in A Major. The sequence ended with the maestro playing 'Pop Goes The Weasel' for his children. Next Jan Peerce and Nadine Connor (see illustration) entered a bare stage and launched into a series of songs and arias. Peerce began with 'O Paradiso' from Meyerbeer's 'L'Africaine', and 'Matinata' by Leoncavallo, followed by Miss Connor who sang an aria from Donizetti's 'Don Pasquale'. They then joined forces for a duet from Donizetti's 'Lucia Di Lammermoor'. Next, Jascha Heifetz was introduced in his comfortable home in California and, accompanied by Emanuel Ray, played Bach's Partita Prelude, Debussy's 'The Girl With The Flaxen Hair', Wienieawski's 'Scherzo Tarantelle' and Paganini's Caprice No 24. The fourth,

and most satisfactory, sequence was a rehearsal session in which Dimitri Mitropoulos conducted the Philharmonic Symphony Orchestra in a performance of the third movement of Liszt's 'Faust' Symphony. **Of Men And Music** was directed by Irving Reis and Alex Hammid, written by Liam O'Brien, Harry Kurnitz, John Paxton and David Epstein, featured Deems Taylor in an introductory segment, and was produced by Rudolph Polk and Bernard Luber.
▽

Call Me Mister (20th Century-Fox) reunited its
dance director Busby Berkeley with its director
Lloyd Bacon for the first time since *42nd Street*
(Warner Bros. 1933), and once again teamed
Betty Grable with Dan Dailey. Not a great deal
(three songs, to be precise) of Harold Rome's
1946 Broadway revue remained in the updated
screen version of it (its new setting was Japan at
the time of the Korean war) and Albert E. Lewin
and Burt Styler's screenplay, based on Rome and
Arnold M. Auerbach's original book, was no
masterpiece. Yet Grable, as an entertainer with
the Civilian Actress Technician Service in Japan,
and Dailey as her GI husband from whom she
has been separated, were in fine form throughout. Storyline had Dailey (right) forging an
assignment paper in order to stage an army
camp show in the hope of winning Grable
(centre) back. They both displayed their respective musical wares on several enjoyable occasions, Grable dominating the scene in an excellent Mack Gordon-Sammy Fain number called
'Japanese Girl Like American Boy'. Other highlights were her and Dailey's dancing of the title
number (by Harold Rome), co-star Danny
Thomas's delightful 'Lament To The Pots And
Pans', written especially for him by Jerry Seelen
and Earl K. Brent, and an energetic dance
routine by a trio of male dancers called The
Dunhills. Apart from 'Love Is Back In Business'
(by Gordon and Fain), an over-elaborate finale,
all the routines were modestly and effectively
staged. Dale Robertson (left), Benay Venuta,
Richard Boone, Jeffrey Hunter and Frank Fontaine were also cast, and it was produced (in
Technicolor) by Fred Kohlmar. Other songs and
musical numbers: *Going Home Train*; *Military
Life* Rome; *I Just Can't Do Enough For You Baby*
Gordon, Fain; *I'm Gonna Love That Guy* Frances
Ash. Bobby Short made an unbilled appearance.

The title of Warner Bros.' **Lullaby Of Broadway**
came, of course, from the Al Dubin-Harry
Warren song indelibly associated with Busby
Berkeley's masterful production number in the
same studio's *Gold Diggers Of 1935*, a sequence
whose memory nothing in the new film could
eclipse. The Earl Baldwin story and screenplay
involved a musical comedy star (Doris Day) who
arrives in New York from London believing that
her mother (Gladys George), now a drunken
singer in a sleazy Greenwich Village nightclub,
is still the Broadway hit she once was. The truth
is kept from Doris by Billy De Wolfe and Anne
Triola, as a song-and-dance team working temporarily as servants for a lovable millionaire
(played by S.Z. Sakall — who else?), until
complications arise with the millionaire's wife
(Florence Bates). The songs, with a couple of
exceptions, were no less familiar than the plot,
but infinitely more welcome. Unfortunately,
LeRoy Prinz, who staged the dance numbers,
could not match Berkeley's delirious invention.
Gene Nelson (illustrated) played the romantic
lead, and the film, produced in gorgeous Techni-
color by William Jacobs, was competently dir-
ected by Roy Del Ruth. Songs and musical
numbers included: *Lullaby Of Broadway*; *You're
Getting To Be A Habit With Me* Al Dubin, Harry
Warren; *Just One Of Those Things* Cole Porter;
Somebody Loves Me George Gershwin, Buddy De
Sylva, Ballard MacDonald; *I Love The Way You
Say Goodnight* Eddie Pola, George Wyle; *Please
Don't Talk About Me When I'm Gone* Sam Stept,
Sidney Clare; *In A Shanty In Old Shanty Town*
Little Jack Little, John Siras, Joe Young; *Zing
Went The Strings Of My Heart* James Hanley.

Though Betty Grable topped the bill in **Meet Me
After The Show** (20th Century-Fox), the real star
was its choreographer, Jack Cole, whose lively
production numbers went some considerable
distance to lend enchantment to an otherwise
arid story about a musical comedy star (Grable,
illustrated centre) and the bickering relationship
she shares with her producer husband (Mac-
Donald Carey). After seven years of marriage the
couple have a serious fall-out, at which point in
the plot (by Erna Lazarus and W. Scott Darling,
screenplay by Mary Loos and director Richard
Sale), Eddie Albert (as a singer) and Rory Calhoun (as a beachcomber), admirers of Miss
Grable, decide to try their chances with her. The
production numbers included 'It's A Hot Night
In Alaska', 'No Talent Joe' and 'I Feel Like
Dancing' (in which co-choreographer Gwen
Verdon also appeared); while the best of an
indifferent batch of Jule Styne-Leo Robin songs
was Grable's 'Bettin' On A Man'. It was produced (in Technicolor) by George Jessel, whose
cast also included Fred Clark, Irene Ryan and
Lois Andrews. Other songs and musical numbers: *Meet Me After The Show*; *Let Go Of My Heart*.

It seemed, at one point, that producer Arthur
Freed would never get MGM's **Royal Wedding**
(GB: **Wedding Bells**) off the ground. Ten days
into shooting, leading lady June Allyson discovered she was pregnant and in the time it took
to find a replacement (Judy Garland), director
Charles Walters moved on to another project.
Garland, however, soon began to behave in her
characteristically unprofessional manner and
was fired. Freed then learned of the availability
of Jane Powell (hitherto the property of producers Joe Pasternak and Jack Cummings) and
decided to give her a chance in what turned out
to be her most prestigious musical to date, and
the one in which she finally came of age. Never
before had she worked so hard or so well, and
her performance as part of a brother and sister
act who travel to London to take part in the
festivities leading up to Princess Elizabeth's
wedding to Philip Mountbatten, was a revelation. Her brother was none other than Fred
Astaire and, while in London, they both fall in
love: he with a music hall dancer (Sarah
Churchill – the role was originally offered to
Moira Shearer who was unavailable); she with a
handsome English lord (Peter Lawford). The
ending had both couples marrying on the same
day as the Princess. Keenan Wynn was featured
in a dual role as twin brothers, with other parts
going to Albert Sharpe, Viola Roache, Henri
Letondal, James Finlayson and Mae Clarke. Stanley Donen made his solo directorial debut with
this one, and it was a first, too, for Alan Jay
Lerner who contributed the serviceable screenplay. The patter, however, was of tertiary importance to the singing and the dancing, and with
an engaging score by Lerner and Burton Lane,
choreography by Nick Castle and orchestrations
by Conrad Salinger and Skip Martin, the musical
side of Freed's production never faltered. Highlights were Astaire's 'Sunday Jumps' number
performed with a hat-stand; the celebrated
'You're All The World To Me' whose melody was
first heard as 'I Want To Be A Minstrel Man' in
Goldwyn's *Kid Millions* (1934) and in which he
dances on the walls and ceiling of a hotel room
(illustrated); as well as the rough-and-ready
duet he did with Powell called 'How Could You
Believe Me When I Said I Love You When You
Know I've Been A Liar All My Life?', and
Powell's touching rendition of 'Too Late Now',
which became a huge hit. An exhilarating
Technicolor entertainment. Other songs and
musical numbers: *Ev'ry Night At Seven*; *Open
Your Eyes*; *The Happiest Day Of My Life*; *I Left My
Hat In Haiti*; *What A Lovely Day For A Wedding*.

Ten specialty acts and a handful of songs were ▷ the main features of **Casa Mañana**, a programmer from Monogram whose skeletal story involved a triangle situation between a would-be singer (Virginia Welles, illustrated), a nightclub owner (Robert Clarke) who wants to make her the star of his new club, and Robert Karns, Clarke's rival in love. Tony Roux, Carol Brewster, Paul Mazey and Jean Richey also had parts in Bill Raynor's nondescript screenplay, with the Rio Bros, Eddie Le Baron and His Orchestra (illustrated), Spade Cooley, Yadira Jiminez, Zaree and Dolores, The Mercer Brothers, Armande and Lita, Betty and Beverley, Olga Perez, and Davis and Johnson roped in for support. Jean Yarbrough directed and it was produced by Lindsley Parsons. Songs and musical numbers included: *Bounce* Olsen and Johnson, Ray Evans, Jay Livingston; *People Like You* Otis Bigelow, Harold Cooke; *I Hear A Rhapsody* Jack Baker, George Fragos, Dick Gasparre; *Fifty Games Of Solitaire On Saturday Night* Ruth and Louis Herscher.

△

Mario Lanza (illustrated) received top billing in the third and most successful film of his erratic career, **The Great Caruso** (MGM). A heavyweight entry in every respect – from Lanza's own (220 lbs) to the box-office gross ($4,500,000), it was the high-water mark of producer Joe Pasternak's career, and the most successful 'long-haired' entertainment ever to emerge from Hollywood. As an authentic biopic of the life of the celebrated Italian tenor Enrico Caruso, it owed more to the imaginations of scenarists Sonya Levien and William Ludwig than it did to truth, and fluctuated between total fiction and gross distortion, even giving Caruso one wife instead of two. Little more than a series of clichés, the film sketched in some obligatory early struggles in which Caruso is seen to be a Neapolitan café singer (cue for 'Mattinata'), then quickly went on to record his triumphs in the opera houses of the world (especially New York's Metropolitan), his marriage, his illness, and his death (during a performance of Flotow's *Martha*). It was all over in 109 minutes that were mainly devoted to the music most closely associated with Caruso's career. In addition to the numerous operatic extracts (staged by the Metropolitan's Peter Herman Adler), a popular hit emerged in 'The Loveliest Night Of The Year', adapted by Irving Aaronson from 'Over The Waves' by Juventino Rosas, and with a new lyric by Paul Francis Webster. Ann Blyth received second billing as Dorothy Benjamin, Caruso's wealthy socialite wife, with other roles going to sopranos Dorothy Kirsten and Jarmila Novotna, Richard Hageman, Carl Benton Reid, Eduard Franz, Ludwig Donath and Alan Napier. There was additional operatic participation by Blanche Thebom, Teresa Celli, Nicola Moscona, Giuseppe Valdengo, Lucine Amara and Marina Koshetz. Directed by Richard Thorpe, it was 40 carat corn, and quite irresistible. The musical supervision and the background score were by Johnny Green. Other operatic extracts and songs: *Vesti La Giubba* (from 'Pagliacci') Leoncavallo; *The Last Rose Of Summer* Thomas Moore, Richard Alfred Milliken; *M'Appari* (from 'Martha') Flotow; *Celeste Aida*; *Numi Pieta*; *O Terra Addio* (from 'Aida') Verdi; *The Sextet* (from 'Lucia Di Lammermoor') Donizetti; *La Donna E Mobile* (from 'Rigoletto') Verdi; *Che Gelida Manina* (from 'La Bohème') Puccini; *E Lucevan Le Stelle* (from 'Tosca') Puccini; *Ave Maria* Bach-Gounod; *Because* Teschemacher, Guy d'Hardelot; *Sweethearts* Victor Herbert, Robert B. Smith.

△

Technicolor added an important dimension to the third screen version of Jerome Kern and Oscar Hammerstein II's **Show Boat** (MGM), previous versions being the bowdlerized Universal offering in 1929, and the same studio's glowing remake of it in 1936. Arthur Freed's production at MGM (see illustration) was less faithful to the original stage show than the middle version, and scenarist John Lee Mahin tidied up the ending by keeping the storyline in the 19th century, and eliminating all references to Magnolia's success as an actress. In Mahin's treatment of the story, Kim, the daughter of Magnolia and Ravenal, remains a child, whereas in Hammerstein's original libretto and in the 1936 screen version, she follows in her mother's footsteps and becomes a Broadway star. As the ending of **Show Boat** (from the novel by Edna Ferber) has never really been satisfactorily resolved, Freed and Mahin can be forgiven for their interference. What their version lacked in narrative weight, it more than compensated for in the neatness of its structure. From its jaunty opening scenes aboard *The Cotton Blossom*, to its tearful finale, MGM's multi-million dollar production unfurled with all the gloss and expertise audiences had come to expect from the studio. Kathryn Grayson, top billed as Magnolia sang better than she acted; Ava Gardner (vocals dubbed by Eileen Wilson) was second-billed as the mulatto Julie and, although beautiful to look at and certainly very moving in the role, could not match the performance in the same part given by Helen Morgan in the 1936 film. Howard Keel played Ravenal, Joe E. Brown Cap'n Andy, Robert Sterling was Steve, William Warfield Joe, Agnes Moorehead Parthenia Hawks and, lending unbridled zest to it all, Marge and Gower Champion as Ellie and Frank. Their two big dances, 'I Might Fall Back On You' and 'Life Upon The Wicked Stage', choreographed by Robert Alton, were both winners. The solid, workmanlike direction was by George Sidney, with Adolph Deutsch in charge of the musical direction. Other songs and musical numbers: *Cotton Blossom* (chorus); *Buck and Wing Dance* (Champions); *Where's The Mate For Me?* (Keel); *Make Believe* (Keel, Grayson); *Can't Help Lovin' Dat Man* (Gardner, reprised Grayson, Gardner); *Mis'ry's Comin' Around* (chorus); *Ol' Man River* (Warfield, chorus); *You Are Love* (Grayson, Keel); *Why Do I Love You?* (Grayson, Keel); *Bill* (Gardner) lyrics P.G. Wodehouse; *After The Ball* (Grayson) by Charles K. Harris.

Jane Powell (2nd right) starred in **Rich Young And Pretty** (MGM), a handsomely packaged (in Technicolor) feather-light *bon-bon* which introduced Vic Damone (2nd left) and Fernando Lamas (left) to moviegoers, and also saw the return to Hollywood of Danielle Darrieux (right). It was all about a lass from Texas (Powell) who, while visiting Paris with her rancher father (Wendell Corey), meets the man of her dreams (Damone) as well as her mother (Darrieux), a lady of independent spirit who deserted her husband many years before for a sophisticated life in Europe. Several attractive songs by Nicholas Brodszky and Sammy Cahn were appliquéd on to Dorothy Cooper and Sidney Sheldon's screenplay (story by Miss Cooper), the catchiest being 'We Never Talk Much' delightfully sung by Miss Darrieux and Mr Lamas (her beau), and later reprised by Powell and Damone who, together with The Four Freshmen, acquitted themselves well in 'How Do You Like Your Eggs In The Morning?'; while from Miss Darrieux there was a sexy rendition of 'There's Danger In Your Eyes, Chérie' (by Jack Meskill and Pete Wendling). The dances were staged by Nick Castle, it was produced by Joe Pasternak with a cast that included Marcel Dalio, Una Merkel, Richard Anderson, Jean Murat and Hans Conried, and directed by Norman Taurog. Other musical numbers: *Wonder Why; Dark Is The Night; Paris; L'Amour Toujour, Tonight For Sure; I Can See You* Brodszky, Cahn; *The Old Piano Roll Blues* Cy Coben; *Deep In The Heart Of Texas* June Hershey, Don Swander.
▽

If Bud Abbott (right) and Lou Costello (centre) were an acquired taste, only the most undemanding of tots was likely to acquire it from **Jack And The Beanstalk**, Warner Bros'. musical fantasy which began in black and white and reverted to Super Cinecolor *á la The Wizard Of Oz* (MGM, 1939), when Costello dreams himself into a fairy-tale world where he is pitted against the giant, played by ex-prizefighter Buddy Baer. Jean Yarbrough directed the Nat Curtis screenplay (from a treatment by Pat Costello) with an impossibly heavy hand, and Alex Gottlieb produced. Also featured were Dorothy Ford (left), Barbara Brown, David Stollery, Patrick the Harp, and James Alexander and Shaye Cogan as the romantic leads. Songs and musical numbers: *He Never Looked Better In His Life; I Fear Nothing; Darlene; Dreamer's Cloth* Lester Lee, Bob Russell.

Twenty-eight disc jockeys, as well as Ginny Simms (centre right), Michael O'Shea, Tom Drake (left), Jane Nigh (right), Russ Morgan (centre left), Lenny Kent, Tommy Dorsey, George Shearing, Nick Lucas, Herb Jeffries, Sarah Vaughan, The Weavers, Jerome Cowan, Foy Willing and The Riders Of The Purple Sage, Red Nichols, Red Norvo, Ben Pollack, Joe Venuti and Jack Fina appeared in **Disc Jockey** (Allied Artists). As each made his presence felt, there was very little room left for plot – and what there was of it concerned the efforts of disc jockey radio promoter O'Shea to make a star out of an unknown singer (Ginny Simms) through recordings and the help of disc jockeys. Clark E. Reynolds thought it all up, Maurice Duke produced, and the direction was by Will Jason. Songs and musical numbers included: *Let's Meander Through The Meadow; Show Me You Love Me* S. Steuben, Roz Gordon; *Nobody Wants Me; After Hours* Gordon; *Disc Jockey; In My Heart* Herb Jeffries, Dick Hazard; *Peaceful Country; Riders Of The Purple Sage* Foy Willing; *Brain Wave* George Shearing; *Oh Look At Me Now* John De Vries, Joe Bushkin; *The Roving Kind* Jessie Cavanaugh, Arnold Stanton.
▽

△

On Moonlight Bay (Warner Bros.), written by Jack Rose and Melville Shavelson from some of Booth Tarkington's evergreen Penrod stories, starred Doris Day as the-girl-next-door who woos and eventually marries boy-next-door Gordon MacRae (illustrated centre with Day); with Leon Ames, Rosemary De Camp and Mary Wickes in support. Apart from 'Love Ya' by Charles Tobias and Peter De Rose sung by Doris, and third-billed Jack Smith, (illustrated right), the songs were all standards culled from the period in which the film was set. Roy Del Ruth directed the William Jacobs Technicolor production and LeRoy Prinz choreographed. Songs and musical numbers: *Moonlight Bay* Percy Wenrich, Edward Madden; *Till We Meet Again* Ray Egan, Richard Whiting; *Pack Up Your Troubles* Felix Powell, George Asaf; *Cuddle Up A Little Closer; Every Little Movement Has A Meaning All Its Own* Otto Harbach, Karl Hoschna; *I'm Forever Blowing Bubbles* Jaan Kenbrovin, John W. Kellette; *Christmas Story* Pauline Walsh; *Tell Me* J. Will Callahan, Max Kortlander.

The highlight of **Excuse My Dust** (MGM), a Technicolorful, Gay Nineties romp in which Red Skelton (left) starred as an automobile inventor, was a cross-country auto race in the best Keystone tradition. But it took a long time coming, and most of the film's running time was devoted to Skelton's unpopular tinkering with his assorted gadgets to the annoyance of the neighbours in general and the father of his sweetheart (a livery stable man) in particular. Sally Forrest was Skelton's pretty inamorata and together they sang 'Spring Is Sprung', one of the better bits of musical embroidery (by Arthur Schwartz and Dorothy Fields, who composed the rest of the score as well). William Demarest played Forrest's ill-tempered father, with Monica Lewis, MacDonald Carey, Raymond Walburn (right), Jane Darwell (centre), Lillian Bronson, Guy Anderson and Paul Harvey completing the cast for producer Jack Cummings. The broad direction was by Roy Rowland and the dances were staged by Hermes Pan. Sally Forrest's vocals were dubbed by Gloria Grey. Other songs and musical numbers: *Lorelei Brown; Get A Horse; That's For Children; I'd Like To Take You Out Dreaming; Going Steady.*
▽

In **Comin' Round The Mountain** (Universal International), Bud Abbott (standing centre left) and Lou Costello (standing right) found themselves searching for hidden treasure, while their scriptwriters Robert Lees and Frederick I. Rinaldo searched for a few fresh ideas and the audiences for their promised share of laughs. Messrs A. and C. found Fort Knox; but there was only dross for the paying customers. A running gag about a love potion soon ran itself into them thar Kentucky hills, and a lot of unentertaining feudin', fussin' and fightin' between the McCoys and the Winfields seemed to dominate the action. Dorothy Shay (2nd right) as a singing Park Avenue hillbilly provided muscial accompaniment throughout, with Kirby Grant, Joe Sawyer (standing left), Glenn Strange, Ida Moore (centre) and Shaye Cogan completing the cast. Howard Christie produced and the director was Charles Lamont. Songs included: *You Broke Your Promise* George Wyle, Irving Taylor, Eddie Pola; *Agnes Clung* Hessie Smith, Dorothy Shay; *Why Don't Someone Marry Mary Ann?* Wilbur Beatty, Britt Wood; *Sagebrush Sadie* Britt Wood.
▽

A melodrama with a musical accompaniment, **The Strip**, produced in black and white by Joe Pasternak, was a low-budget entry from MGM that starred Mickey Rooney as a drummer discharged from the army who arrives in Hollywood where he falls in with bookie James Craig. He meets a dancer-cum-cigarette girl (Sally Forrest), and introduces her to Craig who shows a decided interest in her. Rooney is beaten up, the bookie killed and Forrest fatally wounded. Written by Allen Rivkin, and told largely in flashback, the film relied heavily on its musical interludes to lighten the gloom, and these were supplied by Louis Armstrong, Jack Teagarden, Earl 'Fatha' Hines, Barney Bigard, and guest stars Vic Damone, who sang 'Don't Blame Me' (by Dorothy Fields and Jimmy McHugh) and Monica Lewis, who sang 'La Bota' (by Haven Gillespie II and Charles Wolcott). Rooney banged the drums on several occasions (see illustration), Miss Forrest danced, and the hit song, reprised a number of times, was 'Give Me A Kiss To Build A Dream On' by Bert Kalmar, Harry Ruby and Oscar Hammerstein II (composed in 1935). The dances were staged by Nick Castle, it was directed by Leslie Kardos, and the cast was completed by William Demarest as a nightclub owner, Kay Brown, Tommy Rettig, Tom Powers, Jonathan Cott and Tommy Farrell. Other musical numbers: *Basin Street Blues* (Armstrong, Teagarden) Spencer Williams; *Shadrack* (Armstrong) Robert MacGimsey; *Rose Room* (Armstrong) Harry Williams, Art Hickman; *Ain't Misbehavin'* (Rooney, Armstrong) Andy Razaf, Fats Waller.

Considering television's threat to the industry in the early 50s, it received a surprising 'plug' in **Sunny Side Of The Street** (Columbia), a mediocre vehicle (in Super Cinecolor) for Frankie Laine and Billy Daniels (illustrated), whose plot (by Harold Conrad, screenplay by Lee Loeb) was basically concerned with would-be singer Jerome Courtland's attempt to break into TV via a former sweetheart (Audrey Long) – to the chagrin of his present lady (Terry Moore). About as substantial as a commercial, it was directed by Richard Quine, produced by Jonie Taps, and featured, in support, Toni Arden, Dick Wesson, William Tracy and, in a small part, Lynn Bari. Songs and musical numbers included: *On The Sunny Side Of The Street* Dorothy Fields, Jimmy McHugh; *I'm Gonna Live Till I Die* Al Hoffman, Mann Curtis, Walter Kent; *I May Be Wrong But I Think You're Wonderful* Harry Ruskin, Henry Sullivan; *Let's Fall In Love* Ted Koehler, Harold Arlen; *I Get A Kick Out Of You* Cole Porter.

A light-hearted, thoroughly engaging entertainment from the pens of Virginia Van Upp, Liam O'Brien and Myles Connolly (story by O'Brien and Robert Riskin), **Here Comes The Groom** (Paramount) was also the perfect vehicle for both its star (Bing Crosby) and its producer-director (Frank Capra). The tale of an easy-going roving reporter (Crosby, centre in suit) who adopts a couple of French orphans and is given five days either to find a wife for himself or give up the two children, it co-starred Jane Wyman as the woman he decides on, and Franchot Tone as the Boston millionaire she is just about to marry. Tone may be wealthy, but Crosby is rich in charm – and it's no surprise when, in the end, he gets the girl of his choice. Alexis Smith, James Barton, Connie Gilchrist, Robert Keith, Jacques Gencel, Walter Catlett and Beverly Washburn were also in it; so were Anna Maria Alberghetti, who sang 'Caro Nome' from Verdi's *Rigoletto*, and Dorothy Lamour, Phil Harris, Louis Armstrong and Cass Daley (centre right) who joined Crosby in a number called 'Misto Cristofo Columbo' (by Jay Livingston and Ray Evans). But the hit number was 'In The Cool Cool Cool Of The Evening', by Johnny Mercer and Hoagy Carmichael. The dances were staged by Charles O'Curran. Other songs: *Bonne Nuit*; *Your Own Little House* Livingston, Evans.

Walt Disney's full-length animated cartoon version of RKO's **Alice In Wonderland** (illustrated) was more Disney than Lewis Carroll, its original creator. Though full of clever little touches, and not without entire sequences that worked extremely well (such as 'The Mad Hatter's Tea Party' and 'The Caucus Race') the film, which also borrowed heavily from *Alice Through The Looking Glass*, lacked the surreal and satiric qualities of the book and, visually, as was to be expected, bore no relation to the famous Tenniel illustrations that accompanied the first edition of the text. Still, there was much to enjoy, not least of which were the songs and the delicious characterizations of The Mad Hatter, The March Hare and The Cheshire Cat as interpreted (vocally) by Ed Wynn, Jerry Colonna, and Sterling Holloway. Other voices: Kathryn Beaumont as a very English Alice, Pat O'Malley as The Walrus, The Carpenter and Tweedledum and Tweedledee, Bill Thompson as The White Rabbit and Dodo, Richard Haydn as The Caterpillar, and Verna Felton as The Queen of Hearts. The production supervisor was Ben Sharpsteen and the directors Clyde Geronimi, Hamilton Luske and Wilfred Jackson. It was photographed in Technicolor. Songs included: *Very Good Advice*; *In A World Of My Own*; *All In A Golden Afternoon*; *Alice In Wonderland*; *The Walrus And The Carpenter*; *The Caucus Race*; *I'm Late*; *Painting The Roses Red*; *March Of The Cards* Bob Hilliard, Sammy Fain.

Written by Sid Silvers and Hal Kanter from a story by Sammy Cahn, **Two Tickets To Broadway** (RKO) was the one about a group of hopefuls and their bid for the big-time – except that, contrary to the title, what they have their eyes on is TV. So much for the scenarists' nod in the direction of topicality. Yet, despite an almost absurdly familiar narrative line, it was agreeably cast with Tony Martin as an unemployed tenor, Janet Leigh as his girlfriend, Eddie Bracken (on floor) as a thoroughly incompetent wheeler-dealing agent, Gloria De Haven (centre) as Bracken's singing sweetheart, and Ann Miller (right) as the dancer of the group. Other plus factors were the appearances of Joe Smith and Charles Dale as a couple of delicatessen proprietors, an acrobatic troupe called The Charlivels, seven enjoyable Jule Styne-Leo Robin tunes, and the dance direction of Busby Berkeley. Also appearing was Bob Crosby, on whose TV show agent Bracken hopes to place his enthusiastic hopefuls. Of course, he eventually succeeds. Ann Miller was terrific in a routine called 'Let The Worry Bird Worry For You' (by Styne and Robin), and from Martin there was some heavy vocalizing in the Prologue from Leoncavallo's 'Pagliacci'. He also sang two of his standards, 'There's No Tomorrow' (by Al Hoffman, Leo Corday and Leon Carr) and 'Manhattan' (by Richard Rodgers and Lorenz Hart). James V. Kern directed, and Howard Hughes received the producer's credit, though it was Jerry Wald who was in charge of the Technicolor production. Also cast: Barbara Lawrence (left), Taylor Holmes, Buddy Baer. Other songs and musical numbers: *The Closer You Are*; *Baby, You'll Never Be Sorry*; *Big Chief Hole In The Ground*; *Pelican Falls High*; *It Began In Yucatan* Styne, Robin; *Let's Make Comparisons* Crosby, Sammy Cahn.

Though Esther Williams (illustrated), playing a ▷
carnival performer who is dunked every time a
customer succeeds in hitting a target with a ball,
was billed above Red Skelton in **Texas Carnival**
(MGM), she had very little to do in producer Jack
Cummings's damp squib of a show. She swam
once (in a dream sequence) and that was more
or less it. The same applied to co-stars Howard
Keel and tap-happy Ann Miller, the latter bright-
ening up the decidedly dreary proceedings with
one characteristically exuberant solo called
'It's Dynamite' (by Harry Warren and Dorothy
Fields). For the rest it was left to Skelton to make
what he could of a mistaken identity story (by
Dorothy Kingsley and George Wells, screenplay
by Kingsley) in which he is assumed to be a
millionaire oil and cattle tycoon when, in fact,
he's nothing but a carnival bum, pitching for
Miss Williams. Lasting only 77 minutes, the film
appeared to have been the victim of some drastic
editing which might well explain why the rest of
the cast - including Keenan Wynn (as the
millionaire Skelton's mistaken for), Paula Raymond, Tom Tully and Glenn Strange, seemed
so under-employed. Also appearing: The Red
Norvo Trio, and Foy Willing and His Band. The
score was, to be euphemistic, indifferent; so was
Hermes Pan's dance direction. It was sluggishly
directed by the usually able Charles Walters.
(Technicolor). Other musical numbers included:
Whoa! Emma; *Young Folks Should Get Married*;
Carnie's Pitch Dorothy Fields, Harry Warren;
Clap Your Hands David Rose, Earl Brent; *Deep In
The Heart Of Texas* June Hershey, Don Swander.

△

Judy Canova (right), appearing for the first time
in 'glorious New Trucolor', was the star of
Honeychile (Republic), another hillbilly adventure, set in Cactus Junction, Wyoming, and all
about the efforts of a couple of music publishers
(Eddie Foy Jr, left, and Walter Catlett) to secure
the rights of a song called 'Honeychile' written
by Miss C. The lady doggedly refuses to sell –
until she needs some ready cash to free her
fiancé (Alan Hale Jr) from the clutches of a pair
of crooked bookies who have rigged a chuck-
wagon race. Claire Carleton, Karolyn Grimes,
Brad Morrow, Roy Barcroft, Leonid Kinskey and
Gus Schilling supported, the serviceable screenplay was by Jack Townley and Charles E.
Roberts, Herbert J. Yates produced and the
director was R.G. Springsteen. Songs and musical numbers: *Honeychile* Jack Elliott, Harold
Spina; *Tutti Frutti* Elliott, Ann Canova; *More
Than I Care To Remember* Ted Johnson, Matt
Terry; *Rag Mop* Johnny Lee Wills, Deacon
Anderson.

Loosely based on the life and times of Lotte
Crabtree, that popular little entertainer from
Rabbit Creek, California, **Golden Girl** (20th
Century-Fox), produced by George Jessel in
Technicolor, was first class entertainment that
starred Mitzi Gaynor (centre) as the lady in
question, Dale Robertson as handsome Tom
Richmond of Alabama (the man to whom she
loses her heart but who turns out to be a
Confederate spy); Una Merkel as her disapprov-
ing ma, James Barton as her reprobate father,
and Dennis Day as a timid admirer. The period
atmosphere (1861) was aptly caught in Lloyd
Bacon's stalwart direction and in Seymour
Felix's choreography; and the screenplay, by
Walter Bullock, Charles O'Neal and Gladys
Lehman (from a story by Albert and Arthur
Lewis and Edward Thompson) gave sufficient
idea of what theatrical life 'on the road' must
have been like during the Civil War. Lotte
Crabtree reached the peak of her career when
she played Niblo's Gardens in New York, and
one of the best scenes in the film had her singing
'Dixie' (by Daniel Decatur Emmett) to the
vehement disapproval of her booing audience
when news of the North's victory comes
through. Also cast: Raymond Walburn, Gene
Sheldon, Carmen D'Antonio, Michael Ross and
Harry Carter. Songs and musical numbers:
Carry Me Back To Old Virginny; *Oh, Dem Golden
Slippers* James A. Bland; *California Moon* George
Jessel, Sam Lerner, Joe Cooper; *Sunday Mornin'*
Eliot Daniel, Ken Darby; *Kiss Me Quick And Go
My Honey* Daniel; *Never* Daniel, Lionel Newman;
When Johnny Comes Marching Home Patrick S.
Gilmore; *Believe Me If All Those Endearing Young
Charms* Thomas Moore, Matthew Locke; *La
Donna E Mobile* (from 'Rigoletto') Verdi. ▷

Filmed in a sepia tone, **Purple Heart Diary** (GB:
No Time For Tears), produced for Columbia by
Sam Katzman, directed by Richard Quine and
starring Frances Langford (centre), was a series
of simply presented songs (performed by Langford, Ben Lessy and Tony Romano, all playing
themselves) attached to a perfunctory story
about a trio of performers in the war-torn Pacific
and the pleasure they bring to the troops –
especially an amputee (Brett King) whose feel-
ings of frustration threaten to ruin a romance he
is having with a nurse (Aline Towne). Basically
a PR job for the United Service Organisation
(the entertainment industry's establishment for
troop entertainment), it was written by William
Sackheim and also featured Warren Mills, Larry
Stewart, Joel Marston, Richard Grant and Lyle
Talbot. Songs included: *Hold Me In Your Arms*;
Hi, Fellow Tourists; *Where Are You From?* Johnny
Bradford, Barbara Hayden, Tony Romano;
Bread And Butter Woman Allan Roberts, Lester
Lee; *Tattle-Tale Eyes* John Bradford, Romano. ▷

Ezio Pinza, operatic bass turned Broadway star
(in Rodgers and Hammerstein's *South Pacific*),
made an undistinguished movie debut in **Mr
Imperium** (GB: **You Belong To My Heart**), a
stinker of such proportions that MGM decided to
release it after Pinza's second film, *Strictly
Dishonorable*. But it bombed just the same. Lana
Turner (illustrated left) received top billing in
Edwin H. Knopf's production, playing a singer
(Fran Warren dubbed for her) with a cowboy
quartet who falls in love with a European prince
(Pinza) on the Italian Riviera. The affair is
doomed as Pinza soon becomes king and is not in
a position to marry a commoner. Pinza sang
pleasantly enough, the settings were suitably
sumptuous, and Miss Turner was gorgeously
costumed by Walter Plunkett. The script (by
Knopf and Don Hartman from a play by Knopf)
and direction (by Hartman) did not bear thinking about. Also cast: Marjorie Main, Barry
Sullivan, Sir Cedric Hardwicke, Debbie Reynolds, Keenan Wynn. Songs: *My Love And My
Mule*; *Andiamo*; *Let Me Look At You* Harold Arlen,
Dorothy Fields; *You Belong To My Heart* Ray
Gilbert, Augustin Lara.
▽

Fifties Musicals

Like the Impressionist and post-Impressionist canvases from which it drew its inspiration, the superb ballet that climaxed **An American In Paris** (MGM) was full of light and movement. Nothing of its kind from Hollywood had quite possessed its class, sense of style, and chic. It began at the Beaux Arts Ball where a painter (Gene Kelly), after finding himself separated from the girl he loves (Leslie Caron), wanders, heavy-hearted, out onto a terrace, and begins a sketch with à black crayon. He tears it up. But suddenly there is a breeze and the two halves of the torn sketch come together to form a backdrop against which the artist appears. At his feet he sees a red rose. He picks it up, the black and white background bleeds into colour and the scene changes to the Place de la Concorde, with sets and costumes after Dufy. Then, as the painter sees and pursues the girl he loves, the setting becomes a flower market near La Madeleine, the mood sad but tranquil, the style and decor now paying homage to Renoir. The pastel colours of Utrillo inspire a street scene followed by a spirited George M. Cohanesque dance, this time in a Rousseau setting, performed by four Americans in Paris celebrating the Fourth of July. The. mood changes from exuberance to passion as the painter, filled with longing and regret, dances in and around a fountain in the Place de la Concorde. The scene now changes to the Paris Opera, à la Van Gogh, and after that to Lautrec's Montmartre, where the painter becomes the character of Chocolat. The final sequence sees a return to the fountain, accompanied by a frenzied eruption of music. Everyone disappears and the painter is left alone. Designed by Preston Ames, costumed by Irene Sharaff, and choreographed by Kelly, it was 18 minutes of screen magic, unsurpassed in the boldness of its design and the dazzle of its execution. It took six months to rehearse, a month to shoot, and

cost $450,000. The rest of the film was, in every way, more conventional – telling a rather trite story of an American GI-painter's love for a perfume shop assistant (Caron) and the complications that arise when a wealthy patron of the arts (Nina Foch) tries to ensnare him. The screenplay was by Alan Jay Lerner and what it lacked in originality, it compensated for in the opportunities it provided for Kelly (left), Caron (right), and co-stars Oscar Levant and Georges Guetary to interrupt the narrative with song and dance. The music was by George and Ira Gershwin, whose complete catalogue of songs producer Arthur Freed purchased from the Gershwin estate for $300,000. The best of these were 'I Got Rhythm' sung and danced by Kelly to a group of French children, and 'Tra-La-La', played on the piano (by Levant) and danced by Kelly in a Paris attic. Less successful was the rather self-consciously endearing 'By Strauss' (performed by Kelly, Guetary and Levant), and Levant's dream sequence in which he imagines himself as conductor, soloist and every member of the orchestra in the third movement of Gershwin's Concerto in F. It was a pleasing Walter Mitty-ish idea which somehow did not quite come off. Leslie Caron (making her screen debut) was enchanting, especially in her introductory dance solos to various arrangements of 'Embraceable You'. Contributing incalculably to the overall success of **An American In Paris** was director Vincente Minnelli, whose unerringly sophisticated visual sense made sure that it was always good to look at. The musical direction was by Johnny Green and Saul Chaplin. Other songs and musical numbers: *S'Wonderful* (Kelly, Guetary); *Love Is Here To Stay* (Kelly, Caron); *I'll Build A Stairway To Paradise* (Guetary) lyrics by E. Ray Goetz and Buddy De Sylva; *Nice Work If You Can Get It* (Guetary, Levant); *I Don't Think I'll Fall In Love Today* (Levant); *Liza* (Levant).

△

With a minimal plot – the romance between a Hollywood actress and an Air Force corporal – and a plethora of guest appearances, **Starlift** (Warner Bros.) was a Korean War updating of the stars-and-stripes *Hollywood Canteen* format. The title was derived from Operation Starlift, by which movie performers were flown up to Travis Air Base near San Francisco to entertain outgoing or incoming troops and, as usual, more pleasure was to be gained from spotting familiar faces – Doris Day, Gordon MacRae, Virginia Mayo (illustrated), Gene Nelson, Ruth Roman, James Cagney, Gary Cooper, Virginia Gibson, Phil Harris, Frank Lovejoy, Lucille Norman, Louella Parsons, Randolph Scott, Jane Wyman and Patrice Wymore – than from following the romantic peregrinations of the nominal leads (Janis Paige and Ron Haggerthy). It was written by John Klorer and Karl Kamb, directed by Roy Del Ruth, choreographed by LeRoy Prinz, and produced by Robert Arthur. Songs and musical numbers included: *Liza; S'Wonderful* George and Ira Gershwin; *You Do Something To Me; What Is This Thing Called Love?* Cole Porter; *It's Magic* Sammy Cahn, Jule Styne; *I May Be Wrong But I Think You're Wonderful* Harry Ruskin, Henry Sullivan; *Good Green Acres Of Home* Irving Kahal, Sammy Fain; *You Oughta Be In Pictures* Edward Heyman, Dana Suesse; *You're Gonna Lose Your Gal* Joe Young, James V. Monaco.

Painting The Clouds With Sunshine (Warner Bros.) was yet another adaptation of the Avery Hopwood *Gold Diggers* story which had inspired some of the studio's most memorable musicals in the '30s. Virginia Mayo, Lucille Norman and Virginia Gibson were three showgirls on the make in Las Vegas; Gene Nelson (illustrated), Tom Conway and Dennis Morgan the three guys who convince them that true love is worth more than tiaras; S.Z. Sakall and Wallace Ford provided the inevitable comic relief. The weak screenplay was the work of Harry Clork, Roland Kibbee and Peter Milne. LeRoy Prinz choreographed, the film was produced, in Technicolor, by William Jacobs, and directed by David Butler. Songs and musical numbers: *Painting The Clouds With Sunshine; Tip-Toe Through The Tulips* Al Dubin, Joe Burke; *Vienna Dreams* Irving Caesar, Rudolf Sieczynski; *With A Song In My Heart* Richard Rodgers, Lorenz Hart; *Birth Of The Blues* Buddy De Sylva, Lew Brown, Ray Henderson; *You're My Everything* Harry Warren, Mort Dixon; *Jealousy* Vera Bloom, Jacob Gade; *Man Is A Necessary Evil; Mambo Man* Jack Elliott, Sonny Burke.
▽

1952

△

She's Working Her Way Through College (Warner Bros.) was an adaptation of the James Thurber-Elliott Nugent stage comedy *The Male Animal* (already filmed by the studio in 1942 with Henry Fonda and Olivia de Havilland) with songs added and most of the original plot subtracted. In its new incarnation, the Peter Milne screenplay involved a burlesque star (Virginia Mayo, foreground centre) with ambitions to be a serious actress, who enrols in the drama course at a small mid-west college, and the complications that all too predictably ensue. Ronald Reagan (2nd right) played the professor who injudiciously befriends her, and Phyllis Thaxter (right) his suspicious wife. Also on the campus were Don DeFore (who played in the 1942 version), Gene Nelson (left), Patrice Wymore, Roland Winters, Raymond Greenleaf, The Blackburn Twins and Ginger Crowley. The lacklustre musical numbers were staged by LeRoy Prinz, and the film was produced (in Technicolor) by William Jacobs. Songs and musical numbers: *I'll Be Loving You; The Stuff That Dreams Are Made Of; Give 'Em What They Want; Am I In Love?; Love Is Still For Free; She's Working Her Way Through College* Sammy Cahn, Vernon Duke; *With Plenty Of Money And You* Al Dubin, Harry Warren.

Frank Sinatra starred in **Meet Danny Wilson** (Universal-International), a tuneful platitude about a saloon-room singer's rise to stardom. Alex Nicol played his pianist buddy, and Shelley Winters the gal they both fancy, with Raymond Burr as a racketeer villain who gets what's coming to him in a climactic scene in an empty, floodlit ball park. Sinatra (illustrated) showed positive signs of developing into the fine actor he later became, and his singing was, as usual, terrific. There were nine songs in all including 'A Good Man Is Hard To Find' (by Eddie Green) sung by Sinatra and Miss Winters, and such old favourites as 'I've Got A Crush On You' (by the Gershwins) and 'That Old Black Magic' (by Harold Arlen and Johnny Mercer). Don McGuire wrote it, Leonard Goldstein produced, and it was directed by Joseph Pevney. Other songs: *When You're Smiling* Mark Fisher, Joe Goodwin, Larry Shay; *All Of Me* Seymour Simons, Gerald Marks; *How Deep Is The Ocean?* Irving Berlin; *She's Funny That Way* Neil Moret, Richard Whiting; *You're A Sweetheart* Harold Adamson, Jimmy McHugh; *Lonesome Man Blues* Sy Oliver.

▽

△

There were so many special effects in **The Belle Of New York** (MGM) that it took producer Arthur Freed 24 weeks to complete. Based on the 1897 stage show of the same name (it was a mild flop in New York, but a huge hit in London where, as the first American musical to play the West End, it ran for 674 performances), Freed's version retained the show's turn of the century setting and its basic plot, but Hugh Morton's original book and lyrics were entirely ditched, as was Gustav Kerker's score. Instead Freed commissioned Johnny Mercer and Harry Warren to provide the words and music, and Robert O'Brien and Irving Ellinson to script it (from an adaptation by Chester Erskine). For the lead role of the playboy who, to date, has left five brides stranded at the altar, Freed cast Fred Astaire (illustrated) who, six years earlier, had declined the part, with Vera-Ellen co-starring as the straitlaced Salvation Army lass he finally settles for. Marjorie Main was Astaire's equally straitlaced Aunt on whom he depends for his income. The rest of the cast was completed by Keenan Wynn, Alice Pearce, Clinton Sundberg, Gale Robbins, and Lisa Ferraday. The meagre plot was augmented by nine songs, one of which literally had Astaire dancing solo in the clouds to the tune of 'Seeing's Believing'. Best song, though, was 'Baby Doll' sung and danced by Vera-Ellen and Astaire, and the only number in the score to make it into the pop charts. Pleasing, too, was 'Thank You Mr Currier, Thank You Mr Ives' ('The Bride's Wedding Song') in which Vera-Ellen, against backdrops inspired by Currier and Ives prints, imagines herself dancing through the four seasons with Astaire. The first-class choreography was by Robert Alton, the gorgeous settings by Cedric Gibbons and Jack Martin Smith, and the costumes by Helen Rose. Charles Walters's direction had the lush MGM 'feel' to it, and it was photographed in Technicolor. Other songs and musical numbers: *When I'm Out With The Belle Of New York; Bachelor's Dinner Song; Oops; Naughty But Nice; I Wanna Be A Dancin' Man* Mercer, Warren; *Let A Little Love Come In* Roger Edens.

Fifties Musicals

Singin' In The Rain (MGM) was the story of a matinée idol called Don Lockwood (Gene Kelly) and his romance with chorus girl Kathy Selden (Debbie Reynolds). One of the best, and best written story-lines (by Betty Comden and Adolph Green) to grace a Hollywood musical, it was the perfect subject on which to hang the Arthur Freed-Nacio Herb Brown songs that accompanied it, and a marvellous opportunity to take a light-hearted and often satirical look at the early days of talking pictures. With the exception of two numbers – 'Fit As A Fiddle' (by Freed, Al Hoffman and Al Goodhart) and 'Moses Supposes' (the latter written especially for the film by Roger Edens, Comden and Green) – all the Freed-Brown numbers featured in **Singin' In The Rain** were from earlier MGM movies: 'All I Do Is Dream Of You' sung by Debbie Reynolds (after popping out of an enormous cake at a typical Hollywood party) was first heard in *Sadie McKee* (1934); 'Should I?' was featured in *Lord Byron Of Broadway* (1929); 'Singin' In The Rain' came from *Hollywood Revue Of 1929*; 'I've Got A Feelin' You're Foolin', 'You Are My Lucky Star' and 'Broadway Rhythm', all from *Broadway Melody Of 1936* (1935); 'The Wedding Of The Painted Doll' from *Broadway Melody* (1929); 'You Were Meant For Me' from *Broadway Melody* (1929); 'Would You' from *San Francisco* (1936); 'Good Morning' from *Babes In Arms* (1939), 'Beautiful Girl' (sung here with flair by Jimmy Thompson) from *Going Hollywood* (1933), and 'Broadway Melody' from *Broadway Melody* (1929). Just as most of its music had featured prominently in past films, so everything else in **Singin' In The Rain** drew its inspiration from the movies. In fact most of the film was a compendium of borrowings drawn from a variety of real-life sources and personalities. The scene on the sound stage, for example, with dumb blonde Jean Hagen, in a *tour-de-force* performance, desperately trying to 'speak into the bush' where the microphone has been hidden, had its origins in reality. Douglas Shearer, head of MGM's sound department, was consulted regularly about the hazards of early sound recording, and most of the tribulations suffered by the artists and technicians in **Singin' In The Rain's** reconstruction of those times, actually happened. Roscoe Dexter (Douglas Fowley) the director in that particular scene, was modelled on Busby Berkeley, while R.F. Simpson, the studio boss (Millard Mitchell), was inspired by producer Arthur Freed, Dora Bailey the columnist (played by Madge Blake) was modelled on Louella Parsons, Kelly himself on a composite of several matinée idols (particularly Fairbanks, in the 'Duelling Cavalier' sequences) and Cyd Charisse, in the 'Broadway Ballet', on Louise Brooks. Musically, the ballet, choreographed by Kelly, was the film's most ambitious sequence, also drawing its inspiration from the movies. Entirely new, however, was what Kelly calls the 'Crazy Veil' sequence in which Cyd Charisse danced with a soft piece of voile, and which required the use of three aeroplane motors to control the veil's movement. Choreographically, it was Kelly at his most lyrical, and a highspot in a film crowded with them. In fact, **Singin' In The Rain**, directed and choreographed by Kelly and Stanley Donen, remains an undoubted masterpiece and the finest, most durable musical ever to have come out of Hollywood. If the test of a great musical is that you can see it over and over again without longing for the dialogue to end and the musical numbers to begin, then **Singin' In The Rain** passes *cum laude*. And it is more popular in today's nostalgia-addicted world than it was on its initial release. But even to those not seduced by nostalgia, it remains an invigorating musical, perfect in its reconstruction of a world gone forever, and unforgettable if only for Kelly's joyous dancing in the title number as he abandons himself to a Californian cloudburst, kicks and stamps in a gutterful of water, and climbs halfway up a lamp-post, arms outstretched, and water pouring onto his face, defying adversity. The number, an 'irrepressible ode to optimism' as it has been described by Comden and Green, was the apotheosis of his art, and the climax of an adventurous career. Though the rest of the film never quite equalled the magic of those five glorious minutes, every other number was still head and shoulders above most of the musicals of the fifties. Donald O'Connor has never been as good again, most notably in his justly celebrated 'Make 'Em Laugh' routine, in which he danced, sang, and clowned as if his artistic life depended on the success of it. Every trick in his repertoire was aired afresh and the cumulative effect was devastating in its virtuosity. As for Debbie Reynolds, her dancing in the buoyant 'Good Morning' never for an instant betrayed her lack of experience, and she was a most sympathetic partner for Kelly in the lyrical 'You Were Meant For Me' into which Kelly attempted to inject the perfect romantic atmosphere on a sound stage through the auspices of five hundred kilowatts of stardust and a soft, summer breeze. It was the third time he had used this 'make-believe' device – first with Kathryn Grayson in *Anchors Aweigh* (MGM, 1945), and next in *Summer Stock* (MGM, 1950) where he wooed Judy Garland. The producer was Arthur Freed, Harold Rosson photographed it (in Technicolor), Cedric Gibbons and Randall Duell were the art directors, Walter Plunkett created the costumes, Lennie Hayton was the musical director; Conrad Salinger, Wally Heglin and Skip Martin orchestrated the numbers, and the cast was completed by Rita Moreno, King Donovan, Kathleen Freeman and Mae Clarke. Illustrations: Kelly dances the title number; Inset: Kelly dancing with Cyd Charisse.

△

The life and lyrics of Gus Kahn were the inspiration for Warner Bros.' **I'll See You In My Dreams** which, though it followed the well-trodden path of a hundred other such movie biographies wherein hard-won success in Tin Pan Alley and marital difficulties at home were the underlying factors in the plot, was sensitively directed by Michael Curtiz from a skilful screenplay by Melville Shavelson and Jack Rose, and proved to be a well-deserved box-office hit. Danny Thomas (illustrated), making a bid for the movie stardom that had always eluded him, played Gus, Doris Day (illustrated) was his wife Grace, while Frank Lovejoy, Patrice Wymore, James Gleason, Mary Wickes, Jim Backus and Minna Gombell excelled in support. Louis F. Edelman produced, and the dance director was LeRoy Prinz. Songs and musical numbers – all by Kahn, co-composers listed – included: *Ain't We Got Fun*; *Ukelele Lady* Richard Whiting, Ray Egan; *The One I Love Belongs To Somebody Else*; *I'll See You In My Dreams*; *It Had To Be You*; *Swingin' Down The Lane* Isham Jones; *Makin' Whoopee*; *Yes, Sir, That's My Baby*; *Carolina In The Morning*; *Love Me Or Leave Me* Walter Donaldson; *Pretty Baby* Egbert Van Alstyne, Tony Jackson; *Memories* Van Alstyne; *Nobody's Sweetheart* Ernie Erdman, Billy Meyers, Elmer Schoebel; *My Buddy* Donaldson; *Toot Toot Tootsie* Erdman, Dan Russo; *No, No, Nora* Erdman, Ted Fiorito; *Your Eyes Have Told Me So* Van Alstyne, Walter Blaufuss; *I Wish I Had A Girl* Grace LeBoy Kahn; *San Francisco* Bronislau Kaper; *I Never Knew* Fiorito; *The Carioca* Edward Eliscu, Vincent Youmans; *I'm Through With Love* Fud Livingston, Matt Malneck; *Liza* George and Ira Gershwin; *Shine On Harvest Moon* Jack Norworth, Nora Bayes (not a Kahn composition).

△

Based on a hoary old 1919 play by Walter B. Hare, and brought to the screen in Technicolor, with a scenario by Claude Binyon, Paramount's **Aaron Slick From Punkin Crick** (GB: **Marshmallow Moon**) was a stultifying bore that made little attempt to lampoon the time-worn saga of the innocent country lass who almost loses her farm to a city slicker but is saved in the nick of time by a shy but determined local yokel. Dinah Shore (left) was the hapless heroine, Alan Young (right) the diffident hero, and Robert Merrill the villain. Hisses and boos all round, especially to Mr Binyon whose direction was as leaden as his screenplay. William Perlberg and George Seaton produced, Jay Livingston and Ray Evans contributed several unmemorable songs, and the supporting cast included Adele Jergens, Minerva Urecal, Martha Stewart, Fritz Feld, Veda Ann Borg and Chick Chandler. Songs: *Life Is A Beautiful Thing*; *I'd Like To Baby You*; *My Beloved*; *Marshmallow Moon*; *Why Should I Believe In Love?*; *Purt Nigh But Not Plumb* (sic); *Still Water*; *Saturday Night In Punkin Creek*; *Step Right Up*.

After the enormous success of *The Great Caruso* (MGM) the previous year, Mario Lanza took a backward step, and **Because You're Mine** (MGM), though not exactly a box-office dud, was the least successful of the oversized tenor's four films to date. The plot contrived by Ruth Brooks Flippen and Cy Gomberg, and scripted by Karl Tunberg and Leonard Spigelgass, had Lanza (illustrated) playing an opera star who is drafted into the army. Fortunately his sergeant (James Whitmore) loves classical music and, furthermore, has a sister (Doretta Morrow) who is herself an aspiring young singer. Paula Corday played a temperamental soprano jealous of Lanza's new-found *amour*, with other roles in producer Joe Pasternak's Technicolor production going to Dean Miller, Celia Lovsky, Jeff Donnell, Spring Byington and Curtis Cooksey. There were several operatic extracts in the musical programme and some new songs by an assortment of composers, plus a reprise of Nicholas Brodszky and Sammy Cahn's 'Be My Love' – sung by Miss Morrow over the telephone as part of an audition. The film was directed by Alexander Hall. Songs and operatic excerpts: *Lee-Ah-Loo* John Leeman, Ray Sinatra; *The Song Angels Sing* Paul Francis Webster, Irving Aaronson (melody adapted from 3rd movement of Brahms's Symphony No 3); *You Do Something To Me* Cole Porter; *All The Things You Are* Jerome Kern, Oscar Hammerstein II; *The Lord's Prayer* Albert Hay Malotte; *Granada* Augustin Lara; *Addio Alla Madre* (from 'Cavalleria Rusticana') Mascagni; *Addio* (from 'Rigoletto'); *Il Balen Del Suo Sorriso* and *Miserere* (from 'Il Trovatore') Verdi; *Casta Diva* (from 'Norma') Bellini; *O Paradiso* (from 'L'Africaine') Meyerbeer; *The Sextet* (from 'Lucia Di Lammermoor') Donizetti. ◁

With A Song In My Heart (20th Century-Fox), written and produced by Lamar Trotti and directed by Walter Lang, was a colourful, tear-jerking biopic of Jane Froman whose career as a popular songstress was interrupted when she was badly injured in an aeroplane crash in Lisbon in 1943. Susan Hayward (illustrated right) starred as Miss Froman (with Froman herself doing the singing) and gave one of the best performances in a musical since James Cagney unleashed his George M. Cohan onto the world in *Yankee Doodle Dandy* (Warner Bros. 1942). Starting as a modest radio singer in Cincinnati, Froman worked her way to Broadway stardom in the familiar biopic format, taking time off from vocalizing to undergo a series of operations as a result of the accident. Much of the screenplay was involved with Froman's courageous battle to survive her painful ordeal, in the process of which two men dominate her life: Don Ross (David Wayne, illustrated left), the man who helped shape her career; and John Burn (Rory Calhoun), the pilot who rescued her from the Tagus River when their plane went down. In real life Froman divorced Ross and married the pilot, but in the film she remains married to Wayne. Thelma Ritter was fourth-billed as Clancy, a hospital nurse who becomes a life-long friend of Hayward's, with Helen Westcott, Una Merkel, Richard Allan, Max Showalter, Lyle Talbot and Leif Erickson in support. Also in it, as a handsome young paratrooper with shell-shock, was Robert Wagner. For every tear shed throughout, there was an accompanying song, an American medley of old favourites sung by Hayward at an army camp being the musical highlight. Splendid, too, was Miss Froman's stirring singing of the title number (by Richard Rodgers and Horenz Hart) staged at the Roxy Theatre. The superb musical direction was by Alfred Newman, and the choreography by Billy Daniels. The many other songs and musical numbers included: *Blue Moon* Rodgers, Hart; *Tea For Two* Irving Caesar, Vincent Youmans; *That Old Feeling* Lew Brown, Sammy Fain; *I've Got A Feelin' You're Foolin'* Arthur Freed, Nacio Herb Brown; *They're Either Too Young Or Too Old* Frank Loesser, Arthur Schwartz; *It's A Good Day* Peggy Lee, Dave Barbour; *I'll Walk Alone* Sammy Cahn, Jule Styne; *I'm Thru With Love* Gus Kahn, Fud Livingston, Matt Malneck; *Embraceable You* George and Ira Gershwin; *On The Gay White Way* Ralph Rainger, Leo Robin; *Get Happy* Ted Koehler, Harold Arlen; *Jim's Toasted Peanuts*; *Wonderful Home Sweet Home* Ken Darby; American medley: *Deep In The Heart Of Texas* June Hershey, Don Swander; *Carry Me Back To Old Virginny* James Bland; *Give My Regards To Broadway* George M. Cohan; *Alabamy Bound* Bud Green, Buddy De Sylva, Al Jolson, Joseph Meyer; *Chicago* Fred Fisher; *America The Beautiful* Katherine Lee Bates, Samuel A. Ward; *Dixie* Daniel Decatur Emmett; *California Here I Come* Buddy De Sylva, Jolson, Meyer.
▽

△

Skirts Ahoy! (MGM) starred Esther Williams (centre), Joan Evans (left) and Vivian Blaine (right) as three pretty girls who decide to join the Waves. Scenarist Isobel Lennart's plot, which was red-eyed with tiredness, blearily focused on their respective amorous exploits with Barry Sullivan, Keefe Brasselle and Dean Miller. There were eight new songs by composer Harry Warren (his last score at MGM) and lyricist Ralph Blane; and one ('Oh By Jingo') by Lew Brown and Albert von Tilzer which producer Joe Pasternak dragged in at the last minute for guest stars Debbie Reynolds and Bobby Van who appeared as themselves at a naval show. None of the songs was particularly memorable, though Williams's 'What Makes A Wave?' performed together with the five De Marco Sisters; and 'What Good Is A Gal Without A Guy?' (sung by Williams, Evans and Blaine) were serviceable enough. Two swimming sequences, plus a guest appearance by Billy Eckstine (singing 'Hold Me Close To You') were other minor embellishments in an entertainment that newly defined the word routine. The dances were staged by Nick Castle and the direction was by Sidney Lanfield. Also cast: Mary Foran (seated centre), Jeff Donnell, Margalo Gillmore, Thurston Hall, Russell and Kathy Targay and Roy Roberts. (Technicolor). Other songs and musical numbers: I Get A Funny Feeling; We Will Fight; Hilda Matilda; Glad To Have You Aboard; The Navy Waltz.

Joe Pasternak's expensive Technicolor production of Franz Lehar's The Merry Widow (MGM) couldn't compare in either style or sophistication with Ernst Lubitsch's celebrated 1934 screen version for the same studio. Rewritten by Sonya Levien and William Ludwig so as not to over-tax the limited acting abilities of its star, Lana Turner (vocals by Trudy Erwin), and with Fernando Lamas in support, it emerged as little more than a far-fetched romance between a widowed American millionairess who, on returning to Marshovia, the country of her late husband's birth, meets and falls in love with the dashing Count Danilo. Gone was the sense of fun that permeated the Lubitsch film, and gone was the subtle sexual interplay between the two flirting protagonists. Instead, audiences were left with a rather coarse performance from Turner, an operetta stereotype from Lamas (who, despite the fact that it was written for the widow, sang 'Vilia'), and direction from Curtis Bernhardt that was as heavy as Lubitsch's was light. Jack Cole staged the dances ('The Can-Can' illustrated) and not once approached, in splendour or invention, the climactic 'Merry Widow' waltz from the earlier film. Una Merkel was third-billed as Turner's lady in waiting, with other roles going to Richard Haydn as Baron Popoff, Thomas Gomez as the King of Marshovia, John Abbott as the Marshovian Ambassador, Marcel Dalio as a police sergeant, King Donovan as Nitki and Robert Coote as the Marquis de Crillo. Gwen Verdon (right) was prominent among the dancers. Other musical numbers: Girls, Girls, Girls; I'm Going To Maxim's; Can-Can; Night all lyrics by Paul Francis Webster.

A remake of the Jerome Kern-Dorothy Fields musical Roberta (RKO, 1935), Lovely To Look At (MGM), produced in Technicolor by Jack Cummings, starred Kathryn Grayson, Red Skelton, Howard Keel, Marge and Gower Champion and Ann Miller. In George Wells and Harry Ruby's new adaptation of Alice Duer Miller's story (additional dialogue by Andrew Solt) Skelton played an American comedian who inherits a half interest in a Parisian dress salon. He and pals Keel and Champion travel to Paris where they discover that the salon – run by two sisters (Grayson and Marge Champion) – is almost bankrupt. So Skelton, instead of selling his share of the inheritance in order to raise finances for a Broadway show, decides to take over the running of the salon himself. Helping to flesh out the fragile story were the romances that blossomed between the leading players, Grayson pairing off with Keel, Miller with Skelton and Champion with Champion. Also cast: Zsa Zsa Gabor, Kurt Kasznar, Marcel Dalio and Diane Cassidy. If, musically, the film never quite reached the sublime heights attained in the earlier Astaire-Rogers version, it was not without its good things – notably Miss Miller's torrid 'I'll Be Hard To Handle' (see illustration), Grayson's glorious singing of the miraculous 'Smoke Gets In Your Eyes', and the Champions dancing 'I Won't Dance' (performed in a roomful of fashion dummies). The dances were staged by Hermes Pan, and it was directed by Mervyn LeRoy. Kern composed all the numbers, but with a variety of collaborators. Songs and musical numbers (lyricists listed): Yesterdays (Grayson; ballet danced by Champions); The Touch Of Your Hand (Keel, Grayson); Smoke Gets In Your Eyes (Grayson; danced by Champions) Otto Harbach; LaFayette (Keel, Gower Champion, Skelton) Dorothy Fields; Lovely To Look At (Keel, chorus) Fields, Jimmy McHugh; The Most Exciting Night (Keel); You're Devastating (Keel, Grayson) Harbach, Fields; I Won't Dance (Champions) Fields, McHugh, Harbach, Hammerstein II; I'll Be Hard To Handle (Miller) Fields, Bernard Dougall; Opening Night (chorus) Fields, McHugh (not Kern).

▽

▷

△

Although the title might have suggested a sequel to the previous year's She's Working Her Way Through College – with Virginia Mayo's stripper, her newly won Ph.D demurely concealing her charms, on the way to success in the legitimate theatre – She's Back On Broadway (Warner Bros.) bore no relation to the earlier film, being the routine account of a Hollywood star (Mayo, left) who hopes to shore up a flagging career with a big stage hit, Breakfast In Bed. Not even a strong supporting cast – Steve Cochran as the show's director, Patrice Wymore as a bitchy singer, Frank Lovejoy as a long-suffering producer, and Gene Nelson (right) – could help fill the holes created by Orin Jannings's uneven screenplay or the totally unmemorable score by Bob Hilliard and Carl Sigman. Larry Keating, Paul Picerni, Condos and Brandow, Douglas Spencer and Jacqueline de Wit were also on view, LeRoy Prinz staged the dance numbers (in the studio's new colour process, thoughtfully named WarnerColor), Gordon Douglas directed and Henry Blanke produced. Songs and musical numbers included: I'll Take You As You Are; One Step Ahead Of Everybody; The Ties That Bind; Breakfast In Bed; Behind The Mask Bob Hilliard, Carl Sigman; I Think You're Wonderful.

The original premise of April In Paris (Warner Bros.) – a chorus girl, Ethel Jackson (Doris Day), is sent on a cultural junket to Paris instead of Ethel Barrymore for whom the invitation was intended – was so puerile that the film was quite unable to survive it. A shipboard romance that developed between Day, and Ray Bolger (illustrated centre), playing a State Department official, was rendered implausible by Bolger's strenuous hamming, and apart from the title song by Vernon Duke and E.Y. Harburg, the score was undistinguished. The brightest spot in this otherwise awful David Butler-directed film was the lively staging in the ship's galley of 'I'm Gonna Ring The Bell Tonight'. The production numbers by LeRoy Prinz were numbingly forgettable, and the screenplay by Jack Rose and Melville Shavelson, with parts in it for Eve Miller, George Givot, Paul Harvey and Herbert Farjeon, thoroughly inept. Produced (in Technicolor) by William Jacobs. Songs and musical numbers: It Must Be Good; That's What Makes Paris Paree; Give Me Your Lips; I Know A Place; I Ask You Sammy Cahn, Vernon Duke.

▽

The third and least successful biopic to deal with the life of Stephen Foster (the other two being *Harmony Lane*, Mascot, 1935, and *Swanee River*, 20th Century-Fox, 1939) was Republic's Trucolor production, **I Dream Of Jeanie**. Allan LeMay's screenplay was no more accurate a reflection of how it really was than were the earlier versions, and depicted Foster (Bill Shirley – illustrated) as a thick-skulled, bookkeeping dilettante who dabbled in composition when he wasn't throwing himself at a selfish and unworthy Southern belle (Muriel Lawrence). The girl who eventually nabs him is Lawrence's more appealing sister Jeanie (Eileen Christy). There was, alas, nothing very appealing about the film in general or the performances in particular – with one notable exception: Ray Middleton as Minstrel Man E.P. Christy. Veteran Allan Dwan directed for producer Herbert J. Yates, and the dances were staged by Nick Castle. Also cast: Lynn Bari, Richard Simmons and Rex Allen. Songs included: *My Old Kentucky Home*; *Swanee River*; *Oh Susanna*; *Old Dog Tray*; *Old Folks At Home*; *Ring De Banjo*; *De Camptown Races*; *I Dream Of Jeanie With The Light Brown Hair*; *Come Where My Love Lies Dreaming* Foster.

▽

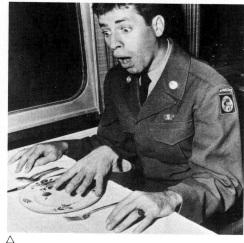

△

The Dean Martin-Jerry Lewis formula (Lewis illustrated) was successfully put to the test once again in **Jumping Jacks** (Paramount). They played a pair of cabaret entertainers who become paratroopers with amusing, if wholly predictable, results. Slight romantic interest was supplied by Mona Freeman, and Robert Strauss (who appeared with the boys in *Sailor Beware*, Paramount, 1951) was again cast as their superior, with other roles in Hal Wallis's production going to Don DeFore, Dick Erdman, Ray Teal, Marcy McGuire and Danny Arnold. Mack David and Jerry Livingston provided the score, and it was directed without restraint by Norman Taurog. Funniest moment: Lewis attempting to pack a parachute in mime. Songs and musical numbers: *Keep A Little Dream Handy*; *Do The Parachute Jump*; *I Can't Resist A Boy In Uniform*; *What Have You Done For Me Lately?*; *I Know A Dream When I See One*; *Big Blue Sky*.

Shortly after having had a growth on her vocal chords removed, Betty Hutton starred in her penultimate film, and her last for Paramount, **Somebody Loves Me**. It was a Technicolor biopic based on the lives of vaudeville headliners Blossom Seeley and her husband Benny Fields. Hutton (right)was of course, Seeley, and Ralph Meeker (left) played Fields. Starting in 1906 on San Francisco's Barbary Coast, the film sketched out Seeley's career through World War 1 (and the volunteer war work she did) to her success on Broadway. It was the usual rags-to-riches story, with the usual dosage of heartache thrown in for the furtherance of the largely fictional storyline – despite which trials and tribulations Seeley, in the person of Hutton continued to face life with a song, and sang a good many of them, including such old favourites as 'Rose Room' (by Harry Williams and Art Hickman), 'Way Down Yonder In New Orleans' (by Henry Creamer and J. Turner Layton), 'Teasing Rag' (by Joe Jordan), 'Dixie Dreams' (by Arthur Johnston, George W. Meyer, Grant Clarke and Roy Turk) and 'On San Francisco Bay' (by Vincent Bryan and Gertrude Hoffman). There were three new songs: 'Love Him', 'Thanks To You', and 'Honey Oh My Honey' by Ray Evans and Jay Livingston, the latter sung by co-star Adele Jergens (as an arrogant vaudeville star). Also cast: Robert Keith as Hutton's agent, Billie Bird as her wise-cracking confidante, and Henry Slate and Sid Tomack as her first partners, a group called The Chez Paree Adorables; also, in an unbilled appearance, Jack Benny doing one of his well-known routines. The film was choreographed by Charles O'Curran, produced by William Perlberg and directed by Irving Brecher who also wrote the screenplay. Other songs included: *Somebody Loves Me* Buddy De Sylva, George Gershwin; *Jealous* Jack Little, Tommy Malie, Dick Finch; *June Night* Cliff Friend, Abel Baer; *I Cried For You* Gus Arnheim, Arthur Freed, Abe Lyman; *I'm Sorry I Made You Cry* N.J. Clesi, Theodore Morse; *Toddling The Todalo* E. Ray Goetz, A. Baldwin Sloane; *Smiles* J. Will Callahan, Lee S. Roberts; *Wang Wang Blues* Gus Mueller, Buster Johnson, Henry Busse; *I Can't Tell You Why I Love You* Will J. Cobb, Gus Edwards.

▽

△

Although much of the material had worn badly, **Where's Charley?** (Warner Bros.), based on the George Abbott-Frank Loesser musical adaptation of Brandon Thomas's venerable farce *Charley's Aunt*, was pleasantly viewable for two reasons: the lively score, and Ray Bolger (centre)who, repeating his Broadway success as the Oxford student obliged to impersonate his own aunt from Brazil ('where the nuts come from') in order that two young lovers might be respectably chaperoned, was determined to prove there was life in the old warhorse yet, and almost single-handedly saved the proceedings from tedium. Also featured were Allyn McLerie, who had played Amy in the stage version, Robert Shackleton, Mary Germaine, Horace Cooper (left), Howard Marion Crawford (right) and, as the real aunt, Margaretta Scott. John Monks Jr wrote the screenplay, David Butler directed, and Michael Kidd – using mainly English chorus girls and boys – choreographed. The Technicolor production was shot in England, partly on location in Oxford. Songs and musical numbers: *Make A Miracle*; *The New Ashmolean Marching Society And Students' Conservatory Band*; *My Darling, My Darling*; *Once In Love With Amy*; *At The Red Rose Cotillon*; *Better Get Out Of Here* Frank Loesser.

△

A public relations job for Columbia Pictures (in and around whose studios much of it was set), **Rainbow Round My Shoulder**, by the same team that brought you *Sunny Side Of The Street* (Columbia, 1951), top-starred Frankie Laine and Billy Daniels, but the plot, such as it was, concerned the efforts of young Charlotte Austin to become a film star against vehement opposition from her socialite grandmother and guardian (Ida Moore). Blake Edwards and Richard Quine wrote it (the latter also directing). Lee Scott was the choreographer (production number illustrated), the supporting cast included Arthur Franz, Eleanore Davis, Lloyd Corrigan, Barbara Whiting and Ross Ford, and the production (in Technicolor) was under the supervision of Jonie Taps. Solid, programmer entertainment. Songs and musical numbers: *There's A Rainbow Round My Shoulder* Dave Dreyer, Billy Rose, Al Jolson; *Bye Bye Blackbird* Mort Dixon, Ray Henderson; *She's Funny That Way* Neil Moret, Richard Whiting; *Wrap Your Troubles In Dreams* Harry Barris, Ted Koehler, Billy Moll; *The Last Rose of Summer* Thomas Moore, R.A. Milliken; *Wonderful, Wasn't It?* Hal David, Don Rodney; *Girl In The Wood* Terry, Neal & Stuart Gilkyson; *Pink Champagne* Bob Wright, George Forrest.

Fifties Musicals

Although the navy had been the inspiration for innumerable hits, most notably MGM's *On The Town* (1949), for some reason musicals with an army setting rarely proved satisfactory, and **About Face** (Warner Bros.) was no exception. Although the principals – Gordon MacRae (centre), Dick Wesson (right) and Eddie Bracken, matched with Virginia Gibson (2nd left), Aileen Stanley Jr (left) and Phyllis Kirk – were likeable enough, the Peter Milne screenplay, recounting the adventures (both military and romantic) of three cadets was derivative and inane. Also featured were Larry Keating, Cliff Ferre, John Baer and, years before his name went up in lights on Broadway, Joel Grey. Roy Del Ruth directed this William Jacobs Technicolor production, which was based on a successful 1936 play, *Brother Rat*, by John Monks Jr and Fred Finklehoffe (already filmed by Warner Bros. in 1938 with Ronald Reagan, Wayne Morris and Eddie Albert). Songs and musical numbers: *If Someone Had Told Me*; *Piano, Bass And Drums*; *No Other Girl For Me*; *I'm Nobody*; *Spring Has Sprung*; *Wooden Indian*; *Reveille*; *Tar Heels*; *They Haven't Lost A Father Yet* Charles Tobias, Peter De Rose.

Husband and wife team Marge and Gower Champion (illustrated centre) played a husband and wife team in **Everything I Have Is Yours** (MGM), the first film in which they enjoyed star billing. Acting, however, was not their particular *forte* and it needed performances stronger than they were able to deliver to rescue producer George Wells's story and screenplay from being just another piece of musical flim-flam. Focusing mainly on the couple's domestic set-up, the plot concerned Gower's gallivanting with Monica Lewis while Marge sits home minding the baby and having day dreams about dancing with her husband. This ploy at least gave choreographers Nick Castle and Mr Champion an excuse for yet one more dance sequence in a film that only came alive when its protagonists were on their toes. On various occasions Champion danced with his wife, with Miss Lewis and even with some toys, while Mrs Champion came into her own in a solo called 'Derry Down Dilly' by Johnny Green and Johnny Mercer. Dennis O'Keefe, Dean Miller, Eduard Franz, John Gallaudet, Diane Cassidy and Elaine Stewart completed the cast, and it was directed by Robert Z. Leonard. (Technicolor). Other songs and musical numbers: *Like Monday Follows Sunday* Green, Clifford Grey, Rex Newman, Douglas Furber; *17,000 Telegraph Poles* Saul Chaplin; *Serenade For A New Baby* Green; *My Heart Skips A Beat* Bob Wright, Chet Forrest, Walter Donaldson; *Everything I Have Is Yours* Harold Adamson, Burton Lane.

330

The one undeniably rousing element in 20th Century-Fox's **Stars And Stripes Forever** (GB: **Marching Along**) was its music. For the rest, it was a tedious reconstruction of incidents in the life of march king John Philip Sousa that plodded listlessly along in producer Lamar Trotti's enervating screenplay. A bewhiskered Clifton Webb (illustrated foreground) was called on to impersonate Sousa, which he did with his usual haughty veneer, and was co-starred with Debra Paget and Robert Wagner who, as a pair of young lovers, shouldered a substantial portion of the 'plot' – he as a horn player in Sousa's band, she as a singer. Ruth Hussey was cast as Sousa's sensible wife with other roles in the Technicolor production going to Finlay Currie (2nd right), Roy Roberts, Tom Browne Henry, Lester Matthews (right) and Maude Prickett. The film was directed by Henry Koster, and contained a ballet sequence staged by Nick Castle and Al White Jr built around Percy Gaunt and Charles Hoyt's popular song, 'The Bowery'. Best moments were a negro choir's singing of 'The Battle Hymn Of The Republic' (by Julia Ward Howe and William Steffe) and a performance of 'Dixie' (by Daniel Decatur Emmett) played by Sousa and his musicians as they enter the Cotton States Exposition in Atlanta. Other musical numbers: *Stars And Stripes Forever*; *El Capitan*; *Washington Post*; *King Cotton* Sousa; *Light Cavalry* Von Suppe; *Turkey In The Straw* (traditional); *Hail To The Chief* John Sanderson.

After the successful box-office returns from *Paleface* (Paramount, 1948), it was inevitable that a sequel would follow, and only surprising that it took so long. But it finally happened, and was called **Son Of Paleface** (Paramount). Bob Hope (illustrated foreground centre) played the son of the late pioneer dentist, Painless Potter, and Jane Russell was a lady bandit whose front (you should pardon the expression) was saloon singing. They were joined by Roy Rogers and Trigger who, playing themselves, offered Hope valiant assistance in tracking down his inheritance. Director Frank Tashlin, together with Robert L. Welch and Joseph Quillan, provided the trio with a gloriously anachronistic screenplay (redolent of some of the more inspired 'Road' films), and there were several new and appealing songs as well as a reprise of Jay Livingston and Ray Evans's world-wide smash, 'Buttons And Bows'. The dances were staged by Josephine Earl, and it was produced, in Technicolor, by Robert L. Welch with a cast that also included Bill Williams, Lloyd Corrigan, Paul E. Burns, Douglass Dumbrille, Harry Von Zell, Iron Eyes Cody, Wee Willie Davis, and Charles Cooley. Other songs and musical numbers included: *There's A Cloud In My Valley Of Sunshine* (Rogers) Jack Hope, Lyle Morraine; *California Rose* (Rogers); *Wing-Ding Tonight* (Hope, Russell); *What A Dirty Shame* (chorus) Jay Livingston, Ray Evans; *Am I In Love?* (Hope, Russell); *Four Legged Friend* (Rogers) Jack Brooks.

George Jessel's Technicolor production for 20th Century-Fox of Damon Runyon's **Bloodhounds of Broadway** owed very little in spirit to the original. But with Mitzi Gaynor (centre) at her exuberant best, heading an agreeable cast that also included Scott Brady, Mitzi Green, Marguerite Chapman, Michael O'Shea, Wally Vernon, Henry Slate, George E. Stone and Charles Buchinsky (later Bronson) this amiable story of how a crooked New York bookie (Brady), who, while lying low in Georgia, meets and is ultimately reformed by a hillbilly (Gaynor) with show-biz aspirations, was a merry enough entertainment in its own right. Gaynor's dancing helped it along most pleasurably and her singing of Eliot Daniel's 'Bye Low' was enchanting. Harmon Jones directed from a screenplay by Sy Gomberg and Robert Sidney choreographed. Other songs: *Jack O'Diamonds* Ben Oakland, Paul Webster; *Broadway Rhythm*; *I've Got A Feelin' You're Foolin'* Arthur Freed, Nacio Herb Brown; *I Wish I Knew* Mack Gordon, Harry Warren.

'A *bona fide* Goldwyn dazzler' was how one critic at the time described Sam Goldwyn's 78th production, **Hans Christian Andersen** (RKO). Weighing in at over four million dollars, $400,000 of it going on a 17-minute ballet sequence, $175,000 on the salary of its star, Danny Kaye, $14,000 on shoes alone and umpteen thousands on the 16 screenplays Goldwyn commissioned over a 15-year period of germination and gestation – it justified the expenditure, and was a visual and aural delight with a tuneful and imaginative score by Frank Loesser. Though critical opinion was divided on the merits of Danny Kaye's performance in the central role, the film grossed over $6,000,000 to become the third biggest money-maker in Goldwyn's history, outdistanced only by *The Best Years Of Our Lives* (1946), and the yet to come *Guys And Dolls* (1955). Kaye's performance was, in fact, just what Moss Hart's gentle screenplay (from a story by Myles Connolly) called for. Toning down the facial tics usually associated with him, the comedian was particularly effective in the musical numbers, especially the enchanting 'Thumbelina' and 'The Ugly Duckling'. Apart from the lengthy ballet sequence (choreographed, as were all the dance sequences, by Roland Petit, whose wife Zizi Jeanmaire, was cast opposite Kaye) Kaye was hardly off the screen. As a disclaimer at the beginning of the film made clear, **Hans Christian Andersen** was not a biography of the great Danish writer, but a fairy tale about a cobbler's unrequited love for a ballerina (Jeanmaire, illustrated centre with Kaye) and how, instead of finding romance, he finds fame as a writer of children's stories. Joey Walsh played Andersen's faithful companion Peter, with other roles under Charles Vidor's direction going to Farley Granger as Jeanmaire's husband Niels, Philip Tonge, John Brown, John Qualen and ballet dancer Erik Bruhn as 'The Hussar' in the Ice-Skating Ballet. Roland Petit also appeared, as The Prince in 'The Little Mermaid' sequence. It was photographed by Harry Stradling (in Technicolor) with Richard Day and Antoni Clave on art direction. Other musical numbers: *The King's New Clothes*; *Inchworm*; *I'm Hans Christian Andersen*; *Wonderful Copenhagen*; *Dream Fantasy*; *Anywhere I Wander*; *Wedding Fantasy*; *No Two People*.
▽

The spectacular water ballets created by Busby ▷ Berkeley for MGM's **Million Dollar Mermaid** (GB: **One Piece Bathing Suit**) saved an otherwise pedestrian biopic that purported to tell the story of Annette Kellerman, the Australian swimming champion who, in the 1920s, found fame and fortune as the aquatic star attraction in the New York Hippodrome, and notoriety as the girl who first introduced the world to the 'daring' one-piece bathing suit and got herself arrested in Boston for doing so. Esther Williams (illustrated foreground centre) in a role tailor-made for her, was top-cast as Miss Kellerman, Victor Mature co-starred as the American promoter she first meets in England, and who, after inducing her to swim 26 miles down the Thames as a publicity stunt, launches her in America. Also cast: David Brian as the manager of the Hippodrome and Mature's rival for Miss Williams's affections, and Walter Pidgeon as Williams's father. But, as was so often the case when Busby Berkeley had a hand in things, he was the real star of the film, with his two elaborately staged sequences again proving that, when it came to pulling out the stops in a musical routine – be it on water or on *terra firma* – he was still the best in the business. Everything else in the film, including Mervyn LeRoy's direction, was anaemic by comparison. It was produced (in Technicolor) by Arthur Hornblow Jr with a cast that included Donna Corcoran, Jesse White, Maria Tallchief, Howard Freeman, Charles Watts and Wilton Graff. The screenplay was by Everett Freeman.

△

Bing Crosby (left) playing a widowed Broadway producer, and Jane Wyman (as his fiancée) appeared together for a second time in **Just For You** (Paramount), a sentimental little piece in Technicolor which found Crosby – between songs – trying to improve his image as a parent. To this end he decides to cut down his production schedule and take his hitherto neglected 18-year-old son (Robert Arthur) and younger daughter (Natalie Wood, centre) on an extended holiday to a country resort. Finding it difficult to communicate with them, he sends for fiancée Wyman, whose presence, far from alleviating the situation, aggravates it when young Robert falls in love with her. After several plot complications via scenarist Robert Carson, whose inconsequential screenplay was adapted from a novel by Stephen Vincent Benet, Robert enlists in the air force and pulls himself together, while Miss Wood is sent to a swanky finishing school run by Ethel Barrymore. The Harry Warren-Leo Robin score was far better than the material deserved. Best numbers: 'Zing A Little Zong', 'I'll Si-Si Ya In Bahia' and 'On The 10.10 From Ten-Ten-Tennessee'. Pat Duggan produced, Elliott Nugent directed, and the supporting cast included Cora Witherspoon (right), Regis Toomey, Ben Lessy and Art Smith. Other songs and musical numbers: *Just For You*; *He's Just Crazy For Me*; *Checkin' My Heart*; *The Maiden Of Guadalupe*; *The Live Oak Tree*; *Call Me Tonight*.

An enjoyable period piece (set in 1904), **Meet Me At The Fair** (Universal International) starred Dan Dailey (left) as a fantasy-prone, easy-going travelling medicine show operator who sets the wheels of Irving Wallace's screenplay (adapted by Martin Beckley from a novel by Gene Markey) in motion when he befriends a runaway orphan (Chet Allen, right) and is soon after accused of kidnapping him. Romance intruded in the shape of Diana Lynn (2nd left), a social worker strongly opposed to Dailey's friendship with the boy. In the end, however, she becomes his ally and wins a successful battle against a crooked district attorney (High O'Brian, 2nd right) who also happens to be her fiancé. Carole Mathews was also in it, as a fairground singer in love with Dailey, and the rest of the cast comprised 'Scat Man' Crothers as Dailey's assistant, Rhys Williams, Russell Simpson, Thomas E. Jackson and George Chandler. The smooth and efficient direction was by Douglas Sirk, the dances were staged by Kenny Williams, and the producer was Albert J. Cohen. Songs and musical numbers: *Meet Me At The Fair* Milton Rosen, Frederick Herbert; *I Was There* F.E. Miller, 'Scat Man' Crothers; *Remember The Time* Kenneth Williams, Marvin Wright; *I Got The Shiniest Mouth In Town* Stan Freeberg; *Bill Bailey Won't You Please Come Home?* Hughie Cannon; *Oh Susanna* Stephen Foster; *Sweet Genevieve* George Cooper, Henry Tucker; *Ave Maria* Schubert; *Ezekiel Saw De Wheel*; *All God's Chillun Got Wings* (traditional).
▽

1953

△

△

Academy Awards

Best Actress
NOMINATIONS INCLUDED: Leslie Caron *Lili* (MGM)

Supporting Actress
NOMINATIONS INCLUDED: Marjorie Rambeau *Torch Song* (MGM)

Direction
NOMINATIONS INCLUDED: Charles Walters *Lili*

Writing (Screenplay)
NOMINATIONS INCLUDED: *Lili* Helen Deutsch
(Story and Screenplay)
NOMINATIONS INCLUDED: *The Band Wagon* (MGM) Betty Comden and Adolph Green

Cinematography (colour)
NOMINATIONS INCLUDED: *Lili* Robert Planck

Art Direction (Set Decoration) (colour)
NOMINATIONS INCLUDED: *Lili* Cedric Gibbons and Paul Groesse; Edwin B. Willis and Arthur Krams

Costume Design (colour)
NOMINATIONS INCLUDED: *The Band Wagon* Mary Ann Nyberg. *Call Me Madam* (20th Century-Fox) Irene Sharaff.

Music
Song
'Secret Love' *Calamity Jane* (WB) Sammy Fain *cm*; Paul Francis Webster *lyr*.
NOMINATIONS INCLUDED: 'My Flaming Heart' *Small Town Girl* (MGM) Nicholas Brodszky *cm*; Leo Robin *lyr*.

Scoring Of A Dramatic Or Comedy Picture
Lili Bronislau Kaper
Scoring Of A Musical Picture
Call Me Madam Alfred Newman
NOMINATIONS INCLUDED: *The Band Wagon* Adolph Deutsch. *Calamity Jane* Ray Heindorf. *5,000 Fingers Of Dr T.* (Kramer, Columbia) Frederick Hollander and Morris Stoloff. *Kiss Me Kate* (MGM) Andre Previn and Saul Chaplin.

The New York Times Annual 'Ten Best'
2nd *Lili*

The Annual Top Moneymaking Films
INCLUDED: *Peter Pan* (Disney, RKO). *Hans Christian Andersen. Gentlemen Prefer Blondes* (20th Century-Fox).- *Scared Stiff* (Paramount). *The Stooge* (Paramount). *The Road To Bali* (Paramount).

Road To Bali (Paramount) was the first *'Road'* film made by the team of Crosby, Hope and Lamour for five years, and although not as spontaneously zany as their last adventure, was nothing to be ashamed of. Messrs Crosby and Hope (illustrated) were, as usual, a couple of vaudevillians on the run, this time finishing up in the South Seas where, together with a sarong-clad Miss L., they become embroiled in a plot involving hidden treasure. Making unbilled guest appearances were Humphrey Bogart (in his 'African Queen' get-up), Bob Crosby (who fires a rifle, explaining that brother Bing promised him 'one shot' in it), Dean Martin, Jerry Lewis, and Jane Russell. Frank Butler, Hal Kanter and William Morrow's screenplay lacked the freshness of some of the earlier *'Road'* films, and if Crosby, Lamour and Hope were definitely getting older, so were the gags. Johnny Burke and Jimmy Van Heusen provided the undistinguished score and Charles O'Curran staged the dances. Produced (in Technicolor) by Harry Tugend, directed by Hal Walker and, in support featured Murvyn Vye, Peter Coe, Ralph Moody, Leon Askin, Donald Lawton and Michael Ansara. Songs: *The Merry-Go-Runaround*; *Chicago Style*; *Hoots Mon*; *To See You*; *Moon-flowers* Burke, Van Heusen; *Chorale For Brass, Piano And Bongo* Stan Kenton, Pete Rugolo.

Although screenwriters Frank Davis, Leonard Stern and Lewis Meltzer dutifully updated narrative elements for the remake of **The Jazz Singer** (Warner Bros.), they were incapable of disguising the sentimentality ingrained in Samson Raphaelson's play which, at this late date, was an irrefutable argument for a return to the silent cinema. Danny Thomas (left) played the cantor's son who, in this version, is a Korean War veteran returning home and discovering, to the distress of his father (Eduard Franz), that he is more attracted by the rewards of Broadway than those of heaven. The basic material proved intractably *schmaltzy*, rendering the movie as much an anachronism as it had originally been epoch-making. Peggy Lee (right), played the girl Thomas loves, Mildred Dunnock, Tom Tully Alex Gerry, Allyn Joslyn and Harold Gordon supported, Michael Curtiz directed, LeRoy Prinz staged the dance numbers, Louis F. Edelman produced (in Technicolor) and it was edited by Alan Crosland Jr, the son of the man who had directed the original version in 1927. Songs and musical numbers included: *Lover* Richard Rodgers, Lorenz Hart; *Just One Of Those Things* Cole Porter; *This Is A Very Special Day* Peggy Lee; *Clover* Mort Dixon, Harry Woods; *Birth Of The Blues* De Sylva, Brown, Henderson; *Living The Life I Love*; *I Hear The Music Now*; *What Are New Yorkers Made Of*; *Hush-A-Bye*; *Oh Moon* Sammy Fain, Jerry Seelen; *I'll String Along With You* Al Dubin, Harry Warren; *Breezin' Along With The Breeze* Richard A. Whiting, Seymour Simons, Haven Gillespie; *If I Could Be With You* Henry Creamer, Jimmy Johnson; *Kol Nidrei* (Hebrew △ traditional).

Paramount sat on **The Stooge** for two years before releasing it in 1953. Though it starred the popular team of Dean Martin and Jerry Lewis (illustrated), the screenplay fashioned for it by Fred Finkelhoffe and Martin Rackin (story by Finkelhoffe and Sid Silvers) veered from the usual formula fare M. and L.'s fans had come to expect in that it introduced an element of mawkishness and sentimentality totally at variance with the team's basic zaniness. The result was an unsatisfying effort in which Martin appeared as a thoroughly conceited and objectionable vaudeville star and Lewis as his good-natured, frequently put-upon stooge. There was an excellent performance from Eddie Mayehoff as Martin's agent, the direction was by Norman Taurog, and it was produced by Hal Wallis with a cast including Marion Marshall, Polly Bergen, Richard Erdman and Frances Bavier. Songs: *A Girl Named Mary And A Boy Named Bill* Mack David, Jerry Livingston; *Who's Your Little Whozis?* Al Goering, Ben Bernie, Walter Hirsch; *Just One More Chance* Arthur Johnston, Sam Coslow; *With My Eyes Wide Open I'm Dreaming* Mack Gordon, Harry Revel; *Louise* Leo Robin, Richard A. Whiting; *I'm Yours* E.Y. Harburg, Johnny Green.

A bargain-basement *On The Town* (MGM, 1949), **All Ashore** (Columbia) starred Mickey Rooney (left), Dick Haymes (right) and Ray McDonald as three sailors on shore leave at Catalina Island. Their adventures (with Rooney playing the fall guy of the trio) formed the basis of Blake Edwards and Richard Quine's screenplay (story by Edwards and Robert Wells) and also involved Peggy Ryan, Jody Lawrance (centre) and Barbara Bates as the available gals, with Fay Roope, Jean Willes, Rica Owen, Patricia Walker and Edwin Parker also cast for producer Jonie Taps. It was photographed in Technicolor, and relied solely on the multi-talented Rooney – seen at his best in a dream sequence in which he imagines he is a brave, mediaeval knight – for its laughs and general entertainment value. The director was co-author Quine. Songs included: *You're A Buddy*; *Boy Meets Girl*; *Heave Ho, My Hearties*; *I Love No One But You* Robert Wells, Fred Karger.
▽

A really lousy script by Walter Bullock was the cardinal fault of **The I-Don't-Care Girl**, a Technicolor biopic from 20th Century-Fox that attempted crudely, and wholly unsatisfactorily, to find out (via flashbacks) what made tempestuous vaudeville star Eva Tanguay tick. Mitzi Gaynor (illustrated) starred (in a role tailor-made for Betty Hutton), but was unable to breathe life into the character, or to make Bullock's hodge-podge of a screenplay seem plausible. Even the number 'I Don't Care' (by Jean Lenox and Harry O. Sutton) which made Tanguay famous, was more convincingly sung by Judy Garland in *In The Good Old Summertime* (MGM 1949). What the film did have going for it (apart from its splendid Technicolor) were three production numbers staged by Jack Cole (though none of them true to the period in which the film was set) and a trio of tap routines (choreographed by Seymour Felix) for Gaynor and co-star David Wayne (as Tanguay's first dancing partner). Cole's work could be seen in 'The Beale Street Blues' (by W.C. Handy), 'I Don't Care' and 'The Johnson Rag' (by Jack Lawrence, Guy H. Hall and Henry Kleinkauf); and Felix's in 'This Is My Favourite City' (by Mack Gordon and Josef Myrow), 'I Don't Care' (a second version) and 'Pretty Baby' (by Gus Kahn, Tony Jackson and Egbert Van Alstyne). Gaynor's other co-stars were Oscar Levant, and Bob Graham, a singer, and the object of Gaynor's affections. Also cast: Craig Hill, Warren Stevens, Hazel Brooks, Marietta Canty and Sam Hearn. Producer George Jessel appeared as himself, the idea behind Bullock's screenplay being to feature Jessel as a producer about to begin a motion picture of Eva Tanguay's life, and seeking out some pertinent facts about the star from those who knew her best. Lloyd Bacon directed. Other songs and musical numbers: *As Long As You Care (I Don't Care)* George Jessel, Joe Cooper; *Oh, You Beautiful Doll* Nat D. Ayer, A. Seymour Brown; *Liebestraum* Liszt; *Piano Concerto No 1* (excerpt) Liszt; *Hello, 'Frisco, Hello* Louis A. Hirsch, Gene Buck; *On The Mississippi* Ballard MacDonald, Harry Carroll, Arthur Fields; *Here Comes Love Again* Jessel, Eliot Daniel; *Little G Minor Fugue* Bach (used to frame *The Johnson Rag* sequence); *Largo Al Factotum* (from 'The Barber Of Seville', also used in *Johnson Rag* sequence) Rossini.

As technically stunning as anything Walt Disney had achieved in the past (or would achieve in the future), **Peter Pan** (RKO) owed more to the imagination of Disney's team of animators than it did to its original creator, J.M. Barrie. Though the storyline was basically unchanged, the characters and their visual realization were all Disney stereotypes – the least successful being Tinker Bell, a sexy nymphet who wouldn't have been tolerated in fairyland for a second. And if the plotting was bold and vigorous something of the magic of Barrie's story was missing. Yet, it was fun while it lasted – the highlight being Captain Hook's encounter with the dreaded crocodile. The music and songs were skilfully integrated into the narrative, and although the score wasn't as memorable as *Cinderella*'s (RKO, 1950), it was perfectly serviceable. Bobby Driscoll's voice was heard as Peter, Kathryn Beaumont's as Wendy, with other vocal characterizations by Hans Conried (Captain Hook), Bill Thompson (Smee), Heather Angel (Mrs Darling), Paul Collins (Mr Darling) Tommy Luske (John), Candy Candido (Indian Chief) and Tom Conway (narrator). It was directed by Hamilton Luske, Clyde Geronimi and Wilfred Jackson and produced, in Technicolor, at a cost of $4,000,000, by Walt Disney. (Peter Pan and Wendy illustrated). Songs: *The Elegant Captain Hook*; *You Can Fly*; *Your Mother And Mine*; *What Makes The Red Man Red?* Sammy Cahn, Sammy Fain; *A Pirate's Life* Oliver Wallace, Erdman Penner; *Tee Dum-Tee Dee* Wallace, Ted Sears, Winston Hibler; *Never Smile At A Crocodile* Frank Churchill, Jack Lawrence.

It is not often that the word 'enchanting' can accurately be applied to a musical, but it was the best way to describe **Lili** (MGM), as well as Leslie Caron's genuinely touching performance in it. Adapted by Helen Deutsch from a story by Paul Gallico, it told the tender tale of a 16-year-old orphan who becomes a waitress with a travelling carnival show. She's fired for spending too much time watching the show's magic act, and is comforted in her grief by a group of puppets, (illustrated, with Caron) operated unbeknownst to the naive Miss Caron, by Mel Ferrer, a cripple whom she loathes, believing him to be cruel and heartless. It is only after Ferrer, who is in love with the waif, slaps her in a jealous rage (for Miss Caron prefers Jean-Pierre Aumont, the show's handsome magician, to him), that she begins to understand that the love exuding from the puppets comes from the love Ferrer feels for her. Bronislau Kaper provided the music for this absorbing, bitter-sweet film and the hit song 'Hi-Lili, Hi-Lo' (performed by the puppets) had a lyric by scenarist Deutsch. The film also contained a delightful dream ballet, choreographed by Charles Walters and Dorothy Jarnac. Walters directed, and it was produced (in Technicolor) by Edwin H. Knopf with a cast that was completed by Zsa Zsa Gabor, Kurt Kasznar, Amanda Blake, Alex Gerry, Ralph Dumke, Wilton Graff and George Baxter. In 1961, a Broadway musical based on the film, and called *Carnival*, reversed the usual procedure of Hollywood always sponging off Broadway. It starred Anna Maria Alberghetti and was a Broadway success, running for 719 performances.

A jolly, brightly-packaged Technicolor offering from MGM that could have done with a slightly more substantial screenplay, **I Love Melvin** starred Donald O'Connor and Debbie Reynolds (centre) in a simple story about a photographer's assistant who rashly promises a would-be film star (Reynolds) that he will put her picture on the cover of *Look* magazine. Such was the lightweight situation concocted by Laslo Vadnay, and which producer George Wells scripted (additional dialogue by Ruth Brooks Flippen), with parts in it for Una Merkel and Allyn Joslyn (as Reynolds's parents), Richard Anderson, Les Tremayne, Noreen Corcoran, Jim Backus, Barbara Ruick, and guest star Robert Taylor. O' Connor and Reynolds's musical comedy talents were exploited in several full-scale production numbers, the three best being 'A Lady Loves', in which Reynolds imagines herself as a famous film star; 'Saturday Afternoon Before the Game', a football routine featuring Reynolds as the football; and 'I Wanna Wander', a knockabout item for the versatile and energetic O'Connor. All the songs were by Mack Gordon and Josef Myrow, and they were excellently staged by Robert Alton. Don Weis's direction drew engaging performances from the two stars. Other songs and musical numbers: *We Have Never Met As Yet*; *Life Has Its Funny Little Ups And Downs*; *Where Did You Learn To Dance?*; *And There You Are.*

EVA TANGUAY

Irving Berlin's mammoth Broadway hit, **Call Me Madam**, gave Ethel Merman (illustrated) the best screen role of her career and she devoured it greedily. As Mrs Sally Adams, 'the hostess with the mostest' and Ambassadress to Lichtenberg, she recreated the part she played 644 times on Broadway in a no-holds-barred performance that left critics and audiences alike breathless. However, for those unfortunate enough to remain unresponsive to the lady's particular brand of scenery-chewing, sock-it-to-'em tactics, the experience must, indeed, have been a painful one. For the film was Merman, and Merman was the film. And anyone else – such as Donald O'Connor (as her press attaché), Vera-Ellen (as the princess O'Connor falls for) and George Sanders (as the Lichtenberg general who proves the hostess has a heart by stealing it), were little more than agreeable appendages to the main business at hand – which is not to discredit O'Connor and Ellen's superb dancing to Robert Alton's notable choreography. Also trying to get a look in were Billy De Wolfe, Helmut Dantine, Walter Slezak, Steve Geray, and Ludwig Stossel. Musically, too, Merman had it all her own way, completely dominating O'Connor in their duet 'You're Just In Love' and overpowering the rest of the cast with her high voltage belting of 'The Hostess With The Mostest', 'International Rag' and 'Can You Use Any Money Today?'. Sanders coped well enough with his solo, 'Marrying For Love', and from Vera-Ellen (her vocals dubbed by Carole Richards) and Donald O'Connor there was a spirited rendition of 'It's A Lovely Day Today'. But it was the redoubtable Merman who carried the movie to success, making one regret that her screen appearances were so few and far between. It was adapted from Howard Lindsay and Russel Crouse's book by Arthur Sheekman, produced (in Technicolor) for 20th Century-Fox by Sol C. Siegel, and directed by Walter Lang. Other songs and musical numbers: *Welcome To Lichtenberg* (chorus); *Mrs Sally Adams* (girls); *The Ocarina* (Vera-Ellen, chorus); *What Chance Have I With Love?* (O'Connor); *Something To Dance About* (O'Connor, Vera-Ellen); *The Best Thing For You* (Merman, Sanders).

Warner Bros. unwisely opted to give Sigmund Romberg's operetta **The Desert Song** another airing (its third on film), but neither the principals, Gordon MacRae and Kathryn Grayson, nor director Bruce Humberstone could do much to conceal the ancient origins of the material. MacRae (foreground centre) played the Riff chieftain (no longer referred to as 'The Red Shadow', doubtless because, in a period jumpy with McCarthyism, the adjective had too many communistic associations) who saves the French garrison from the wicked Sheik Youssef (Raymond Massey) and wins the hand of the general's daughter (Grayson). It may have worked back in 1926 (the show's original libretto was by Lawrence Schwab, Otto Harbach, Frank Mandel, Sigmund Romberg and Oscar Hammerstein II) but, 27 years later, in Roland Kibbee's idiotic screenplay, it was a case of too little, too late. Also featured were Steve Cochran (as a legionnaire), Ray Collins, Dick Wesson (foreground left) and Allyn McLerie. The musical numbers, including a weird houri dance for McLerie, were staged by LeRoy Prinz, and the film was produced, in Technicolor, by Rudi Fehr. Songs and musical numbers: *The Desert Song*; *Long Live The Night*; *The Riff Song*; *Romance*; *One Alone*; *One Flower* Romberg, Hammerstein; *Gay Parisienne* Jack Scholl, Serge Walter.

Dangerous When Wet (MGM) didn't offer very much by way of plot (its star, Esther Williams, right, spends most of her time preparing to swim across the English Channel), but it was brimful of attractive people and attractive performances. Handsome Fernando Lamas played an amorous and wealthy peddler of French champagne, Jack Carson was a producer-cum-travelling salesman. Charlotte Greenwood (left) Williams's high-kicking Ma, William Demarest her Pa, and Barbara Whiting and Donna Corcoran her sisters. The score was by Arthur Schwartz and Johnny Mercer, and contained a pip of a number in 'I Got Out Of Bed On The Right Side' as well as the pleasant 'Ain't Nature Grand' sung, at various stages, by practically every member of the cast. In addition, there was a lengthy animated dream sequence directed by Fred Quimby, William Hanna and Joseph Barbera, featuring Tom and Jerry, as well as a live-action Miss Williams – the highlight of the film. Dorothy Kingsley's screenplay was slightly better than serviceable, the 'dramatic' climax being the Channel swim itself. It was directed by Charles Walters for producer George Wells, and the cast was completed by Denise Darcel, Bunny Waters, Henri Letondal, Paul Bryer, Jack Raine, Richard Alexander, Tudor Owen and Ann Codee. (Technicolor). Other songs: *I Like Men*; *Liquapep*; *Fifi*; *In My Wildest Dreams*.

William Lundigan, Jane Greer (illustrated), Mitzi Gaynor, Gloria De Haven and David Wayne starred in **Down Among The Sheltering Palms** (20th Century-Fox), a minor musical whose lush and exotic Pacific island background provided the scene for a really weather-beaten story (by Edward Hope, screenplay by Claude Binyon, Albert Lewin and Burt Styler) in which a decorous officer (Lundigan), while attempting to see that his GIs keep their distance from the island's bevy of local lovelies, finds himself ensnared by an American newspaper columnist (Greer), an amorous civilian (De Haven) and one of the native islanders (Gaynor). Wayne played Lundigan's sidekick, and together they sang the best tune in the show, 'I'm A Ruler Of A South Sea Island' (by Harold Arlen and Ralph Blane, who wrote all the new songs). From Miss Greer came 'Who Will It Be When The Time Comes?', Gaynor's high point was 'What Makes De Difference?' while Gloria De Haven gave out with 'All Of Me' (by Seymour Simons and Gerald Marks). The dances were staged by Seymour Felix, it was produced in Technicolor by Fred Kohlmar, and directed by Edmund Goulding. Other musical numbers included: *Down Among The Sheltering Palms* Abe Olman, James Brockman; *When You're In Love* Arlen, Blane.

Betty Grable (left) didn't so much as show an ankle in **The Farmer Takes A Wife** (20th Century-Fox), a Technicolor remake of the 1935 version which had starred Janet Gaynor in the Grable role and Henry Fonda in the role played in the musical version by Dale Robertson (right). Based on a novel by Walter D. Edmonds, and a stage play by Frank B. Elser and Marc Connelly, its folksy story, set on the Erie Canal in 1850, concerned Molly Larkin (Grable), a cook on a canal boat owned by Jotham Klore (John Carroll), and her romance with driver Daniel Harrow (Robertson), much to rival Carroll's aggressive disapproval. To give it the zest it so pitifully lacked, it needed a screenplay far racier than the one Walter Bullock, Sally Benson and Joseph Fields provided, and performances of more conviction than its leads were capable of. Its redeeming feature was its score by Harold Arlen and Dorothy Fields, especially a number called 'We're In Business' sung by Grable and Robertson, as well as by practically every one else in a cast that also included Thelma Ritter, Eddie Foy Jr, Gwen Verdon, Charlotte Austin, Kathleen Crowley and Merry Anders. Jack Cole was in charge of the dance direction, Frank P. Rosenberg produced, and Henry Levin called the shots. Other songs and musical numbers: *On The Erie Canal*; *We're Doing It For The Natives In Jamaica*; *When I Close My Door*; *Today I Love Everybody*; *Somethin' Real Special*; *With The Sun Warm Upon Me*; *Can You Spell Schenectady*.

Sol Hurok always loved music, but as he had no performer's talents the only way he could participate in the art he so passionately adored was to become an impresario, a fact which was duly celebrated in a gaudy biopic from 20th Century-Fox called **Tonight We Sing**. Barring some domestic upheavals when his wife (Anne Bancroft) temporarily walks out on him, the film concentrated mainly on Hurok's entrepreneurial activities with such stars as Chaliapin (Ezio Pinza, here illustrated as Mussorgsky's *Boris Godounov*), Anna Pavlova (Tamara Toumanova), and the great violinist Eugene Ysaye (Isaac Stern), thus providing the cue for an outpouring of glorious music. As Hurok himself, David Wayne gave one of the least convincing performances of his indifferent career, but then, apart from the music, nothing about George Jessel's synthetic, Technicolor production was overburdened with anything as weighty as conviction. Harry Kurnitz and George Oppenheimer pasted the script together from incidents related in a book written by Hurok and Ruth Goode, and it was unimaginatively directed by Mitchell Leisen. Also cast: Byron Palmer (with vocals dubbed by Jan Peerce), Roberta Peters, Oscar Karlweis (as Hurok's partner), Mikhail Rasumny (as Hurok's valet), Steve Geray, Walter Woolf King and John Meek (as Hurok aged 10). The musical direction was by Alfred Newman, choral direction by Ken Darby, and ballet choreography by David Lichine. Musical extracts: *Le Cygne* (Toumanova) Saint-Saëns; *Sempre Libera* (Peters) from Verdi's 'La Traviata'; *Jewel Song* (Peters) from Gounod's 'Faust'; *Qu'Attendez-Vous Encore* (Pinza, Palmer) from 'Faust'; *Vous Qui Faites L'Endormie* (Pinza, Palmer) from 'Faust'; *Love Duet* (Palmer, Peters) from Act 1 of Puccini's 'Madam Butterfly'; *Andante Le Triste Vero* (Palmer) from 'Madam Butterfly'; *Addio Fiorito Asil* (Palmer) from 'Madam Butterfly'; *Mattinata* (Palmer) Leoncavallo; *Valse Caprice in E Flat* (Stern) Anton Rubinstein; *Processional* (from 'Boris Godounov') Mussorgsky.

Chart-topper Rosemary Clooney (right) made a pleasing screen debut in **The Stars Are Singing**, slamming home such Jay Livingston-Ray Evans hits as 'I Do I Do I Do', 'Haven't Got A Worry To My Name' and 'Lovely Weather For Ducks'; and Ross Bagdasarian and William Saroyan's 'Come On-A-My-House' (a big hit which had established Clooney as a major singing star in 1951). Musically, she was well assisted by Anna Maria Alberghetti (left) and Lauritz Melchior, though as far as the story (by Paul Hervey Fox) was concerned, she received no assistance at all from scenarist Liam O'Brien. A trifle about a group of undiscovered talents (Clooney in company with dancer Tom Morton and comedian Bob Williams) who do their best to promote the career of a young Polish soprano (Alberghetti), it relied for dramatic emphasis solely on the fact that Miss Alberghetti had entered the States illegally. Still, all the performances were agreeable enough, the songs were first class, and Bob Williams's celebrated act with a recalcitrant dog called Red Dust, was hilarious. The Technicolor production was by Irving Asher, whose cast also included Fred Clark, John Archer, Mikhail Rasumny, Lloyd Corrigan and Don Wilson, and the seasoned direction was by Norman Taurog. Other songs, musical numbers and operatic extracts: *My Heart Is Home* (Alberghetti, Melchior); *My Kind Of Day* (Alberghetti); *Feed Fido Some Rruff* (Clooney, Alberghetti, Morton, Williams); *New Father* (Morton) Livingston, Evans; *Voices Of Spring* (Alberghetti) Johann Strauss; *Una Voce Poco Fa* (Alberghetti) from Rossini's 'Barber of Seville'; *Because* (Melchior) Edward Teschemacher, Guy d'Hardelot; *Ah! Fors'è Lui Che L'Anima* (Alberghetti) from Verdi's 'La Traviata'; *Vesti La Giubba* (Melchior) from Leoncavallo's 'Pagliacci'.

As he had done on so many occasions in the past, the legendary Busby Berkeley came to the rescue of a musical desperately in need of a few good ideas. This time it was on **Small Town Girl** (MGM) that he worked his special brand of alchemy, turning a routine song-and-dance show into a good one. The simple story was of a millionaire playboy (Farley Granger) who, after being given a 30-day sentence for speeding through the quiet streets of small-town Duck Creek, falls out of love with his fiancée (Ann Miller) and into love with the daughter (Jane Powell) of the local Judge. Apart from Berkeley's inventive dance direction, the film was also blessed with Bobby Van, as a small-town clerk aching for a career in the theatre. Van stopped the show with a dance routine called 'Take Me To Broadway' performed entirely in energetic hops, and was the freshest talent on display. There was reliable work too, from Ann Miller, whose 'I've Got To Hear That Beat' was effectively staged by Berkeley in a set whose floor comprised dozens of holes through which appeared the disembodied hands of over fifty musicians, each of them holding a musical instrument. (illustrated). Other musical highlights included Jane Powell singing 'Small Towns Are Smile Towns', and guest star Nat King Cole's 'My Flaming Heart'. All the songs were by Nicholas Brodszky and Leo Robin, with Andre Previn as the musical director. Joe Pasternak produced, it was photographed in Technicolor, and the director was Leslie Kardos. Also cast: S.Z. Sakall, Billie Burke, Fay Wray, Dean Miller, William Campbell, Philip Tonge. Other songs and musical numbers: *Fine Fine Fine*; *The Fellow I'd Follow*; *Lullaby Of The Lord*; *My Gaucho*.

An imaginative musical fantasy, **The 5,000 Fingers Of Dr T** (Columbia) was a Stanley Kramer production that was always interesting to look at but, in the end, not particularly successful dramatically. All about a youngster (Tommy Rettig, centre) who'd rather be out with the rest of his chums playing baseball than practising the piano for his teacher Dr Terwilliker, it took the form of an elaborate and extended dream sequence set in a nightmarish land dominated by the evil Dr T. who runs a piano school for 500 boy prisoners and whose dungeon, below his uninviting fortress dwelling, houses a group of unfortunate creatures imprisoned for having the audacity to play musical instruments other than pianos. In the best sequence in the film the hapless prisoners, grown green and mouldy with age, perform a bizarre ballet (choreographed by Eugene Loring) that made for genuinely original cinema. The Dr T. of the title (as well as Dr Terwilliker) was played – with a delicious sense of the sinister – by Hans Conried, (left foreground), with Peter Lind Hayes (right foreground) top cast as a plumber who, together with young Rettig, comes to the aid of Rettig's mother (Mary Healy), another of the dreaded Doctor's victims. It was thought up by humorist Ted Geisel (better known as Dr Seuss, under which name he was credited as co-author of the screenplay with Allan Scott) and directed by Roy Rowland, whose grip on the unorthodox material was variable. Dr Seuss also wrote the lyrics for the show's songs, and the music was by Frederick Hollander. The imaginative art direction was by Rudolph Sternad. (Technicolor). Songs: *The Kid's Song*; *Ten Happy Fingers*; *Get Together Weather*; *Dream Stuff*; *The Dressing Song (My Do-Me-Do-Duds)*; *Dungeon Elevator*; *Hypnotic Duel*; *Victorious*.

Fifties Musicals

The Band Wagon (MGM) was the apotheosis ▷
of the backstage musical. Betty Comden and
Adolph Green's witty screen play (written
around songs by Howard Dietz and Arthur
Schwartz) was able to include the line 'Gosh,
with all this raw talent around, why can't us
kids get together and put ourselves on a show',
which was both tongue in cheek and lump in the
throat. It was not only a sophisticated tribute to
all those innocent backstage movies that had
preceded it, but was also a brilliantly double-
edged tribute to its star, Fred Astaire. Exactly
twenty years since Astaire (left) made his film
debut in *Dancing Lady* (MGM), producer Arthur
Freed gave him what could be considered his
finest role in the best film he ever made. Behind
the titles, Fred's talismanic top hat and cane are
seen, but as the film opens we hear that 'perhaps
the most famous top hat and stick of our
generation' are being auctioned off. They belong,
in the movie's context, to fading Hollywood
musical star, Tony Hunter (Astaire), persuaded
by his friends Nanette Fabray and Oscar Levant
(playing two Broadway librettists modelled on
Comden and Green), to make a come-back on the
Great White Way. They have asked ballet dancer
Gabrielle Gerard (Cyd Charisse, centre, in her first
starring role) to co-star, and theatrical *wunder-
kind* Jeffrey Cordova (Jack Buchanan) to direct.
Buchanan, in a role originally meant for Clifton
Webb, played it to perfection, and his top hat and
white tie duo, 'I Guess I'll Have To Change My
Plan', with Fred, was a delightful moment of
Anglo-American harmony, a harmony achieved
in the plot only after various trials and tribulations. Buchanan, who is first seen as Oedipus
Rex, tries to turn the show into a modern Faust
which results in a huge flop, giving rise to one of
director Vincente Minnelli's best visual jokes – a
close-up of an enormous egg. Other outstanding
visual moments: the machine in the penny
arcade opening up after Astaire kicks it at the end
of his energetic 'A Shine On Your Shoes' number,
and Fred, Buchanan and Fabray as tiny babies
in the hilarious 'Triplets'. Oliver Smith (from
Broadway) designed the sets, including those for
the brilliant Mickey Spillane-inspired 'Girl Hunt'
ballet which was a high-water mark in a genre
that the Freed unit had virtually invented: Alan
Jay Lerner (uncredited) wrote Astaire's spoof
narration, Roger Edens adapted themes from
Dietz–Schwartz songs, and Michael Kidd choreographed (dazzlingly). In the ballet, Astaire was a
private eye caught up with 'bad, dangerous'
blonde/brunette Cyd Charisse who (her vocals
dubbed by India Adams) proved an exciting
partner for Astaire. She seemed to bring out an
erotic quality in his dancing, especially in the
exquisite 'Dancing in the Dark', with its Central
Park setting which recalled some of the more
lyrical of the Astaire-Rogers dances in the
thirties. There was only one new song in the film,
'That's Entertainment', written in 30 minutes by
Schwartz and Dietz in answer to Freed's request
for a 'There's No Business Like Show Business'
type number, and it summed up perfectly what
the film was all about. Completing the cast were
James Mitchell (foreground right) Robert Gist,
Thurston Hall, and LeRoy Daniels. Ava Gardner
made a guest appearance. Other songs and
musical numbers: *By Myself* (Astaire); *I Love
Louisa* (Astaire, Levant, Charisse, Fabray, chor-
us); *New Sun In The Sky* (Charisse); *Louisiana
Hayride* (Fabray, chorus); *You And The Night And
The Music* (chorus); *High And Low* (orchestra);
Something To Remember You By (chorus); *Beggar's
Waltz* (Charisse, corps de ballet).

The screenplay fashioned by Charles Lederer for ▷
20th Century-Fox's version of Joseph Fields and
Anita Loos's smash musical comedy **Gentlemen
Prefer Blondes** (from Loos's celebrated novel)
was spot-on for three-quarters of its playing
time, but deteriorated sadly towards the end. A
pity, for until its decline and fall, this lavishly
produced (by Sol C. Siegel) yarn about a couple
of big girls from Little Rock was smashing
entertainment. Fortunately, its two stars, Marilyn Monroe (right, as Lorelei Lee, in the role
created on Broadway by Carol Channing) and
Jane Russell (left) as Dorothy, both giving their
best performances to date, never for an instant
faltered. And in the witty dance sequences
created for them by choreographer Jack Cole,
they were sensational – particularly Monroe,
who benefited greatly from Cole's really classy
staging of the film's best song, 'Diamonds Are A
Girl's Best Friend' (by Jule Styne and Leo Robin,
who wrote the original Broadway score). Russell
was at her best in Hoagy Carmichael-Harold
Adamson's 'Ain't There Anyone Here For Love',
staged by Cole in a ship's gymnasium, and
featuring a couple of dozen of the world's most
beautifully built men. Together the girls did 'Bye
Bye Baby', and the stunning opening number,
'A (Two) Little Girl(s) From Little Rock' (the two
remaining Styne-Robin songs held over from the
stage production), as well as another Car-
michael-Adamson contribution called 'When
Love Goes Wrong'. On each occasion they
ignited the screen with their particular brands of
sex appeal, their combustible presences enrich-
ing the studio coffers by over $5,000,000.
Charles Coburn was delightful as a diamond
millionaire Monroe temporarily sets her sights
on. Tommy Noonan (as Monroe's fiancé) gave
his usual interpretation of a 'nebbish', Elliott Reid
played a private detective hired by Noonan's
millionaire father (Taylor Holmes) to see that his
son and Monroe remain apart, and young
George Winslow as a precocious six-year-old
called Henry Spofford III, gave the best supporting performance of all. The direction, unham-
pered by subtlety, was by Howard Hawks.

There was an air of desperation about Paramount's **Scared Stiff**, an inferior remake of Bob
Hope's 1940 comedy *The Ghost Breakers* (Paramount). It starred Dean Martin and Jerry Lewis
(illustrated) as the hapless victims of a haunted
house, and Lizabeth Scott as the gal that got
them there. As part of the desperation tactics
employed by producer Hal Wallis, Carmen Miranda was drawn into the sorry business too,
and, in unbilled guest appearances, so were Bing
Crosby and Bob Hope. But nothing and no one
could save the show from disaster. Herbert
Baker and Walter DeLeon wrote it (from the play
by Paul Dickey and Charles W. Goddard), the
musical numbers were staged by Billy Daniels
and included 'San Domingo' and 'Song of The
Enchilada Man' (by Jerry Livingston and Mack
David) performed by Martin, Lewis and Miranda
as well as 'Mama Yo Quiero' (by Al Stillman, and
Jaraca and Vincente Paiva) in which Lewis
mimed (indifferently) to a recording made by
Miranda, and the supporting cast included
George Dolenz, Dorothy Malone, William Ching,
Paul Marion, Jack Lambert and Tom Powers. It
was directed by George Marshall, who was more
successful when he directed it the first time
round. Other songs and musical numbers: *You
Hit The Spot* Mack Gordon, Harry Revel; *I Don't
Care If The Sun Don't Shine* David; *I'm Your Pal*
David, Livingston; *When Somebody Thinks You're* ◁
Wonderful Harry Woods.

A small-scale, but pleasant little Technicolor offering, **Cruisin' Down The River** (Columbia) used flashbacks to recall a long-standing feud between riverboat owner Cecil Kellaway and a gambler called Beauregard Clemment (Dick Haymes) who wins Kellaway's boat from him. Years later, Beau III (also played by Haymes) offers to return the riverboat but Kellaway proudly refuses. A compromise is reached and, with the help of Kellaway's granddaughter (Audrey Totter) and servant (Billy Daniels), the boat – called the 'Chattahoochee Queen' – is turned into a floating nightclub. It was written by Blake Edwards and Richard Quine, choreographed by Lee Scott, directed by Jack Corrick and produced by Jonie Taps, with a cast that also included Connie Russell, Douglas Fowley, Larry Blake, Johnny Downs, Benny Payne, The Bell Sisters, specialty dancer Erze Ivan, and The Lee Scott Dancers (illustrated). Songs and musical numbers included: *Cruisin' Down The River* Eily Beadell, Nell Tollerton; *There Goes That Song Again* Sammy Cahn, Jule Styne; *Pennies From Heaven* Johnny Burke, Arthur Johnston; *Sing You Sinners* Sam Coslow, W. Frank Harling; *Swing Low Sweet Chariot* (traditional); *Father Dear Father* Emmet G. Coleman

June Haver's last movie before entering a convent was **The Girl Next Door** (20th Century-Fox), a piece of inconsequentiality in which she starred opposite Dan Dailey. Plot by L. Bus-Fekete and Mary Helen Fry (screenplay by Isobel Lennart) was an elongated cliché in which Haver (left), a musical comedy star eager for the quiet life, becomes romantically involved with a widower (Dailey, right) who also happens to be a newspaper strip cartoonist by profession. In this instance music spoke louder than words, with Haver seen and heard at her best in Mack Gordon and Josef Myrow's 'Nowhere Guy' – Messrs Gordon and Myrow supplying all of the songs. Dennis Day was cast as Haver's business manager, with other roles in Robert Bassler's Technicolor production going to Billy Gray, Cara Williams, Natalie Schaefer and Clinton Sundberg. It was directed by Richard Sale and choreographed by Richard Barstow. UPA supplied a cartoon sequence which made no impact at all. Other songs and musical numbers: *If I Love You A Mountain*; *I'd Rather Have A Pal Than A Gal – Anytime*; *We Girls Of The Chorus*; *The Great White Way*; *A Quiet Little Place In The Country*; *You're Doing Allright*; *The Girl Next Door*; *You Walk By*.
▽

The only major hit song to emerge from a Dean Martin-Jerry Lewis film was 'That's Amore' by Harry Warren and Jack Brooks, and it was featured in **The Caddy** (Paramount), a middling effort about a couple of show business celebrities who originally started out as professional golfers. As scripted by Edmund Hartmann and Danny Arnold, there weren't that many laughs *per se*, but Lewis (right, with Martin), pretending on one occasion to be an elegant Continental swell and, on another, an English man of letters, proved himself a mimic of superb ability. Donna Reed and Barbara Bates were the girls in their lives, and the cast was completed by Joseph Calleia, Fred Clark, Clinton Sundberg, Howard Smith, Marshall Thompson, Marjorie Gateson, Frank Puglia and Lewis Martin. Norman Taurog directed, and it was produced by Paul Jones. Other songs: *What Would You Do Without Me?*; *It's A Whistling Kinda Morning*; *The Gay Continental*; *It Takes A Lot Of Little Likes To Make One Big Love*; *You're The Right One* Warren, Brooks.
▽

△

Like *On Moonlight Bay* (1951), **By The Light Of The Silvery Moon** (Warner Bros.) offered more turn-of-the-century nostalgia in which plot – the travails of a small-town girl (Doris Day, illustrated), to keep her father (Leon Ames) from the clutches of a group of actresses who wish to lease the local theatre, and the problems this causes her steady beau (Gordon MacRae) – was decidedly subservient to the chance of hearing the principals sing an impressive roster of long-established standards. The supporting cast – Rosemary De Camp, Mary Wickes and Billy Gray – were recruited from the earlier film, imparting a cosy family aspect to the wholesome proceedings which David Butler directed for producer William Jacobs and which was choreographed by LeRoy Prinz. (Technicolor). Songs and musical numbers: *By The Light Of The Silvery Moon* Gus Edwards, Edward Madden; *I'll Forget You* Ernest R. Ball, Annalu Burns; *Your Eyes Have Told Me So* Gus Kahn, Egbert Van Alstyne, Walter Blaufuss; *Be My Little Baby Bumble Bee* Stanley Murphy, Henry I. Marshall; *If You Were The Only Girl In The World* Clifford Grey, Nat D. Ayer; *Ain't We Got Fun* Kahn, Ray Egan, Richard A. Whiting; *King Chanticleer* Ayer.

Rhonda Fleming (centre) starred in **Those Redheads From Seattle** (Paramount), a 3-D musical with 2-D characters and a 1-D plot, concerning a mother (Agnes Moorehead) who takes her four daughters (Fleming, Teresa Brewer, right, Cynthia Bell, left, and Kay Bell) to the Yukon to join their father (Frank Wilcox) in the gold rush. Wilcox, however, is killed before his family arrives, forcing the girls to turn to assorted work until the romantic problems they encounter along the way are all satisfactorily resolved. Gene Barry co-starred opposite Fleming as a saloon keeper, with other roles in director Lewis R. Foster, Geoffrey Homes and George Worthington Yates's screenplay going to singer Guy Mitchell, Jean Parker, Roscoe Ates, John Kellogg, and Walter Reed. It was produced, in Technicolor, by William H. Pine and William C. Thomas. Songs and musical numbers: *Baby Baby Baby* Mack David, Jerry Livingston; *Mr Banjo Man* Jay Livingston, Ray Evans; *I Guess It Was You All The Time* Johnny Mercer, Hoagy Carmichael; *Chick-A-Boom* Bob Merrill; *Take Back Your Gold* M.H. Rosenfeld, Louis W. Pritzkow.

So This Is Love (GB: **The Grace Moore Story**), a satisfactory biography of soprano Grace Moore related, in flashback, her rise from a rural childhood in Tennessee to a wildly successful debut at New York's Metropolitan Opera House, where her Mimi in *La Boheme* commanded no fewer than 28 curtain calls. Although the John Monks Jr screenplay trod the familiar path of the Hollywood biopic (and omitted Miss Moore's tragic death in a plane crash), it made for an entertaining and convincing narrative, benefiting enormously from Kathryn Grayson's ability (as Miss Moore) to move easily from popular to operatic standards. The singer's first love was played by newcomer Merv Griffin, later to become famous as the host of a TV talk show; while the suitor whom she finally rejects for the greater glory of her career was Douglas Dick. Walter Abel played her father, with Rosemary De Camp, Jeff Donnell, Fortunio Bonanova (illustrated, with Grayson) Ann Doran, Joan Weldon and Mabel Atherton (as *diva* Mary Garden) also cast, Gordon Douglas directed, LeRoy Prinz staged the musical sequences and Henry Blanke produced (in Technicolor) for Warner Bros. Songs: *Time On My Hands* Harold Adamson, Mack Gordon, Vincent Youmans; *Remember* Irving Berlin; *I Wish I Could Shimmy Like My Sister Kate* Armand J. Piron, Peter Bocage; *Ciribiribin* Harry James, Jack Lawrence, A. Pestalozza; *The Kiss Waltz*; extracts from Mozart's *The Marriage Of Figaro*, Gounod's *Faust*; Puccini's *La Boheme*.
▽

1954

Best Picture

NOMINATIONS INCLUDED: *Seven Brides For Seven Brothers* (MGM) produced by Jack Cummings.

Best Actor

NOMINATIONS INCLUDED: James Mason *A Star Is Born* (Transcona, WB).

Best Actress

NOMINATIONS INCLUDED: Dorothy Dandridge *Carmen Jones* (Preminger, 20th Century-Fox) Judy Garland *A Star Is Born*.

Writing (Motion Picture Story)

NOMINATIONS INCLUDED: *There's No Business Like Show Business* (20th Century-Fox) Lamar Trotti

(Screenplay)

NOMINATIONS INCLUDED: *Seven Brides For Seven Brothers* Albert Hackett, Frances Goodrich and Dorothy Kingsley.

(Story and Screenplay)

NOMINATIONS INCLUDED: *The Glenn Miller Story* (U-I) Valentine Davies and Oscar Brodney.

Cinematography (colour)

NOMINATIONS INCLUDED: *Seven Brides For Seven Brothers* George Folsey

Art Direction (Set Decoration) (colour)

NOMINATIONS INCLUDED: *Brigadoon* (MGM) Cedric Gibbons and Preston Ames; Edwin B. Willis and Keogh Gleason. *Red Garters* (Paramount) Hal Pereira and Roland Anderson; Sam Comer and Ray Moyer. *A Star Is Born* Malcolm Bert, Gene Allen and Irene Sharaff; George James Hopkins.

Costume Design (colour)

NOMINATIONS INCLUDED: *Brigadoon* Irene Sharaff. *A Star Is Born* Jean Louis, Mary Ann Nyberg and Irene Sharaff. *There's No Business Like Show Business* Charles LeMaire, Travilla and Miles White.

Sound Recording

The Glenn Miller Story Leslie I. Carey, sound director.
NOMINATIONS INCLUDED: *Brigadoon* Wesley C. Miller, sound director.

Film Editing

NOMINATIONS INCLUDED: *Seven Brides For Seven Brothers* Ralph E. Winters

Music
Song

NOMINATIONS INCLUDED: 'Count Your Blessings Instead Of Sheep' *White Christmas* (Paramount) Irving Berlin. 'The Man That Got Away' *A Star Is Born* Harold Arlen *cm*; Ira Gershwin *lyr*.

Scoring Of A Musical Picture

Seven Brides For Seven Brothers Adolph Deutsch and Saul Chaplin
NOMINATIONS INCLUDED: *Carmen Jones* Herschel Burke Gilbert. *The Glenn Miller Story* Joseph Gershenson and Henry Mancini. *A Star Is Born* Ray Heindorf. *There's No Business Like Show Business* Alfred Newman and Lionel Newman.

Honorary Award

To Danny Kaye, for his unique talents, his service to the Academy, the motion picture industry and the American people.
(statuette)

The New York Times Annual 'Ten Best'

1st *The Glenn Miller Story*. 5th *Seven Brides For Seven Brothers*.

The Annual Top Moneymaking Films

INCLUDED: *White Christmas*. *The Glenn Miller Story*. *Seven Brides For Seven Brothers*. *Living It Up* (Paramount).

One of the best, most endearing, and enduring biopics to emerge from Hollywood, **The Glenn Miller Story** (Universal International) was, in every respect, a fitting tribute to one of the greatest of the Big Band bandleaders. And, in James Stewart (right), producer Aaron Rosenberg found just the right man to portray him. A lovingly scripted (by Valentine Davies and Oscar Brodney) rags-to-riches account of Miller's rise to eminence (ending with his untimely death in 1944, when the military plane on which he was travelling from England to France, went missing), it was not merely a simple-minded excuse for a series of musical interpolations, but a well-told account of an interesting life, and particularly successful in the way it showed Miller struggling for, and ultimately achieving, the special 'sound' which characterized his most celebrated arrangements. June Allyson (left) had the best role of her career as Mrs Miller, and there was good work too from Irving Bacon and Kathleen Lockhart as Miller's parents, as well as from Henry Morgan, Charles Drake, George Tobias, Marion Ross, Barton MacLane, Sig Rumann, James Bell and Katherine Warren. Also appearing – as themselves – were Louis Armstrong and Gene Krupa (marvellous together in 'Basin Street Blues' by Spencer Williams), Frances Langford, Ben Pollack, The Archie Savage Dancers and The Modernaires. The musical numbers were staged by Kenny Williams; Joseph Gershenson and Henry Mancini were in charge of the musical direction, and it was sensitively directed by Anthony Mann (Technicolor). Stewart's trombone playing was dubbed by Murray MacEachern. Musical numbers included: *Moonlight Serenade* Mitchell Parish, Miller; *In The Mood* Andy Razaf, Joe Garland; *Tuxedo Junction* Buddy Feyne, Erskine Hawkins, William Johnson, William Dash; *Little Brown Jug* J.E. Winner; *Adios* Eddie Woods, Enric Madriguera; *String of Pearls* Eddie DeLange, Jerry Grey; *Pennsylvania 6-5000* Gray, Carl Sigman; *Stairway To The Stars* Mitchell Parish, Matt Malneck, Frank Signorelli; *American Patrol* E.H. Meacham; *I Know Why*; *Chattanooga Choo Choo* Mack Gordon, Harry Warren; *Bidin' My Time* George and Ira Gershwin; *I Dreamed I Dwelt In Marble Halls* Alfred Bunn, Michael Balfe; *St Louis Blues March* arrangement of W.C. Handy's *St Louis Blues* by Ray McKinley, Perry Burgett, Jerry Gray, Glenn Miller.
▽

◁ **Top Banana** (United Artists) was a filmed transcript of the 1951 stage show of the same name. Shot at the Winter Garden Theatre, New York, by producers Al Zugsmith and Ben Peskay and directed by Alfred E. Green, its chief attraction was its star Phil Silvers (illustrated). Playing a character reputedly modelled on comedian Milton Berle, Silvers, as a TV clown with his own show, is ordered by his sponsors to introduce some love interest into the programme. He does so by hiring a pair of young lovers (Judy Lynn, Danny Scholl). Then, much to his dismay, watches as a real love affair develops between them, for he, too, has fallen in love with his ingenue. Hy Kraft wrote the burlesque-inspired book, Johnny Mercer the songs, and it was presented by Harry M. Popkin. Others in the cast were Rose Marie, Jack Albertson, Johnny Coy, Joey and Herbie Faye, Walter Dare Wahl, Bradford Hatton and Dick Dana. Songs and musical numbers included: *A Word A Day*; *If You Want To Be A Top Banana*; *I Fought Every Step Of The Way*; *Sans Souci*; *Only If You're In Love*; *The Man Of The Year This Week*; *My Home Is In My Shoes*.

Performing talent rather than cinematic technique – it was one of the early ventures into CinemaScope – was on display in **New Faces** (20th Century-Fox), a flatly filmed version (with a silly plot appended) of Leonard Sillman's successful Broadway revue which, directed by John Murray Anderson, opened in 1952 and ran for 365 performances. In a cast ranging in quality from brilliant to superb, the stand-out (and most durable) performer was Eartha Kitt (illustrated) who sang 'Bal, Petit Bal' (by F. Lemarque) and gave new meaning to the word 'Monotonous' in a song of the same name by Arthur Siegel and June Carroll. In the filmed version of the show, Kitt's popularity resulted in her being given three additional numbers: 'Uskadara' (adapted from a Turkish folk song), 'C'Est Si Bon' (by Jerry Seelen and Henri Betti) and 'Santa Baby' (by Joan Javits, Phil Springer and Tony Springer). She devoured them all. June Carroll made quite an impression too in a marvellous ballad of infidelity by Murray Grand and Elisse Boyd called 'Guess Who I Saw Today', and, from pint-sized Robert Clary, came the poignant 'I'm In Love With Miss Logan', and 'Lucky Pierre' (both by Ronny Graham). Alice Ghostley's 'Boston Beguine' (by Sheldon Harnick) was another stand-out number; so was 'Penny Candy' (by Siegel and Carroll) sung by June Carroll and danced by Carol Lawrence. There were some excellent sketches too, notably a take-off of Arthur Miller's *Death Of A Salesman*; a wicked send-up of Truman Capote as an effete Southern writer in an item written and performed by Ronny Graham; and Michael Brown's 'Lizzie Borden', performed by about half the company led by Paul Lynde, who featured prominently in the show. The film was directed by Harry Horner, produced by Edward L. Alperson, Berman Swartz and Leonard Sillman, and scripted by various writers including Mel Brooks. The choreography was by Richard Barstow. Also in it were: Virginia de Luce, Bill Mullikin, Rosemary O'Reilly, Allen Conroy, Jimmy Russell, George Smiley, Polly Ward, Johnny Laverty, Elizabeth Logue, Faith Burwell and Clark Ranger. Other items: *Take Off The Mask* Alice Ghostley, Ronny Graham; *Waltzing In Venice*; *Raining Memories*; *He Takes Me Off His Income Tax* Graham; *We've Never Seen You Before* Graham, P. DeVries.

A stagy western spoof in vibrant colour and with a parcel of songs by Jay Livingston and Ray Evans, **Red Garters** (Paramount) always promised a great deal more than it delivered. By inverting every horse-opera cliché, such as the cavalry failing to arrive at the last moment, and the hero failing to score in the climactic shoot-out etc. etc. Michael Fessier's screenplay drew a certain amount of laughs from its subject. But it wasn't strong enough to underline producer Pat Duggan's satirical point of view; nor were the songs or Nick Castle's staging of them, particularly memorable. Which left a talented and energetic cast, headed by Rosemary Clooney (featured centre) as a saloon songstress and Jack Carson as the sheriff, and the man she intends to land, working overtime to create something out of very little. They partially succeeded, with help from co-stars Guy Mitchell (as a cowboy who feuds with Gene Barry), Pat Crowley, Joanne Gilbert (Whose 'Love Is Greater Than I Thought' was one of the show's better tunes), Frank Faylen, Reginald Owen, Cass Daley, Richard Hale and, in a fairly minor role, Buddy Ebsen. Clooney succeeded, in one of the film's best sequences, in creating a hit with 'Brave Man'. The leaden direction was by George Marshall. Other songs and musical numbers: *Bad News*; *Red Garters*; *Meet A Happy Guy*; *A Dime And A Dollar*; *Man And Woman*; *Good Intentions*; *Vaquero*; *Lady Killer*; *Specialty Dance*; *Big Doin's*.

Rhapsody, from a novel by Henry Handel Richardson, came to the screen in CinemaScope and colour, in an adaptation by Ruth and Augustus Goetz and a screenplay by Fay and Michael Kanin, with a cast headed by Elizabeth Taylor (centre, double image), Vittorio Gassman (left) and John Ericson (right). Lavishly presented by MGM and set in such picturesque spots as Zurich and Paris, it told the novelettish story of an extremely wealthy young woman (Taylor) and the romantic problems she encounters with a handsome violinist called Paul Bronte (Gassman). The fact that Miss Taylor insists on nibbling his ears while he practises may have had something to do with Gassman's decision to leave her and devote himself to his career, whereupon Taylor – on the rebound – marries pianist John Ericson and makes his life a misery. But it all came right in the end, with Taylor seeing the error of her spoilt and selfish ways. A soap opera adorned with generous chunks of musical war horses, most notably the Tchaikovsky *Violin Concerto* and the Rachmaninov *Piano Concerto No 2*, it was directed by Charles Vidor for producer Lawrence Weingarten with a cast that also included Louis Calhern, Michael Chekhov, Barbara Bates, Richard Hageman, Richard Lupino, Celia Lovsky, Stuart Whitman and Madge Blake. Michael Rubin dubbed Gassman's violin sequences, and Claudio Arrau played the piano for Ericson.

With *Gentlemen Prefer Blondes* (20th Century-Fox, 1953) very much in mind, producer Edmund Grainger flung together **The French Line** (RKO), a tawdry spin-off of the Marilyn Monroe-Jane Russell hit with Russell (foreground centre left) heading a cast that included Gilbert Roland, Arthur Hunnicutt, Mary McCarty (foreground centre right) and Joyce MacKenzie. A mistaken identity plot involved an inordinately wealthy Texan oil heiress (Russell), seen in various stages of *déshabille*, who takes an ocean trip to Gay Paree after being jilted shortly before her wedding. Roland, as a musical comedy star, turns out to be the man of Russell's dreams, though Hunnicutt, as her drawling Texan guardian, was clearly the better actor. Also cast: Paula Corday, Scott Elliott, Craig Stevens, Laura Elliot, Jayne Mansfield (debut) and Michael St Angel. It was written by Mary Loos and Richard Sale from a story by Matty Kemp and Isabel Dawn, Lloyd Bacon directed, and Billy Daniels staged the dances. The film was photographed in Technicolor and initially released in 3-D. Songs and musical numbers: *Comment Allez-Vous?*; *What Is This That I Feel?*; *Well I'll Be Switched*; *Any Gal From Texas*; *With A Kiss*; *Wait Till You See Paris*; *The French Line*; *By Madame Fuelle*; *Lookin' For Trouble*; *Poor Andre* Josef Myrow, Ralph Blane, Robert Wells.

A story of a group of theatrical entertainers stranded in Miami, **Lucky Me** – Warner Bros.' first musical in CinemaScope – was a singularly undistinguished effort whose trite screenplay (by James O'Hanlon, Robert O'Brien, and Irving Ellison, story by O'Hanlon), sabotaged the combined efforts of Doris Day (left), Robert Cummings, Phil Silvers (right), Eddie Foy Jr, Nancy Walker and Martha Hyer, all of whom looked, in the CinemaScope close-ups, as if they were peering into a giant letter box. Jack Donohue directed it, LeRoy Prinz staged the numbers, and it was produced by Henry Blanke in Warnercolor. Songs and musical numbers: *Lucky Me*; *Superstition Song*; *I Speak To The Stars*; *Take A Memo To The Moon*; *Bluebells Of Broadway*; *High Hopes*; *Men*; *Love You Dearly*; *I Wanna Sing Like An Angel* Sammy Fain, Paul Francis Webster.

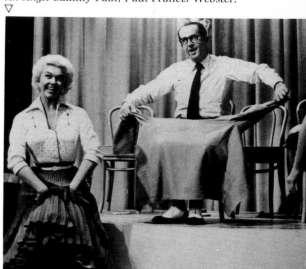

Fifties Musicals

Deep In My Heart (MGM), an all-star biopic of Hungarian-born composer Sigmund Romberg, was produced in Technicolor by Roger Edens, directed by Stanley Donen and, as Sigmund Romberg, starred the versatile Jose Ferrer. Less felicitously cast was the insipid Doe Avedon as Mrs Romberg. Taking the usual liberties with the facts, scenarist Leonard Spigelgass, working from a biography of the composer by Elliott Arnold, came up with the usual ladder-of-fame narrative, showing the composer's step-by-step rise to Broadway eminence after humble beginnings as a musician in a modest Second Avenue café owned by Anna Mueller (a winning performance from opera star Helen Traubel). A song plugger (flashily played by David Burns) persuades Romberg to up-tempo his approach to music, and the result is 'The Leg Of Mutton Rag', Romberg's first commercial success (gloriously performed by Ferrer and Traubel). A string of minor songs in minor shows for the Shubert brothers followed, until *Maytime* – whose success resulted in two Broadway productions of it appearing at the same time. Slightly padding out the non-existent plot was Romberg's romance with Miss Avedon which did, at least, give rise to the best scene in the film: a run-through at a Catskill resort of a new (fictitious) Romberg show called *Jazz A Doo* with all the parts in it being played by Ferrer. Other musical highlights included Ann Miller's dancing of 'It' (not from *Artists And Models* as the film claimed, but from *The Desert Song*, lyrics by Otto Harbach and Oscar Hammerstein II) and Cyd Charisse and James Mitchell's erotic *pas de deux* to 'One Alone' from *The Desert Song* (lyrics Harbach, Hammerstein II). Gene Kelly and his brother Fred (as the O'Ryan

brothers, illustrated centre – Fred left) danced together for the first and last time in a film in 'I Love To Go Swimmin' With Wimmen' (from *Dancing Around* though no such dancers and no such song existed in that particular 1914 production; the number – lyrics by Ballard Mac-Donald – was in fact written for *Love Birds*, 1921, but dropped). Ferrer (excellent throughout as Romberg) joined his real-life wife Rosemary Clooney in 'Mr and Mrs' (lyrics by Cyrus Wood). Merle Oberon was cast as lyricist Dorothy Donnelly, Walter Pidgeon was J.J. Shubert, Paul Henreid Florenz Ziegfeld, and Tamara Toumanova Gaby Deslys, Paul Stewart and Jim Backus completed the cast, and the remaining guest stars were Jane Powell and Vic Damone (who sang 'The Road To Paradise' solo and 'Will You Remember' from *Maytime*, lyrics by Rida Johnson Young, with Powell), William Olvis (singing 'Serenade' from *The Student Prince*, lyric by Dorothy Donnelly), Howard Keel (in 'Your Land And My Land', lyrics by Donnelly, from *My Maryland*) and Tony Martin and Joan Weldon (in 'Lover Come Back To Me' from *The New Moon*, lyric by Oscar Hammerstein II). The choreography was by Eugene Loring. Other songs, musical numbers with their lyricists: *You Will Remember Vienna* (Traubel) Hammerstein II; *Auf Wiedersehn* (Traubel) Herbert Reynolds; *Softly As In A Morning Sunrise* (Toumanova, Traubel) Hammerstein II; *When I Grow Too Old To Dream* (Ferrer, chorus) Hammerstein II; *Stout-Hearted Men* (Traubel) Hammerstein II; *Riff Song* (orchestral); *The Desert Song* (orchestral); *One Kiss* (orchestral); *Deep In My Heart* (chorus) Donnelly; *I Love To Say Hello* (Toumanova) Alex Gerber.

The problems Mario Lanza continued to have with his weight led, ultimately, to his relinquishing the role of Prince Karl in Joseph Pasternak's CinemaScope production of Sigmund Romberg's **The Student Prince** (MGM) to Edmund Purdom (illustrated centre left). Lanza's voice, however, was used in the vocals, with slightly disconcerting results in view of Purdom's tall, slim, rather 'pretty' good looks. Still, after the first half hour or so, audiences began to accept the fact that the Prince's face and the voice emanating from it weren't a perfect match, and settled back to enjoy the glorious outpouring of melody which was the film's *raison d'être*, no one in 1954 being able to take seriously the operetta romance between a handsome aristocrat and a workaday barmaid in 1894 Heidelberg. Ann Blyth (left) was pleasant on both eye and ear as the barmaid Kathie, and there were several stereotyped performances from Louis Calhern as The King of Karlsburg, Edmund Gwenn as the prince's tutor and S.Z. Sakall as a hotelier. Also cast: Betta St John (centre right) as the princess Purdom finally marries, John Williams, John Ericson (right), John Hoyt, Evelyn Varden and Richard Anderson. In addition to such Romberg classics as 'Deep In My Heart', 'Golden Days', 'The Drinking Song' and 'Serenade', were three new ones by Nicholas Brodszky and Paul Francis Webster: 'Beloved', 'Summertime In Heidelberg' and 'I'll Walk With God', as well as the traditional 'Gaudeamus Igitur'. Most unfortunate scene in the film to a present-day viewer: a group of brightly caparisoned students interlocking arms and warbling: 'Come boys, let's all be gay boys'! It was written by William Ludwig and Sonya Levien (based on the operetta by Dorothy Donnelly and a play by William Meyer-Foerster) and directed by Richard Thorpe (Anscocolour).

△

White Christmas (Paramount) grossed $12,000,000 and was the top money-making film of 1954. With a score by Irving Berlin, and with Bing Crosby and Danny Kaye – the latter fresh from his triumph in Paramount's *Knock On Wood* – heading the cast, it was bespoke entertainment for all the family. Kaye, in fact, was a replacement for Donald O'Connor who had injured his leg, which led to the additional casting of John Brascia to partner Vera-Ellen (which he did very well) in several of the dance numbers. A throwback to the days of *Holiday Inn* (Paramount, 1942) and *Blue Skies* (Paramount, 1946), its screenplay, by Norman Panama, Melvin Frank and Norman Krasna, featured Crosby (standing centre right) and Kaye (standing centre left) as – would you believe – a song-and-dance team who, after first meeting while on active service, become pals as well as two of the big names in show business. Deciding to take time off in the company of showgirls Rosemary Clooney (left of Kaye) and Vera-Ellen (right of Crosby), they travel to a New England ski resort only to discover that its owner (Dean Jagger) who had been their general in the army is on the verge of bankruptcy because there hasn't been any snow that year. So they stage a mammoth Christmas benefit for him. It's a roaring success, snow suddenly begins to fall, and the film ends with the resort being saved from closure, and with Crosby and Kaye happy in the arms of Clooney and Vera-Ellen respectively. Fortunately the Berlin songs – most notably 'Sisters', first sung by Clooney and Vera-Ellen, and then by Crosby and Kaye miming to the girls' voices – were a lot better than the plot and, as there were quite a few of them, they helped pass the time agreeably enough. Robert Alton choreographed the two big production numbers, 'I'd Rather See A Minstrel Show' and 'Choreography', though far more effective were the modestly staged 'The Best Things Happen When You're Dancing', performed by Kaye and Vera-Ellen, and Clooney's 'Love, You Didn't Do Right By Me', whose male line-up featured a young George Chakiris. Michael Curtiz directed and it was produced in Vistavision (the first film to use it) and Technicolor by Robert Emmett Dolan with a cast that included Mary Wickes, Anne Whitfield, Grady Sutton and Sig Rumann. Other songs and musical numbers: *White Christmas* (Crosby, Kaye, Clooney, Vera-Ellen); *The Old Man* (Crosby, Kaye); *Gee, I Wish I Was Back In The Army* (Crosby, Kaye, Clooney, Vera-Ellen); *Snow* (Crosby, Kaye, Clooney, Vera-Ellen); *Count Your Blessings Instead Of Sheep* (Crosby, Clooney); *What Can You Do With A General* (Crosby); *Abraham* (Vera-Ellen, Brascia); *Mandy* (Vera-Ellen, Brascia, ensemble); *Heat Wave*; *Let Me Sing*; *Blue Skies* (Crosby, Kaye).

Another bumper musical extravaganza featuring a further batch of Irving Berlin standards, **There's No Business Like Show Business** (20th Century-Fox) was, perhaps, the splashiest of the year's musicals, and – with a cast that included Ethel Merman (top starred), Donald O'Connor, Marilyn Monroe, Dan Dailey, Johnnie Ray (his debut) and Mitzi Gaynor – one of the most entertaining in a seen-it-all-before kind of way. It dealt with the joys and heartaches experienced by a vaudeville family called the Donahues, with Merman and Dailey as Ma and Pa, and Ray, Gaynor and O'Connor as their talented offspring. Though the film ran 117 minutes, not a great deal actually happened in Phoebe and Henry Ephron's screenplay (from a story by Lamar Trotti) other than an alcohol-prone O'Connor having a turbulent on-off love affair with nightclub singer Monroe and (in the film's most nauseating scenes) Johnnie Ray deciding to become a priest. Berlin's 'Alexander's Ragtime Band' was made the subject of the film's big production number, being interpreted by various members of the Donahue family in a number of different ways. Thus Dailey and Merman performed it as heavily accented Swiss might; O'Connor did it Scottish, Gaynor gave it a bit of the 'oo-la-la', while Ray made of it something quite unbelievably lugubrious. Marilyn Monroe did a sexy version of 'Heat Wave', and from O'Connor came some nifty dancing with 'A Man Chases A Girl Until She Catches Him'. Monroe's routines were staged by Jack Cole and all the others by Robert Alton, it was produced in CinemaScope and Colour by Sol C. Siegel, directed by Walter Lang and, in secondary roles, featured Richard Eastham, Hugh O'Brian, Rhys Williams, Lee Patrick, Eve Miller, Robin Raymond and Lyle Talbot. Illustration shows left to right: Merman, Dailey, Gaynor, O'Connor, Monroe. Other songs and musical numbers: *There's No Business Like Show Business* (Merman, Dailey, O'Connor, Ray, Gaynor, Monroe); *When The Midnight Choo Choo Leaves For Alabam* (Merman, Dailey, Gaynor, O'Connor); *Let's Have Another Cup Of Coffee* (Merman); *Play A Simple Melody* (Merman, Dailey); *After You Get What You Want You Don't Want It* (Monroe); *You'd Be Surprised* (Dailey); *A Sailor's Not A Sailor* (Merman, Gaynor); *A Pretty Girl Is Like A Melody* (Merman, Dailey); *Remember* (chorus); *Lazy* (Gaynor, O'Connor, Monroe); *If You Believe* (Ray); *Marie* (trio).
▽

1955

Best Actor
NOMINATIONS INCLUDED: James Cagney *Love Me Or Leave Me* (MGM)

Best Actress
NOMINATIONS INCLUDED: Eleanor Parker *Interrupted Melody* (MGM).

Supporting Actress
NOMINATIONS INCLUDED: Peggy Lee *Pete Kelly's Blues* (Mark VII, WB)

Writing (Motion Picture Story)
Love Me Or Leave Me Daniel Fuchs
(Screenplay)
NOMINATIONS INCLUDED: *Love Me Or Leave Me* Daniel Fuchs and Isobel Lennart
(Story and Screenplay)
Interrupted Melody William Ludwig and Sonya Levien
NOMINATIONS INCLUDED: *It's Always Fair Weather* (MGM) Betty Comden and Adolph Green. *The Seven Little Foys* (Paramount) Melville Shavelson and Jack Rose.

Cinematography (colour)
NOMINATIONS INCLUDED: *Guys And Dolls* (Goldwyn, MGM) Harry Stradling. *Oklahoma!* (Hornblow, Magna Corp.) Robert Surtees.

Art Direction (Set Decoration)
(For the first time, set designers as well as art directors of a winning film received a full-size Academy statuette, instead of a certificate or plaque.)
(colour)
NOMINATIONS INCLUDED: *Daddy Long Legs* (20th Century-Fox) Lyle Wheeler and John DeCuir; Walter M. Scott and Paul S. Fox. *Guys And Dolls* Oliver Smith and Joseph C. Wright; Howard Bristol.

Costume Design (colour)
NOMINATIONS INCLUDED: *Guys And Dolls* Irene Sharaff. *Interrupted Melody* Helen Rose.

Sound Recording
Oklahoma! Todd-AO Sound Dept.; Fred Hynes, sound director
NOMINATIONS INCLUDED: *Love Me Or Leave Me* Wesley C. Miller, sound director.

Film Editing
NOMINATIONS INCLUDED: *Oklahoma!* Gene Ruggiero and George Boemler

Music
Song
NOMINATIONS INCLUDED: 'I'll Never Stop Loving You' *Love Me Or Leave Me* Nicholas Brodszky *cm*; Sammy Cahn *lyr*. 'Something's Gotta Give' *Daddy Long Legs* Johnny Mercer.

Scoring Of A Musical Picture
Oklahoma! Robert Russell Bennett, Jay Blackton and Adolph Deutsch
NOMINATIONS INCLUDED: *Daddy Long Legs* Alfred Newman. *Guys And Dolls* Jay Blackton and Cyril J. Mockridge. *It's Always Fair Weather* Andre Previn. *Love Me Or Leave Me* Percy Faith and George Stoll.

The New York Times Annual 'Ten Best'
8th *It's Always Fair Weather*. 9th *Oklahoma!*

The Annual Top Moneymaking Films
INCLUDED: *The Lady And The Tramp* (Disney, RKO). *A Star Is Born. Pete Kelly's Blues. There's No Business Like Show Business.*

With a more assured director than Gordon Douglas and a sharper script than that provided by Julius J. Epstein and Lenore Coffee, **Young At Heart** (Warner Bros.), a musical remake of the Claude Rains-John Garfield melodrama, *Four Daughters* (1938), might just have worked. Certainly, the unusual teaming of Doris Day (right) as a respectable New England Miss with Frank Sinatra (left) as the embittered songwriter she marries on the rebound, promised more than it delivered, though perhaps their respective styles could never have fruitfully co-existed. Doris's two sisters (the fourth sister was dropped for this version) were charmingly played by Dorothy Malone and Elizabeth Fraser; Gig Young was the composer on whom she originally set her sights, and Ethel Barrymore and Robert Keith her aunt and father. It was produced, in Warnercolor (print by Technicolor), by Henry Blanke. Songs and musical numbers: *Young At Heart* Johnny Richards, Carolyn Leigh; *Hold Me In Your Arms* Ray Heindorf, Charles Henderson, Don Pippin; *Ready, Willing And Able* Floyd Huddleston, Al Rinker, Dick Gleason; *Till My Love Comes To Me* lyrics Paul Francis Webster, music adapted by Ray Heindorf from Mendelssohn's 'On Wings of Song'; *There's A Rising Moon (For Every Falling Star)* Sammy Fain, Webster; *Someone To Watch Over Me* George and Ira Gershwin; *Just One Of Those Things* Cole Porter; *One For My Baby* Harold Arlen, Johnny Mercer; *You, My Love* Mack Gordon, Jimmy Van Heusen.
▽

1956

Academic Awards

Best Picture
NOMINATIONS INCLUDED: *The King And I* (20th Century-Fox) produced by Charles Brackett

Best Actor
Yul Brynner *The King And I*

Best Actress
NOMINATIONS INCLUDED: Deborah Kerr *The King And I*

Direction
NOMINATIONS INCLUDED: Walter Lang *The King And I*

Writing (Motion Picture Story)
NOMINATIONS INCLUDED: *The Eddy Duchin Story* (Columbia) Leo Katcher. *High Society* (MGM) Edward Bernds and Elwood Ullman (withdrawn from final ballot)

Cinematography (colour)
NOMINATIONS INCLUDED: *The Eddy Duchin Story* Harry Stradling. *The King And I* Leon Shamroy.

Art Direction (Set Decoration) (colour)
The King And I Lyle Wheeler and John DeCuir; Walter M. Scott and Paul S. Fox.

Costume Design (colour)
The King And I Irene Sharaff

Sound Recording
The King And I 20th Century-Fox Studio Music Dept.; Carl Falkner, sound director. NOMINATIONS INCLUDED: *The Eddy Duchin Story* Columbia Studio Sound Dept.; John Livadary, sound director.

Music
Song
NOMINATIONS INCLUDED: 'True Love' *High Society* Cole Porter

Scoring Of A Musical Picture
The King And I Alfred Newman and Ken Darby
NOMINATIONS INCLUDED: *The Best Things In Life Are Free* (20th Century-Fox) Lionel Newman. *The Eddy Duchin Story* Morris Stoloff and George Duning. *High Society* Johnny Green and Saul Chaplin. *Meet Me In Las Vegas* (MGM) George Stoll and Johnny Green.

Honorary Award
To Eddie Cantor for distinguished service to the film industry. (statuette)

The New York Times Annual 'Ten Best'
2nd *The King And I*

The Annual Top Moneymaking Films
INCLUDED: *Guys And Dolls* (Goldwyn, MGM). *The King And I. High Society. The Eddy Duchin Story.*

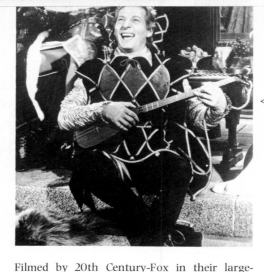

Filmed by 20th Century-Fox in their large-screen CinemaScope 55 process (altogether more successful than Todd-AO), Rodgers and Hammerstein's most tuneful musical, **Carousel**, offered audiences an ear and eyeful of well packaged sentimentality as Gordon MacRae and Shirley Jones re-enacted what was originally Ferenc Molnar's bitter-sweet fantasy *Liliom*. All about a carnival barker called Billy Bigelow (MacRae) who marries a cotton mill girl (Jones), is killed in an attempted robbery, then, years later, is briefly allowed to return to earth to redeem himself and to see his now grown-up daughter, it stuck faithfully to Molnar's original story while, at the same time, undergoing a change of locale from Budapest to New England. Containing some of Rodgers's finest music, it remains one of the most poignant of all Broadway musicals but, at the same time, because of the tightrope it treads between whimsy and *schmaltz*, one of the most difficult to pull off successfully. For most of the time the screen version, with a scenario by Phoebe and Henry Ephron (adapted from the stage show by Oscar Hammerstein II, from an adaptation of Molnar's play by Benjamin F. Glazer), skilfully negotiated the stickier moments in the narrative, thanks mainly to the vigorous, whole-hearted performances of a company that included Cameron Mitchell, Barbara Ruick, Claramae Turner, Robert Rounseville, Susan Luckey, Jacques D'Amboise and Gene Lockhart, as well as the sheer energy generated by Rod Alexander's choreography, especially in the exuberant 'June Is Bustin' Out All Over' (production number illustrated). Charles E. Clarke's Eastmancolor photography was superb; so was the full-bodied playing of the 20th Century-Fox studio orchestra under the direction of Alfred Newman and Ken Darby. Other songs and musical numbers: *Carousel Waltz* (orchestra); *When I Marry Mister Snow* (Ruick); *If I Loved You* (MacRae, Jones); *When The Children Are Asleep* (Rounseville, Ruick); *Soliloquy* (MacRae); *Stonecutters Cut It On Stone* (Mitchell, chorus); *What's The Use Of Wondrin'* (Jones); *A Real Nice Clambake* (Rounseville, Ruick, Mitchell, Turner); *You'll Never Walk Alone* (Jones, Turner); *Carousel Ballet* (Luckey, D'Amboise).
▽

◁ Ye olde mediaeval plotte involving, among other things, wicked olde usurpers to the throne, formed the riotous content of **The Court Jester** (Paramount). The second best thing about it was its total lack of inhibition in matters farcical; the first was the happy casting of Danny Kaye (illustrated) as the titular hero of the piece. Beginning as a potboy to a forest leader, Kaye champions an heir to the throne of England and, in the guise of court jester, gains access to the court of evil Basil Rathbone, whom he schemes to overthrow. Angela Lansbury was cast as Princess Gwendolyn, Glynis Johns was Maid Jean, with other parts in producer-directors Norman Panama and Melvin Frank's knock-about screenplay going to Cecil Parker, Mildred Natwick (as necromancer Griselda), Robert Middleton, Michael Pate, Herbert Rudley, Noel Drayton, John Carradine, Alan Napier and Hermine's Midgets. The songs were by Mrs Danny Kaye (Sylvia Fine) and Sammy Cahn, and the choreography by James Starbuck. (Vistavision and Technicolor). Songs and musical numbers: *Life Could Not Better Be*; *Outfox The Fox*; *I'll Take You Dreaming*; *My Heart Knows A Love Song* Fine, Cahn; *Maladjusted Jester* Fine.

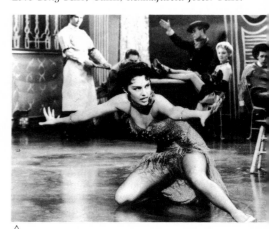
△

Long-legged, loose-limbed Cyd Charisse (illustrated), billed second to Dan Dailey, was the best thing in and about MGM's **Meet Me In Las Vegas** (GB: **Viva Las Vegas**). A simple-minded little yarn, gaudily accoutred in CinemaScope and Eastmancolor, it was set in and about The Sands Hotel, Nevada, and told what happens when a gambling rancher (Dailey) discovers that all he has to do to win at roulette is take hold of ballerina Charisse's hand. Joe Pasternak's high-gloss production gave potential visitors to Vegas a pretty good idea of what the place looks like; Isobel Lennart's screenplay was not without its quota of gags and wisecracks, and the dance routines, by Hermes Pan and Eugene Loring (the latter responsible for the 'Frankie and Johnny Ballet', lyrics by Sammy Cahn), danced by Charisse, John Brascia and Liliane Montevecchi, and sung offstage by Sammy Davis Jr, were entertaining enough. Agnes Moorehead appeared as Dailey's mother, with other parts under Roy Rowland's commonplace direction going to Lili Darvas, Jim Backus, Paul Henreid and Oskar Karlweis. Making guest appearances were Lena Horne, Frankie Laine, Jerry Colonna, Mitsuko Sawamura, Frank Sinatra, Tony Martin and Debbie Reynolds. Other songs and musical numbers: *The Gal With The Yaller Shoes* (Dailey); *If You Can't Dream* (Horne); *My Lucky Charm* (Dailey and Japanese child); *Hell Hath No Fury* (Laine) Sammy Cahn, Nicholas Brodszky; *Rondo Brilliante* (Charisse) Mendelssohn; *Sleeping Beauty* (excerpt, Charisse) Tchaikovsky.

With **The Benny Goodman Story**, Universal-International attempted to do for the clarinettist what *The Glenn Miller Story* (1954) had done for the trombonist but, unfortunately, although the production team was to some extent the same, the results were not nearly as successful. Labouring under a plodding and unimaginative screenplay by Valentine Davies, who also directed, was a cast headed by Steve Allen (right) – making his motion picture debut as Goodman – Donna Reed (left) as his wife, and Berta Gersten as his mother. Also: Herbert Anderson, Robert F. Simon, Sammy Davis Jr, Dick Winslow, Barry Truex, David Kasday, Hy Averback and Wilton Graff. The familiar story of the slum kid who makes good, forms his own swing band, struggles a bit, becomes a successful impresario, then marries into society, its best moments had nothing whatsoever to do with the narrative, but were the result of the copious amount of music appended to it. And, with the participation of Harry James, Gene Krupa, Martha Tilton, Lionel Hampton, Ziggy Elman and Kid Ory – the music was in good hands. It was produced, in Technicolor, by Aaron Rosenberg. Steve Allen's clarinet playing was dubbed by Goodman himself. Musical numbers included: *Let's Dance* Fanny Baldridge, Gregory Stone, Joseph Bonine; *Down South Camp Meeting* Irving Mills, Fletcher Henderson; *It's Been So Long* Walter Donaldson, Harold Adamson; *Bugle-Call Rag* Elmer Schoebel, Billy Meyers, Jack Pettis; *Goody, Goody* Johnny Mercer, Matt Malneck; *Don't Be That Way* Goodman, Mitchell Parish, Edgar Sampson; *Shine* (Harry James) Cecil Mack, Lew Brown, Ford Dabney; *Sing, Sing, Sing* (James, Krupa) Louis Prima; *Stompin' At The Savoy* Goodman, Sampson, Chick Webb, Andy Razaf; *One O'Clock Jump* Count Basie; *Memories Of You* (trio) Eubie Blake, Andy Razaf; *And The Angels Sing* (Tilton) Johnny Mercer, Ziggy Elman; *China Boy* Dick Winfree, Phil Boutelje; *Moonglow* Will Hudson, Eddie DeLange, Irving Mills; *Avalon* Al Jolson, Vincent Rose; *Sensation Rag* E.B. Edwards; *Original Dixieland One Step* (Allen, Ory) Nick La Rocca; *On The Sunny Side Of The Street* (Teddy Wilson) Jimmy McHugh, Dorothy Fields; *King Porter Stomp* Jelly Roll Morton; *Roll 'Em* Mary Lou Williams; *Clarinet Concerto* Mozart.

A vintage MGM musical, **High Society**, with a melodious score by Cole Porter, was a Technicolor remake of Philip Barry's *The Philadelphia Story*, first seen as a Broadway play in 1939, then as an MGM film the following year starring Katharine Hepburn, Cary Grant and James Stewart. The musical remake boasted an equally glittering cast with Bing Crosby (left) top-starred as C.K. Dexter Haven, and Grace Kelly (centre) as his ex-wife, a Philadelphia heiress on the verge of marrying husband number two (John Lund). Frank Sinatra (right) was third-billed as a newspaper reporter assigned to cover Miss Kelly's impending marriage, with Celeste Holm also in it as his chic assistant. The rest of the cast was completed by Louis Calhern, Sidney Blackmer, Margalo Gillmore, Lydia Reed, Richard Keene, Hugh Boswell and, prominently featured as himself, Louis Armstrong. John Patrick's screenplay stuck closely to the guide-lines laid down in Barry's play, with Crosby successfully wooing Kelly away from Lund to ensure a happy ending. All the performances under Charles Walters's direction sparkled, the undoubted musical highlight being Crosby and Armstrong's memorable foray into 'Now You Has Jazz', with Sinatra and Holm's 'Who Wants To Be A Millionaire?' running a close second. Sol C. Siegel produced. Other songs: *High Society Calypso* (Armstrong); *Little One* (Crosby); *True Love* (Crosby, Kelly); *You're Sensational* (Sinatra); *I Love You Samantha* (Crosby, Armstrong); *Well, Did You Evah* (Crosby, Sinatra); *Mind If I Make Love To You?* (Sinatra).

Dean Martin and Jerry Lewis's final film as a team was **Hollywood Or Bust** (Paramount), the bust of the title belonging to Anita Ekberg who, although appearing only towards the end of the film, was referred to throughout as the star film-fan Jerry Lewis most wants to meet. How, in the company of bookie Dean Martin, and Pat Crowley (both illustrated) a girl they encounter while motoring from New York to Hollywood, he finally succeeds in doing so, formed the undernourished content of Erna Lazarus's screenplay. Fortunately director Frank Tashlin managed to endow it with a sense of humour not apparent in the dialogue, his staging of the title number being almost surreal as hordes of pretty, waving girls decorate the roadside from coast to coast. A few comic routines – such as Lewis attempting to fix Miss Crowley's broken-down car, and his skirmish with an aggressive bull – hardly extended the comedian's gifts, nor did the songs written by Sammy Fain and Paul Francis Webster for Martin stretch him as a crooner. In short, predictable entertainment (Vistavision and Technicolor). Maxie Rosenbloom and Jack McElroy completed the cast for producer Hal Wallis. Other songs: *A Day In The Country*; *Let's Be Friendly*; *It Looks Like Love*; *The Wild And Woolly West*. ▷

Gene Kelly began work on **Invitation To The Dance** (MGM) as early as 1952. It was to be a specialized, yet popular, film in four separate parts, utilizing the talents of some of Europe and America's best dancers. Four years later it was finally released having, in the interim, shed sequence number three, in which Kelly and several other dancers interpreted, through the medium of dance, a dozen popular songs. The first of the three remaining ballets was 'Circus'. Composed by Jacques Ibert, it was the tale of a love-sick Pierrot (Kelly) who falls to his death from a high-wire trapeze while trying to impress the girl he loves (Claire Sombert), who loves another (Igor Youskevitch). The second segment, 'Ring Around The Rosy', had music by Andre Previn and was a *La Ronde* type of story which traced the history of a bracelet given by a doting husband to his wife who, in turn, gives it to an artist, who gives it to a model whence it passes to a crook, a nightclub siren, a crooner, a hat-check girl, a sailor, a whore and, finally, back to the husband. It was danced by Kelly (right), Tamara Toumanova (left), Tommy Rall, Claude Bessy, Diane Adams, Igor Youskevitch, Paddy Stone and Irving Davies. The third and final item was 'Sinbad The Sailor', with music from Rimsky-Korsakov's *Scheherazade*. It combined live-action with animated cartoon figures, featured Kelly as a sailor, young David Kasday as a genie, and Carol Haney as Scheherazade. Of the three sections, the middle, being closest in spirit to a typical large scale MGM production number, was the most successful, with some marvellous dancing in it from Tommy Rall. The finale was effective, too, while the first, despite an excellent *pas de deux* by Kelly and Claire Sombert, was relentlessly mannered and pretentious. In it Kelly strove to be the kind of classical dancer he patently was not and the strain showed. The cartoon sequences were directed by Fred Quimby, William Hanna and Joseph Barbera; Kelly served throughout as both choreographer and director, with Arthur Freed in charge of the production. It was photographed in Technicolor by Joseph Ruttenberg and F.A. Young.

△

Not only was **The Pajama Game** (Warner Bros.) – set in a pajama factory and all about a 7½ cents wage dispute – one of the best and most profitable musicals of the decade, it also furnished proof that it was possible to transfer a Broadway hit to the screen almost intact without its becoming stage-bound in the process. Directors George Abbott and Stanley Donen so skilfully opened out the material that one soon forgot its theatrical origins. The 'Once-A-Year Day' picnic scene, for example, was a real movie-stopper, with the camera, no less mobile than Bob Fosse's marvellous dancers, swooping, panning, tracking and practically performing cartwheels. But just as memorable were numbers with an apparently much smaller potential for movie pyrotechnics, such as 'I'll Never Be Jealous Again', sung by Eddie Foy Jr and Reta Shaw as the camera itself seems to do a soft-shoe shuffle over the factory floor; or the hilarious tango 'Hernando's Hideaway' (with Carol Haney). Numbers like these demonstrated that, in a truly cinematic musical, the camera is not a spectator but a performer. Doris Day (left) gave her most enchanting performance ever as the head of the factory's grievance committee, conspiring to look both sexy and wholesome in pajamas, and John Raitt (right) repeated his role as the workshop superintendent, and dancers Buzz Miller and Kenneth LeRoy accompanied Haney in 'Steam Heat'. The screenplay was by George Abbott and Richard Bissell (from the latter's novel *Seven And A Half Cents*) and the superlative score, which included the hit ballad 'Hey, There', by Richard Adler and Jerry Ross. This rejuvenating movie was produced by Abbott and Donen, with Fred Brisson, Robert E. Griffiths and Harold Prince as associate producers. Other musical numbers included: *The Pajama Game*; *I'm Not At All In Love*; *Small Talk*; *There Once Was A Man*; *Seven And A Half Cents*; *Racing With The Clock*.

△

The efforts of a former fan dancer (Virginia Field) to live down her past and, together with her two teenage children (Cary Vinson, right, and Judy Busch), to find acceptance in the small town of Springville, was what **Rockabilly Baby** (20th Century-Fox) was all about. Average programmer material with a cast that also included Douglas Kennedy, Irene Ryan, Ellen Corby, Marlene Willis (left), singer Luis Amando and, as himself, Les Brown, it whiled away 82 minutes painlessly enough, featured six songs, and sufficient plot complications (screenplay by Will George and William Driskill) to engage one's attention without undue strain. It was produced and directed by William F. Claxton. Songs: *We're On Our Way*; *Why Can't I?*; *Is It Love?*; *I'd Rather Be*; *My Calypso Baby* Paul Dunlap; *Teenage Cutie* Dick Kallman.

Elvis Presley (illustrated) signed up with MGM for **Jailhouse Rock**, the best of his three films to date, in which he played an ex-jail-bird (imprisoned on a manslaughter charge) who becomes a rather unlovable pop star on his release. Very much a Presley vehicle from first to last, the film wasted the talents of co-star Judy Tyler (a Broadway singer who, tragically, died shortly after the film's completion), with whom Presley forms a record company and falls in love; and Mickey Shaughnessy as Presley's prison cell-mate and a former folk singer. Completing the cast were Vaughn Taylor, Jennifer Holden and Anne Neyland. Presley's songs were by Jerry Lieber and Mike Stoller, the two best being the title number, sung in prison, and 'Treat Me Nice'. It was produced in CinemaScope and black and white by Pandro S. Berman and the director was Richard Thorpe. Other songs: *Young And Beautiful*; *I Wanna Be Free*; *Don't Leave Me Now*; *Baby I Don't Care* (all sung by Presley).

Yet another case of a minor talent helplessly trying to impersonate a major one, Warner Bros.' **The Helen Morgan Story** (GB: **Both Ends Of The Candle**) was doomed to failure by the casting of Ann Blyth (illustrated) as the great torch singer of the twenties. Although director Michael Curtiz vividly recaptured both the squalor of the carnival sideshows in which Helen Morgan began her career, and the glittering speakeasies which saw her rise to stardom, he could not disguise the void at the centre of the film. Nor was he aided by a routine biopic screenplay by Oscar Saul, Dean Reisner, Stephen Longstreet and Nelson Gidding. Paul Newman played the unscrupulous hustler who helps launch Morgan's career, and Richard Carlson the married man to whom she becomes disastrously attached. Gene Evans, Alan King, Cara Williams and Virginia Vincent led the solid supporting cast. Although Miss Blyth was the possessor of a soprano voice, she was dubbed by Gogi Grant. The producer was Martin Rackin, and the songs and musical numbers were staged by LeRoy Prinz. They included: *Bill* Jerome Kern, P.G. Wodehouse; *Can't Help Lovin' Dat Man*; *Don't Ever Leave Me*; *Why Was I Born?* Kern, Oscar Hammerstein II; *If You Were The Only Girl In The World* Clifford Grey, Nat D. Ayer; *I Can't Give You Anything But Love* Dorothy Fields, Jimmy McHugh; *Avalon* Vincent Rose, Al Jolson; *Breezin' Along With The Breeze* Haven Gillespie, Seymour Simons, Richard Whiting; *Someone To Watch Over Me*; *I've Got A Crush On You*; *Do Do Do* George and Ira Gershwin; *Body And Soul* Edward Heyman, Robert Sour, Frank Eyton, John Green; *I'll Get By* Roy Turk, Fred Ahlert; *The Love Nest* Otto Harbach, Louis A. Hirsch.

▽

1958

Academy Awards
Best Picture
Gigi (MGM) produced by Arthur Freed

Direction
Vincente Minnelli *Gigi*

Writing (Screenplay)
based on material from another medium
Gigi Alan Jay Lerner

Cinematography
After a one-year change in 1957, two awards again given for cinematography achievement
Gigi Joseph Ruttenberg
NOMINATIONS INCLUDED: *South Pacific* (Magna Corp., 20th Century-Fox) Leon Shamroy

Art Direction (Set Decoration)
(black and white or colour)
Gigi William A. Horning and Preston Ames; Henry Grace and Keogh Gleason

Costume Design
(black and white or colour)
Gigi Cecil Beaton

△

Some splendid aerial shots of Rome – gorgeous in Technirama and colour – the unexpected sight of Mario Lanza (illustrated) doing impersonations of Dean Martin, Frankie Laine, Louis Armstrong and Perry Como, plus the haunting strains of 'Arrivederci Roma' (by Renato Rascel and Carl Sigman) powerfully sung by Lanza, were the best things about **The Seven Hills Of Rome** (MGM). The worst were its glossy selection of clichés in which Lanza was featured as an American TV star who journeys to Rome in pursuit of his heiress girlfriend (Peggie Castle) after a lovers' quarrel, meets pretty Maria Alassio, and only towards the end of the film realizes he loves *her* rather than Miss Castle. Composer Rascel was second-billed as Lanza's Roman cousin, with other roles in producer Lester Welch's predominantly Italian cast going to Celia Matania, Rossella Como, Amos Davoli, Guido Celano and Carlo Rizzo. The director was Roy Rowland, and it was written by Art Cohn and Giorgio Prosperi. Other songs: *Seven Hills Of Rome*; *Never Till Now* John Green, Paul Francis Webster; *Earthbound* Jack Taylor, Clive Richardson, Bob Muset; *Come Dance With Me*; *Lolita*; *There's Gonna Be A Party Tonight*; *Italian Calypso*; *Questa o Quella* (from 'Rigoletto') Verdi; *Imitation Routine*; *Temptation* Arthur Freed, Nacio Herb Brown; *Jezebel* Wayne Shanklin; *When The Saints Go Marching In* (trad.); *Memories Are Made Of This* Terry Gilkyson, Richard Dehr, Frank Miller.

Sound
No longer categorized as Sound Recording
South Pacific Todd-AO Sound Dept., Fred Hynes, sound director

Film Editing
Gigi Adrienne Fazan

Special Effects
Tom Thumb (MGM) Tom Howard

Music
Song
'Gigi' *Gigi* Frederick Loewe *cm*; Alan Jay Lerner *lyr*.

Scoring Of A Musical Picture
Gigi Andre Previn
NOMINATIONS INCLUDED: *Damn Yankees* (WB) Ray Heindorf, *Mardi Gras* (20th Century-Fox) Lionel Newman. *South Pacific* Alfred Newman and Ken Darby

Honorary Award
To Maurice Chevalier for his contributions to the world of entertainment for more than half a century. (statuette)

The New York Times Annual 'Ten Best'
2nd *Gigi*. 7th *Damn Yankees*

The Annual Top Moneymaking Films
INCLUDED: *South Pacific*

Pop idol Tommy Sands (illustrated) made his screen debut in **Sing Boy Sing** (20th Century-Fox) whose screenplay by Claude Binyon, from a story by Paul Monash, was a cross between *Loving You* (Paramount, 1957) and *The Jazz Singer* (Warner Bros. 1927). As was the case in the Presley film, Sands was a simple lad from Dixie who is promoted to stardom by a ruthless manager (Edmond O'Brien). Its *Jazz Singer* overtones intruded when, with his preacher grandfather (John McIntire) on the verge of dying, Sands returns home, determined to forsake the $300,000 a year he could be earning in the glare of the spotlights, and becomes a preacher himself. But his heart isn't in it, and it is his wise old Aunt Caroline (Josephine Hutchinson) who, in an impassioned speech, implores him to lead his own life. Giving a performance that was both credible and likeable, Sands made the best of Binyon's familiar but serviceable screenplay, sang a dozen songs (including 'Rock Of Ages') pleasantly, and generally proved himself to be more than just another pretty face. His supporting cast included Nick Adams, Lili Gentle, Diane Jergens and Jerry Paris. It was produced and directed by Henry Ephron. Songs: *Sing Boy Sing*; *Gonna Talk With My Lord*; *Who Baby?*; *Crazy 'Cause I Love You*; *Bundle Of Dreams*; *Your Daddy Wants To Do Right*; *Just A Little Bit More*; *That's All I Want From You*; *People In Love*; *Soda-Pop Song*; *Would I Love You*.
▽

Merry Andrew (MGM) was basically a one-idea ▷ show – the idea being to present an English schoolmaster's hilariously inept adventures as a performer in a circus. Danny Kaye (left) was the teacher turned ringmaster-cum-tumbler-cum-trapeze artist, and it all began when he set out from school one day on an archaeological dig in search of an ancient statue of Pan. What he unearths instead, is Pier Angeli (right), a member of Gallini's Circus, who attracts him even more than the study of antiquities. It was amiable albeit uninspired fare, enlivened by several Saul Chaplin-Johnny Mercer songs, the best being a number called 'Salud' featuring Kaye, Angeli and Salvatore Baccaloni (as the circus owner), plus several excellent dancers all energetically responding to director Michael Kidd's assertive choreography. Based on a Paul Gallico story with a screenplay by Isobel Lennart and I.A.L. Diamond, it also featured Robert Coote, Noel Purcell, Patricia Cutts, Rex Evans, Tommy Rall, Walter Kingsford and Rhys Williams, and was produced by Sol C. Siegel in CinemaScope and Metrocolor. Other songs and musical numbers: *Pipes Of Pan*; *Chin Up Stout Fellows*; *Everything Is Tickety Boo*; *You Can't Always Have What You Want*; *Square Of The Hypotenuse*; *Here's Cheers*.

△

Another fair lady from the team of Alan Jay Lerner and Frederick Loewe, **Gigi** was the last of the great MGM musicals and it justly deserved its eight Academy Awards. The delightful story of a young girl reared by her grandmother and her great-aunt to follow the family tradition by becoming a courtesan, it starred Leslie Caron (right, giving the performance of her career) as Gigi. Louis Jourdan (left) as the handsome, outrageously eligible Gaston Lachaille who scandalizes Gigi's family by actually proposing marriage to her, Maurice Chevalier as his wordly grandfather Honoré, and Hermione Gingold and Isabel Jeans as Gigi's grandmother and great-aunt respectively. Set in *fin de siécle* Paris, it was brilliantly costumed by Cecil Beaton, directed by Vincente Minnelli and scripted by Alan Jay Lerner from the novel by Colette with grace and elegance. In fact, **Gigi** was a stylish triumph from start to finish which sadly – but gloriously – marked the end of an era. (Its producer Arthur Freed would make only one more musical, *Bells Are Ringing*, MGM 1960.) If **Gigi** was one of Freed's finest achievements, it also showed Minnelli on top of his form. For sheer sustained visual opulence and the brilliant use it made of colour,

the film ranks with his work on *Meet Me In St Louis* (MGM, 1944) and *An American In Paris* (MGM, 1951). Musically, too, it was perfection; the highlight of its ravishing and extraordinarily durable score being whatever number you may care to choose: be it the rousing 'The Night They Invented Champagne' (Caron, Jourdan, Gingold), the incomparable 'Gigi' (Jourdan), the tender 'Say A Prayer For Me Tonight' (Caron), Chevalier's jaunty ode to old age 'I'm Glad I'm Not Young Anymore' or, perhaps best of all, the touching 'I Remember It Well', magnificently performed by Chevalier and Gingold on the terrace of a Deauville Hotel against a calculatedly romantic sunset. The richly textured orchestrations throughout were by Conrad Salinger, with Andre Previn in charge of the musical direction. Leslie Caron's vocals were dubbed by Betty Wand, and the cast was completed by Eva Gabor, Jacques Bergerac and John Abbott. It was magnificently photographed in Metrocolor and CinemaScope by Joseph Ruttenberg. Other songs: *Thank Heaven For Little Girls* (Chevalier); *It's A Bore* (Jourdan, Chevalier); *The Parisians* (Caron); *Waltz At Maxim's* (*She's Not Thinking Of Me*) (Jourdan); *Gossip* (chorus).

SHIRLEY MacLAINE in
"SWEET CHARITY" A PANAVISION
OHN McMARTIN · CHITA RIVERA · PAULA KELLY
STUBBY KAYE
MONTALBAN as The Actor
AVIS JR as Big Daddy

LEE
MARVIN   CLINT   JEAN
EASTWOOD SEBERG
PAINT YOUR WAGON

△

Brought to the screen with enough fidelity to maintain the original's quality and flavour, but given sufficient cinematic flair to work purely as film, **Gypsy** was the finest stage-to-film transcription of all the Broadway hits slavishly adapted for the big screen during the sixties and early seventies. The original stage show, with its Arthur Laurents book (adapted from Gypsy Rose Lee's memoirs) and brilliant Jule Styne-Stephen Sondheim score, was the apotheosis of the Broadway musical in its integration of story, character, music and dance, and has become a milestone in the history of the American musical theatre. Leonard Spigelgass's screenplay subtly added depth and texture to the characterizations, plus an immeasurable amount of substance and wit. Other plus factors in the film were producer-director Mervyn LeRoy's loving recreation of a bygone theatrical era, and his use of a perfect cast. The central role of Mama Rose, the stage mother to end them all, had been played on Broadway by Ethel Merman, and where Merman had been volcanic, Rosalind Russell, the screen Rose, was merely dynamic, with Miss Russell accurately conveying Rose's unflagging energy and zeal, her almost frightening ambition and, at the same time, the enthusiasm, warmth and humour that made it feasible that her children loved her while being frustrated by her. As the candy-man Herbie, who becomes Rose's manager, lover, companion and trouble shooter, Karl Malden maintained his masculinity and an attractive simplicity while playing second fiddle to Rose, whose inability to commit herself to marriage finally forces him to desert her. Natalie Wood as the child-woman Louise, later Gypsy (see illustration), was at her loveliest, perfectly capturing the note of gaucheness and vulnerability of the youngster; while her transformation into a sophisticated, determinedly independent (and beautiful) woman, was breathtaking. LeRoy's production, progressing from the heyday of vaudeville, through its dying gasps, to the gaudy world of burlesque, was theatrically stylized, sometimes to bewitching effect – notably in a steamy back alley where one of the chorus boys (Paul Wallace) demonstrates his dreamed-of nightclub act to an adoring Louise. Only after Rose has decided that she will make Louise into a star, does the film momen-

tarily flag, and partial blame must rest with the distributors who cut the lively trio 'Together, Wherever We Go'. The lapse is brief, however, and with the act's erroneous booking into a seedy burlesque house, the stage is set for Louise's debut as a stripper – on which subject she is the recipient of some hilarious tuition from three hardened professionals (Faith Dane, Betty Bruce and Roxanne Arlen) in one of the show's standout numbers, 'You Gotta Have A Gimmick'. Apart from the mentioned excision, the original score was left intact, from the excitingly orchestrated overture (conducted on screen by composer Styne) to Russell's devastating 'Rose's Turn' in which her hopes, regrets, frustrations, her bitterness, and her pent-up desires to be a performer, come blazing out in a musical *tour-de-force*. Russell was partially dubbed by Lisa Kirk in a skilful 'ghosting' blend, and this mesmeric finale, along with other show stoppers like the forceful 'Some People' and the defiantly optimistic 'Everything's Coming Up Roses', were given their full measure of authority. Louise's sister, June (Ann Jillian) bursting onto the Ziegfeld stage with 'Broadway, Broadway', June and Louise's plaintive waltz duet 'If Mama Was Married', and 'Louise's increasingly confident renditions of 'Let Me Entertain You' – the *leit-motif* which transforms itself from 'cute' kiddies' number into Gypsy's artful, sexually suggestive accompaniment to her striptease act were other notable numbers. Frank P. Perkins was the musical supervisor, Harry Stradling was responsible for the evocative photography (Techni-rama and Technicolor) and Robert Tucker choreographed. One must, however, acknowledge the debt that the whole creative team owed to Jerome Robbins who directed and choreographed the stage original. The cast was completed by Diane Pace and Suzanne Cupito (June and Louise as children), Harry Shannon, Parley Baer, Jean Willes, Louis Quinn, George Petrie, Ben Lessy and Guy Raymond. Other numbers: *Small World* (Russell); *Baby June And Her Newsboys* (Cupito, Pace, boys); *Mr Goldstone, I Love You* (Russell, ensemble); *Little Lamb* (Wood); *All I Need Is The Girl* (Wallace, with Wood); *Dainty June And Her Farmboys* (Jilliann, Wood, boys); *Cow Song* (Jillian); *You'll Never Get Away From Me* (Russell, Malden).

Made entirely on location in Europe by Walt Disney Productions, **Almost Angels** (GB: **Born To Sing**) set out to show that there was nothing 'softie' about the numerous youngsters who comprise the famed Vienna Boys' Choir, and that basically they are as regular a bunch of kids as you'd expect to find back home in the States even though one scene showed them dressed up as little girls! Still, the singing was glorious – and there was even something of a plot (by R.A. Stemmle, screenplay by Vernon Harris) concerning a choir boy (Peter Weck) whose voice breaks on the eve of a major tour. Hans Holt, Fritz Eckhardt, Bruni Lobel, Gunther Phillipp, Vincent Winter (illustrated), Sean Scully and Denis Gilmore were also in it, the choreographer was Norman Thomson, the musical director Heinz Schreiter (with Helmuth Froschauer conducting the Vienna Philharmonic Orchestra), and Peter V. Herald was the production supervisor. Steve Perrin directed. The Technicolor production was released by Buena Vista. Songs: *Blue Danube*; *Emperor Waltz*; *Vienna Bonbons*; *Vienna Blood*; *Stadt Und Land*; *Lustiger Rat*; *Tritsch-Tratsch Polka*; *Roses From The South* Johann Strauss II; *Radetsky March* Johann Strauss Sr; *Chicken And The Trout* Froschauer; *Rose On The Meadow*; *The Linden Tree* Franz Schubert; *Cradle Song* Johannes Brahms; *Der Postillon*; *Well Then, The Time Has Come*; *Gay Is The Gypsy Life*; *Winter Is Almost Over*; *Greensleeves* (traditional).

▽

Busby Berkeley was the Second Unit director on ▷
Billy Rose's Jumbo (MGM), the last film on which he worked. An old-fashioned circus extravaganza based on Rose's mammoth 1935 stage production at New York's Hippodrome, it came nowhere near Cecil B. De Mille's *The Greatest Show On Earth* (Paramount, 1952) in quality, spectacle or excitement, and was little more than an excuse for a series of pleasant but undistinguished circus routines and musical numbers. These were tacked on to a familiar plot which featured Doris Day (left) as the daughter of an all-but-bankrupt circus owner (Jimmy Durante, centre right) whose only bankable asset is his elephant Jumbo; and Stephen Boyd (right) as the son of a rival circus owner (Dean Jagger) who infiltrates Durante's circus with sabotage on his mind, but finishes up on Durante's side, and in love with his daughter. The score, by Richard Rodgers and Lorenz Hart, retained the bulk of the numbers originally featured in the 1935 stage presentation, the most imaginatively staged being 'Over And Over Again' performed by Doris Day and several trapeze artists under the Big Top. 'Why Can't I', sung by Day and co-star Martha Raye (as the circus's resident comedienne, centre left) was lifted from Rodgers and Hart's *Spring Is Here* (1929) and, from *The Boys From Syracuse* (1938), came 'This Can't Be Love' (Day). The finale was supplied by Roger Edens and was called 'Sawdust, Spangles And Dreams'. Using material originally written by Rodgers and Hart, it was effectively belted out by the film's four principals, as was the opening, 'The Circus Is On Parade'. Despite the energy and the enthusiasm that went into the project, **Jumbo**, directed by Charles Walters, was somewhat less than jumbo entertainment. The screenplay was by Sidney Sheldon, based on a musical play by Ben Hecht and Charles MacArthur. Joseph Waring, Lynn Wood, Charles Watts, James Chandler, Robert Burton, Wilson Wood, Norman Leavitt and Grady Sutton completed the cast for producers Joe Pasternak and Martin Melcher (Mr Doris Day). The score was orchestrated by Conrad Salinger who, after completing the arrangements for the song 'Little Girl Blue' committed suicide. Other songs and musical numbers: *My Romance*; *The Most Beautiful Girl In The World*.

Except for an ingenious use of backgrounds by ▷ Matisse, Modigliani, Toulouse-Lautrec, Cézanne and Van Gogh, the UPA cartoon **Gay Purr-ee** (illustrated), released by Warner Bros., was derivative of Disney but inferior to the best of his studio's output. The screenplay by Chuck and Dorothy Jones (about a country cat Mewsette, town cat Jaune-Tom, and their misadventures with some city slickers led by smooth, sleek Meowrice) was pleasant if unoriginal, but the Harold Arlen-E.Y. Harburg score didn't quite hit the right note for children and the dubbing by several famous voices – Judy Garland, Robert Goulet, Red Buttons, Hermione Gingold and Mel Blanc – was perhaps not sufficient an attraction for their parents. Paul Frees and Morey Amsterdam were also heard. It was directed (in Technicolor) by Abe Levitow for executive producers Henry J. Saperstein and Lee Orgel. Songs: *Paris Is A Lonely Town*; *The Money Cat*; *Take My Hand, Paree*; *Mewsette*; *Little Drops Of Rain*; *Roses Red, Violets Blue*; *Bubbles*; *The Horse Won't Talk*.

Elvis Presley's fourth film in 1962 was **Girls! Girls! Girls!** (Paramount) and in it he took to the open seas as an impecunious charter boat pilot (illustrated). Laurel Goodwin supplied the romantic interest as a wealthy girl pretending to be a working girl with other parts in Edward Anhalt and Allan Weiss's thoroughly undistinguished screenplay going to Stella Stevens (wasted as a torch singer – although she did have three songs of her own to sing, including 'The Nearness Of You' by Ned Washington and Hoagy Carmichael, and 'Never Let Me Go' by Jay Livingston and Ray Evans), Jeremy Slate, Guy Lee, Benson Fong, Beulah Quo, Robert Strauss, Frank Puglia, Lili Valenti and Barbara and Betty Beall. The film was more convincing musically than dramatically, its numerous songs (staged by Charles O'Curran) being its *raison d'être*. Hal Wallis produced (in Panavision and Technicolor) and Norman Taurog directed. Songs and musical numbers: *Girls, Girls, Girls* Jerry Leiber, Mike Stoller; *Return to Sender*; *We're Coming In Loaded* Otis Blackwell, Winfield Scott; *A Boy Like Me, A Girl Like You*; *Song Of The Shrimp*; *Earth Boy*; *The Walls Have Ears* Sid Tepper, Roy C. Bennett; *Thanks To The Rolling Sea*; *Because Of Love*; *Where Do You Come From?* Ruth Batchelor, Bob Roberts; *We'll Be Together, Mama* Charles O'Curran, Dudley Brooks; *I Don't Wanna Be Tied* Bill Giant, Bernie Baum, Florence Kaye; *I Don't* ◁ *Want To* Janice Torre, Fred Spielman.

△

1964

Academy Awards

Best Picture
My Fair Lady (WB) produced by Jack L. Warner
NOMINATIONS INCLUDED: *Mary Poppins* (Disney, Buena Vista) produced by Walt Disney and Bill Walsh

Best Actor
Rex Harrison *My Fair Lady*

Best Actress
Julie Andrews *Mary Poppins*
NOMINATIONS INCLUDED: Debbie Reynolds *The Unsinkable Molly Brown* (MGM)

Supporting Actor
NOMINATIONS INCLUDED: Stanley Holloway *My Fair Lady*

Supporting Actress
Gladys Cooper *My Fair Lady*

Direction
George Cukor *My Fair Lady*
NOMINATIONS INCLUDED: Robert Stevenson *Mary Poppins*

Writing (Screenplay)
based on material from another medium
NOMINATIONS INCLUDED: *Mary Poppins* Bill Walsh and Don DaGradi. *My Fair Lady* Alan Jay Lerner

Cinematography (colour)
My Fair Lady Harry Stradling
NOMINATIONS INCLUDED: *Mary Poppins* Edward Colman. *The Unsinkable Molly Brown* Daniel L. Fapp

Art Direction (Set Decoration) (colour)
My Fair Lady Gene Allen and Cecil Beaton; George James Hopkins
NOMINATIONS INCLUDED: *Mary Poppins* Carroll Clark and William H. Tuntke; Emile Kuri and Hal Gausman. *The Unsinkable Molly Brown* George W. Davis and Preston Ames; Henry Grace and Hugh Hunt.

Costume Design (colour)
My Fair Lady Cecil Beaton
NOMINATIONS INCLUDED: *Mary Poppins* Tony Walton. *The Unsinkable Molly Brown* Morton Haack.

Sound
My Fair Lady Warner Bros. Studio Sound Dept.; George R. Groves, sound director
NOMINATIONS INCLUDED: *Mary Poppins* Walt Disney Studio Sound Dept.; Robert O. Cook, sound director. *The Unsinkable Molly Brown* MGM Studio Sound Dept.; Franklin E. Milton, sound director

Film Editing
Mary Poppins Cotton Warburton
NOMINATIONS INCLUDED: *My Fair Lady* William Ziegler

Special Visual Effects
Mary Poppins Peter Ellenshaw, Hamilton Luske and Eustace Lycett

Music
Song
'Chim Chim Cher-ee' *Mary Poppins* music and lyrics by Richard M. Sherman and Robert B. Sherman
NOMINATIONS INCLUDED: 'My Kind Of Town' *Robin And The 7 Hoods* (WB) Jimmy Van Heusen *cm*; Sammy Cahn *lyr*.

Score (Substantially Original)
Mary Poppins Richard M. Sherman and Robert B. Sherman

Scoring Of Music (Adaptation or Treatment)
My Fair Lady Andre Previn
NOMINATIONS INCLUDED: *Mary Poppins* Irwin Kostal. *Robin And The 7 Hoods* Nelson Riddle. *The Unsinkable Molly Brown* Robert Armbruster, Leo Arnaud, Jack Elliot, Jack Hayes, Calvin Jackson and Leo Shuken.

The New York Film Critics Awards
Best Motion Picture
My Fair Lady

Best Actor
Rex Harrison *My Fair Lady*

The New York Times Annual 'Ten Best'
7th *Mary Poppins*. 8th *My Fair Lady*

The Annual Top Moneymaking Films
INCLUDED: *The Unsinkable Molly Brown*. *My Fair Lady*. *Viva Las Vegas* (MGM). *Sword In The Stone* (Disney, Buena Vista).

A colourful tourist brochure for Mexico's famous holiday resort, **Fun In Acapulco** (Paramount) tied its exotic locale to a story and screenplay (by Allan Weiss) that featured Elvis Presley (illustrated) as a trapeze artist who, after a tragic incident in which he is responsible for a colleague being seriously maimed, arrives in Acapulco to start life afresh. A shoe-shine lad (Larry Domasin) hears Presley singing, volunteers to become his manager, and finds him a job as a singer-cum-lifeguard at a plush Acapulco hotel. Between songs, Presley became romantically attached to Ursula Andress and a lady bullfighter (Elsa Cardenas), settling in the end for the former, and even managing to overcome his understandable fear of heights by diving off the famous 136 ft cliff at La Quebrada. A light-hearted, lightweight entertainment that left Presley fans light-headed at the physical, romantic and vocal accomplishments of their hero, it also featured Paul Lukas, Alejandro Rey, Robert Carricart and Terry Hope, was directed by Richard Thorpe and glossily produced by Hal Wallis. (Technicolor). Songs: *Bossa Nova Baby* Jerry Leiber, Mike Stoller; *Fun In Acapulco* Ben Weisman, Sid Wayne; *Vino Dinero Y Amor*; *Mexico*; *The Bullfighter Was A Lady* Sid Tepper, Roy C. Bennett; *(There's) No Room To Rhumba In A Sports Car* Fred Wise, Dick Manning; *El Toro* Bill Giant, Bernie Baum, Florence Kaye; *Marguerita* Don Robertson; *I Think I'm Gonna Like It Here* Don Robertson, Hal Blair; *You Can't Say No In Acapulco* Sid Feller, Dolores Fuller, Lee Morris; *Guadalajara* Tito Guizar.

After his fun in Acapulco, Elvis Presley (centre) found himself in hillbilly territory in **Kissin' Cousins** (MGM), a poor man's *Li'l Abner* (Paramount, 1959) in which he played a dual role: an Air Force officer sent to Tennessee to persuade a stubborn hillbilly family to lease their property to the government as a missile launching site; and the blonde backwoods cousin who hates his guts. GI Elvis spends much of his time romancing Yvonne Craig (right); while his cousin sets his sights on shapely Cynthia Pepper. Several songs and dances later, Gerald Drayson Adams and director Gene Nelson's screenplay reached a happy ending for everyone. Two Elvis's for the price of one should have been the bargain offer of the year, but Sam Katzman's Panavision and Metrocolor Production, indifferently directed by Nelson with choreography to match by Hal Belfer, arrived with a dull thud. Also cast: Arthur O'Connell, Glenda Farrell, Jack Albertson, Pamela Austin, Donald Woods. Songs: *Kissin' Cousins* Fred Wise, Randy Starr; *Kissin' Cousins* (No 2); *There's Gold In The Mountains*; *One Boy, Two Little Girls*; *Catchin' On Fast*; *Tender Feeling* Bill Giant, Bernie Baum, Florence Kaye; *Smokey Mountain Boy* Lenore Rosenblatt, Victor Millrose; *Anyone (Could Fall In Love With You)* Bennie Benjamin, Sol Marcus, Louis A. De Jesus; *Barefoot Ballad* Dolores Fuller, Lee Morris; *One Is Enough* Sid Tepper, Roy C. Bennett; *Echoes Of Love* Bob Roberts, Paddy McMains; *(It's A) Long Lonely Highway* Doc Pomus, Mort Shuman (all sung by Elvis).

◁

Julie Andrews made a spectacular movie debut ▷ in **Mary Poppins** (Buena Vista), an appropriately spectacular screen entertainment which, if it did nothing else, served to point an admonishing finger at Jack Warner's temerity (and timidity) in overlooking its star for the plum role of Eliza Doolittle in his production of *My Fair Lady*. **Mary Poppins** set Miss Andrews firmly on the road to international stardom, and heaped adulation on Disney and his creative team of movie magicians. Probably the best, most inventive, original screen musical of the decade, it was as near perfect a realization of the Mary Poppins stories created by P.L. Travers as was possible, with Andrews (right) as the embodiment of the much beloved nanny who takes over the running of the father-dominated Banks household to the delight and wonderment of both the adults and the children. Contributing hugely to the magic purveyed throughout its 140-minute running time were, of course, its special effects, which made **Mary Poppins** the best live-action film in Disney studio's history. Animation played a part in it too, most notably in the scenes in which Mary Poppins, accompanied by young Karen Dotrice and Matthew Garber as Jane and Michael Banks, and co-star Dick Van Dyke (left) as chimney sweep Bert, walks into a typically Disneyesque cartoon land full of frolicking barnyard animals. Another highlight was a cartoon fox hunt to the accompaniment of 'Jolly Holiday', one of the several memorable Richard M. and Robert B. Sherman songs composed especially for the film. Best of all, though, were Van Dyke's two marvellous dances, first with animated penguins, then with several chimney sweeps (and Miss Andrews) across the rooftops of London. Technically they were as fine an achievement as anything Disney had ever done, and choreographically a delight (the dance directors were Marc Breaux and Dee Dee Wood). Other musical highlights included the tongue-twisting 'Supercalifragilisticexpialidocious' sung by Andrews and Van Dyke, 'Chim Chim Cheree' (Van Dyke) and 'A Spoonful Of Sugar' (Andrews). David Tomlinson and Glynis Johns were splendid as Mr and Mrs Banks, with other parts in co-producer Bill Walsh and Donald Da Gradi's screenplay going to Ed Wynn (as Uncle Albert), Hermione Baddeley, Elsa Lanchester, Arthur Treacher, Reginald Owen, Reta Shaw and Jane Darwell. It was photographed in Technicolor by Edward Colman, the special effects were by Peter Ellenshaw, the musical director was Irwin Kostal, and the overall director Robert Stevenson. Other songs and musical numbers: *The Perfect Nanny* (Dotrice, Garber); *Sister Suffragette* (Johns); *The Life I Lead* (Tomlinson); *Stay Awake* (Andrews, Van Dyke, Wynn); *Feed The Birds* (Andrews); *Fidelity Fiduciary Bank* (Van Dyke, Tomlinson); *Let's Go Fly A Kite* (Johns, Tomlinson).

Having already journeyed to Acapulco and Tennessee in 1964, Elvis Presley's third movie ▷ stopover of the year was Las Vegas in MGM's **Viva Las Vegas** (GB: **Love In Las Vegas**), the best and most successful of all Presley's musicals so far. Apart from the man of the moment himself (playing a singing racing car driver who arrives in Vegas to take part in the Grand Prix only to discover that he has engine trouble), the film co-starred Ann-Margret (right) as the swimming instructress he falls for, and with whom he shares a quartet of better-than-average numbers: the title song (by Doc Pomus); 'The Lady Loves Me' (by Sid Tepper and Roy C. Bennett), 'What'd I Say?' (by Ray Charles) and 'The Climb'. The two stars were dynamite together and helped inject into Sally Benson's flimsy screenplay more personality and zest than its meagre ration of plot deserved. David Winters's choreography brought out the best in both Elvis and his leading lady; so did George Sidney's assured direction. It was photographed in Panavision and Metrocolor for producers Sidney and Jack Cummings and, in other roles, featured Cesare Danova as Presley's racing rival, as well as William Demarest, Jack Carter and Nicky Blair. Other songs and musical numbers: *I Need Somebody To Lean On* Doc Pomus; *Come On, Everybody* Stanley Chianese; *Today, Tomorrow and Forever* Bill Giant, Bernie Baum, Florence Kaye; *If You Think I Don't Need You* Bob 'Red' West; *Appreciation*; *My Rival* Marvin More, Bernie Wayne.

Elvis Presley fetched up as handyman to carnival owner Barbara Stanwyck in **Roustabout** (Paramount), his main purpose in scenarist Anthony Lawrence and Allan Weiss's very thin story being to boost business by drawing the crowds with his singing. Which he does most satisfactorily, until a *fracas* with one of the customers results in his accepting a job at a rival carnival. Presley's departure spells gloom and doom for Stanwyck, but all ends happily when his girlfriend, Joan Freeman (illustrated left, with Presley), finally persuades him to return. Leif Erickson, Sue Ane Langdon, Pat Buttram, Joan Staley, Dabs Greer and Steve Brodie were also in it, Joseph Lilley was musical director, the numbers were staged by Earl Barton, and it was photographed in Techniscope and Technicolor by Lucien Ballard. The good-looking production was by Hal Wallis whose director, John Rich, succeeded in making the most of the least. Songs and musical numbers: *Roustabout*; *Poison Ivy League*; *One Track Heart* Bill Giant, Bernie Baum, Florence Kaye; *Little Egypt* Jerry Leiber, Mike Stoller; *Wheels On My Heels*; *It's A Wonderful World* Sid Tepper, Roy C. Bennett; *It's Carnival Time* Ben Weisman, Sid Wayne; *Carny Town* Fred Wise, Randy Starr; *Hard Knocks*; *There's A Brand New Day On The Horizon* Joy Byers; *Big Love, Big Heartache* Fuller, Morris, Hendrix (all sung by ◁ Presley).

Made specifically with youth appeal in mind, producer Joe Pasternak's **Looking For Love** (MGM) combined music and romance in a light-as-air plot that had Connie Francis (illustrated) as a switchboard operator with show business aspirations determinedly pursuing lanky Jim Hutton, but realizing after their first kiss that he isn't for her. The final romantic accounting in Ruth Brooks Flippen's flippant screenplay had Francis finally pairing with a grocery assistant called Cuz Rickober (Joby Baker) leaving Hutton free to fall into the arms of her room-mate (Susan Oliver). There were seven songs in the film, including a reprise (yet again) of Nicholas Brodszky and Sammy Cahn's 'Be My Love' – and they were all sung by Miss Francis. Johnny Carson, Yvette Mimieux, George Hamilton, Paula Prentiss and Danny Thomas made guest appearances, with Barbara Nichols, Jay C. Flippen, Jesse White, Charles Lane and Joan Marshall completing the cast. The director was Don Weiss and it was choreographed by Robert Sidney. A Euterpe Inc.-Franmet Production in Panavision and Metrocolor. Other songs: *Looking For Love*; *Let's Have A Party*; *When The Clock Strikes Midnight* Hank Hunter, Stan Vincent; *Whoever You Are I Love You* Peter Udell, Gary Gold; *This Is My Happiest Moment* Ted Murray, Benny Davis; *I Can't Believe That You're In Love With Me* Jimmy McHugh, Clarence Gaskill.

Jack Warner, who personally supervised the filming of **My Fair Lady** (Warner Bros.), faced almost as many problems in transferring Alan Jay Lerner and Frederick Loewe's blockbuster musical (based, of course, on Shaw's *Pygmalion*) to the screen as did Professor Higgins in turning Eliza Doolittle from a cockney flowerseller into a lady. The initial difficulty lay in the casting: Warner, judging Julie Andrews insufficiently familiar to movie audiences, opted for Audrey Hepburn (a mistake he was later to rue, with the phenomenal success of Miss Andrews in *Mary Poppins* and in *The Sound Of Music*). For Higgins, he had decided on Cary Grant, who wisely declined, remarking that not only would he not play the part, he would not even bother to see the film if someone other than Rex Harrison (right) were chosen. Thus it was that the film became, apart from its other qualities, quite simply a document recording one of the greatest of all musical comedy performances, with familiarity breeding, for Harrison, an even more subtly attuned reading of the role and, for the spectator, an ever increasing admiration. Miss Hepburn (left), on the other hand, made a game attempt but was visibly a lady all the time, which removed much of the story's credibility. Still, with Cecil Beaton's sets and costumes and Hermes Pan's choreography, **My Fair Lady** proved indestructible. George Cukor directed tastefully, making a real show-stopper out of 'Get Me To The Church On Time' with the sublime Stanley Holloway as Doolittle (another second choice: Warner preferred James Cagney!), while other highlights included the 'Ascot Gavotte', whose elegant Edwardian ladies and gentlemen were decked out by Beaton in glorious black and white; 'The Rain In Spain' (Hepburn, Harrison and Wilfrid Hyde-White as Colonel Pickering) and, perhaps most memorable of all, Harrison's unexpectedly touching rendition of 'I've Grown Accustomed To Her Face'. Gladys Cooper was cast as Mrs Higgins, Isobel Elsom as Mrs Eynsford Hill and Jeremy Brett as her lovesick son Freddy. The film, with a screenplay by Alan Jay Lerner, was beautifully photographed in Super Panavision and Technicolor by Harry Stradling. Audrey Hepburn's vocals were dubbed by Marni Nixon. Other songs and musical numbers: *With A Little Bit Of Luck* (Holloway, chorus); *Why Can't The English Teach Their Children How To Speak?* (Harrison); *Show Me* (Hepburn, Brett); *I Could Have Danced All Night* (Hepburn); *Just You Wait, 'Enry 'Iggins* (Hepburn); *Wouldn't It Be Luverly* (Hepburn, chorus); *I'm An Ordinary Man* (Harrison); *Embassy Waltz* (orch.); *On The Street Where You Live* (Brett); *You Did It* (Harrison, Hyde-White); *Without You* (Hepburn); *Servants' Chorus* (chorus); *A Hymn To Him* (Harrison).

Meredith Willson's 1960 Broadway hit, **The Unsinkable Molly Brown**, reached the screen via MGM with Debbie Reynolds in the role created on stage by Tammy Grimes. Harve Presnell, making his movie debut, co-starred as Johnny Brown, the role he played on Broadway, and if the pairing wasn't exactly explosive, neither was the film. Rather, it was a solid workmanlike transfer from stage to screen of a solid workmanlike piece of Broadway carpentry that didn't have an original idea in its head. The story of a hoydenish foundling from Colorado who strikes it rich after marrying handsome Harve – its main plot emphasis centred on *nouveau riche* Molly's fight to become accepted into snobby Denver society. She embarks on a self-improvement tour of Europe, and her new-found sophistication, plus her heroism while returning to the States on the *Titanic*, changes her backwoods status overnight and, after nearly losing her man, she not only wins back his love, but also the undivided approval of the Denverites. Reynolds gave her all, but was unable to hide the fact that she was acting her head off. Presnell, on the other hand, underplayed to the point of vapidity. Just the right note of exuberance, however, was struck by Peter Gennaro's choreography – seen at its buoyant best in a number (not in the stage show) called 'He's My Friend', as well as in the infectious 'Belly Up To The Bar Boys' (illustrated, with Reynolds). Helen Deutsch's screenplay stuck fairly closely to Richard Morris's original book, and had featured parts in it for Ed Begley as Reynolds's foster father, Hermione Baddeley and Jack Kruschen as two of Begley's colourful cronies, Martita Hunt and Vassili Lambrinos. Also: George Mitchell, Harvey Lembeck, Fred Essler, Gus Trikonis, Grover Dale and Hayden Rorke. Laurence Weingarten produced (in CinemaScope and Metrocolor) and it was directed, with verve substituting for inspiration, by Charles Walters. Other songs and musical numbers: *I'll Never Say No; I Ain't Down Yet; Colorado My Home; Soliloquy; Dolce Far Niente* (background); *Up Where The People Are* (shorter version of Broadway original).

If Warner Bros.' **Robin And The 7 Hoods** had been as amusing an experience for audiences as it patently was for the cast, it would have broken box-office records. A Robin Hood parody whose basic joke was that the skulduggery took place in gangland Chicago *circa* 1928, it was marred by the self-indulgent fooling of such talents as Frank Sinatra (left), Dean Martin (right), Sammy Davis Jr, Peter Falk and (as Allen A. Dale) Bing Crosby (centre), and by a rambling screenplay by David R. Schwartz. Edward G. Robinson made an extremely brief guest appearance (he was killed off before you could say 'Edward G. Robinson'), with Barbara Rush, Victor Buono, Hank Henry, Allen Jenkins and Jack La Rue also in it. Unfortunately, director Gordon Douglas made little effort to keep The Clan in check, and the film's most deserved credit was William H. Daniels's for his brilliant colour photography. A P.E. Production, it was filmed in Technicolor and Panavision and produced by Sinatra, with Howard W. Koch as executive producer. The songs were by Jimmy Van Heusen and Sammy Cahn – the two best being Sinatra's 'My Kind Of Town', and 'Style' – stylishly sung and danced by Sinatra, Crosby and Martin. Other songs and musical numbers: *All For One* (Falk); *Don't Be A Do-Badder* (Crosby); *Any Man Who Loves His Mother* (Martin); *Mr Booze* (Sinatra, Crosby, Martin, Davis); *Bang Bang* (Davis); *Charlotte Couldn't Charleston* (Chorus); *Give Praise* (Chorus).

Producer Sam Katzman, who was nothing if not a trend follower, caught on to the currently popular (and profitable) craze for the Watusi with MGM's **Get Yourself A College Girl** (GB: **The Swingin' Set**), billing music-makers The Dave Clark Five, The Animals, The Jimmy Smith Trio, Stan Getz, Astrud Gilberto, The Standells and Roberta Linn and Freddie Bell and The Bell Boys, above both the title and his dramatic cast – which showed precisely in which direction his priorities lay. And – considering the unutterable banality of Robert E. Kent's story and screenplay (about a goodlooking student in an exclusive girls' school who endangers her tenure there when it is discovered that she is the composer of several hit tunes, but who is saved from dismissal by a descendant of the school's founder, now a would-be senator badly in need of some young folks' votes) – who could blame him? Mary Ann Mobley (a former Miss World, right) played the undergraduate tunesmith and Willard Waterman was the would-be senator, with other roles under Sidney Miller's perfunctory direction going to Chad Everett, Joan O'Brien, Nancy Sinatra (left), Chris Noel and Fabrizio Mioni. Hal Belfer staged the numbers. (Metrocolor). Songs included: *Get Yourself A College Girl* Sidney Miller, Fred Karger; *The Swingin' Set* Donnie Brooks, Miller, Karger.

1965

Fort Lauderdale during Easter was the setting of Elvis Presley's latest romp, **Girl Happy** (MGM), and although art directors George W. Davis and Addison Hehr saw fit to provide the Florida landscape with mountains, at least the music was authentic Presley, and his fans gave it the thumbs up. Storyline had Presley (illustrated) being hired by a Chicago nightclub owner (Harold J. Stone) to look after his over-exuberant daughter (Shelley Fabares, illustrated) for the duration of her Fort Lauderdale vacation, which was easier said than done. Harvey Bullock and R.S. Allen's screenplay won no awards for originality or invention, but it provided a solid enough foundation on which to balance the show's twelve musical numbers – the best being 'She's Evil' sung by Presley and Fabares, and Presley's 'Wolf Call' (by Bill Giant, Bernie Baum and Florence Kaye). Nita Talbot, as a stripper, also did well by a number called 'Good News' (by Sam Cooke) in which she was covered in newspaper. It was produced by Joe Pasternak in Panavision and Metrocolor, with a cast that included Gary Crosby (left), Joby Baker (2nd left),

A modest but entertaining biopic of country and western singer Hank Williams, **Your Cheatin' Heart** (MGM) starred George Hamilton (left) as the composer-singer (his vocals were dubbed by the subject's son, Hank Williams Jr) and Susan Oliver (right) as Audrey, the girl he meets while performing in a travelling medicine show, and marries. A familiar rags to riches story, its screenplay, by Stanford Whitmore, alternated the joy and the tragedy that featured so prominently in Williams's life, providing an excellent part for Red Buttons as Shorty Younger, the trouper who became Williams's life-long friend and who tried desperately to rehabilitate him when success robbed him of his touch with the common folk and drove him to drink. Arthur O'Connell played Fred Rose, the music publisher who gave Williams his first important break, with other roles under Gene Nelson's caring direction going to Shary Marshall, Chris Crosby, Rex Holman, Hortense Petra and Roy Engel. The producer, for Four Lead Productions, was Sam Katzman. Songs: *Your Cheatin' Heart*; *Hey, Good Lookin'*; *I Saw The Light*; *Jambalaya*; *Ramblin' Man*; *I'm So Lonesome I Could Cry*; *Cold Cold Heart*; *Kaw-Liga*; *I Can't Help It*; *Long Gone Lonesome Blues*; *You Win Again* all by Williams.

Mary Ann Mobley, Jimmy Hawkins (right) and Jackie Coogan; the choreographer was David Winters and it was directed by Boris Sagal. Other songs and musical numbers: *Girl Happy* Doc Pomus, Norman Meade; *Cross My Heart And Hope To Die* Ben Weisman, Sid Wayne; *Do Not Disturb*; *Spring Fever* Giant, Baum, Kaye; *Fort Lauderdale Chamber Of Commerce*; *Puppet On A String* Sid Tepper, Roy C. Bennett; *I've Got To Find My Baby*; *The Meanest Girl In Town* Joy Byers; *Startin' Tonight* Lenore Rosenblatt, Victor Millrose; *Do The Clam* Weisman, Wayne, Dolores Fuller.

Louis M. Heyward's screenplay for American International's **Sergeant Deadhead** centred on the switch made by bumbling airman Frankie Avalon when, after changing personality during a space trip following a guardhouse breakout, he becomes a snooty extrovert. At the end of the film's 89-minute running time, he is rehabilitated back into his old, likeable self, in which guise he and co-star Deborah Walley are paired to provide the final clinch. Far more interesting than the youngsters were some of the older members of the cast, especially Fred Clark and Eve Arden (both illustrated) as a WAF commander and his sweetheart, the latter doing well by Guy Hemric and Jerry Styner's 'You Should've Seen The One That Got Away'. Cesar Romero, Gale Gordon and Reginald Gardiner were also in it (as a trio of inspectors who come to witness a missile launch); so were Harvey Lembeck, John Ashley and Buster Keaton. James H. Nicholson and Samuel Arkoff produced (in Pathecolor and Panavision), it was choreographed by Jack Baker, and the director was Norman Taurog. Other songs and musical numbers: *Sergeant Deadhead*; *The Difference In Me Is You*; *Let's Play Love*; *Two-Timin' Angel*; *How Can You Tell?*; *Hurry Up And Wait* Hemric, Styner.

△

Though Rodgers and Hammerstein's monumentally successful **The Sound Of Music** (20th Century-Fox) – which has grossed over $80,000,000 to date – was a decided improvement on the long-running Broadway hit from whence it came, the mawkish sentimentality it oozed from every frame of its 174-minute running time made it difficult to enjoy without the uneasy feeling that one's emotions were being mercilessly manipulated. Yet, as a piece of old-fashioned popular entertainment with both eyes firmly on the box-office cash registers of the world, it was a shrewdly professional piece of work, stunningly presented, and crafted with awesome expertise. It also starred Julie Andrews (centre left) who, alone in a cast that included an unsympathetic and wooden Christopher Plummer (centre), as well as Eleanor Parker (as the Baroness), Richard Haydn (as Max Detweiler), Peggy Wood (as Mother Abbess) and Charmian Carr (as Liesl), managed to wade through the molasses of Ernest Lehman's screenplay (from the book by Howard Lindsay and Russel Crouse) while keeping her head above it all. She played Maria, the postulant nun who forsakes the abbey for a position as governess to the seven children (illustrated) of martinet widower Captain Von Trapp (Plummer), and remains on in his household (after the obligatory set-backs) to become his wife. It was Andrews's extraordinarily assured and appealing central performance – coupled with some magnificent Todd-AO and Color by De Luxe aerial views of Salzburg (the story's setting), photographed by Ted McCord, that was largely responsible for the film's enormous success. Marc Breaux and Dee Dee Wood choreographed the simple but effective dance routines, Boris Leven, the art director, made excellent use of Salzburg's architectural landmarks, and the production and direction were by Robert Wise. Completing the cast: Heather Menzies, Nicolas Hammond, Duane Chase, Angela Cartwright, Debbie Turner, Kym Karath, Anna Lee, Portia Nelson, Ben Wright, Daniel Truhitte, Norma Varden, Gil Stuart, Marni Nixon, and Evadne Baker. Christopher Plummer's vocals were dubbed by Bill Lee. Songs and musical numbers: *The Sound Of Music* (Andrews); *Praeludium* (nun's chorus); *Morning Hymn And Alleluia* (nun's chorus); *Maria* (Lee, Nixon, Nelson, Baker); *I Have Confidence In Me* (Andrews); *Sixteen Going On Seventeen* (Carr, Truhitte); *Climb Every Mountain* (Wood); *Lonely Goatherd* (Andrews, Baird Marionettes); *Do-Re-Mi* (Andrews, children); *Something Good* (Andrews, Plummer); *Edelweiss* (Plummer, Andrews, children); *So Long, Farewell* (children); *Processional* (orchestra); *My Favourite Things* (Andrews).

I'll Take Sweden (United Artists), was a self-conscious effort on behalf of its writers – Nat Perrin, Bob Fisher and Arthur Marx – to be 'with it'. Bob Hope played a widowed oil company executive who, to free his perfectly contented daughter (Tuesday Weld) from the clutches of her impoverished boyfriend (Frankie Avalon), gets himself transferred to Sweden. In Sweden the situation, as far as the harassed Hope is concerned, is even worse, for, in that country's climate of free love, Weld is soon taken up by a suave lecher (Jeremy Slate) of whom papa disapproves even more than he did of Avalon. As for Hope himself, he too finds himself romantically involved – with an interior decorator (Dina Merrill). Avalon (centre) sang the title number (by Diane Lampert and Ken Lauber) as part of a lakeside production number, Hope sang 'Nothing Can Compare With You' (by 'By' Dunham), a group called The Vulcans were featured in 'Watusi Joe' (by Jimmie Haskell and Jim Economides) and Miss Weld was heard but once in 'Give It To Me' (by Haskell and Dunham). Edward Small and Alex Gottlieb were the producer and associate producer of this tedious Technicolor frolic, with Frederick De Cordova directing. Also cast: Rosemarie Frankland, Walter Sande, John Qualen, Peter Bourne, Fay De Witt, Alice Frost and Roy Roberts. Other songs: *Killin' Polka*; *Mad Latina*; *Take It Off*; *Tell Me, Tell Me* Jimmie Haskell, 'By' Dunham; *The Bells Keep Ringin'*; *Peep Show*; *There'll Be Rainbows Again* Dunham, Bobby Beverly; *Would Ya Like My Last Name* Kenneth Lampert, Diane Lampert.

▽

◁

Elvis Presley's **Tickle Me** (Allied Artists) certainly didn't tickle the fancy of the critics who justifiably consigned it to the trash can where it belonged. The story of a rodeo rider who signs on as a horse wrangler at an expensive Arizona dude ranch-cum-beauty spa, it thrust its star among a bevy of lovelies (see illustration), while at the same time involving him in a plot to rescue a cache of gold from a bunch of crooks. Jocelyn Lane was the rightful owner of the hidden fortune, Julie Adams the owner of the dude ranch, with other parts in Elwood Ullman and Edward Bernds's silly screenplay falling to Jack Mullaney, Merry Anders, Connie Gilchrist, Edward Faulkner, Bill Williams and Louis Elias. There were nine songs, all of which came from previous Presley albums and all of which were staged by David Winters. It was produced by Ben Schwalb in Panavision and Color by De Luxe, and directed by Norman Taurog with the accent on slapstick. Songs: *(It's A) Long, Lonely Highway*; *Night Rider* Doc Pomus, Mort Shuman; *It Feels So Right* Ben Weisman, Fred Wise; *Dirty Dirty Feeling* (English version of *Si Seulement!*) Jerry Leiber, Mike Stoller; *(Such An) Easy Question* Otis Blackwell, Winfield Scott; *Put The Blame On Me* Norman Blagman, Kathleen G. Twomey, Wise; *I'm Yours* Don Robertson, Hal Blair; *I Feel That I've Known You Forever* Pomus, Alan Jeffreys; *Slowly But Surely* Sid Wayne, Weisman.

▽

Box-office wise, it appeared that Elvis Presley (illustrated) could do no wrong. His films from 1957 to 1965 grossed in excess of $175,000,000 – even with such dyed-in-the-wool stinkers as **Harum Scarum** (GB: **Harum Holiday**). A frightful *mélange* of this and that from MGM, it featured Presley as a movie star who is kidnapped by a group of assassins while on a personal appearance tour of the Middle East. In no time at all he finds himself decked out like Rudolph Valentino in *The Sheikh*, and involved in a plot to kill the king. Gerald Drayson Adams's screenplay, trading in one absurdity after another, must have given even the lad from Memphis's most ardent admirers a bit of a headache; ditto Gene Nelson's plodding direction. Mary Ann Mobley co-starred as a princess, with other roles in this Technicolored, Four Leaf Production going to Fran Jeffries, Michael Ansara, Jay Novello, Philip Reed, Theo Marcuse, Dick Harvey, and Busby Berkeley's favourite midget, Billy Barty. The dances were staged by Earl Barton. Songs and musical numbers: *Harum Scarum* Peter Andreoli, Vince Poncia Jr, Jimmie Crane; *Golden Coins*; *Go East, Young Man*; *Shake That Tambourine*; *Animal Instinct*; *Wisdom Of The Ages*; *Mirage* Bill Giant, Bernie Baum, Florence Kaye; *Hey Little Girl*; *So Close, Yet So Far (From Paradise)* Joy Byers; *My Desert Serenade* Stanley Jay Gelber; *Kismet* Sid Tepper, Roy C. Bennett.

1966

Academy Awards

Music
Scoring Of Music (Adaptation or Treatment)
A Funny Thing Happened On The Way To The Forum (United Artists) Ken Thorne
NOMINATIONS INCLUDED: *The Singing Nun* (MGM) Harry Sukman

Despite the five golden Gershwin oldies featured in MGM's **When The Boys Meet The Girls**, the film was a depressing retread of *Girl Crazy* – first seen as an RKO film in 1932, then as a vehicle for Mickey Rooney and Judy Garland from MGM in 1943. Connie Francis (left) and Harve Presnell (right) were top-starred as a couple who run a dude ranch for divorcées, with Sue Ane Langdon as the 'other' woman. Fred Clark, Frank Faylen and Joby Baker were in it too; so were Sam The Sham and The Pharaohs, Herman's Hermits, Louis Armstrong and, playing a number called 'Aruba', which he wrote himself, Liberace. It was produced in Panavision and Metrocolor for Four Leaf Productions by Sam Katzman, choreographed by Earl Barton, and directed by Alvin Ganzer. Robert E. Kent wrote it from the stage musical *Girl Crazy* by Guy Bolton and John McGowan. Songs and musical numbers: *But Not For Me* (Francis, Presnell); *I Got Rhythm* (Francis, Presnell, Armstrong); *Bidin' My Time* (Herman's Hermits); *Embraceable You* (Presnell); *Treat Me Rough* (Langdon) George and Ira Gershwin; *When The Boys Meet The Girls* (Francis) Jack Keller, Howard Greenfield; *Mail Call* (Francis) Fred Karger, Ben Weisman, Sid Wayne; *Monkey See, Monkey Do* (Sam and Pharaohs) Johnny Farrow; *Listen People* (Herman's Hermits) Graham Gouldman; *Throw It Out Of Your Mind* (Armstrong) Armstrong, Bill Kayle.
▽

The problem in bringing the Bert Shevelove-Larry Gelbart-Stephen Sondheim Broadway hit, **A Funny Thing Happened On The Way To The Forum** (United Artists) to the screen, was finding a cinematic counterpart for the stage show's near perfect construction. It was a problem only partially solved by director Dick Lester, whose approach to the material was to drop several of the original songs and to impose a completely new rhythm and pace onto the convoluted story of Pseudolus, a house slave in ancient Rome, who hopes to win his freedom by organizing things so that his young master and an innocent courtesan in a neighbouring bawdy house can elope. Lester also indulged in a series of sight gags, jump cuts and (as in the Beatles films), flashy editing, often to the detriment of Melvin Frank and Michael Pertwee's deliciously anachronistic screenplay. Very much a hit and miss affair in which the hits, fortunately, outnumbered the misses, it scored a bull's eye everytime where its performances were concerned, with the larger-than-life Zero Mostel (right) heading a glorious cast that included Phil Silvers (left), Michael Crawford and Annette Andre (as the suitably simple-minded young lovers), Michael Hordern, Leon Greene and, best of all, Jack Gilford (centre right) as the aptly named slave Hysterium. Buster Keaton (centre left), in his last film appearance, was in it too. The one cherishable musical moment was the brilliant 'Everybody Ought To Have A Maid' ('sweeping out, sleeping in') sung by Mostel, Silvers, Gilford and Hordern. Ethel and George Martin staged the numbers, the production and costumes were designed by Tony Walton, and it was produced in Color by De Luxe by Melvin Frank. Other songs and musical numbers: *Comedy Tonight* (Mostel); *Lovely* (Mostel, Crawford, Andre, Gilford); *Bring Me My Bride* (Greene); *The Dirge* (Greene).

British pop group Herman's Hermits (illustrated, leader Peter Noone, foreground) received star billing in **Hold On!** (MGM), a witless encumbrance which found the five Hermits being shadowed, while on a tour of the USA, by a space agency scientist (Herbert Anderson) out to check their credentials and to see whether they are worthy enough to have a nose-cone named after them. Female interest was supplied by Sue Ane Langdon as a pushy starlet out to make the headlines, and by Shelley Fabares as Noone's other half. Also cast: Bernard Fox, Harry Hickock, Hortense Petra and Mickey Deems. Sam Katzman produced in Panavision and Metrocolor and Arthur Lubin directed from a screenplay by James B. Gordon. Wilda Taylor choreographed. Songs and musical numbers: *Hold On!*; *A Must To Avoid*; *All The Things I Do For You Baby*; *Where Were You When I Needed You?* P.F. Sloan, Steve Barri; *Make Me Happy*; *The George And Dragon*; *Got A Feeling*; *We Want You, Herman*; *Wild Love*; *Gotta Get Away* Fred Karger, Sid Wayne, Ben Weisman; *Leaning On A Lamp Post* Noel Gay.
▽

Elvis Presley's 22nd film in ten years was **Spinout** (GB: **California Holiday**), and in it he played the leader of a touring musical combo who prefers his Dusenberg to the quartet of girls who inundate his life – namely millionaire's daughter Shelley Fabares, best-selling authoress Diane McBain, Deborah Walley and, briefly, Dodie Marshall (left, with Presley). In the end he marries all four of them. Theodore J. Flicker and George Kirgo were actually paid for writing it, the eight musical numbers were staged by Jack Baker, and it was directed by Norman Taurog with a cast that also included Jack Mullaney, Will Hutchins, Warren Berlinger, Jimmy Hawkins, Cecil Kellaway and Una Merkel. A Euterpe Picture distributed by MGM, it was produced in Panavision and Metrocolor by Joe Pasternak. Songs and musical numbers: *Stop, Look, Listen* Joy Byers; *Adam And Evil* Fred Wise, Randy Starr; *All That I Am*; *Am I Ready*; *Smorgasbord* Sid Tepper, Roy C. Bennett; *Never Say Yes* Doc Pomus, Mort Shuman; *Beach Shack* Bill Giant, Florence Kaye, Bernie Baum; *I'll Be Back* Sid
◁ Wayne, Ben Weisman.

△

Sixteen years after the death of Gertrude Lawrence, 20th Century-Fox accorded her a colourful accolade of sorts in **Star!**, a glittering $12,000,000 worth of celluloid biography in which they cast Julie Andrews as the legendary Gertie – not because she was ideal for the part, but because she happened to be the hottest star around at the time. And it says much for Miss Andrews that, despite the polarities in temperament of the two ladies, she did a most credible and creditable job. Like many show-biz stories, this one began in poverty – in Clapham, London, where Gertrude Lawrence was born. Scenarist William Fairchild's handling of his subject's early struggles during her music hall and chorus girl days was the best thing in a long (165 minutes), familiar, rags-to-riches chronicle that tended to run out of dramatic steam in direct ratio to its star's rise to fame. Which is not to say that the film was short on narrative incident. On the contrary, it was just that the sight of a successful but destructively selfish Gertie becoming the toast of two continents was less compelling than the zestful struggles she faced before her career took off. Fortunately, though, the film was also a veritable sardine-tin of musical numbers on to which one could anchor one's restless spirits. And with such composers as Noel Coward (played by Daniel Massey), Cole Porter and the Gershwins providing many of the tunes, the numbers (choreographed by Michael Kidd) were decidedly welcome in their own right. Julie Andrews (illustrated, as Coward's 'Parisian Pierrot') sang virtually all the songs, generally solo, sometimes with one of her male co-stars or accompanied by dancers. There were many musical standouts, three of which were Miss Andrews's renditions of Kurt Weill and Ira Gershwin's 'Jenny' and Cole Porter's 'The Physician' – both a far cry from the *Mary Poppins – Sound Of Music* image generally associated with her – and Daniel Massey's urbane presentation of Noel Coward's 'Forbidden Fruit'. Richard Crenna was second-billed as Richard Aldrich, Gertie's forceful, sympathetic and supportive second husband, with other parts going to Jenny Agutter (Gertie's daughter), Bruce Forsyth as her music hall-performer father, Beryl Reid as her mother, as well as Michael Craig, Robert Reed, John Collin, Alan Oppenheimer, Richard Karlin and Lynley Laurence. The production was designed by Boris Leven, photographed in Todd-AO and Color by De Luxe by Ernest Laszlo, produced

by Saul Chaplin, and directed by Robert Wise. Songs and musical numbers: *Star!* Jimmy Van Heusen, Sammy Cahn; *Piccadilly* Walter Williams, Bruce Seiver, Paul Morande; *Oh It's A Lovely War* J.P. Long, Maurice Scott; *My Garden Of Joy* Saul Chaplin; *'n Everything* Buddy De Sylva, Gus Kahn, Al Jolson; *Burlington Bertie From Bow* William Hargreaves; *Limehouse Blues* Philip Brahm, Douglas Furber; *Someone To Watch Over Me*; *Dear Little Boy*; *Do Do Do* George and Ira Gershwin; *Someday I'll Find You*; *Has Anybody Seen Our Ship?* Coward; *My Ship* Kurt Weill, Ira Gershwin. The film also contained an extract from Noel Coward's play *Private Lives*. Interesting sideline: After the film's release, and its failure to garner the hoped-for box-office returns, it was shortened and re-released under a new title, *Those Were The Happy Days*. It remained, however, a financial failure in both versions.

△

Though the fictitious storyline attached to United Artists' **The Night They Raided Minsky's** (GB: **The Night They Invented Striptease**) told of an innocent lass (Britt Ekland) from the Amish country – an area inhabited by a puritan religious sect – who arrives in New York's East Side hoping to find fame as a dancer, but finds it, instead, as the inventor of the strip tease (the top of her dress accidentally falls off while she is in the middle of a 'bible dance' at Minsky's famous burlesque theatre), the film's strength derived not from its plot but from its sleazy atmosphere, and the period nostalgia it evoked. It also benefited from the performances of Jason Robards (right) as Minsky's fast-talking 'straight man', his comedian rival Norman Wisdom (left), and Bert Lahr as a retired comedian responsible for introducing Miss Ekland (centre) into the seltzer bottle, bawdy skit, beefy chorus line world of burlesque. Completing the excellent cast were Forrest Tucker, Harry Andrews (as Ekland's father), Joseph Wiseman, Denholm Elliott, Elliott Gould and Jack Burns. The lively, affectionate screenplay (unburdened by such strictures as good taste) was by Arnold Schulman, Sidney Michaels and Norman Lear (the latter producing for Bud Yorkin-Norman Lear Productions), and William Friedkin directed. The narration was spoken and the title song (by Lee Adams and Charles Strouse) performed by Rudy Vallee, and the choreography was by Danny Daniels. Songs and musical numbers: *The Night They Raided Minsky's*; *A Perfect Gentleman*; *Take Ten Terrific Girls*; *You Rat, You*; *Penny Arcade*; *How I Loved Her*; *Wait For Me (love theme)* Adams, Strouse.

Although the E.Y. Harburg-Burton Lane musical fantasy **Finian's Rainbow** (Warner Bros.) clocked up more than seven hundred performances on stage, its unique blend of blarney, social comment and sheer Broadway know-how was a decidedly tricky substance to recapture on film and it eluded Francis Ford Coppola, still a relative newcomer to Hollywood, who directed it. Harburg's plotline (which he and co-librettist Fred Saidy adapted and slightly updated for the screen) concerned a whimsically naive Irish immigrant living in Rainbow Valley, Missitucky, somewhere near Fort Knox, who argues that America's riches have blossomed as a result of the country's buried gold underground at Fort Knox, and decides to reap the same reward by 'planting' a crock of gold he had once stolen from a leprechaun. A sub-plot involving a racist southern senator who, abusing one of the three wishes granted by the gold, is turned into a black, further emphasized the moral of the tale: that gold *is* a base metal and people constitute the world's true wealth. Fred Astaire (left), as Finian McLonergan, looked like an oversized leprechaun and would have been ideal for the role ten years earlier; Petula Clark (right) played his daughter and Don Francks the object of her affections. Tommy Steele, Barbara Hancock, Keenan Wynn, Al Freeman Jr, Jester Hairston, Avon Long, Roy Glenn and Ronald Colby were also to be seen, it was choreographed by Hermes Pan, and produced in Technicolor and Panavision by Joseph Landon. Songs and musical numbers: *How Are Things In Glocca Morra?*; *If this Isn't Love*; *Look To The Rainbow*; *Old Devil Moon*; *Something Sort Of Grandish*; *The Begat*; *This Time Of The Year*; *That Great Come-And-Get-It Day*; *When The Idle Poor Become The Idle Rich*; *When I'm Not Near The Girl I Love*; *Rain Dance Ballet*.
▽

◁ A sort of *Hellzapoppin'* 1968 style, **Head** (Columbia) took the synthetically manufactured and patently untalented pop group, the Monkees (illustrated), through a series of psychedelic-type situations best experienced under the influence of marijuana. A few amusing moments – such as an assault on a Coca Cola machine, and a sequence in which the pop group appear as dandruff in guest-star Victor Mature's hair – revealed a certain visual imagination in producer-director Bob Rafaelson's approach to the plotless material (he also 'wrote' it together with co-producer Jack Nicholson). But for the most part it was a free-wheeling, hit-or-miss affair. Also cast: Annette Funicello, Timothy Carye, Logan Ramsay, Abraham Sofaer, Vito Scotti, and female impersonator T.C. Jones. Nicholson and Rafaelson also appeared – as themselves – and Toni Basil choreographed. (Technicolor). Songs and musical numbers: *Porpoise Song* Gerry Goffin, Carole King; *Circle Sky* Michael Nesmith; *As We Go Along* King, Toni Stern; *Daddy's Song* Nilsson; *Long Title: Do I Have To Do This All Over Again?*; *Can You Dig It?* Peter Tork.

Owing more to *The Happiest Millionaire* (Buena Vista, 1967) than *Mary Poppins* (Buena Vista, 1964), Buena Vista's **The One And Only Genuine Original Family Band** (see illustration) was another clanger from the Disney stable whose uninviting subject was the political race between Grover Cleveland and Benjamin Harrison. Based on the autobiography of Laura Bower Van Nuys, of Rapid City, South Dakota (who was one of the children featured in the story), its screenplay, by Lowell S. Hawley, attempted to draw mileage from the fact that grandpa Walter Brennan was an ardent Democrat while the rest of his brood were staunch Republicans. Hawley's attempts were unsuccessful, and his failure reflected badly in Brennan's tiresome performance, as well as on the perfomances of Buddy Ebsen and Janet Blair in the thankless roles of Ma and Pa Bower. Lesley Ann Warren and John Davidson (stale from their failure in *The Happiest Millionaire*) were the young lovers, with other parts in Bill Anderson's flaccid, Technicolor production going to Kurt Russell, Steve Harmon, Richard Deacon, Wally Cox, Debbie Smith, Goldie Hawn, Bobby Riha and Smitty Wordes. Trying unsuccessfully to hang it all together was director Michael O'Herlihy, the Sherman brothers provided the lack-lustre score, and the dull choreography was by Hugh Lambert. Songs and musical numbers: *The One And Only Genuine Original Family Band*; *Dakota*; *Drummin' Drummin' Drummin'*; *Let's Put It Over With Grover*; *Ten Feet Off The Ground*; *'Bout Time*; *The Happiest Girl Alive*; *Oh Benjamin Harrison*; *West Of Wide Missouri*.
▽

1969

Academy Awards

Best Picture
NOMINATIONS INCLUDED: *Hello, Dolly!* (20th Century-Fox) produced by Ernest Lehman

Best Actor
NOMINATIONS INCLUDED: Peter O'Toole *Goodbye, Mr. Chips* (MGM)

Direction
NOMINATIONS INCLUDED: Arthur Penn *Alice's Restaurant* (United Artists)

Cinematography
NOMINATIONS INCLUDED: *Hello, Dolly!* Harry Stradling Sr.

Art Direction (Set Decoration)
Hello, Dolly! John DeCuir, Jack Martin Smith and Herman Blumenthal; Walter M. Scott, George Hopkins and Raphael Bretton.
NOMINATIONS INCLUDED: *Sweet Charity* (Universal) Alexander Golitzen and George C. Webb; Jack D. Moore.

Costume Design
NOMINATIONS INCLUDED: *Hello, Dolly!* Irene Sharaff *Sweet Charity* Edith Head.

Sound
Hello, Dolly! Jack Solomon and Murray Spivack

Film Editing
NOMINATIONS INCLUDED: *Hello, Dolly!* William Reynolds

Score Of A Musical Picture (Original or Adaptation)
Hello, Dolly! Lennie Hayton and Lionel Newman
NOMINATIONS INCLUDED: *Goodbye, Mr. Chips* Leslie Bricusse and John Williams. *Paint Your Wagon* (Paramount) Nelson Riddle. *Sweet Charity* Cy Coleman.

The New York Times Annual 'Ten Best'
INCLUDED: *Alice's Restaurant*.

The Annual Top Moneymaking Films
INCLUDED: *Funny Girl* (Columbia). *Finian's Rainbow* (Warner Bros.-Seven Arts).

With MGM's musical remake of their wonderful 1939 weepie, **Goodbye, Mr Chips**, audiences were ready to cry 'Good riddance!', and who could blame them? James Hilton's best seller about the shy, retiring and soon to be retired schoolmaster looking back over his life was totally unsuited to big-budget musical treatment, nor was the enterprise helped one bit by Peter O'Toole's unconvincing and unappealing performance in the title role (it could not be mentioned in the same breath as Robert Donat's in the earlier version), or by Leslie Bricusse's thoroughly undistinguished score. Petula Clark (illustrated, with O'Toole) played the musical comedy star whom Chips marries to the dismay of headmaster Michael Redgrave; with George Baker, Jack Hedley and Sian Phillips offering stalwart, but futile support. Terence Rattigan wrote the screenplay, Herbert Ross directed, and Arthur P. Jacobs produced (in Panavision and Metrocolor). Songs and musical numbers: *Fill The World With Love*; *Where Did My Childhood Go?*; *London Is London*; *And The Sky Smiled*; *Apollo*; *When I Am Older*; *Walk Through The World*; *What Shall I Do With Today?*; *What A Lot Of Flowers*; *Schooldays*; *When I Was Younger*; *You And I*.

Based on the hit recording, 'The Alice's Restaurant Massacree', in which Arlo Guthrie (right), son of Woody, recounted incidents from his past, including an arrest for littering and his fleeting induction into the US Army – **Alice's Restaurant** (United Artists), written by Venable Herndon and its director, Arthur Penn, was a strikingly original, often hauntingly beautiful account of life in the sixties as experienced by a young man at odds with society. Guthrie's early years – his short-lived college career, his home life and his friendships, especially with a young couple called Alice and Ray Brook who live in a deconsecrated church in Stockbridge and own a restaurant that becomes a haven for hippies – was handled with charm and insight. The Brooks were superbly played by Pat Quinn and James Broderick, with other parts in Hillard Elkins and Joe Manduke's commendable production going to Geoff Outlaw, Tina Chen (left), Kathleen Dabney, Shelley Plimpton, and, as themselves, Pete Seeger and Police Chief William Obanhein. Although basically Guthrie could not be called an actor, he knew how to make his likeable presence felt, and supplied most of the songs. It was stunningly photographed by Michael Nebbia in Color De Luxe. Songs: *Alice's Restaurant Massacree*; *Chilling Of The Evening*; *Ring Around A Rosy Rag*; *Now And Then*; *I'm Going Home*; *Motorcycle Song*; *Highway In The Wind* (Guthrie) Arlo Guthrie; *Amazing Grace* (choir); *Songs For Ageing Children* (Joni Mitchell) Mitchell; *The Pastures Of Plenty* (Pete Seeger) Woody Guthrie.
▽

1970

Academy Awards

Costume Design
NOMINATIONS INCLUDED: *Darling Lili*
(Paramount) Donald Brooks and Jack Bear.

Music
Song
NOMINATIONS INCLUDED: 'Whistling Away
The Dark' *Darling Lili* Henry Mancini *cm*;
Johnny Mercer *lyr*.

Original Song Score
NOMINATIONS INCLUDED: *Darling Lili* Henry
Mancini and Johnny Mercer. *A Boy
Named Charlie Brown* (Mendelson-Melendez.
Cinema Center Films, National General) Rod
McKuen, John Scott Trotter, Bill Melendez,
Al Shean and Vince Guaraldi

Jean Hersholt Humanitarian Award
Frank Sinatra

The Annual Top Moneymaking Films
INCLUDED: *Hello, Dolly!* (Chenault, 20th
Century-Fox).

The Aristocats (Buena Vista) cost the Walt
Disney organization $4,000,000 to draw, and it
was worth every cent. The delightful story of a
'catnapping' (the victims being a mama cat and
her three offspring, Toulouse, Berlioz and Marie)
perpetrated by a greedy, evil old butler who'd
rather his mistress left her fortune to him than to
her cats (illustrated), its strength, and most of its
fun, lay in the instantly recognizable 'human'
elements embodied in the animals on display.
Apart from the feline family around which Tom
Rowe and Tom McGowan's amusing little story
revolved, other characters who featured prominently included a group of Bohemian hip-cat
musicians headed by Scat Cat, the romantic
alley cat O'Malley, a mouse called Roquefort, a
pair of hounds named Napoleon and Lafayette
and, most endearing of all, a couple of spinster
geese called Agatha and Abigail. Lending their
voices to these creations were Phil Harris, Eva
Gabor, Sterling Holloway, Scatman Crothers,
Paul Winchell, Lord Tim Hudson, Carole Shelley, Hermione Baddeley, Nancy Kulp, Dean
Clark, Liz English, Gary Dubin and Pat Buttram.
It was produced in Technicolor by Wolfgang
Reitherman and Winston Hibler, with Reither-
man directing from a screenplay by Larry Clem-
mons. Songs and musical numbers: *The Aristo-
cats* (title song sung by Maurice Chevalier); *She
Never Felt Alone* (Gabor); *Scales And Arpeggios*
(Gabor and 'kittens') Richard M. and Robert B.
Sherman; *Thomas O'Malley Cat* (Harris) Terry
Gilkyson; *Everybody Wants To Be A Cat* (Harris,
Crothers) Floyd Huddlestone, Al Rinker.

The sight of Julie Andrews doing a strip-tease
gave **Darling Lili** (Paramount) what little novelty
value it had. For most of its 136-minute running
time, producer-director Blake Edwards's multi-
million dollar extravaganza was an utter bore
that mixed music, melodrama, adventure, and
romance to indigestible effect. The Mata Hari
story of a World War I stage star who also
happens to be a German spy called Lili Smith,
it top-cast Julie Andrews (illustrated) as the
darling of the title, co-starred Rock Hudson (as
an American air squadron commander who
knows all about her treacherous activities but
loves her just the same) with Jeremy Kemp,
Lance Percival, Michael Witney, Jacques Marin,
Andre Marianne and Gloria Paul in support. It
was written by Edwards and William Peter
Blatty who failed to bring a point of view to their
material resulting in their star's performance
carrying even less conviction than the screenplay and the indifferent numbers written for the
star by Henry Mancini and Johnny Mercer.
Musically speaking, the film temporarily flickered into life only when Andrews was belting
out some well-worn World War I favourites
such as 'Pack Up Your Troubles In Your Old Kit
Bag' by Felix Powell and George Asaf, 'It's A
Long Way To Tipperary' by Jack Judge and
Harry Williams, and 'Keep The Home Fires
Burning' by Ivor Novello and Lena Guilbert-
Ford. Physically, the production looked far
better than it sounded, its French and Belgian
exteriors appearing especially inviting in Russell
Harlan's splendid Technicolor photography.
Hermes Pan choreographed. Songs and musical
numbers: *Darling Lili*; *Smile Away Each Rainy
Day*; *Whistling Away The Dark*; *Little Birds*; *A Girl
In No-Man's Land*; *I'll Give You Three Guesses*;
Skol; *Your Goodwill Ambassador*.

Not even Barbra Streisand could save **On A
Clear Day You Can See Forever** (Paramount)
from being the confused mish-mash it was
under Vincente Minnelli's unusually faltering
direction. Based on the stage show (book and
lyrics by Alan Jay Lerner and music by Burton
Lane), its theme was reincarnation as demonstrated by heroine Streisand who, when not
under co-star Yves Montand's hypnotic spell, is
just plain Daisy Gamble from Flatbush, Brooklyn.
Under hypnosis, however, she regresses to the
18th century, taking on the persona of a breathtaking aristocratic beauty called Melinda Wain-
whistle whose childhood was spent in an orphan-
age (see illustration, Streisand centre). Though
Lerner's screenplay differed a great deal from his
book for the stage version – and, indeed, was a
distinct improvement on it – it was, nonetheless,
the victim of some brutal editing which rendered
much of the narrative unintelligible. Another
victim of the editor's scissors was Jack Nicholson

as Streisand's guitar-strumming hippy-type ex-
step-brother, whose one song (as well as an
elaborate production number) was completely
eliminated from the final release print. Larry
Blyden played Streisand's boring fiancé, with
other parts in the Howard W. Koch-Alan Jay
Lerner production going to Bob Newhart, Simon
Oakland, John Richardson, Pamela Brown and
Irene Handl. The numbers were staged by
Howard Jeffrey without much flair, the best being
Montand's visually quite interesting 'Come Back
To Me'. Streisand's singing of the half a dozen
numbers retained for her from the original
Broadway production (which had starred the
volatile Barbara Harris) was dynamic, and pro-
vided the only bright spots in a dull and top-
heavy show. (Panavision and Technicolor) Other
songs: *He Isn't You*; *Go To Sleep*; *Hurry, Its Lovely
Up Here*; *Love With All The Trimmings*; *Melinda*; *On
A Clear Day You Can See Forever*; *What Did I Have
That I Don't Have?*

In a misguided attempt to recreate the phenomenal success of *The Sound Of Music* (20th Century-Fox, 1965), producers Virginia and Andrew Stone poured into their vast Super Panavision 70 and Color De Luxe screen version of the 1944 Broadway success **Song Of Norway** (ABC) about as much treacle as it could comfortably contain, and then some. A monument to kitsch (including cartoon and puppet sequences), the only element to emerge unscathed was its sublime Norwegian scenery — a setting appropriate to the story it told of the life and times of composer Edvard Grieg. Heading a cast whose multi-national flavour resembled something out of the United Nations, was Toralv Maurstadt as the maestro himself and Florence Henderson (illustrated) as his wife Nina, with other roles in Stone's cliché-cramped screenplay (based on the musical by Milton Lazarus from a play by Homer Curran) being caricatured to the hilt by Frank Poretta, Harry Secombe, Robert Morley, Edward G. Robinson, Oscar Homolka, Christina Schollin and Elizabeth Larner. The music was by Grieg and the lyrics by Bob Wright and Chet Forrest — the same team who put words to Borodin's music in *Kismet*. Lee Theodore was responsible for the energetic but numbingly familiar dance routines, Davis Boulton for the picture-postcard views of the fjords and mountains, and John Ogden for the piano playing. Andrew Stone directed. Songs and musical numbers: *Solveig's Song*; *Piano Concerto In A Minor*; *Life Of A Wife Of A Sailor*; *Freddy And His Fiddle*; *A Rhyme And A Reason*; *Strange Music*; *Song Of Norway*; *Ribbons And Wrappings*; *The Little House*; *When We Wed*; *At Christmastime*; *In The Hall Of The Mountain King*; *Wrong To Dream*; *Hill Of Dreams*; *Hymn Of Betrothal*; *Be A Boy Again*; *Hand In Hand*; *Three There Were*; *The Solitary Wanderer*; *I Love You*.

Based on the NBC television series for children, **Pufnstuf** (Universal) was a totally forgettable, and soon forgotten, musical fantasy about a little boy (Jack Wild, illustrated) and his adventures with a dragon, a gopher and various witches (most notably Martha Raye and Mama Cass). Also featured were Billy Hayes, Roberto Gamonet, Sharon Baird and Johnny Silver; it was produced by Si Rose, who also wrote the screenplay with John Fenton Murray, and directed by Hollingsworth Morse. Songs and musical numbers: *Pufnstuf*; *Angel Raid*; *Charge*; *Fire In The Castle*; *Happy Hour*; *Leaving Living Island*; *Rescue Racer To The Rescue*; *Witchiepoo's Lament*; *Different* Charles Fox, Norman Gimbel.

1971
Academy Awards

Best Picture
NOMINATIONS INCLUDED: *Fiddler On The Roof* (Mirsch, United Artists) produced by Norman Jewison

Best Actor
NOMINATIONS INCLUDED: Topol *Fiddler On The Roof*

Supporting Actor
NOMINATIONS INCLUDED: Leonard Frey *Fiddler On The Roof*

Direction
NOMINATIONS INCLUDED: Norman Jewison *Fiddler On The Roof*

Art Direction (Set Decoration)
NOMINATIONS INCLUDED: *Bedknobs And Broomsticks* (Disney, Buena Vista) John B. Mansbridge and Peter Ellenshaw; Emile Kuri and Hal Gausman. *Fiddler On The Roof* Robert Boyle and Michael Stringer, Peter Lamont.

Costume Design
NOMINATIONS INCLUDED: *Bedknobs And Broomsticks* Bill Thomas

Sound
Fiddler On The Roof Gordon K. McCallum and David Hildyard

Cinematography
Fiddler On The Roof Oswald Morris

Special Visual Effects
Bedknobs And Broomsticks Alan Maley, Eustace Lycett and Danny Lee

Music
Song
NOMINATIONS INCLUDED: 'The Age Of Not Believing' *Bedknobs And Broomsticks* music and lyrics by Richard M. Sherman and Robert B. Sherman

Scoring (Adaptation and Original Song Score)
Fiddler On The Roof John Williams NOMINATIONS INCLUDED: *Bedknobs And Broomsticks* Richard M. Sherman, Robert M. Sherman and Irwin Kostal. *The Boy Friend* (MGM) Peter Maxwell Davies and Peter Greenwell. *Willy Wonka And The Chocolate Factory* (Paramount) Leslie Bricusse, Anthony Newley and Walter Scharf.

The Annual Top Moneymaking Films
INCLUDED: *The Aristocats* (Disney, Buena Vista).

Another entertaining full-length animated cartoon, but not really for children, **Shinbone Alley**, with a screenplay by Mel Brooks and Joe Darion (based on characters created by Don Marquis, and on Darion's book of the 1957 Broadway musical), told of the misadventures of a cockroach called archy (a reincarnation of a poet who does his free verse writing on an old typewriter belonging to a newspaper columnist, but cannot manage the key that provides the capital letters) and his unrequited romance with Mehitabel (illustrated) a friendly neighbourhood cat who claims her soul once belonged to Cleopatra. Eddie Bracken (who played archy on Broadway) lent only his voice on this occasion, while Carol Channing was heard as Mehitabel (Eartha Kitt played the role on stage). The other voices on the sound track belonged to Alan Reed, Ken Sanson, Hal Smith, Joan Gerber, Sal Delano and The Jackie Ward Singers. The music and lyrics were by George Kleinsinger and Joe Darion, the best number being an item called 'Flotsam and Jetsam'. An Allied Artists release of a Fine Arts Films Production, it was produced (in Technicolor) by Preston M. Fleet and directed by John David Wilson. Other songs: *Toujours Gai*; *A Woman Wouldn't Be A Woman*; *Cheerio My Deario*.

Roald Dahl's **Willie Wonka And The Chocolate Factory** (based on his story *Charlie And The Chocolate Factory*) was the tale of a young lad called Charlie who, together with four obnoxious children, is given a chance to tour a magic chocolate factory while, at the same time, having his character tested by Willy Wonka, the factory's rather eccentric owner. In theory, and with all its obvious ingredients for success, it should have been ideal family entertainment. And had it been made by the Walt Disney studios it probably would have been. The Stan Margulies-David Wolper production, however, filmed in Bavaria and released by Paramount, was as hard to swallow as a toffee. Lacking visual flair, creative imagination and a hummable song or two (the thoroughly mundane score was by Anthony Newley and Leslie Bricusse), it simply failed to come to life, resulting in a lot of very bored six-year-olds wondering what on earth it was all about. Gene Wilder (illustrated centre) worked hard as Wonka, but to no avail; young Peter Ostrum was Charlie and Jack Albertson was his grandpa Joe, with other parts under Mel Stuart's galumphing direction going to Roy Kinnear, Julie Dawn Cole, Leonard Stone, Denise Nickerson, Dodo Denney, Paris Themmen, Michael Bollner and Ursula Reit. Howard Jeffrey choreographed, and it was photographed in Technicolor by Arthur Ibbetson. Songs and musical numbers: *Candy Man*; *Cheer Up Charlie*; *I've Got A Golden Ticket*; *Pure Imagination*; *Oompaloompa-doompa-dee-doo*; *I Want It Now*.

The latest in a spate of stage-to-screen transfers ▷
was **Fiddler On The Roof** (Mirisch-United
Artists) which, at 3,242 performances, was one
of the longest running Broadway musicals of all
time. Producer-director Norman Jewison clearly
had no choice but to replace the stage show's
stylized, Chagall-inspired settings with the real
thing, but the consequence was that the whole
conception of the show as originally directed
and choreographed by Jerome Robbins, underwent a change which was not, unfortunately,
for the better. On stage, **Fiddler On The Roof** was
a work of art that was a tribute to the American
musical comedy theatre. On screen, in Panavision 70 and Technicolor (and at 180 minutes), it
was merely another big-budget Broadway
transfer whose 'opening up' served only to
minimize its impact. Also missing from the
screen version was the sheer exuberance and
exhilaration engendered by Robbins's choreography. Director Jewison seemed to cut away
from the dances at all the wrong moments with
the result that at no time were audiences swept
up by the infectious rhythms of Jerry Bock and
Sheldon Harnick's memorable score as they had
been in the theatre. Israeli actor Chaim Topol
(illustrated) who played the role of the milkman
Tevye with great charisma and success on the
London stage (it was created on Broadway, most
memorably, by Zero Mostel) brought immense
charm to his screen performance, but not much
conviction or authority. Norma Crane as his
wife Golde was even less convincing, which left
the acting honours to Molly Picon as Yente the
Matchmaker and Leonard Frey as Motel the
tailor. The rest of the cast included Paul Mann as
Lazar Wolf the Butcher, Rosalind Harris, Michele Marsh, and Neva Small as Tevye's eldest
daughters Tzeitel, Hodel and Chava, Michael
Glaser as Perchik, Patience Collier as Grandma
Tzeitel and Tutte Lemkow as the Fiddler (violin
dubbed by Isaac Stern). The village of Anatevka
in which this simple Sholem Aleichem tale
about a milkman, his wife, and five dowryless
daughters, takes place (in 1905), was designed
by Robert Boyle and photographed by Oswald
Morris at Pinewood Studios, England, and on
location in Yugoslavia. It was written by Joseph
Stein with admirable fidelity to his stage play,
and choreographed by Robbins, Tom Abbott
and Sammy Bayes. The musical director was
John Williams. Songs and musical numbers:
Prologue – Fiddler On The Roof (Stern); *Tradition*
(Topol, chorus); *Matchmaker, Matchmaker* (Har-
ris, Marsh, Small, Edwards, Candy Bonstein); *If I
Were A Rich Man* (Topol); *Sabbath Prayer* (Topol,
Crane, chorus); *To Life* (Topol, Mann, chorus);
Miracle Of Miracles (Frey, Harris); *Tevye's Dream*
(Topol, Collier, chorus); *Sunrise, Sunset* (Topol,
Crane, chorus); *Wedding Celebration And Bottle
Dance* (chorus); *Do You Love Me?* (Topol, Crane);
Far From The Home I Love (Marsh); *Chava Ballet*
(Harris, Marsh, Small); *Anatevka* (Topol, Crane,
Picon, Mann, chorus).

More successful on every level than *Willie
Wonka* was the latest entry from the Disney
stable, **Bedknobs And Broomsticks** (Buena
Vista). Written by producer Bill Walsh and Don
DaGradi (from the book by Mary Norton) it
employed animation and special effects to
superb advantage in telling its story of three
Cockney children who, during World War II, are
evacuated to the seaside home of Eglantine Price
– a lady who, it transpires, is an apprentice witch
studying witchcraft by correspondence in the
hope of using her newly acquired craft against
the Germans. Suddenly life for the three Cockney kids couldn't be rosier, and after learning
the art of·magic themselves, they perform all
sorts of wonderful tricks – such as flying to
London on a bedstead. It was sheer enchantment in the best, most inventive Disney tradition, with Angela Lansbury (illustrated) in fine
form as the would-be witch. Her co-star was
David Tomlinson as Emelius Browne – phoney
founder of the Emelius Browne College of Witchcraft, with Roddy McDowall, Sam Jaffe, John
Ericson, Bruce Forsyth, Tessie O'Shea, Reginald
Owen, Arthur E. Gould-Porter and Ben Wrigley
in support. The three children were played by
Cindy O'Callaghan, Roy Snart and Ian Weighill.
Alan Maley, Eustace Lycett and Danny Lee were
in charge of the special effects and Ward Kimball
of the animation; the songs were by the prolific
Sherman brothers, Donald McKayle choreographed, it was photographed in Technicolor by
Frank Phillips, and directed with a gleeful sense
of fun by Robert Stevenson. Songs and musical
numbers: *The Old Home Guard*; *Eglantine*; *Portobello Road*; *Portobello Street Dance*; *The Beautiful
◁ Briny*; *Substitutiary Locomotion*.

Though Sandy Wilson's **The Boy Friend** (MGM-
EMI) began life as a delectable stage show which
satirized the musicals of the twenties, it finally
reached the screen as a homage to the Hollywood musicals of the early thirties – and involved two 'Boy Friends'; one being performed by
a tacky provincial repertory company, the other
imagined – by a Hollywood producer sitting in
the stalls – as a big Busby Berkeley-style musical.
The idea (devised by producer-director Ken
Russell) was ingenious and might, indeed, have
worked, except that visually there was little
difference between the two versions. Former
model Twiggy (left) made an enchanting debut
as the young unknown forced on opening night
to replace the star (an uncredited Glenda Jackson hugely enjoying it all), and she was pleasantly partnered by former Royal Ballet dancer
Christopher Gable (right, who also choreographed). Max Adrian played the company's
flyblown impresario and Vladek Sheybal the
Hollywood producer, with Bryan Pringle,
Barbara Windsor, Antonia Ellis, Georgina Hale,
Moyra Fraser and long-legged Tommy Tune in
support. The confused and confusing adaptation
and screenplay were by director Russell, and the
evocative sets by Tony Walton. Songs and
musical numbers: *I Could Be Happy*; *Perfect
Young Ladies*; *The Boy Friend*; *Won't You Charles-
ton With Me?*; *Fancy Forgetting*; *Sur La Plage*; *A
Room In Bloomsbury*; *Safety In Numbers*; *It's
Never Too Late To Fall In Love*; *Poor Little Pierrette*;
Riviera; *The You Don't Want To Play With Me
Blues* Sandy Wilson; *All I Do Is Dream Of You*;
You Are My Lucky Star Nacio Herb Brown,
Arthur Freed; *Any Old Iron* Charles Collins, E.A.
Shepherd, Fred Terry.

1972

△
Enjoyment of **Lady Sings The Blues** (Paramount) was largely dependent on how much (or how little) one knew about its subject – the great blues singer Billie Holiday – and on whether or not one responded to Diana Ross (illustrated) in her debut screen performance as the lady in question. For audiences *au fait* with the depressing facts of Holiday's sad and often turbulent existence (which ended in 1959 when she was 44 years old), her unhappy romances, her losing battle with drugs etc. etc., there was more to offend than to admire in this travesty of the truth. On the other hand, Diana Ross fans, and those with no knowledge of the facts, were amply catered for in Jay Weston and James S. White's basically old fashioned, forties-type biopic, crisply scripted (but loosely adapted) by Terence McCloy, Chris Clark and Suzanne de Passe from the book by Miss Holiday and William Duffy, with only the merest nod in the direction of verisimilitude. Musically the many standards sung by Miss Ross lacked the authenticity of the Holiday era, sounding more like Motown than Harlem. Billy Dee Williams co-starred as Louis McKay (in reality Holiday's third husband but the only man in her life in the film), with other parts under Sidney J. Furie's competent direction going to Richard Pryor, James Callahan, Paul Hampton, Sid Melton, Virginia Capers, Yvonne Fair, Scatman Crothers, Harry Caesar and Robert L. Gordy. (Panavision and colour). Songs: *Lady Sings The Blues* Holiday, H. Nichols; *T'Ain't Nobody's Bizness If I Do* Porter, Grainger, Graham Prince, Clarence Williams; *All Of Me* Seymour Simons, Gerald Marks; *The Man I Love*; *Our Love Is Here To Stay* George and Ira Gershwin; *Them There Eyes* Maceo Pinkard, William Tracy, Doris Tauber; *I Cried For You* Abe Lyman, Gus Arnheim, Arthur Freed; *Mean To Me* Roy Turk, Fred Ahlert; *What A Little Moonlight Can Do* Harry Woods; *Lover Man (Oh Where Can You Be?)* Jimmy Davis, Jimmy Sherman, Roger 'Ram' Ramirez; *You've Changed* Bill Carey, Carl Fischer; *Gimme A Pigfoot And A Bottle Of Beer* 'Kid' Wesley, 'Sox' Wilson; *Good Morning Heartache* Irene Higginbotham, Ervin Drake, Dan Fisher; *My Man* Channing Pollock, Maurice Yvain; *Strange Fruit* Lewis Allan; *God Bless The Child*; *Don't Explain* Holiday, Arthur Herzog Jr.

△
Broadway's musical version of the events leading up to the signing of the Declaration of Independence, **1776**, was reverentially brought to the screen by its original director Peter L. Hunt together with most of the original creative team, assembled in Hollywood by producer Jack L. Warner for Columbia. The stage version had conquered Broadway for 1,217 performances, but the Panavision screen emphasized the piece's pretensions: its coy, self-congratulatory pomposity, its flaccid score and arch lyrics. Peter Stone's script, from his original libretto, still had some gripping moments of drama as the congressional members wrangled and manoeuvred to assert their points of view, but couldn't disguise the fact that the chief protagonist John Adams (William Daniels, left) was something of a bore, or that the mood shifted uneasily as great figures of history like Benjamin Franklin (Howard Da Silva, right) and Thomas Jefferson (Ken Howard) were diminished and trivialized in the name of humour; while numbers like 'Mama, Look Sharp' (about war's young casualties) and 'Molasses to Rum' (about the North's double standards regarding slavery) proclaimed their messages with high-toned solemnity. When not being overtly serious, Sherman Edwards's lyrics were twee, with titles like 'Piddle, Twiddle and Resolve' and lines like 'He plays the violin, he tucks it right under his chin'. Not surprisingly, the film failed to repeat its Broadway success. Harry Stradling Jr photographed it. Onna White was in charge of the minimal choreography and Ray Heindorf supervised the music. The cast included Donald Madden, John Cullum, Blythe Danner (centre), Roy Poole, David Ford, Virginia Vestoff and Ron Holgate. Other songs: *But, Mr Adams*; *The Lees of Old Virginia*; *Sit Down, John*; *Till Then*; *Yours, Yours, Yours*; *The Egg*; *Is Anybody There?* Edwards.

Seventies Musicals

The main trouble with the screen version of the Dale Wasserman-Mitch Leigh-Joe Darion long-running (2,338 performances) hit musical **Man Of La Mancha** (a Produzioni Europee Associate Production, released by United Artists in Color by De Luxe), was that the three leads – Peter O'Toole (left) who was cast to play the triple roles of Don Quixote, Miguel de Cervantes and Alonso Quijana, Sophia Loren (Dulcinea and Aldonza), and James Coco (Sancho Panza, right) – couldn't sing. They were first class in bringing to life scenarist Wasserman's words, but sabotaged Leigh's music and Darion's lyrics in no uncertain terms. A terrible shame this, since the songs were the show's only redeeming feature in the face of the plodding and pretentious book, matched by Arthur Hiller's heavy-handed direction (he also produced). Rounding out the cast were Harry Andrews, John Castle, Brian Blessed, Ian Richardson, Julie Gregg, Rosalie Crutchley and Gino Conforti. Gillian Lynne's choreography was deficient in flair and the musical direction, by Laurence Rosenthal, lacked sparkle. Songs and musical numbers: *It's All The Same*; *The Impossible Dream*; *Barber's Song*; *Man Of La Mancha*; *Dulcinea*; *I'm Only Thinking Of Him*; *I Really Like Him*; *Little Bird, Little Bird*; *The Dubbing*; *Life As It Really Is*; *Aldonza*; *A Little Gossip*; *The Psalm*; *Golden Helmet of Mambrino*.
▽

Resisting the tendency to 'open out' the musical numbers as he had done in *Sweet Charity* (Universal, 1969) Bob Fosse, in his *tour de force* **Cabaret** (Allied Artists), went to the other extreme in the film version, and confined almost all of them to the small stage of a smoky, crowded cabaret in Berlin just before the outbreak of hostilities in the late thirties. It was part of a radical re-assessment of the Joe Masteroff-John Kander-Fred Ebb stage show on which it was based and, like everything else in the movie, was a distinct improvement on its Broadway counterpart. All the songs (several were specially written for the film by its composers Kander and Ebb) commented on the action as opposed to being integrated into it; the screenplay, by Jay Presson Allen and Hugh Wheeler (the latter billed as 'research consultant') based on John van Druten's play *I Am A Camera* and Christopher Isherwood's *Goodbye To Berlin*, was much sounder in both content and construction than Masteroff's book for the stage show; and, with Liza Minnelli (illustrated) cast as Sally Bowles (a fifth rate American singer ekeing out a living in a decadent, sexually ambiguous *milieu*) the central character sprang vividly and memorably to life. The fact that the hugely talented Miss Minnelli was called upon to play a performer of no conspicuous ability whatsoever – and got away with it without throwing the entire plotline off balance, was a remarkable testament to her unique qualities as an actress and as a star 'presence'. She shared the majority of the songs with Joel Grey, who repeated his mesmeric stage performance as the cabaret's cynical MC – the most effectively staged (by Fosse) of these being 'Money, Money' and 'Mein Herr', both written

specially for the film. Other musical highlights were an explosive performance of the title number by Minnelli and, from Grey, 'Wilkommen', the lascivious 'Two Ladies' about the attractions of a *ménage à trois*, and the nauseating, sinister, anti-semitic but compelling 'If You Could See Her' danced with an organza-clad chimpanzee. Michael York co-starred as the young bisexual writer from Britain who fetches up in digs with Minnelli in Berlin, and through whose eyes the era is witnessed; Helmut Griem was the wealthy, irresponsible playboy with whom they both have affairs, and Marisa Berenson and Fritz Wepper a young Jewish department-store heiress and her sweetheart. It was dazzlingly photographed (in Technicolor) by Geoffrey Unsworth, with Ralph Burns in charge of the musical direction and orchestrations. Cy Feuer was responsible for the production. Other songs and musical numbers: *Maybe This Time* (Minnelli); *Sitting Pretty* (orchestra); *Tiller Girls* (Grey, girls); *Heiraten* (Greta Keller – voice only); *Tomorrow Belongs To Me* (boys' chorus).

Compared with his ridiculous big-screen account of the champagne life of waltz king Johann Strauss II called, with mind-blowing originality, **The Great Waltz** (MGM), Andrew L. Stone's *Song Of Norway* (ABC 1970) was positively sublime! For his latest venture into biopic territory, which he also wrote and directed (sample dialogue: Strauss to Offenbach, 'I admire your versatility . . . operettas, waltzes, fast gallops, quadrilles . . . how *do* you do it?') he cast Horst Bucholz (illustrated) as the composer of 'The Blue Danube', Mary Costa as his wife, Yvonne Mitchell as his mother, Nigel Patrick as Strauss senior, Rossano Brazzi as Baron Tedesco and James Faulkner as Josef Strauss, plus the voice of Kenneth McKellar. Bob Wright and Chet Forrest provided the lyrics to Strauss's immortal melodies, and the three-quarter time choreography was by Onna White. Musical programme: *The Blue Danube Waltz*; *Tritsch-Tratsch Polka*; *Louder and Faster (Leichtes Blut)*; *Pitter Patter Polka (Thunder And Lightning)*; *Love Is Music (Wine, Women And Song)*; *Say Yes* (from 'The Gypsy Baron'); *Crystal and Gold*; *Six Drinks*; *Nightfall*; *Warm*; *Who Are You* Johann Strauss II; *The Radetzky March* Johann Strauss Sr; *With You Gone (Brennende Liebe)* Josef Strauss.

1973

Considering the generally mediocre quality of the latter-day Joseph Barbera and William Hanna cartoons, Paramount's **Charlotte's Web** – based on the celebrated children's classic by E.B. White which tells of a spider called Charlotte who unselfishly devotes her life to saving a piglet called Wilbur from the slaughterhouse – was a welcome surprise and an unexpected pleasure. Its charm was enhanced by the vocal participation of Debbie Reynolds as Charlotte and Henry Gibson as Wilbur, as well as Paul Lynde, Rex Allen, Martha Scott, Dave Madden, Danny Bonaduce, Agnes Moorehead and Pam Ferdin. The ubiquitous Sherman brothers provided the score, it was scripted by Earl Hamner Jr. and directed by Charles A. Nichols and Iwao Takamoto. Songs: *Charlotte's Web*; *A Veritable Smorgasbord*; *There Must Be Something More*; *I Can Talk*; *Chin Up*; *Mother Earth And Father Time*; *We've Got Lots In Common*; *Deep In The Dark*; *Zuckerman's Famous Pig*.

Another animated feature for youngsters everywhere, **Robin Hood** (see illustration), from the Disney stable, retold yet again the story of the bold adventurer who robbed the rich to give to the poor – but this time featured the birds and animals of Sherwood forest rather than its two-legged denizens. Hence Robin, in Larry Clemmons and Ken Anderson's new story and conception, became a wily fox, Little John a bear, Allan-a-Dale a rooster (who also served as the film's narrator), and evil Prince John a scrawny lion. Under the inventive direction of its producer Wolfgang Reitherman, and with vocal characterizations supplied by Brian Bedford (Robin), Andy Devine (Friar Tuck), Peter Ustinov (Prince John), Roger Miller (Allan-a-Dale), Phil Harris (Little John) and Pat Buttram (the Sheriff of Nottingham), the film was an unmitigated delight. (Technicolor). Songs: *Whistle Stop*; *Oo-de-Lolly*; *Not In Nottingham* Roger Miller; *Love* Floyd Huddleston, George Bruns; *Phoney King Of England* Johnny Mercer.

Probably the worst musical of the decade, Ross Hunter's tacky remake of Frank Capra's 1937 classic **Lost Horizon** (Columbia) lumbered its elephantine way on to the Panavision screen, trampling underfoot such talented performers as Peter Finch, Liv Ullman, Sally Kellerman, George Kennedy, Michael York, Charles Boyer and John Gielgud who not only couldn't sing and dance, but on this painful occasion, couldn't act either. Larry Kramer's screenplay, based on the novel by James Hilton (in which a group of plane passengers survive a crash in the Tibetan mountains, are rescued by an inscrutable Oxford graduate and led to the magical Shangri-La), borrowed liberally from Robert Riskin's 1937 screenplay, but ultimately choked itself on too much philosophizing. Charles Jarrott's direction was stodgy, Hermes Pan's choreography (number led by Bobby Van, illustrated) embarrassingly coy, Burt Bacharach and Hal David's score feeble, and Jerry Wunderlich's sets unimaginative. Also cast: Olivia Hussey, James Shigeta, Sian Phillips. Songs and musical numbers: *Lost Horizon*; *Share The Joy*; *The World Is A Circle*; *Living Together Growing Together*; *I Might Frighten Her Away*; *If I Could Go Back*; *Where Knowledge Ends*; *Question Me An Answer*.

Although there were some striking and innovative moments in producers Norman Jewison and Robert Stigwood's visually exciting cinematic version of Tim Rice and Andrew Lloyd Webber's **Jesus Christ Superstar** (Universal), it failed to repeat the success of the best-selling album of the same name, or the London version of the stage show based on the album. With a screenplay by Melvyn Bragg and Jewison that tacked a rather pretentious show-within-a-show format on to Rice's original book, direction (by Jewison) that displayed an imagination more frenzied than fertile, and performances that were mixed both in quality and in style – the film emerged as an eclectic hodge-podge with no discernible rhyme or reason for many of the visual images that accompanied the loud and plenteous score. Fortunately, many of those images were tellingly photographed in Technicolor by Douglas Slocombe (on location in Israel), and much of the score was stirringly conveyed under Andre Previn's direction. It was just that when all the diverse elements in the production merged, the overall effect was less than the sum of its parts. Ted Neeley (illustrated) was top-cast as Jesus, but lacked the charisma of co-star Carl Anderson as Judas; Yvonne Elliman (left) had her moments as Mary Magdalene, the best being her singing of 'I Don't Know How To Love Him' (one of the most durable songs to emerge from the show), with other roles going to an over-the-top Barry Dennen as Pontius Pilate, a swishy Joshua Mostel (son of Zero) who, as King Herod, couldn't quite manage to pull off the show-stopping 'Herod's Song'. Bob Bingham (Caiaphas), Larry T. Marshall (Simon Zealotes), Kurt Yaghjian (Annas) and Philip Toubus (Peter). Robert Iscove choreographed, often inventively. Musical highlights included 'What's The Buzz' (Neeley, Elliman and chorus) and 'Hosanna' (Neeley, Bingham and chorus). Other songs and musical numbers: *Heaven On Their Minds*; *Strange Thing, Mystifying*; *Then We Are Decided*; *Everything's Alright*; *This Jesus Must Die*; *Simon Zealotes*; *Poor Jerusalem*; *Pilate's Dream*; *The Temple*; *Damned For All Time*; *Blood Money*; *The Last Supper*; *Gethsemane (I Only Want To Say)*; *The Arrest*; *Peter's Denial*; *Pilate And Christ*; *Could We Start Again, Please*; *Judas's Death*; *Trial Before Pilate*; *Superstar*; *Crucifixion*; *John 1941*.

Jesus Christ was also the subject of **Godspell** (Columbia), a much more nimble-footed entertainment than *Jesus Christ Superstar*, in which Jesus was portrayed (androgynously) by Victor Garber as a clown-like flower child living (and dying) in Manhattan. As written by its director David Greene, and John-Michael Tebelak (based on Tebelak's off-Broadway production) **Godspell**, with its stunning Technicolor photography (by Richard G. Heimann), its exciting choreography (by Sammy Bayes, see illustration) and its tuneful razz-a-matazz approach to its subject, was more a glorification of show-business and of Manhattan than it was of the life of Christ. In essence the only religious thing about it was its dedication to and worship of Broadway razzle-dazzle. Everything it stood for was brilliantly encapsulated in a production number called 'All For The Best', performed by Garber and David Haskell (playing John the Baptist) as a soft-shoe shuffle in front of a Times Square advertising billboard composed entirely of pattern-making light bulbs. The other high spot in Stephen Schwartz's score was Robin Lamont's singing of the show's hit song 'Day By Day'. Edgar Lansbury produced, and his cast included Jerry Sroka, Lynne Thigpen, Katie Hanley, Gilmer McCormick, Joanne Jonas, Merrell Jackson and Jeffrey Mylett. Other songs and musical numbers: *O Bless The Lord My Soul*; *Prepare Ye The Way Of The Lord*; *Turn Back O Man*; *Beautiful City*; *Save The People*; *All Good Gifts*; *Light Of The World*; *Alas For You*; *On The Willows* Schwartz; *By My Side* Jay Hamburger, Peggy Gordon.

Produced by Arthur P. Jacobs for Readers' Digest, and released by United Artists, Mark Twain's **Tom Sawyer**, filmed on location in Missouri, was an engaging slice of mid-western Americana that suffered on occasion from some rather antiseptic direction (by Don Taylor), a self-conscious striving for wholesomeness and a tendency to cuteness. Its plus factors, however, were its De Luxe Color photography (by Frank Stanley), a pleasing score by the Sherman brothers (who also provided an imaginative screenplay) and the performances of Johnny Whitaker as Tom (illustrated 2nd left), Celeste Holm as Aunt Polly, Warren Oates as Muff Potter, newcomer Jeff East as Huck Finn (left) and Jodie Foster as Becky Thatcher. Musically, the best moments were Holm's singing of the title tune, and a number called 'Freebootin' (sung by Whitaker and East), dedicated to the art of doing nothing. A large-scale production number (choreographed by Danny Daniels) depicting the Hannibal, Mo. holiday picnic drenched the screen in nostalgia for a gone but not forgotten era (the 1840s) in American history. Completing the cast were Kunu Hank, Lucille Benson, Henry Jones, Noah Keen, Dub Taylor, Richard Eastham, Joshua Hill Lewis and Susan Joye. Other songs: *River Song* (the film's theme, sung by Charley Pride on soundtrack); *Gratifaction*; *A Man's Gotta Be (What He's Born To Be)*; *If'n I Was God*; *How Come? Hannibal Mo (Zouree)*; *Aunt Polly's Soliloquy*.

▽

1974

Academy Awards

Music
Song

NOMINATIONS INCLUDED: 'Little Prince' *The Little Prince* (Paramount) Frederick Loewe

cm: Alan Jay Lerner *lyr.*

Scoring
Original Song Score and/or Adaptation
NOMINATIONS INCLUDED: *The Little Prince* Alan Jay Lerner, Frederick Loewe; Angela Morley and Douglas Gamley. *Phantom Of The Paradise* (20th Century-Fox) Paul Williams and George Aliceson Tipton.

The Annual Top Moneymaking Films
INCLUDED: *That's Entertainment* (MGM). *Robin Hood* (Disney, Buena Vista, re-issue)

△

Presented by the American Film Theatre, **Lost In The Stars** (from the 1949 Maxwell Anderson-Kurt Weill musical of the same name fashioned from South African Alan Paton's powerful novel *Cry, The Beloved Country*) emerged as a dated melodrama. Daniel Mann's uneasy direction brought no conviction to the moving story of a black preacher's travels – and travails – through the shanty townships of Johannesburg in search of his son who has committed a murder and is hiding from the law. Mann failed completely to reconcile the 'stagey' Broadway feel of the property to the more naturalistic demands of the cinema, and the performances fell, likewise, uncomfortably short of conviction. Brock Peters (right) starred as the Reverend Kumalo, Clifton Davis was his fugitive son, Melba Moore (left) the son's girlfriend, and Paul Rogers a white bigot whose own son was the victim of the killing. Also cast: Raymond St Jacques, Paula Kelly (who staged the one dance sequence in the film), H.B. Barnum III, Jitu Cumbuka and Alan Weeks. It was written for the screen by Alfred Hayes, and was produced by Ely Landau. The one saving grace of this travesty was its superb score. Songs included: *Lost In The Stars*; *Cry The Beloved Country*; *Little Gray House*; *Trouble Man*; *Bird Of Paradise*; *Big Mole*; *Train Go Now To Johannesburg*.

When MGM decided to re-open its Ali Baba cave of treasures with a compilation film of extracts from its musicals entitled **That's Entertainment**, box-office tills were set ringing everywhere. And no wonder! Although much of the linking commentary (by such narrators as Fred Astaire, Gene Kelly, Bing Crosby, Peter Lawford, Liza Minnelli, Donald O'Connor, Debbie Reynolds, Mickey Rooney, Frank Sinatra, James Stewart and Elizabeth Taylor) was embarrassingly self-congratulatory and banal, and one might cavil at some of the films and stars included (or omitted), **That's Entertainment** fully lived up to its title, making the spectator feel like a child let loose in a toy factory. Here again – under the same roof, as it were – one could see the enormous wedding-cake number from *The Great Ziegfeld* (1936), a segment of the brilliant ballet from *An American In Paris* (1951), the joyous 'Atchison, Topeka and Santa Fe' number with Judy Garland and Ray Bolger from *The Harvey Girls* (1945), a couple of delirious water-ballets from *Bathing Beauty* (1944) and *Million Dollar Mermaid* (1952) (illustrated, with Esther Williams) and, of course, perhaps the single most enchanting moment of the whole genre, Gene Kelly 'singin' and dancin' in the rain'. There were some rarities too, such as the charming if inadequate rendering by Clark Gable of 'Puttin' On The Ritz' from *Idiot's Delight* (1939), The Gumm Sisters singing *'La Cucaracha'*, and Cary Grant and Jean Harlow's duet 'Did I Remember' from *Suzy* (1936). But producer Jack Haley Jr (son of the Tin Man from *The Wizard Of Oz*, 1939) wisely judged that what audiences were looking for was a chance to wallow in a shared cinematic past, when both they and Hollywood were younger – the sort of movie, in fact, that sends you out singing – even in the rain. Haley wrote the narration, and the executive producer was Daniel Melnick.

▽

A really risible rock adaptation of Shakespeare's *Othello*, **Catch My Soul** (Cinerama) was burdened by an unintentionally hilarious screenplay by Jack Good, based on his stage show of the same name, in which the bard's immortal tragedy was transposed from Venice to the American South West, and in which the Moor became a black evangelist, Desdemona his flower-power wife and Iago the dyspeptic leader of a hippie commune with a Satan complex. Richie Havens (illustrated right) was Othello, Lance LeGault Iago and Season Hubley (left) Desdemona, with Tony Joe White (Cassio) and Susan Tyrrell (Emilia) in support. Good produced it with Richard Rosenbloom, and the director was Patrick McGoohan. Songs and musical numbers: *Othello*; *Working On A Building* Tony Joe White; *Wash Us Clean*; *Eat The Bread, Drink The Wine*; *Book Of Prophecy*; *Catch My Soul* White, Jack Good; *That's What God Said*; *Chug A Lug*; *I Found Jesus* Delaney Bramlett; *Looking Back* White, Bramlett; *Open Our Eyes* Leon Lumkins; *Lust Of The Blood*; *Put Out The Light* Ray Pohlman, Good; *Tickle His Fancy* Emil Dean Zoughby, Good; *Run Shaker Life* (traditional).

▽

Unquestionably everybody's favourite aunt from modern fiction is – or should be – **Mame** (Warner Bros.) who began life in Patrick Dennis's best-selling novel *Auntie Mame*, later surfaced in a smash-hit Broadway play and an equally successful film, a Broadway musical and finally, the film version of the musical. A dazzling line-up of great ladies have incarnated, in one form or another, the flamboyant *grande dame*: Rosalind Russell, Angela Lansbury, Dolores Gray, Ginger Rogers, Bea Lillie, Constance Bennett, Eve Arden, Greer Garson, Sylvia Sidney and Juliet Prowse – and for the film musical Lucille Ball was chosen. Although possessing just as much pazazz as her predecessors, Lucy's infinite variety had been somewhat withered by age, notwithstanding the gallant efforts of photographer Philip Lathrop to envelop her in the softest of focuses, and those of choreographer Onna White to keep her on the sidelines of the more frenetic musical numbers. The rather mechanically regimented choreography,

in fact, proved an asset only in the catchy title number (illustrated, Ball centre), in which red-coated, black-toppered huntsmen energetically hopped, skipped and jumped around the slightly blurry star. Beatrice Arthur was splendidly decadent as Mame's actress friend Vera Charles (a role she played on Broadway); Robert Preston charming as her Southern beau, Jane Connell (also from Broadway) was marvellous as Agnes Gooch, and Bruce Davison, Kirby Furlong, Doria Cook, John McGiver and Joyce Van Patten gave solid support. It was written for the screen by Paul Zindel (from the musical by Jerome Lawrence, Robert E. Lee, and Jerry Herman, who composed the catchy score), directed by Gene Saks and produced (in Panavision) by Robert Fryer and James Cresson. Musical numbers: *Mame*; *If He Walked Into My Life*; *Bosom Buddies* (excised in GB); *It's Today*; *Loving You*; *My Best Girl*; *Gooch's Song (What Do I Do Now?)*; *Open A New Window*; *The Man In The Moon*; *We Need A Little Christmas Now*; *St Bridget*; *The Letter*.

△

△

Having succeeded the previous year with their *Tom Sawyer*, The Readers' Digest and producer Arthur P. Jacobs did the obvious and musicalized Mark Twain's **Huckleberry Finn** (United Artists). The results were disastrous. It bore no relation in mood and atmosphere to Twain's original, and the Sherman brothers' screenplay (they also wrote the instantly forgettable tunes) was cloying, and the film deadly dull. It was directed by J. Lee Thompson, who deserved a special Oscar for his under-achievement in turning a hitherto fool-proof property into a dud; and starred Jeff East (illustrated) – whose performance was nowhere near as effective as it had been in *Tom Sawyer* – as Huck, Paul Winfield as Jim, Arthur O'Connell as Colonel Grangerford, Natalie Trundy as Mrs Loftus and, best of all, Harvey Korman and David Wayne as the roguish King and Duke. At least they breathed some fresh air into a stale and stuffy entertainment. It was photographed in Panavision and Color De Luxe and choreographed by Marc Breaux. Songs and musical numbers: *Freedom*; *Huckleberry Finn*; *Someday Honey Darlin'*; *Cairo, Illinois*; *Rose In A Bible*; *Royalty*; *Royal Nonesuch*; *What's Right, What's Wrong*; *Rotten Luck*.

Loosely based on Gaston Leroux's classic chiller *The Phantom Of The Opera*, Brian De Palma's rock musical parody **Phantom Of The Paradise** (20th Century-Fox) concerned a disfigured musician whose song has been plagiarised by a sinister *entrepreneur*, and who takes his revenge by haunting the latter's 'Paradise' discothèque. Glittery and energetic, the film caught the disco craze as it was just starting and became something of a cult. Paul Williams (illustrated), who also wrote the score, played the impresario, William Finley the crazed Phantom and Jessica Harper the young singer desired by both. Also appearing were George Memmoli, Gerrit Graham and the singing group of Jeffrey Comanor, Archie Hahn and Harold Oblong. De Palma wrote his own screenplay, and the film was a Harbor Productions presentation produced (in Color De Luxe) by Edward R. Pressman. The undertaking provoked a lawsuit brought by Universal, the holders of the film rights to Leroux's original property. Songs and musical numbers: *Goodbye, Eddie, Goodbye*; *Faust*; *Upholstery*; *Special To Me*; *Old Souls*; *Somebody Super Like You*; *Life At Last*; *The Hell Of It*; *The Phantom's Theme (Beauty And The Beast)*.

1975

△

Funny Lady, a Ray Stark production for Columbia-Warner, took up the story of vaudevillian Fanny Brice where William Wyler's *Funny Girl* (1968) left off, proving that even in the lives of the greatest stars there wasn't always enough material for two biopics. It related how Brice, having finally worked gambler Nicky Arnstein (Omar Sharif reprising from the earlier movie) out of her system, meets up with showman Billy Rose (James Caan) during the tough Depression years and, somewhat on the rebound, marries him; subsequently, his infidelities and her professional commitments draw them apart. Barbra Streisand, needless to say, was once again perfectly cast as Brice: a star playing a star (illustrated). Director Herbert Ross, while unable to breathe life into the emotional episodes of Jay Presson Allen and Arnold Shulman's screenplay, managed to invest the backstage sequences with real glitter, even if the production numbers – particularly the Vincent Youmans-Edward Eliscu-Billy Rose Song, 'Great Day', which Streisand sang with writhing black girls at her feet – were often ponderously over-elaborate. Also cast (though, with Streisand around, it was a very dogged performer indeed who got his face in edgeways) were Roddy McDowall, Ben Vereen, Carole Wells, Larry Gates and Heidi O'Rourke. Betty Walberg choreographed, and the film was photographed in Eastmancolor by the great James Wong Howe. Other songs and musical numbers: *Blind Date; So Long, Honey Lamb; How Lucky Can You Get?; Isn't This Better?; Let's Hear It For Me* (specially written for the film by John Kander, Fred Ebb); *More Than You Know* Youmans, Eliscu, Rose; *It's Only A Paper Moon* Harold Arlen, E.Y. Harburg, Rose with *I Like Him/I Like Her*, by Kander and Ebb, sung as a counter melody; *I Found A Million Dollar Baby In A Five And Ten Cent Store* Harry Warren, Mort Dixon, Rose; *Beautiful Face, Have A Heart* James V. Monaco, Fred Fisher, Rose; *If You Want The Rainbow, You Must Have The Rain* Oscar Levant, Dixon, Rose; *I Caught A Code In My Dose* Arthur Fields, Fred Hall, Rose; *Am I Blue?* Harry Akst, Grant Clarke, Rose; *Clap Hands, Here Comes Charley* Joseph Meyer, Ballard MacDonald, Rose; *Me And My Shadow* Al Jolson, Dave Dreyer, Rose; *If I Love Again* Jack Murray, Ben Oakland.

Though Peter Bogdanovich had gained both critical and commercial favour with earlier essays into movie nostalgia (*The Last Picture Show* (Columbia, 1971), *What's Up Doc* (Warner Bros. 1972) and *Paper Moon* (Paramount, 1973), he was to discover to his cost with **At Long Last Love** (20th Century-Fox) that the 30s could be a dangerous age. A pastiche of the Astaire-Rogers musicals, it was as lavishly mounted as one had a right to expect from its $6,000,000 budget and, filtered through Laszlo Kovacs's brilliant photography, its Long Island mansion, sparkling lawns and vintage automobiles looked exactly as *Top Hat* (RKO, 1935) or *The Gay Divorcée* (RKO 1934) might have done if shot in colour. There were 16 marvellous Cole Porter songs, some of them unfamiliar. And if the plot – the change-partners romancing of smooth playboy (Burt Reynolds, left), carefree deb (Cybill Shepherd, right), Broadway star (Madeline Kahn) and immigrant gambler (Duilio Del Prete) – was only workmanlike, it was no worse than those of

▽

innumerable well-loved and enduring Hollywood musicals. All that was lacking – but it proved to be everything – were Fred and Ginger themselves. Both Reynolds and Shepherd had charming screen presences, but their dancing was flat-footed in an embarrassingly literal sense, the wisecracks dreamt up by director-writer Bogdanovich for the secondary characters (played by such usually reliable foils as Eileen Brennan, Mildred Natwick and John Hillerman) were more cracked than wise, and the whole sorry spectacle was a resounding and deserved flop at the box office. Songs and musical numbers: *At Long Last Love; Just One Of Those Things; I Get A Kick Out Of You; You're The Top; It's De-Lovely; From Alpha To Omega; A Picture Of Me Without You; Well, Did You Evah?; Friendship; Find Me A Primitive Man; Let's Misbehave; But In The Morning, No; Most Gentlemen Don't Like Love; Which; I Loved Him (But He Didn't Love Me)* Porter; *Poor Young Millionaire* music Bogdanovich, Artie Butler, lyrics Porter.

Robert Altman's **Nashville** (Paramount) wove a rich tissue of narrative and musical strands as it traced the overlapping lives of 24 people in the Tennessee capital of country-and-western during the campaign of a Presidential candidate, whose assassination brings the film to a dramatic end. In spite of the dangers inherent in such an undertaking, it was a triumph for its director and his familiar repertory company of actors, many of whom themselves wrote the songs they sang. The film, by its very nature, boasted no star roles but, out of a huge cast, particularly noteworthy were Ronee Blakely as a singer on the verge of a breakdown, Gwen Welles as a starlet reduced to stripping at stag suppers, Shelley Duvall as a spaced-out groupie, Keith Carradine as a heartless Don Juan, Lily Tomlin as the mother of deaf-mute children, and Henry Gibson as the smooth *eminence grise* of country-and-western. Also to be seen were Ned Beatty, Karen Black, Allen Nichols (left), Barbara Harris (right), Michael Murphy, Keenan Wynn and, as Opal from the BBC, Geraldine Chaplin. It was ▽

scripted by Joan Tewkesbury (though, reportedly, everyone involved had a hand) and produced, in Panavision, by Altman, with Martin Starger and Jerry Weintraub as executive producers. Songs and musical numbers: *200 Years* Richard Baskin, Henry Gibson; *Yes, I Do* Baskin, Lily Tomlin; *Down To The River* Ronee Blakely; *Let Me Be The One* Baskin; *Sing A Song* Joe Raposo; *The Heart Of A Gentle Woman* Dave Peel; *Bluebird* Blakely; *The Day I Looked Jesus In The Eye* Baskin, Robert Altman; *Memphis; Rolling Stone; I Don't Know If I Found It In You* Karen Black; *For The Sake Of The Children* Baskin, Richard Reicheg; *Keep A' Goin'* Baskin, Gibson; *Swing Low Sweet Chariot* (arr. Millie Clements); *Tapedeck In His Tractor (The Cowboy Song); My Idaho Home; Dues* Blakely; *I Never Get Enough* Baskin, Ben Raleigh; *Rose's Cafe* Allan Nicholls; *Old Man Mississippi* Juan Grizzle; *My Baby's Cookin' In Another Man's Pan* Jonnie Barnett; *One, I Love You* Baskin; *I'm Easy; Honey; It Don't Worry Me* Keith Carradine; *Since You've Gone* Gary Busey; *Trouble In The USA* Arlene Barnett.

Richard O'Brien's long-running stage musical *The Rocky Horror Show* was adapted and 'opened out' for the screen and called **The Rocky Horror Picture Show** (20th Century-Fox), a high camp blend of Gay Liberation and B-movie Gothick about an innocent young couple who stumble into the annual convention of transvestite aliens from the far-out (in both senses) planet of Transylvania. Tim Curry (left) reprised the role of Frank'n'Furter which he had created in the theatre, Susan Sarandon and Barry Bostwick were the 'straights', and O'Brien himself played the disconcerting butler Riff Raff. Also appearing were Jonathan Adams, Nell Campbell, Peter Hinwood (right), Charles Gray and Meatloaf. Director Jim Sharman also wrote it, and Michael White produced. Songs and musical numbers: *Science Fiction Double Feature; Wedding Song; Over At The Frankenstein Place; The Time Warp; Sweet Transvestite; The Sword Of Damocles; Charles Atlas Song; What Ever Happened To Saturday Night; Toucha Toucha, Touch Me; Eddie's Teddy; Planet Schmanet; It Was Great When It All Began; I'm Going Home; Super-Heroes* O'Brien.

With the combined talents of director Stanley Donen, composer Frederick Loewe, lyricist Alan Jay Lerner and choreographer Bob Fosse, Paramount's **The Little Prince** ought to have been a knockout. In the event, it was a leaden exercise in tweeness which, like aviator Richard Kiley's plane, never got off the ground. The basic problem was that Antoine de Saint-Exupéry's book – about a pilot grounded in the desert and his adventures among the stars with a space-travelling tot was – notwithstanding its status as a children's classic – a fragile little tale that failed to respond to Donen's tricksy optical effects or the relentless mugging of such performers as Gene Wilder, Joss Ackland, Clive Revill and Victor Spinetti. Nor was the Lerner-Loewe score – to put it mildly – one of their best and only Fosse (right) as the Snake scored in his 'Snake In The Grass' routine. The Little Prince was played by a six-year-old charmer called Steven Warner (left), with Graham Crowden and dancer Donna McKechnie also cast. Lerner wrote the screenplay and the film was produced (in Technicolor) by Donen, with A. Joseph Tandet as associate producer. Songs and musical numbers: *It's A Hat; I Need Air; I'm On Your Side; Be Happy; You're A Child; I Never Met A Rose; Why Is The Desert (Lovely To See)?; Closer And Closer And Closer; Little Prince (From Who Knows Where).* ▽

1976

Academy Awards

Cinematography
NOMINATIONS INCLUDED: *A Star Is Born* (First Artists, WB) Robert Surtees

Sound
NOMINATIONS INCLUDED: *A Star Is Born* Robert Knudson, Dan Wallin, Robert Glass and Tom Overton

Music
Song
'Evergreen' (Love Theme from *A Star Is Born*) *A Star Is Born* Barbra Streisand *cm*; Paul Williams *lyr*.

Original Song Score and Its Adaptations or Best Adaptation Score
NOMINATIONS INCLUDED: *A Star Is Born* Roger Kellaway

Folk-singer Leadbelly (real name Huddie Ledbetter) died at the age of 60 in 1949, after a violent life in which he served sentences on two chain gangs (one of them, in Texas, for murder), and spent a further year in prison in 1939 for stabbing a man. The singer's early life and hard times were the subject of Gordon Parks's good to look at, but ultimately synthetic and over prettified (photography by Bruce Surtees) biopic, called **Leadbelly** (Paramount). In keeping with Parks's glossy conception of the production was Roger E. Mosley's (right) somewhat passionless performance in the central role, though the vocals by HiTide Harris were first-class. Paul Benjamin was fine as Leadbelly's sharecropper father, with good work, too, from Madge Sinclair as a madame and Loretta Greene as the singer's serious love interest. Also cast: Albert P. Hall, Art Evans, James E. Broadhead and John Henry Faulk. It was written by Ernest Kinoy, and produced (in Eastmancolor) by Marc Merson, with David Frost as executive producer.

After William A. Wellman's straight version of 1937 and George Cukor's musical version of 1954 (Cukor's *What Price Hollywood*, made in 1932, also treated of the same material), it was almost inevitable that **A Star Is Born** (Warner Bros.) would be updated into the world of rock music. With a literate screenplay by John Gregory Dunne, Joan Didion and director Frank Pierson (based on the story by William Wellman and Robert Carson), the Barbra Streisand-Kris Kristofferson starrer succeeded surprisingly well in extracting viable dramatic mileage from the now rather too-familiar story of an ill-starred showbiz couple, her meteoric rise to fame a perfect mirror-image of his precipitous decline into failure and alcoholism. While in no way eclipsing the superlative Cukor version with Judy Garland and James Mason, it was a considerable achievement in an era of undistinguished disco musicals, and neither Streisand nor Kristofferson (illustrated) disgraced their prestigious predecessors – that it received a lambasting from the critics on its release was due more to Streisand's reputation for megalomania than to any crippling defects in the film, which grossed a very healthy $37,100,000. It was produced by Jon Peters for Barwood-First Artists and, in secondary roles, featured director Paul Mazursky, Gary Busey, Oliver Clarke, Vanetta Fields, Clydie King

and Martin Heflin. Songs and musical numbers: *Watch Closely Now*; *Spanish Lies*; *Hellacious Acres*; *Woman In The Moon*; *With One More Look At You* Paul Williams, Kenny Ascher; *Queen Bee* Rupert Holmes; *Everything* Holmes, Williams; *Lost Inside Of You* Leon Russell, Streisand; *Evergreen* Williams, Streisand; *I Believe In Love* Kenny Loggins, Alan Bergman, Marilyn Bergman; *Crippled Crow* Donna Weiss.

MGM's sequel to their hugely successful *That's Entertainment* (1974), **That's Entertainment, Part Two,** was originally announced as *That's Entertainment, Too,* and the decision of producers Saul Chaplin and Daniel Melnick to revert to the less jokey title perhaps reflects an avowal on their part that there was rather less entertainment on offer this time around. Not that there wasn't a great deal of pleasure to be derived from seeing or re-seeing clips from almost a hundred of the studio's most delightful movies, but audible above the familiar voices of the MGM stock company and the inimitably lush orchestrations was the distinct screech of a barrel being scraped. Rarities were, well, rare – and often, as with Arthur Freed's rendering of his own 'Wedding Of The Painted Doll', ludicrously truncated; and the montages of non-musical films were, in the context, quite misguided. Saddest of all however, were the witless linking passages which featured Gene Kelly and Fred Astaire. Better to recall the real highlights – Maurice Chevalier singing 'Girls Girls Girls' in *The Merry Widow* (1934), Garland (centre right) and Margaret O'Brien (centre left) in 'Have Yourself A Merry Little Christmas' from *Meet Me In St Louis* (1944) or Bobby Van's joyous hop dance 'Take Me To Broadway' from *Small Town Girl* (1953) – whose undimmed enchantment, coupled with the ineptitude of the film that framed them, only served the more forcibly to remind us that the MGM musical was, sadly, well and truly dead.

With a reportedly enormous budget (the Russian portion of which remains a mystery), one of Hollywood's most stylish directors, George Cukor, and three 'generations' of female stars – Ava Gardner, Elizabeth Taylor and Jane Fonda – the American-Soviet co-production of Maurice Maeterlinck's **The Blue Bird** must have seemed a wonderful idea. But, considering the meagre distribution it has had in the West, 20th Century-Fox (who had filmed a non-musical version of the play with Shirley Temple in 1941) no doubt learned, along with Mytyl and Tyltyl, the two infant protagonists of the movie, that the Blue Bird of Happiness (and profit) is to be found right there at home. Cukor was hamstrung by sub-standard studio facilities, and his customary taste and flair were totally absent from this grotesque hodge-podge of ballet (see illustration), cartoons, inadequate special effects and hideous decor. Edith Head decked out the female leads in amusingly garish costumes, but her years of experience had obviously not prepared her for 'clothing' the roles of Water, Bread, Milk, and other staple items called for by Maeterlinck's arch and irrevocably dated fantasy. The songs by Andrei Petrov and Irwin Kostal (English lyrics by Tony Harrison) were negligible, reaching a nadir of absurdity with Robert Morley in Heaven singing 'You're In The Hands Of Fate' to a group of yet-to-be-born children. The film was produced in colour by Paul Maslansky and also starred George Cole, Cicely Tyson, Mona Washbourne and Richard Pearson.

1977

Academy Awards

Best Actor
NOMINATIONS INCLUDED: John Travolta *Saturday Night Fever* (Paramount)

Costume Design
NOMINATIONS INCLUDED: *A Little Night Music* (Sascha-Wien/Elliot Kastner, New World Pictures) Florence Klotz

Music
Song
NOMINATIONS INCLUDED: 'Candle On The Water' *Pete's Dragon* (Disney, Buena Vista) music and lyrics by Al Kasha and Joel Hirschhorn. 'Someone's Waiting For You' *The Rescuers* (Disney, Buena Vista) Sammy Fain *cm*; Carol Connors and Ayn Robbins *lyr*.

Original Song Score
and Its Adaptation or Best Adaptation Score
A Little Night Music Jonathan Tunick
NOMINATIONS INCLUDED: *Pete's Dragon* Al Kasha Joel Hirschhorn and Irwin Kostal.

The Annual Top Moneymaking Films
INCLUDED: *A Star Is Born* (First Artists, WB). *The Rescuers*.

In **Outlaw Blues**, a Warner Bros. release of a Fred Weintraub-Paul Heller Production, Peter Fonda played a prison inmate determined to track down the country-and-western star (James Callahan) who plagiarized his blues number and turned it into a hit. Totally undistinguished, and with songs so feeble one imagined Fonda would have been delighted to rid himself of them, it was directed by Richard T. Heffron from a screenplay by B.W.L. Norton and produced by Steve Tisch with a cast that also included Susan Saint James (illustrated), as a back-up singer employed by Callahan, but fired after she refuses to comply with his advances. Michael Lerner, Steve Fromholz, Richard Lock-Miller and Matt Clarke. Songs: *Outlaw Blues* John Oates; *Jailbirds Can't Fly* Harlan Sanders, R.C. O'Leary; *Whisper In A Velvet Night* Lee Clayton; *I Dream Of Highways*; *Beyond These Walls*; *Water For My Horses* Hoyt Axton.

A brilliant but flawed pastiche of forties musicals, Martin Scorsese's **New York, New York** (United Artists) traced the separate careers and mutual marital difficulties of an embittered jazz saxophonist (Robert De Niro, right) and a rising singer (Liza Minnelli, left) against the background of the changeover from big bands to bebop. Over ninety minutes were excised from the original running time of four hours (including a full-scale production number 'Happy Endings' by John Kander and Fred Ebb), some of the cuts painfully unbalancing the narrative, and Jazz purists objected to the numerous inaccuracies in style and chronology. Nevertheless, it was an impressive directorial effort by Scorsese, who managed to recapture the more seductive textures of forties movies and, together, the two principals were outstanding. In her rendering of the catchy title number (by Kander and Ebb), Minnelli's eerie resemblance to her mother, Judy Garland, added yet more authenticity. Also featured were Lionel Stander, Barry Primus, Mary Kay Place, Diahnne Abbot and Georgie Auld (who dubbed De Niro's saxophone playing). The moody photography (in Panavision and Technicolor) was the work of Laszlo Kovacs, the film was written by Earl Mac Rauch and Mardik Martin (from a story by Mac Rauch) and produced by Irwin Winkler and Robert Chartoff. Other songs and musical numbers: *There Goes The Ball Game*; *But The World Goes Round* Kander, Ebb; *Opus One* Sy Oliver; *You Brought A New Kind Of Love To Me* Sammy Fain, Irving Kahal, Pierre Norman; *Once In A While* Michael Edwards, Bud Green; *You Are My Lucky Star* Arthur Freed, Nacio Herb Brown; *It's A Wonderful World* Jan Savitt, Johnny Watson, Harold Adamson; *The Man I Love* George and Ira Gershwin; *Just You, Just Me* Jesse Greer, Raymond Klages; *Blue Moon* Richard Rodgers, Lorenz Hart; *Honeysuckle Rose* Fats Waller, Andy Razaf; *Don't Be That Way* Benny Goodman, Edgar Sampson, Mitchell Parish; *Flip The Dip*; *Game Over* Georgie Auld; *V-J Stomp*; *Hazoy*; *Once Again Right Away*; *Bobby's Dream* Ralph Burns; *For All We Know* J. Fred Coots, Sam M. Lewis; *Taking A Chance On Love* Vernon Duke, John Latouche, Ted Fetter.

The Rescuers (Buena Vista), Walt Disney's 22nd animated feature was the captivating story of two mice. One of them, Bianca, is a member of the Mouse Rescue Aid Society whose organization operates from the basement of the United Nations Building; the other, Bernard, the society's shy caretaker who volunteers to rescue Penny, an orphan girl, from an evil witch. The adventure – structured by Larry Clemmons and a team of writers from two stories by Margery Sharp – was quintessential Disney with its familiar combination of animal kingdom fantasy and genuine terror – the swamp setting where Penny is held captive was as scary as anything ever perpetrated by the Disney animators. Five songs and some really stunning animation, notably in a magical sequence featuring a rather goofy bird called Orville, and in the scenes involving Evinrude, a helpful dragonfly, contributed to the film's success; so did the vocal characterizations of Bob Newhart and Eva Gabor as the two mice, Geraldine Page as the wicked witch, Michelle Stacy as Penny, Jim Jordan as Orville and James Macdonald as Evinrude. Also: Joe Flynn, Jeanette Nolan, Pat Buttram and John McIntire. It was produced in Technicolor by Wolfgang Reitherman (executive producer Ron Miller), with Reitherman also serving as co-director with John Lounsbery and Art Stevens. Songs and musical numbers: *The Journey*; *Rescue Aid Society*; *Tomorrow Is Another Day* Carol Connors, Ayn Robbins; *Someone's Waiting For You* Sammy Fain, Connors, Robbins; *The US Air Force* Robert Crawford.

The main asset of Disney's live action plus animation fantasy **Pete's Dragon** (Buena Vista) was Elliott, the cartoon dragon itself (illustrated) – an endearingly clumsy, 12ft-tall creature with a mumbling voice (supplied by Charlie Callas, no relation to Maria) and the gift of instant invisibility. As soon as Elliott was off the screen, however, longueurs set in which not even such lively presences as Jim Dale, Mickey Rooney, Red Buttons and Shelley Winters could alleviate. Malcolm Marmorstein's screenplay (from a story by veteran Seton I. Miller and S.S. Field) concerned little orphan Pete (Sean Marshall) who flees his cruel foster family to find love and understanding from a sweet lighthouse keeper's daughter (played by pop singer Helen Reddy); and the setting in turn-of-the-century Maine gave Disney's draughtsmen plenty of opportunity to show their skills in the re-creation of a small New England town. But it was Elliott's show. The film was sluggishly directed by Don Chaffey, and produced by Ron Miller and Jerome Courtland with undistinguished choreography by Onna White and Martin Allen. Animator Ken Anderson was the creator of Elliott. Songs and musical numbers: *Candle On The Water*; *I Saw A Dragon*; *It's Not Easy*; *Every Little Piece*; *The Happiest Home In These Hills*; *Brazzle Dazzle Day*; *Boo Bop Bopbopbop (I Love You Too)*; *There's Room For Everyone*; *Passamashloddy*; *Bill Of Sale* Al Kasha and Joel Hirschhorn.
▽

◁ **Saturday Night Fever** (Paramount) was a somewhat mechanical story about an inarticulate New York youth with a dead-end job who comes to life once a week at a local disco when he is acclaimed as a star. John Badham's flashily competent direction, the screenplay by Norman Wexler (from a story by Nik Cohn) with its accurate rendering of working-class speech patterns, and the complacent Dolby muzak of the Bee Gees all guaranteed that the Robert Stigwood-produced film would turn out to be a sleek and professional Hollywood package. That it also happened to become a phenomenal success at the box office and, more curiously, a genuinely moving depiction of the realities and aspirations of underprivileged youth, was entirely due to the presence of John Travolta (illustrated, with Karen Lynn Gorney), who became a star overnight. Both on and off the dance floor, Travolta exuded a charismatic sexuality that made him one of the key icons of the seventies, and even spectators unsympathetic to youth culture found themselves under his spell. Also cast were Barry Miller, Joseph Cali, Paul Pape and Bruce Ornstein. Kevin McKormick was the executive producer. Songs and musical numbers: *How Deep Is Your Love*; *Night Fever*; *Staying Alive*; *You Should Be Dancing*; *More Than A Woman*; *If I Can't Have You*; *Jive Talkin'* Barry, Robin and Maurice Gibb; *A Fifth Of Beethoven* adapted from Beethoven's Fifth Symphony by Walter Murphy; *Calypso Breakdown*; *Open Sesame* R. Bell, Kool and The Gang; *Boogie Shoes* H.W. Casey, R. Finch; *Disco Inferno* Leo Green, Ron Kersey; *Manhattan Skyline*; *Night On Disco Mountain* adapted from Mussorgsky's 'Night On The Bare Mountain', by David Shire; *Salsation*.

△

Four years after Universal's enormous success with *The Sting* (1973) the studio mounted a tribute to Scott Joplin, the composer whose ragtime music contributed greatly to the success of that film. Called, quite simply **Scott Joplin**, it starred Billy Dee Williams (illustrated) in the title role, with other parts in Don Hough's downbeat production going to Clifton Davis, Godfrey Cambridge, De Wayne Jessie, Mabel King, Taj Mahal, Spo-De-Odee, Eubie Blake, The Commodores, David Healy, Samuel Fuller and Art Carney. After a buoyant first half, Christopher Knopf's screenplay was plunged into gloom as it narrated Joplin's decline and eventual death, destitute and syphilitic, in 1917. The harrowing nature of the material was conveyed with great honesty (despite the meagre 20-day shooting schedule) in Jeremy Paul Keegan's atmospheric direction. With the exception of Harold Johnson's 'Hangover Blues', all the music featured was by Joplin.

With its impressive pedigree (an Ingmar Bergman film) and its refined operetta-like score by the talented Stephen Sondheim, **A Little Night Music** had been a critical success on Broadway and, somewhat surprisingly in view of its rather esoteric flavour, a resounding commercial hit too. Its transfer to the screen required uncommon delicacy, and the Sascha-Wien-New World production's choice of the original stage director Harold Prince probably seemed the safest guarantee of maintaining the show's charm and humour, and its wistfully mocking message of transience and human foolishness. But Prince and his producer, Elliott Kastner, made several fundamental errors, ejecting from the score memorable numbers ('Liaisons'; 'The Miller's Son') while retaining the lugubrious 'Soon' and 'Later' which slowed the film's pace to a halt in the early stages. Two of the best of the remaining numbers had their impact blunted by their staging: 'A Weekend In The Country' was weakened by choppy editing and interrupted choruses, and the show's hit song, the gorgeous 'Send In The Clowns' was sung by the heroine *across* a room to her lover. But there was still much to enjoy. What remained of Sondheim's score was lovely to listen to (especially in Jonathan Tunick's sublime orchestrations), the screenplay by Hugh Wheeler from his own libretto (which had been based on Bergman's 'Smiles of a Summer Night') was literate and ultimately moving. Arthur Ibbetson's colour photography captured the elegiac beauty of turn-of-the-century Viennese opulence and the leading players, Elizabeth Taylor (right) as the actress Desirée, Len Cariou (left) as the newly-married lawyer who rekindles their old affair, Lesley-Ann Down as his virginal wife, Diana Rigg as the haughty wife of Desirée's current lover, and Hermione Gingold as Desirée's mother, were all fine – though Taylor's singing of the film's big song only *just* got by. The film's musical highlight, in fact, turned out to be one of the lesser numbers, 'Every Day A Little Death', performed by Rigg and Down then reprised solo by Rigg. Two of the show's numbers were revised by Sondheim for the film: the duet 'The Glamorous Life' was re-written as a solo for Desirée's daughter (Chloe Franks) and the 'Night Waltz (The Sun Won't Set)' was given new lyrics, retitled 'Love Takes Time' and became the film's theme. Laurence Guittard, Christopher Guard, Heinz Marecek and Lesley Dunlop were also in key roles, and the choreography was by Patricia Birch. An entertainment of limited and perhaps rarefied appeal, it played so few engagements that many who would have found much to enjoy in it were, alas, never given the chance to find out. Other songs and musical numbers: *Now*; *You Must Meet My Wife*; *It Would Have Been Wonderful*.

1978

Academy Awards

Best Actor

NOMINATIONS INCLUDED: Gary Busey *The Buddy Holly Story* (Innovision-ECA Entertainment, Columbia)

Cinematography

NOMINATIONS INCLUDED: *The Wiz* (Universal) Oswald Morris

Art Direction

NOMINATIONS INCLUDED: *The Wiz* Tony Walton, Philip Rosenberg; Edward Stewart, Robert Drumheller

Costume Design

NOMINATIONS INCLUDED: *The Wiz* Tony Walton

Sound

NOMINATIONS INCLUDED: *The Buddy Holly Story* Tez Rudloff, Joel Fein, Curly Thirlwell, Willie Burton

Music
Song

'Last Dance' *Thank God, It's Friday* (Columbia) music and lyrics by Paul Jabara

NOMINATIONS INCLUDED: 'Hopelessly Devoted To You' *Grease* (Paramount) music and lyrics by John Farrar. 'When You're Loved' *The Magic Of Lassie* (Wrather, International Picture Show Co.) music and lyrics by Richard M. Sherman and Robert B. Sherman

The Annual Top Moneymaking Films

INCLUDED: *Grease*. *Pete's Dragon* (Disney, Buena Vista).

John Travolta consolidated his *Saturday Night Fever* (Paramount, 1977) success with **Grease** (Paramount), a Robert Stigwood-Allan Carr production of the long-running Broadway hit. Adapted by Carr from Jim Jacobs and Warren Casey's fifties-style book (screenplay by Bronte Woodard), it was designed specifically as a mammoth showcase for the good looks and sex appeal of its super-star lead and, as such, was a triumphant success. Though contemporary in its language and in its approach to its subject (high school romance) the film tapped a decided vein of nostalgia by virtue of its fifties setting, and the casting of such stalwarts as Eve Arden, Joan Blondell, Edd Byrnes, Sid Caesar, Alice Ghostley and Dody Goodman. Frankie Avalon was also in it (as part of a dream sequence) and there was a certain nostalgia about his token appearance as well. All about how Travolta's (right) summer romance with co-star Olivia Newton-John (left) sours when they find themselves attending the same high school, its infectious high spirits were the results of Patricia Birch's jet-propelled choreography, Woodard's racy (if somewhat loosely constructed) screenplay, an instantly accessible score by Jim Jacobs and Warren Casey (augmented by Barry Gibb, John Farrar, Louis St Louis and Scott J. Simon), and the attractive performances from a cast whose younger members included the marvellous Stockard Channing, Jeff Conaway, Barry Pearl, Michael Tucci, Kelly Ward and Didi Conn. It was stunningly photographed in Panavision and Metrocolor by Bill Butler. Songs and musical numbers: *Grease*; *Summer Nights*; *Hopelessly Devoted To You*; *You're The One That I Want*; *Sandy*; *Beauty School Dropout*; *Look At Me I'm Sandra Dee*; *Greased Lightnin'*; *It's Raining On Prom Night*; *Alone At A Drive-In Movie*; *Blue Moon*; *Rock'n Roll Is Here To Stay*; *Those Magic Changes*; *Hound Dog*; *Born To Hand-Jive*; *Tears On My Pillow*; *Mooning*; *Freddy My Love*; *Rock 'n' Roll Party Queen*; *There Are Worse Things I Could Do*; *We Go Together*; *Love Is A Many Splendoured Thing*.

▽

Paramount's **American Hot Wax**, an affectionate tribute to the rock'n'roll era, was marred by the too reverent treatment accorded its central character, the charismatic disc jockey Alan Freed. The movie glossed over his involvement in the payola racket, preferring to present him as the first martyr of youth culture. Otherwise, it all seemed pleasantly nostalgic (though, given the volume at which the incessant rock music was played, audiences may have felt the need of another kind of wax), with such guest stars as Buddy Holly, Chuck Berry, Jerry Lee Lewis (illustrated), Bobby Darin, Little Richard, The Everly Brothers, and Screamin' Jay Hawkins to confer 50s authenticity. Tim McIntire successfully impersonated Freed, and was supported by Fran Dreecher, Jay Leno and Laraine Newman. It was produced by Art Linson (in Metrocolor), and directed by Floyd Mutrux. Among some 40 songs featured were: *Hot Wax Theme* Kenny Vance, Paul Griffin, Ira Newborn; *Rock And Roll Is Here To Stay* David White; *Reelin' And Rockin'*; *Roll Over Beethoven*; *Sweet Little Sixteen* Chuck Berry; *Why Do Fools Fall In Love* Frank Lymon, Morris Levey; *That Is Rock And Roll* Jerry Leiber, Mike Stoller; *Whole Lotta Shakin' Goin' On* Dave Williams, Sunny David; *Great Balls Of Fire* Jack Hammer, Otis Blackwell.

△

The story of a 'creative' disc jockey battling with commercial pressures, **FM** (Universal) portrayed FM radio stations in a rather sentimentalized manner and offered, as musical support, the usual catchall soundtrack medley of rock numbers (in Dolby sound). Michael Brandon played the station Q-SKY Deejay, with Eileen Brennan, Cassie Yates (illustrated), Alex Karras, Cleavon Little and Martin Mull also featured. Photographer John A. Alonzo directed this Rand Holston production (in Technicolor) from a screenplay by Ezra Sacks. Over 30 songs were heard, including: *FM*; *Do It Again*; *FM Reprise* Walter Becker, Donald Fagen; *Livingston Saturday Night* Jimmy Buffett; *The Key To My Kingdom* Maxwell Davis, Claude Baum, Joe Josea; *Green Grass And High Tides* Hugh Thomasson; *Life In The Fast Lane* Joe Walsh, Don Henley, Glenn Frey; *Bad Man* J.D. Souther, Frey; *Tumbling Dice* Mick Jagger, Keith Richard; *Poor Poor Pitiful Me* Warren Zevon; *Love Me Tender* Elvis Presley Vera Matson; *Life's Been Good* Joe Walsh; *Cold As Ice* Mick Jones, Lew Gramus; *Feels Like The First Time* Jones; *Slow Ride* Dave Peverett; *Night Moves* Bob Seger; *Sentimental Lady* Bob Welch; *Fly Like An Eagle* Steve Miller; *Just The Way You Are* Billy Joel; *Lido Shuffle* Boz Scaggs; *Hollywood* Scaggs, Michael Omartin; *Your Smiling Face* James Taylor; *We Will Rock You* Brian May, Freddy Mercury; *More Than A Feeling* T. Scholz.

A fantasy fashioned around some 30 or so Beatles hits as performed, in the main, by Peter Frampton and The Bee Gees, **Sgt. Pepper's Lonely Hearts Club Band** (Universal) involved several somewhat bizarre characters in a plot to steal the musical instruments belonging to Sgt. Pepper's band, whose leader, in company with the Bee Gees, is Pepper's grandson, Bill Shears (Frampton, left). They don't succeed. End of plot (by Henry Edwards, who also scripted). A musical mish-mash overloaded with electronic visual effects, an insistent soundtrack and no sense of direction (by Michael Schultz), it also featured Frankie Howerd, Paul Nicholas, Donald Pleasence (as a Robert Stigwood-type music business genius), Dianne Steinberg (right), Sandy Farina, Alice Cooper, Stargard, Billy Preston, Earth, Wind and Fire and, as Mayor Kite, George Burns. The songs were by John Lennon, Paul McCartney and George Harrison, and the choreography by Patricia Birch. Among the numerous stars making 'guest' appearances were Peter Allen, Stephen Bishop, Keith Carradine, Carol Channing, Donovan, Jose Feliciano, Peter Noone, Helen Reddy, Chita Rivera, Johnny Rivers, Sha-Na-Na, Aerosmith, Del Shannon, and Connie Stevens. It was produced, in Technicolor, by Robert Stigwood. Songs and musical numbers: *Sgt. Pepper's Lonely Hearts Club Band* (Bee Gees, Nicholas); *With A Little Help From My Friends* (Peter Frampton, Bee Gees); *Fixing A Hole* (Burns); *Getting Better* (Frampton, Bee Gees); *Here Comes The Sun* (Farina); *I Want You (She's So Heavy)* (Bee Gees, Dianne Steinberg, Nicholas, Pleasence, Stargard); *Good Morning, Good Morning* (Nicholas, Frampton, Bee Gees); *Nowhere Man* (Bee Gees); *Polythene Pam* (Bee Gees); *She Came In Through The Bathroom Window* (Frampton, Bee Gees); *Sgt. Pepper's Lonely Hearts Club Band* (Reprise) (Frampton, Bee Gees); *Mean Mr Mustard* (Frankie Howerd); *She's Leaving Home* (Bee Gees, Jay MacIntosh, John Wheeler); *Lucy In The Sky With Diamonds* (Steinberg, Stargard); *Oh! Darling* (Robin Gibb); *Maxwell's Silver Hammer* (Steve Martin); *Because* (Alice Cooper, Bee Gees); *Strawberry Fields Forever* (Farina); *Being For The Benefit Of Mr Kite* (Maurice Gibb, Frampton, Bee Gees, Burns); *You Never Give Me Your Money* (Nicholas, Steinberg); *Got To Get You Into My Life* (Earth, Wind and Fire); *When I'm 64* (Farina); *Come Together* (Aerosmith); *Golden Slumbers* (Frampton); *Carry That Weight* (Bee Gees); *The Long And Winding Road* (Frampton); *A Day In The Life* (Barry Gibb, Bee Gees); *Get Back* (Preston); *Sgt. Pepper's Lonely Hearts Club Band* (Finale, full cast).

I Wanna Hold Your Hand (Universal) was a 'day in the life of . . . ' film: in this case, a day in the life of four New Jersey teenagers bound for New York to catch the Beatles' debut on the Ed Sullivan Show in 1964. That the cinema audience was to be denied a glimpse of the four Liverpudlians was evident from the famous quartet's absence from the cast list, added to which tyro director Robert Zemeckis (a friend and protégé of Steven Spielberg) was more maladroit than amusing in his handling of dissociated shots of legs and shoulders intended to denote their charismatic presence. As a nostalgic celebration of Beatlemania, therefore, it failed to deliver the goods and, as a youth movie, one would be forgiven for supposing it had been made by characters just as dopey as those portrayed in the film by Nancy Allen, Wendy Jo Sperber, Susan Kendall Newman and Theresa Saldana (foreground). Bobby Di Cicco, Marc McClure and Eddie Deezen were also featured. It was scripted by Zemeckis and Bob Gale, and produced by Tamara Asseyev and Alex Rose (with Gale as associate producer and Spielberg as executive producer). Songs and musical numbers included: *I Want To Hold Your Hand*; *Please, Please Me*; *I Saw Her Standing There*; *Thank You Girl*; *Misery*; *Love Me Do*; *Do You Want To Know A Secret?*; *P.S. I Love You*; *From Me To You*; *There's A Place*; *She Loves You* John Lennon, Paul McCartney; *Boys* Carl Perkins; *Twist And Shout* Phil Medley, Bert Berns; *Till There Was You* Meredith Willson; *Money* Janie Bradford, Berry Gordy Jr; *Please Mr Postman* Brian Holland, Freddy C. Gorman.

The magic of Lassie was to be found in films like *Lassie Come Home* (MGM, 1943) and not in **The Magic Of Lassie** (International Picture Show), a heavy-handed throwback in which a crooked businessman steals the canine star from her young owner to force the boy's grandfather (James Stewart) to sell some prize-winning vineyards. Suitable for all children from eight to eight-and-a-half, its sole attraction for anyone outside that age group was the presence of Stewart, Mickey Rooney (illustrated right) and Alice Faye, each of whom sang one of Robert M. and Richard B. Sherman's sugary numbers, as does Lassie herself, whose celebrated collieratura voice was dubbed in by Debby Boone (Pat's daughter). Also featured were Pernell Roberts, Stephanie Zimbalist, Michael Sharrett and The Mike Curb Congregation. The ludicrous script was by Jean Holloway and the Sherman brothers. A Jack Wrather presentation, it was directed by Don Chaffey and produced by Bonita Granville Wrather and William Beaudine Jr. Songs: *A Rose Is Not A Rose* (sung by Alice Faye and, on a jukebox, the voice of Pat Boone); *That Hometown Feeling*; *Thanksgiving Prayer*; *When You're Loved*; *There'll Be Other Friday Nights*; *Brass Rings and Daydreams*; *Travelling' Music*; *Nobody's Property*; *I Can't Say Goodbye*; *Banjo Song*.

Bob Dylan (illustrated right, with Roger McGuinn) both directed and starred in **Renaldo And Clara** (Lombard Street Films), a long meandering, self-indulgent account of his 1975/76 tour with the Rolling Thunder Revue, intercut with fictional, semi-improvised scenes in which Dylan, his wife Sara, Joan Baez, Ronee Blakely, Ronnie Hawkins (playing 'Bob Dylan') and such luminaries of counterculture as Allen Ginsberg and Sam Shepard acted out the lyrics of the songs. For addicts only. Dylan also wrote the scenario (with additional dialogue by Shepard) and the film was produced by Mel Howard. Of the 47 songs featured, 22 were by Dylan. They included: *Isis I Want You*; *It Ain't Me Babe*; *Knockin' On Heaven's Door*; *Hurricane*; *Romance In Durango*; *One Too Many Mornings*; *One More Cup Of Coffee*; *Sara*; *Patty's Gone To Laredo*; *Just Like A Woman*; *A Hard Rain's A-Gonna Fall*; *Sad-Eyed Lady Of The Lowlands*; *When I Paint My Masterpiece*. Other songs included: *Chestnut Mare* Roger McGuinn; *Diamonds And Rust* Joan Baez; *Suzanne* Leonard Cohen; *Need A New Sun Rising* Ronee Blakely; *Salt Pork West Virginia* Jack Elliott; *Kaddish* Allen Ginsberg; *Cucurrucucu Paloma* Thomas Mendez; *Time Of The Preacher* Willie Nelson.

Buried somewhere under the rubble of Sidney Lumet's catastrophically misguided all-black remake of *The Wizard Of Oz* (MGM, 1939) – now abbreviated to **The Wiz** (Universal) – was author Frank Baum's reassuring message that, be it ever so humble, there's no place like home. The other underlying messages were that black is not always beautiful, and big is not always better. Though based on the hit Broadway musical of the same name, Joel Schumacher's screenplay transposed the action from Kansas to New York City, where Dorothy the heroine (Diana Ross) becomes a 24-year-old Harlem school teacher whose encounter with a snow-storm while chasing after her dog Toto, results in her disappearing into a vortex of snow crystals only to re-emerge in another part of Manhattan. Miss Ross's adventures in a Tony Walton-designed New York (the interiors were shot at the historic Astoria Studios and on location in and around Manhattan) more or less paralleled those young Judy Garland had in the earlier film, with only one thing missing: a sense of wonderment. Though no expense was spared in creating contemporary Oz out of New York City, Lumet's direction substituted noise and overblown spectacle for genuine creativity, suc-ceeding only in making the least out of the most. But even more fatal was the casting of Diana Ross, who, as Dorothy (illustrated centre), was far too mature for Baum's innocent heroine, and lacked vulnerability. More happily, though by no means definitively, cast were Michael Jack-son as Scarecrow (2nd left), Nipsey Russell as the Tin Man (right), and Ted Ross as the Cowardly Lion (left); Richard Pryor (under-used) was the Wiz himself and, best of all, Mabel King as the evil witch Evilene who, together with the Flying Monkeys employed in her Sweatshop, stopped the show with their galvanic 'Don't Bring Me No Bad News' number. Lena Horne appeared at the end of the film as Glinda the Good Witch, and gave her all to the black pride number 'Believe In Yourself'; with other roles in Rob Cohen's production (executive producer Ken Harper) going to Theresa Merritt (as Aunt Em), Thelma Carpenter, Stanley Greene and Clyde J. Barrett. The several large-scale production numbers were staged by Louis Johnson (and performed by the Louis Johnson Dance Theatre). It was photographed, by Oswald Morris, in Panavision and Technicolor. Other songs and musical numbers (all by Quincy Jones and Charlie Smalls): *Brand New Day*; *Home*; *He's The Wizard*; *The Feeling That We Have*; *Soon As I Get Home*; *You Can't Win*; *What Would I Do If I Could Feel*; *Slide Some Oil To Me*; *I'm A Mean Old Lion*; *Be A Lion*; *Ease On Down The Road*; *Emerald City*; *So You Wanted To See The Wizard* Charlie Smalls; *Liberation Agitato*; *The Wiz*; *Can I Go On?*; *March Of The Munchkins*; *Good Witch Glinda*; *Is This What Feeling Gets?* (*Dorothy's Theme*); *Now Watch Me Dance*; *Popper Girls*; *End Of The Yellow Brick Road*; *A Sorry Phoney* Quincy Jones.
▽

△

A very patent attempt to cash in on the pheno-menal success of *Saturday Night Fever* (1977), **Thank God It's Friday** (Casablanca/Motown/ Columbia) took place one Friday night in a Hollywood disco nightclub, aptly named The Zoo, and narrated the adventures, both profes-sional and romantic, of its proprietors, per-formers and clients. Apart from a couple of amusing moments (the cod Gene Kelly dance performed by Chuck Vennera in a parking-lot, for example), it was totally forgettable teenage fodder. Written by Barry Armyan Bernstein and directed by Robert Klane, it starred Valerie Landsburg, Terri Nunn and Donna Summer, and also featured Phil Adams (illustrated centre), Ray Vitte, Mark Lonow, Andrea Howard and The Commodores. It was produced (in Metrocolor) by Rob Cohen, with Neil Bogart as executive producer. The plethora of songs and musical numbers included: *After Dark* Simon Soussan, Sabrina Soussan; *Find My Way* J. Melfi; *It's Serious* Gregory Johnson, Larry Blackman; *Let's Make A Deal* Michael Smith; *Romeo And Juliet* Alec Costadinos; *You're The Reason I Feel Like Dancing* H. Johnson; *From Here To Eternity* Giorgio Moroder, Pete Bellotte; *Dance All Night* Willie Hutch; *Love Masterpiece* H. Davis, J. Powell, A. Posey; *I'm Here Again* B. Sutton, M. Sutton, Kathy Wakefield; *Disco Queen* Paul Jabara; *Trapped In A Stairway* Jabara, Bob Esty; *Do You Want The Real Thing*; *You Can Always Tell A Lady By The Company She Keeps* Esty, D.C. LaRue; *Thank God It's Friday*; *You Are The Most Precious Thing In My Life* A.R. Costadinos; *I Wanna Dance* P. Bellotte; *Meco's Theme* Harold Wheeler; *Floyd's Theme* D. St Nicklaus; *Down To Lovetown* Don Daniels, Michael Sutton, Kathy Wakefield; *Lovin', Livin', And Givin'* Kenneth

Stover, Pam Davis; *Sevilla Nights* N. Skorsky, J.M. Descarano, J. C. Petit; *Love To Love You Baby*; *Try With Your Love* Donna Summer, Moroder, Belotte; *Je t'àime* Serge Gainsbourg, arranged by Thor Baldursson.

△

The odd omission of the singer's death in a plane crash in 1959 made **The Buddy Holly Story** (Innovasions – ECA) the kind of routine rags-to-riches show-biz narrative that had, in the past, served indiscriminately for musical comedy fic-tion, as well as film or opera star biopics. Robert Gittler's screenplay (based on the book *Buddy Holly, His Life And Music* by John Coldrosen) eschewed few of the genre's clichés, but the casting of Gary Busey (left) in the title role added immeasurably to the sense of authenticity – the gangling, buck-toothed actor not only resem-bled Holly physically but managed to recapture a voice and stage presence one had supposed inimitable. (Unusually for such films, Busey was not dubbed.) Co-stars were Don Stroud and Charles Martin Smith, with Conrad Janis, Wil-liam Jordan and Maria Richwine (as Holly's wife) also featured. Steve Rash directed and Freddy Bauer produced (with associate producer Frances Avrut-Bauer and executive producers Edward H. Cohen and Fred T. Kuehnert). Songs and musical numbers: *Rock Around With Ollie Vee* Sonny Curtis; *That'll Be The Day*; *Peggy Sue* Jerry Allison, Holly, Norman Petty; *Rave On*; *Oh Boy* Sonny West, Bill Tilghman, Petty; *It's So Easy*; *Maybe Baby*; *True Love Ways* Holly, Petty; *Words Of Love* Holly; *Listen To Me* Charles Hardin, Petty; *Every Day I Have The Blues* Peter Chatman; *Well, All Right* Frances Faye, Don Raye, Dan Howell; *Chantilly Lace* J.P. Richard-son; *Whole Lotta Shakin' Goin' On* Dave Williams, Sunny David; *You Send Me* L.C. Cooke.

1979

Academy Awards

Best Picture

NOMINATIONS INCLUDED: *All That Jazz* (Columbia/20th Century-Fox) produced by Robert Alan Aurthur

Best Actor

NOMINATIONS INCLUDED: Roy Scheider *All That Jazz*

Best Actress

NOMINATIONS INCLUDED: Bette Midler *The Rose* 20th Century-Fox

Best Supporting Actor

NOMINATIONS INCLUDED: Frederic Forrest *The Rose*

Direction

NOMINATIONS INCLUDED: Bob Fosse *All That Jazz*

Writing

Screenplay Written Directly For The Screen
NOMINATIONS INCLUDED: *All That Jazz* Robert Alan Aurthur, Bob Fosse

Cinematography

NOMINATIONS INCLUDED: *All That Jazz* Giuseppe Rotunno

Art Direction

All That Jazz Art Direction – Philip Rosenberg, Tony Walton; Set Decoration – Edward Stewart, Gary Brink

Costume Design

All That Jazz Albert Wolsky

Sound

NOMINATIONS INCLUDED: *The Rose* Theodore Soderberg, Douglas Williams, Paul Wells, Jim Webb

Film Editing

All That Jazz Alan Heim
NOMINATIONS INCLUDED: *The Rose* Robert L. Wolfe, C. Timothy O'Meara

Music

Best Original Song Score and its Adaptation, or Best Adaptation Score
All That Jazz Adaptation Score by Ralph Burns
NOMINATIONS INCLUDED: *The Muppet Movie* (Jim Henson Production. Lord Grade/Martin Starger Presentation) Original Song Score by Paul Williams, Kenny Ascher, adapted by Paul Williams

Best Original Song

NOMINATIONS INCLUDED: 'The Rainbow Connection' *The Muppet Movie* Music and lyrics by Paul Williams and Kenny Ascher

The Annual Top Moneymaking Films

INCLUDED: *The Muppet Movie*

△

A reverential biopic, heavily reminiscent of the fifties in style, which blinkered much of the truth and failed to ask some of the more provocative and probing questions concerning the rise and fall of its subject's staggeringly influential career, **Elvis** (Dick Clark Motion Pictures) was a superficial account of the life and times of Elvis Presley Super Star, which began and ended in Las Vegas in 1969 (the year of Presley's comeback performance in that city) and, in between, repeated certain well-documented facts about his impoverished hillbilly existence in Mississippi, his early professional struggles, his erratic movie career, his spell in the army, and his marriage to Priscilla Beaulifil which ended when he decided to make a theatrical comeback. Presley's life, and life-style, in the seventies were completely omitted. Doing as well as they could by producer Anthony Lawrence's superficial screenplay were Kurt Russell (illustrated) as Presley, Shelley Winters as his mother, Bing Russell as his father, Season Hubley as Priscilla,

Pat Hingle as Colonel Parker, Abi Young as Natalie Wood, Felicia Fenske as Lisa Marie Presley, Randy Gray as the boy Elvis, and Charlie Hodge as himself. Russell's 'Presley' vocals were dubbed by Ronnie McDowell. It was photographed in Metrocolor and directed by Dick Clark. Songs included: *Mystery Train* Sam C. Phillips, Herman Parker Jr; *The Wonder Of You* Baker Knight; *That's Alright Mama* A. Crudup; *Blue Moon Of Kentucky* Bill Munroe; *Old Shep* R. Foley, E.M. Jones; *Heartbreak Hotel* Mae Boren Axton, Tommy Durden, Presley; *Rip It Up* Robert A. Blackwell, John Marascalco; *Love Me Tender* Presley, Vera Matson; *Are You Lonesome Tonight* Roy Turk, Lou Handman; *Crying In The Chapel* Artie Glenn; *Until It's Time For You To Go* Buffy Sainte-Marie; *Pledging My Love* Ferdinand Washington, Don D. Robey; *Suspicious Minds* Fred Zambon; *Burning Love* D. Linde; *Blue Suede Shoes* Carl Lee Perkins; *Finale: Dixie-Battle Hymn Of The Republic* Julia Ward Howe, music attributed to William Steffe; and a concert medley.

△

After the generation-gap comedy *Taking Off* (1971), and his version of a key novel of the sixties, Ken Kesey's *One Flew Over The Cuckoo's Nest* (1976), the choice of Czech director Milos Forman to bring the Galt MacDermot-Gerome Ragni-James Rado counter-culture musical hit **Hair** (United Artists) to the screen, was more logical than it first appeared. On to the heterogeneous sketches and vignettes that comprised the original, Michael Weller's screenplay grafted a slight but serviceable plotline concerning a young Oklahoma cowboy's arrival in New York to report to his army unit for service in Vietnam, and his involvement with a group of hippie dropouts; but it could not assuage the uneasy suspicion that it was either too soon or too late to revive this monument to Flower Power. Nevertheless, there was much to enjoy – Twyla Tharp's brilliant choreography sent the cast dancing through New York's Central Park (see illustration) with vigour, and Forman had plenty of striking visual ideas, such as the

psychedelic church wedding and the lovely sequence when the horses of mounted policemen at a Central Park 'be-in' high-step to the music. John Savage played the young draftee and Beverly D'Angelo was a mixed-up deb, with other parts going to Treat Williams, Annie Golden, Melba Moore, Dorsey Wright, Don Dacus, Cheryl Barnes and the Twyla Tharp Dance Foundation. It was a CIP-Film-Productions feature produced (in Technicolor and Panavision) by Lester Persky and Michael Butler. Songs and musical numbers: *Aquarius; Colored Spade; Aint' Got No; Black Boys/White Boys; Electric Blues; Old-Fashioned Melody; The Flesh Failures; 3-5-0-0; Somebody To Hold; Sodomy; Donna; Hashish; Manchester; Abie Baby; Fourscore; I'm Black; Air; Party Music; My Conviction; I Got Life; Hair; LBJ; Hare Krishna; Where Do I Go; Walking In Space; Easy To Be Hard; Good Morning Starshine; What A Piece Of Work Is Man; Somebody To Love; Don't Put It Down; Let The Sunshine In* MacDermot, Ragni, Rado.

After their worldwide success on TV it was inevitable that the Muppets (illustrated) would transfer to the big screen, and the basic plotline of **The Muppet Movie** (ITC) – Kermit the Frog and Fozzie Bear journey across America, with various other members of the cloth menagerie hitching rides *en route* to Hollywood – appeared to offer a satisfactory peg on which to hang the usual ration of sketches, songs and guest appearances. Unfortunately, too many lugubrious songs held up the action; and of the guests – who included Edgar Bergen, Milton Berle, James Coburn, Dom DeLuise, Elliott Gould, Bob Hope, Madeline Kahn, Carol Kane, Cloris Leachman, Steve Martin, Richard Pryor, Telly Savalas, ▽

Orson Welles and Paul Williams – only Mel Brooks emerged with any honour (perhaps because he's something of a Muppet himself). The Jerry Juhl-Jack Burns screenplay, moreover, made certain elementary miscalculations, notably by allowing Kermit to requite Miss Piggy's affections, and the film was slackly directed by James Frawley. Jim Henson (the creator of the original TV series) produced, with Martin Starger as executive producer. Songs and musical numbers: *The Rainbow Connection*; *Frog's Legs So Fine*; *Movin' Right Along*; *Can You Picture That?*; *Never Before*; *Something Better*; *This Looks Familiar*; *I'm Going To Go Back There Some Day* Paul Williams, Kenny Ascher.

Bette Midler (illustrated) made an astonishing screen debut in **The Rose** (20th Century-Fox), a loosely disguised biopic of the late Janis Joplin. Set in the mid sixties against the background of an unpopular war and the radically changing social and personal values of American society, it charted the decline of Rose, a successful rock singer (Midler) whose small-town Florida background has failed to provide her with the emotional security she needs to cope with her public acclaim. A wild, undisciplined lady whose unconventional life-style renders permanent relationships impossible, Rose takes to drink to see her through her nights and, after ruining her chances of having what promises to be the most successful love affair of her life (with a professional soldier who has deserted after two tours in Vietnam), she overdoses herself with heroin and dies during a standing room only 'homecoming' concert in Florida. Frederic Forrest (excellent) played the soldier, and was billed third behind a rather morose and under-used Alan Bates as Midler's unsympathetic, fed-up-to-the-gills, commercially minded manager. Harry Dean Stanton, Barry Primus, David Keith and Sandra McCabe were also in it; so were female impersonators Michael Greer, Claude Sacha, Michael St Laurent, and Sylvester and Pearl White who, in one of the film's best scenes – set in a Greenwich Village nightclub – appear as Bette Midler (*à la* Rose), Barbra Streisand, Bette Davis, Mae West and Diana Ross, and invite Midler to join their act. Mark Rydell's pyrotechnic direction disguised the fact that the film, despite its raunchy dialogue (screenplay by Bill Kerby and Bo Goldman), was pretty old fashioned. So, of course, did Midler's courageous, no-holds-barred central performance. It was costumed by Theoni V. Aldredge, choreographed by Toni Basil, photographed by Vilmos Zsigmond in 70mm and Color De Luxe, and produced by Marvin Worth and Aaron Russo. Songs: *Let Me Call You Sweetheart* Leo Friedman, Beth Slater Whitson; *The Rose* Amanda McBroom; *Stay With Me* Jerry Ragavoy, George Weiss; *Camellia* Stephen Hunter; *The Night We Said Goodbye* Bill Elliott; *Evil Lies* Greg Prestopino, Carol Locatell; *Sold My Soul To Rock'n'Roll* Gene Pistilli; *Keep On Rockin'* Sammy Hagar, John Carter; *Fire Down Below* Bob Seger; *I've Written A Letter To Daddy* Larry Vincent, Henry Tobias, Mo Jaffe; *When A Man Loves A Woman* C. Lewis, A. Wright; *Midnight In Memphis* Tony Johnson; *Whose Side Are You On?* Kenny Hopkins, Charley Williams. ▽

Directed by Allan Arkush, **Rock'n'Roll High** ▷
School (New World) was a noisy throw-back to the fifties campus musical and something of an anachronism in 1979. Set in the Vince Lombardi High School and all about an avid fan of The Ramones pop group and her clash with a high school administration dedicated to stamping out rock'n'roll – it starred P.J. Soles as the fan (and an aspiring songwriter) and Vincent Van Patten as her secret admirer, with other roles going to May Woronov, Clint Howard, Dey Young and The Ramones (illustrated with Soles, centre), the latter performing several of their biggest hits. These included: 'Blitzkrieg Bop', 'Teenage Lobotomy', 'Pinhead', 'Sheena Is A Punk Rocker' and two new ones they wrote especially for the film, 'I Want You' and 'Rock'n'Roll High School'. In addition to those of The Ramones, the film featured nineteen other songs, including Paul McCartney's 'Did We Meet Somewhere Before?', Fleetwood Mac's 'Albatross' and 'Jigsaw Puzzle Blues', Alice Cooper's 'School's Out', Chuck Berry's 'School Days', Todd Rundgren's 'A Dream Goes Forever', MC5's 'High School', Eddie and the Hot Rods' 'Teenage Depression', The Paley Brothers' 'C'mon Let's Go' and 'You're The Best', Bent Fabric's 'Alley Cat', Devo's 'Come Back Jonee', Nick Lowe's 'So It Goes', Brian Eno's 'Spirits Drifting', 'Alternative 3', 'M386' and 'Energy Fools The Magician', The Velvet Underground's 'Rock'n'roll' and Brownsville Station's 'Smoking In The Boys' Room'. Siana Lee Hale was responsible for the choreography, it was written by Richard Whitley, Russ Dvonch and Joseph McBride from a story by Allan Arkush and Joe Dante. The film was produced by Michael Finnell (the executive producer was 'B' picture king Roger Corman).

△

All That Jazz (Columbia-20th Century-Fox) was the first musical whose subject was death. A self-indulgent though undeniably effective, often brilliant, examination of the life and death of its creator Bob Fosse (and a brutally unglamorous look at the tensions and pressures of life in the commercial theatre), it parted company from reality only in that director-choreographer Fosse, unlike his cinematic incarnation Joe Gideon, lived, after suffering a thrombosis, to tell the tale here told. Basically concerned with the period in Fosse's life (circa 1974) when he was overworking himself on the Broadway-bound musical *Chicago*, and the film *Lenny* (United Artists, 1974), it picked at the knots of the subject's life-style with unflinching honesty and candour. Special emphasis was laid on Fosse's insatiable sexual appetite, his treatment of people as mere objects, his quest for artistic perfection, and his obsessional avoidance of the conventional and ordinary. The choreographer's life (and death) was viewed as a massive production number – a device which cued in several typically Fosse routines, every one of them dazzling in both conception and execution. Fosse himself was convincingly played by Roy Scheider (illustrated), his wife (based on dancer Gwen Verdon, whose voice was heard in one of the numbers) by Leland Palmer, his young daughter by Erzsebet Foldi, and his then mistress by Ann Reinking. Cliff Gorman appeared as the star of Gideon's movie 'The Stand-Up' (actually *Lenny*), with Ben Vereen as an unctuous TV host and Jessica Lange (in the guise of a flirtatious showgirl) as Death herself. Robert Alan Aurthur produced (executive producer Daniel Melnick) in Panavision and Technicolor and, together with Fosse, wrote the screenplay. Songs and musical numbers: *On Broadway* B. Mann, C. Weill, Jerry Leiber, Mike Stoller; *Take Off With Us* Stan Lebowsky, F. Tobias; *Everything Old Is New Again* Peter Allen, Carol Bayer Sager; *South Mt Sinai Parade* Ralph Burns; *After You've Gone* Henry Creamer, J. Turner Layton; *There'll Be Some Changes Made* W.B. Overstreet, Billy Higgins; *Who's Sorry Now?* Ted Snyder, Burt Kalmar, Harry Ruby; *Some Of These Days* Shelton Brooks; *Going Home Now* Ralph Burns; *Bye Bye Love* Felice and Boudleux Bryant.

1980

Academy Awards

Original Score
NOMINATIONS INCLUDED: *Fame* (MGM) Michael Gore

Original Song
NOMINATIONS INCLUDED: 'Fame' *Fame* Michael Gore *cm*; Dean Pitchford *lyr*

Writing (Screenplay) – material written directly for the screen
NOMINATIONS INCLUDED: *Fame* Christopher Gore

Film Editing
NOMINATIONS INCLUDED: *Fame* Gerry Hambling

Set against the background of Manhattan's High School of the Performing Arts, director Alan Parker's **Fame** (MGM) couldn't quite make up its mind whether it wanted to be a traditional musical or a drama of social significance. The result was an unsatisfying melding of romanticism and realism, whose patchwork quilt of a screenplay (by Christopher Gore) traded in clichés as it itemised the hopes and dreams of eight young men and women over a period of four formative years. Most prominently featured were Irene Cara as an ambitious and gifted singer, Paul McCrane as a confused, vulnerable gay; Gene Ray (illustrated, foreground) as a rebellious, illiterate but stunning black dancer; Maureen Teefy as a mother-dominated young Brooklyn Jewess; Lee Carreri as a musician with a penchant for 'synthesized' music and, most talented of all, Barry Miller as a hip Puerto Rican who hides the truth of his squalid family background by lying about it. Also cast: Tresa Hughes (as the mother), Anne Meara, Laura Dean, Antonia Franceschi, Eddie Barth, Boyd Gaines and Albert Hague. Choreographed by Louis Falco whose two big numbers were, frankly, a mess; and the producers were David De Silva and Alan Marshall. Songs and musical numbers: *Red Light*; *Fame*; *I Sing the Body Electric* Michael Gore, Dean Pitchford; *Dogs In The Yard* Dominic Bugatti, Frank Musker; *Hot Lunch Jam* Gore, Robert F. Colesberry, Lesley Gore; *Out Here On My Own* Michael and Lesley Gore; *Is It Okay If I Call You Mine?* Paul McCrane.

▽

Unlike Al Jolson, Neil Diamond, who also made ▷ his movie debut playing a cantor's errant son, could hardly lay claim to being the world's greatest entertainer. Still, his performance as Jess Rabinovitch in **The Jazz Singer**, EMI's remake of Samson Raphaelson's famous play, was nothing to be ashamed of. Like Jolson, Diamond's personality is not exactly ingratiating, and although it strained at plausibility to ask audiences to believe in him as an assistant cantor, he projected a positive presence, both physically and vocally. Fortunately, not too much time is spent in the synagogue and, just as Jolson (and Danny Thomas in the 1953 Warner Bros. remake of the story) abandoned religion for the glitter of show business, much to poppa's disapproval, so Diamond takes off in search of a new life as a pop singer. He succeeds, and, in the end, even poppa joins in the standing ovation. Catlin Adams was cast as Diamond's wife, and Lucie Arnaz co-starred as the manager of a famous recording star (Paul Nicholas) and the woman Diamond leaves his wife for. As the aggrieved cantor Laurence Olivier (left, with Diamond) hammed it up in much the same way that Warner Oland did in the original 1927 version, with other roles in Jerry Leider's $15,000,000 production going to Franklyn Ajaye, Sully Boyar, Mike Kellin and Janet Brandt. It was written by Herbert Baker and Stephen H. Foreman (who, in one sequence, and true to the spirit of the original, had Diamond in blackface), and the director was Richard Fleischer. Songs: *You Baby Baby*; *Jerusalem*; *America* Neil Diamond; *Love On The Rocks*; *On The Robert E. Lee*; *Summer Love*; *Louise*; *Songs of Life* Diamond, Gilbert Becaud; *Hello Again* Diamond, Alan Lindgren; *Amazed And Confused* Diamond, Richard Bennett.

◁ A premeditated attempt on behalf of producer Allan Carr to recapture the lost innocence of MGM's youth-orientated musicals of the forties, **Can't Stop The Music** (EMI) updated the 'let's put on a show' formula, substituting a disco beat for swing, and Steve Guttenberg (as an aspiring composer) for Mickey Rooney. Valerie Perrine also appeared, as a top New York model, and Guttenberg's platonic best friend. The stars of the show, however, and its *raison d'être* were Village People (illustrated, with Perrine), who in the movie, are recruited by Perrine to help promote Guttenberg's music. In real life they are the creation of Jacques Morali who also wrote most of the film's music including (with lyricists Henry Belolo and Victor Willis) Village People's massive hit, 'Y.M.C.A.' The number was excitingly choreographed by Arlene Phillips, whose contribution to Carr's multi-million dollar box-office dud was its only saving grace. Nancy Walker, a veteran of three MGM musicals of the forties, directed a cast that included Tammy Grimes (wasted), Bruce Jenner, Paul Sand, Barbara Rush, Altovise Davis, June Havoc, The Ritchie Family, Hot Gossip, and Marilyn Sokol in the kind of ugly-duckling role so often played by Nancy Walker herself. It was written by Bronte Woodard and Allan Carr. Other songs and musical numbers: *Give Me a Break* Morali, Belolo, Ritchie Family; *The Sound of the City*; *Samantha*; *I'm A Singing Juggler*; *Sophistication* Morali, Belolo, Phil Hurtt; *Liberation*; *I Love You To Death*; *Can't Stop The Music* Morali, Belolo, Hurtt, Beauris Whitehead; *Magic Night*; *Milkshake* Morali, Belolo, Willis; *Macho Man* Morali, Belolo, Willis, Whitehead; *Danny Boy* Frederick E. Weatherly.

Eighties Musicals

Hal Ashby, Arthur Penn and Mike Nichols were ▷ all, at one time or another, set to direct **Popeye** (Paramount/Walt Disney), the live-action, all-singing, all-dancing version of the Famous E. C. Segar cartoon strip. And Dustin Hoffman and Lily Tomlin were tipped for the roles of the spinach-munching Popeye, and Olive Oyl. In the event, the director who finally saw the project through to completion was Robert Altman, and the stars were Robin Williams (right) and Shelley Duvall, both of whom did admirably in bringing their subjects to real life. The film itself – which had Popeye as a shipwrecked sailor arriving in the small harbour town of Sweethaven, saving Olive from marriage to Bluto, and finding both his long lost father and some hidden treasure – was less successful. While undoubtedly true in spirit and essence to the frantic knockabout style of the original cartoons, the overall effect when translated into live action was disquieting. And ear-pummellingly noisy. There were some nifty sight gags which every now and then bulldozed their way through the general tumult, but the movie might have been far more digestible had the Harry Nilsson songs been more tuneful. Ray Walston (left) appeared as Poopdeck Pappy and Paul Dooley as Wimpy, with other parts going to Richard Libertini, Donald Moffatt, MacIntyre Dixon, Roberta Maxwell and Donovan Scott. It was choreographed by Sahron Kinney, Lou Wills and Hovey Burgess, the latter responsible for Robin Williams' dances. Jules Feiffer scripted, and it was produced by Robert Evans. Songs and musical numbers: *I Yam What I Yam*; *He Needs Me*; *Swee' Pea's Lullaby*; *Sweethaven*; *Blow Me Down*; *Everything Is Food*; *Sailin'*; *It's Not Easy Being Me*; *He's Large*; *I'm Mean*; *Kids* Nilsson; *I'm Popeye The Sailor Man* Sam Lerner.

△
A great deal of hardware was sacrificed in the service of **The Blues Brothers** (Universal), a frenetic but entertaining musical farce which traced the violent misfortunes of the titular heroes (John Belushi, right, and Dan Aykroyd, left) as they attempt, after Belushi's release from jail, to re-establish their erstwhile musical combo by persuading its former members to jettison their present jobs and regroup themselves. It's anything but a smooth ride though, for the orgy of destruction unleashed by the Blues Boys wherever they go, puts them on practically every 'wanted' list in the state of Illinois. Messrs Belushi and Aykroyd (a sort of latter day Abbott and Costello), plus a supporting cast that included James Brown, Aretha Franklin, Kathleen Freeman, Carrie Fisher, John Candy, Henry Gibson, Steve Lawrence, Ray Charles, Twiggy, and Cab Calloway (singing his immortal 'Minnie The Moocher', which he wrote with Irving Mills) did wonders for Aykroyd and John Landis's knockabout screenplay. The storyline itself was straight out of the forties, but the language in which it was couched belonged distinctly to the eighties; so did the zesty direction by Landis who, to judge from the number of cars that are destroyed in the film's 133 minutes, clearly bears a grudge against the motor industry. Carlton Johnson choreographed several lively but not particularly distinguished routines, and the producer was Robert K. Weiss. Songs and musical numbers: *She Caught The Katy* Taj Mahal, Yank Rachel; *Peter Gunn Theme* Henry Mancini; *Gimme Some Lovin'* Steve Winwood, Muff Winwood, Spencer Davis; *The Old Landmark* A.M. Brunner; *Quando, Quando, Quando* Tony Renis, A. Testa; *Boom Boom* John Lee Hooker; *Think* Aretha Franklin, Ted White; *Shake Your Tailfeathers* A and P and D and E Love, Z. Phillips, T. Judy; *Theme From Rawhide* Dimitri Tiomkin, Ned Washington; *Stand By Your Man* Tammy Wynette, Billy Sherill; *Can't Turn You Loose* Otis Redding; *Time Is Tight* Booker T; *Everybody Needs Somebody To Love* Jerry Wexler, Bert Berns, Solomon Burke; *Sweet Home Chicago* Woody Payne; *Jailhouse Rock* Jerry Leiber, Mike Stoller.

◁ Like *Can't Stop The Music*, **Xanadu** (Universal), which starred Olivia Newton-John (left) and Gene Kelly (centre), was a throwback to the Hollywood musical of the forties, its particular inspiration being Columbia's *Cover Girl* (1944), in which Kelly had also appeared. But with this casting duplication (in both films Kelly was called Danny McGuire) the similarities ended. Richard Christian Danus, Michael Kane and Marc Reid Rubel's mind-bogglingly inept fantasy also featured Michael Beck (right) as a frustrated artist who, while in the process of searching for a mysterious and beautiful muse (Newton-John) meets a wealthy but embittered clarinettist (Kelly – uneasy in the role) and persuades him to invest his money in a spectacular disco nightclub. With Gene on hand to appeal to the mums and dads, and Olivia to their children, **Xanadu's** producer Lawrence Gordon was clearly hedging his bets. The gamble, however, misfired (Olivia could hardly be called charismatic) and, apart from Kenny Ortega and Jerry Trent's lively staging of the musical numbers, the show was decidedly deficient in goodies. Sandra Katie Hanley, Fred McCarren and Ren Woods completed the cast (Coral Browne and Wilfrid Hyde-White's voices were heard in a fantasy sequence towards the end), and the director was Robert Greenwald. Songs and musical numbers: *I'm Alive; The Fall; Don't Walk Away; All Over The World* (sung by the Electric Light Orchestra) Jeff Lynne; *Xanadu* (Newton-John) Lynne; *Magic* (Newton-John); *Suddenly* (Newton-John, Cliff Richard); *Dancing* (Newton-John, The Tubes); *Suspended In Time* (Newton-John); *Whenever You're Away From Me* (Newton-John, Gene Kelly) John Farrar.

1981

Academy Awards

Writing (Screenplay) – adaptation
NOMINATIONS INCLUDED: *Pennies From Heaven*
(MGM) Dennis Potter

Costume Design
NOMINATIONS INCLUDED: *Pennies From Heaven*
Bob Mackie

Sound
NOMINATIONS INCLUDED: *Pennies From Heaven*
Michael J. Kohut, J.M. Harding, Richard
Tyler, Al Overton

Made in the UK, and not exactly a formula Hollywood musical, **The Great Muppet Caper** (ITC) nevertheless boasted the American creative talents of its successful predecessor, *The Muppet Movie* (ITC, 1979). The script (by Tom Patchett, Jay Tarses, Jerry Juhl and Jack Rose) placed Kermit the Frog, Fozzie Bear, and porcine superstar Miss Piggy in a Muppet extravaganza of jewel theft, grand passion and mistaken identity. Though enhanced by a series of droll movie parodies (notably an Esther Williams-style water ballet (illustrated) choreographed *à la* Busby Berkeley for Miss P), the narrative was sluggish, and few of the guest stars – who included Diana Rigg, Charles Grodin, John Cleese, Robert Morley, Peter Ustinov, Jack Warden and Peter Falk – managed to make much of an impression. Jim Henson, the original Muppeteer, directed competently if impersonally, the music and lyrics were by Joe Raposo, Anita Mann choreographed, and the film's producers were David Lazer and Frank Oz. Songs and musical numbers: *A Movie; The Big Bus; Happiness Hotel; Lady Holiday; Steppin' Out With A Star; The Apartment; Night Life; The First Time It Happens; Couldn't We Ride; Piggy's Fantasy ('Miss Piggy'); Homeward Bound; The Great Muppet Caper; a) The Heist b) The Muppet Fight Song c) Muppets To The Rescue.*

△

A reworking by Dennis Potter of his successful British TV serial of the same name, **Pennies From Heaven** (MGM) switched locales from Britain to America but retained the period (the mid-thirties) of the original. All about a sheet-music salesman working in Depression-hit Chicago, the film took an extraordinarily bleak look at his dreary, workaday life and unsatisfactory marriage, and juxtaposed that bleakness with a fantasy existence – in which all the characters burst into song – inspired by the sunny lyrics he carried with him in his bag. It was a brilliant conception, brilliantly realised by director Herbert Ross, with the best moment of all occurring towards the end when the salesman, to escape the proliferating troubles that are befalling him (including a murder rap), slips into a cinema to see *Follow The Fleet* (RKO, 1936) and physically projects himself into the 'Let's Face

The Music And Dance' (Irving Berlin) routine. The salesman was quite exceptionally well played by Steve Martin (centre), Jessica Harper was his love-shy wife, and Bernadette Peters the schoolteacher he meets on one of his trips, and with whom he has a serious affair. Also cast: Vernel Bagneris, John McMartin, John Karlen, Jay Garner, Robert Fitch, Tommy Rall and, in a special guest appearance, Christopher Walken, whose solo strip dance in a bar was one of the best things in this exciting and adult musical. It was produced by Herbert Ross and Nora Kaye, photographed by Gordon Willis, and choreographed with immense visual flair by Danny Daniels, who superimposed the actual songs of the period (sung by the artists who recorded them) over the action. Also contributing to the musical programme were Marvin Hamlisch, and Billy May who arranged and conducted most of the routines. As much a homage to the Hollywood musical as a salutary evocation of a grim period in America's history, **Pennies From Heaven** was sadly underrated on its release, played to poor business, and quickly disappeared from the circuits. Songs and musical numbers: *The Clouds Will Soon Roll By* Harry Woods, George Brown; *My Honey Says Yes* Con Conrad, Cliff Friend; *I'll Never Have To Dream Again* Isham Jones, Charles Newman; *Roll Along Prairie Moon* Ted Fiorito, Harry Macpherson, Albert Von Tilzer; *Did You Ever See A Dream Walking?* Mack Gordon, Harry Revel; *Pennies From Heaven* Johnny Burke, Albert Johnston; *It's The Girl* Abel Baer, Dave Oppenheim; *Love Is Good For Anything That Ails You* Cliff Friend, Matt Malneck; *Let's Put Out The Lights And Go To Sleep* Herman Hupfeld; *It's A Sin To Tell A Lie* Billy Mayhew; *I Want To Be Bad* Buddy De Sylva, Lew Brown, Ray Henderson; *Life Is Just A Bowl Of Cherries* Henderson, Brown; *Let's Misbehave* Cole Porter; *Serenade In The Night* Cesare A. Bixio, B. Cherubini, Jimmy Kennedy; *Fancy Our Meeting* Phil Charig, Joseph Meyer, Douglas Furber; *The Glory Of Love* Billy Hill.

1982

An anachronism redolent of the musicals assembled by *schmaltz* merchant Joe Pasternak for Mario Lanza in the fifties, **Yes, Giorgio** (MGM) was a major disaster from the studio that once gave the world *Singin' In The Rain* (1952). A vehicle for the overweight opera star Luciano Pavarotti (left), it was barely able to sustain its running time as it told the story of Giorgio Finzi, a world famous tenor who, while on a concert tour of the United States, falls in love with a beautiful throat specialist (Kathryn Harrold, right) after she treats him for a 'crisis of the voice'. Trouble is, she doesn't particularly like opera, and he's a married man with a family. A relationship of sorts does, however, develop (though not on a physical basis), but it is doomed, and the film ends unhappily with the lady doctor realising that Giorgio will never desert his family for another woman. It was such unadulterated piffle from start to finish, that even the operatic extracts failed to make it in any way palatable. Eddie Albert co-starred as Giorgio's manager, with other roles under Franklin J. Schaffner's blush-making direction going to Paola Borboni, James Hong, Beulah Quo, Norman Steinberg and Kathryn Fullen. Norman Steinberg wrote it (from a novel by Ann Piper) and Peter Fetterman produced. Songs and operatic arias: *If I Were In Love* Alan and Marilyn Bergman, John Williams; *Una Furtiva Lagrima* (from 'L'Elisir D'Amore') Donizetti; *La Donna E Mobile* (from 'Rigoletto') Verdi; *Cielo E Mar* (from 'La Gioconda') Ponchielli; *Donna Non Vidi Mai* (from 'Manon Lescaut') Puccini; *Nessun Dorma* (from 'Turandot') Puccini; *Ave Maria* Schubert; *O Sole Mio* Di Capua; *Santa Lucia* (traditional); *Mattinata* Leoncavallo; *Funiculi Funicula* Denza; *I Left My Heart In San Francisco* Douglass Cross, George Cory.

△

▽

Rarely can a movie have been as misnamed as Francis Coppola's **One From the Heart** (American Zoetrope), a $30,000,000 *hommage* to the whole tradition of the musical. A huge and visually resplendent spectacle, it lacked for nothing except – like the Tin Man in *The Wizard Of Oz* (MGM, 1939) – a heart. Though the project originated from a wish on its director's part, after the budgetary and meteorological ordeal of his Vietnam War epic, *Apocalypse Now* (United Artists, 1979), to switch to a comedy-drama of modest dimensions, somewhere along the line its simple, over-familiar plot (a not-so-young estranged couple based in Las Vegas indulge in a little casual romancing on the side before their final reconciliation) got inflated out of existence. The four principals, played with varying degrees of charm by Frederic Forrest, Teri Garr, Raul Julia and Nastassia Kinski (illustrated), were lost in the vast expanses of Dean Tavoularis' admittedly stunning studio recreation of the gaudy Nevada resort; while Coppola seemed to have been too busy tinkering with all his wonderful new video technology (for which the movie was intended as a showcase) to bother with directing his actors. The dance numbers, reportedly supervised by Gene Kelly, were embarrassingly reminiscent of Peter Bogdanovich's *At Long Last Love* (20th Century-Fox, 1975), and the songs (by Tom Waits who, with Crystal Gale, also sang most of them), though intermittently tuneful, would more appropriately have graced a hotel lounge than a Hollywood musical. Armyan Bernstein was responsible for the story and screenplay, it was produced by Gray Frederickson and Fred Roos (executive producer Bernard Gersten), and featured Lainie Kazan and Harry Dean Stanton in support. All in all, the venture was a grossly squandered opportunity and an appalling waste of talent, whose failure was pounced upon by the critics and reflected at the box office where it registered as one of the most calamitous flops in screen history. Songs and musical numbers: *Once Upon A Town*; *The Wages Of Love*; *Is There Any Way Out Of This Dream?*; *Picking Up After You*; *Old Boyfriends*; *Broken Bicycles*; *I Beg Your Pardon*; *Little Boy Blue*; *The Tango* (instrumental); *Circus Girl* (instrumental); *You Can't Unring A Bell*; *This One's From The Heart*; *Take Me Home*; *Presents* (instrumental).

Eighties Musicals

Very much in the style of Ernst Lubitsch and Billy Wilder, Blake Edwards' **Victor/Victoria** (MGM/UA), a remake of a 1933 German UFA comedy called *Viktor Und Viktoria*, scintillated for all of its 133-minute running time. Set in Rodger Maus' sumptuous studio-bound Paris in 1934, it starred Julie Andrews as an impoverished chanteuse whose chance meeting in a bistro one snowy evening with an outrageously gay nightclub entertainer (Robert Preston), also down on his luck, soon leads to fame and fortune for them both. For Preston (centre left), having heard Miss Andrews audition at the very club from which he has recently been fired, has the brilliant notion of masquerading her as a man. Not just *any* man, but the world's greatest female impersonator. The ploy succeeds stunningly and, in no time at all, Miss Andrews alias Victor (centre right) becomes the toast of Gay Paree. There are problems, of course, and they come mainly in the shape of James Garner, a Chicago gangster who sees Miss Andrews' act and immediately falls in love with her, only to be shattered when he is assured that the 'she' is really a 'he'. Using this potentially farce-laden situation to maximum comic effect, Edwards'

breezy screenplay (conceived by Hans Hoemburg and originally scripted for the UFA version by Reinhold Schunzel) drew non-stop laughter and was especially remarkable in that most of the gags in it were repeated twice – and even three times – without the law of diminishing returns taking its toll. The film also carried a live-and-let-live message of sorts: that it is wrong to categorize people into sexual stereotypes. Paddy stone's dance routines did the Henry Mancini-Leslie Bricusse score proud, and were as witty as the screenplay into which they were skilfully sandwiched. Robert Preston's unrestrained performance as 'the old queen' was a joy, and there was a peach of a characterization from Lesley Ann Warren (whose number, 'Chicago Illinois' was one of the highspots) as Garner's sex-pot moll. Alex Karras was featured as Garner's bodyguard, and the rest of the cast included John Rhys-Davies, Peter Arne, Sherloque Tanney and Graham Stark. Blake Edwards and Tony Adams produced. Other songs and musical numbers: *Crazy World*; *You And Me*; *The Shady Dame From Seville*; *Alone In Paris* (instrumental); *King's Can-Can* (instrumental); *Le Jazz Hot*; *Cat And Mouse* (instrumental); *Gay Paree*. ▷

◁ The main trouble with **Annie** (Columbia) – 'the movie of Tomorrow' as its slogan proclaimed – was director John Huston's total inability to perceive the material in musical comedy terms. Daunted, no doubt, by the gargantuan $35 million budget allocated by producer Ray Stark, Huston had little choice but to deliver a 'big event', and the same kind of unwieldy, top-heavy elephantiasis that afflicted Sidney Lumet's *The Wiz* (Universal, 1978) was very much in evidence throughout this disappointing occasion. Also contributing to the film's leaden texture was the insensitive way in which the dance numbers were photographed and edited. The musical sequences were created by executive producer Joe Layton, but staged and choreographed by Arlene Phillips, so it was difficult to know precisely at whose feet to lay the blame. After a nationwide search of Scarlett O'Hara proportions, a 10-year-old girl named Aileen Quinn (right) from Pennsylvania was chosen to play the part of little orphan Annie, the other major roles going to a less comfortably cast Albert Finney (left) as Daddy Warbucks, and to the vivacious Carol Burnett as Miss Hannigan, a fool-proof part if ever there was one. Ann Reinking was wasted as billionaire Warbucks' secretary; nor was justice done to the talents of Tim Curry, Bernadette Peters and Geoffrey Holder. It was written by Carol Sobieski, who found places for four songs (music by Charles Strouse, lyrics by Martin Charnin) that were not in the original Broadway show. Songs and musical numbers included: *Maybe*; *It's A Hard-Knock Life*; *I Think I'm Gonna Like It Here*; *Tomorrow*; *Easy Street*; *You're Never Fully Dressed Without A Smile*; *Little Girls*; *I Don't Need Anything But You*.

When Paramount's 1977 hit *Grease*, took a mammoth $96 million at the box office to become one of the most successful musicals in Hollywood's history (and one of the ten top money-making films of all time) a sequel was inevitable. **Grease 2** was its title, and it in no way equalled the pulling power of its energetic predecessor. Not only was it five years too late, but leading players Maxwell Caulfield (right, from Britain) and Michelle Pfeiffer (left) lacked the box-office clout of John Travolta and Olivia Newton-John, the stars of the first version. Add to this a virtually plotless screenplay (in which Pfeiffer's predilection for leather-clad bikers forces new boy Caulfield to prove himself in this area) and the reasons for the public's lack of enthusiasm become apparent. The film's saving grace was director/choreographer Patricia Birch's lively dance routines, particularly the one set in a bowling alley. Adrian Zmed, Christopher McDonald, Peter Frechette, Leif Green and Lorna Luft (centre) were in it too; so were Tab Hunter, and old-timers Eve Arden, Sid Caesar and Dody Patterson. Ken Finkleman wrote it, and it was produced by Robert Stigwood and Allan Carr. Songs and musical numbers: *Back to School Again*; *Who's That Guy?*; *(Love Will) Turn Back The Hands Of Time* Louis St Louis, Howard Greenfield; *Charaders* St Louis, Michael Gibson; *Girl For All Seasons*; *Rock-A-Hula Luau (Summer Is Coming)* Dominic Bugatti, Frank Musker; *Score Tonight* Bugatti, Musker, St Louis; *Prowlin'* Bugatti, Musker, Christopher Cerf; *Brad* Cerf; *Reproduction*; *Cool Rider* Dennis Linde; *We'll Be Together* Bob Morrison, Johnny MacRae; *Do It For Our Country* Rob Hegel; *Our Day Will Come* Bob Hilliard, Mort Garson; *Rebel Walk* Duane Eddy, Lee Hazlewood.

▽

Appendixes

The three appendixes were compiled because it was considered necessary at least to mention the films they contain if the book were to act as a comprehensive reference guide to the genre. In each case, the listing is chronological, and provides details of title, studio, director, stars, and a brief précis of content for each film. Appendixes 2 and 3 deal with specific areas of the musical and the inclusion of all the titles in them is not especially contentious. Appendix 1, however, covers what, for want of a better term, have been called 'fringe' musicals – films which, for one reason or another, were considered worthy of inclusion in the book, but not as main entries. The choice, as explained in the author's note on page 9, was necessarily subjective and, doubtless, arguments will rage among readers who may well not agree with all the distinctions made. It will be noticed that Elvis Presley's movies inhabit the main section of the book and not the pop appendix. This decision was taken because Presley was a unique phenomenon, both as a star, and in the number of main features in which he appeared. For the rest, the basic material of Appendix 2 was deemed to be of a different flavour to the rest of the main entries, as well as potentially offering a bulk of written material which would have caused the book as a whole to burst through any reasonable confines. The entries in Appendix 3 offer no elements in common with the body of the book, other than music and the use of celluloid.

Appendix 1 – Fringe Musicals – page 424

A chronological listing of films considered important for inclusion in the book, but not sufficiently 'musical' in their basic concept to merit a main entry. Wherever possible, relevant or notable musical information is provided.

Appendix 2 – Miscellaneous Pop Musicals – page 430

From 1956 a proliferation of youth-orientated 'pop' musicals flooded the market, reflecting the current trends of hit-parade music. Thus, there were Rock'n'Roll movies, Twist and Calypso movies, and what came to be known as 'Beach Party' movies. In style, convention and flavour they were radical departures from the Hollywood of, say, *42nd Street*, *Easter Parade* or *Funny Girl*. These pop movies, however, were (and are) undoubtedly part of the musical genre.

Appendix 3 – Documentaries – page 432

The fifties also saw the emergence of the documentary musical – the filming and recording of musical events at the time they were actually happening. Subject matter ranged over a wide spectrum, from international festivals of folk-dancing, through jazz at Newport, to fund-raising and 'protest' concerts. The artists captured for posterity included virtually every singer – male and female, black and white, and every group, who ever made an impact on the country-and-western, rock or soul music scenes over a period of twenty years or so. In style and presentation the documentaries ranged from poorly shot and badly edited exploitation movies (for example *Celebration At Big Sur*, 1971; *Janis*, 1975), to the superbly made and often inventive accounts of major musical events, such as *Jazz On A Summer's Day*, 1959, and *Woodstock*, 1970.

Indexes

In an attempt to make the searching of so extensive a list of references a little easier for the reader, this index has been divided into categories and becomes several indexes under the separate headings FILM TITLES, SONG AND MUSIC TITLES, PERFORMERS, COMPOSERS AND LYRICISTS and OTHER CREATIVE PERSONNEL. These cover material from the decade chapters only (that is, pages 18 to 415 inclusive); the introductory pages and the appendixes have not been indexed. Each index is alphabetically arranged in the usual way but, where a film or song title begins with an arabic numeral, for example *52nd Street*, it will be found under F, as if it were *Fifty-second Street*. Where appropriate, a few names appear in more than one index: Bob Fosse, for example, is listed both as a performer and under 'other creative personnel'.

Index 1 — Film Titles — page 434

All references to a specific film are listed. The page number which refers to that film's main entry is indicated by the use of bold type. If no bold page number is listed for a particular film, this denotes that it is merely mentioned in passing in another film's entry.

Index 2 — Song and Music Titles — page 436

The distinction between songs and music arises because of the many musical numbers without words (for example, 'The Frug' from *Sweet Charity*), and the featuring of instrumental music from the classical repertoire.

Index 3 — Performers — page 447

Where a performer is illustrated in the still which accompanies the account of a film, the relevant page number appears in italic type. It is perhaps appropriate to mention that many Hollywood actors and actresses used different spellings or presentations of their names at different times; we have opted for standardization based on majority usage.

Index 4 — Composers and Lyricists — page 455

Unfortunately, in certain cases, all research has failed to identify the composers of some musical numbers; such numbers are therefore mentioned without credits. This means that the page references listed for each composer or lyricist will not necessarily yield a comprehensive checklist of their output for the genre.

Index 5 — Other Creative Personnel — page 459

This is a mixed listing, and only reference to the entries themselves will provide the information as to the role the individual played. Included in this category are directors, producers (and associate producers), screenwriters, original story writers, editors, art directors, set and costume designers, cameramen, special effects men, sound recordists, choreographers and dance directors, and musical directors and orchestrators. This is not to suggest that the account of every film in the main text carries credits for photography, sound recording, special effects, or even design; such personnel have been mentioned only where their contribution to the film was especially noteworthy. On the other hand, every film is credited with a director and a writer, and most of them with a producer.

Index 6 — New Films, 1980 Onwards — page 463

This edition of the book contains a number of films that have been released since the first edition was published. These are not included in the above indexes but are indexed separately. This supplementary index contains *Popeye* (1980) and musicals released in 1981 and subsequently.

Fringe Musicals

1929

QUEEN OF THE NIGHTCLUBS (Warner Bros.)
The attempts of a successful nightclub entertainer (Texas Guinan) to prevent her jealous rivals from doing the dirty on her. Eddie Foy Jr, Jack Norworth, George Raft, Lila Lee; directed by Bryan Foy.

RED HOT RHYTHM (Pathe)
Songwriter (Alan Hale) of dubious reputation makes a living by fleecing other composers and publishing their works. Kathryn Crawford, Josephine Dunn; directed by Leo McCarey. (Technicolor sequences.) Songs included: *At Last I'm In Love* Robert Emmet Dolan, Walter O'Keefe.

THE BROADWAY HOOFER (GB: DANCING FEET) (Columbia)
A dancer (Marie Saxon) takes a sabbatical in a small country town and falls for the fourth-rate hoofer-manager (Jack Egan) of a burlesque show that is passing through. Directed by George Archainbaud.

1930

LOVE COMES ALONG (Radio Pictures)
Sailor falls in love with a stranded actress in Cuba. Bebe Daniels, Lloyd Hughes, Montague Love; directed by Rupert Julian. Songs included: *Until Love Comes Along*; *Night Winds* Oscar Levant, Sidney Clare.

MELODY MAN (Columbia)
Famous Viennese composer (John Sainpolis) flees to America with his daughter (Alice Day) after murdering his wife's lover in a jealous rage, and discovers jazz. Fifteen years later he returns to Europe to face trial. William Collier Jr; directed by Roy William Neill. Songs included: *Broken Dreams* Ballard McDonald, Arthur Johnston, Dave Dreyer.

MAN TROUBLE (Fox)
Tough cabaret owner (Milton Sills) falls in love with a girl (Dorothy Mackaill) who, in turn, falls in love with a crooning newspaper man (Roscoe Karns). Directed by Berthold Viertel. Songs included: *You Got Nobody to Love*; *Now I Ask You* James Hanley, Joseph McCarthy.

LILIES OF THE FIELD (Warner Bros.)
Corinne Griffith, after suffering an ugly divorce, becomes a gold digger and is arrested for vagrancy. Of interest for Roy Mack's staging of production numbers in a nightclub. Ralph Forbes; directed by Alexander Korda. Songs included: *I'd Like To Be A Gypsy* Herb Magidson, Ned Washington, Michael Cleary.

CHECK AND DOUBLE CHECK (RKO)
Amos 'n' Andy (as a couple of taxi drivers) spend a night in a haunted house and find a vital property deed without which young lovers Sue Carol and Charles Norton cannot marry. Freeman F. Gosden, Charles J. Correll; directed by Melville Brown. Songs included: *Three Little Words* Bert Kalmar, Harry Ruby; *Old Man Blues* Irving Mills, Duke Ellington.

1931

MEN OF THE SKY (Warner Bros./First National)
A French spy (Irene Delroy) in World War I, her aviator lover (Jack Whiting) and father (John Sainpolis), are discovered and shot; directed by Alfred E. Green. Songs included: *Every Little While*; *Boys March*; *Stolen Dreams*; *You Ought to See Sweet Marguerite* Jerome Kern, Otto Harbach.

JUNE MOON (Paramount)
Adaptation of a stage play by Ring Lardner and George Kaufman about a numbskull (Jack Oakie) with ambitions to become a Tin Pan Alley lyric writer. Frances Dee, June MacCloy; directed by Edward Sutherland. Songs included: *June Moon*; *Montana Moon* Lardner, Kaufman.

1932

DANCERS IN THE DARK (Paramount)
Bandleader Jack Oakie tries to save his pal from the clutches of a dancehall girl (Miriam Hopkins) but falls in love with her himself. William Collier Jr. George Raft; directed by David Burton. Songs included: *St. Louis Blues* W.C. Handy.

HORSE FEATHERS (Paramount)
The Marx Brothers' third feature film and the first to have an original screenplay (by Harry Ruby, Bert Kalmar and S.J. Perelman) abounded in visual and verbal non-sequiturs and featured Groucho as Wagstaff, the new president of Huxley College. Directed by Norman McLeod. Songs included: *I'm Against It*; *Everyone Says 'I Love You'* Kalmar, Ruby.

THE DEVIL'S BROTHER (GB: FRA DIAVOLO) (MGM)
Unsuccessful attempt to give Auber's romantic operetta the slapstick treatment. What remained of Auber's score was competently handled by Dennis King. Stan Laurel, Oliver Hardy, Thelma Todd; directed by Hal Roach and Charles Rogers.

NIGHT WORLD (Universal)
60 minute programmer, set in a New York nightclub, and involving an alcoholic customer (Lew Ayres), a friendly chorus girl (Mae Clarke) and the affair the owner's (Boris Karloff) wife (Dorothy Revier) is having with the cabaret's dance director (Russell Hopton). Hedda Hopper, George Raft; directed by Hobart Henley. The choreography (complete with overhead shots) was by Busby Berkeley.

BLONDE VENUS (Paramount)
Marlene Dietrich learns that husband Herbert Marshall needs $1500 to cure him of radium poisoning; she becomes a singer on the New York stage and, during her husband's absence abroad, has an affair with socialite Cary Grant. Marshall's unexpected return begins a melodramatic chain of events that leads to Dietrich's downfall and subsequent rehabilitation. Dickie Moore, Gene Morgan; directed by Josef von Sternberg. Musical numbers: *Hot Voodoo*; *You Little So And So* Sam Coslow, Ralph Rainger; *I Couldn't Be Annoyed* Leo Robin, Richard A. Whiting.

1933

CAVALCADE (Fox)
Screen version of Noël Coward's hit play chronicling the ups and downs of the Marryot family over a period of 33 years – from 1899 to 1932. Diana Wynyard. Clive Brook. Herbert Mundin. Una O'Connor, Ursula Jeans, Beryl Mercer; directed by Frank Lloyd. Songs included: *Twentieth Century Blues*.

DIPLOMANIACS (RKO)
Rhymed dialogue in song was the novelty in this Wheeler and Woolsey programmer in which Messrs W. and W. are handed a couple of million dollars by the Indians to journey to Geneva in an attempt to make the peace delegates stop fighting. Marjorie White. Phyllis Barry. Louis Calhern; directed by William Seiter. Songs included: *Sing To Me* Edward Eliscu. Harry Akst.

1934

KING KELLY OF THE USA (Monogram)
An American producer (Guy Robertson) falls for a princess (Irene Ware) aboard a Transatlantic ocean liner. Edgar Kennedy; directed by Leonard Fields. Songs included: *Right Next Door To Love*; *Believe Me* Bernie Grossman, Joe Sanders.

THE LOUDSPEAKER (GB: THE RADIO STAR) (Monogram)
A railway station express man (Ray Walker) yearns to become a radio star. Jacqueline Wells; directed by Joseph Santley. Songs included: *Who but You?*; *Doo Ah Doo Ah Doo Ah Know What I'm Doing?* Lew Brown, Harry Akst.

LOVETIME (Fox)
Sentimental story of the life and loves of composer Franz Schubert, with Nils Asther starring. Several Schubert melodies featured as background music. Pat Paterson, Herbert Mundin; directed by James Tinling.

BRIGHT EYES (Fox)
Shirley Temple's first starring vehicle, involving a custody battle over an orphan, contained the song that helped make her famous: *On The Good Ship Lollipop* by Sidney Clare and Richard Whiting. James Dunn, Lois Wilson; directed by David Butler.

FASHIONS OF 1934 (Warner Bros.)
A New York couturier (William Powell) pilfers the latest fashion designs from Paris, then passes them off as his own. Production number was directed by Busby Berkeley, and featured 50 girls draped in ostrich feathers being formed into a galleon 60ft long. They were also transformed into human harps. Bette Davis; directed by William Dieterle. Songs: *Spin A Little Web Of Dreams*; *Broken Melody* Irving Kahal, Sammy Fain.

COCKEYED CAVALIERS (RKO)
After appropriating the clothes of the King's inebriated physician and his assistant, Bert Wheeler and Robert Woolsey run amok in a routine mistaken identity plot. Noah Beery, Thelma Todd; directed by Mark Sandrich. Songs included: *And The Big Bad Wolf Was Dead*; *Dilly Dally* Val Burton, Will Jason.

STINGAREE (Radio Pictures)
Romantic tale, featuring operatic arias, based on a character created by E.W. Hornung, of an Australian Robin Hood who captures the heart of an opera singer (Irene Dunne). Richard Dix, Mary Boland; directed by William Wellman. Songs included: *Tonight Is Mine* Gus Kahn, W. Franke Harling; extracts from Gounod's *Faust* and Flotow's *Martha*.

ONE HOUR LATE (Paramount)
Trials and tribulations of a shipping clerk (Joe Morrison) whose naive stenographer sweetheart (Helen Twelvetrees) enjoys flirting innocently with her boss (Conrad Nagel). Arline Judge, Ray Walker; directed by Ralph Murphy. Songs included: *A Little Angel Told Me So*; *Last Roundup* Sam Coslow, Lewis Gensler, Leo Robin.

RAINBOW OVER BROADWAY (Chesterfield)
Unpopular stepmother (Grace Hayes) to a Kansas City family journeys to New York, with the family, to resume her career as a singer. Frank Albertson, Lucien Littlefield; directed by Richard Thorpe. Songs included: *I Must Be In Love With Love*; *Dance My Blues Away* Elizabeth Morgan, Harry Von Tilzer.

1935

THE NITWITS (Radio Pictures)
Confused whodunnit featuring Wheeler and Woolsey as a couple of cigar salesmen who find themselves involved in the murder of a music publisher. Fred Keating, Betty Grable; directed by George Stevens. Songs included: *Music In My Heart* Dorothy Fields, Jimmy McHugh; *You Opened My Eyes* L. Wolfe Gilbert, Felix Bernard.

THIS IS THE LIFE (Fox)
A vaudeville starlet (Jane Withers), dressed as a boy, runs away from her theatrical commitments and befriends a man (John McGuire) wanted by the police. Directed by Marshall Neilan. Songs included: *Gotta New Kind Of Rhythm; Sandy And Me* Sidney Clare, Sammy Stept.

KING SOLOMON OF BROADWAY (Universal)
Melodrama with nightclub background in which Edmund Lowe (as King Solomon), operates a nightclub for jailed gangster Edward Pawley, and loses the club while gambling with a trio of racketeers. Dorothy Page, Pinky Tomlin; directed by Alan Crosland. Songs included: *That's What You Think* Tomlin; *Flower In My Lapel* Con Conrad, Herb Magidson.

MANHATTAN MOON (GB: SING ME A LOVE SONG) (Universal)
Dorothy Page played a dual role: a temperamental entertainer, and the lookalike who deputizes for her at all social engagements. Ricardo Cortez supplied the romantic interest as a nightclub proprietor who falls for Page in her guise as a socialite; directed by Stuart Walker. Songs included: *Manhattan Moon; First Kiss* Arthur Morton, Betty Trivers.

THE MELODY LINGERS ON (United Artists)
Story of a concert pianist's (Josephine Hutchinson) self-sacrifice for her child (David Scott). George Houston; directed by David Burton. Music from Bizet's *Carmen*.

AFTER THE DANCE (Columbia)
Melodramatic programmer about an escaped convict (George Murphy) who befriends a cabaret girl, joins her act and becomes a sensation, but is two-timed by a rival dancer who tips off the police. Nancy Carroll; directed by Leo Bulgakov. Songs included: *Without You I'm Just Drifting; Tomorrow Night* Harry Akst.

THE LITTLE COLONEL (20th Century-Fox)
Little Shirley Temple is instrumental in reuniting her mother (Evelyn Venable) with her estranged grandfather (Lionel Barrymore). Directed by David Butler. Songs: *Love's Young Dream* Thomas Moore; *Stair Dance* (with Bill Robinson).

THE LITTLEST REBEL (20th Century-Fox)
Shirley Temple saves her father (John Boles) from a prison sentence during the Civil War by calling on President Lincoln. Directed by David Butler. Songs: *Believe Me If All Those Endearing Young Charms* Thomas Moore, Matthew Locke; *Polly Wolly Doodle* (with Bill Robinson).

HERE COMES COOKIE (GB: THE PLOT THICKENS) (Paramount)
Gracie Allen's father (George Barbier) temporarily places his considerable fortune at her disposal as a means of discouraging a male gold digger who is out to ensnare his other daughter. George Burns; directed by Norman McLeod. Songs included: *Lazy Moon* Bob Cole, J. Rosamond Johnson; *Vamp Of The Pampas* Leo Robin. Richard Whiting.

1936

POPPY (Paramount)
W.C. Fields's adopted daughter (Rochelle Hudson), after pretending to be a phony heiress, turns out to be a real one after all. Richard Cromwell, Lynne Overman; directed by Edward Sutherland. Songs included: *Poppy* Sam Coslow, Frederick Hollander; *A Rendezvous With A Dream* Leo Robin. Ralph Rainger.

DEVIL ON HORSEBACK (Grand National)
Crooning gaucho (Del Campo) with the soul of a Mexican Robin Hood vies with the son of a coffee millionaire (Fred Keating) for the affections of Lily Damita. Directed by Crane Wilbur. Songs included: *So Divine; Out Of The Hills; The Love Fiesta; Oh Bella Mia* Harry Tobias, Jack Stern.

1937

THE GIRL SAID NO (Grand National)
A bookie (Robert Armstrong) tries to become a producer to get even with a dance-hall hostess (Irene Hervey) who, one passionate evening, gave him the shakedown. He concocts a revenge scheme (involving some Gilbert and Sullivan players) that will land Hervey in showbusiness, by which ploy he hopes to retrieve the money he spent on her. Paula Stone, William Danforth; directed by Andrew L. Stone. Musical extracts from Gilbert and Sullivan's *The Mikado; Patience; Pirates Of Penzance; Ruddigore*.

BLONDE TROUBLE (Paramount)
Lyric writer Johnny Downs comes to Broadway via Schenectady to find fame and fortune, but after one of his songs becomes a radio hit, finds himself Hollywood-bound. Remake of Paramount's 1931 *June Moon*. Eleanore Whitney, Lynne Overman, Benny Baker, William Demarest; directed by George Archainbaud. Songs included: *It Was All In Fun* Burton Lane, Ralph Freed.

THANKS FOR LISTENING (Conn)
Pinky Tomlin starred as the innocent stooge for a gang of high class clip artists, headed by Aileen Pringle. Maxine Doyle, Claire Rochelle; directed by Marshall Neilan. Songs included: *The Love Bug Will Bite You; I Like To Make Music* Tomlin, Connie Lee.

HIGH FLYERS (RKO)
Wheeler and Woolsey pose as aviators, get tangled in a smuggling plot, and effect the capture of the culprits. Lupe Velez, Margaret Dumont, Jack Carson; directed by Edward Cline. Songs included: *Keep Your Head Above Water* Herman Ruby, Dave Dreyer.

HAWAIIAN BUCKAROO (20th Century-Fox)
Western with an Hawaiian setting in which Smith Bellew and sidekick Benny Burt, after finding employment with Evalyn Knapp on her ranch, save her from the machinations of a crooked foreman (George Regas). Directed by Ray Taylor. Songs included: *Hawaiian Memories; I Left Her On The Beach At Waikiki* Harry MacPherson, Albert von Tilzer, Eddie Grant.

THE KING AND THE CHORUS GIRL (Warner Bros.)
Fernand Gravet (making his American debut) falls head over heels for Folies Bergère chorus girl (Joan Blondell). Jane Wyman, Edward Everett Horton; directed by Mervyn LeRoy. Musical numbers staged by Bobby Connolly, including *For You; On The Rue De La Paix* Ted Koehler, Werner Heymann.

PICK A STAR (MGM)
Rowdy comedy with songs about two star-struck sisters (Patsy Kelly and Rosina Lawrence) in Hollywood. Laurel and Hardy appeared briefly in two sequences. Jack Haley, Mischa Auer, Lyda Roberti; directed by Edward Sedgwick. Musical numbers included: *Without Your Love* Johnny Lange, Fred Stryker.

WAY OUT WEST (MGM)
Western of sorts in which Laurel and Hardy help Rosina Lawrence to rescue her gold mine from villainous James Finlayson. Directed by James W. Horne. Songs included: *Commence To Dancing* J.L. Hill; *The Trail Of The Lonesome Pine* Harry Carroll, Ballard MacDonald.

WALLABY JIM OF THE ISLANDS (Grand National)
The adventures of the roistering skipper of a pearl-fishing brig in the South Seas. George Houston, Ruth Coleman; directed by Charles Lamont. Songs included: *Ia-O-Ra-Na; Hi-Ho-Hum* Felix Bernard, Irving Bibo.

SWING HIGH, SWING LOW (Paramount)
An adaptation of George M. Watters and Arthur Hopkins's play *Burlesque*, it charted the up-and-down career of a trumpet player (Fred MacMurray). Carole Lombard was the woman in his life. Charles Butterworth, Dorothy Lamour; directed by Mitchell Leisen. Songs included: *If It Isn't Pain Then It Isn't Love* Leo Robin, Ralph Rainger; *Panamania* Al Siegel, Sam Coslow.

1938

YOU AND ME (Paramount)
The story of a gangster (George Raft) who marries a girl (Sylvia Sidney) with a criminal past herself. An almost Brechtian hybrid of social drama, comedy and German Expressionism. Directed by Fritz Lang. Songs included: *You Can't Get Something For Nothing; The Right Guy For Me* Sam Coslow, Kurt Weill.

FOOLS FOR SCANDAL (Warner Bros.)
An impoverished French marquis (Fernand Gravet) instals himself as cook and butler to a film star (Carole Lombard) as a means of compromising her. Directed by Mervyn LeRoy. Rodgers and Hart provided the songs, most of which were removed from the final release print. Those that survived included: *There's A Big Boy In Harlem; How Can You Forget*.

STOLEN HEAVEN (Paramount)
Two jewel thieves (Olympe Bradna and Gene Raymond) are innocently harboured by an old, broken-down concert pianist (Lewis Stone) until they are ferreted out by the law. Glenda Farrell, Porter Hall; directed by Andrew L. Stone. Music by Wagner, Liszt, Moskowski, Chopin, Grieg and Strauss.

SWISS MISS (20th Century-Fox)
Laurel and Hardy, as a couple of waiters in an Alpine hotel, become involved with a composer (Walter Woolf King) who is trying to get away from his wife (Della Lind); directed by John G. Blystone.

THE GIRL FROM MEXICO (RKO)
Slapstick comedy with songs about an unknown Mexican singer (Lupe Velez) who is brought to New York by a radio executive (Donald Woods). Leon Errol; directed by Leslie Goodwins. Musical numbers included: *Negra Consentida* Joaquin Pardave; *Chiapanecas* Romero, Garuse, De Torre.

1939

SHE MARRIED A COP (Republic)
Film producers Jerome Cowan and Jean Parker fool Irish singing cop (Phil Regan) into falsely believing that he has landed the romantic lead in a new film. Regan marries Parker before she can reveal the deception. Directed by Sidney Salkow. Songs included:

ESCAPE TO PARADISE (RKO)
Bobby Breen, operating a motocycle taxi service in a South American seaport, guides Kent Taylor around the town and into romance with Maria Shelton, and then gets him into trouble by representing him as a buyer of maté leaves. Directed by Erle C. Kenton. Songs included: *Tra la La* Nilo Menendez. Eddie Cherkose.

1940

VILLAGE BARN DANCE (Republic)
Though Doris Day (not to be confused with the more famous Warner Bros. star) loves engineer Richard Cromwell, in order to save the merchants in her town from bankruptcy, she decides to marry wealthy industrialist Robert Baldwin. In the nick of time news reaches her that a radio show put on by the locals has been bought for sponsorship. George Barbier, Esther Dale, Andrew Tombes, radio personalities Lulubelle and Scotty, Barbara Allen (Vera Vague), Don Wilson and the Texas Wanderers; directed by Frank McDonald. Songs included: *What Are Little Girls Made Of* Scotty Wiseman, John Lair; *Howdy Neighbour* Eddie Cherkose.

GRAND OLE OPRY (Republic)
The Weaver family (Leon, Frank and June) starred in a familiar story of locals outwitting city slickers. The family manage to get Leon Weaver elected as governor after the usual difficulties encountered with crooked politicians. Roy Acuff's Smoky Mountain Boys, George Dewey Hay, and Uncle Dave Macon and Dorris supplied hillbilly music. Directed by Frank McDonald.

COMIN' ROUND THE MOUNTAIN (Paramount)
More Ozarkian humour, with Bob Burns returning to his backwoods Tennessee family after a brief sojourn in the city and being elected mayor of the town. Una Merkel, Jerry Colonna, Don Wilson; several tunes, purporting to be authentic music from the Tennessee hill country, were supplied by a hillbilly radio aggregate comprising Pat Barrett, Harold Peary, Bill Thompson, Cliff Arquette and Mirandy. Directed by George Archainbaud.

UP IN THE AIR (Monogram)
Frankie Darro, a radio station page boy, helps the cops discover who murdered singer Lorna Gray and cowboy Gordon Jones. Marjorie Reynolds, Mantan Moreland; directed by Howard Bretherton. Songs included: *By The Looks Of Things*; *Something Or Other* Edward Kay, Harry Tobias.

1941
ANDY HARDY'S PRIVATE SECRETARY (MGM)
Andy Hardy (Mickey Rooney) finally graduates from high school and finds himself with a new roadster and a secretary. Eighteen-year-old Kathryn Grayson, making her debut, played the secretary and, in the course of the film, sang a Cole Porter ballad, Strauss's 'Voices of Spring' and the mad scene from Donizetti's 'Lucia di Lammermoor'. Lewis Stone, Fay Holden, Ann Rutherford; directed by Howard B. Seitz.

VANISHING VIRGINIAN (MGM)
Kathryn Grayson, in her second feature, played authoress Rebecca Yancey whose Southern girlhood this family saga was all about. Frank Morgan (top starred), Spring Byington, Natalie Thompson. Douglass Newland; directed by Frank Borzage. Songs included: *The World Was Made For You*; *Evening By The Moonlight*; *Bill Bailey* (all sung by Grayson).

SMILIN' THROUGH (MGM)
Third version (the other two were in 1922 and 1932) of Jane Cowl and Jane Murfin's play in which a World War I Irish lassie (Jeanette MacDonald) finds her marriage to a young man (Gene Raymond) opposed by her elderly guardian (Brian Aherne) because of an incident in the past in which suitor Raymond's father slew guardian Aherne's bride. Ian Hunter, Frances Robinson; directed by Frank Borzage. (Technicolor). Songs included: *Drink To Me Only With Thine Eyes*; *A Little Love A Little Kiss* Leo Silesu, Adrian Ross; *Smilin' Through* Arthur Penn.

NEW WINE (United Artists)
Ilona Massey attempts to see that Franz Schubert (Alan Curtis) receives the recognition he deserves. Binnie Barnes, Albert Basserman (as Beethoven), Billy Gilbert, Sterling Holloway; directed by Reinhold Schunzel. The music included two songs (one *Ave Maria*) and extracts from symphonies by Schubert.

COUNTRY FAIR (Republic)
As soon as hillbilly June Clyde agrees to marry a fast-talking campaign manager (Eddie Foy Jr) for an aspirant governor (William Demarest), she sets out with a will to electioneer for his rival (Harold Peary). Harold Huber, Guinn Williams, Lulubelle Wiseman, The Vass Family, Simp Phonies; directed by Frank McDonald. Songs included: *Mornin' On The Farm* Jack Elliott.

HARD-BOILED CANARY (Paramount)
When the burlesque house in which little Susanna Foster is appearing as a singer of operatic arias is raided, she is spirited off by a pair of press agents (Allan Jones and Lynne Overman) to a summer music school in the mountains. Margaret Lindsay, Grace Bradley, William Collier Sr; directed by Andrew L. Stone. Extracts from Bizet's *Carmen* and Gounod's *Faust*.

LET'S GO COLLEGIATE (GB: FAREWELL TO FAME) (Monogram)
Frankie Darrow and Jackie Moran, a couple of college kids, have promised their sweethearts that their boatcrew will be top-notch, but their ace crew member is drafted, so they pick a muscular truck driver (Frank Sully) off the street to impersonate the drafted boatman. Marcia Mae Jones, Keye Luke, Mantan Moreland, Gale Storm; directed by Jean Yarbrough. Songs included: *Look What You've Done To Me*; *Sweet Sixteen* Harry Tobias, Edward Kay.

ICE-CAPADES (Republic)
Backstage yarn involving a newsreel cameraman (James Ellison) who, after muffing an assignment at Lake Placid, fakes it with shots of the Central Park pond in New York. Jerry Colonna and skating stars Belita, Vera Hruba Ralston, Dorothy Lewis. Songs included: *Forever And Ever* Sol Meyer, George R. Brown, Jule Styne; *Sophisticated Lady* Duke Ellington.

IT STARTED WITH EVE (Universal)
A hat-check girl (Deanna Durbin) becomes the fiancée of a millionaire (Robert Cummings). Charles Laughton was a crusty old millionaire who is about to die in the opening scene, but actually lives on for the duration of the picture. Remade in 1964 as *I'd Rather Be Rich*. Directed by Henry Koster. Songs included: *Clavelitos* Valverde; *Going Home* Dvorak.

SING FOR YOUR SUPPER (Columbia)
The heartbreaks of a struggling bandleader (Charles 'Buddy' Rogers). Jinx Falkenburg; directed by Charles Barton. Songs included: *Why Is It So* Sammy Cahn, Saul Chaplin.

GLAMOUR BOY (Paramount)
Story of a once famous child star (Jackie Cooper), now a soda-jerk in a Hollywood drug store, who coaches the studio's newest child prodigy (Darryl Hickman) in a remake of one of his (Cooper's) early hits. Susanna Foster, Walter Abel; directed by Ralph Murphy. Songs included: *The Magic Of Magnolias*; *Love Is Such An Old-Fashioned Thing* Frank Loesser. Victor Schertzinger.

1942
CALL OUT THE MARINES (RKO)
Messrs. Victor McLaglen and Edmund Lowe join the Marines as sergeants and compete for the attentions of a café girl (Binnie Barnes), only to discover that she is an enemy agent. Directed by Frank Ryan and William Hamilton. Songs included: *Call Out The Marines*; *Light Of My Life* Mort Greene, Harry Revel.

THE YANKS ARE COMING (PRC)
Arrogant bandleader Henry King, who thinks any soldier without a commission is a chump, finds his band rebelling against his arrogance by enlisting *en masse*. Mary Healy, Little Jackie Helier, Maxie Rosenbloom, Parkyakarkus; directed by Alexis Thurn-Taxis. Songs included: *I Must Have Priorities On Your Love*; *Don't Fool Around With My Heart*.

1943
ALL BY MYSELF (Universal)
After being jilted by her lover (Neil Hamilton) who has fallen for a singer (Rosemary Lane), Evelyn Ankers blackmails a doctor (Patric Knowles) into posing as her fiancé. Also Tip, Tap and Toe and The Loumell Morgan Trio; directed by Felix Feist. Songs included: *All By Myself* Inez James, Buddy Pepper; *You're Priceless* Morey Amsterdam, T. Ramona.

THE GIRL FROM MONTEREY (PRC)
Programmer with a boxing background about a Mexican girl (Armida) and her romance with a light-heavyweight champion (Terry Frost). Edgar Kennedy, Veda Ann Borg; directed by Wallace Fox. Songs included: *Last Night's All Over*; *The Girl From Monterey* Louis Herscher.

THE AMAZING MRS HOLLIDAY (Universal)
War-time story in which Deanna Durbin played the spirited survivor of a small mission in China and foster mother to nine waifs of uncertain origin. Edmond O'Brien, Barry Fitzgerald; directed by Bruce Manning. Songs included: *Vissi d'Arte* (from Tosca) Puccini; *The Old Refrain*.

GET GOING (Universal)
Grace McDonald arrives in Washington from New England, lands Robert Paige, and uncovers the headquarters of a spy ring. Barbara Jo Allen (Vera Vague); directed by Jean Yarbrough. Songs included: *Got Love*; *Hold That Line* Everett Carter, Milton Rosen.

SO'S YOUR UNCLE (Universal)
Programmer with Jan Garber and Jack Teagarden and their orchestras, The Delta Rhythm Boys, Mary O'Brien and the Tailor Maids, lending musical support to a far-fetched yarn in which playwright Donald Woods finds himself impersonating his uncle. Musical interludes take place in a nightclub sequence. Billie Burke, Elyse Knox; directed by Jean Yarbrough. Songs included: *That's The Way It Goes* Everett Carter, Milton Rosen; *Don't Get Around Much Anymore* Duke Ellington, Bob Russell.

CHATTERBOX (Republic)
Joe E. Brown played a radio cowboy, Judy Canova the woman he marries in the last reel. Directed by Joseph Santley. Songs included: *Mad About Him, Sad About Him, How Can I Be Glad Without Him Blues* Larry Marks, Dick Charles; *Sweet Lucy Brown* Leon and Otis Rene.

IT AINT HAY (GB: MONEY FOR JAM) (Universal)
Remake of Damon Runyon's *Princess O'Hara* (Universal, 1935) as an Abbott and Costello vehicle in which the two comedians, by mistake, find themselves owners of a prize racehorse called Tea Biscuit. The usual complications ensue. Grace McDonald, Cecil Kellaway, Eugene Pallette; directed by Erle C. Kenton. Songs included: *Sunbeam Serenade*, *Hang Your Troubles On A Rainbow* Harry Revel, Paul Francis Webster.

SARONG GIRL (Monogram)
Burlesque queen (Ann Corio), an orphan, has to dredge up a mother if she is to remain out of jail when police close her show. Mary Gordon, Mantan Moreland, Irene Ryan, Johnny 'Scat' Davis; directed by Arthur Dreifuss. Songs included: *Woogie Hula* Louis Herscher, Andy Iola Long; *Darling Nellie Gray* Benjamin, Russell Hanby.

LADY OF BURLESQUE (GB: STRIPTEASE LADY) (United Artists)
Backstage melodrama involving murder and suicide. Based on Gypsy Rose Lee's novel *The G-String Murders*. Barbara Stanwyck, Michael O'Shea; directed by William Wellman. Songs included: *Take It Off The E String*; *So This Is You* Sammy Cahn, Harry Akst.

LAUGH YOUR BLUES AWAY (Columbia)
Ex-rich dowager (Isobel Elsom) tries to marry off her son (Douglas Drake) to the daughter (Phyllis Kennedy) of a wealthy Texas cattleman (Dick Elliott). Jinx Falkenburg (top-starred) and Bert Gordon appeared as a pair of jobless actors attempting to emulate a Russian count and countess. Directed by Charles Barton. Songs included: *Prairie Parade* Larry Marks, Dick Charles.

HI DIDDLE DIDDLE (United Artists)
Martha Scott and sailor Dennis O'Keefe find their 48-hour honeymoon fraught with frustrating interruptions. Adolphe Menjou (top-billed), Pola Negri, Billie Burke, June Havoc; directed by Andrew L. Stone. Songs included: *Loved Too Little Too Late*; *Big Sombrero* Foster Carling, Phil Boutelje.

HOOSIER HOLIDAY (Republic)
The Hoosier Hotshots, a hillbilly novelty band, appearing as the Baker Boys, find themselves opposed by the head of the draft board (Thurston Hall) when they decide to quit their farm and enlist. George D. Hay, Dale Evans, George Byron, Emma Dunn, The Music Maids, George 'Shug' Fisher; directed by Frank McDonald. Songs included: *Hoosier Holiday*; *Grandaddy Of Boogie Woogie* Johnny Marvin, Charles Henderson.

NEARLY EIGHTEEN (Monogram)
Aspiring singer (Gale Storm) attempts to find a niche for herself in show business, discovering, in the process, that she is too young to seek employment as a café singer, and too old to become a student in a noted music academy. Rick Vallin, Bill Henry, Luis Alberni; directed by Arthur Dreifuss. Songs included: *Smiles For Sale*; *Walking On Air*.

OH MY DARLING CLEMENTINE (Republic)
A group of itinerant hillbilly entertainers, managed by Frank Albertson, wind up in a snobby town in Dixie, and attempt to put on a show. Roy Acuff, Harry 'Pappy' Cheshire, Lorna Gray, Irene Ryan; directed by Frank McDonald. Music provided by Acuff and other hillbilly stars.

TRUE TO LIFE (Paramount)
Story of a writer (Dick Powell) of a family radio serial who moves in with an all-American family for inspiration. Mary Martin, Franchot Tone, Victor Moore; directed by George Marshall. Songs included: *There She Was; The Old Music Master* Hoagy Carmichael, Johnny Mercer.

CINDERALLA SWINGS IT (RKO)
All about Guy Kibbee's attempts to interest a Broadway producer in a small-town classical singer (Gloria Warren). Directed by Christy Cabanne. Songs included: *I Heard You Cry Last Night* Ted Grouya, Jerrie Kruger; *The Flag's Still There* George Jessel, Ben Oakland.

1944

LOUISIANA HAYRIDE (Columbia)
Judy Canova, movie-struck hick, outsmarts con-men Richard Lane and George McKay, and achieves her ambition to make it in pictures. Ross Hunter; directed by Charles Barton. Songs included: *Rainbow Road; You Gotta Go Where The Train Goes* Kim Gannon, Walter Kent.

A WAVE, A WAC AND A MARINE (Monogram)
Story of a Hollywood agent (Henny Youngman) who mistakenly signs a pair of under-studies (Elyse Knox and Anne Gillis) believing them to be the real stars of a Broadway show. Sally Eilers; directed by Phil Karlstein. Songs included: *Time Will Tell; Gee, I Love My G.I. Guy* Eddie Cherkose, Jacques Press, Freddie Rich.

GIRL RUSH (RKO)
Wally Brown and Alan Carney, comics in a San Francisco show c.1840, join the gold rush and wind up in the womanless town of Red Creek where they promise to recruit girls both as entertainers and as wives for the miners. Frances Langford; directed by Gordon Douglas. Songs included: *Rainbow Valley; If Mother Could Only See Us Now* Harry Harris, Lew Pollack.

SING NEIGHBOUR SING (Republic)
Young lothario (Brad Taylor) poses as a distinguished, elderly English psychologist in a small college town – until the real psychologist appears. Ruth Terry, Virginia Brissac, Roy Acuff and His Smoky Mountain Boys, Lulubelle and Scotty; directed by Frank McDonald. Songs included: *Blake Song; Phrenology* Jack Elliott, R. Dale Bates.

SONG OF RUSSIA (MGM)
Famous American conductor (Robert Taylor) tours Russia during World War II and falls in love with a young Russian pianist (Susan Peters) whom he marries. Directed by Gregory Ratoff. Music included a thematic serenade by Jerome Kern and E.Y. Harburg called *And Russia Is Her Name.*

HI BEAUTIFUL (GB: PASS TO ROMANCE) (Universal)
Remake of *Love In A Bungalow* (Universal, 1937). Romance between a caretaker of a model home (Martha O'Driscoll) and the soldier (Noah Beery Jr) she meets after he is unable to find accommodation at a hotel. Couple win a marital contest for the 'Happiest GI' pair but are, in fact, unmarried. Hattie McDaniel; directed by Leslie Goodwins. Songs included: *Don't Sweetheart Me* Charles Tobias, Cliff Friend; *Best Of All* Allie Wrubel.

ROSIE THE RIVETER (GB: IN ROSIE'S ROOM) (Republic)
Programmer about four wartime factory workers forced to live in one room because of the housing shortage; the men and women have to take turns. Jane Frazee, Frank Albertson, Vera Vague; directed by Joseph Santley. Songs included: *Rosie The Riveter* Redd Evans, John Jacob Loeb; *Why Can't I Sing A Love Song?* Harry Akst, Sol Meyer.

THREE LITTLE SISTERS (Republic)
A young soldier corresponds with his 'dream girl' whom he has never seen. In her letters, the girl describes her luxurious life in a family mansion with her two sisters. In reality, the sisters wash clothes for local villagers, and the girl is an invalid in a wheelchair. Mary Lee, Ruth Terry, Cheryl Walker; directed by Joseph Santley. Songs included: *Don't Forget The Little Girl Back Home; Sweet Dreams Sweetheart* Kim Gannon, Walter Kent.

MY BEST GAL (Republic)
A father (Frank Craven) tries to interest his daughter (Jane Withers) in the family's show-biz traditions; she tries to interest a backer in a musical written by Jimmy Lydon. Directed by Anthony Mann. Songs included: *Upsy Downsy; Where There's Love* Kim Gannon, Walter Kent.

EVER SINCE VENUS (Columbia)
A young man (Ross Hunter) invents a new kind of lipstick, sets out to market it and, in the process, falls in love with his secretary (Ann Savage). Ina Ray Hutton, Hugh Herbert; directed by Arthur Dreifuss. Songs included: *Wedding Of The Samba And The Boogie* Bernie Wayne, Ben Raleigh; *Glamour For Sale* Lester Lee, Harry Harris.

FOOTLIGHT GLAMOUR (Columbia)
Blondie and Dagwood Bumstead find themselves involved in the theatrical aspirations of a tool manufacturer's daughter (Ann Savage). Penny Singleton, Arthur Lake; directed by Frank Strayer. Songs included: *Bamboola; What's Under Your Mask, Madame?* Ray Evans, Jay Livingston.

JIVE JUNCTION (PRC)
To forget his grief after the death of his aviator father overseas, young Dickie Moore switches from classical to popular music and entertains the servicemen stationed nearby. Tina Thayer, Gerra Young; directed by Edward G. Ulmer. Songs included: *We're Just In Between*; Bell song from Delibes' *Lakme.*

MEN ON HER MIND (PRC)
An ambitious singer (Mary Beth Hughes) refuses to let love and marriage interfere with her career. Edward Norris, Ted North; directed by Wallace Fox. Songs included: *Heaven On Earth* Lee Zahler, Pat O'Dea.

NATIONAL BARN DANCE (Paramount)
When turned down by radio executive Robert Benchley for an audition, Charles Quigley and the National Barn Dance troupe pose as servants in Benchley's home and stage an impromptu show with positive results. Jean Heather, Mabel Paige, The Hoosier Hotshots, Lulubelle and Scotty, The Dinning Sisters; directed by Hugh Bennett. Songs included: *When Pa Was Courtin' Ma; Angels Never Leave Heaven.*

IN SOCIETY (Universal)
Bud Abbott and Lou Costello invade high society's horsey set with predictably chaotic results. Marion Hutton; directed by Jean Yarbrough. Songs included: *My Dreams Are Getting Better All The Time* Mann Curtis, Vic Mizzy; *What A Change In The Weather* Kim Gannon, Walter Kent.

LOST IN A HAREM (MGM)
In sets left over from *Kismet* (MGM, 1944), Abbott and Costello, as a pair of stranded magicians, find themselves up against wicked ruler Douglass Dumbrille and buxom Marilyn Maxwell; Jimmy Dorsey and His Band. Directed by Charles Riesner. Songs included: *What Does It Take?; It Is Written* Don Raye, Gene De Paul.

1945

THE BELLS OF ST MARY'S (RKO)
Bing Crosby, as Father O'Malley, comes to rescue the financially embarrassed parochial school run by Sister Ingrid Bergman. Henry Travers; directed by Leo McCarey. Songs included: *The Bells Of St Mary's* Douglas Ferber, A. Emmett Adams; *Adeste Fidelis.*

SWINGIN' ON A RAINBOW (Republic)
Songwriter Jane Frazee arrives in New York to seek vengeance on a bandleader who has stolen one of her songs, and falls in love with lyric writer Brad Taylor. Harry Langdon; directed by William Beaudine.

ABBOTT AND COSTELLO IN HOLLYWOOD (MGM)
Abbott and Costello, as a porter and a barber at a Hollywood studio, decide to enter the talent agency business. Frances Rafferty; directed by S. Sylvan Simon. Songs included: *I Hope The Band Keeps You Playing; Fun On The Wonderful Midway* Ralph Blane, Hugh Martin.

I LOVE A BANDLEADER (Columbia)
A housepainter (Phil Harris) suffers an amnesia attack and thinks he's a bandleader. Eddie (Rochester) Anderson; directed by Del Lord. Songs included: *Eager Beaver* Sammy Cahn, Jule Styne.

FRISCO SAL (Universal)
New England girl (Susanna Foster) finds employment in a Barbary Coast saloon while searching for the murderer of her brother. Turhan Bey; directed by George Waggner. Songs included: *Beloved* George Waggner, Edward Ward; *Good Little Bad Little Lady* Jack Brooks.

IT'S A PLEASURE (RKO)
Romantic tribulations of an exhibition skater (Sonja Henie) and an ice-hockey star (Michael O'Shea). (Technicolor). Directed by William A. Seiter. Songs included: *Romance* Walter Donaldson.

MASQUERADE IN MEXICO (Paramount)
Dorothy Lamour, a nightclub entertainer, finds herself suspected of a jewel theft in Mexico City. Arturo de Cordova, Patric Knowles; directed by Mitchell Leisen. Songs included: *Forever Mine* Bob Russell, Eddie Lisbona, Maria T. Lara; *Masquerade In Mexico* Ben Raleigh, Bernie Wayne.

EVE KNEW HER APPLES (Columbia)
Radio star (Ann Miller) is mistaken for a murderess, in the process of which she falls in love with a reporter (William Wright). Robert Williams, Ray Walker; directed by Will Jason. Songs included: *An Hour Never Passes; I've Waited A Lifetime.*

BECAUSE OF HIM (Universal)
Deanna Durbin has to convince actor Charles Laughton that she is an accomplished actress, capable of being his leading lady. Franchot Tone; directed by Richard Wallace. Songs included: *Lover* Richard Rodgers, Lorenz Hart; *Danny Boy.*

TAHITI NIGHTS (Columbia)
American bandleader (Dave O'Brien) arrives on a Tahitian island to discover that arrangements are underway for him to marry a princess (Jinx Falkenburg) of one of the tribes. Mary Treen, Florence Bates, The Vagabonds; directed by Will Jason. Songs included: *Let Me Love You Tonight* Mitchell Parish, René Touzet.

THE BIG SHOW-OFF (Republic)
Nightclub pianist Arthur Lake tries to score with singer Dale Evans by pretending that he is the unknown masked wrestler. Lionel Stander, George Meeker, Anson Weeks and His Orchestra; directed by Howard Bretherton. Songs included: *Cleo From Rio; Hoops My Dear* Dave Oppenheim, Roy Ingraham.

CRIMSON CANARY (Universal)
Five jazz bandsmen are about to depart from a smalltown night spot for San Francisco when the female vocalist is mysteriously murdered. Whodunnit? Noah Beery Jr, Lois Collier, John Litel; directed by John Hoffman. Songs included: *The Walls Of Jericho; One Meat Ball (And No Spaghetti)* Hy Zaret, Lou Singer.

1946

QUEEN OF BURLESQUE (PRC)
Murder mystery set against burlesque background. Evelyn Ankers, Carelton Young; directed by Sam Newfield. Songs included: *How Can I Tell You?; Flower Song* Gene Lucas, Al Stewart.

SPECTER OF THE ROSE (Republic)
Pretentious tale of ballerina Viola Essen's love for a mad and murderous dancing genius (Ivan Kirov). The several ballet sequences were choreographed by Tamara Geva. Judith Anderson, Michael Chekhov; directed by Ben Hecht.

I'VE ALWAYS LOVED YOU (GB: CONCERTO) (Republic)
Professional rivalry between a male chauvinist orchestral conductor (Philip Dorn) and a young pianist (Catherine McLeod) whose career he ruins by conducting his orchestra too loudly, thus drowning her efforts at the piano during Rachmaninov's *Piano Concerto No 2*. Directed by Frank Borzage. Music by Chopin, Beethoven, Mendelssohn, Wagner and Bach. Song: *I've Always Loved You* Aaron Goldmark, Ludwig Flato.

BETTY CO-ED (GB: THE MELTING POT) (Columbia)
After interrupting her career as a carnival singer to enrol as a student at Upton College, Jean Porter finds nothing but snobbery and hostility from the president (Shirley Mills) of the campus sorority. Directed by Arthur Dreifuss. Songs included: *Put The Blame On Mame*; *You Gotta Do What You Gotta Do* Doris Fisher, Allan Roberts.

MURDER IN THE MUSIC HALL (Republic)
During a performance of an ice revue, a former director of an ice show is found murdered. Vera Hruba Ralston and the show's conductor (William Marshall) attempt to solve the crime before the police inspector (William Gargan) does. Directed by John English. Songs included: *My Wonderful One*; *Mess Me Up*.

BREAKFAST IN HOLLYWOOD (GB: THE MAD HATTER) (United Artists)
Screen version of Tom Breneman's popular radio show with three separate stories interwoven into the narrative line, and all taking place on the same day. Bonita Granville; directed by Harold Schuster. Songs included: *It Is Better To Be Yourself* Nat King Cole; *If I Had A Wishing Ring* Marla Shelton, Louis Alter.

IDEA GIRL (Universal)
Songplugger Julie Bishop arranges amateur song contest and other stunts which, while helping to put the song publishers for whom she works on the map, also gives them problems. Jess Barker, George Dolenz, Alan Mowbray; directed by Will Jason. Songs included: *I Don't Care If I Never Dream Again*; *I Can't Get You Out Of My Mind* Jack Brooks, Edgar Fairchild.

IN OLD SACRAMENTO (Republic)
Romance between a music hall belle (Constance Moore) with rigid ethical standards, and a gentleman gambler who doubles as a notorious stagecoach robber (William Elliott). Hank Daniels, Ruth Donnelly, Eugene Pallette, Lionel Stander; directed by Joseph Kane. Songs included: *Speak To Me Of Love* Bruce Siever, Jean Lenoir; *The Man Who Broke The Bank At Monte Carlo* Fred Gilbert.

DING DONG WILLIAMS (RKO)
Studio music director (Felix Bressart) hires a clarinettist (Glenn Vernon) to compose a score for him, only to discover that Vernon cannot read or write a note of music. Marcy McGuire, Anne Jeffreys, 11-year-old pianist Richard Korbel, Bob Nolan and The Sons of The Pioneers; directed by William Berke. Songs included: *I Saw You First*; *Candlelight And Wine* Harold Adamson, Jimmy McHugh.

1947

IT HAPPENED ON FIFTH AVENUE (Monogram-Allied Artists)
A gentlemanly vagabond (Victor Moore) establishes residence in a millionaire's mansion each winter during the latter's absence, and surrounds himself with homeless war veterans. Don DeFore, Gale Storm, Ann Harding, Charlie Ruggles; directed by Roy Del Ruth. Songs included: *Speak My Heart*; *That's What Christmas Means To Me* Harry Revel.

WHEN A GIRL'S BEAUTIFUL (Columbia)
Young promotion man (Marc Platt) in a model agency submits a composite photograph of all a model's best features, then has to find a girl to fit the picture. Adele Jergens; directed by Frank McDonald. Songs included: *I'm Sorry I Didn't Say I'm Sorry*; *When A Girl's Beautiful* Allan Roberts, Lester Lee.

THE SECRET LIFE OF WALTER MITTY (Goldwyn-RKO)
Zany reworking of Thurber's story of a mother's boy (Danny Kaye) who, after spending most of his time day-dreaming of wild adventures from which he always emerges the hero, finds himself actually involved in just such an adventure. Songs: *Symphony For Unstrung Tongue (The Little Fiddle)*; *Anatole Of Paris* Sylvia Fine.

1948

A FOREIGN AFFAIR (Paramount)
Sparkling comedy with songs in which Jean Arthur is sent to investigate conditions in post-war Berlin, falls in love with John Lund and encounters a rival in Marlene Dietrich. Directed by Billy Wilder. Songs included: *Black Market*; *Ruins of Berlin*; *Iowa Corn Song* Frederick Hollander.

THE PALEFACE (Paramount)
Western send-up in which a dentist (Bob Hope) thanks to the help of Calamity Jane (Jane Russell) becomes a hero. Directed by Norman Z. McLeod. Songs included: *Buttons And Bows*; *Meetcha Round The Corner* Ray Evans, Jay Livingston.

VARIETY TIME (RKO)
An entertaining compendium of dance routines, musical numbers, short comedies and silent film clips. Jack Paar, Freddie Carle and His Orchestra, Edgar Kennedy, Pat Rooney, Jesse and James, Leon Errol, Lynn, Royce and Vanya, and Hans Conried. Directed by Hal Yates. Songs and musical numbers included: *Carle Boogie* Frankie Carle; *The Daughter Of Rosie O'Grady* Monte Brice, Walter Donaldson; *Babalu* Bob Russell, Marguerita Lecuona.

1949

MY FRIEND IRMA (Paramount)
Complications resulting from dim-witted Marie Wilson's decision to desert her layabout boyfriend (John Lund) for a singing orange juice stall-keeper (Dean Martin). Martin and Jerry Lewis's debut. Diana Lynn, Don DeFore; directed by George Marshall. Songs included: *Here's To Love*; *Just For Fun* Ray Evans, Jay Livingston.

THE SUN COMES UP (MGM)
Sentimental tale of bitter war widow Jeanette Mac-Donald (her last film) who finds life worth living again after she mothers orphan Claude Jarman Jr. Lloyd Nolan, Percy Kilbride, Lewis Stone, Margaret Hamilton, Lassie; directed by Richard Thorpe. Songs included: *Un Bel Di* from Puccini's 'Madame Butterfly'; *Songs My Mother Taught Me* Dvorak; *Romance* Anton Rubinstein, Paul Bourget.

1950

DOUBLE CROSSBONES (Universal)
Set in the colonial settlement of Charlestown in the Carolinas, the story involved the adventures of Donald O'Connor, as an apprentice shopkeeper, who is erroneously arrested for trafficking with pirates. Helena Carter; directed by Charles T. Barton. Songs included: *Percy Had A Heart*; *Song Of Adventure* Lester Lee, Dan Shapiro.

EVERYBODY'S DANCIN' (Lippert)
A phoney promoter with a heart of gold (Spade Cooley) tries to revive public interest in a behind-the-times dance-hall. Richard Lane, Barbara Woodall, Ginny Jackson and 10 musical groups. Directed by Will Jason.

FANCY PANTS (Paramount)
Echoing *Ruggles Of Red Gap* (Paramount, 1935), the story had Bob Hope playing an American actor playing an English butler (in the Wild West) to wealthy, status-seeking Lucille Ball. Bruce Cabot; directed by George Marshall. Songs included: *Home Cookin'*; *Fancy Pants* Ray Evans, Jay Livingston.

MY FRIEND IRMA GOES WEST (Paramount)
Marie Wilson and friends, on a trip to Hollywood in the company of Dean Martin and Jerry Lewis, stop over in Las Vegas to seek employment as entertainers. John Lund, Corinne Calvet, Diana Lynn; directed by Hal Walker. Songs included: *Baby Obey Me*; *Fiddle And Guitar Band*; *Querida Mia* Ray Evans, Jay Livingston.

LOVE HAPPY (United Artists)
The last film the Marx Brothers made as a team starred Harpo as a food thief who has unwittingly stolen a sardine-tin containing some valuable diamonds and Groucho as a detective out to catch him. Chico Marx, Ilona Massey, Vera-Ellen, Raymond Burr, Marion Hutton, Bruce Gordon and, in a brief appearance, Marilyn Monroe. Directed by David Miller. Songs included: *Willow Weep For Me*; *Mama Wants To Know*; *Love Happy* Ann Ronell.

1951

TWO GALS AND A GUY (United Artists)
Programmer that set out to spoof TV, but ended up as a routine backstage yarn chronicling the desperate efforts to find someone to take the place of the star female lead in a TV show. Robert Alda, Janis Paige, James Gleason, and The Three Suns instrumental trio; directed by Alfred E. Green. Songs included: *Laugh And Be Happy*; *So Long For Now* Hal David, Marty Nevins.

DOUBLE DYNAMITE (RKO)
Frank Sinatra as a shy bank clerk suspected of stealing $75,000. Low spot in the career of all concerned. Jane Russell, Groucho Marx; directed by Irving Cummings. Songs included: *It's Only Money*; *Kisses And Tears* Sammy Cahn, Jule Styne.

THE LEMON DROP KID (Paramount)
Bob Hope as a bookie whose incompetence lands him in trouble with a gangster. Marilyn Maxwell; directed by Sidney Lanfield. Songs included: *It Doesn't Cost A Dime To Dream*; *They Obviously Want Me To Sing* Ray Evans, Jay Livingston.

STRICTLY DISHONORABLE (MGM)
Opera star Ezio Pinza marries Janet Leigh for the sake of her reputation, after which the young wife, with the help of her husband's mother (Esther Minciotti), successfully attempts to put the marriage on a more conventional footing. Directed by Melvin Frank and Norman Panama (from the play by Preston Sturges). Songs included: *Everything I Have Is Yours* Harold Adamson, Burton Lane; *I'll See You In My Dreams* Gus Kahn, Isham Jones.

AT WAR WITH THE ARMY (Paramount)
Dean Martin played a sexually confident sergeant in pursuit of the girls, with Jerry Lewis as an incompetent private who spends most of his time on KP duty. Mike Kellin, Jimmy Dundee, Dick Stabile, Angela Green, Polly Bergen; directed by Hal Walker. Songs included: *The Navy Gets The Gravy And The Army Gets The Beans*; *You And Your Beautiful Eyes*; *Tanda Wanda Hoy* Mack David, Jerry Livingston.

THE MILKMAN (Universal)
Mindless tale about a milk delivery man (Jimmy Durante) whose firm gets him a job accompanying the idiot son (Donald O'Connor) of the director of a rival concern on his milk round. Joyce Holden, William Conrad, Piper Laurie, Henry O'Neill; directed by Charles T. Barton. Songs included: *Girls Don't Want My Money* Durante, Jack Barnett; *It's Bigger Than Both Of Us*; *Early Morning Song* Sammy Fain, Barnett; *That's My Boy* Durante, Barnett.

GI JANE (Lippert)
Tom Neal is an impresario about to go into the army who has a dream about the life ahead of him in which he populates a remote desert post with a platoon of WACS. Jean Porter, Iris Adrian, Jimmy Dodd, Jean Mahoney, Jimmy Lloyd; directed by Reginald Le Borg.

FOOTLIGHT VARIETIES (RKO)
Musical revue compiled from old and new footage, compered by Jack Parr and featuring Liberace, The Sportsmen, Grace Romanos, Buster West and Frankie Carle and His Orchestra; directed by Hal Yates. Songs and musical numbers included: *La Paloma* Sebastian Yradier; *Goodnight Ladies E.P.* Christy; *Liberace Boogie.*

YES SIR, MR BONES (Lippert)
A small boy wanders into a home for old minstrels, wants to know all about them, and via a flashback to an old river showboat, is shown how a group of minstrels prepared for a performance. Cotton and Chick Watts, Scatman Crothers, F.F. Miller, Billy Green, The Hobnobbers; directed by Ron Ormond. Songs included: *I Want To Be A Minstrel Man; Stay Out Of The Kitchen; Is Your Rent Paid Up In Heaven?*

1952

THE WAC FROM WALLA WALLA (GB: ARMY CAPERS) (Republic)
Judy Canova gets into the WACS by mistake and becomes a heroine when she corners some heavies who are trying to steal data on guided missiles. Stephen Dunne; directed by William Witney. Songs included: *Lovey; If Only Dreams Came True* Jack Elliott.

HAS ANYBODY SEEN MY GAL? (Universal)
Delightful comedy with songs, set in the twenties, in which millionaire Charles Coburn becomes a lodger in the home of a family descended from an erstwhile sweetheart of his. Family are unaware of his wealth. Piper Laurie, Gigi Perreau, Rock Hudson; directed by Douglas Sirk. (Technicolor) Songs included: *Gimme A Little Kiss; Will Ya Huh?* Roy Turk, Jack Smith, Maceo Pinkard; *When The Red Red Robin Comes Bob-Bob-Bobbin' Along* Harry M. Woods.

SAILOR BEWARE (Paramount)
Dean Martin and Jerry Lewis enter the armed forces with hilarious results. Leif Erickson, Marion Marshall, Don Wilson, Skip Homeier, an unbilled appearance by Betty Hutton, and guest star Corinne Calvet; directed by Hal Walker. Songs included: *Sailor's Polka; Today, Tomorrow, Forever; Never Before* Jerry Livingston, Mack David.

GLORY ALLEY (MGM)
Feeble psychological drama with music, set in a New Orleans Bourbon Street bar with Leslie Caron miscast as the loyal girlfriend of war-time 'coward' Ralph Meeker. Louis Armstrong's appearance was its only redeeming feature. Kurt Kasznar, Gilbert Roland; directed by Raoul Walsh. Songs included: *St Louis Blues* W.C. Handy; *Glory Alley* Mack David, Jerry Livingston.

SOUND OFF (Columbia)
Mickey Rooney plays a nightclub entertainer who suddenly finds himself in the army. Anne James; directed by Richard Quine. (Super Cinecolor). Songs included: *My Lady Love* Lester Lee, Bob Russell; *Blow Your Own Horn* Rooney.

BELLES ON THEIR TOES (20th Century-Fox)
Sequel to *Cheaper By The Dozen* (20th Century-Fox) recounting the further adventures of the Gilbreth family, but without papa Clifton Webb. Myrna Loy, Jeanne Crain, Debra Paget, Jeffrey Hunter; directed by Henry Levin. (Technicolor). Songs included: *Whispering* John Schonberger, Richard Coburn, Vincent Rose; *When You Wore A Tulip* Jack Mahoney, Percy Wenrich.

1953

TAKE ME TO TOWN (Universal)
Ann Sheridan is a lady with a past, who while hiding out from the Federals in a Northwest lumber town, takes advantage of an offer from three young boys who think she would make a good mother while their timberman father (Sterling Hayden) is away from home. Directed by Douglas Sirk. (Technicolor) Songs included: *Oh, You Red-Head* Frederick Herbert, Milton Rosen; *Take Me To Town* Lester Lee, Dan Shapiro.

LET'S DO IT AGAIN (Columbia)
Remake of the studio's 1937 comedy *The Awful Truth* about a philandering composer (Ray Milland) whose wife (Jane Wyman) decides to teach him a lesson by embarking on an affair. Tom Helmore, Don Ameche, Leon Ames, Karin Booth, Mary Treen; directed by

Alexander Hall. Songs included: *Call Of The Wild; Give Me A Man Who Makes Music* Lester Lee, Ned Washington.

LATIN LOVERS (MGM)
Tropical romance involving a millionairess (Lana Turner) who can't decide whether to settle for a man (John Lund) even richer than she is, or a poor but charming Brazilian (Ricardo Montalban). Directed by Mervyn LeRoy. (Technicolor) Songs included: *I Had To Kiss You; A Little More Of Your Amor* Nicholas Brodszky, Leo Robin.

GERALDINE (Republic)
John Carroll plays a musical instructor studying folk music at a western college, and Stan Freberg a top recording star who hears one of Carroll's musical discoveries and wants to record it. Mala Powers, Jim Backus, Kristine Miller; directed by R.G. Springsteen. Songs included: *Geraldine* Sidney Clare, Victor Young; *Wintertime Of Love* Edward Heyman, Young.

1954

THE COUNTRY GIRL (Paramount)
About an alcoholic actor (Bing Crosby) who is given a chance for a comeback by a young director (William Holden), and the mistaken belief that the actor's wife (Grace Kelly) is the reason behind his alcoholism. Directed by George Seaton. Songs: *The Pitchman; Live And Learn; The Search Is Through* Ira Gershwin, Harold Arlen.

KNOCK ON WOOD (Dena Productions, released Paramount)
Danny Kaye played a vaudeville ventriloquist whose dummy has been stuffed with secret documents, all of them vitally important to a nest of spies. Leon Askin, Abner Biberman, Steve Geray, Mai Zetterling, Diana Adams, Torin Thatcher; directed by Norman Panama and Melvin Frank. Songs and musical numbers: *Knock On Wood; All About You* Monohan O'Han.

1955

HOW TO BE VERY VERY POPULAR (20th Century-Fox)
Remake of *She Loves Me Not* (Paramount, 1934) in which Betty Grable and Sheree North flee from a San Francisco nightclub after the murder of a Chinese striptease artist and fetch up in an ivy-covered men's college. Robert Cummings, Charles Coburn; directed by Nunnally Johnson. (CinemaScope. Color by De Luxe). Songs included: *Shake, Rattle And Roll; Bristol Bell* Ken Darby, Lionel Newman; *How To Be Very, Very Popular* Jule Styne, Sammy Cahn.

1956

I'LL CRY TOMORROW (MGM)
Uncompromising account of singer Lillian Roth's 16-year battle with booze. Susan Hayward excellent in the lead; so was Jo Van Fleet as her pushy mother. Richard Conte, Eddie Albert; directed by Daniel Mann. Songs included: *Sing You Sinners* Sam Coslow, W. Frank Harling; *Happiness Is Just A Thing Called Joe* E.Y. Harburg, Harold Arlen.

THAT CERTAIN FEELING (Paramount)
About a cartoonist (Bob Hope) whose lack of confidence results in his hiring himself out as a 'ghost' to a comic-strip artist. Eva Marie Saint, George Sanders, Pearl Bailey; directed by Norman Panama and Melvin Frank. Songs included: *That Certain Feeling* George and Ira Gershwin; *Zing Went The Strings Of My Heart* James Hanley.

HE LAUGHED LAST (Columbia)
Gangster spoof of the twenties (told in flashback) about what happens when a singer-dancer (Lucy Marlow) inherits the money and the enterprises of an underworld czar (Alan Reed). Frankie Laine, Anthony Dexter; directed by Blake Edwards. (Technicolor) Songs included: *Strike Me Pink; Save Your Sorrows* Arthur Morton.

MAGIC FIRE (Republic)
Biopic of composer Richard Wagner, filmed on location

in Germany, with Alan Badel as Wagner. Yvonne de Carlo, Peter Cushing, Frederick Valk, Valentina Cortese; directed by William Dieterle. Music included abbreviated extracts from Wagner's music dramas.

PARDNERS (Paramount)
Dean Martin and Jerry Lewis spoof the traditional Western in a remake of Bing Crosby's 1936 *Rhythm On The River* (Paramount). Martin played a ranch foreman, Lewis a pampered millionaire from New York who becomes sheriff. Jeff Morrow and John Baragrey were the heavies; Lori Nelson and Jackie Loughery the female interest; directed by Norman Taurog. Songs included: *Me 'n' You 'n' The Moon; Buckskin Beauty* Sammy Cahn, Jimmy Van Heusen.

1959

SOME LIKE IT HOT (United Artists)
After witnessing a Chicago gangland slaying similar to the St Valentine's Day Massacre, musicians Tony Curtis and Jack Lemmon disguise themselves as a couple of broads and, for safety, join an all-girl band in Florida. Marilyn Monroe, George Raft, Pat O'Brien, Joe E. Brown; directed by Billy Wilder. Songs included: *I Wanna Be Loved By You* Bert Kalmar, Harry Ruby; *Runnin' Wild* Joe Grey, Leo Wood, A. Harrington Gibbs.

1960

CINDERFELLA (Paramount)
The familiar fairy tale, but with a switch of sex of the central character. Jerry Lewis, Ed Wynn, Judith Anderson, Anna Maria Alberghetti; directed by Frank Tashlin. (Technicolor) Songs included: *Somebody; Let Me Be A People* Harry Warren, Jack Brooks.

THE SUBTERRANEANS (MGM)
Film of Jack Kerouac's celebrated 'beatnik' novel. George Peppard as Olympic gold medallist Leo Percepied, Leslie Caron as the mixed-up girl he falls in love with while searching for a meaning to life in San Francisco's Bay area. Janice Rule, Roddy McDowell, Anne Seymour, Jim Hulton; music by André Previn, performed by, among others, Art Farmer, Shelly Manne, Red Mitchell, Dave Bailey. An Arthur Freed production; directed by Ranald MacDougall.

1961

WHERE THE BOYS ARE (MGM)
Youth-orientated melodrama with songs, set during Easter vacation in Fort Lauderdale, Florida, and involving four college girls in search of love and romance. George Hamilton, Dolores Hart, Paula Prentiss, Jim Hutton, Yvette Mimieux, Connie Francis; directed by Henry Levin. (Metrocolor, CinemaScope) Songs included: *Where The Boys Are; Turn On The Sunshine* Neil Sedaka, Howard Greenfield.

101 DALMATIONS (Buena Vista)
Full-length Disney cartoon about an English couple, their brood of dogs, and a lady 'dognapper' whose hobby is making coats out of Dalmatians' skins. Songs included: *Cruella De Ville; Dalmation Plantation* Mel Leven.

THE LADIES' MAN (Paramount)
Jerry Lewis played a houseboy in a Hollywood boarding house for girls run by Helen Traubel. Directed by Jerry Lewis. Songs included: *Don't Go To Paris* Harry Warren, Jack Brooks.

ALL HANDS ON DECK (20th Century-Fox)
Naval comedy with songs. Pat Boone, Buddy Hackett (as a wealthy and eccentric American Indian), Dennis O'Keefe (as the ship's commander), Gale Gordon, Barbara Eden; directed by Norman Taurog. (Cinema-Scope and Color Deluxe). Songs included: *All Hands On Deck; I've Got It Made* Jay Livingston, Ray Evans.

1964

THE LIVELY SET (Universal)
James Darren has to choose between hot-rod racing or college. Remake of *Johnny Dark* (Universal, 1954). Pamela Tiffin; directed by Jack Arnold. (Eastmancolor) Songs included: *If You Love Him; Casey Wake Up.*

I'D RATHER BE RICH (Universal)
Remake of Universal's 1941 release *It Started With Eve*. Sandra Dee has to find a fiancé to satisfy the last wish of her ailing grandfather (Maurice Chevalier). Robert Goulet, Andy Williams; directed by Jack Smight. (Eastmancolor) Songs included: *Almost There*; *Where Are You?* Harold Adamson, Jimmy McHugh.

THE PLEASURE SEEKERS (20th Century-Fox)
Three girls seek romance in Spain. Retread of *Three Coins In The Fountain* (20th Century-Fox, 1954). Carol Lynley, Ann-Margret, Pamela Tiffin, Tony Franciosa; directed by Jean Negulesco. (CinemaScope and Color by De Luxe) Songs included: *The Pleasure Seekers*; *Something To Think About* Sammy Cahn, Jimmy Van Heusen.

1966
MADE IN PARIS (MGM)
Fashion designer's assistant (Ann-Margret) goes to Paris and falls for couturier Louis Jourdan. Directed by Boris Sagal. Songs included: *Paris Lullaby* Sammy Fain, Paul Francis Webster; *Skol Sister* Quincy Jones.

1968
LIVE A LITTLE, LOVE A LITTLE (MGM)
Photographer Elvis Presley, working for conservative publisher Rudy Vallee as well as for a girlie magazine, expends a lot of energy trying to ensure that each of his respective bosses doesn't find out about the other. Michele Carey; directed by Douglas Laurence. (Panavision and Metrocolor) Songs included: *A Little Less Conversation* Billy Strange, Scott Davis; *Almost In Love* Randy Starr, Luiz Bonfa.

FOR SINGLES ONLY (Columbia)
Adventures of a group of young men and women in an apartment block restricted to unmarried people under thirty years of age. John Saxon, Mary Ann Mobley, Milton Berle; directed by Arthur Dreifuss. (Pathe Color) Songs included: *Kee Ka Roo* Walter Wanderley, Bobby Worth; *Take A Chance With Me* Wanderley.

1969
THE TROUBLE WITH GIRLS (MGM)
Presley's 30th film found him as the manager of a combination entertainment educational travelling show. Marilyn Mason; directed by Peter Tewksbury. (Panavision, Metrocolor) Songs included: *Clean Up Your Own Back Yard* Scott Davis, Billy Strange.

1970
NORWOOD (Paramount)
Glen Campbell, a Vietnam veteran, sets out from Texas to New York to find fame as a TV singer. *En route* he encounters, among several other people, a pregnant Kim Darby with whom he falls in love. Cass Daley, Jack Haley Sr. Directed by Jack Haley Jr. (Technicolor) Songs included: *Ol' Norwood's Comin' Home* Marie Mitchell Torok, Ramona Reed.

1972
SNOOPY COME HOME (National General)
Schulz's Snoopy leaves home to find Lila, his original owner, who writes from a hospital that she needs him. Featuring the voices of Bill Melendez (Snoopy), Johanna Baer (Lila), Chad Webber, Robin Kohn, Stephen Shea, David Carey; directed by Bill Melendez. Songs by Richard M. And Robert B. Sherman.

1976
BOUND FOR GLORY (United Artists)
Superbly evocative biography of folk singer Woody Guthrie (David Carradine) featuring Guthrie's own compositions. Ronny Cox, Melinda Dillon; directed by Hal Ashby. (Color) Songs included: *So Long It's Been Good To Know Yuh*; *This Land Is Your Land*; *Talking Dust Bowl Blues*; *Pastures Of Plenty*.

SPARKLE (Warner Bros.)
Story of a rock'n'roll sister act who determine to escape their Harlem background. Irene Cara, Lonette McKee, Dwan Smith, Mary Alice, Beatrice Winde, Philip M. Thomas, Dorian Harewood, Paul Lambert; directed by Sam O'Steen.

THE FIRST NUDIE MUSICAL (Paramount)
Second generation Hollywood producer (Stephen Nathan), after making a few flop porno flicks, decides to make a porno musical *á là* the 1930's. Cindy Williams, Bruce Kimmel, Leslie Ackerman; directed by Kimmel, who also wrote the score. (De Luxe Color).

1977
THE TURNING POINT (20th Century-Fox)
Dance-orientated drama about the effect a visit of a famous ballerina (Anne Bancroft) has on erstwhile friend (Shirley MacLaine), who has opted for domesticity rather than a dancing career, and regrets it. Bancroft fears old age and regrets not having had a family. Tom Skerritt, and ballet dancers Mikhail Baryshnikov, Leslie Browne, Antoinette Sibley; directed by Herb Ross. (Color by DeLuxe).

1978
GOIN' COCONUTS (Osmond Distribution Co.)
Extension of Donny and Marie Osmond's TV show, with a plot which finds Marie in possession of a necklace the show's baddies want. Herbert Edelman, Kenneth Mars, Ted Cassidy; directed by Howard Morris. (Color DeLuxe).

SEXTETTE (Crown International Pictures)
In this very poor movie, privately financed by a pair of her millionaire fans, Mae West (aged 87) starred as a beautiful movie star whose wedding night is interrupted by a summit conference being held in the same hotel. Timothy Dalton, Dom De Luise, Tony Curtis, George Hamilton, Walter Pidgeon, Rona Barret, Ringo Starr. Directed by Ken Hughes.

MOVIE MOVIE (Warner Bros.)
Second half of this 'double feature', called BAXTER'S BEAUTIES OF 1933, spoofs the Busby Berkeley backstage musical of the early thirties (with particular reference to *42nd STREET* (Warner Bros. 1933). Rebecca York was the Ruby Keeler character, Barry Bostwick, Dick Powell, and George C. Scott. Warner Baxter. Trish Van Devere, Barbara Harris; Michael Kidd choreographed; directed by Stanley Donen.

1979
A PERFECT COUPLE (20th Century-Fox)
On-off relationship between a wealthy, family-dominated Greek antique dealer (Paul Dooley), and a pop singer (Marta Heflin). Directed by Robert Altman. Songs included: *Hurricane* Tom Berg, Ted Neely, Allan Nichols; *Fantasy* Allan Nichols.

1980
COAL MINER'S DAUGHTER (Universal)
How coal miner's daughter Loretta Lynn (Sissy Spacek) made it from Butcher Holler to Nashville, with help from her husband Doolittle (Tommy Lee Jones) and folk singer Patsy Cline (Beverly D'Angelo); directed by Michael Apted. Songs included: *I'm A Honky Tonk Girl*; *You Ain't Woman Enough To Take My Man* Loretta Lynn.

Miscellaneous Pop Musicals

1956
ROCK AROUND THE CLOCK (Columbia)
First rock 'n' roll film, featuring Bill Haley and His Comets, The Platters, Tony Martinez and His Band. Storyline involved efforts of a dance band manager (Johnny Johnston) to promote them all. Lisa Gaye, Alix Talton. Directed by Fred Sears.

ROCK ROCK ROCK (Vanguard)
Twenty numbers tied to plot involving college girl's (Tuesday Weld) efforts to find money for new dress for Spring prom. Teddy Randazzo, Jacqueline Kerr, Frankie Lymon, The Teenagers, Chuck Berry, disc jockey Alan Freed (and Connie Francis dubbing for Weld). Directed by Will Price.

1957
DON'T KNOCK THE ROCK (Columbia)
Group of rock exponents attempt to overcome small town's hostility to their music. Bill Haley and His Comets, Little Richard, Dave Appel and The Appeljacks, Alan Freed, The Treniers. Directed by Fred Sears.

CARNIVAL ROCK (Howco)
David J. Stewart, owner of a run-down nightclub, is madly in love with singer Susan Cabot, but she only has eyes for gambler Brian Hutton. Dick Miller, Iris Adrian, Jonathan Haze with musical support from The Platters, David Houston, Bob Luman, The Shadows, and The Blockbusters; directed by Roger Corman.

ROCK ALL NIGHT (American International)
Two murderers (Russell Johnson, Jonathan Haze) apprehended by guy (Dick Miller) only 5'1" tall, proving it takes more than height to make a man a man. Abby Dalton, The Platters. Directed by Roger Corman.

CALYPSO HEAT WAVE (Columbia)
Unscrupulous juke box czar (Michael Granger) buys his way into record company to disapproval of partners (Johnny Desmond, Merry Anders), George E. Stone, Darla Hood, Jeanette Dana, The Treniers, The Hi-Los, Mac Niles, The Calypsonians. Directed by Fred Sears.

UNTAMED YOUTH (Warner Bros.)
Two sisters (Mamie Van Doren, Lori Nelson) are sent to a prison farm whose inmates are all rock 'n' roll addicts. John Russell, Don Burnett. Directed by Howard W. Koch.

MR ROCK 'N' ROLL (Paramount)
Disc jockey Alan Freed sets out to convince sceptical editor that rock 'n' roll is beneficial to its young adherents. Carol Hendricks, Joe Prentiss, Al Fisher, Lionel Hampton and His Band, Frankie Lymon and The Teenagers, The Moonglows, Little Richard. Directed by Charles Dubin.

ROCK PRETTY BABY (Universal International)
High school music combo leader (John Saxon) has problems when parents refuse to lend him $300 for new guitar. Luana Patten, Edward C. Platt, Fay Wray, Rod McKuen. Directed by Richard Bartlett.

CALYPSO JOE (Allied Artists)
Romantic difficulties beset airline hostess (Angie Dickinson) and TV star (Edward Kemmer). Laurie Mitchell, Claudia Drake, Lord Flea and His Calypsonians, Duke of Iron, The Easy Riders, Herb Jeffries' Calypsomaniacs. Directed by Edward Dein.

SHAKE RATTLE AND ROCK (American International)
TV personality (Tom Connors) attempts to set up rock 'n' roll centre for underprivileged kids against opposition from reactionary reformers. Lisa Gaye, Sterling Holloway, Douglass Dumbrille, Margaret Dumont, Fats Domino. Directed by Edward L. Cahn.

BOP GIRL GOES CALYPSO (United Artists)
Rock singer (Judy Tyler) switches to Calypso at urging of psychologist (Bobby Troup). Maro Wood, Lucien Littlefield, The Mary Kaye Trio, The Goofers, The Cubanos, Nino Tempo, Lord Flea and His Calypsonians. Directed by Howard W. Koch.

JAMBOREE (GB: DISC JOCKEY JAMBOREE) (Warner Bros.)
Studio's first attempt to capture the youth market with story about a pair of singing sweethearts (Paul Carr, Freda Holloway) and their once married agents (Kay Medford, Robert Pastine). Fats Domino, Buddy Knox, Jodie Sands, Slim Whitman, Jerry Lee Lewis, Frankie Avalon, Count Basie and His Orchestra. Directed by Roy Lockwood.

1958

THE BIG BEAT (Universal)
Classical recording company is taken over by the boss's son (William Reynolds), a rock fanatic. Andra Martin, Gogi Grant, Jeffrey Stone, Hans Conried, Buddy Bregman, Fats Domino, The Four Aces, George Shearing, Harry James, The Mills Brothers. Directed by Will Cowan.

KEEP IT COOL, also known as **LET'S ROCK** (Columbia)
Popular ballad singer (Julius La Rosa) loses favour with his fans when he refuses to board the rock bandwagon. Phyliss Newman, Conrad Janis, Joy Harman, Paul Anka, Danny and The Juniors, Della Reese, Wink Martindale. Directed by Harry Foster.

SUMMER LOVE (Universal)
Tribulations of teenage love involving a young musician (John Saxon) whose affair with girlfriend Judy Meredith is threatened when he and his combo are given their first job away from home. John Wilder, Rod McKuen, Fay Wray, directed by Charles Haas.

SENIOR PROM (Columbia)
About a college girl (Jill Corey) and the two men in her life – snobby Tom Laughlin and pop singer Paul Hampton. Jimmy Komack, Barbara Bostock, Frieda Inescort, Ed Sullivan, Louis Prima, Keely Smith, Sam Butera and The Witnesses, Mitch Miller, Connie Boswell, Bob Crosby. Directed by David Lowell Rich.

1961

TEENAGE MILLIONAIRE (United Artists)
Teenage millionaire orphan (Jimmy Clanton) attempts to enter show biz against wishes of his aunt (ZaSu Pitts). Rocky Graziano, Diane Jergens, Chubby Checker, Bill Black's Combo, Dion. Directed by Lawrence F. Doheny.

HEY LET'S TWIST (Paramount)
The successful efforts of a couple of Italian brothers (Joey Dee, Teddy Randazzo) to turn their father's ice-cream parlour into a haven for twist addicts. Dino de Luca, The Starliters, Kay Armen, The Peppermint Loungers. Directed by Greg Garrison.

1962

TWIST AROUND THE CLOCK (Columbia)
Unemployed agent (John Cronin) 'discovers', and attempts to promote, The Twist. Mary Mitchell, Maura McGiveny, Chubby Checker, Dion, Vicki Spencer, The Marcels. Directed by Oscar Rudolph (remake of *Rock Around The Clock*).

TWIST ALL NIGHT (American International)
Louis Prima and partners Sam Butera and The Witnesses need money to pay rent on their nightspot after it is invaded by a group of non-spending teenagers. June Wilkinson, Ty Perry, Gertrude Michael. Directed by William J. Hole.

DON'T KNOCK THE TWIST (Columbia)
About a TV producer (Gene Chandler) and his romantic entanglements with a dress designer (Mari Blanchard). Chubby Checker, Vic Dana, Linda Scott, The Carroll Brothers, The Dovells. Directed by Oscar Rudolph.

TWO TICKETS TO PARIS (Columbia)
On-off romance aboard the liner *SS France* between Joey Dee and Jeri Lynne Fraser, with Dee specializing in dancing the Twist. Gary Crosby, Kay Medford, Lisa James, Charles Nelson Reilly, Sal Lombardo, Jeri Archer, Jay Burton, The Starliters. Directed by Greg Garrison.

1963

BEACH PARTY (American International)
Anthropologist Robert Cummings studies the sex habits of Malibu Beach *habitués*. Dorothy Malone, Frankie Avalon, Annette Funicello. Directed by William Asher.

THE YOUNG SWINGERS (Associated Producers Inc/20th Century-Fox)
Inane youth-orientated movie about a lady real estate agent (Jo Helton) and her attempts to replace a nightclub, owned by a group of youngsters, with an office block. Her niece (Molly Bee) opposes her. Rod Lauren, Ray Dennis, Dodie Warren, Rusty Wescoatt and The Sherwood Singers. Directed by Maury Dexter.

1964

SURF PARTY (20th Century-Fox)
A trio of Arizona girls arrive at the coast in search of the brother of one of them. Bobby Vinton, Patricia Morrow, Jerry Summers, Jackie De Shannon, The Astronauts, The Routers. Directed by Maury Dexter.

BIKINI BEACH (American International)
Publisher Keenan Wynn's attempts to evict surfers from beach where he wants to build community for senior citizens. Frankie Avalon (in dual role as a surfer and a bespectacled British pop singer), Annette Funicello, Harvey Lembeck, Don Rickles, Boris Karloff, Rene Riano, Little Stevie Wonder, The Exciters Band, The Pyramids. Directed by William Asher.

MUSCLE BEACH PARTY (American International)
Frankie Avalon heads group of surfers who clash head-on with group of muscle men led by Rock Stevens, when latter invade beach territory belonging to former. Luciana Paluzzi, Annette Funicello, Don Rickles, Jody McCrea, Peter Lorre, Little Stevie Wonder, The Del Tones. Directed by William Asher.

PAJAMA PARTY (American International)
A Martian (Tommy Kirk) is sent to earth to pave the way for forthcoming invasion, but falls in love with Annette Funicello instead. Elsa Lanchester, Harvey Lembeck, Jody McCrea, Jesse White, Buster Keaton, Dorothy Lamour, Rene Riano. Directed by Don Weiss.

1965

BEACH BLANKET BINGO (American International)
Pot-pourri of surfing, sky-diving and mermaids. Frankie Avalon, Annette Funicello, Deborah Walley, Harvey Lembeck, Buster Keaton, Don Rickles, Bobbi Shaw, Jody McCrea. Directed by William Asher.

A SWINGIN' SUMMER (United Screen Artists)
Three youngsters and local lifeguard help save a Californian dance pavilion threatened with closure. William Wellman Jr, Quinn O'Hara, James Stacy, Martin West, Raquel Welch, Mary Mitchell. Directed by Robert Sparr.

THE GIRLS ON THE BEACH (Lebin Brothers Production, distributed by Paramount)
Adventures of three co-eds whose sorority beach house is in danger of closure through lack of funds. Noreen Corcoran, Linda Marshall, Anna Capri, Martin West, Steve Rogers, Aron Kincaid, The Beach Boys, The Crickets. Directed by William Witney.

SKI PARTY (American International)
Set in snow-bound Sun Valley, and all about the rivalry between Frankie Avalon, Dwayne Hickman and Aron Kincaid for Yvonne Craig and Deborah Walley. To discover the secret of Kincaid's charms, Avalon and Hickman pretend to be women. The Hondells, James Brown and The Fame Flames, Lesley Gore. Directed by Alan Rafkin.

WILD ON THE BEACH (Lippert Inc. Production, distributed by 20th Century-Fox)
Battle for possession of a beach house between Lee Sullivan and Frankie Randall. Jackie and Gale, The Astronauts, Sonny and Cher. Directed by Maury Dexter.

WINTER-A-GO-GO (Columbia)
How the plan for the proposed renovation of a ski lodge on Lake Tahoe is impeded by 'heavy' Walter Maslow. William Wellman Jr, Beverly Adams, The Nooney Rickett Four, Joni Lyman and The Reflections. Directed by Richard Benedict.

HOW TO STUFF A WILD BIKINI (American International)
A mysterious redhead (Beverly Adams) appears from nowhere to fill a bikini which has been floating aimlessly in mid-air. Frankie Avalon, Annette Funicello, Mickey Rooney, Buster Keaton, Harvey Lembeck, Dwayne Hickman, Brian Donlevy. Directed by William Asher.

1966

WILD WILD WINTER (Universal)
College heart-throb (Gary Clarke) finds himself competing in championship ski contest. Chris Noel, Don Edmonds, Suzie Kaye, Jay and The Americans, The Beau Brummels, Dick and Dee Dee, The Astronauts. Directed by Lennie Weinrib.

NASHVILLE REBEL (American International)
A newly-wedded aspiring country singer (Waylon Jennings) saves his marriage and his career from a conniving talent agent. Gordon Oas-Heim, Mary Frann, Cece Whitney, Tex Ritter, Henny Youngman, Faron Young. Directed by Jay Sheriden.

OUT OF SIGHT (Universal)
Butler (Jonathan Daly) to a rock 'n' roll star sets out to prevent a man with a hatred of rock music (John Lawrence) from sabotaging forthcoming music fair. Karen Jensen, Carole Shelyn, Robert Pine, Gary Lewis and The Playboys, Freddie and The Dreamers. Directed by Lennie Weinrib.

FIREBALL 500 (American International)
Frankie Avalon as a cocky racing driver competes with Fabian for the attentions of Annette Funicello. Harvey Lembeck, Chill Wills, Julie Parrish. Directed by William Asher.

THE COOL ONES (Warner Bros.)
As a publicity stunt, impresario (Roddy McDowell) plays matchmaker to a rising pop singer (Debbie Watson) and a failing crooner (Gil Peterson). Phil Harris, Robert Coote, George Furth, The Bantams, Glen Campbell, The Leaves, T.J. and The Fourmations. Directed by Gene Nelson.

THE GHOST IN THE INVISIBLE BIKINI (American International)
A corpse (Boris Karloff) is visited in his coffin by his erstwhile sweetheart (Susan Hart) and told he will only get to heaven if he performs a good deed in the next 24 hours. Tommy Kirk, Basil Rathbone, Deborah Walley, Aron Kincaid, Nancy Sinatra, Francis X. Bushman, Patsy Kelly. Directed by Don Weis.

1967

THE CATALINA CAPER (Crown International)
Last of the 'beach party' series in which Tommy Kirk helps a group of frugging teenyboppers on Catalina to nab a couple of gangs of art thieves. Del Moore; directed by Lee Sholem. (Color).

1969

THAT TENNESSEE BEAT (20th Century-Fox)
A guitar-playing petty thief (Earl Richards) is rehabilitated and becomes a successful country musician on the Nashville theatre circuit. Sharon De Bord, Dolores Faith, Minnie Pearl, Merle Travis, Jim Reader. Directed by Richard Brill.

1971

ZACHARIAH (Cinerama)
Rock-western-cum-morality tale in which John Rubinstein and Don Johnson set off to become gunfighters, but, in the end, resume more productive, mature lives. Pat Quinn (as Belle Starr) Elvin Jones, Doug Kershaw and musical support from Country Joe and The Fish, The James Gang, The New York Rock Ensemble, and White Lightnin'; directed by George Englund.

1972

PAYDAY (Cinerama Releasing Corp.)
All about the last 36 hours in the life of a country and western singer (Rip Torn), Elayne Heilveil, Anna Capri, Michael C. Gwynne; directed by Daryl Duke. Songs by Shel Silverstein, Ian and Sylvia Tyson, Bobby Smith, Tommy McKinney.

Documentaries

1954

THE WORLD DANCES (Festival Pictures)
70-minute film recording folk music and folk dancing groups from over twenty nations. Directed by Brooke L. Peters.

1956

SATCHMO THE GREAT (United Artists)
Louis Armstrong and His Band on tour in Europe and Equatorial Africa, with stopover dates in Stockholm, Paris, London and the Gold Coast. Climax at Lewisohn Stadium, New York, where band joined the Philharmonic Orchestra in a performance of W.C. Handy's 'St Louis Blues'. This footage originally shot for Ed Murrow's TV show, 'See It Now'.

ROCKIN' THE BLUES (Austin Productions)
A poorly produced melée of all-black acts (e.g. Flournoy Miller and Mantan Moreland, The Harptones, The Hurricanes, The Miller Sisters, Linda Hayes etc.) to exploit the then up-and-coming rock craze. Directed by Arthur Rosenblum.

1959

JAZZ ON A SUMMER'S DAY (Hillcrest)
A superbly photographed account of the July 1956 Newport, Rhode Island, Jazz Festival, capturing on celluloid artists of the calibre of Thelonius Monk, Anita O'Day, Dinah Washington, Gerry Mulligan, Chico Hamilton, Louis Armstrong, Jack Teagarden, Mahalia Jackson, Chuck Berry, George Shearing etc. Directed by Bert Stern.

1960

SING A SONG FOR HEAVEN'S SAKE (Marathon Pictures)
A musical revue by some fifty artists, performing some thirty songs, at a Gospel meeting in Nashville, Tennessee. Directed by Ulf Van Court.

1964

THE T.A.M.I. SHOW (American International Pictures)
A musical revue featuring such artists as The Beach Boys, Marvin Gaye, Lesley Gore, The Rolling Stones, Gerry and The Pacemakers, Billy J. Kramer and The Dakotas, The Supremes, at the Teenage Awards Music International. Staged at the Santa Monica Civic Auditorium in October, 1964. Directed by Steve Binder.

1966

THE BIG T.N.T. SHOW (American International)
Top artists performing their hit recordings at the Hollywood Moulin Rouge. The compere was David McCallum, the performers included Roger Miller, Joan Baez, Ray Charles, Donovan, Petula Clark, The Byrds, The Lovin' Spoonful, Ike and Tina Turner, The Ronettes, Bo Diddley etc. Directed by Larry Peerce.

MUSIC CITY USA (Gemini Pictures)
Disc Jockey T. Tommy and a group of his friends taking a look at music in Nashville, including the Record World Awards, and visiting a country and western nightclub where they hear, among many others, Webb Pierce, The Wilburn Brothers, Loretta Lynn, Dave Dudley, Jean Shepard, Warner Mack, Charlie Louvin and His Band, The Osborne Brothers, Lorene Mann, Hillous Butrum, Vincent Youmans Jr. Produced and directed by Preston Collins and James Dinet.

1967

SPREE (Producers Equity Corporation)
A poorly photographed and clumsily edited journalistic look at the Las Vegas casinos and some of their better known cabaret performers such as Vic Damone, Jayne Mansfield, Juliet Prowse, Mickey Hargitay, Constance Moore. Directed by Mitchell Leisen and Walon Green.

COUNTRY WESTERN HOEDOWN (Jam Art Pictures)
A musical revue consisting of country and western acts – e.g. Pee Wee King, Redd Stewart, Little Eller Long, Red Murphy, Neal Burris, Bonnie Sloan, Shorty Hayes etc – performing on barn dance stages throughout America, including at the Grand Ole Opry, Nashville. Directed by William R. Johnson.

FESTIVAL (Peppercorn-Wormser Inc.)
Footage (in black and white) of the Newport Folk Festivals of 1963-6, including interviews with performers and fans explaining the appeal of folk music. The plethora of artists on show included Joan Baez, Theodore Bikel, Mike Bloomfield, The Blue Ridge Mountain Dancers, Paul Butterfield Blues Band, Johnny Cash, Judy Collins, Cousin Emmy, Donovan, Bob Dylan, Mimi Farina, The Freedom Singers. Directed by Murray Lerner.

1968

YOU ARE WHAT YOU EAT (Commonwealth United)
A *pot-pourri* of scenes depicting America's contemporary youth revolution, with the major portion devoted to rock and folk performers such as Tiny Tim, Peter Yarrow, Barry McGuire, Super Spade, Harper's Bizarre, The Electric Flag, Carol Wayne, John Simon, The Family Dog, David Crosby etc. etc. Directed by Barry Feinstein.

1969

MONTEREY POP (Leacock Pennebaker Inc.)
A record of the 1967 Monterey International Pop Festival, emceed by Brian Jones of The Rolling Stones. A combination of heavy rock and the voguish serenity of 'flower children' which featured, among many others, Janis Joplin, The Mamas and The Papas, Canned Heat, Hugh Masekela, Jefferson Airplane, Grace Slick, Eric Burdon and The Animals, The Who, Country Joe and The Fish, Otis Redding, Simon and Garfunkel, Ravi Shankar, Jimi Hendrix. Directed by D.A. Pennebaker.

JOHNNY CASH! THE MAN, HIS WORLD, HIS MUSIC (Verite Productions)
Top country and western star Johnny Cash on a concert tour with his wife and other artists. Interviews and recording sessions with Carl Perkins and Bob Dylan featured. Directed by Robert Elfstrom.

1970

THE NASHVILLE SOUND (The Nashville Company/Aurora Publishers/Amram Nowak Associates)
Nearly 40 top country and western artists performing in Nashville, together with footage of interviews, the Country Music Association Disc Jockey Convention, and a young singer, Herbie Howell, embarking on his career. Some of those appearing included Archie Campbell, Johnny Cash, Skeeter Davis, Lester Flatt, Bubba Fowler, Loretta Lynn, Bill Monroe, Tracy Nelson and Mother Earth, Dolly Parton, Charley Pride, Del Reeves, Jeannie C. Riley, Tex Ritter, Earl Scruggs. Directed by Robert Elfstrom and David Hoffman.

ELVIS – THAT'S THE WAY IT IS (MGM)
Interviews, studio rehearsals, concert preparation and show numbers from live performances (mostly in Las Vegas) make up this creatively edited account of superstar Elvis Presley, and also features other artists such as Charley Hodge, Glen Hardin, Millie Kirkham, The Sweet Inspirations, The International Hotel Orchestra. Directed by Denis Sanders.

WOODSTOCK (Warner Bros.)
Superbly photographed and inventively edited account of the now legendary rock festival held near Bethel, N.Y., in 1969 and attended by 500,000 people. Raw footage includes interviews and candid coverage with and of the audience, local farmers, the army, the police. Drug sub-culture and anti-Vietnam sentiments well-caught, and perfectly blended with outstanding musical performances. Stunning montage of colours and images, and notable use of creative split-screen, multi-panel and variable-frame techniques. A milestone in rockumentary film making, the artists appearing included Richie Havens, Joan Baez, Crosby, Stills, Nash and Young, The Who, John Sebastien, Joe Cocker, Sha-Na-Na, Country Joe and The Fish, Arlo Guthrie, Santana, Sly and The Family Stone, Jimi Hendrix etc. Directed by Michael Wadleigh.

GIMME SHELTER (Maysles Films)
Candid footage of the 1969 Rolling Stones American tour, which ended with the fatal stabbing of a black youth by a 'Hell's Angel' at Altmont. Among artists appearing with The Stones were The Jefferson Airplane and Grace Slick, The Flying Burrito Brothers, Ike and Tina Turner. Directed by David and Albert Maysles and Charlotte Zwerin.

GROUPIES (Maron Films)
A revealing but confused exposé, highlighting the drug-taking habits and sexual codes of the teenage girls (and boys) who camp-follow rock musicians – in this case Joe Cocker, Alvin Lee, Dry Creek Road, Terry Reid, Keith Webb, Peter Shelly, Spooky Tooth, Luther Grosvenor, Ten Years After – throughout America. Directed by Robert Dorfman and Peter Nevard.

IT'S YOUR THING (Paramount)
Straight, poorly photographed account of a marathon festival of commercial soul music, held at New York's Yankee Stadium in 1969. Among the performers appearing were Patty Austin, The Edwin Hawkins Singers, Jackie 'Moms' Mabley, Ike and Tina Turner, Brooklyn Bridge etc. Directed by Mike Garguilo.

JOAN – CARRY IT ON (Maron Films)
Folk singer Joan Baez and her non-violent activist husband, David Harris, featured in candid interviews (shot in black and white), preceding his three-year jail sentence for non-cooperation with the Draft Board; Baez, meanwhile, although pregnant, goes on a summer concert tour. Produced and directed by James Coyne, Robert C. Jones and Christopher Knight.

MAD DOGS AND ENGLISHMEN (MGM)
A nationwide American concert tour in 1970 by Joe Cocker and an entourage of 42 musicians, singers, their wives, girlfriends and children. Produced and directed by Pierre Adidge.

1971

PETE SEEGER . . . A SONG AND A STONE (Theatre Exchange Activities)
A concert at Brandeis University, by the legendary folk singer Pete Seeger, intercut with sequences from TV shows and peace rallies, with Seeger explaining his views on politics, pollution and militarism. Other artists included Johnny Cash, Mike Seeger, Don McClean etc. Directed by Robert Elfstrom.

MEDICINE BALL CARAVAN (Warner Bros.)
A well-photographed chronicle of a cross-country bus junket by 150 youths, including artists B.B. King, Doug Kershaw, Alice Cooper, The Youngbloods, Delaney and Bonnie, Sal Valentino, Stoneground – who, to advertise alternative life-styles, staged small rock concerts along the way. Directed by Francois Reichenbach.

SOUL TO SOUL (Cinema Releasing Corporation)
Santana, Willie Bobo, Roberta Flack, Les McCann, Eddie Harris, The Staple Singers, Voices of East Harlem, Damas Choir, Amoa Azangio, Kumasi Drummers, Wilson Pickett, Ike and Tina Turner performing in rock, jazz and gospel concert held in Ghana in honour of the country's 14th anniversary. Directed by Denis Sanders.

SWEET TORONTO (Pennebaker Productions)
Cinema Verité filmization of selected performances from the 12-hour Toronto Rock 'n' Roll Festival held in September, 1969, where the performers included Bo Diddley, Jerry Lee Lewis, Chuck Berry, Little Richard, The Plastic Ono Band with John Lennon and Yoko Ono etc. Directed by D.A. Pennebaker.

CELEBRATION AT BIG SUR (20th Century-Fox)
Mediocre, and badly photographed, coverage of the 1969 Big Sur Folk Festival, where performers included Joan Baez, David Crosby, Mimi Farina, Joni Mitchell, Greg Reeves, Dallas Taylor, The Struggle Resistance Band etc. No director credited.

1972

THE CONCERT FOR BANGLADESH (20th Century-Fox)
A modest and well-photographed record of George Harrison's Madison Square Garden benefit concert for the Bangladesh refugees, where artists giving their services included Eric Clapton, Bob Dylan, Billy Preston, Leon Russell, Ravi Shankar, Ringo Starr, Badfinger, Jesse Davis, Claudia Linnear. Directed by Saul Swimmer.

FILLMORE (20th Century-Fox)
A nostalgic look at the Fillmore rock concerts from 1965 to 1972, and the final office closure of impresario Bill Graham who created them and spawned the now defunct 'San Francisco' sound. Among the featured artists were Santana, The Grateful Dead, Cold Blood, Hot Tuna, The Rowan Brothers, Quicksilver Messenger Service, The New Riders of the Purple Sage, It's A Beautiful Day. Directed by Richard T. Heffron.

1973

SAVE THE CHILDREN (Paramount)
122-minute record of a black rock show in the summer of 1972 at the Black Exposition in Chicago, sponsored by Operation PUSH. Much of the music interpolated into montages of contemporary black progress and urban living. Among the performers captured on film were The Temptations, The Main Ingredient, Isaac Hayes, Zulema, The Cannonball Adderly Quintet, Sammy Davis Jr, Roberta Flack, Quincy Jones and Nancy Wilson. Directed by Stan Lathan.

JIMI HENDRIX (Warner Bros.)
A homage to Jimi Hendrix who died from an overdose of drugs at the age of 27. Over twenty interviews, as well as footage from live performances at the Woodstock and Monterey Festivals etc., and participation by – among others – Pete Townshend, Eric Clapton, Paul Carusa, Dick Cavett, Al Hendrix, Little Richard, Edie Kramer, Mick Jagger, Jennifer Dean, Alan Douglas and Germaine Greer. Directed by Joe Boyd, John Head and Gary Weis.

LET THE GOOD TIMES ROLL (Columbia/Warner)
A compilation rock 'n' roll concert culled from several 1972 stage shows, as well as newsreel, feature film and television footage from the '50's. Artists included Chuck Berry, Fats Domino, Little Richard, Chubby Checker, Bo Diddley, The Shirelles, The Five Satins, Bill Haley and The Comets, Richard Nader. Directed by Sid Lewin and Robert Abel.

WATTSTAX (Columbia)
A benefit concert in aid of the coloured Californian community of Watts at the Los Angeles Memorial Coliseum. Sociological comment and interviews interpolated with music by black artists of the Stax record label such as Richard Pryor, Isaac Hayes, The Staple Singers, Luther Ingram, Johnny Taylor, The Emotions, Rufus Thomas, Reverend Jesse Jackson, Louise McCord, Debra Manning, Eric Mercury, Ernie Hines, Little Sonny etc. Directed by Mel Stuart.

ELVIS ON TOUR (MGM)
Elvis Presley's 1972 stage act, spliced with interviews, rehearsals, backstage banter and TV footage of the legendary star and his supporting artists. Produced and directed by Pierre Adidge and Robert Abel.

1974

LADIES AND GENTLEMEN, THE ROLLING STONES (Dragon Aire)
A 20-minute segment of film showing an audience filing into an auditorium precedes 15 deafening numbers, plus off-stage footage, culled from the Stones's 1972 American tour. Directed by Rollin' Binzer.

SING SING THANKSGIVING (Varied Directions)
A provocative filmed account of a rock concert held for the inmates of Sing Sing prison in November, 1972. As well as Joan Baez, Mimi Farina, B.B. King, Jimmy Walker, Joe Williams, The Voices of East Harlem, Tito Butler etc., several acts were performed by the prisoners themselves. Directed by David Hoffman and Harry Wiland.

1975

JANIS (Universal)
A slipshod assembly of footage from rock concerts in Woodstock, Monterey, Calgary and London, spliced with interviews, make up this homage to Janis Joplin who died of an overdose of drugs and alcohol in 1970. Directed by Howard Alk and Seaton Findlay.

1976

SALSA (Fania Records Inc.)
An account with additional footage, of a Latin American pop concert at the Yankee Stadium, New York, and part of another concert in San Juan, Puerto Rico. As well as a host of Latin American artists, including Celia Cruz and Jose Feliciano, film clips of Desi Arnaz, Al Jolson and Carmen Miranda were used. Directed by Jerry Masucci and Leon Gast.

VOLUNTEER JAM (Roger Grods Productions)
The Volunteer Jam concert held in October, 1975, at Middle Tennessee University. Backstage footage and a slow motion sequence of Charlie Daniels on horseback. Directed by Stanley Dorfman.

1977

THE GRATEFUL DEAD (Monarch/Noteworthy)
Concert footage and animated sequences, plus nostalgic examination of the West Coat music scene. Technically proficient rockumentary, featuring the veteran rock combo of the title. Jefferson Airplane, Janis Joplin, Quicksilver Messenger Service and Bill Graham also appeared.

1978

THE LAST WALTZ (United Artists)
An outstanding record of the farewell concert given by The Band on Thanksgiving Day, 1976, at Winterland, San Fransisco, after performing together, and as Bob Dylan's backing group, for 16 years. Among the personalities appearing were Rick Danko, Joni Mitchell, Neil Diamond, Emmylou Harris, Muddy Watters, Ringo Starr, Lawrence Ferlinghetti, Martin Scorsese etc. Directed by Martin Scorsese.

1979

THE LAST OF THE BLUE DEVILS (Cinegate)
Story of the music that emerged from Kansas City in the twenties and thirties when the Mid-Western watering-hole became the centre of an intense concentration of nightlife. Artists appearing included: Count Basie and his Orchestra, Bennie Motten and his Orchestra, Joe Turner, Jay McShann, Charlie Parker, The Oklahoma Blue Devils. Directed by Bruce Ricker.

1980

DIVINE MADNESS (Warner Bros.)
Filmed account of Bette Midler's dynamic stage show at the Pasadena Civic Auditorium, also featuring 'The Harlettes' – Jocelyn Brown, Ula Hedwig and Diva Gray; directed by Michael Ritchie. Songs included: *Shiver Me Timbers* Tom Waits; *I Shall Be Released* Bob Dylan; *Stay With Me* Jerry Ragovoy, George Weis.

Film Titles

Song and Music Titles

Performers

PERFORMERS

Composers and Lyricists

Other Creative Personnel

New Films, 1980 Onwards

Film Titles

Annie **420**
Apocalypse Now 419
At Long Last Love 419
Follow The Fleet 418
Grease 421
Grease 2 421
Great Muppet Caper, The **418**
Muppet Movie, The 418
One From The Heart **419**
Pennies From Heaven **418**
Popeye **416**
Singin' In The Rain 419
Victor/Victoria **420**
Viktor Und Viktoria **420**
Wiz, The **420**
Wizard Of Oz, The 419
Yes, Giorgio **419**

Song and Music Titles

Alone In Paris 420
Apartment, The 418
Ave Maria 419
Back To School Again 421
Big Bus, The 418
Blow Me Down 416
Broken Bicycles 419
Cat And Mouse 420
Charaders 421
Chicago, Illinois 420
Circus Girl 419
Clouds Will Soon Roll By, The 418
Cool Rider 421
Couldn't We Ride 418
Crazy World 420
Did You Ever See A Dream Walking? 418
Do It For Our Country 421
Easy Street 420
Everything Is Food 416
Fancy Our Meeting 418
First Time It Happens, The 418
Funiculi Funicula 419
Gay Paree 420
Girl For All Seasons 421
Glory Of Love, The 418
Great Muppet Caper, The 418
Happiness Hotel 418
He Needs Me 416
He's Large 416
Hey, A Movie 418

Homeward Bound 418
I Beg Your Pardon 419
I Don't Need Anything But You 420
I Left My Heart In San Francisco 419
I Think I'm Gonna Like It Here 420
I Want To Be Bad 418
I Yam What I Yam 416
If I Were In Love 419
I'll Never Have To Dream Again 418
I'm Mean 416
I'm Popeye The Sailor Man 416
Is There Any Way Out Of This Dream? 419
It's A Hard-Knock Life 420
It's A Sin To Tell A Lie 418
It's Not Easy Being Me 416
It's The Girl 418
Kids 416
King's Can-Can 420
Lady Holiday 418
Le Jazz Hot 420
Let's Face The Music And Dance 418
Let's Misbehave 418
Let's Put Out The Lights And Go To Sleep 418
Life Is Just A Bowl Of Cherries 418
Little Boy Blue 419
Little Girls 420
Love Is Good For Anything That Ails You 418
Mattinata 419
Maybe 420
My Honey Says Yes 418
Night Life 418
O Sole Mio 419
Old Boyfriends 419
Once Upon A Town 419
Our Day Will Come 421
Pennies From Heaven 418
Picking Up After You 419
Piggy's Fantasy 418
Presents 419
Prowlin' 421
Rebel Walk 421
Reproduction 421
Rock-A-Hula-Luau (Summer Is Coming) 421
Roll Along Prairie Moon 418
Sailin' 416

Santa Lucia 419
Score Tonight 421
Serenade In The Night 418
Shady Dame From Seville, The 420
Steppin' Out With A Star 418
Swee' Pea's Lullaby 416
Sweethaven 416
Take Me Home 419
Tango, The 419
This One's From The Heart 419
Tomorrow 420
(Love Will) Turn Back The Hands Of Time 421
Wages Of Love, The 419
We'll Be Together 421
Who's That Guy? 421
You And Me 420
You Can't Unring A Bell 419
You're Never Fully Dressed Without A Smile 420

Composers and Lyricists

Baer, Abel 418
Bergman, Alan 419
Bergman, Marilyn 419
Berlin, Irving 418
Bixio, Cesare A 418
Bricusse, Leslie 420
Brown, George 418
Brown, Lew 418
Bugatti, Dominic 421
Burke, Johnny 418
Cerf, Christopher 421
Charig, Phil 418
Charnin, Martin 420
Cherubini, B 418
Conrad, Con 418
Cory, George 419
Cross, Douglass 419
De Sylva, Buddy 418
Denza, Luigi 419
Di Capua, Eduardo 419
Douizetti, Gaetano 419
Eddy, Duane 421
Fiorito, Ted 418
Friend, Cliff 418
Furber, Douglas 418
Gale, Crystal 419
Garson, Mort 421
Gibson, Michael 421

Gordon, Mack 418
Greenfield, Howard 421
Hamlisch, Marvin 418
Hazlewood, Lee 421
Hegel, Rob 421
Henderson, Ray 418
Hill, Billy 418
Hilliard, Bob 421
Hupfeld, Herman 418
Johnston, Albert 418
Jones, Isham 418
Kennedy, Jimmy 418
Leoncavallo, Ruggiero 419
Lerner, Sam 416
Linde, Dennis 421
Macpherson, Harry 418
MacRae, Johnny 421
Malneck, Matt 418
Mancini, Henry 420
Mayhew, Billy 418
Meyer, Joseph 418
Morrison, Bob 421
Musker, Frank 421
Newman, Charles 418
Nilsson, Harry 416
Oppenheim, Dave 418
Ponchielli, Amilcare 419
Porter, Cole 418
Puccini, Giacomo 419
Raposo, Joe 418
Revel, Harry 418
Schubert, Franz 419
St Louis, Louis 421
Strouse, Charles 420
Verdi, Guiseppe 419
Von Tilzer, Albert 418
Waits, Tom 419
Williams, John 419
Woods, Harry 418

Performers

Albert, Eddie 419
Andrews, Julie 420
Arden, Eve 421
Arne, Peter 420
Bagneris, Vernel 418
Borboni, Paola 419
Burnett, Carol 420
Caesar, Sid 421
Caulfield, Maxwell *421*
Cleese, John 418
Curry, Tim 420
Dixon, MacIntyre 416
Dooley, Paul 416
Duvall, Shelley 416
Falk, Peter 418
Finney, Albert *420*
Fitch, Robert 418

Forrest, Frederic 419
Frechette, Peter 421
Fullen, Kathryn 419
Gale, Crystal 419
Garner, James 420
Garner, Jay 418
Garr, Teri 419
Green, Leif 421
Grodin, Charles 418
Harper, Jessica 418
Harrold, Kathryn *419*
Hoffman, Dustin 416
Holder, Geoffrey 420
Hong, James 419
Hunter, Tab 421
Julia, Raul 419
Karlen, John 418
Karras, Alex 420
Kazan, Lainie 419
Kinski, Nastassia *419*
Lanza, Mario 419
Libertini, Richard 416
Luft, Lorna *421*
McDonald, Christopher 421
McMartin, John 418
Martin, Steve *418*
Maxwell, Roberta 416
Moffatt, Donald 416
Morley, Robert 418
Newton-John, Olivia 421
Patterson, Dody 421
Pavarotti, Luciano *419*
Peters, Bernadette 418, 420
Pfeiffer, Michelle *421*
Preston, Robert, *420*
Quinn, Aileen *420*
Quo, Beulah 420
Rall, Tommy 418
Rhys-Davis, John 420
Rigg, Diana 418
Scott, Donovan 416
Stanton, Harry Dean 419
Stark, Graham 420
Steinberg, Norman 419
Tanney, Sherloque 420
Tomlin, Lily 416
Travolta, John 421
Ustinov, Peter 418
Waits, Tom 419
Walken, Christopher 418
Walston, Ray *416*
Warden, Jack 418
Warren, Lesley Ann 420
Williams, Esther 418
Williams, Robin *416*
Zmed, Adrian 421

Other Creative Personnel

Adams, Tony 420
Altman, Robert 416
Ashby, Hal 416
Berkeley, Busby 418
Bernstein, Armyan 418
Birch, Patricia 421
Bogdanovich, Peter 418
Burgess, Hovey 416
Carr, Allan 421
Coppola, Francis 418
Daniels, Danny 418
Edwards, Blake 420
Evans, Robert 416
Feiffer, Jules 416
Fetterman, Peter 419
Finkleman, Ken 421
Frederickson, Gray 418
Gersten, Bernard 418
Henson, Jim 418
Hoemburg, Hans 420
Huston, John 420
Juhl, Jerry 418
Kaye, Nora 418
Kelly, Gene 418
Kinney, Sahron 416
Layton, Joe 420
Lazer, David 418
Lubitsch, Ernst 420
Lumet, Sidney 420
Mann, Anita 418
Maus, Rodger 420
May, Billy 418
Nichols, Mike 416
Oz, Frank 418
Pasternak, Joe 419
Patchett, Tom 418
Penn, Arthur 416
Phillips, Arlene 420
Piper, Ann 419
Potter, Dennis 418
Roos, Fred 418
Rose, Jack 418
Ross, Herbert 418
Schaffner, Franklin J. 419
Schunzel, Reinhold 420
Segar, E. C. 416
Sobieski, Carol 420
Stark, Ray 420
Steinberg, Norman 419
Stigwood, Robert 421
Stone, Paddy 420
Tarses, Jay 418
Wilder, Billy 420
Willis, Gordon 418
Wills, Lou, 416

THE HOLLYWOOD MUSICAL THE HOLLYWOOD MUSICAL